Rick Steves®

SWITZERLAND

D0034695

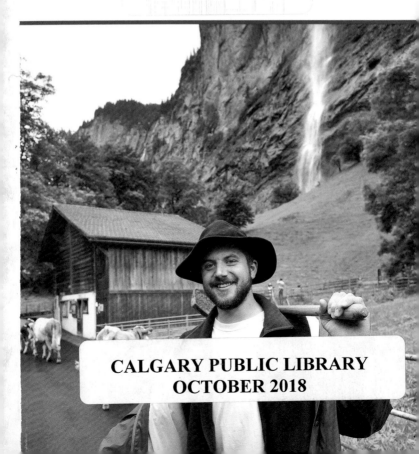

CONTENTS

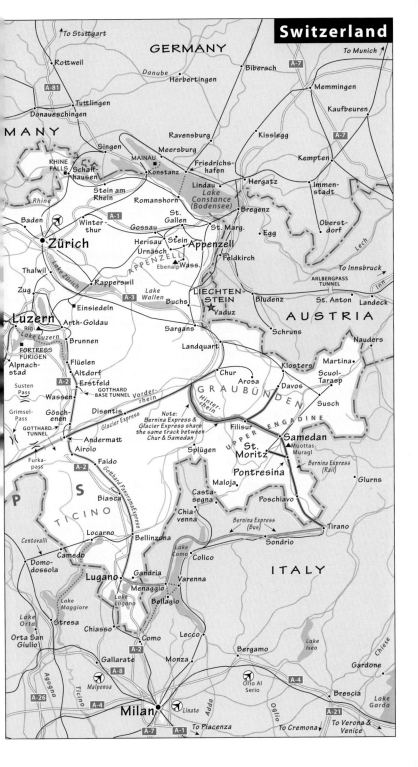

Schilthorn, Berner Oberland

Kramgasse, Bern

Grüetzi!

Bernina Express

Chapel Bridge, Luzern

...me to Rick Steves' Europe

...ed living—maximum thrills per minute and
...great sources of legal adventure. Travel is free-
...s, and we need it.

...ed a passion for Eu-
...as a teen and have
...it ever since—through
...public television and
...s, and travel guide-
...r the years, I've taught
...of travelers how to best
...pe's blockbuster sights—
...rience "Back Door" dis-
...that most tourists miss.
...s book offers you a bal-
...mix of cities and villages, mountaintop hikes and lake
..., thought-provoking museums and sky-high gondola
...And it's selective—rather than listing dozens of moun-
...etaways, I recommend only the best ones. My self-guid-
...useum tours and city walks give insight into Switzerland's
...ant history and today's living, breathing culture.

...I advocate traveling simply and smartly. Take advantage
...my money- and time-saving tips on sightseeing, transpor-
...tion, and more. Try local, characteristic alternatives to ex-
...ensive hotels and restaurants. In many ways, spending more
...money only builds a thicker wall between you and what you
...raveled so far to see.

We visit Switzerland to experience it—to become temporary locals. Thoughtful travel engages us with the world, as we
learn to appreciate other cultures and new ways to measure
quality of life.

Judging from the positive feedback I receive from readers, this book will help you enjoy a fun, affordable, and rewarding vacation—whether it's your first trip or your tenth.

Gute Reise! Happy travels!

Rick Steves

Ric

SWITZE

Welcom

Travel is intensif
one of the last
dom. It's reces
I discove
ropean trave
been sharing
my tours,
radio show
books. Ov
thousands
enjoy Eur
and exp
coveries
Th
anced
cruise
rides.
tain
ed m
vibr

of
ta
p

FRANCE
• Freiburg
GERMANY
Rhine R.
Lake
Constance
• Basel
Zürich •
APPENZELL
Appenzell •
LIECHTENSTE
Jura
Mountains
Ebenalp
⊛ Vaduz
Luzern
▲ Rigi
AUSTRIA
Neuchâtel •
Bern ⊛
Pilatus ▲
Rhine R.
• Chur
Lake
Luzern
Murten •
Interlaken
GRAUBÜNDEN
• Gruyères
BERNER
Alps
UPPER
ENGADINE
VAUD
OBERLAND
TICINO
St. • Samedan
Lausanne
Gstaad
Moritz Pontresina
Lake
Geneva
• Montreux
Rhône R.
Alps
Locarno
• Tirano
Geneva
• Martigny
• Zermatt
Lugano •
• Menaggio
Chamonix •
Matterhorn
Lake
Lake
Lugano
Lake
Como
▲ Mt.
Blanc
Maggiore
40 Kilometers
40 Miles
ITALY
• Milan

N

INTRODUCTION

Little, mountainous, efficient Switzerland is one of Europe's most appealing destinations. Wedged neatly between Germany, Austria, France, and Italy, Switzerland melds the best of all worlds—and adds a healthy dose of chocolate, cowbells, and cable cars. Fiercely independent and decidedly high-tech, the Swiss stubbornly hold on to their quaint traditions, too. Join cheesemakers in a high valley, try to call the shepherds on an alphorn, and hike through some of the world's most stunning mountain scenery.

This book breaks Switzerland into its top big-city, small-town, and rural attractions. It gives you all the information and sugges-

tions necessary to wring the maximum value out of your limited time and money. If you plan three weeks or less in Switzerland, this lean and mean little book has all the information you need...unless you're a skier. (This is a fair-weather book—it focuses on the highlights of summertime fun—but for basic info for a winter visit, see the Switzerland in Winter chapter.)

Experiencing Europe's culture, people, and natural wonders economically and hassle-free has been my goal throughout my life of traveling, tour guiding, and writing. With this guidebook, I pass on to you the lessons I've learned.

This book covers the predictable biggies while mixing in a healthy dose of Back Door intimacy. Along with Luzern, the Matterhorn, and the Glacier Express, you'll experience windswept Roman ruins and ramble through traffic-free alpine towns. I've been selective, including only the top destinations. For example, the country is dotted with alpine villages—but Gimmelwald is a cut above.

The best is, of course, only my opinion. But after spending much of my life exploring and researching Europe, I've developed a sixth sense for what travelers enjoy. Just thinking about the places featured in this book makes me want to yodel.

ABOUT THIS BOOK

Rick Steves Switzerland is a personal tour guide in your pocket. This book is organized by destinations. Each is a mini vacation on its own, filled with exciting sights, strollable neighborhoods, affordable places to stay, and memorable places to eat. In the following chapters, you'll find these sections:

Planning Your Time suggests a schedule for how to best use your limited time.

Orientation has specifics on public transportation, helpful hints, local tour options, easy-to-read maps, and tourist information.

Sights describes the top attractions and includes their cost and hours.

Self-Guided Walks take you through interesting neighborhoods, pointing out sights and fun stops.

Sleeping describes my favorite hotels, from good-value deals to cushy splurges.

Eating serves up a buffet of options, from inexpensive *Stübli* to fancy restaurants.

Connections outlines your options for traveling to destinations by train and bus. In car-friendly regions, I've also included route tips for drivers.

The **Switzerland in Winter** chapter provides tips for enjoying the Alps in snow, and describes some uniquely Swiss holiday traditions.

The **Switzerland: Past & Present** chapter introduces you to some key people and events in this nation's complicated past, making your sightseeing that much more meaningful.

The **Practicalities** chapter near the end of this book is a traveler's tool kit, with my best advice about money, sightseeing, sleeping, eating, staying connected, and transportation.

The **appendix** has the nuts and bolts: useful phone numbers and websites, a holiday and festival list, recommended books and films, a climate chart, a handy packing checklist, and survival phrases in German, French, and Italian.

Throughout this book, you'll find money- and time-saving tips

Top Destinations in Switzerland

ZÜRICH APPENZELL
LUZERN & CENTRAL SWITZ.
BERN & MURTEN
— BOAT
BERNER OBERLAND
LAKE GENEVA & FRENCH SWITZ.
UPPER ENGADINE
❹
❶
ZERMATT & THE MATTERHORN
❷
LUGANO ❸ BUS

Scenic Rail Journeys:
❶ Golden Pass
❷ Gotthard Panorama Express
❸ Bernina Express
❹ Glacier Express

for sightseeing, transportation, and more. Some businesses—especially hotels and walking tour companies—offer special discounts to my readers, indicated in their listings.

Browse through this book, choose your favorite destinations, and link them up. Then have a great trip! Traveling like a temporary local, you'll get the absolute most of every mile, minute, and dollar. And, as you visit places I know and love, I'm happy that you'll be meeting some of my favorite Swiss people.

Planning

This section will help you get started planning your trip—with advice on trip costs, when to go, and what you should know before you take off.

TRIP COSTS

Five components make up your trip costs: airfare, surface transportation, room and board, sightseeing and entertainment, and shopping and miscellany.

Airfare to Europe: A basic round-trip flight from the US to Zürich can cost, on average, about $1,000-2,000 total, depending on where you fly from and when (cheaper in winter). If Switzerland is part of a longer trip, consider saving time and money in Europe by flying into one city and out of another; for instance, into Zürich and out of Paris. Overall, Kayak.com is the best place

Budget Tips

Switzerland is pricey, but there are ways to stretch your dollars. For example, you can cut down on restaurant costs by having scenic picnics or seeking out self-service cafeterias (often attached to department or grocery stores), which offer good food at a fraction of the cost of dining out.

Many expensive alpine lifts offer discounted "early bird" tickets for the first (and sometimes last) trip of the day. Train trips get cheaper when you choose the right rail pass (for help, see page 403); the Swiss Travel Pass is a swinging deal for most travelers, covering more than just trains.

Save on Sightseeing with the Swiss Travel Pass

The Swiss Travel Pass offers consecutive-day or flexipass coverage of Switzerland's trains, boats, and buses, a 50 percent discount off most lifts, and fully covers the cable car to the Schilthorn peak near Mürren (about $490 for 15-day consecutive pass in second class). It also doubles as a Swiss Museum Pass (which otherwise costs about $170), covering admission to 500 museums or so on the days your pass is valid (the standard Swiss Museum Pass is good for a year). To get the most out of a flexipass, use it to visit a museum, ride a lake boat, or take a lift either on the same day you arrive at that destination or on the day you depart.

to start searching for flights on a combination of mainstream and budget carriers.

Transportation in Europe: For a two-week whirlwind trip of most of my recommended destinations by public transportation, allow $700 per person. This covers a second-class, 15-consecutive-day Swiss Travel Pass, plus high-mountain trains and lifts, and reservation fees for scenic trains. You can purchase a Swiss Travel Pass before you leave home, or wait until you arrive in Switzerland—they're also sold at local train stations.

If you plan to rent a car, allow at least $250 per week, not including tolls, gas, and supplemental insurance; figure on an additional $250 for mountain lifts sans car. If you need the car for three weeks or more, leasing can save you money on insurance and taxes. If you are going to other places in Europe, don't hesitate to consider flying, as budget airlines are often cheaper than taking the train (check www.skyscanner.com for intra-European flights). For more on public transportation and car rental, see "Transportation" in Practicalities.

Room and Board: You can manage comfortably in Switzerland on $170 a day per person for room and board (more in big cities). This allows $25 for lunch, $40 for dinner, $5 for chocolate, and $100 for lodging (based on two people splitting the cost of a

The following sights, described in this book, are covered by the Swiss Travel Pass and the Swiss Museum Pass (for a full list, see www.museumspass.ch):

Zürich: Swiss National Museum and Rietberg Museum

Luzern: Rosengart Collection, Depot History Museum, Bourbaki Panorama, Glacier Garden, Richard Wagner Museum, Museum of Art Luzern, and Museum of Natural History, plus Fortress Fürigen Museum nearby in Stansstad (Swiss Transport Museum is 50 percent off with the pass)

Bern: Museum of Fine Arts and Paul Klee Center

Near Murten: Roman Museum in Avenches

Interlaken: Museum of Tourism

Near Interlaken: Ballenberg Open-Air Folk Museum in Brienz

Zermatt: Matterhorn Museum

Appenzell Region: Appenzell Museum and Appenzell's two modern art museums, and folk museums in Stein and Urnäsch

Lausanne: Collection de l'Art Brut, Olympic Museum, and City History Museum

Lake Geneva Region: Château de Chillon

French Swiss Countryside: Gruyères Castle, H. R. Giger Museum, and Tibet Museum

$200 double room that includes breakfast). Students and tightwads can enjoy Switzerland for as little as $70 a day ($40 for a hostel bed, $30 for supermarket meals and snacks).

Sightseeing and Entertainment: Figure about $10-15 per sight, and about $80 for each major alpine lift. Though hiking is free, lifts to some of the best high-altitude trails aren't. An overall average of $50 a day works for most. Don't skimp here. After all, this category is the driving force behind your trip—you came to sightsee, enjoy, and experience Switzerland.

Shopping and Miscellany: Figure $5 per coffee, beer, and ice-cream cone. Shopping can vary in cost from nearly nothing to a small fortune. Good budget travelers find that this category has little to do with assembling a trip full of lifelong memories.

SIGHTSEEING PRIORITIES
So much to see, so little time. How to choose? Depending on the length of your trip, and taking geographic proximity into account, here are my recommended priorities:

3 days: Berner Oberland

5 days, add: Luzern and Central Switzerland

7 days, add: Bern and Lake Geneva area, connecting them with Golden Pass scenic rail journey

10 days, add: Zermatt and Appenzell, linking them with the
                Glacier Express train
14 days, add: Lugano and Upper Engadine area, connecting
                with Bernina Express and Gotthard Panorama
                Express train rides
16 days, add: Zürich and Murten
21 days, add: More day trips (French Swiss countryside),
                more hikes, and time to slow down

This includes nearly everything on the map and itinerary in the "Switzerland's Best Two-Week Trip by Train" sidebar (later in this chapter), plus modifications for a longer or shorter trip. If you don't have time to see it all, prioritize according to your interests. The "Switzerland at a Glance" sidebar (later) can help you decide where to go.

WHEN TO GO

The summer "tourist season" runs roughly from May through September, though in mountainous areas, it doesn't start until sometime in June. High summer (July-Aug) has its advantages: the best weather, snow-free alpine trails, very long days (light until after 21:00), and the busiest schedule of tourist fun. In late May, June, September, and early October, travelers enjoy fewer crowds, mild weather, and the ability to grab a room almost whenever and wherever they like.

During the *Zwischenzeit* ("between time"—that is, between summer and ski seasons, roughly April, early May, late Oct, and Nov), the cities are pleasantly uncrowded, but mountain resort towns such as Zermatt and Mürren are completely dead (most hotels and restaurants are closed, and the weather is iffy).

During ski season (Dec-March), mountain resorts are crowded and expensive, while cities are quieter (some accommodations and sights are either closed or run on a limited schedule). The weather can be cold and dreary, and nighttime will draw the shades on your sightseeing before dinner. But Christmastime traditions (such as colorful markets and special holiday foods) can warm up your trip at this chilly time of year.

Pack warm clothing for the Alps, no matter when you go—the weather can change suddenly.

Before You Go

Check this list of things to arrange while you're still at home. For more information on these topics, see the Practicalities chapter (and www.ricksteves.com, which has helpful travel tips and talks).

Make sure your passport is valid. If it's due to expire within six months of your ticketed date of return, you need to renew it.

Switzerland at a Glance

▲▲**Zürich** Bustling cosmopolitan city—Switzerland's largest by far—with upscale shops and a charming riverside old-town quarter full of pointy church spires and pealing bells.

▲▲**Luzern and Central Switzerland** Touristy yet worthwhile town of historic wooden bridges, picturesque streets, and vintage steamships that ply lovely Lake Luzern, ringed by mountains with stunning vistas accessible by high-altitude lifts.

▲▲▲**Bern** Cozy capital of Switzerland tucked in a sharp river bend, with arcaded shopping promenades, medieval clock towers, and museums devoted to Albert Einstein and artist Paul Klee.

▲▲**Murten** Quaint, small, walled town sitting right next to the German/French linguistic fault line, with nearby Roman ruins and museum in Avenches.

▲▲▲**Gimmelwald and the Berner Oberland** Rustic village spectacularly perched on a cliff in this mountainous region—popular for its alpine towns and scenic hikes, lifts, and train rides. Touristy Interlaken is the gateway.

▲▲**Zermatt and the Matterhorn** Glitzy ski resort that sports some traditional old-fashioned touches, in a valley at the foot of the famous Matterhorn.

▲▲**Appenzell** The most traditional Swiss region, known for pastoral scenery, small towns, cows, folk museums, and, just a cable-car ride away, a rustic cliffside retreat at Ebenalp.

▲▲**Lake Geneva and French Switzerland** Small-but-sophisticated lakeside city of Lausanne, Switzerland's best castle experience at Château de Chillon, the cute cheesemaking center of Gruyères, and pleasant scenery in the surrounding countryside.

▲**Lugano** Leading city of Italian-speaking Switzerland, with a tidy—if dull—urban core, scenic boat trips on Lake Lugano, and mountain lifts to lakeside peaks.

▲**Upper Engadine** Romansh-speaking mountain resort region, anchored by three towns: touristy Pontresina, humble Samedan, and swanky St. Moritz.

▲▲**Scenic Rail Journeys** Four famous train rides, each offering panoramic views and crisscrossing the country.

Switzerland's Best
Two-Week Trip by Train

Day	Plan	Sleep in
1	Arrive Zürich Airport, head to Appenzell	Appenzell or Ebenalp
2	All day for Appenzell and Ebenalp	Appenzell or Ebenalp
3	Leave early for Luzern	Luzern
4	Luzern	Luzern
5	Boat, then train to Lugano along Gotthard Panorama Express route	Lugano
6	Bernina Express to Upper Engadine area	Pontresina
7	Upper Engadine (Pontresina, St. Moritz, and Samedan)	Pontresina
8	Take Glacier Express; if weather's good, head for Zermatt; if weather's bad, consider going straight to Lausanne (see below)	Zermatt
9	Zermatt and hikes, Matterhorn-view lifts	Zermatt
10	If weather's good, spend more time in Zermatt and go late to Lausanne; if weather's bad, leave early for Lausanne	Lausanne
11	Take the Golden Pass to the Berner Oberland. If weather's good, go early; if weather's bad, linger in Lausanne/Lake Geneva area and leave late	Gimmelwald or Mürren
12	All day for lifts and hikes in the Berner Oberland	Gimmelwald or Mürren
13	More time in the Berner Oberland	Gimmelwald or Mürren
14	Early to Bern, then on to Zürich	Zürich
15	More time in Zürich, or fly home	

Notes

Zermatt isn't worth the trip in bad weather. If your reservations are flexible, consider skipping that leg and going straight to Lausanne (take the Glacier Express only to Brig, then change for Lausanne).

To connect Luzern and Lugano, follow the Gotthard Panorama Express route, but don't spend extra for the official tourist package-trip.

If you have extra time in Switzerland, I'd suggest spending it in (listed in order of priority): Murten and Bern, Zürich, Lausanne and the Lake Geneva area, Lugano (relaxing) or the Luzern area (day trips). For a short trip of a week or so, I'd just focus on the Berner Oberland, Luzern, and Bern.

Rail Pass: The best rail pass for this itinerary is a Swiss Travel Pass, specifically for 15 consecutive days ($490 second class,

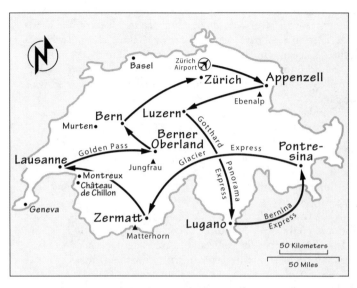

$775 first class, prices are per adult age 28 or older, confirm latest prices at www.ricksteves.com/rail; figure an additional $100 total in reservation fees for all four scenic rail journeys). This pass doesn't cover most higher mountain lifts, but it usually earns you a 50 percent discount.

By Car: Although this itinerary is designed for public transportation, it can be done by car with a few modifications. Obviously, you won't take the scenic rail trips. Instead, drive from Appenzell straight to the Upper Engadine area, then continue through Tirano and on to Lugano (via Lake Como in Italy). From Lugano, drive to Zermatt (crossing again through Italy) and resume the above itinerary, visiting Luzern at the end before returning to Zürich. The French Swiss countryside and the area around Murten merit more time if you have a car.

Beyond Switzerland: Switzerland, right in the middle of Western Europe, splices neatly into a multicountry trip by car or train. For instance, the Appenzell region is a likely gateway to Germany's Bavaria or Austria's Tirol. Italy's Lake Como is a stone's throw from Lugano (in fact, the Bernina Express bus drives right alongside it)—and Milan is not much farther. If you're in Lausanne, you're literally looking at France (across Lake Geneva), and a handy train ride whisks you to Lyon or Chamonix. And big Swiss cities are efficiently connected by fast trains to destinations in all of these countries and beyond.

Allow up to six weeks to renew or get a passport (www.travel.state.gov).

Arrange your transportation. Book your international flights. Figure out your main form of transportation within Switzerland: It's worth thinking about buying train tickets online in advance, getting a rail pass, renting a car, or booking cheap European flights. (You can wing it once you're there, but it may cost more.)

Book rooms well in advance, especially if your trip falls during peak season (July and August) or any major holidays or festivals (see page 417).

To take one of the popular **scenic trains** during high season (July-Aug), you may want to reserve ahead. See the Scenic Rail Journeys chapter for details and advice.

Consider travel insurance. Compare the cost of the insurance to the cost of your potential loss. Check whether your existing insurance (health, homeowners, or renters) covers you and your possessions overseas.

Call your bank. Alert your bank that you'll be using your debit and credit cards in Europe. Ask about transaction fees, and get the PIN number for your credit card. You don't need to bring Swiss francs for your trip; you can withdraw them from cash machines in Europe.

Use your smartphone smartly. Sign up for an international service plan to reduce your costs, or rely on Wi-Fi in Europe instead. Download any apps you'll want on the road, such as maps, translation, transit schedules, and Rick Steves Audio Europe (see sidebar).

Rip up this book! Turn chapters into mini guidebooks: Break the book's spine and use a utility knife to slice apart chapters, keeping gummy edges intact. Reinforce the chapter spines with clear wide tape; use a heavy-duty stapler; or make or buy a cheap cover (see Travel Store at www.ricksteves.com), swapping out chapters as you travel.

Pack light. You'll walk with your luggage more than you think. Bring a single carry-on bag and a daypack. Use the packing checklist in the appendix as a guide.

Travel Smart

If you have a positive attitude, equip yourself with good information (this book), and expect to travel smart, you will.

Read—and reread—this book. To have an "A" trip, be an "A" student. Note opening hours of sights, closed days, crowd-beating tips, and whether reservations are required or advisable. Check the latest at www.ricksteves.com/update.

Be your own tour guide. As you travel, get up-to-date info

∩ Rick Steves Audio Europe ∩

My Rick Steves Audio Europe app makes it easy to download audio content to enhance your trip. Enjoy my audio tours of many of Europe's top destinations and a library of insightful travel interviews from my public radio show with experts from Switzerland and around the globe. The app and all of its content are entirely free. (And new content is added about twice a year.) You can download the app via Apple's App Store, Google Play, or Amazon's Appstore. For more info, see www.ricksteves.com/audioeurope.

on sights, reserve tickets and tours, reconfirm hotels and travel arrangements, and check transit connections. Visit local tourist information offices (TIs). Upon arrival in a new town, lay the groundwork for a smooth departure; confirm the train, bus, or road you'll take when you leave.

Outsmart thieves. Pickpockets abound in crowded places where tourists congregate. Treat commotions as smokescreens for theft. Keep your cash, credit cards, and passport secure in a money belt tucked under your clothes; carry only a day's spending money in your front pocket. Don't set valuable items down on counters or café tabletops, where they can be quickly stolen or easily forgotten.

Minimize potential loss. Keep expensive gear to a minimum. Bring photocopies or take photos of important documents (passport and cards) to aid in replacement if they're lost or stolen.

Guard your time and energy. To avoid long lines, follow my crowd-beating tips, such as making advance reservations, or sightseeing early or late. Buy a "Good Morning Ticket" for the Jungfraujoch in the Berner Oberland, and you'll beat the hordes and save 25 percent.

Be flexible. Even if you have a well-planned itinerary, expect changes, strikes, closures, sore feet, bad weather, and so on. Your Plan B could turn out to be even better. For example, you might plan on three days split between the city of Bern and the mountainous Berner Oberland region. If it's raining as you approach the area, head for Bern. If it's sunny, make a beeline for the mountains, then hit Bern on your way out of the area. To help decide, tune in to websites and TV stations that show the weather in various parts of the country. Many high-altitude observation decks have 24-hour online cameras that pan slowly back and forth, showing you exactly what you'll see when you get up top (for example, www.swisspanorama.com for the Berner Oberland, www.zermatt.ch for Zermatt).

Attempt the language. Many Swiss—especially in the tourist trade and in cities—speak English, but if you learn some Italian, German, or French, even just a few phrases, you'll get more smiles and make more friends. Practice the survival phrases near the end of this book, and even better, bring a phrase book.

Connect with the culture. Interacting with locals carbonates your experience. Enjoy the friendliness of the Swiss people. Ask questions; most locals are happy to point you in their idea of the right direction. Set up your own quest for the richest hot chocolate, cheeriest window box, biggest cowbell, or most densely packed stack of firewood. When an opportunity pops up, make it a habit to say "yes."

Switzerland...here you come!

SWITZERLAND

Switzerland is one of Europe's richest, best organized, most expensive countries. Like the Boy Scouts, the Swiss count cleanliness, neatness, punctuality, tolerance, independence, thrift, and hard work as virtues...and they love pocketknives. The country is an enjoyable mix of bucolic peace and daring adventure. Around every alpine turn, you feel you could get a glimpse of Heidi milking a cow or James Bond schussing past on skis.

Nearly half of Switzerland—Europe's most mountainous country—consists of uninhabitable rocks and rugged Alps. It

seems that any flat land (and quite a bit of hilly land) is cultivated into tidy little farms. While landlocked, Switzerland has more than its share of clear rivers and big, beautiful lakes with a striking mountain backdrop (such as Lake Geneva, Lake Murten, Lake Luzern, and Lake Lugano—all covered in this book).

Despite the country's small size, Switzerland is unusually diverse. Its wild geography has kept people apart historically, helping its many regions maintain their distinct cultural differences. Switzerland has four official languages: German, French, Italian, and Romansh.

And yet, regardless of which language is spoken, the entire country is unmistakably Swiss. Everyday things like the grocery store, train station, or familiar products have the same signage and logos, but in different languages. And everywhere you go, you'll notice a dedication to order and organization that distinguishes Swiss culture. It's refreshing to visit a predictable

The abbreviation for Swiss Federal Railways—in German, French, and Italian

SWITZERLAND

Switzerland: Western Europe's Linguistic Crossroads

You'd be forgiven for thinking of Switzerland as a "German" country. The heart of Switzerland, with about three-fifths of the population and most of the famous cities and sights, is linguistically (as well as culturally) Germanic. But even here, Germans and Austrians don't feel quite at home. As if keeping alive an archaic code for insiders, the Swiss speak to each other in the lilting, fun-to-listen-to Swiss German, a.k.a. *Schwyzertütsch,* then switch seamlessly to standard German (or English) when interacting with outsiders.

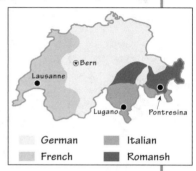

German   Italian
French   Romansh

Surrounding the German-speaking core is a more colorful Romance language-speaking fringe—French (to the west), Italian (to the south), and Romansh (tucked in the southeastern mountains). Switzerland's biggest canton, officially trilingual, is its linguistic melting pot: the southeastern region called Graubünden (in German), Grigioni (in Italian), and Grischun (in Romansh).

Subtle differences in cuisine, climate, and landscape seem to match the linguistic boundaries. German-speaking Switzerland enjoys a vigorous efficiency reminiscent of Germany's. The pace in genteel French-speaking Switzerland is a bit mellower, the cuisine and lifestyle more refined, resembling France's. And the relatively balmy Italian-speaking canton of Ticino comes with a touch of chaos and lust for life that's not far removed from Italy proper (which surrounds it on three sides). You can spend a week in Switzerland and feel almost as if you've traveled from Paris to Munich to Rome...without ever crossing a border.

place where, once you've got the gist of things in one city, you generally know what to expect in the next.

That sort of orderliness doesn't happen by itself. The Swiss jealously guard their way of life. If you accidentally drop a scrap of paper on the ground, someone might cross the street to be sure you pick it up. As if belonging to an exclusive club that's careful about admitting new members, the Swiss strike some visitors as a bit standoffish—polite but not gregarious, welcoming but perhaps a bit suspicious. If you find the Swiss to be a little buttoned-down, remember that the payoff is a beautiful country where the trains run on time, the streets are clean, and every flower petal is perfectly in place.

While it's one of Europe's most progressive "big-government" countries—with high taxation, ample social services, and liberal drug policies—Switzerland also has a sometimes surprising conservative streak. Traditional mindsets persist in the remote mountain hamlets—for example, women weren't guaranteed the right to vote in federal elections until 1971 (and were still barred from local elections in one region until 1990).

Historically, Switzerland is one of Europe's oldest democracies. Born when three states (cantons) united in 1291, over time the Swiss Confederation grew to the 26 cantons of today. The "CH" decal on cars doesn't stand for chocolate...but for "Confoederatio Helvetica," the country's official title (using the Latin name avoids linguistic controversy). The country is named for the Celtic Helvetii tribe that lived here back in Roman times. (Stamp collectors know to identify a Swiss stamp by looking for the word *Helvetia*.) The confederation's government is decentralized, and cantonal loyalty is very strong.

Similar to US states, each canton is semi-independent. Just as we debate "states' rights," the Swiss wrangle with just how much autonomy to allow cantons. Considering that each comes with not only its own political concerns, but also its own dialect and cultural heritage, cantonal independence is particularly important and delicate.

With the exception of the Protestant Reformation and an almost bloodless civil war in 1847, Swiss history has been pretty quiet...and that's just how the Swiss like it. They're happy to be high and dry in the mountains, watching from above the fray as the tides of history swirl around them (for an overview, see the Switzerland: Past & Present chapter). Stubbornly independent, or maybe just smart, Switzerland loves its neutrality and stayed out of both world wars. But it's far from lax when it comes to national defense—on the contrary, the Swiss are legendary for their military readiness. A vast reserve army and a countryside embedded with hidden fortresses have earned Switzerland its unique ability to preserve its right to self-determination well into the 21st century, even though it's surrounded by bigger, stronger nations. Through the tumult of the 20th century, no foreign invaders dared to try cracking this nut.

Even so, for more than a century and a half, a different kind of invasion—of tourists—has descended on Switzerland each summer (for hiking season, all summer long but busiest July-Aug) and each winter (for ski season, roughly Christmas through Easter). You'll share the trails and lifts with a deluge of international visitors—from Europe, the US, and the rest of the world. Partly because several Bollywood movies have used the Swiss Alps as a stand-in

SWITZERLAND

Switzerland Almanac

Official Name: The *Confoederatio Helvetica,* or Switzerland, has a different name in each of its four official languages: *Schweizerische Eidgenossenschaft* (German), *Confédération Suisse* (French), *Confederazione Svizzera* (Italian), and *Confederaziun Svizra* (Romansh). Locals shorten those to "die Schweiz," "la Suisse," "la Svizzera," and "la Svizra."

Population: Switzerland has 8.2 million people (similar to the population of Virginia); 65 percent speak German as their main language, 23 percent speak French, 8 percent speak Italian, and about 1 percent speak Romansh. About 22 percent of Swiss residents are not Swiss citizens; these range from EU businesspeople to immigrant workers. The populace is 38 percent Catholic, 27 percent Protestant, 6 percent other Christian, 5 percent Muslim, and 24 percent other or unspecified.

Latitude and Longitude: 47°N and 8°E, similar latitude to Quebec, Canada.

Area: 16,000 square miles; twice the size of New Jersey, or half the size of South Carolina.

Geography: Switzerland sits at the crossroads between northern and southern Europe. The Alps are Europe's high point and continental divide, from which the major rivers flow—Rhine, Rhône, Danube, and Po. Switzerland's highest point is the 15,200-foot Monte Rosa (specifically, the summit called Dufourspitze), along the Italian border. Though Switzerland is mostly mountainous, the center of the country consists of rolling hills and large lakes.

Biggest Cities: One in seven Swiss lives in or near Zürich (pop. 380,000 in the city; 1.2 million in the metropolitan area). Geneva has 192,000 people, and Basel has 167,000. The capital is Bern (pop. 129,000).

Economy: Like a fine watch, Switzerland's economy just keeps on ticking. The gross domestic product is $494 billion. Its per-capita

for Kashmir, Switzerland is popular with tourists from India. And Middle Eastern visitors flock here to escape the heat. Locals report a spike in Middle Eastern tourists in the weeks leading up to the sacred, month-long observance of Ramadan...when their numbers drop to virtually zero, as Muslims go back home to spend time with their families.

Though not a European Union member—in part because its agricultural lobby doesn't want competition from more efficiently produced EU products—Switzerland conforms to EU standards to be able to conduct business easily. Major Swiss moneymakers include banking, insurance, watches (from top-of-the-line pieces to inexpensive Swatches), chemicals and pharmaceuticals, choco-

GDP of $59,400 is among Europe's highest (about equal to the US). The franc is strong, workers are highly skilled, and unemployment is less than half the European Union average. Blessed with hydropower and using nuclear technology, Switzerland generates 99 percent of its electricity with virtually no oil.

Currency: 1 Swiss franc (CHF) = 100 rappen/centimes = about $1.

Government: Founded in 1291 as a confederation of cantons, the country is still a model of federalism, balancing the needs of its different linguistic/ethnic groups. No single political party (or two or even three parties) dominates. The president, chosen by the legislature, serves for just one calendar year. The two-house Federal Assembly consists of the 46-seat Council of States and the 200-seat National Council, elected for four-year terms.

Flag: Switzerland's white cross on a distinctively square red background may have been the inspiration for the red-on-white symbol of the International Red Cross. It's one of only two recognized flags that are perfect squares (the other being the flag of Vatican City).

The Average Swiss: He or she has 1.5 children and will live to be 82. A typical Swiss man serves at least 260 days of compulsory service in the military. The average woman earns almost 20 percent less than her similar male counterparts, and often doesn't return to the workforce after having children. He or she travels about 1,400 miles a year on a train, the equivalent of crossing the country six times. Every month, the average Swiss drinks almost a quart of alcohol and eats more than a pound and a half of chocolate.

late (Nestlé is the biggest producer), tourism, and precision instruments. Swiss-made equipment helps produce everything from clothing to ballpoint-pen tips to parts for the Mars Exploration Rover. Swiss ingenuity is nowhere more apparent than in the famous Swiss Army knives, which come in sizes big and small, with as many—or as few—tools as any armchair MacGyver could need.

Perhaps owing to its financial strength, Switzerland is one of Europe's most expensive countries. A night on the town can be a major splurge. Locals call sitting on the pavement around a bottle of wine "going out." Double rooms with bath for less than $175 are rare. Even dormitory beds are expensive. If your budget is tight, be sure to chase down hostels (many have private rooms for couples

Understanding the Alps

Switzerland's snowy, rugged mountains are its claim to fame—and most likely a main reason for your visit. Fortunately, you don't have to be a mountain climber to see the Alps up close, as the Swiss transportation system is as remarkable as its mountains. Its cog railways, gondolas, and cable cars whisk you up into the type of scenery that's only accessible in some countries by ropes, pitons, and crampons.

The Alps were formed by the collision of two continents. About 100 million years ago, the African plate began pushing north against the stable plates of Europe and Asia. In the process, the sediments of the ancient Tethys Ocean (which once occupied the general real estate of the modern Mediterranean) became smooshed between the landmasses. Shoving all this material together made the rocks and sediments fold, shatter, and pile on top of each other; over millennia this growing jumble built itself up into today's Alps. Up in the mountains, look for folds and faults in the rocks that hint at this immense compression, which is still happening today: The Alps continue to rise by at least a millimeter each year (while erosion wears them down at about the same rate).

The current shape of the mountains and valleys is the handiwork of at least five ice ages over the last two million years. Glaciers flowed down the mountain valleys, scooped out Switzerland's beautiful alpine lakes, and carried rocks far away from where they had formed. The Alps were the first mountains extensively studied by geologists, and many of the geological terms that describe mountains originated here. Once you learn how to recognize a few of the landforms shaped by glaciers, you can easily spot these features when you visit other alpine areas. Study glacier exhibits to train your eye to recognize what you're seeing.

Glaciers are big and blunt, so they make simple, large-scale marks on the landscape. If a valley is U-shaped (with steep sides and a rounded base), it likely was scoured out by a glacier. Switzerland's Lauterbrunnen Valley and California's Yosemite Valley are classic examples.

A **cirque** (French for "circus") is the amphitheater-like depression carved out at the upper part of a valley by a glacier. If two adjacent cirques erode close to each other, a sharp steep-sided ridge forms, called an **arête** (French for "fishbone"). Cirques and arêtes are common in mountains with glaciers. More rarely, when three or more cirques erode toward one another, a pyramidal peak is created, called a **horn.** The Matterhorn is the world's most famous example. Glaciers flowed down all sides of this mountain, scooping material away and creating the distinctive sharp peak.

A common feature left behind by retreating glaciers is a **moraine,** a pile of dirt and rocks carried along on the glacier as it advanced, then dumped as the glacier melted. The Lindenhof in Zürich, a hilltop square once crowned with forts to defend the town, perches on a moraine.

Alpine glaciers can only originate above the snowline, so if you see any of these landforms (U-shaped valleys, cirques, horns, or moraines) in lower elevations, you know that the climate there used to be colder. The warming climate has profoundly affected the glaciers of Switzerland, which have lost at least a third of their volume since the 1950s. Some studies project that at that rate most glaciers in Switzerland could virtually disappear by the end of the century, affecting water storage and hydroelectric power generation.

In higher elevations, mountainsides have become less stable due to the melting of permafrost. A heat wave in 2003 caused several rockfalls on the Matterhorn, resulting in trail closures and the evacuation of dozens of climbers trapped on the summit. The ski resort of Pontresina built a dam in 2002 to protect the town from a potential landslide from its nearby mountain.

Another consequence of the warming climate is that winter weather no longer reliably produces snow at altitudes that it did in the past—which is bad news for Switzerland's huge ski industry. Seeing a future of ever-warmer winters, the Swiss are putting their ingenuity to the test. This goes beyond snow machines: Many resorts are investing hugely in new spas, convention centers, and other attractions that don't require snow.

With their acute awareness of their alpine climate's fragility, the Swiss are especially keen to explore green technology—even high up in the Alps. Now when they build mountain refuges, the favored design isn't necessarily a rustic stone-hut chalet, but a high-tech building that depends on solar power. Switzerland's technological innovation can help keep its mountains white and its valleys green.

and families), and keep your eyes peeled for *Matratzenlagers* ("mattress dorms"). Hiking is free, though most major alpine lifts cost at least $50.

Switzerland has more than its share of cosmopolitan cities. My favorites—Zürich, Luzern, Bern, Lausanne, and Lugano—are covered in this book. Each one offers an enticing, I-could-live-here glimpse of the appealing and uniquely Swiss urban quality of life: efficient trams and buses gliding around town, manicured pedes-

trian zones teeming with locals enjoying their cities, crystal-clear rivers and lakes made accessible by scenic cruise boats, eclectic restaurants offering a tasty range of both Swiss and international cuisine, and low-key but generally compelling museums. While Switzerland lacks a world-class metropolis on par with Paris or Rome, all of these cities are engaging—especially if bad weather keeps you from heading for the hills.

But let's face it: Travelers don't flock to Switzerland for its cities. Spend most of your time getting high in the Alps. You can climb onto a train in one of Switzerland's most bustling stations and, within an hour or two, step off into an idyllic time-warp world where traditional culture still thrives. Alpine villages (such as Gimmelwald) and towns (such as Appenzell) give you a taste of rural Switzerland, and are the perfect base for pastoral countryside hikes or riding lifts to dramatic cut-glass alpine panoramas.

If you're in the countryside on a Sunday, you'll most likely enjoy traditional music, clothing, and culture. At the end of a day of hiking, you can retreat to a village enclave preserving a colorful, rustic, rural way of life.

Because the Swiss have chosen (at great cost) to protect their agricultural sector against competition from imports, the government subsidizes families who raise cows and make cheese the old-fashioned way. In the spring and again in the fall, you might be lucky enough to see a parade of cows on their way up to or back down from the high-mountain pastures.

The cows have also had a big impact on Swiss cuisine—especially cheese. Two of the most revered Swiss cheeses are the smooth Gruyère (from the town of Gruyères) and the stinky Appenzeller (from the region of Appenzell). In these areas, you can watch the cheese being made—just as it has been for centuries...or at modern facilities using technology to carry out the same age-old processes (including robots that tenderly rub and flip each aging wheel of

cheese). Cheese shops (*Käserei* in German) sell a fragrant festival of mold, perfect for picnicking or for making two famous Swiss culinary specialties: fondue (a pot of cheese melted into wine) or raclette (cheese melted over potatoes and other vegetables). But after a few days of cheese plates for breakfast, cheese sandwiches for lunch, and cheese specialties for dinner, even the biggest cheese lovers might find they need a dairy detox.

Switzerland's public transportation system is tops, whether you want to go across the country or straight up into the mountains. The country is crisscrossed with fine autobahns and arguably Europe's most efficient rail system. Boats ply the tranquil waters of the country's many lakes, and PostBuses (operated by the post office) pick you up in the rare situations that trains let you down. You can even go *through* the mountains, thanks to long tunnels (but you'll miss the views). Try the variety of fun cogwheel trains, funiculars, and cable cars that deliver you—no matter the season—from sunny valleys up to dizzying heights and snowy vistas.

Switzerland's best attraction might just be hiding between the cities and the villages: In this land of dramatic mountains and picture-perfect farms, perhaps more than anywhere else in Europe, the journey is the destination. The Swiss Railway markets several scenic journeys that run along the country's prettiest routes, many with special panoramic trains designed to maximize views (for details, see the Scenic Rail Journeys chapter). But don't let the tourist hype give you tunnel vision. A sunny day spent on a train just about anywhere in Switzerland can rank as a memorable trip-capper.

From its famous efficiency, to its unique mingling of the modern and the traditional, to its flat-out spectacular scenery, Switzerland delights the Swiss...and their visitors.

ZÜRICH

Zürich is one of those cities that tourists tend to skip right through. Since it's a transportation hub, people fly in or change trains here, but don't give stopping a serious thought. The local graffiti jokes: *Zürich = zu reich, zu ruhig* ("too rich, too quiet"). But even though you won't find a hint of Swiss Miss in Switzerland's leading city, Zürich is rewarding and worth getting to know.

In prehistoric times, people lived on pilings near the shores of Lake Zürich. Later, the Romans founded a city here as a customs post. Roman Turicum eventually became Zürich. It gained city status in the 10th century, and by the 19th century it was a leading European financial and economic center. Today, thanks largely to Switzerland's long-term economic and political stability, Zürich is a major hub of international banking. Assuming you've got the money to enjoy it, Zürich is by many measures the world's most livable city. Its 380,000 people (1.4 million in greater Zürich) are known for their wealth and hard work. Zürich is the only place in Switzerland where I've seen men in ties running in the streets.

PLANNING YOUR TIME

While Luzern and Bern provide more charming urban experiences, Zürich is worth a quick look. With two weeks in Switzerland, I'd spend a day here. Begin by visiting the impressive Swiss National Museum (sometimes called Landesmuseum on maps and brochures), then wander along the river, using my self-guided walk, and take a river/lake cruise. With less time, do only the walk.

Orientation to Zürich

Zürich is draped around the northern tip of the long, skinny Lake Zürich (Zürichsee). The grand Bahnhofstrasse cuts through the city's glitzy shopping center, connecting the train station with the lakefront (a 15-minute walk away). Across the Limmat River is the Niederdorf neighborhood—a vibrant, cobbled, Old World zone of colorful little shops, cafés, and restaurants.

TOURIST INFORMATION

The helpful TI is off the great hall of the train station, near the fat blue angel hanging from the ceiling (Mon-Sat 8:00-20:30, Sun 8:30-18:30; Nov-April Mon-Sat 8:30-19:00, Sun 9:00-18:00; tel. 044-215-4000, www.zuerich.com). Make this your first stop upon arrival in Zürich. They sell Swiss Travel Passes, local transit passes, and tickets to special events around town.

For a whirlwind visit, consider the TI's **ZürichCARD,** which covers transportation by train, tram, bus, and boat (including trips to the airport and up to the Uetliberg viewpoint; additional 5-CHF surcharge for boat trips); admission to most of the city's museums; half off the TI's city walking tour (described later, under "Tours in Zürich"); and freebies in many restaurants (24 CHF/24 hours, 48 CHF/72 hours, sold at TI). The one-day card pays for itself if you do the walking tour and one museum.

ARRIVAL IN ZÜRICH

By Train: The slick **train** station is at the north end of downtown. Many platforms are underground; to orient yourself, follow signs for tracks 3-17, which dead-end at the great hall of the station.

In the hall (with your back to the tracks), the ticket office is to your left (Mon-Fri 7:00-20:30, Sat-Sun 8:00-19:30); the TI is also just ahead to your left. Exiting through the front doors—straight ahead—brings you to the river (cross it to reach many recommended hotels). Lockers are down one flight below the big fat angel, and a pricey WC (with showers) is down two flights. A Migros supermarket with long hours is in the maze-like shopping mall one level down. The right-hand doors of the hall lead to tram stops and Bahnhofstrasse, while the left-hand doors lead toward the Swiss National Museum.

By Plane: If arriving at Zürich Airport, see the end of the chapter.

GETTING AROUND ZÜRICH

Much of Zürich is walkable. But given that the city is laced by trams, buses, and boats, consider getting a day pass. All forms of transportation are covered by the same ticket and must be purchased at ticket machines (at most stops and at the train station) before boarding. You can also purchase tickets at the TI, where the staff can help you understand your options. Those riding any form of transportation without a stamped ticket will be fined a steep 100 CHF.

The ticket options are endless and quite confusing. When heading from the train station to your hotel, consider a *short-distance* ticket (2.70 CHF; check listed stops to make sure yours is covered) or a single one-hour ticket (4.40 CHF). A 24-hour day pass (8.80 CHF) is a good investment if spending a full day in Zürich. Add the boat surcharge ticket (good for one day) for 5 CHF and take as many boat rides as you like.

Most of your sightseeing will take place in the central zone (zone 110). Trams #4 and #11 run north and south along Limmatquai and Bahnhofstrasse, respectively, and are the most convenient for tourists. Journeys to the Uetliberg viewpoint (zone 155) and to the airport (zone 121; by tram #10 or train) cost extra, as they're outside the central zone. The Swiss Travel Pass and Zürich-CARD, described earlier, cover all local transportation (but all ticket holders must pay a 5-CHF surcharge when traveling by boat). For transit information, visit www.zvv.ch or call 0848-988-988.

HELPFUL HINTS

Medical Help: The **Permanence** drop-in clinic on the main floor of the train station offers on-the-spot medical aid (daily 7:00-22:00, Bahnhofplatz 15, tel. 044-215-4444, www.permanence.ch). The **Bahnhof Apotheke** next door is convenient if you need a pharmacy (Mon-Sat 7:00-24:00, closed Sun). A dentist is on the lower level.

Laundry: Expresswäscherei Selfservice, next to the Kinkelstrasse tram stop for trams #9 and #10, is a short ride from downtown (daily 7:00-22:00, Winterthurstrasse 62, mobile 079-346-4032 or 076-305-1111).

Parking: The Central parking garage, on Seilergraben, is close to downtown (34 CHF/day, tel. 044-229-5050, www.pls-zh.ch).

Shopping on Sunday: Though most stores are closed on Sunday, the vast mall under the train station is wide open.

Tours in Zürich

Walking Tours

The TI's two-hour **guided walk** is similar to the self-guided walk in this chapter (25 CHF, half-price with ZürichCARD; leaves from TI April-Oct daily at 15:00; Nov-March Wed and Sat-Sun at 11:00, Sat also at 15:00). Unfortunately, this tour is given in

German and English at the same time—sometimes it may be just in English, other times it may be a few words of English sprinkled amid German commentary. It depends on who signs up.

Bus Tours

If you'd rather ride than walk, consider a bus tour. Two companies offer a similar 2-hour tour for 34 CHF and leave from the bus lot behind the train station. **Best of Switzerland Tours** runs a "Best of Zürich City Tour," which includes a live guide who switches between German and English, and a short journey on a cogwheel train (April-Oct daily at 10:00, 13:00, and 15:30; Nov-March daily at 13:00; tel. 044-710-5050, www.switzerland-tours.ch). **Gray Line** offers a "Zürich Experience City Tour," which has larger groups and recorded headphone commentary (daily at 9:45, 12:00, and 14:00 year-round; tel. 044-383-7878, www.meiertours.ch).

ZÜRICH

Zürich Walk

If you're blitzing Zürich from the train station, this self-guided walk is a great way to connect the city center's main sights. It criss-crosses the river en route to the boat dock for a lazy lake-cruise finale (or a quick tram ride back to the station). Allow about an hour.

❶ Train Station

Step inside the main concourse of this major European hub. It handles 2,000 trains a day, including InterCity expresses to many major capitals. To keep up with Europe's ever-faster transportation expectations, the station's tracks have been tunneled deep underground so trains can zip through the city rather than being

hampered by an old-fashioned facility where tracks dead-end at the station. Built in 1870, its vast main hall was once lined with six tracks. Today, this hall is a community-events venue busy with concerts, exhibitions, and even "beach" volleyball—and a farmers market (Wed 10:00-20:00). The station sits above a modern, underground shopping mall (Mon-Fri until 21:00, Sat-Sun until 20:00).

Above you hangs the fat blue angel, Zürich's "Guardian Angel," protecting all travelers. The angel (sculpted by French-American artist Niki de St. Phalle) was placed here in 1997 to celebrate the 150th anniversary of the Swiss rail system. Crossing the street to the angel's right would bring you to the **Swiss National Museum** (Schweizerisches Nationalmuseum). It's the best museum in town, offering an essential introduction to Swiss history. Consider touring this museum before starting the walk (see listing, later).

• *Exit the station hall to the fat angel's left, following a passage leading to Bahnhofplatz (also well-signed).*

❷ Bahnhofplatz

Mile-long Bahnhofstrasse, stretching from the train station to the lake, is lined with all the big-name shops. Cross the street (watch for silent trams), but before heading down the street, stop on Bahnhofplatz and look back at the station.

The station facade is a huge triumphal **arch,** built in 1871 to symbolize the triumph of industry. In the Industrial Age, Zürich emerged as Switzerland's leading city. Sitting atop the arch and presiding over all this triumph is Helvetia, the personification of Switzerland (she's waving a Swiss flag). The Helvetii were the Celtic tribe that the Romans defeated in 58 B.C. to gain control of what is now Switzerland. Helvetia was adopted as a symbol of the Swiss confederation in 1848 (a Swiss version of France's Marianne), when the diverse cantons that banded together to create Switzerland needed some symbol of unity to transcend all their linguistic and regional differences. The same word was put to use in the Latin name for the new federal state *(Confoederatio Helvetica).* Today, this neutral name is used when there's a need to avoid favoring any of the country's four languages—thus the "CH" on Swiss license plates, in Web addresses, and in the abbreviation for the country's currency (CHF).

Helvetia is flanked by allegories of river travel (the goddess sitting on the boat) and rail travel (another goddess sitting on a train), reminding us that Zürich has long been a transportation hub. Zürich's river, the Limmat, starts from the lake and eventually flows into the Rhine and then (at Rotterdam) out to sea.

The statue in the foreground honors **Alfred Escher,** the Swiss politician who, in the mid-19th century, spearheaded the creation of the infrastructure—railways, universities, and banks—that allowed Switzerland to function efficiently within its mountains and connected this country with the rest of Europe. Without Escher, it's quite possible Switzerland would never have become such an economic powerhouse. Infrastructure!

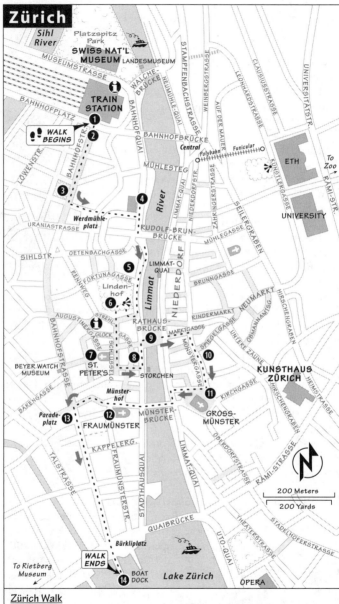

ZÜRICH

Zürich Walk

1. Train Station
2. Bahnhofplatz
3. Bahnhofstrasse to Pestalozzi Park
4. Police Department
5. Schipfe
6. Lindenhof
7. St. Peter's Church
8. Weinplatz & Roman Bath
9. Rathausbrücke
10. Conditorei Schober
11. Grossmünster
12. Fraumünster
13. Paradeplatz
14. Lake Zürich

• *Start strolling down Bahnhofstrasse. In two blocks (on the right), you'll see a park.*

❸ Bahnhofstrasse to Pestalozzi Park

Bahnhofstrasse was built in the 1860s when the newfangled train station needed a suitable approach road. Long before there was a train station, this would have been the moat

lining the town's 13th-century fortifications. Today, you can stroll the entire lane from here to the lakefront, lined with department stores, elegant shops, and banks. This city is all about the service industry: banking, insurance, conferences, and education (it's home to several important universities).

The only park along this pedestrian- and tram-only boulevard is dedicated to a famous Swiss educational reformer, Johann Heinrich Pestalozzi (1746-1827). He promoted the then-radical notions that good education should focus on the whole child (not just on specific skills) and should be available to everyone (not only the sons of rich families).

Parks like this are rare in central Zürich because of sky-high property values—Swiss real estate is among the most expensive in the world. In the park's far corner gurgles a green, Parisian-style **fountain.** Hundreds of fun and fresh fountains are sprinkled around town, spouting water that's as good as bottled mineral water (the city regularly checks its quality). This is a blessing in a town where restaurants charge for a glass of tap water. Tourist brochures brag that Zürich is Europe's most "fountainous" city.

• *From the green fountain, cross the street and head two blocks down Werdmühlestrasse. Then follow white* Stadtpolizei *signs up and around to the river side of the grand building facing the water, Zürich's...*

❹ Police Department (Stadtpolizei)

Enter the big police building at Bahnhofquai 3 for a peek at a fine example of Swiss Art Nouveau, called *Jugendstil* in German (free,

open daily 9:00-11:00 & 14:00-16:00). The Swiss artist Augusto Giacometti painted the arched vaults of the building's entry hall in the 1920s. Awash in vibrant orange and red, with flowery motifs, the "Hall of Flowers" reflects the relief and joy the artist felt when World War I ended.

Switzerland's Clear-Headed Drug Policy

Like many of its neighbors, Switzerland has a progressive drug policy that aims to reduce the overall harm to its society, rather than focus on punishing users. Even by European stan-

dards, the country's approaches to soft and hard drugs are unusually pragmatic.

Switzerland's policy has swung harder and softer in recent years. When polls showed that more than 30 percent of Swiss people had used marijuana, the parliament decided to decriminalize the drug, rather than criminalize a third of its population. But, while not want-

ing to clog its prisons with petty pot smokers, the country doesn't want to be known as another Holland, either. So the laws, which vary between cantons, remain a bit ambiguous: The Swiss can possess and use pot, but they can't sell it. Each spring, there's a push for stricter control. Word gets out that Switzerland is no haven for pot, and then things ease up. Now medical marijuana shops can legally sell very weak strains of marijuana that contain less than 1 percent THC. Smoking this gets you relaxed but not high.

Unlike marijuana, hard drugs remain absolutely illegal. Still, Swiss laws treat addicts as people needing medical help, rather than as criminals. Even in classy Zürich, you can see evidence of this policy. For instance, across the river from the station, on the far side of the Walche-Brücke bridge, there's a big, nondescript vending machine bolted to the railing selling safe, government-subsidized syringes to heroin junkies. Go ahead, buy a box—it's about the cheapest souvenir you can purchase in Zürich.

(Augusto's nephew, Alberto, is the more famous Giacometti, well-known for his tall, skinny statues.)

• *From the door of the police building, head to the right, upstream along the river. (Notice the towering old observatory off to your right.) Ahead of you, the inviting* **Schweizer Heimatwerk** *shop shows off Swiss folk crafts. It originated long ago as a place for farmers and mountain folk to showcase and retail the handiwork that the boredom of their long winters inspired. From there, go down the stairs and continue walking upstream. You'll pass curious and arty little shops and come to a delightful riverside square. (High above you on the right is a viewpoint on a bluff. That's Lindenhof, where we're heading.)*

❺ Schipfe

Back when the city's trade depended on river traffic, this small street was Zürich's harbor. Today it retains its old river-merchant ambience. You'll pass a fun waterfront eatery (the recommended Restaurant Schipfe 16) and an arcade.

• *Follow the river down along the arcade. Twenty yards before the ugliest bridge in Switzerland, head right, away from the river, and up the stairs. Keep going uphill, eventually reaching Pfalzgasse, which leads steeply to a park with fine views.*

❻ Lindenhof

Important forts and strategic buildings stood on this bluff from Roman times through the ninth-century Carolingian era. The statue commemorates the local women who cleverly defended the town in 1292. Their men were engaged in another battle when the Habsburgs encircled the city. The women put on armor and made like a big, rowdy army, tricking the Habsburgs into thinking the whole city was prepared to attack.

In the early 13th century, Zürich became a free city of the Holy Roman Empire, meaning it was relatively autonomous and self-ruling. The townspeople destroyed the fort here and established a law forbidding any new construction. The citizens realized that whoever lived on this hill would control the city—and they didn't want any more such rulers. Today, this is a people's square, where locals relax under linden trees (for which the square is named) and enjoy the commanding city view.

Look out and survey Zürich. The **university** (behind the green spire) is the largest in Switzerland, with 25,000 students. Left of that is Zürich's renowned **technical college,** the ETH (Eidgenössische Technische Hochschule—the Federal Institute of Technology), with 15,000 students. The ETH has graduated 25 Nobel Prize winners, including Albert Einstein and Wilhelm Röntgen (who discovered X-rays). The ETH terrace offers a great city viewpoint (which you can visit later by riding the little Polybahn funicular). Lining the opposite side of the river, the **Niederdorf** is a lively district of restaurants, cafés, and bars. On a clear day, you can see the Alps beyond the twin domes of the Grossmünster.

• *Descend the stairs at the back corner of the park, just beyond where you entered, to a little square with a fountain. Ahead, down Glockengasse, is a restaurant called The Golden Bell. Walk around it down a lane (Robert-Walser-Gasse) on the left. You'll pass a characteristic eatery, Reblaube Gaststube, made famous by visits from Goethe in 1779. He'd meet here for long, wine-fueled discussions with the minister of...*

❼ St. Peter's Church (St. Peterskirche)

Founded in the seventh century, this church—Zürich's oldest—

has one of Europe's largest clock faces (28 feet in diameter). The town watchman used to live above the clock. If he spotted a fire, he would ring the alarm and hang a flag out of the window facing the blaze. This system seems to have worked—Zürich never suffered a devastating fire.

• *Continue past the church on Schlüssel-gasse and take the first left, down the narrow Thermengasse ("Bath Lane"). Here we meet a bit of Roman Zürich. Glass cases on the wall contain artifacts, and under your feet are the excavations of a* **Roman bath,** *discovered by accident in 1984. You're standing over studs that elevated the floor, which was heated from below.*

The lane empties out on...

❽ Weinplatz

This pleasant spot was a wine market in centuries past (look for the happy grape picker on the fine little fountain). Note the dock here for the riverboat-bus (described later, under "Sights in Zürich"; this stop is called Storchen). The city's first bridge was built where the ❾ **Rathausbrücke** stands today.

• *Cross the bridge, passing the 17th-century, Renaissance-style Town Hall (which faces a fancy Neoclassical police station), and walk a block straight uphill along Marktgasse, which brings you into the bustling...*

▲▲Niederdorf

A district of colorful streets, fun shopping, restaurants, and nightlife, the Niederdorf neighborhood continues to the left along narrow Niederdorfstrasse, which was the leading commercial street before the old city wall was torn down to create Bahnhofstrasse. You can explore this area now...or, better yet, tonight (you'll find some dining suggestions later, under "Eating in Zürich").

Now, go in the opposite direction (right), heading up **Münstergasse.** Art enthusiasts know that, in 1916, the "anti-art" Dada movement was started at the Cabaret Voltaire (#26) by a group of rebellious young artists and writers. Although the Dada movement picked up steam, the cabaret itself lasted only until 1917: Complaints about excessive nightly noise forced its closure. At #19, pop into Schwarzenbach, a delightful specialty grocery store that's been operating here for more than 100 years. They still sell things the old-fashioned way (in loose bags, by weight). Inhale. Pick up 100 grams of dried bananas from Togo or whatever appeals. Across the street is Zürich's popular ❿ **Conditorei Schober,** a venerable chocolate shop that feels like a time warp, with a fine perch from which to enjoy a cup of coffee or hot chocolate. Across the lane to the left of it is a Swiss schnapps shop that many will find interesting.

• *Farther up Münstergasse is the...*

⑪ Grossmünster

Literally the "big cathedral," this is where Huldrych Zwingli—whose angry religious fervor made Martin Luther seem mellow—sparked the Reformation in German-speaking Switzerland. The domes of its towers (early examples of Neo-Gothic) are symbols of Zürich. They were rebuilt following a 1781 fire, and after much civic discussion, were left a plain stone color.

Cost and Hours: Church-free, daily 10:00-18:00, off-season until 17:00; tower climb-4 CHF, closes 1 hour earlier than church; cloister-free, Mon-Fri 10:00-17:00, closed Sat-Sun; pick up English story of the Swiss Reformation, www.grossmuenster.ch.

Visiting the Church: Step inside and sit down. Let the strength and purity of the 12th-century Romanesque architecture have its way with you. The simple round arches seem strong, and the pulpit—surrounded by none of the old Catholic ornamentation—gave you almost no alternative other than to be riveted by Zwingli's fiery sermons. Zwingli's reforms led to a clean sweep of Catholic decor in 1519.

In the front are three **choir windows** by Augusto Giacometti (c. 1933). Mary and the Baby Jesus (at her feet) meet two of the three kings bearing their gifts, while angels hover above with offerings of flowers. You can (prayerfully) walk to just below the windows for a closer look. While there, check out the 1531 Zürich Bible. (Like Luther, Zwingli was a fan of having the Bible available in the people's language—which is what got them in hot water with the Church.) In the dank **crypt** (stairs below altar), you'll see an original 15th-century statue of Charlemagne (a copy now fills its niche on the river side of the church exterior). For a sweeping city view, climb the 187 steps to the top of the **Karlsturm,** one of the church's twin towers.

Leaving the church, go right and into the corner, where a door leads to a fine Romanesque **cloister** ringed with fanciful 12th-century carvings. Upon entering, take 10 steps to the left and meet the sculptor (self-portrait on the highest arch).

• *Cross back over the river to the tall-steepled church with "1732" on the tower.*

⑫ Fraumünster

This ▲▲ church was founded along with a convent in 853, when Zürich was little more than a village. The current building, which

sits on the same footprint as its predecessor, dates from 1250. With the Reformation of Zwingli, the church was taken by the Zürich town council in 1524 and—you know the drill—gutted to fit Zwingli's taste. Today, it's famous for its windows by Marc Chagall.

Cost and Hours: 5 CHF, includes excellent audioguide; Mon-Sat 10:00-18:00, Sun 12:00-18:00, Nov-March until 17:00; occasional evening concerts, www.fraumuenster.ch.

Visiting the Church: The Fraumünster's claim to fame is a collection of 30-foot-tall stained-glass windows by Chagall (1887-1985), the Russian-born French artist. While there's more to see in the church, understandably, most visitors are here for the Chagall windows. The included audioguide explains the entire church—including the historic crypt with fine and well-described artifacts (stairs from near the altar). But most importantly, grab a seat in the front of the church with the five Chagall windows towering above you and enjoy the entire audioguide description.

In 1967, Zürich's art museum hosted a Chagall retrospective. It so impressed the Fraumünster's pastor that he offered the world-famous artist a commission. To his surprise, the 80-year-old Chagall accepted. He designed the windows to stand in the church's spacious choir zone behind the altar—a space where he intuitively felt his unique mix of religious themes could flourish.

For the next three years, Chagall threw his heart and soul into the project, making the sketches at his home on the French Riviera, then working in close collaboration with a glassmaking factory in Reims, France. After the colored panes were made, he outlined the figures in black, which were then baked into the glass. Chagall spent weeks in Zürich overseeing the installation, completed in 1970.

Chagall's inimitable painting style—deep colors, simple figures, and shard-like Cubism—is perfectly suited to the medium of stained glass. Blending Jewish and Christian traditions, he created a work that can make people of many faiths comfortable.

The five windows depict Bible scenes, culminating in the central image of the crucified Christ. From left to right, they are as follows:

The Prophets (red): The prophet Elisha (bottom) looks up to watch a horse-drawn chariot carry his mentor Elijah off to heaven. Farther up, Jeremiah (blue in color and mood) puts his hand to

Switzerland's Zwingli Reformation

Today's Evangelical Reformed Church of Switzerland was founded by Huldrych Zwingli (1484-1531), who preached in Zürich from
1519 through 1531. A follower of the humanist philosopher Erasmus
of Rotterdam, Zwingli believed that the Holy Scriptures should be
preached freely—in the people's language, rather than in Latin. In
1522, most of German-speaking Switzerland embraced Zwingli's
ideas...and that required leaving the Roman Catholic Church.

In 1517, when Zwingli was 33, German church reformer Martin
Luther posted his revolutionary *95 Theses* (which questioned the
practice of selling forgiveness, salvation, church offices, and so
on). Within two years, sellers of indulgences were refused entry
to Zürich. As the Reformation swept Switzerland, things heated
up. In 1523, rioters were storming churches, and authorities called
for an orderly removal of all images in Zürich houses of worship
(except stained-glass windows, which were destroyed).

The new, reformed Swiss church let priests marry. (Zwingli, like Luther, promptly took advantage of this freedom.) Fancy
Masses were replaced by simple services. At Zürich's main church,
the Grossmünster, preachers studied Latin, Greek, and Hebrew in
order to translate the Bible into the people's German. In 1531, the
Zwingli Bible, a complete translation into Swiss German, was published. It's still used today (like the King James Bible is in English).

Zwingli gave the Swiss church an unusual austerity: no altar,
no pictures, and for a while, not even any music. Church services focused on preaching. Holy Communion was celebrated only
on holidays. This puritanical simplicity permeated Swiss society
in general. Zwingli was no fan of the "separation of church and
state." Pushing for a theocracy, he established an ironclad city

his head and ponders the destruction of wicked Jerusalem. Up in
heaven (top), a multicolored, multifaceted God spins out his creation, sending fiery beams down to inspire his prophets on earth.
This window is artificially lit, as it's built into an interior wall.

Jacob (blue—Chagall's favorite color): Jacob (bottom, riding
a skateboard amid the deep blue) dreams of a ladder that snakes
up to heaven, with red-tinged angels ascending and descending,
symbolizing the connection between God above and Jacob's de-
scendants (the Children of Israel) below.

Christ (green): The middle, and biggest, window depicts the
central figure in God's plan of salvation—Jesus Christ, who, as
the Messiah, fulfills the promises of the Old Testament prophets.
Mother Mary suckles Baby Jesus (bottom) amid the leafy family
tree of Jesus' Old Testament roots. The central area is an indistinct
jumble of events from Christ's life, leading up to his Crucifixion.
The life-size ascendant Christ is crucified in a traditional medieval

law: The government's duty was to oversee public worship, and only preaching that was true to the Bible was to be tolerated.

But Zwingli's reforms were by no means universally supported. The Reformation was a messy process. The Protestant movement split over the proper role of baptism. Luther and Zwingli split over the Eucharist (is Christ's body really *in* the bread, or there only in a spiritual sense?). And, as old-school Catholics predicted, putting the Bible into the hands of regular people brought chaos—enabling every Tom, Dick, and Hans to "carve his own path to hell." Switzerland became embroiled in a religious civil war, as Protestant cantons fought Catholic ones. In 1531, while fighting as a "citizen soldier," Zwingli was killed in battle. His friend and partner Heinrich Bullinger succeeded him as the leader of German-speaking Swiss Protestantism.

Bullinger collaborated with John Calvin as Swiss Protestantism matured. The Protestant focus on preaching promoted the translation and interpretation of the Bible. Everyone was reading the Bible directly, which promoted literacy. The Reformation provided a basis for the autonomous community spirit, strong work ethic, and high literacy of a prosperous Switzerland for the future. The Swiss church became a place where equals would meet and worship God. As in other Protestant countries, Zwingli's heritage included transferring the notion of social charity from a church phenomenon to the responsibility of any self-respecting modern state. The foundations of Swiss democracy and its present social policies are rooted in Zwingli's teaching. And these Swiss reformers planted the seeds of what became the Presbyterian Church in the United States.

pose, but he's surrounded by a circle that seems to be bearing him, resurrected, to heaven. Chagall signed and dated the work (1970).

Zion (yellow): King David (bottom right) strums his harp and sings a psalm, while behind him stands his mistress Bathsheba, who gave birth to Solomon, the builder of Jerusalem's temple. At the end of history, an angel (top) blows a ram's horn, announcing the establishment of a glorious New Jerusalem, which descends (center), featuring rust-colored, yellow, and green walls, domes, and towers.

The Law (blue): Moses, with horns of light and the Ten Commandments (top), looks sternly down on law-breaking warriors on horseback wreaking havoc. At the bottom, an angel (in red) embraces the prophet Isaiah (very bottom) and inspires him to foretell the coming of the messiah (in red, above the angel).

Everyone comes away with a different interpretation of this complex work, which combines images from throughout the Bible. Some feel that the tall, skinny windows seem to emphasize the vertical connection between heaven above and earth below, both bathed in the same colored light. Some think Chagall used colors symbolically: Blue and green represent the earth; red and yellow, heavenly radiance. But all recognize that the jumble of images—evoking the complexity of God's universe—reaches its Point Omega in the central window, celebrating the idea of salvation through Christ's Crucifixion.

• *From the church, veer left into the square (away from the river). This is the Münsterhof, the original courtyard of a fortified convent that was made into a traffic-free public space in 2016. Head toward the blue building (Restaurant Zunfthaus zur Waag, once the wool and linen weavers' guild). Follow the small lane to its left, passing (or walking through) the recommended Zeughauskeller restaurant (500 years ago the city armory, it has a weapons theme for its decoration today—including what they call an "authentic replica" of William Tell's crossbow). As you round the corner you'll hit busy...*

⑬ Paradeplatz

Survey the scene, a triumph of urban planning and people-friendly vision: The train station is a 10-minute walk to your right up Bahnhofstrasse, and the lake is a few minutes to your left, down the classiest stretch of Bahnhofstrasse. On the square is **Sprüngli,** Zürich's top café for the past century. Its "Luxemburgerli" *macarons*—little

cream-filled, one-inch *macaron*-meringue treats—are a local favorite (you can buy just a couple; if you buy 100 grams, you'll get a selection of 12). Sprüngli also sells elegant sandwich lunches, either in its café (upstairs/outside) or to go (perfect for a lakeside snack). Across the square is Credit Suisse, with a luxurious ground floor full of fancy shops. If you like, detour a block back up Bahnhofstrasse to #31 and visit the fine little **Beyer Clock and Watch Museum,** in the basement of the elegant Beyer watch shop (8 CHF, ZürichCARD valid but not Swiss Travel Pass, Mon-Fri 14:00-18:00, closed Sat-Sun).

• *Turning left, follow Bahnhofstrasse past a few more elegant shops and mighty banks to the boats and riverside terrace at Bürkliplatz. We'll finish this walk at...*

⑭ Lake Zürich (Zürichsee)

Lake Zürich is 17 miles long, 2.5 miles wide, and—because it's relatively shallow—warm enough for swimming in the summer. From here, you can enjoy the lakeside promenade (a fine strolling path stretching 3 miles in either direction; left is sunnier and more interesting) or a short cruise. To go back to the station, catch tram #11 (from the inland side, across the street) or the Limmat riverboat. Both cruise and riverboat options are described next.

Sights in Zürich

Cruises on Limmat River and Lake Zürich

A boat ride down the Limmat River or on Lake Zürich is a nice addition to your visit. Small riverboat-buses take commuters and joy-riding visitors up and down the river and to points nearby on the lake. Big, romantic ships take tourists on longer rides around Lake Zürich. All boats are run by ZSG and do not include commentary (tel. 044-487-1333, www.zsg.ch).

Riverboat-Buses: These low-to-the-water boats (designed to squeeze under the bridges) start where the Swiss National Museum and the Platzspitz Park meet on the banks of the Limmat River. On their one-hour trip, boats make several stops down the river to Bürkliplatz (pier #6), and then do a quick loop around the lake before returning to their starting point. They can be handy for connecting the museum and the lake (9.40 CHF; can buy ticket on boat in cash but best to purchase ahead of time; covered by 24-hour day pass and ZürichCARD with 5-CHF surcharge; April-mid-Oct daily 2/hour, more during peak season; first boat generally at 13:00 Mon-Fri, 10:00 Sat-Sun; last boat generally at 21:00).

Big Lake-Only Excursion Boats: These start at Bürkliplatz and go farther down the lake. The basic 1.5-hour "short round trip" goes as far as Erlenbach (8.80 CHF, covered by 24-hour day pass and ZürichCARD with 5-CHF surcharge; April-Oct daily 2/hour 9:10-19:40, fewer off-season, buy tickets near pier #3, boats depart from pier #1-#6). They also offer longer trips and jazz and dinner cruises.

The Big Lake Zürich Ride: A good and scenic half-day excursion is to ride the boat all the way to Rapperswil (at the far end of Lake Zürich), enjoy that town for lunch, and then catch the train back to Zürich. Get details at the TI.

Tips for Swiss Travel or Eurail Pass holders: Regular departures are free with a Swiss Travel Pass and half-price with a Eurail pass; however, all ticket holders pay a 5-CHF surcharge for boat excursions. Doing the lake cruise on the day you arrive or depart—when you're already using a flexi-day for your train transportation—can be a smart plan.

▲▲Swiss National Museum (Schweizerisches Nationalmuseum)

By the late 19th century, it was clear that the world was changing, and the Swiss wanted to protect their unique heritage. A national competition was held, Zürich won, and it created the country's national museum. Located in a Neo-Gothic castle, this massive and interesting museum (sometimes called Landesmuseum, its original name) provides a solid background on Swiss history and identity. If Zürich is your first stop in Switzerland, visiting here for a primer on all things Swiss can help put the rest of your trip in context. Even if you're not staying the night in Zürich, the museum (just across the street from the train station) can be a worthwhile rainy-day excursion from other cities (especially if you have a train pass) or a quick stop while passing through.

Cost and Hours: 10 CHF, covered by Swiss Travel Pass and ZürichCARD; Tue-Sun 10:00-17:00, Thu until 19:00, closed Mon; audioguide-5 CHF, mandatory bag check in free lockers, Museumstrasse 2, café in courtyard, tel. 044-218-6511, www.nationalmuseum.ch.

Visiting the Museum: The museum is well-designed and well-described in English. Review the floor plan you'll get with your ticket to understand the layout. Main exhibits are organized thematically.

The archaeology rooms make it clear there were people here long before William Tell. The history section takes you from Roman times, through the birthing pains of the Swiss nation, medieval weaponry, lots of church art, the Reformation, and right up to fascinating modern times—with exhibits on early tourism, women earning the vote (very late), Switzerland during World Wars I and II (including its controversial neutrality), and immigration through the ages (including today's challenges).

An exhibit chronicling Switzerland's economic development covers the early industrial age and the creation of its impressive infrastructure, and explains how this mountainous corner of Europe ended up with so much money (banking, year-round tourism, precision manufacturing, and neutrality).

There's a huge collection of folk costumes, animals of the Alps, and a fun look at Swiss icons, from chocolate to Swatch.

▲▲Kunsthaus Zürich

It's worth the tram/bus ride up here to see Switzerland's top collection of fine art. The renovated modern wings are great, but you'll find most of the gems in the historical rooms, with works by Swiss artists (Alberto Giacometti, Johann Heinrich Füssli, and Ferdinand Hodler), as well as international greats such as Munch, Picasso, Kokoschka, Beckmann, Corinth, Monet, and Chagall. More recent generations are also represented, with pieces by Rothko, Merz, Twombly, Beuys, Bacon, and Baselitz.

Cost and Hours: 16 CHF, includes audioguide, free on Wed, not covered by Swiss Travel Pass; Tue-Sun 10:00-18:00, Wed-Thu until 20:00, closed Mon; mandatory bag check downstairs—lockers require a 2-CHF coin; café; tram #3, #5, #8, or #9, or bus #31 to Kunsthaus stop, Heimplatz 1; tel. 044-253-8484, www.kunsthaus.ch.

Rietberg Museum

Filling historic villas set in a beautiful park, this museum houses art from Asia, Africa, the Americas, and the South Pacific.

Cost and Hours: 14 CHF, covered by Swiss Travel Pass; Tue-Sun 10:00-17:00, Wed until 20:00, closed Mon; audioguide-5 CHF, tram #7 from station (direction: Wollishofen) to Museum Rietberg stop, Villa Wesendonck, Gablerstrasse 15, tel. 044-415-3131, www.rietberg.ch.

Zürich Zoo

With 360 species, an impressive Madagascar rainforest hall, and a huge indoor exhibit, the city's zoo is a kid-friendly, fun place to see locals at play.

Cost and Hours: 26 CHF, daily 9:00-18:00, Nov-Feb until 17:00, tram #6 from Bahnhofstrasse in front of the station (direction: Zoo), ride to last stop, Zürichbergstrasse 221, tel. 044-254-2500, www.zoo.ch.

Uetliberg

For an interesting 1.5-hour excursion high above the city and lake, take the little red/orange S10 excursion train that climbs from the main train station to this little mountain peak (17.60 CHF four-zone *Tageskarte* covers your round-trip and gives you 24 hours of free transport around town, also covered by ZürichCARD; 2-3/hour, runs 6:30-24:00, 25 minutes, www.zvv.ch). From the Uetliberg station, it's a moderately steep, 10-minute climb up a paved pedestrian road to a hotel and a tall observation tower overlooking the city. The view is particularly striking at sunset.

Sleeping in Zürich

High season in Zürich is May, June, September, and October. In this business-oriented city, rooms tend to be cheaper on weekends and pricier during festivals and conventions (September can be particularly busy). Most hotels have "dynamic pricing," with rates closely tied to fluctuating demand. For the best deals, check hotel websites and book direct in advance.

Most of my listings are near the busy train station, ideal for those passing through or leaving on an early-morning train or plane. To avoid nighttime noise, ask for a room on a high floor.

NEAR THE TRAIN STATION

With this efficient neighborhood as your home base, you're a quick stroll away from the train station, Swiss National Museum, riverboat-bus dock, a huge underground mall of services and shops (under the station), and the Niederdorf restaurant and nightlife zone. From the station, exit through the front doors of the great hall and cross the river.

$$$$ Hotel Leoneck offers 80 traditional rooms with small bathrooms and a tasteful touch of Swiss kitsch. Consider booking a comfort room for a bit more space. The large lobby and its restaurant/bar are a nice place to relax (family rooms, some rooms with balconies, elevator, air-con, limited pay garage parking, Leonhardstrasse 1, tel. 044-254-2222, www.leoneck.ch, info@leoneck.ch). From the Walchebrücke bridge, it's a 12-minute uphill walk (faster if you take the many stairs), or take tram #10 from the station (direction: Flughafen Zürich) two stops to Haldenegg. You can also take tram #10 directly from the airport (30 minutes).

$$$ Hotel Bristol, well run by Martin Hämmerli and his staff, has 56 modern rooms that are handy to the train station. He loves our readers and gives a 12-percent discount when you book direct by email (RS%, pay laundry, elevator, fans, Stampfenbachstrasse 34, tel. 044-258-4444, www.hotelbristol.ch, info@hotelbristol.ch).

$$$ Hotel Arlette is stuck in a time warp, with 28 comfortable, no-frills rooms. The central location makes up for the sometimes gruff reception staff (elevator, air-con, Stampfenbachstrasse 26, tel. 044-252-0032, www.hotelarlette.ch, hotel@hotelarlette.ch, Schlotter family).

Behind the Train Station: Unlike the earlier listings, these sister hotels are on the same side of the river as the train station. **$$$$ Walhalla Hotel** has 48 modern rooms and mobile phones for guest use (fans, elevator, just behind train station—exit near track 17 to Limmatstrasse 5, tel. 044-446-5400, www.walhalla-hotel.ch, info@walhalla-hotel.ch). **$$$ Walhalla Guest House,** around the corner at Konradstrasse 13, rents 33 smaller, cheaper rooms, with tiny modular bathrooms and funky Route 66-themed decor (check-in and breakfast in main building, fans, elevator, www.walhalla-guesthouse.ch).

ZÜRICH

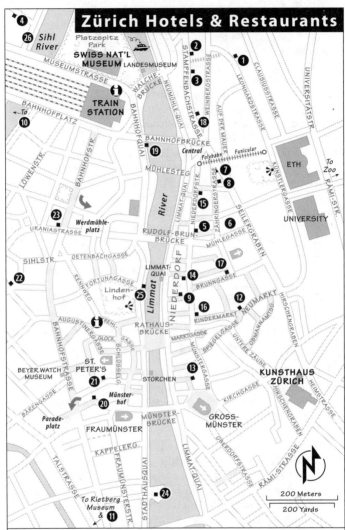

Zürich Hotels & Restaurants

Accommodations
1 Hotel Leoneck
2 Hotel Bristol
3 Hotel Arlette
4 Walhalla Hotel
5 Hotel Alexander
6 Alexander Guest House & Raclette Stube
7 Hotel du Théâtre
8 Hotel Marta
9 City Backpacker Hotel Biber
10 To Dakini's B&B & EasyHotel
11 To Youth Hostel

Eateries & Other
12 Wirtschaft Neumarkt
13 Rest. Mère Catherine
14 Rest. Swiss Chuchi
15 Rheinfelder Bierhalle & Johanniter
16 Raclette Factory
17 Café Zähringer
18 Commihalle Italian Restaurant
19 Supermarket
20 Zeughauskeller
21 Rest. zum Kropf
22 Hiltl Veggie Rest.
23 Manora Cafeteria
24 Rest. Bauschänzli
25 Rest. Schipfe 16
26 Bus Tours

NIEDERDORF DISTRICT

The atmospheric, cobblestoned old town of Zürich is only slightly farther from the station than the previous listings. During the day, it's busy with shoppers and workers on lunch breaks; at night, restaurants and clubs keep the pedestrian streets vibrant and noisy. From the train station, cross the Bahnhofbrücke bridge (to your right as you leave the main hall), go through the square called Central, and head to the right along Niederdorfstrasse.

$$$$ Hotel Alexander is a good 41-room business-class hotel in a busy central location offering a decent value, especially if you book well in advance (RS%, family rooms, air-con, elevator, Niederdorfstrasse 40, tel. 044-251-8203, www.hotel-alexander. ch, info@hotel-alexander.ch). They also run the **$$$ Alexander Guest House** a block away at Zähringerstrasse 16, housing 20 twin-bedded rooms with modern bathrooms and cheaper prices (breakfast extra, check in at Hotel Alexander, www.alexander-guesthouse.ch).

$$$$ Hotel du Théâtre occupies a renovated little trapezoid-shaped theater around the corner from Central square. The 50 thespian-themed rooms are dark but comfortable, with triple-paned windows that keep out most of the street noise (save money by skipping breakfast, a few rooms have air-con, elevator, Seilergraben 69, tel. 044-267-2670, www.byfassbind.com, info@hotel-du-theatre.ch).

$$$$ Hotel Marta, on a side street near Central square, is run by a nonprofit foundation that assists women with disabilities in finding employment. The 39 sparse yet modern rooms vary in size and quietness. The hotel's website describes them with unusual honesty and lets you choose (elevator, fans, Zähringerstrasse 36, tel. 044-269-9595, www.hotelmarta.ch, info@hotelmarta.ch).

¢ City Backpacker Hotel Biber, buried in the middle of the Niederdorf action three floors above a restaurant, offers the cheapest backpacker beds in the old center, with a cool, rough-at-the-edges ambience aimed at young travelers who don't mind climbing lots of narrow stairs. Families will feel more comfortable at the official hostel (private rooms, towels and sheets extra, no breakfast, lockers, kitchen, pay laundry, terrace, street noise at night, no curfew, reception open daily 8:00-12:00 & 15:00-22:00, 8-minute walk from station at Niederdorfstrasse 5, tel. 044-251-9015, www. city-backpacker.ch, sleep@city-backpacker.ch).

FARTHER FROM THE CENTER

You can sleep a little more cheaply if you're willing to compromise a bit on rooms and location. The first two listings are located in an area known for its bar scene.

$$ Dakini's B&B, run by well-traveled Susanne Seiler, rents eight creatively decorated rooms on three floors above a café in a lively urban neighborhood. Each floor has a shared bathroom and a kitchen (no elevator, Brauerstrasse 87, tel. 044-291-4220, mobile 078-661-8374, www.dakini.ch, sleep@dakini.ch). From the station, take bus #31 (direction: Schlieren Zentrum) to the Bäcker-anlage stop, then walk a half-block back along Feldstrasse and turn right on Brauerstrasse.

$ EasyHotel is a decent value in this pricey town, with 33 small, modern rooms located away from all the sights, a 15-minute walk from the station. There are several catches: It has four floors but no elevator (except for a luggage dumbwaiter); no common space aside from the basement computer room; most bathrooms are teeny, modular installations with opaque glass that might make the modest a bit uncomfortable; and rooms are cleaned after four nights (credit-card surcharge, no breakfast, Zwinglistrasse 14, tel. 043-322-0551, www.easyhotel.com, zuerich@easyhotelschweiz. ch). From the station: bus #31 (direction: Schlieren Zentrum) to Kanonengasse stop, walk a block down Kanonengasse with back to train station, then right on Zwinglistrasse to #14.

¢ Zürich Youth Hostel is big (290 beds), modern, and well-equipped with lots of services, and in a pleasant neighborhood near the lake that's easy to reach from the station. Its 30 rooms with private bath compete favorably with hotels (fair-trade breakfast, lunch or dinner extra, packed lunch, elevator, lockers, laundry, no curfew, pay parking, Mutschellenstrasse 114, tel. 043-399-7800, www.youthhostel.ch/zuerich, zuerich@youthhostel.ch). From the station, take tram #7 (direction: Wollishofen) to Morgental, then walk back 5 minutes along Mutschellenstrasse.

Eating in Zürich

While famously expensive and formal, Zürich has a good variety of places to eat memorably. And, if you know your options, you don't need to go broke to eat well. My recommendations range, including romantic and traditional Swiss places, cheesy raclette bars, beer halls and beer gardens (both sloppy and elegant), a nice French spot, a hippie café, and a famous, venerable vegetarian place. And they are within a 10-minute walk of each other. The Swiss love their cheese but are almost comically sensitive about it stinking up their clothing (they don't like the smell unless they're actually eating the cheese). It seems that restaurants either do cheese or don't do cheese. In the finer places, reservations can be wise. Read the entire list and then...*Guten Appetit!*

ZÜRICH

NIEDERDORF DISTRICT

Niederdorf is Zürich's dining district, and the traffic-free Niederdorfstrasse is its restaurant row. The countless eateries lining this main drag don't offer the best values, though the people-watching is hard to beat. Many of Zürich's venerable guild houses—no longer economic powers—are now convivial traditional restaurants. And, just a block or two away, you'll feel like you're far from the tourist crush and rubbing elbows with a smarter clientele.

$$$$ Wirtschaft Neumarkt, tucked away in the old town, is packed with in-the-know locals eating well under chestnut trees in their big "summer night dream garden." The creative, international menu uses healthy, organic ingredients. The interior is classic Swiss, and the garden creates a wonderful backyard feel. Alex enjoys greeting guests and being sure they get the most out of his menu (lunch specials, always a vegetarian plate, Mon-Sat 11:30-14:00 & 18:00-24:00, closed Sun, extensive wine list and good beer on tap, Neumarkt 5, tel. 044-252-7939, www.wirtschaft-neumarkt.ch).

$$$$ Restaurant Mère Catherine is a little oasis of Provençal elegance tucked away in the old town, popular for its south-of-France menu and good wines by the glass. Both the interior and its tiny courtyard are delightful and cozy (daily 11:30-22:15, Nägelihof 3, tel. 044-250-5940).

$$$ Restaurant Swiss Chuchi is a big and busy place along the main drag, popular with tourists and locals for their fun and wide selection of traditional cheese and meat fondues. The 30-CHF fondue and raclette is perfectly splittable if you order another dish or a salad (daily 11:30-24:00, indoor and outdoor seating, follow your nose to Rosengasse 10 on Hirschenplatz, tel. 044-266-9666, www.swiss-chuchi.ch).

$$$ Raclette Stube is the place to go if you want your clothes to smell like good Swiss cheese for days to come. In a bright, modern mountain chalet interior they do only the cheese specialties: raclette and fondue (nightly from 18:00, Zähringerstrasse 16, tel. 044-251-4130).

Budget Eating in the Niederdorf

$$ Rheinfelder Bierhalle is a cheap and sloppy beer hall with a cheap and sloppy clientele enjoying cheap and sloppy grub. The interior is characteristic, and there are plenty of tables on the pedestrian street that are perfect for enjoying the action (daily 9:00-24:00, Niederdorfstrasse 76, tel. 044-251-5464). **Johanniter,** next door, is another sloppy beer hall-type place that might deserve a look before you sit down in Rheinfelder.

$$ Raclette Factory, the IHOP of melted Swiss cheese, serves your choice on a variety of potatoes with the traditional onion and

ZÜRICH

pickle. The fun menu offers 9-CHF half-portions at a great savings. Their big, open windows ventilate the place, making it less cheesy inside. It's a fun perch, overlooking the action in the heart of the Niederdorf district (daily 11:00-22:00, Rindermarkt 1, tel. 044-261-0410).

$$$ Café Zähringer is an artsy, bohemian co-op with a passion for serving reasonably priced, healthy food. Linger in the stay-awhile interior, or enjoy the leafy seating with the older hippies out on the square (daily special served all day, always good veggie and vegan plates, breakfasts, organic produce, salads, also meat dishes and wok dishes, famously good coffee, kitchen open daily 11:30-15:00 & 17:30-23:00, Zähringerplatz 11, tel. 044-252-0500, www.zaehringer.ch).

NEAR THE TRAIN STATION

$$$ Commihalle Italian Restaurant, a fresh and modern place with dressy if plain decor that caters to locals, is near several recommended hotels. Part of a popular chain, their 40-CHF "Tavolata" special—ideal for big eaters—gets you an antipasto buffet, pasta dish, main meat dish, and dessert-buffet finale (available Tue-Sat 18:30-21:30). You can dine inside or out on a menu that offers plenty of pasta but no pizza, and always a good vegetarian option (daily 11:00-24:00, Stampfenbachstrasse 8, tel. 044-250-5960, www.commihalle.ch).

Supermarkets: A convenient, midsized, long-hours **Migros** supermarket is in the underground mall at the train station, near the Landesmuseum (Swiss National Museum) entrance/exit. Around the corner (also under the station) is the **Migros Takeaway,** which sells big portions of daily main dishes, packaged to go for about 10 CHF (both open daily until 22:00). A much larger **Co-op** supermarket is kitty-corner from the station by the Bahnhofbrücke bridge (Mon-Sat until 22:00, closed Sun).

ON OR JUST OFF BAHNHOFSTRASSE

$$$ Zeughauskeller fills an atmospheric 500-year-old armory with medieval battle gear (including an "authentic reproduction" of William Tell's crossbow) and the wonderful energy of happy eaters enjoying typical German-Swiss cuisine. Their fun, accessible menu offers big (splittable) portions, traditional dishes, and lots of soft meats. *Kalbsgeschnetzeltes*—diced veal with mushrooms in cream sauce—is a local favorite and house specialty (served with *Rösti* for 37 CHF). While it has outdoor seating, the interior has all the character and stays cool even when it's hot. It's touristy yet fun, and you may find yourself sharing a table (weekday lunch specials, daily 11:30-23:00, plenty of beer and wine, kid-friendly, near Paradeplatz at Bahnhofstrasse 28, tel. 044-220-1515, www. zeughauskeller.ch).

$$$ Restaurant zum Kropf serves traditional Zürich cuisine in a grand and dressy beer hall with a sophisticated yet cozy atmosphere (Mon-Sat 11:30-23:00, closed summer weekends and first half of Aug, tel. 044-221-1805, next to Zeughauskeller at In Gassen 16).

$$$ Hiltl Vegetarian Restaurant is a popular treat for vegetarians. In 1898, Ambrosius Hiltl was fighting rheumatoid arthritis. His doctor said, "No more meat," so Ambrosius established what may have been Europe's first vegetarian restaurant. Over a century later, it's still in the family and a Zürich institution. The vast and appetizing buffet is what people come for. Choose your seating section from three zones: regular self-service (plain tables); self-service in the bar area (your food will be weighed at a 10 percent discount); and fancier dining with table service. Food is sold by weight and can add up quickly—generally running 25-30 CHF per plate. For self-service, find the cashier to get weighed and pay. For table service, weigh your food and present your ticket to waitstaff. Tap water is free. The à la carte menu comes with delightful salads, curries, and fancy fruit juices. Hiltl's food is legendary for its freshness and lack of preservatives (buffet open daily 6:00-23:00, 2 blocks off Bahnhofstrasse where it kinks, Sihlstrasse 30, tel. 044-227-7000, www.hiltl.ch).

$$ Manora Cafeteria, on the fifth floor of the Manor department store on Bahnhofstrasse, is reliably good, fast, and always affordable. Choose from a fresh salad bar (big plate for 12.50 CHF) or a variety of main dishes. Take advantage of the free tap water. They offer a fun 6-CHF breakfast buffet. A few outdoor tables have a nice rooftop view. As it can be crowded with locals, eat early or late (Mon-Sat 9:00-20:00, closed Sun, Bahnhofstrasse 75).

ALONG THE WEST BANK OF THE RIVER

$$ Restaurant Bauschänzli is a leisurely beer garden with a huge buffet line, lots of picnic-table seating, and a fine riverside setting. A block inland from the boat docks at Bürkliplatz, it fills a small island on the river. Its fun-loving and popular self-serve restaurant offers a great beer-garden experience—like a Munich *Biergarten* without the kraut—and it's reasonably priced. Help yourself to the salad bar (6.50 CHF for a small plate) and the beer and wine from big casks (grab the glass or carafe of your choice). A little vocabulary is helpful: *Bürl* is a roll; *Beilage* is a vegetable side dish; *Penache* is a Radler (beer with lemonade). It's open from mid-April through mid-September in good weather only (daily 11:00-23:00, Stadthausquai 2, tel. 044-212-4919, www.bauschaenzli.ch). Live music (daily 15:00-17:00 & 19:00-22:30) has people up and dancing and gives it a Lawrence Welk-party feel. For a little peace, grab a table at the quieter tip of the island. The small restaurant section, off to the side, is more expensive. (While it tries to be elegant, the sloppy and noisy beer-garden fun splashes over the little fence.)

$$$ **Restaurant Schipfe 16,** gorgeously and peacefully situated on the river with an old-town view, is part of a city-run organization providing work for hard-to-employ people. It was originally a soup kitchen, but the location was just too charming to stay that way, so it was turned into a restaurant open to everyone. Don't expect polished service; instead, feel good that you're contributing to a worthy cause and enjoying healthy and decent food at a great price. The menu is small—always with a fish, meat, and veggie dish. The best seats are right along the river (two-course daily specials, Mon-Sat 10:00-22:00, closed Sun, Schipfe 16, tel. 044-211-2122, www.stadt-zuerich.ch/schipfe, reservations smart).

Zürich Connections

BY TRAIN
From Zürich by Train to: Luzern (2/hour, 45 minutes, more with transfer), **Interlaken** (2/hour, 2 hours, transfer in Bern, but 3-hour trip with transfer in Luzern is more scenic), **Bern** (2/hour, 1 hour, more with transfers), **Murten** (2/hour, 2 hours, change in Bern or Neuchâtel), **Appenzell** (2/hour, 2 hours, change in Gossau), **Lausanne** (hourly direct, 2 hours, more with change in Bern), **Zermatt** (hourly, 3.5 hours, change in Visp), **Chur** (2-3/hour, 1.5 hours), **Lugano** (1-2/hour, 2 hours), **Berlin** (hourly, 8 hours, 1 transfer; one direct overnight option, 10 hours), **Munich** (3/day direct, 4 hours; or go by bus from Sihlqual bus terminal, 3/day, 4 hours, reserve through train system), **Frankfurt** (every 2 hours, 4 hours, more with change in Basel), **Vienna** (4/day direct, 8 hours; 1 night train, 10 hours), **Paris** (5/day direct, 4 hours, more with transfers). Train info: Toll tel. 0900-300-300, www.sbb.ch.

BY PLANE
Smooth, compact, and user-friendly, **Zürich Airport** (airport code: ZRH) has three levels and is an eye-opening introduction to Swiss efficiency. On the ground floor are the baggage claim and the train station (with train info and a ticket desk). The main level has a top-end food court, Migros and Co-op supermarkets, fancy souvenir shops, a post office, mobile-phone shops, banks, ATMs, and lockers. The upper level has departures, TI, and lockers. Eateries and ATMs are plentiful before and after the security checkpoint, and there's free Wi-Fi. For flight information, visit www.zürich-airport.com (avoid calling their expensive information number). (avoid calling their expensive information number).

If you're leaving Switzerland by air with **tax-free purchases** in your checked luggage, let the staff know at check-in and you'll be directed (with your bag) to a customs office that will certify your purchases and put your bags on the belt. If you have tax-free goods in your hand luggage, you'll visit a different customs office located inside security.

Getting Between the Airport and Downtown: From the station underneath the airport, trains whisk you to **downtown Zürich** in about 10 minutes (6.80 CHF for three-zone single ticket, 13.60 CHF for three-zone 24-hour day pass, leaves every 10 minutes 5:00-24:00). You can also ride tram #10 into town (takes longer, same ticket as the train). Your ticket into Zürich is also good for one hour on all city public transportation. Either option is much cheaper than the 60-CHF taxi ride.

Sleeping at the Airport: Since most of my recommended accommodations are near the station, and the train connection to the airport is so fast and frequent, there's little reason to sleep at the airport. But if you really want to stay close to the airport, choose a hotel within a few miles that has a free shuttle service, such as the **Ibis Zürich Messe-Airport** or the **Best Western in Glattbrugg.**

Zürich Airport Connections: From the airport you can take the train to **Luzern** (hourly, 1 hour, more with change at Zürich main station), **Interlaken** (2/hour, 2.5 hours, change in Bern and sometimes Spiez), **Bern** (2/hour, 75 minutes), **Murten** (hourly, 2 hours, change in Bern or Neuchâtel), **Appenzell** (2/hour, 2 hours, change in Gossau), **Lausanne** (2/hour, 2.5 hours), **Zermatt** (hourly, 3.5 hours, change in Visp), **Chur** (2/hour, 2 hours, change at Zürich main station), **Lugano** (2/hour, 2.5 hours, change at Zürich main station and sometimes Arth-Goldau), **Munich** (4/day direct, 4 hours, more with transfers).

ZÜRICH

LUZERN & CENTRAL SWITZERLAND

Luzern has long been Switzerland's tourism capital. Situated on the edge of a lake, with a striking alpine panorama as a backdrop, Luzern was a regular stop on the Grand Tour route of Europe during the Romantic era, entertaining visitors such as Mark Twain, Goethe, and Queen Victoria. And with a charming old town, a pair of picture-perfect wooden bridges, a gaggle of fine museums, and its famous weeping lion, there's still enough in Luzern to earn it a place on any Swiss itinerary. Luzern also makes a fine home base for exploring the surrounding region, known as Central Switzerland (Zentralschweiz).

PLANNING YOUR TIME

Luzern is worth at least a full day and two nights. Fun excursions within easy reach of Luzern include boating on Lake Luzern, riding cog railways to mountain summits—the world's steepest, up Mount Pilatus, and Europe's oldest, up Mount Rigi—and exploring Swiss military history at Fortress Fürigen.

Luzern

Luzern (loot-SAIRN, "Lucerne" in English) is a charming midsize city with about 80,000 residents (and a metropolitan area sprawling to more than 200,000). The town grew up around a monastery and is said to have been founded here because an angel shone a heavenly spotlight on the site (the name "Luzern" is derived from *lucerna*, Latin for "lamp").

Luzern sits where the Reuss ("royce") River flows out of Lake Luzern. Its English name is Lake Lucerne, but German-speaking Swiss call it the Vierwaldstättersee—"Lake of Four Forest States," since it lies at the intersection of four of Switzerland's cantons (political units similar to US states).

South of the river is the train station and the bustling new town (Neustadt), and north of the river is the quaint, traffic-free old town (Altstadt). The river is spanned by a series of pedestrian bridges, including two classic wooden ones: the Chapel Bridge, with its famous stone water tower, and the Mill Bridge. Museums, restaurants, and hotels are scattered on both sides of the river.

To get the most out of a full day in Luzern, begin with the TI's two-hour walking tour, or follow the self-guided walk in this chapter. Then hit the museums that interest you most: Art buffs flock to the Rosengart Collection for its Picasso exhibit; historians will enjoy the Depot History Museum; and gearheads will have a ball at the Swiss Transport Museum. In the early evening, take a peaceful boat trip on Lake Luzern, then wander the town's scenic bridges at sunset.

Orientation to Luzern

TOURIST INFORMATION

Luzern's helpful, modern TI is right inside the train station (Mon-Fri 8:30-19:00, Sat 9:00-19:00, Sun 9:00-17:00; shorter hours in off-season; Zentralstrasse 5, tel. 041-227-1717, www.luzern.com). Pick up the free, informative *City Guide.* The TI provides a free room-booking service (with some great last-minute deals), offers free use of its public computer and Wi-Fi, and sells the Swiss Travel Pass, public transport tickets, and tickets to activities around town, such as boat trips.

Sightseeing Passes: The **Swiss Travel Pass** covers most of Luzern's attractions. If you don't have the pass, consider the **Lucerne Museum Card,** sold only at the TI, which gives you entry into all of Luzern's museums over a two-day period (36 CHF); it pays for itself if you visit the Swiss Transport Museum and one other museum. When you check into your hotel, you should receive a free **Visitors Card** *(Gästekarte),* probably affixed to a copy of the *City Guide* brochure. The card gives 10-20 percent discounts at most of Luzern's sights and activities. You should also receive a **Mobility Ticket** *(Passepartout),* which gives you free public transportation by bus and train in the city center (zone 10).

ARRIVAL IN LUZERN

Luzern's waterfront **train station** is user-friendly. The TI is along track 3, as are pay lockers. The SBB ticket counters are upstairs—

take the escalator by track 10 (Mon-Fri 6:40-21:00, Sat-Sun until 20:00; international-travel windows close two hours earlier). Most other important services are downstairs in an underground shopping mall called RailCity. There you'll find pricey WCs (including showers), ATMs, a convenient self-service cafeteria, a Co-op grocery store, and other shops and restaurants. These can be particularly convenient on Sundays when many shops are closed.

Luzern's **lake boats** dock directly in front of the train station. Between the boat docks and the station entrance are platforms for Luzern's city buses, which fan out in every direction from the station.

HELPFUL HINTS

Medical Help: Permanence is a welcoming drop-in medical clinic located downstairs in the train station (daily 7:00-23:00, tel. 041-211-1444, www.permanence.ch).

Festivals: The **Lucerne Festival** draws classical musicians and fans each year from mid-August to mid-September (www.lucernefestival.ch).

Markets: On Tuesdays and Saturdays a farmers market borders both sides of the river near the main bridge (7:00-12:00). On Saturdays from May through October, a flea market stretches along the river from the Jesuit Church to the Mill Bridge, and on the first Saturday of the month, craft stalls set up on Weinmarkt in the old town.

Wi-Fi: The area around the train station and riverfront has free Wi-Fi provided by the local power company (EWL); connect to the "luzern.wlan" network, open your browser, click on "Verbinden," select English, and enter your mobile phone number to get a 4-digit PIN via text message.

Laundry: Take your dirty laundry to **Jet Wasch,** a 10-minute walk from the train station (full service only; Mon-Fri 8:00-12:00 & 14:00-18:00, Sat 9:00-16:00, closed Sun, Bruchstrasse 28, tel. 041-240-0151, www.jetwasch.ch). They will pick up or deliver to your hotel for an extra fee.

Bike Rental: You can rent bikes at the train station and enjoy Luzern's delightful lakeside cycling paths (27 CHF/half-day, 35 CHF/day, 5 CHF less with Eurail pass or Swiss Travel Pass; at SBB ticket office upstairs in station—signage gives no indication they have bikes, but they do; ask for maps with possible routes; www.sbb.ch/mobilitaet).

Parking: The best downtown parking garage is **Parkhaus Kesselturm** at Burgerstrasse 20 (25 CHF/day if you prepay, choose "season ticket" on payment machines, tel. 041-240-3255, www.parking-luzern.ch). Avoid the train-station garages, which cost 50 CHF/day.

Luzern and Central Switzerland at a Glance

▲▲**Luzern** Pretty, pristine lakeside city boasting excellent museums, painted bridges, and a handful of historic sights. See page 49.

▲▲**Lake Luzern** Oddly shaped lake at the very heart of Switzerland, traversed by vintage steamships and surrounded by steep hillsides, gravity-defying villages, and snowy peaks. See page 75.

▲**Mount Pilatus** Craggy mountain hunkering south of Luzern, with sublime views, luge ride, ropes course, and a range of hiking options. See page 76.

▲**Mount Rigi** Long ridge across the lake from (and east of) Luzern, famous for its sunrise vistas and Europe's first cogwheel train. See page 81.

▲**Fortress Fürigen** Underground bunker southeast of Luzern giving you a peek at Switzerland's hidden defense system. See page 84.

Cinema: In Switzerland, movies are shown in their original language with subtitles. The Bourbaki Panorama building has several screens (www.kinoluzern.ch).

Water Fountains: Luzern is proud of its clean drinking water and its more than 200 public fountains—each with a fun design—that spout potable water. In the summer, make like the locals, who take full advantage of these fountains, refilling their water bottles again and again.

GETTING AROUND LUZERN

Except for the Swiss Transport Museum, all of the Luzern sights, hotels, and restaurants recommended in this chapter are within walking distance of the station. However, buses can be handy time-savers. The TI's free city map and *City Guide* brochure both include a map of bus routes and onboard displays to help you navigate.

For getting around town, you'll need either a *short-distance* ticket (2.50 CHF; check listed stops to make sure yours is covered) or a single one-hour ticket (4.10 CHF). A 24-hour day pass (8.20 CHF) is a good investment if you're spending a full day in Luzern. If you're spending the night, save your money: You'll receive a **Mobility Ticket** *(Passepartout)* upon check-in at your hotel, which entitles you to free use of buses and trains in the city center (zone 10) throughout your stay.

Most destinations in this chapter (except a portion of the trip from Luzern to Alpnachstad, on the way to Mount Pilatus) are in the central zone (zone 10); trips outside this zone cost more. You can buy tickets from the touchscreen machines at stops or ask at the TI, where the helpful staff can help you make the best choice. All public transit in Luzern is covered by the Swiss Travel Pass. Transit info: www.vbl.ch.

Tours in Luzern

Walking Tour
A two-hour English-only tour is offered every morning in summer. It covers the same route as my "Reuss River Stroll," later, but with more stories (18 CHF, departs from TI at 9:45, daily May-Oct).

Tourist Train
This tacky little train does a 40-minute circuit of the city's sights, departing from Hotel Schweizerhof Luzern (12 CHF, kids-5 CHF, buy tickets from driver, headphone commentary; April-Oct daily, runs June-Aug hourly 11:00-19:00, less frequent in spring and fall; closed Nov-March; tel. 041-220-1100, www.citytrain.ch).

Boat Tour
The one-hour Scenic Panorama-Yacht Cruise, worth ▲, is a lazy, picturesque sightseeing loop with a well-done audio tour in English (25 CHF, 15 CHF with Eurail pass, half-price with Swiss Travel Pass, buy tickets as you board; daily June-mid-Sept, departs every 75 minutes from 10:15 to 19:00, fewer cruises mid-Sept-May; snack bar onboard and picnics welcome; departs from Pier 7 in front of the Hotel Schweizerhof Luzern, tel. 041-367-6767, www.lakelucerne.ch).

Local Guide
Ursula Korner is a good guide (180 CHF/2 hours, mobile 079-479-8261, ursula.korner@ko5ive.com). The TI has a list of other guides, who are likely to charge more.

Reuss River Stroll

This self-guided orientation stroll, worth ▲▲, gives you a brief overview of the town. You'll walk up along the Reuss River, across one of Luzern's famous wooden bridges, then back through the old town.

• *Begin at Bahnhofplatz, the busy zone between the lake and the train station. Stand in front of the big stone arch.*

❶ **Bahnhofplatz:** This is the transportation hub of Luzern—and all of Central Switzerland. From the area in front of the station, buses zip you anywhere in town.

Along the lakefront, you can catch a boat for a lazy cruise around Lake Luzern. And underneath you is the extensive RailCity shopping mall, honeycombed with pedestrian passageways leading to different parts of town. The big stone **arch** was the entrance of the venerable old train station—built in the late 19th century when (thanks to the advent of steam-powered trains) Switzerland became a top tourist spot, with Luzern as its main attraction. But it burned down in 1971 and was replaced with the modern station. Today, the arch hides vents for the huge underground parking lot below. This is a popular evening meeting spot for city teens (and street people). A visit to the free WCs here is a reminder why for some, a free toilet is a blessing... and for others it's not.

• *The huge modern building with the big overhanging roof (on your right, with your back to the station) is the...*

❷ **Culture and Convention Center (Kultur- und Kongresszentrum):** This building, finished in 1998 by Parisian architect Jean Nouvel, features a concert hall that hosts the Luzern Festival, one of Switzerland's biggest music events. It also holds the **Luzern Museum of Art** (Kunstmuseum Luzern; described later, under "Sights in Luzern").

Lake water is pumped up, through, and out of this building; if you were to wander around its far side, you'd see open channels that go right through the middle of the structure, as well as a big pond. The architect claims the design recalls earlier times, when this area was swampland...but it more likely recalls his own original plans for the building. Nouvel wanted to put the center out in the middle of the lake. When he was voted down by the people of Luzern, he decided to surround it with water anyway. The plaza under the roof (which reflects the lake and weather, further incorporating the building into the surrounding environment) is a busy community space popular for open-air concerts.

• *Now walk in the opposite direction from the conference center, across the busy street. Stroll Bahnhofstrasse along the river until you have a good view of Luzern's most famous landmark, the wooden...*

❸ **Chapel Bridge (Kapellbrücke):** Luzern began as a fishing village. By the 13th century, with traffic between northern and southern Europe streaming through the nearby Gotthard

Pass, Luzern became a bustling trading center. In the first half of the 14th century, this bridge was built at an angle as part of the town ramparts, designed to connect the town's medieval fortifications. The octagonal stone **Water Tower** (Wasserturm, pictured here) was built around 1300.

In the 17th century, the bridge was decorated with paintings depicting the development of the town, as well as its two patron saints. In 1993, a leisure boat moored under the bridge caught fire, and before long, Luzern's wooden landmark was in flames. (A plaque before the start of the bridge tells the story.) When you venture onto the bridge, you'll notice the wood is a lighter color—that is, newer—in the middle. Chapel Bridge was painstakingly rebuilt, but many of its famous paintings were lost. Those still remaining under the wooden roof at the ends of the bridge are restorations of the 17th-century originals; those in the middle were in storage during the fire and were therefore saved. Many burnt and charred paintings are still in their original spots. Boats are no longer allowed under the bridge, it's now strictly nonsmoking, and tiny security cameras are everywhere.

LUZERN

• *Wander out onto the bridge.*

Study the colorful **paintings** overhead. The coats of arms on the paintings tell you which aristocratic families sponsored them. Painting #1 features a legendary and formidable giant, an icon of Luzern you'll see all over town. This big boy dates back to the Middle Ages, when mammoth bones discovered locally were mistakenly identified as the bones of a 15-foot-tall human giant. Painting #2 shows an angel shining a divine light on the place where the town would be born, and where, in the eighth century, a monastery was founded. (The name Luzern means, roughly, "city of light.") Painting #3 shows Luzern circa 1400—see how the bridge was already part of the city fortifications. Painting #6 shows a bigger city, as it looked in 1630. Paintings #9 and #10 remain charred black—a reminder of the tragic fire. In the middle of the bridge (just after the shop), a painting features the town's patron saint, Mauritius (a plaque mid-bridge, near #48, tells why he matters to Luzern). The bridge was part of the city defense system, so the "window"

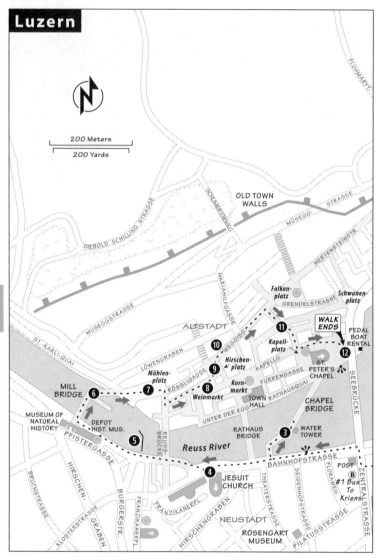

Luzern

openings facing the lake are smaller than those on the inland side, giving defenders more cover from lakeside attacks.

• *Return to the train-station end of the bridge, and continue down the river. Enter the big, white church.*

❹ **Jesuit Church (Jesuitenkirche):** This was the first major Baroque church in Switzerland, circa 1670 (free, Tue-Wed and Fri-Sun 6:30-18:30, Mon and Thu 9:30-18:30). It's dedicated to the great missionary Francis Xavier, a co-founder of the Jesuit order, who's shown on the facade baptizing Asians (depicted looking like

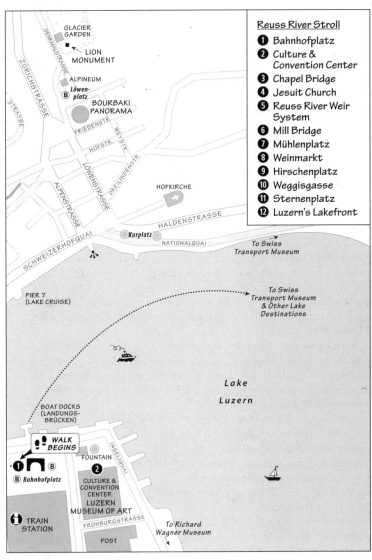

Native Americans). Luzern's music school uses the church's pipe organ for practice—if you're lucky, you may catch an impromptu concert.

Even though Luzern was a relatively small town back then, the pope wanted to establish a strong presence in Central Switzerland to empower the area's Catholics during the tense times following the Protestant Reformation. The interior of the church once dripped with Baroque stucco. It's been retouched in the lighter Rococo style (c. 1750). Rich as it looks, there's no real marble here—what you see on the altar, pulpit, and side-chapel altars is stucco made from ground-up marble laid smoothly and economically upon a wooden foundation.

The decorations on the ceiling celebrate the life (and afterlife) of Xavier. After the missionary dies, you see him heaven-bound (in the center). In an exuberant setting that includes both this church and Luzern's landmark Chapel Bridge, the pope's representative and the townsfolk gather to wish him Godspeed. Xavier's cart is pulled by an elephant, a leopard, and a camel, all commemorating his mission trips to the exotic Far East. Riding his chariot into heaven, he anticipates a hero's welcome.

In the second side chapel on the right, you can meet the only Swiss saint: Brother Klaus, a 15th-century hermit who lived in the nearby mountains. He was a great peacemaker between the cantons and is considered the original Swiss isolationist. Since Klaus' time, Switzerland has employed this ethic of avoiding pointless entanglement in foreign squabbles. The statue wears Klaus' original robe. His walking stick is in a case just over the altar.

• *Back outside, continue strolling downriver toward Luzern's other wooden bridge. You'll pass the recommended Opus wine bar/restaurant and iron pedestrian bridge (at the narrowest crossing spot, marking the location of Luzern's first bridge in the 12th century). Stop at the spiky fence partially damming up the river.*

❺ **Reuss River Weir System:** This big river flowing out of the lake may seem wild, but it's been tamed. Lake Luzern's main source of water is snowmelt, which trickles in from streams coming off the surrounding mountains. The water drains out of the lake here on its way to the Rhine. Luzern is responsible for controlling the flow of water and preventing the flooding of lakeside villages by maintaining the lake level. In the mid-19th cen-

tury, the city devised and built a simple yet ingenious extendable dam (*Nadelwehr,* "spiked weir"). When the water is highest (in the spring), they remove the wooden spikes to open the flow; as the summer wears on and the water level drops, they gradually broaden the dam (by extending the wooden pickets) to keep the flow steady. In the winter, they close the dam entirely to keep the lake level high enough for boats. It's a dangerous process—workers, tethered by the safety cable overhead, pull up the chain to hoist the metal skeleton of the platform on the riverbed.

• *Continuing down the river, you'll pass the Depot History Museum on your left (described later, under "Sights in Luzern") before coming to the wooden...*

❻ Mill Bridge (Spreuerbrücke): Unlike the rebuilt Chapel Bridge, this one's original—and the city is determined to keep it

that way (try to find the low-profile security cameras). Before you cross the bridge, pause to appreciate the first of the bridge's fine 17th-century paintings, which shows Luzern's favorite giant again, with the blue-and-white city and cantonal banners under the double eagle of the Holy Roman Empire—a reminder that the emperor granted free status to the city. The flip side shows Judgment Day, with some going to heaven and others to hell. As you cross the bridge, notice that each painting includes a kind of Grim Reaper skeleton—always very busy with the death thing. Townsfolk crossed the bridge daily, and these scenes provided vivid reminders that nobody, in any walk of life, can escape death (an especially poignant message in times of war and plague, when these were painted). Like the other wooden bridge, this bridge was part of the city fortification—its downstream defending wall is higher.

Midway across is a little 16th-century chapel, built to ensure divine protection against destruction by flood. A line of family crests on the door frame acknowledges the volunteers who, over the years, have kept the chapel decorated according to the season. Since 1987, this has been the work of Frau Segesser. While you're paused here, notice the serious woodwork of the bridge construction.

The far end of the bridge was designed to accommodate wagons delivering grain or whatever else was to be milled. Once upon a time, three mills churned here—this was the medieval industrial center of Luzern. The "Spreu" in the bridge's name means "chaff" (the sheath surrounding the wheat), which was separated from the wheat at the mill. You can see sketches of these mills as you leave the bridge (on the red wall on the left). A turbine that generated power in 1889 sits quiet on the left, but the tradition of harnessing water power continues here. Beneath you, underwater, is a modern hydroelectric plant that creates enough power for 1,000 households.

• *After crossing the bridge, turn right to find yourself in...*

❼ Mühlenplatz: This traffic-free square marks the entrance to the old town. Riverside benches make a good place for a picnic lunch or snack. On the square, at #11, the mural shows the city back when the water mills were hard at work.

• *At the top of the square (under the Swiss Marilyn Monroe), head right on Kramgasse, then take the first left onto Weinmarktgasse, which leads to...*

❽ Weinmarkt: In medieval Luzern, this square served as a marketplace for wine (as the name implies). Enjoy the fine wall paintings all around. At first glance, the big mural on the green building at the top of the square seems to depict the Last Supper, but it's actually the Wedding Feast at Cana, where Jesus turned water into wine. Across the square is a building with a secret message hiding in the strange zigzags on its modern shutters. Start at the top left and read: W-E-I-N-M-A-R-K-T. The soldiers on the fine 15th-century fountain are there to remind visitors that this town is tough and strong.

• *Leave the square on the far left side, then walk several yards to...*

❾ Hirschenplatz: History lingers long after things change—especially on this square. Its namesake, the Hirschen ("Deer") Hotel, is gone but its elaborate golden sign will always hang here. Across from that, guess who used to have a shop in the big green building? Yep—the jeweler. (See all the rings?) Notice the until-death-do-us-part ring at far left, and that high above, Cupid has shot his arrow. To the right of that building, a painting declares *"Goethe logierte hier 1779."* Goethe—the "German Shakespeare"—visited Luzern and stayed in a hotel on this corner. It was the city's top hotel at the time...I bet it was named the Golden Eagle. To the left of the jewelers, the grand facade on the Dornach House, from 1899, celebrates the 400-year anniversary of the last battle against the Habsburgs. Switzerland has enjoyed a durable understanding that there can be disagreements—but no wars—with its historically aggressive and militaristic neighbors.

Continue out of the square (opposite where you entered) onto the busy ❿ **Weggisgasse.** As you stroll, consider that every building in the old town—whether new or rebuilt—is required to offer residential apartments to prevent this historic zone from becoming only office space and touristy shops.

• *After two blocks, you'll come to the Manor department store, with the recommended, tasty, and convenient Manora self-service cafeteria on the top floor. (There are great, free city views from its rooftop terrace.) Turn right after Manor and walk one block and around the corner to...*

⓫ Sternenplatz: This tiny square is dominated by the colorful facade of the Restaurant Fritschi. The paintings feature characters and symbols from Luzern's annual Mardi Gras celebration—the city's biggest event, called Fasnacht here. Pictured near the top of the building are Mr. and Mrs. Fritschi—the cheerleaders of the festival, celebrating Fasnacht by wearing masks and throwing oranges. Flanking them are their trusty servants, a nanny and a jester. Below them is the story of Fasnacht: The cock calls at 5:00 in the morning the Thursday before Ash Wednesday (on the left), and the people get up to frighten winter away. Mr. and Mrs. Fritschi arrive on their wagon to kick off the festivities (on the right). Flying around the scene are oranges—traditionally tossed by the Fritschis to their adoring fans. Once rare here in winter, oranges are special to the festivities, as they mark the beginning of spring.

Continue down the street at the bottom of the square (Hans-Holbein-Gasse), and you'll come upon a colorful fountain with more Fasnacht fun. This is where the locals gather—often more than 10,000 strong—at five in the morning to kick off the biggest party of the year—six days long.

⓬ Luzern's Lakefront: Continue to the riverfront, walking around **St. Peter's Chapel,** the namesake of Chapel Bridge. You're back at the bridge, having made the full circle. Enjoy the classic Luzern view: the Chapel Bridge and Water Tower, with Mount Pilatus hovering in the background. *From here, cross over to the lakeside and stroll to the left...*

Any swans out? Residents say they originated as a gift from French King Louis XIV in appreciation for the protection he got from his Swiss guards. Today, local children (and tourists) make sure the swans get their daily bread.

The lakefront promenade was built in the mid-1800s when tourists were mostly aristocrats on the Grand Tour, and Luzern was one of the requisite stops. This part of the bay was filled in and fancy resort hotels went up—giving this city the nickname "Monte Carlo of Switzerland."

• *Your town walk is finished. From here you have several options: You can catch the one-hour lake cruise (from Pier 7, described earlier under "Tours in Luzern"). You can cross the street and peruse the ritzy Swiss watches at the flagship Bucherer store (selling envy since 1888). You can walk along the lake to the Swiss Transport Museum. Or you can cut inland to the Lion Monument.*

Sights in Luzern

If you'll be doing a lot of sightseeing here, review your options for saving money: Many Luzern sights are covered by the Swiss Travel Pass; the Lucerne Museum Card gives you free entry to all the museums listed here and quickly saves you money; your stamped Visitors Card (free from your hotel) gives you 10-20 percent discounts at many attractions—remember to ask when buying tickets.

MUSEUMS

Luzern is charming enough that simply strolling the streets and bridges and cruising the lake is enough for a happy day of sightseeing. But the city also offers some fine museums, especially if you're into modern art.

▲Rosengart Collection (Sammlung Rosengart)

In the 1930s and 1940s, wealthy resident Siegfried Rosengart palled around with all-star modern artists, financing and collecting their works. At an early age his daughter Angela took an interest in her father's work and eventually became his business partner. This museum displays the fruits of their labor. Angela, now in her 90s, visits the museum daily and still has an art gallery in town.

Cost and Hours: 18 CHF, covered by Swiss Travel Pass, daily April-Oct 10:00-18:00, Nov-March 11:00-17:00, mandatory bag check; well-written little 2.50-CHF English booklet—or borrow English info sheets when you buy your ticket; a few blocks from the train station in the new town up Pilatusstrasse at #10, tel. 041-220-1660, www.rosengart.ch.

Visiting the Museum: The building's three floors boast works from the big names of the late 19th and early 20th centuries, with an emphasis on the art of Pablo Picasso and Paul Klee. The ground and first floors feature an extensive **Picasso** collection focusing on his later works, including 32 paintings and some 100 drawings, watercolors, and graphic and sculptural works. Rosengart was Picasso's leading Swiss art dealer and helped him place a number of works in national and international museums.

On the upper floor are several dozen black-and-white candid photographs of Picasso (from a rotating collection of 200) by American David Douglas Duncan. This exhibit makes the museum a ▲▲▲ experience for Picasso fans. I've seen a pile of Picassos, but never have I gotten as personal with him as I did here. Duncan's intimate photos of the artist and his family capture the very human personality of this larger-than-life genius. The photos—taken in Picasso's later years, and many featuring his wife Jacqueline—provide insight into his artistic process, as well as his lifestyle, showing him at work and at play. The excellent English descriptions (borrow when you buy your ticket) are essential for getting the stories behind the photos.

The first floor also has some Impressionist and Modernist works by Braque, Monet, Renoir, Miró, Chagall, Cézanne, Matisse, Modigliani, and Pissarro, as well as a small room with a video about the museum (subtitled in English).

In the basement are 125 small works by **Paul Klee,** displayed chronologically by room number so you can follow the evolution of his career. Watch as Klee discovers colors and blossoms from a doodler and, at times, watercolor artist into a mature painter.

▲Depot History Museum (Depot Historisches Museum)

This cluttered old museum is a "depot" for the accumulated bric-a-brac of Luzern's past. It's housed in one of Luzern's oldest surviving buildings, which was long used to store military weapons and uniforms. Their collection is too big to display traditionally, so they've come up with an innovative and fun concept: Throw all of their archived stuff together and display it on three crowded floors. You'll wander through shelves of old weapons, stained-glass windows, sculptures, and old-fashioned tourism posters. Each shelf (sometimes each item) is labeled with a barcode—use your scanner (included with entry) on whichever one you're interested in. You can then read about its history in English on your handheld screen. Don't miss the modern and chilling guillotine on the ground floor—last used in 1940.

Cost and Hours: 10 CHF, covered by Swiss Travel Pass, Tue-Sun 10:00-17:00, closed Mon, Pfistergasse 24, tel. 041-228-5424, www.historischesmuseum.lu.ch.

▲Swiss Transport Museum (Verkehrshaus)

This "Swiss Smithsonian," across the lake from the train station, includes hundreds of exhibits in an enormous complex, covering virtually all modes of transportation. It's pricey and a little overwhelming, but overall, it's an amazing display of Swiss ingenuity and craftsmanship. If you're in town for only one day, skip this and enjoy the museums and ambience in the Old Town. But with a second day or younger kids in tow, or if you're  obsessed with trains, planes, and automobiles, this museum can provide endless hours of entertainment. Come early and spend the whole day.

Cost and Hours: 30 CHF, half-price with Swiss Travel Pass, daily April-Oct 10:00-18:00, Nov-March until 17:00, café,

Lidostrasse 5, tel. 041-370-4444, recorded info tel. 0848-852-020, www.verkehrshaus.ch.

Getting There: From downtown, it's a 30-minute **walk** to the museum, most of it along a beautiful promenade that's pleasant even if you're not going to the museum (described earlier, under "Luzern's Lakefront"). To make a beeline to the museum, take **bus** #6, #8, or #24 from the station and get off at the Verkehrshaus stop (2.50 CHF; the stop is announced, plus you'll see the huge, barrel-shaped theater). For a more scenic approach in summer, catch a **boat** in front of the train station (direction: Verkehrshaus, 1-2/hour, 10 minutes, 6 CHF).

Visiting the Museum: The museum's five main halls are arranged in a circle around an open central area. Pick up a map and use the white line on the floor as a guide to help you find your way. Most exhibits are at least partly translated into English. As you enter, check the schedule of demonstrations (ranging from car crash tests to airport X-ray machines; usually in English on request).

The first building is a long shed packed with train engines and tram cars. You'll learn that hydropower generates 90 percent of the electricity for Swiss trains, and you'll appreciate the evolution of Swiss trains and tunnels over the last century.

The second hall is a car enthusiast's dream, with two floors devoted to road transport. One wall is stacked floor to ceiling with 80 vehicles dating from 1860 to 2005, mostly cars and motorcycles. Interactive screens let you zoom in on any vehicle for insights into its design and history.

The third building covers boats and submarines on the lower two floors, and shows off some Swiss cable cars. Be sure to seek out the **"Swissarena"** on the top floor. This is an enormous (more than 2,000 square feet), up-to-date aerial photograph of Switzerland. Spread out on the floor like laminated linoleum, this photo map is detailed enough to show virtually every single building within the country's borders. It's impressive even if you've Google-Earthed. Slide on the Swiss-flag slippers, borrow a map and magnifying glass, and glide across Switzerland, looking for the places you've visited so far.

The next hall is the Hans Erni Museum, showcasing works of a well-known local 20th-century painter and illustrator (they have nothing to do with transport, but are worth a quick peek).

The fifth and final building covers flight (airplanes below, space travel above). The helicopter and airplane simulations are included in your entry price (expect lines). There's also a relaxing parasailing simulator, where you can lie on a smoothly gliding platform and peer down at the countryside below.

Two vintage Swissair planes are parked in the open area in the center of the museum (a DC-3 and a Convair 990). You'll also find a miniature train that little kids can ride (small fee), and a high-tech swingset. Simulators, games, giant slides, and interactive exhibits can easily keep children busy all day.

Extras: Three other attractions share the grounds with and have the same hours as the Transport Museum: a planetarium, the Swiss Chocolate Adventure, and the IMAX-esque Filmtheater. Each costs 15-18 CHF to enter (small discount with Transport Museum ticket, see website for showtimes, www.verkehrshaus. ch). The Chocolate Adventure, a chocolate museum structured as a 20-minute amusement-park ride, is entertaining, but I prefer the less expensive and more authentic chocolate factories at Broc and Lugano.

Richard Wagner Museum

This museum is a 10-minute walk along the lakefront, south of the train station and housed in a building where the composer once lived.

Cost and Hours: 10 CHF, covered by Swiss Travel Pass, April-Nov Tue-Sun 10:00-17:00, closed Mon and Dec-March, café, Richard Wagner Weg 27, tel. 041-360-2370, www.richard-wagner-museum.ch.

Luzern Museum of Art (Kunstmuseum Luzern)

Located in the lakefront cultural center by the train station, this museum features special exhibits of contemporary art—generally changing a couple times a year and advertised by a big poster on the wall.

Cost and Hours: 15 CHF, covered by Swiss Travel Pass, Tue-Sun 10:00-17:00, Wed until 20:00, closed Mon, Europaplatz 1, tel. 041-226-7800, www.kunstmuseumluzern.ch.

Museum of Natural History (Natur-Museum)

With an emphasis on interactive exhibits, this is a great place to bring kids.

Cost and Hours: 8 CHF, covered by Swiss Travel Pass, Tue-Sun 10:00-17:00, closed Mon, near the end of the Mill Bridge (Spreuerbrücke) next to the Depot History Museum at Kasernen-platz 6, tel. 041-228-5411, www.naturmuseum.ch.

LÖWENPLATZ

North of the old town, Löwenplatz was a big deal back in the early days of tourism. Its three sights (the lion, Glacier Garden, and Bourbaki Panorama) were a destination in the Romantic Age. It remains a bucket-list stop for tour groups but has the tired air of a tourist trap. I enjoy dropping by for a thought-provoking peek at old-time tourism here; behind the tacky souvenir shops, the sights do retain some of their Victorian-era charm.

Getting There: It's a 10-minute walk from the old town or a short bus ride across the river from the station (take bus #1, #19, #22, or #23 north from the train station to the Löwenplatz stop). Across from the bus stop is the round Bourbaki Panorama. The lion and the Glacier Garden are one long block farther up the hill.

▲Lion Monument (Löwendenkmal)

This free, famous monument remains an essential stop if you're visiting Luzern—if only because when you get back home, everyone will ask you, "Did you see the lion?"

Open from sunrise to dusk, the huge sculpture (33 feet long by 20 feet tall) is carved right into a cliff face, over a reflecting pool in a peaceful park—the site of a sandstone quarry when it was carved in 1821. Though it's often overrun with tour groups, a tranquil moment here is genuinely moving: The mighty lion rests his paws on a shield, with his head cocked to one side, tears streaming down his cheeks. In his side is the broken-off end of a spear, which is slowly killing the noble beast. (Note the angle of the spear, which matches the striations of the rock face, subtly suggesting more spears raining down on the lion.) This heartbreaking figure represents the Swiss mercenaries who were killed or executed in 1792 defending the French king in the French Revolution. The inscription reads, *Helvetiorum fidei ac virtuti*—"To the loyalty and bravery of the Swiss." While a local artist carved it in 14 months, it was designed by the great Danish Neoclassical sculptor Bertel Thorvaldsen.

Bourbaki Panorama

Here's your chance to get right in the middle of a great painting—literally. In the 19th century, before the dawn of cinema, modern people were hungry for visual entertainment. Panorama theaters like this were built all over Europe and hosted various gigantic paintings, which were rolled up and taken on road trips. This 360-degree painting (a 33-foot-tall wraparound canvas with a circumference of 360 feet) tells the story of one of the culminating events of the Franco-Prussian War—the flight of thousands of French soldiers to Switzerland in 1871.

The Bourbaki Panorama was painted by Edouard Castres, who was actually there on that frigid morning as a Red Cross volunteer.

The 1881 painting was thoroughly refurbished in 2000, when several life-size figures were added to the foreground.

After Prussia won the war against France, some French soldiers were determined to surrender to the neutral Swiss rather than the enemy Germans. For three days in February of 1871, a hungry, weary 87,000-man army led by the panorama's namesake, General Charles-Denis Bourbaki, trudged through the snow and across the Swiss border, near Neuchâtel. Once in Switzerland, they gave up their weapons and surrendered to the Swiss—who, the story goes, took excellent care of the French, nursing them back to health before sending them home with a hefty bill for their stay. The free booklet explains it all and makes for a good souvenir.

Upon arrival, ask for the English version of the historical soundtrack. Spend your waiting time enjoying the first-floor background exhibit. When the English narration starts, be on the second-floor viewing platform to savor all 360 degrees of drama.

Cost and Hours: 12 CHF, includes a tablet guide, covered by Lionpass combo-ticket and Swiss Travel Pass; daily April-Oct 9:00-18:00, Nov-March 10:00-17:00; Löwenplatz 11, tel. 041-412-3030, www.bourbakipanorama.ch.

Glacier Garden (Gletschergarten)

This complex is a strange sort of miniature theme park with an eclectic hodgepodge of exhibits, most loosely relating to alpine geology. Although the various pieces don't quite hang together (such as the fun but out-of-place Hall of Mirrors), it can add up to a pleasant, if overpriced, activity.

Cost and Hours: 15 CHF, covered by Lionpass combo-ticket and Swiss Travel Pass, daily April-Oct 9:00-18:00, Nov-March 10:00-17:00, Denkmalstrasse 4, tel. 041-410-4340, www.gletschergarten.ch.

Visiting the Garden: You'll walk through the **glacier-grinded grounds** that give the garden its name. While geologists might get a thrill out of this, it was just a bunch of holes to me. Then the **museum,** with exhibits about glacial processes and a dramatic slideshow, gives you an idea of what this area once looked like. Downstairs are huge 3-D reliefs of late-18th-century Luzern, and the Alps and lakes of Central Switzerland. The **Amrein's House** is an old chalet with some original furnishings and models of traditional Swiss buildings. As you leave, you have the option of hiking up the steep **Tower Walk,** which leads to another old chalet and an observation tower.

You'll finish with the **Hall of Mirrors.** Made in 1896 for a national exhibition in Geneva, it's a delightfully low-tech fun house. You'll grope your way through twisting corridors—with mirrors on all sides—decorated like a Disneyfied Alhambra. It's confusing,

LUZERN

dizzying, and claustrophobic, but goofy fun. As you run into yourself (literally) again and again, you'll lament the poor sap who has to clean the smudge marks off all those mirrors. As you leave, giggling and nauseated, you may find yourself wondering, "So, what exactly did that have to do with glaciers?"

Sleeping in Luzern

Luzern is busiest—and most expensive—in summer. Spring and fall bring lower prices, and winter has rock-bottom rates. Luzern has erected yellow-and-brown signs throughout the city pointing you to most hotels. None of the hotels listed below have air-conditioning. To avoid nighttime street noise, ask for a room high up.

IN THE CENTER

$$$$ Hotel des Alpes is a good bet if you want to sleep right on the river in the old town, next door to Luzern's iconic Chapel Bridge and water tower. The 45 classic rooms are bright and fresh; pricier riverfront rooms come with beautiful views. The reception entrance is on the backside of the building (a few rooms have balconies, elevator, fans, Furrengasse 3, tel. 041-417-2060, www.desalpes-luzern.ch, info@desalpes-luzern.ch).

$$$$ Hotel Waldstätterhof fills a fine 19th-century building across the street from the train station (on the land side with no water views). This central location comes with quite a bit of noise (especially on the weekends). Its 96 bright, spacious, and modern rooms have all the amenities, and its rates are reasonable for the high level of comfort (family rooms, elevator, quieter rooms face the courtyard, pay parking—reserve ahead, Zentralstrasse 4, tel. 041-227-1271, www.hotel-waldstaetterhof.ch, info@hotel-waldstaetterhof.ch).

$$$$ Hotel Krone Luzern, facing one of Luzern's quaint squares, is a good bet if you want to sleep right in the center. The 25 spacious rooms are modern and crisp, a stark contrast to the rather outdated reception and corridors (family rooms, elevator, pay parking, Weinmarkt 12, tel. 041-419-4400, www.alstadthotels.ch, info@alstadthotels.ch).

$$$ Schlüssel Hotel, well run by Marija, offers 10 tastefully decorated rooms with personal touches that make you feel at home. This recently renovated building, first opened as a hotel in 1545, takes pride in its long history. It's well-located on a small square near the river and houses several restaurants (discount if you skip breakfast, family rooms, a few rooms have balconies, elevator, Franziskanerplatz 12, tel. 041-210-1061, www.schluessel-luzern.ch, welcome@schluessel-luzern.ch).

$$$ Stern Luzern is a solid value, offering 15 small but bright rooms over a popular restaurant a couple of doors from the Schlüssel Hotel (family rooms, tiny elevator, Burgerstrasse 35, enter at Franziskanerplatz 4, check-in desk at restaurant entrance, tel. 041-227-5060, www.sternluzern.ch, info@sternluzern.ch).

OUTSIDE THE CENTER

$$$ Ibis Styles Luzern City has 115 modern rooms with colorful accents. It's near the action, but away from much of the noise (family rooms, elevator, Friedenstrasse 8, tel. 041-418-4848, www.ibis.com, h8549@accor.com). It's a 15-minute walk from the train station, or take bus #1—direction: Maihof, get off at Löwenplatz and walk down Friedenstrasse; the hotel faces the Bourbaki Panorama.

$$ Hotel Alpha, once a convent-run boarding house for village girls, is now a respectable hotel for value-minded travelers who don't mind being away from the center. It offers 47 big, bright, dorm-style rooms, most with the toilet down the hall, though 11 have private baths. Although it's located in a nice residential area, it still has some street noise from the nearby school and playing field—even at night (many doubles are twins, family rooms, elevator, fans available upon request, comfy lounges and TV room, pay parking—reserve ahead, Zähringerstrasse 24, at intersection with Pilatusstrasse, tel. 041-240-4280, www.hotelalpha.ch, info@hotelalpha.ch). It's a 10-minute walk or an easy two-stop bus ride from the train station: Take bus #12 or #18, get off at Pilatusplatz, and continue down Pilatusstrasse.

$$ The Bed and Breakfast, lovingly run by Isabelle, offers 13 bright, spacious rooms—three with private bathrooms, other 10 rooms share eight bathrooms—in her grandmother's former home. This is a perfect spot for those looking for a more personal experience and don't mind being a bit away from the center. The kind staff and cozy garden will make you wish you were staying longer (closed Nov-Feb, family rooms, Taubenhausstrasse 34, tel. 041-310-1514, www.thebandb.ch, info@thebandb.ch). It's a 15-minute walk from the train station, or take bus #1—direction: Kriens-Obernau, get off at Eichhof and walk 100 yards down Taubenhausstrasse).

$$ Ibis Budget Luzern City's 128 tight, cookie-cutter rooms are worth considering if you're on a budget and don't mind being in a soulless neighborhood near the train tracks. You get a narrow double bed, sometimes with a bunk bed above it, plus an opaque shower cabinet that opens straight into the room (air-con, breakfast extra, pay parking, Kellerstrasse 6, tel. 041-367-8000, www.ibis.com, h6782@accor.com). It's a 10- to 15-minute walk from the train station, or take bus #4 three stops to Brünigstrasse.

¢ Backpackers Luzern is calm and well-run, sharing a modern, blocky building with student dorms *(Studentenheim)* in a peaceful residential area a 15-minute walk south of the train sta-

tion. The place has 30 rooms (each with a balcony), shared toilets and showers, a pair of kitchens for guests, a welcoming lounge, and no curfew. The walk to the center is mostly along the lake, through pretty parks and next to a fine beach (sheets included, towel extra, no breakfast but nice kitchen, elevator, full-service pay laundry, reception open 7:30-10:00 & 16:00-23:00, Alpenquai 42, tel. 041-360-0420, www.backpackerslucerne.ch, info@backpackerslucerne.ch). By bus, take #6, #7, or #8 from the station four stops to Weinbergli, then walk left five minutes to the hostel.

Eating in Luzern

While eateries along the river are pricey and a bit touristy, if you have one evening in Luzern, that's where you'll make the best memories. I've listed several places with great riverfront settings, two trendier foodie places in the new town (with no tourists), and some good budget options. Reservations are smart at nice places. For a memorable evening on a budget, consider catching the last one-hour sightseeing boat on the lake (19:00) and enjoying a picnic dinner while you cruise.

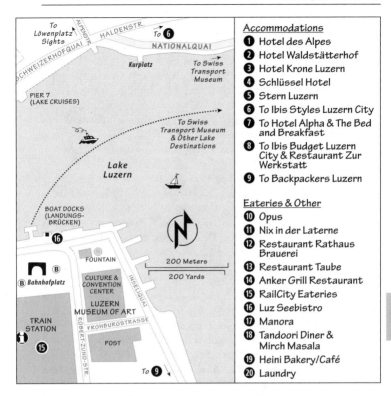

Accommodations
1. Hotel des Alpes
2. Hotel Waldstätterhof
3. Hotel Krone Luzern
4. Schlüssel Hotel
5. Stern Luzern
6. To Ibis Styles Luzern City
7. To Hotel Alpha & The Bed and Breakfast
8. To Ibis Budget Luzern City & Restaurant Zur Werkstatt
9. To Backpackers Luzern

Eateries & Other
10. Opus
11. Nix in der Laterne
12. Restaurant Rathaus Brauerei
13. Restaurant Taube
14. Anker Grill Restaurant
15. RailCity Eateries
16. Luz Seebistro
17. Manora
18. Tandoori Diner & Mirch Masala
19. Heini Bakery/Café
20. Laundry

LUZERN

DINING IN STYLE

$$$$ Opus, next to the big Jesuit Church, is both a trendy wine bar and a good restaurant. Pair your wine with meat, fish, and vegetarian dishes with international flair; the lush and varied salad bar ("antipasti buffet"—the midsized plate piled high makes a light and healthy dinner); or your choice of dried meats and cheeses (sold by weight, choose and cut your own fresh bread to go with it). They always have a couple dozen bottles of wine open and available by the glass. Sit in the upscale, colorful interior; in the extremely romantic wine cellar with candlelight reflecting in the bottle-lined walls; or out front, under the church and next to the river (daily 9:00-24:00, Bahnhofstrasse 16, tel. 041-226-4141, www.restaurant-opus.ch).

$$$$ Nix in der Laterne has a romantic, dressy interior and great outside seats right on the fast-rushing river. Nikki is Swiss-Austrian, and so is his cuisine. Daily options are listed on a chalkboard; ask your server for details. Their budget option: *tarte flambée*—a savory tart where you can mix and match a dozen toppings (22-CHF weekday lunches, daily 11:00-24:00, Reusssteg 9, tel. 041-240-2543, www.nixinderlaterne.ch).

ALONG THE RIVER

$$$ Restaurant Rathaus Brauerei is a lively microbrewery on the river under the Town Hall. While the beer hall is plain, there are plenty of outdoor seats—both under arches and on the river. It's a local favorite for its Seidel Rathausbier, which you can only get here. Special seasonal brews are on the menu board, along with salads, "gourmet" pretzel sandwiches (your light and affordable option), Germanic main courses, and the daily three-course special (open long hours daily, Unter der Egg 2, tel. 041-410-6111, www. rathausbrauerei.ch).

$$$$ Restaurant Taube, popular for serving "grandma's cooking," is known for its ham-and-cheese *Rösti*. While the food is fine, the interior is forgettable. I'd only eat here to take advantage of their amazing riverside seating (21-CHF two-course weekday lunches, daily 11:30-14:00 & 17:30-22:30, Burgerstrasse 3, tel. 041-210-0747, www.taube-luzern.ch).

IN THE NEW TOWN

Both of these places are in a more workaday district, closer to the train station than the river and away from the tourist zone. And each is patronized by a smart local clientele.

$$$$ Restaurant Zur Werkstatt is a fun, inventive approach to eating: There's communal seating and one three-course menu that changes each week (58 CHF, 48-CHF vegetarian option). This "food workshop" invites you to become part of the experience, and the open kitchen allows you to watch the action and take in the enticing aromas. It's the perfect splurge for the adventurous eater with plenty of time—and who's ready for creative cuisine served by people passionate about food (Mon-Sat 11:30-13:30 and 17:00-24:00, closed Sun, Waldstätterstrasse 18, tel. 041.979.0303, www. zurwerkstatt.ch).

$$$$ Anker Grill Restaurant fills an old ballroom of the once-venerable Hotel Anker with an eclectic blend of old and new—mixing crystal glassware with hip music and low lighting. It's a fun and youthful place with an open kitchen and a diverse menu focused on fresh, local ingredients and tasty grilled meats (daily 11:30-10:00, Pilatusstrasse 36, tel. 041-220-8800, www. hotel-restaurant-anker.ch).

FAST AND AFFORDABLE

In the Train Station's "RailCity": As in every big Swiss city, the train station comes with a "RailCity" mall bursting with places to eat. All are bright, efficient chains catering to locals with more money than time. Near the TI, a **Migros Daily** serves prepared food (daily 6:00-22:00). Just down the escalator you'll find a string of creative **fast-food places** with small standup tables (kebabs, salads, burgers, and currywurst) and a big **Co-Op supermarket** (daily 6:00-22:00). Upstairs is **$$ Tibits Vegetarian Restaurant,** a self-serve salad bar nestled in a modern, peaceful spot above the tracks (other veggie dishes available, daily 6:30-23:00). For a more relaxing and atmospheric meal near the station, head across the street to the lakeside **$$ Luz Seebistro** (daily 7:30-23:00, Schifflandungsbrücke 1).

Self-Service Cafeterias: $$ Manora, a cafeteria on the fifth floor of the Manor department store in the old town, is ideal for a tasty, efficient lunch. Fill a plate at the salad bar or choose among a variety of main dishes (including *Beilage*—starches and veggies). In good weather, climb the stairs to the outdoor terrace, with great views over the rooftops of Luzern to the lake and Mount Pilatus. This place is packed with locals and can get crowded during peak times—eat early or late, and send your travel partner up top to claim an outdoor table while you buy the food (Mon-Wed 9:00-18:30, Thu-Fri 9:00-21:00, Sat 8:00-16:00, closed Sun, free Wi-Fi, Weggisgasse 5).

Indian Food: In the old town **$ Tandoori Diner** sells budget Indian meals (meat or vegetarian; chose from your choice of eight combos—see photos and they'll dish it up immediately, Mon-Sat 11:30-21:30, closed Sun, Löwengraben 4, tel. 041-340-5296). **$$ Mirch Masala,** two doors away and run by the same folks, is a bit more elegant (15-CHF lunch buffet, Mon-Sat 11:30-14:00 and 17:30-22:30, Sun 16:30-22:30, Löwengraben 8, tel. 041-410-6308).

Bakery: $ Heini Bakery/Café, on Falkenplatz a half-block down from the Manor department store, is popular with the local lunch crowd for its weekday salad bar, sandwiches, quiches, and delectable pastries. There's both indoor and outdoor seating (Mon-Sat 7:00-18:30, Sun 9:00-17:00, Hertensteinstrasse 66, tel. 041-412-2020).

Luzern Connections

Luzern is well-situated, with convenient connections to anywhere in the country. Note that Luzern is on both the Golden Pass and the Gotthard Panorama Express scenic rail routes (see the Scenic Rail Journeys chapter).

From Luzern by Train to: Zürich (2/hour, 50 minutes), **Zürich Airport** (hourly direct, 1 hour, more with change at Zürich main station), **Bern** (hourly direct, 1 hour, more with transfer), **Interlaken** (hourly direct, 2 hours), **Lausanne** (hourly direct, 2 hours, more with transfer), **Appenzell** (hourly, 3 hours, change in Herisau), **Lugano** (2/hour, 2.5 hours, some with change in Arth-Goldau), **St. Moritz** (1-2/hour, 4.5 hours, at least 2 changes; 6.5

hours via Glacier Express route, 2-5 changes including Göschenen and Andermatt), **Zermatt** (1-2/hour, 3.5 hours, changes in Bern and Visp; 5.5 hours via Glacier Express route, 2-3 changes including Göschenen). Train info: toll tel. 0900-300-300 (pricey 1.20 CHF/minute), www.rail.ch.

Central Switzerland Day Trips

Luzern is perched on the edge of a scenic lake and ringed by family-friendly mountain peaks that are easily conquerable—for a price. All of this makes the city a perfect springboard for alpine excursions. Three side-trips are especially popular and worthwhile: two famous and accessible mountains—Mount Pilatus and Mount Rigi—and the hidden military fortress of Fürigen. All three attractions can be reached by boat and mountain lifts from Luzern. One other less-touristy mountain nearby, Mount Stanserhorn, requires a short train ride to the base but rewards the effort with the world's first double-decker cable car.

PLANNING YOUR TIME

Of the mountains I list, Mount Pilatus has more variety to offer, Mount Rigi appeals more to serious hikers, and Mount Stanserhorn has fewer crowds. For a fun, relaxed day (especially in good weather), focus on Mount Pilatus.

Note that the fortress is open only on weekends from April through October. While it's possible to combine Mount Pilatus and the fortress into one jam-packed day trip (best if you start with an early-morning gondola up), you'll have little time to savor the scenery.

For all these side-trips, you can choose whether to go both out and back by train, or to travel one way by boat (slower and more expensive than the train). Confirm all schedules and logistics before embarking.

For a spin around the lake, you can take a short or longer cruise any time of year.

Tell-Pass: If you're home-basing in Luzern for several days and don't have a rail pass, consider the Tell-Pass. This pass covers up to 10 consecutive days of free rides on lifts, boats, and several area train lines (180-300 CHF depending on number of days; buy at TIs, train stations, and boat docks; cheaper 110-220-CHF version Nov-March when schedules are sparser, www.tellpass.ch). A Tell-Pass doesn't make sense if you have a consecutive-day Swiss Travel Pass (as opposed to a flexipass).

Lake Luzern

Lake Luzern—the most touristed in Switzerland—has a variety of boat routes and destinations (35 stops in all). Cruises range from a one-hour sampler tour (around Luzern's "harbor") to a full-blown, 5.5-hour exploration (to Flüelen, at the far end of the lake, and back). Some routes are round-trip dinner or sightseeing cruises, but most boats have scheduled stops and are designed for you to get out, explore, and then take the next boat back. Romantics will want to hitch a ride on one of the old-fashioned paddleboat steamers.

Boats leave from the lake piers in front of the Luzern train station. In addition to the dockside office (Pier 1), the Luzern TI also sells tickets. Both can offer advice on which trip best fits your schedule. Tickets can be purchased onboard as well.

Regular departures are free with a Swiss Travel Pass and half-price with a Eurail pass. It can be smart to do the lake cruise on the day you arrive or depart—when you're already using a flexi-day for your train transportation. If you're already planning to take the Gotthard Panorama Express to Lugano (see page 330), there's little point in doing another lake excursion.

BOATING OPTIONS

All boats are operated by the Lake Lucerne Navigation Company (tel. 041-367-6767, www.lakelucerne.ch). For a quick trip, consider the **"panorama yacht"** *Saphir*, which goes on a villa-and-castle cruise, making a one-hour, 25-CHF round-trip sightseeing swing around Luzern's corner of the lake.

For more dramatic scenery, sail an hour across the lake on the scheduled **boat to Weggis or Vitznau** (where the Mount Rigi ascent starts), then back to Luzern (38 CHF round-trip to Weggis, 45 CHF to Vitznau). For most, a two-hour circle is enough lake scenery.

An **exciting full-day option** is to sail from Luzern to Flüelen (3 hours), then catch the hourly train from there to Arth-Goldau, where you can ride the blue cogwheel train to the Rigi summit on your way back to Luzern.

You can also get out on the lake under your own power. **Pedal boats** can be rented at Schwanenplatz, just across the bridge from the Luzern train station (20 CHF/30 minutes, 30 CHF/hour; 5 CHF more on weekends).

LUZERN

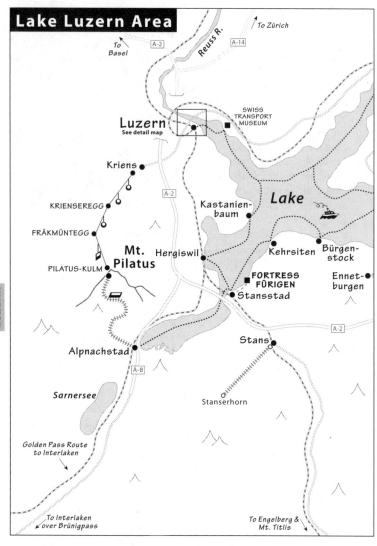

Mount Pilatus

Looming behind Luzern, Pilatus (7,000 feet), worth ▲, is a dramatic backdrop to the city and also an enjoyable destination. While legend dictates that it's named for Pontius Pilate—whose body is supposedly in one of its lakes, kicking up a fuss if disturbed—it more likely comes from a Latin word meaning "cloudy." It's also said to be infested with dragons.

There are two parts to your visit. First you have to get from

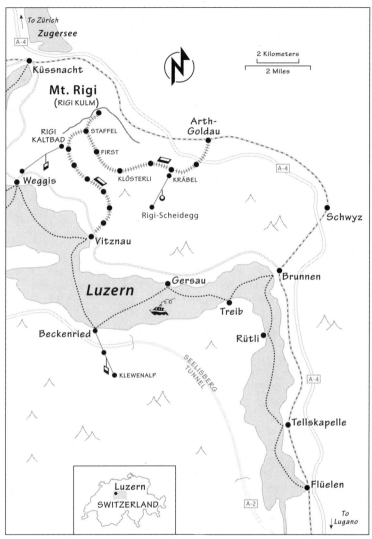

LUZERN

Luzern to the mountain's base. Then you can ride either a **cogwheel train,** or a combination of a **gondola and a cable car** to the summit (called "Pilatus Kulm"). The cogwheel train runs from Alpnachstad up the east side, straight to the summit—its 48 percent grade is the world's steepest. The other ascent—by gondola and then cable car—runs from Kriens up the north side, with a chance to stop at Fräkmüntegg for a luge ride or ropes course.

For maximum views, go up one way, down the other—in good weather, the view's spectacular on both sides in both directions. In most cases, I'd take the cogwheel train up, as it's a bit more dramatic to ride it uphill than down (and the gondola ride down catches more afternoon light). However, if you want to do the luge at Fräkmüntegg, it makes more sense to take the gondola and cable car up.

Information: For more advice, ask at your hotel or Luzern's TI. For more detailed information, visit www. pilatus.ch.

SUMMITING MOUNT PILATUS

Figure four hours for the total round-trip from Luzern—consider leaving before noon to reach the summit with time to spare. The schedules and prices listed here are for May through mid-October (the cogwheel train does not operate off-season).

Cost: A round-trip to the top and back, no matter how you go, costs 72 CHF from the base of the mountain (with your choice of cogwheel train or gondola/cable car for each leg; does not include transportation between Luzern and the mountain). Swiss Travel Pass and Eurail pass holders get a 50 percent discount (36 CHF round-trip). Don't throw your ticket away when you board, as you'll have to scan it several times until you exit at the last station.

By Train: The cogwheel train leaves from the lakeside town of Alpnachstad. To reach Alpnachstad from Luzern, take either the S5 train (2/hour, 20 minutes, 7.80 CHF one-way, part of this journey not covered by the Visitors Card—buy 3.70-CHF ticket from Hergiswil to Alpnachstad) or the boat, which leaves from the dock opposite the train station (7/day, 1-2 hours, 27 CHF one-way). The cogwheel train runs mid-May-mid-Nov only (daily, first train up at 8:10; last train up at 17:10, last train down at 17:45; longer operating times late June-late Aug and shorter operating times in Nov, 30 minutes up, 40 minutes down; for the best views, take a downhill-facing seat with your left shoulder against the window).

By Gondola/Cable Car: The gondola leaves from Kriens, a suburb of Luzern. To reach Kriens, catch city bus #1, which departs frequently from Luzern train station; its stop is on the other side of the busy street from where most of the bus platforms are located (15-minute ride, direction: Kriens, stop: Zentrum Pilatus). After getting off the bus, cross the busy street and walk 10 minutes uphill to the gondola station, following *Pilatus* signs. (To return to Luzern from the gondola station, follow the white signs for *Luzern bus* and hop on bus #1; you don't want the bus stop in front of the gondola terminal.)

The gondola runs continuously from Kriens to Fräkmüntegg (30-minute trip). At the Krienseregg station, halfway through the gondola trip, you have the option to hop out (there's a recreational area with trails and a playground). At Fräkmüntegg, you leave the gondola; it's another seven minutes in a cable car to the observation platform at Pilatus Kulm. Unlike the cogwheel train, the gondola and cable car run all year, except for two weeks' maintenance in fall (first ascent from Kriens at 8:30, April–mid-Oct last descent from Pilatus at 17:30, off-season last descent at 16:30).

Round-Trip "Deal": The Golden and Silver Round Trip tickets won't save you any money, but they will simplify your journey with just one ticket that includes all transportation from Luzern to the summit and back.

ACTIVITIES ON PILATUS
At Fräkmüntegg

This spot, on the north slope of Pilatus, is a summer-fun zone. If the weather's good, stop here to zip down the nearly mile-long Fräkigaudi, Switzerland's longest **luge ride** (8 CHF per ride, automated machine takes cash and credit cards, kids under 8 must be accompanied by an adult, open daily mid-April–late Oct 10:00–17:00, closes if rainy, mandatory bag check, expect lines on sunny weekends, www.rodelbahn.ch).

At the fun **Suspension Rope Park** (Seilpark), you can test your agility high up on 10 rope courses with varying degrees of difficulty (28 CHF includes three hours on the course plus material and instruction, family discounts—different course for kids under 8, late April–mid-Oct daily 10:00–17:00, www.pilatus-seilpark.ch).

At the Summit

The visitors center has a good information office, souvenir shop, snack bars, and several restaurants (generally open 11:00–15:00). Above the information office is a self-service cafeteria, but nicer options exist at the Hotel Pilatus-Kulm on the other side of the

outdoor terrace with both indoor and outdoor dining areas.

LUZERN

LUZERN

Luge Lesson

Taking a wild ride on a summer luge (pronounced "loozh") is a quintessential alpine experience. In German, it's called a *Sommerrodelbahn* ("summer toboggan run"). To try one of Europe's great accessible thrills (around 8 CHF), take the lift up to the top of a mountain, grab a wheeled sled-like go-cart, and scream back down the mountainside on a banked course. Then take the lift back up and start all over again.

Luge courses are highly weather-dependent, and can close at the slightest hint of rain. If the weather's questionable, call ahead to confirm that your preferred luge is open. Stainless-steel courses are more likely than concrete ones to stay open in drizzly weather.

Operating the sled is simple: Push the stick forward to go faster, pull back to apply brakes. Even a novice can go very, very fast. Most are cautious on their first run, speed demons on their second...and bruised and bloody on their third. A woman once showed me her travel journal illustrated with her husband's dried five-inch-long luge scab. He had disobeyed the only essential rule of luging: Keep both hands on your stick. To avoid a bumper-to-bumper traffic jam, let the person in front of you get as far ahead as possible before you start. You'll emerge from the course with a windblown hairdo and a smile-creased face.

Key Luge Terms

Lenkstange	lever
drücken / schneller fahren	push / go faster
ziehen / bremsen	pull / brake
Schürfwunde	scrape
Schorf	scab

Hiking: Stop by the information office to pick up a map. All walks leave from the summit, Pilatus Kulm, and lead to great viewpoints.

From the outdoor terrace, Oberhaupt (marked with a cross) looms above you and is just a five-minute climb. Those with a bit more energy can continue on a 15-minute loop that goes along the ridge above Hotel Pilatus-Kulm toward the biggest radar station in Switzerland (housed in an off-limits military zone), down some steep stairs, around the other side of the mountain through tunnels and various viewpoints in the rock, and eventually back to the visitors center.

A 10-minute hike above Hotel Bellevue takes you up to **Esel** ("Donkey," commemorating the pre-cable-car days, when Queen Victoria came up to Pilatus on the back of a donkey). Below Esel hides an impressive part of Switzerland's anti-aircraft defense system. Find the gray, round structures within the imitation rock. Modern missiles behind the camouflage point to the skies.

Hiking to **Tomlishorn** (35 minutes), you'll spot more camouflaged military installations. Stop at the yellow *Echo* sign and shout your message out to the world. Somebody out there keeps yelling it back.

A 1.5-hour hike leads to the 6,700-foot cross-capped summit of **Matthorn** (not Matterhorn). This hike is moderately strenuous—generally uphill, with lots of ups and downs. A visitors' book invites you to sign and leave your impressions on this breathtaking spot.

Sleeping at the Summit: You can spend the night on the summit of Pilatus, lingering outside to enjoy the views with the marmots and mountain goats. The information office in the visitors center serves as the reception desk for both hotels. Prices listed here are for "half-board," meaning they include breakfast and dinner. **$$$ Hotel Pilatus-Kulm,** with 30 rooms, is a historic building from 1900. **$$$ Hotel Bellevue** is a modern, round building with 20 slightly cheaper rooms—clean and bright, with Nordic-style furniture. The hotels share contact information: Tel. 041-329-1212, www.pilatus.ch, hotels@pilatus.ch.

Mount Rigi

This long, shelf-like mountain, across the lake from Luzern, provides sweeping views of Central Switzerland (and, on a clear day,

Germany and France, too). Even though it's at a lower altitude than Pilatus (5,900 feet), this so-called "Queen of the Mountains" boasts the oldest cog railway in Europe (from 1870) and claims to offer the best vistas in the area. The top can be busy between 10:00 and 15:00.

You can reach the top of Rigi, called Rigi Kulm, from either its "front" (west) or "back" (east) side. Hourly cogwheel trains chug up to the summit from base stations on both sides (hikers can hop off partway up or down). The west side also has a cable-car option.

If you're staying in Luzern, coming up the west side makes

the most sense, as it gives you an excuse to take a scenic boat ride to the base of the mountain. This route also has better views than the east face and lets you go one direction by train and the other by cable car.

Information: All details on transport and activities on Rigi are helpfully collected at www.rigi.ch.

SUMMITING MOUNT RIGI

Figure five to six hours for the total round-trip from Luzern. The schedules and prices listed here are for April through mid-October (boats and the Vitznau-Rigi Kulm train run less frequently in winter). Trains run hourly, so a missed connection can be a big waste of time; check schedules before you go.

Cost: No matter how you go, the price from the base of the mountain to Rigi Kulm is 45 CHF one-way, 72 CHF round-trip, plus the cost of getting from Luzern to the cogwheel train or cable-car stations at the base of the mountain. With a Swiss Travel Pass, the whole trip is free, from Luzern all the way to the top of Rigi. With a Eurail pass, everything is half-price (but you'll have to use one of your flexi-days).

From the West: From Luzern's dock, hourly boats leave for the cable car station at Weggis (38 CHF round-trip, 45-minute ride), then continue to the cogwheel train station at Vitznau (45 CHF round-trip, one-hour ride).

To simplify things, buy your Rigi Kulm ticket at the boat dock (117 CHF, includes all transport to/from Mount Rigi). From **Weggis dock,** it's a 15-minute walk uphill to the cable-car (Luftseilbahn), where a 10-minute ride lifts you up to **Rigi Kaltbad** (2/hour; Mon-Fri 6:45-19:10, Sat-Sun from 8:10). From there you connect to the red cogwheel train to reach the tippy-top, or you can hike up in about one hour. From **Vitznau,** the red cogwheel train chugs to the summit, stopping halfway in Rigi Kaltbad (hourly, 30 minutes up, 40 minutes down, daily 9:15-19:15, June-early Sept until 22:05, for the best views up, sit on the side closest to the station). For more flexibility, I recommend taking the train up (since it's more dramatic as an uphill ride) and the cable car down. Either way, you get to the summit in the same amount of time (1.5 hours from Luzern).

From the East: If you're visiting Rigi from Zürich, Lugano, or other points to the north, east, and south, it makes sense to ascend the "back" side of the mountain, from the town of Arth-Goldau, which is on Switzerland's main rail line. From Arth-Goldau, a blue cogwheel train takes you up to the summit (hourly, daily 8:00-17:10, July-Aug until 18:10, 45-minute ride).

LUZERN

ACTIVITIES ON RIGI

A small information office, souvenir shop, and snack bar border the train tracks. To reach the top of the mountain, it's a steep, five-minute climb past the Rigi Kulm Hotel (full-service restaurant and self-service cafeteria, generally open 11:30-14:00).

The mountain is laced with more than 60 miles of hiking trails and other attractions to while away an afternoon. All are well-described in the *Rigi Explorer Guide,* available at Luzern's TI and on the Rigi website (www.rigi.ch).

Hiking: Serious hikers can do the whole thing on foot (well-marked trails start at Weggis, Vitznau, and Arth-Goldau; about 3-4 hours uphill from Weggis or Vitznau), but I'd save my legs for a shorter walk up top, where the views are. The classic Rigi hike between the summit at Rigi Kulm and the cable-car station at Rigi Kaltbad takes one hour. (I prefer it as a downhill stroll; you can shorten the walk by meeting the train at the scenic Staffel stop.)

Rigi has a few other good hiking options, including a 45-minute walk down from the summit to a working cheese farm *(Alp-käserei Chäserenholz);* from there you can cross the hill to the Staffel train stop to avoid the steep hike back up to the summit. For a longer hike from the *Alpkäserei,* continue down Rigi's "back" ridge to the Obere Schwändihütte, then across the mountain to the Klösterli stop, where you can visit the cute Chapel of Maria-of-the-Snow before hopping on the blue cogwheel train (1.5 hours from the summit to Klösterli stop). You can also hike along sections of the Mark Twain trail, which traces his route up the mountain (as described in *A Tramp Abroad),* with excerpts from his account signposted along the way.

Sleeping at or near the Summit: Stay overnight and watch the sun rise, accompanied only by the sounds of the wind and the ringing of a few cow bells. **$$$$ Rigi Kulm Hotel** is the only inn set just below the summit, with 33 rooms and stunning views (tel. 041-880-1888, www.rigikulm.ch, hotel@rigikulm.ch, Käppeli family). **$$$$ Rigi Kaltsbad Mineral Bath & Spa,** between Vitznau and Rigi Kulm, has 52 rooms and is a nice place to rejuvenate with its indoor and outdoor pools and bathing areas (tel. 041-399-8181, www.hotelrigikaltbad.ch, info@hotelrigikaltbad.ch).

LUZERN

Mount Stanserhorn

Mount Stanserhorn (6,000 feet) is less touristy than the other mountain options I list and provides equally stunning views. At the summit there is a revolving self-service restaurant and plenty of hiking options for all levels, including a 30-minute walk around the peak.

In the late 19th century, a funicular train took visitors from the town of Stans to Mount Stanserhorn's summit in three sections. One of these old-time trains still operates along the first section of track, but the second and third sections have been replaced by the world's first double-decker cable car, the Cabrio. Those on the open upper deck get 360-degree views of the Alps and at least 10 nearby lakes. Another option is to hike from Stans to the summit (4.5 hours).

Stanserhorn is near Fortress Fürigen, listed next—consider combining both into a nice day trip from Luzern.

Cost: 74 CHF round-trip from base to summit. Swiss Travel Pass holders and Eurail pass holders get a 50 percent discount (37 CHF round-trip).

Getting There: From Luzern, take the train to Stans (3/hour, 20 minutes), then walk 10 minutes to the mountain's base to catch the funicular up to the summit. Boats also run between Luzern and Stansstad, adjacent to Stans (see details in "Fortress Fürigen" section below; from Stansstad, take bus #323 to the train station in Stans, 4-minute ride).

Information: For more advice, ask at your hotel or Luzern's TI. For more detailed information, visit www.stanserhorn.ch.

Fortress Fürigen

The Fortress Fürigen (Festung Fürigen) shows you another face of the country, part of the reason why Switzerland has been able to remain peaceful and neutral: its elaborate and secret system of bunkers and fortresses. Unfortunately, this fascinating exhibit, worth ▲, is open only on weekends, April through October.

Cost and Hours: 7 CHF, covered by Swiss Travel Pass, April-Oct Sat-Sun 11:00-17:00, closed Mon-Fri and Nov-March, tel. 041-618-7340, www.nidwaldner-museum.ch (click on "Festung Fürigen").

Getting There: Fortress Fürigen is just outside the lakefront town of Stansstad, not far from Luzern. It's an easy trip from Luzern on the S4 **train** (2/hour, 17 minutes). From the train station in Stansstad, walk 15-20 minutes, following the brown signs to *Festungsmuseum* or the yellow hiking signs to *Kehrsiten* (down Bahnhofstrasse to Stanserstrasse, cross and follow signs, right on Achereggstrasse, left on Kehrsitenstrasse passing swimming-pool sign, tennis courts, parking lot, small cove with marina, and finally winding along the lake under cliffs for a couple hundred yards). A bakery and a grocery store along the way are good for lunch.

You can also get to Stansstad from Luzern by **boat** (7/day, 1 hour). From Stansstad's boat dock, walk 10 minutes up to the main street (Achereggstrasse) and keep left, following the brown signs for *Festungsmuseum*.

Drivers arriving in Stansstad can follow white signs to *Kehrsiten* and the lakeside parking lot (free WC, 5-minute walk along lake to museum entrance).

VISITING THE FORTRESS

The fortress consists of an underground bunker that's invisible from the outside. Enter through an innocent-looking wooden shed. Ask for the brochure (with map) and loaner English booklet as you go in. The bunker is always chilly, but no worries: Visitors without jackets are loaned original Swiss Army coats. Allow an hour to visit the various parts of the bunker.

The fortress is a petting zoo of 20th-century weaponry. Visitors can fiddle with—and even aim—heavy guns, knowing all the ammo is now imaginary. Think of the photo op: you, in a Swiss military uniform, aiming a cannon. Besides the machine gun and artillery emplacements, the highlights of the exhibit include the 200-yard-long main tunnel, the ammunition room, and the troops' living and eating quarters. The radio room was placed near the entrance to assure clear reception. The living quarters were gas-proof, complete with specially sealed doors and devices to monitor the air for poison.

Fortress Fürigen was built in 1941 as part of a new military strategy (see sidebar). In case of a Nazi invasion, the Swiss government would retreat to a secret bunker near Brünig in the Berner Oberland, and Swiss troops would abandon the border regions and fall back around this alpine stronghold. The fortress at Fürigen was meant to protect roads and rail lines that led from Luzern and Zürich along Lake Luzern into the Berner

Swiss Military Readiness

Strolling through a peaceful Swiss village—charming pastoral greenery studded with rustic farmhouses between an Alp and a lake—my friend walked with me to the door of a nondescript barn. He said, "Stand here," and slid open the door to reveal a solitary, mighty gun—pointing right at me. Crossing a field, kicking a stray soccer ball back to a group of happy grade-schoolers, we came to another barn. This time I noticed the "wooden" door was actually metal, with a clever paint job. Inside was a military canteen, now sell-

ing snacks to civilians, and a steel ladder leading down into a military-gray world that felt like a vast submarine. A network of passages, just big enough for heavily armed soldiers to race down single file, led to a series of gun barns and subterranean command rooms with charts locating other installations in the area.

Switzerland may be famous for its neutrality, but it's anything but lax defensively. Travelers marvel at how Swiss engineers have conquered their Alps with the world's most-expensive-per-mile road system. But no one designs a Swiss bridge or tunnel without also designing its destruction. Each comes with built-in explosives, so, in the event of an invasion, the entire country can be blasted into a mountain fortress.

Even today, you can't get a building permit without an expensive first-class bomb shelter worked into the plan. Old tank barriers (nicknamed "Toblerones" for their shape) stand ready to be dragged across the roads to slow any invasion. Sprawling hospitals are dug into mountains, still ventilated to be kept dry and ready for use. And halfway up alpine cliffs, Batcave-type doors can slide open, allowing fighter jets to zoom into action from hidden airstrips cut out of solid rock. If you're approaching a mountain pass by car, look for the explosive patches ominously checkering the roads near the summit.

The end of the Cold War in 1989 brought changes even to neutral Switzerland. Western armies began cutting back on their military spending, and Switzerland followed suit, with deep cuts in its defense budget. The Swiss Army met its tighter budget in part by closing many of the 15,000 hidden fortresses that protected the country's strategic roads, train lines, and mountain passes. Some of the forts, such as Fürigen, have been turned into tourist attractions no more formidable than medieval castles.

Oberland. Fürigen (the name comes from a village on top of the cliff) was one of the smaller fortresses of its type. After World War II, they were retooled with a new focus: the threat of the Soviet Union and nuclear war.

The big guns in the fortress could shoot more than six miles, while the machine guns protected the immediate access routes to the bunker. This fortress could house and feed 100 people for three weeks. But in 1990, with the end of the Cold War, the practical Swiss decommissioned the fortress, refit it with vintage WWII and early Cold War gear, and opened it to the curious public. It's now administered by the local historical museum.

BERN & MURTEN

Enjoy urban Switzerland in the charming, compact capital of Bern. Ramble the ramparts of Murten, Switzerland's best-preserved medieval town, and resurrect the ruins of an ancient Roman capital in nearby Avenches.

PLANNING YOUR TIME

On a quick trip, big Bern and little Murten—about a half-hour apart by train or car—are each worth a half-day. Either makes a fine day trip or overnight stop. Murten, while easy by train, is even better by car.

Bern is a convenient stop between other Swiss destinations (such as going from the Berner Oberland to Murten or Zürich). If you're day-tripping, put your bag in a locker at the Bern station, spend a few hours taking my self-guided "Heart of Bern" walk and visiting some museums, then catch a late-afternoon train to your next stop. You could combine the destinations in this chapter by ending your busy Bern day in Murten, where you can spend the evening wandering the walls and savoring a lakeview dinner. In the morning, linger in Murten or move on to your next destination.

Bern

Stately but human, classy but fun, the Swiss capital is the most rewarding place to experience urban Switzerland. Window-shop along streets lined with cozy, covered arcades, and people-watch in the lively market square. Enjoy Bern's excellent museums, quaint-for-a-capital ambience, and delightful river scene. In this city (and canton), look for flags "bearing" the symbol of the local mascot—a roaring bear.

The city, founded in 1191, has managed to avoid war damage and hasn't burned down since a great fire swept through in 1405. After the fire, wooden buildings were no longer allowed, and Bern took on its gray-green sandstone complexion (with stones quarried from nearby). During its 12th- and 13th-century growth spurt, the frisky town grew through two walls. Looking at the map of the city contained within a bend of the Aare River, you can get a sense of how it started with a castle at the tip of the peninsula, and ex-panded with a series of walls—each defending an ever-bigger city from its one land-accessible side. The clock tower marks the first wall (1218). A generation later, another wall was built (in 1256, at today's prison tower). The final wall—where today's train station sits—was built in 1344.

In 1353, the surrounding canton (also called Bern) became

the eighth to join the Swiss Federation. Today, Canton Bern is Switzerland's second-largest, both in area (after Graubünden) and population (after Zürich). Since 1848, the city of Bern has been the Swiss capital. It's small for a capital (129,000 people, or 360,000 with the suburbs—two-thirds Protestant and one-third Catholic). Though firmly German-speaking, it's strategically located near French-speaking regions, and you'll also hear French around town.

Its pointy towers, sandstone buildings, colorful fountains, and riverside setting make Bern one of Europe's finest surviving medieval towns.

Orientation to Bern

User-friendly Bern is packed into a peninsula bounded by the Aare River. The train station is located where the peninsula connects to the mainland. From there, a handy main drag leads gradually downhill, straight through the middle of town past most of the major sights, to the tip of the peninsula (across a bridge and finally to the Bear Park and a rose garden). Allow 30 minutes to walk from the station to the Bear Park; see the self-guided walk later in this chapter.

Tourist Information: The main TI is on the ground floor inside the **train station** (daily 9:00-19:00, tel. 031-328-1212, www.bern.com). If you're planning to follow my self-guided walk, pick up the TI's leaflet on the clock tower (Zytglogge-Turm). A second TI is near the **Bear Park** (Mon-Fri 8:00-18:00, Sat 10:00-16:00, Sun 10:00-12:00).

ARRIVAL IN BERN

By Train: Bern's bustling train station is a thriving three-story mall. The trains almost get lost. On the upper level, you'll find a Migros grocery store (daily 8:00-21:00) and a pharmacy (daily 6:30-22:00). The ground floor has the TI, ticket office (Mon-Fri 6:15-21:00, Sat-Sun until 20:00), and pay lockers (down a corridor behind the TI). The lower level has pay WCs (with showers), a Co-op grocery store, and a big Migros takeaway deli.

Trams and buses fan out from the square in front of the station. While most listed sights and accommodations are within walking distance, hopping a bus or tram can be smart (and, with the Bern Ticket provided by your hotel, it's free).

By Car: The old town is essentially car-free (only service vehicles and public transit allowed), so leave your car near the train station *(Bahnhof)*. Drivers approaching by freeway should follow *Bern Zentrum* signs, then *Bahnhof* and *Bahnhof Parking* to find the huge parking garage behind the station (4.30 CHF/hour, 36 CHF/day, www.parking-bern.ch). While not the cheapest option, it's the easiest for a quick visit. From here, you're just an elevator ride away from the TI and the streets of Switzerland's capital. If you visit the Paul Klee Center, you can park there all day (till midnight) for 7 CHF on days the museum is open. From there take bus #12 into the town center.

HELPFUL HINTS

Blue Monday: Most of Bern's museums are closed on Mondays. But you can still follow my self-guided walk, tour the cathedral (and climb its tower), tour the Zytglogge-Turm, watch the parliament in action (generally possible Mon afternoons), ogle the beasts at Bear Park, and go for a swim in the river.

Market: An outdoor market with clothes, gifts, and other merchandise fills the lower end of Bärenplatz several times per week (year-round Tue 8:00-18:00 and Sat 8:00-16:00, plus April-Oct Wed and Fri 9:00-20:00, www.marktbern.ch).

Wi-Fi: There's free Wi-Fi at the **train station** (network name: SBB-Free; to log in you'll need a mobile phone that can receive texts). You could also try **the Museum of Fine Arts,** the **Co-op** or **Migros** cafeterias, or any branch of **McDonald's** or **Starbucks.**

Bookstore: Stauffacher is huge, with an entire floor of English books, including a fine selection of writing on Switzerland, and a café (Mon-Fri 9:00-19:00, Thu until 20:00, Sat until 17:00, closed Sun, a block from the train station at Neuengasse 37—for location see "Bern Hotels & Restaurants" map, later, tel. 031-313-6363, www.stauffacher.ch).

Laundry: Jet Wash, a self-service launderette, is a quick, three-stop bus ride from the station (Mon-Sat 7:00-21:00, Sun 9:00-18:00, take bus #20 from platform G at station to the Lorraine stop, then find Dammweg 43 on the left, mobile 077-417-9502, www.jetwash.ch).

GETTING AROUND BERN

The city is walkable, though the buses and trams can be handy. Buy a *Kurzstreckebillet* (short-haul ticket-2.60 CHF) or *Einzelbillett* (standard single ticket-4.60 CHF), depending on the how far you're going. The *Kurzstreckebillet* is good for five stops, which will take you from the train station to Bear Park. A day pass is 13 CHF (buy tickets from touch-screen machines at stops, credit cards accepted, info at tel. 031-321-8844, www.bernmobil.ch).

Your hotel or hostel will give you a card called the **Bern Ticket** that covers local transit; when you arrive in town, your lodging confirmation serves as your transit ticket until you get the card at check-in. All public transit in Bern is also covered by the Swiss Travel Pass.

BERN & MURTEN

Tours in Bern

Walking Tours

These leave daily from April through October at 11:00 from the TI at the train station; Sat only in the off-season (1.5 hours, 23 CHF, reserve the day before to ensure the guide speaks English). The TI also offers a four-hour **iPod audioguide** (18 CHF, discount with Swiss Travel Pass).

Local Guide

Marie-Thérèse Lauper is a charming and hardworking independent guide who offers special rates for individuals and small groups (mobile 079-700-0880, www.bern-guide.ch, info@bern-guide.ch).

Heart of Bern Walk

Follow this self-guided walk to explore central Bern. You'll start at the train station and finish at the Bear Park at the far end of town, where you can catch a bus back to the station. Along the way, visit a bakery or supermarket to put together a picnic, which you can eat at a terrace behind the cathedral or near Bear Park.

❶ Train Station

The station is essentially a bright and airy shopping mall, with a TI and all the shops you could need—all open on Sunday. For a grand perch, ride the escalator to the top floor directly above the red circle benches. A huge board listing departures illustrates why so many Swiss urbanites choose not to own a car.

With your back to the big departures board, step outside onto the big square called Bahnhofplatz. The old town was sealed off here with a fortified wall, which was replaced in the 19th century by the train station. Today all city buses and trams come and go from the station.

Bern's vision is to create a car-less city. The striking glass-topped bus station, designed by renowned Spanish architect Santiago Calatrava, makes riding the bus a bit more elegant.

Across the square stands the **Holy Ghost Church** (Heiliggeistkirche). Notice the gray-green Bernese sandstone, quarried nearby, used for the church and surrounding buildings. Because this stone is porous and easily eroded by water, Bern's buildings are designed with characteristic oversize eaves. As dictated by city law, even newer buildings (like these) are built with the same stone (though generally just a thin veneer) to maintain architectural harmony.

• *Cross Bahnhofplatz, walk 50 yards, and turn left (around the church) onto Spitalgasse. This marks the start of one long street (with four names).*

The spine of both the peninsula and our walk, this street rambles down-hill through the heart of town to the bridge and Bear Park.

Notice the first of Bern's 11 historic **fountains,** the Bagpiper. These colorful 16th-century fountains are Bern's trademark. The city commissioned them for many reasons: to brighten the cityscape of gray-stone buildings, to show off the town's wealth, and to remind citizens of great local heroes and events. They also gave 16th-century artists something to work on after the Reformation deprived them of their most important patron, the Catholic Church.

Shopping opportunities abound under the more than three miles of arcades that line Bern's lanes. Stores run the gamut from affordable to high-end (generally open 9:00-18:30, Thu until 21:00, Sat until 16:00, closed Sun). In German, the slang for the corridor under these arcades is *Rohr* (pipe). To stroll through the town is to *rohren* (go piping).

• *Continue* "rohren" *down Spitalgasse until you reach...*

❷ Bärenplatz

The street runs under the **Prison Tower** (Käfigturm)—once a part of the city wall (c. 1256). Renovated in the 1640s, the tower served as a prison until 1897 (*Käfig* means "cage"). Notice how the hand on the clock really is a hand—and how it was built in a slower-paced era, when just an hour-hand told time precisely enough. The bears on the tower are part of Bern's coat of arms (with the double-eagle reminder that Bern was part of the Holy Roman Empire in the early Middle Ages). Live bears await you at the end of this walk.

As each of the town's successive walls and moats was torn down, Bern was left with an elongated swath of land that's now a people-friendly "square" like this one. **Bärenplatz** is a top place to be seen in the evening.

To the left (50 yards), you'll see the **Dutch Tower** (Hollän-derturm). Swiss soldiers were famous mercenaries—guns for hire who fought all over Europe. Returning from a battle in the Netherlands, the soldiers brought back the habit of smoking. But back in the 18th century, smoking tobacco was forbidden within the city walls of Bern, so they hid in this tower to smoke discreetly. Locals joke that now that a new, modern-day smoking ban has come to Bern, this tower may regain its historic function.

Farther left at the far end of the square is a modern, mossy **fountain** by the Swiss surrealist Meret Oppenheim. Made in 1983, it symbolizes growth and life, and is supposed to demonstrate communication between an object of art and the beholder. It worked well...too well, in fact, as most citizens immediately communicated their dislike and wanted it destroyed. But Bern's politicians proved braver than expected, and the fountain survived. Time has trans-

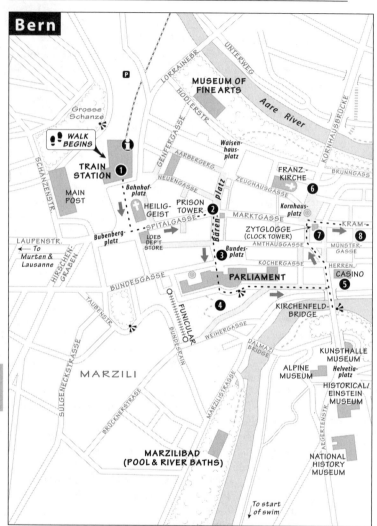

formed Oppenheim's gray concrete column into a multicolored pillar decorated with moss, grass, and flowers. Residents do like it in the winter, when it's covered with ice. The grand building beyond the fountain—once the city orphanage—is the police station.

• *With your back to the modern fountain, stroll to the south end of Bären-platz, filled with market stalls, lined with fun places to eat (see "Eating in Bern," later), and hiding a massive underground parking lot. The big building you'll see at the end of the square is the...*

❸ Parliament (Bundeshaus)

You may brush elbows with some high-powered legislators, but

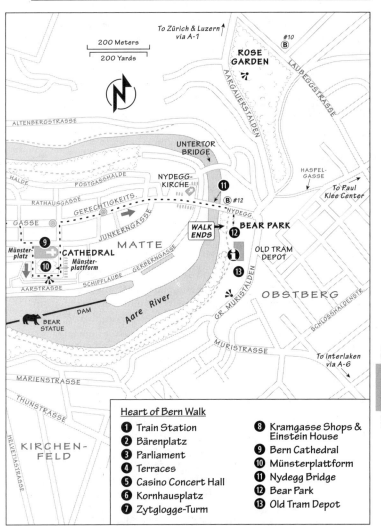

To Zürich & Luzern via A-1

ROSE GARDEN

Ⓑ #10

LAUBEGGSTRASSE

AARGAUERSTALDEN

ALTENBERGSTRASSE

UNTERTOR BRIDGE

HALDE

POSTGASSHALDE

NYDEGG-KIRCHE

HASPEL-GASSE

To Paul Klee Center

RATHAUSGASSE

GERECHTIGKEITS-

Ⓑ #12

NYDEGG

Ⓚ 11

GASSE

JUNKERNGASSE

WALK ENDS

Ⓚ 12 **BEAR PARK**

Ⓚ 9

CATHEDRAL

MATTE

OLD TRAM DEPOT

Münster-platz

Münster-plattform

Ⓚ 13

GERBERNGASSE

Ⓚ 10

AARSTRASSE

SCHIFFLAUBE

GR. MURISTALDEN

OBSTBERG

DAM

Aare River

SCHLOSSHALDENSTR.

BEAR STATUE

MURISTRASSE

To Interlaken via A-6

MARIENSTRASSE

THUNSTRASSE

KIRCHEN-FELD

HELVETIASTRASSE

BERN & MURTEN

Heart of Bern Walk

❶ Train Station
❷ Bärenplatz
❸ Parliament
❹ Terraces
❺ Casino Concert Hall
❻ Kornhausplatz
❼ Zytglogge-Turm
❽ Kramgasse Shops & Einstein House
❾ Bern Cathedral
❿ Münsterplattform
⓫ Nydegg Bridge
⓬ Bear Park
⓭ Old Tram Depot

---

you wouldn't know it—everything looks very casual for a national capital. Check out the statuary: The woman on the top of the building represents political independence, the one on the left (under the "1291"—when the first three cantons bound together to found the nucleus of Switzerland) stands for freedom, and the one on the right (under 1848, when the people got their constitution assuring democracy) symbolizes peace. The fine granite plaza in front of the parliament (built in 2004 to replace a parking lot) is a favorite spot for demonstrations and markets. The 26-squirt fountain (one for each canton) is a real kid-pleaser (and makes for fun photos) on a hot summer day. Facing the square on the left is the Swiss National

Bank—this country's Fort Knox, with half the Swiss gold stock buried under the square (the rest is in Zürich).

Walk through the passageway to the right of parliament and drop into the **welcome center** at the back of the building, where you can pick up some of their generous literature on the Swiss government. Its bicameral system was inspired by the US Constitution, with one big difference: Executive power is shared by a committee of seven, with a rotating ceremonial president and a passion for consensus. This is a mechanism to avoid power grabs by any single individual...a safeguard that the Swiss love (and enjoy bragging about lately).

Touring the Parliament: When parliament is in session, the **galleries** are open to the public, so you can watch the action (free; generally Mon afternoon, Tue and Thu mornings, and all day Wed; leave ID at entrance, lines can be long, no photos). When parliament is not in session, you can take a free, guided, hour-long **tour** of the building (English tours normally mid-July-mid-Aug Mon-Sat at 14:00, Sat-only in off-season, no tours early Sept-early Oct; reserve up to 3 days ahead at www.parlament.ch—click "Services and Media" then "Guided Tours," tel. 058-322-9022).

• *Beyond the back of the parliament building are...*

❹ Terraces

From here, you have a commanding view over the Aare River and Bern's biggest swimming pool, the **Marzilibad.** On a clear day, you can see the Eiger, Mönch, and Jungfrau—the highest peaks in the Berner Oberland—and, in the foreground, the far less imposing "mountain" of Bern, the **Gurten** (with the view tower poking up above its forested summit). The Gurten is the city's favorite recreation spot, offering music festivals in summer and modest skiing opportunities for children in winter. On a hot day the river is speckled with locals doing the "Bern float" in the water.

Stroll along the terrace walls a few hundred yards to **Kirchenfeld Bridge.** Walk out to the center for great river views (a big museum complex, including the Einstein Museum, is just across the bridge; described later, under "Sights in Bern"). The ❺ **Casino** isn't for gamblers—it's the home of Bern's Symphony Orchestra.

• *Backtrack across the bridge, and with your back to the river, follow the tram tracks up to another swath of land created by the removal of a city wall to Theaterplatz and then...*

❻ Kornhausplatz

This square is ornamented by the colorful fountain of an **Ogre** (*Chindlifresser*, "child-eater"). Two legends try to explain this grue-some sight. It's either a folkloric representation of the Greek god Chronos, or a figure that was intended to scare children off the former city walls.

The building behind on the left used to be the granary and now houses the modern public library and the huge **Kornhauskeller** restaurant. If the restaurant is open, wander down the stairs and head inside—even if you're not eating here, you must take a peek at this magnificent subterranean place. Once the vast city wine cellar—now a recommended restaurant—this space was built in high Baroque style (1718) and renovated with paintings inspired by the Pre-Raphaelites in 1897. The 12 columns (in the upper level) show traditional costumes of Bernese women.

• *Back on Kornhausplatz, step under the clock tower where Marktgasse becomes Kramgasse to see the fancy clock ornamenting its downhill side.*

❼ Zytglogge-Turm

Bern's famous clock tower was part of the original wall marking the first gate to the city (c. 1250). The clock, which dates back to

1530, performs four minutes before each hour: The happy jester comes to life, Father Time turns his hourglass, the rooster crows (in German, that's "kee-kee-ree-kee" rather than "cock-a-doodle-doo"), and the golden man on top hammers the bell. Apparently, this little spectacle was considered quite entertaining five centuries ago. The word *Zytglogge* is local dialect. The Standard German equivalent, which doesn't actually exist, would be *Zeitglocke* (literally "time bell").

To pass the time waiting for the action, read the plaque explaining what's so interesting about the fancy old clock (for example, the golden hour hand is an hour behind for half the year because of the modern innovation of Daylight Saving Time). You can determine the zodiac, today's date, and the stage of the moon—look at the black-and-gold orb.

Under the clock are the old regional measurements (Swiss foot, the bigger Bernese foot, and the *Elle*, or "elbow," which was the distance from the elbow to the fingertip) and the official meter and double meter. It took a strong leader like Napoleon to bring consistency to measurements in Europe, and he replaced the many goofy feet and elbows of medieval Europe with the metric system used today (c. 1800).

BERN & MÜRTEN

Touring the Tower: Enthusiasts can tour the medieval mechanics—early Swiss engineering at its best—and see the bellows that enable the old rooster to crow (15 CHF, 50-minute tour, April-Oct daily at 14:30, buy ticket at the door).

• *Continue your stroll down the main drag. At this point, you enter the oldest part of town, where bigger department stores are replaced by quainter shops and galleries on...*

❽ Kramgasse

Bern has wide streets like this one, but not many true squares. In the Middle Ages, craftsmen exhibited their goods on the sidewalks

under simple roofs. Eventually, these were formalized, buildings were expanded, and arcades evolved. Today, though the arcades are privately owned, owners must keep them clean and allow public access.

Most shops are underneath the arcades, but don't miss the ones in the **cellars** that you can access only from the main road. The cellars, marked by old-time hatches, were originally for storing household goods, and later, wine. People said "merry Bern" was floating on wine, just as Venice was floating on water. The merry times ended in 1798, when the French invaded (and drank all the wine). The cellars were once again used for household goods, and the city got a new nickname: "sad Bern." Napoleon's soldiers not only liberated Bern from its wine, but also from the tremendous treasury the city was known for. Napoleon used money looted from Bern to finance his Egyptian crusade.

• *About 200 yards below the clock tower, on the right at Kramgasse 49, is the home of a very smart man.*

The apartment that Albert Einstein called home between 1903 and 1905—the years when he formulated the theory of relativity while working in obscurity at the Patent Office—is now the **Einstein House** museum. Einstein and his wife Mileva welcomed their first child in this one-bedroom apartment, and shared a kitchen and bathroom with the neighbors. Inside, you can see period furniture, including Einstein's Patent Office desk, and a few photos and manuscripts. Another apartment one floor farther up has been turned into an informative—if dry—exhibit

on Einstein's life. This quick, inexpensive visit (well-described in English with a few historic artifacts and a 20-minute video—

request English) is just about the right amount of Einstein for most visitors. It doesn't do much for me, but I guess everything's relative (6 CHF; daily 10:00-17:00, closed late Dec-Jan; tel. 031-312-0091, www.einstein-bern.ch). Die-hard fans should consider visiting the Einstein Museum's more extensive exhibit (triple the price but free with Swiss Travel Pass), located within Bern's Historical Museum (see page 106).

A bit farther down, in the cellar of #37 (next to the Samson fountain), is **Hanftheke Bern** (*hanf* means hemp), a marijuana shop. In Switzerland, marijuana with less than 1 percent THC (the psychoactive component of cannabis) is legal. This strain is high in cannabidiols, which make you very relaxed...but you can't get high on it. The person behind the counter is happy to explain the local approach to pot.

• *Twenty yards below the Samson fountain (he's fighting a lion to demonstrate his strength), at #29, turn right through the narrow tunnel-lane, Münstergässchen, to the...*

❾ Bern Cathedral (Berner Münster)

Bern's 15th-century Catholic-turned-Protestant cathedral is capped with a 330-foot-tall tower, the highest in Switzerland (finished in 1893). The late-Gothic church was dedicated to St. Vincent of Zaragoza.

The church's **main portal,** with its striking gold-leaf highlights, seems pretty un-Protestant. It probably survived because its theme, the Last Judgment, showed that no matter how rich you are or what rank you have in Church hierarchy, anyone can end up in hell (an idea Protestants dug). Condemned people are popping in the flames like lottery balls. Notice the humorous details in the commotion of people heading to hell (especially what the little green devil is doing to the sinful monk).

Step inside. The plain interior was once adorned with 26 separate little chapels and altars dedicated to Mary and various saints. An ornate screen separated the priests from the worshippers. But when the Reformation came to town in 1528, all this was swept away. The iconoclasts believed that images distracted worshippers from focusing on God, so they destroyed the distasteful decoration. The new center of attention was the pulpit, where Protestant preachers shared the word of God—not in Latin, but in the people's language.

Those Protestant iconoclasts didn't manage to trash the church's precious painted keystones. Sixty feet up and hard to see, they still decorate the ceiling of the choir. They feature 78 saints and other Christian VIPs. You can also see some surviving 15th-century stained glass in the apse. The organ filling the back wall dates from 1729.

Albert Einstein in Bern

The man who changed how we see our universe made his greatest discoveries during the eight years he lived in Bern (1901-1909).

Raised in Germany, Albert Einstein (1879-1955) went to college in Zürich, hoping to land a job teaching math and physics. But the young grad's GPA and résumé were mediocre, so instead he took a job in Bern's Patent Office, inspecting and registering inventions.

Twenty-three-year-old Albert and his new bride Mileva (his brainy college sweetheart) rented a second-floor apartment at Kramgasse 49 (today's Einstein House), where Mileva soon gave birth to their first son, little Hans Albert. Einstein punched the clock at the Patent Office and spent his spare time reading, hiking the Bernese countryside, and thinking. At night, he'd join with his mates—the self-named "Olympia Academy"—to smoke, drink beer, and talk math and philosophy. Outwardly, he led an ordinary life, but his thoughts were always on science's Big Questions. At home, in pubs, or at work he'd scribble down equations and ideas, filing them in his self-described "Department of Theoretical Physics"—a desk drawer in his office.

Then, one warm spring day, as Einstein walked on the outskirts of Bern, it all started coming together. So began his *annus mirabilis*—the miracle year of 1905—in which the 26-year-old unknown amateur physicist quickly wrote five papers that would shock and perplex the world. Published in a major physics journal, they touched on a variety of subjects—such as how molecules move and how light can appear as either a wave of energy or as a beam of tiny particles.

The most famous and unsettling paper, his theory of special relativity, described a world in motion. A person on a moving train and someone who's stationary see the world from different perspectives—that's the classic principle of relativity described by Galileo and Newton. But Einstein said there's an exception to the rule—light, whose speed always remains constant whether it's on a moving train or on the ground. So a person on a moving train and one at rest will never agree on what they observe...yet they're both right. The discrepancies only become obvious as the train travels close to the speed of light. Then, while the person on the train thinks everything is normal, the one on the ground sees the train shrink, train clocks slow down, and the person on the train stops aging!

Einstein's papers initially drew little interest and a measure of skepticism. (Einstein did get a promotion in the Patent Office—from "technical expert third class" to "technical expert second class.") But over time, other physicists grasped the significance of Einstein's work, seeing how he took earlier findings, wove them together, and did the math that explained it all. Subsequent experiments proved that, in fact, even Einstein's most bizarre assertions were correct. Time on a fast-moving jet really does slow down (hence, those interminable intercontinental flights).

Einstein was invited to lecture at the local university, though he was still working nine-to-five at the Patent Office. In his spare time, he worked on his next project, general relativity. He theorized that gravity is not a force that attracts things but a curving of space—like a bowling ball on a soft mattress—that affects the motion of nearby objects. In 1909, Einstein's growing reputation won him a job offer to teach in Zürich, and he quit the Patent Office and left Bern for good.

Einstein would never again approach the creative level of his days in Bern. (In 1922, he won the Nobel Prize for his work done during the 1905 *annus mirabilis*.) Albert and Mileva split, and he married a cousin. When Hitler took power in Germany (1933), Einstein—a pacifist and a Jew—left Europe for America. His curly black hair had turned white, and his aging face later became a pop-culture icon of genius—complete with pipe, moustache, basset-hound eyes, and halo of frizzy white hair (which he back-combed in order to look sufficiently unkempt).

In 1939, Einstein wrote a letter to President Franklin Delano Roosevelt warning that scientists (including some in Germany) could soon discover a way to release an enormous amount of energy. The research was based on a principle he'd outlined back in 1905—that energy is equivalent to mass times the speed of light squared (a very big number). And so, $E = mc^2$ became the principle behind the atomic bomb—a very big bang from an idea hatched in the pubs and arcaded streets of Bern.

If you're curious to learn more, Bern has two sights about its brightest mind: the Einstein House in the town center and the Einstein Museum just across the river (both described in this chapter).

BERN & MURTEN

Cost and Hours: Free to enter cathedral; Mon-Sat 10:00-17:00, Sun 11:30-17:00; mid-Oct-April Mon-Fri 12:00-16:00, Sat 10:00-17:00, Sun 11:30-16:00; audioguide-5 CHF, tel. 031-312-0462, www.bernermuenster.ch.

Climbing the Tower: You can pay 5 CHF to huff up the spiral staircase (over 300 steps) to a viewpoint at the base of the lacy see-through steeple (same hours as cathedral). From this 210-foot-high vantage point, you enjoy a behind-the-scenes look at the varied courtyards and rooftop gardens hidden behind the conformist building facades. Don't forget to turn around to appreciate an up-close look at the tower's carved figures. Marie-Therese Lauper works up here every day, watching over the church, answering questions, and giving visitors a chance (on their way down) to peek at the cathedral's **bells**—including the largest bell in Switzerland, a 10.5-ton beauty cast in 1611 and called Susanne (named by a bellringer after his sizeable girlfriend). This bell was so heavy that it took eight men to swing her. If you're up here when the Prayer Bell rings, you may feel the tower sway.

• *Head behind the cathedral to a terrace overlooking the river, the...*

❿ Münsterplattform

Starting in the 14th century, this terrace was built from all kinds of "recycled" stones from older buildings. Archaeologists have even unearthed some heads of statues that were victims of Reformation iconoclasts. Look down on the Aare. (Is that a bear out on the dam?) Just right of the weir is the recommended **Schwellenmätteli Restaurant lounge,** where a trendy local crowd enjoys cocktails over the rushing river on nice days. Directly below, notice the security nets. The platform used to be the favorite place for suicides—to the terror of people living below. Twin 18th-century pavilions grace the square. On the right is a tiny branch of the city library (providing park-goers with books, *boules*, and table tennis). And in the far left is a café offering a scenic spot under a chestnut tree for a bite or a drink on a sunny day. This little park is frequented by pot smokers, and nobody seems to care. Behind the café, the elevator (a "vertical tram") has been carrying passengers up and down since 1896 (1.20 CHF).

With your back to the river, exit on the right and return to the main drag (now called Gerechtigkeitsgasse) via Kreuzgasse.

A block downhill, on the **Fountain of Justice,** a blindfolded figure triumphs over the mayor, pope, sultan, and emperor. Along this stretch of the street, a grate reveals a bit of the canal that used to flow open down the middle of the peninsula, providing people with a handy disposal system, place to wash, and the medieval equivalent of a fire hose.

At the end of the street on the right, just before the bridge, look for the red *Nette Toilet* sign on the window of the Junkere Café-Bar. The city government pays local bars to let the public use their WCs—so feel free to pop in and use the toilet.

• *From here, you reach...*

❶ Nydegg Bridge

Look downstream. To your left, a church sits on the site of the original town castle. The small bridge below is the oldest in Bern (and, until 1844, was the only bridge crossing the Aare here). Above on the ridge, just behind and to the right of the pointy spire, is the Rosengarten restaurant (described in "Eating in Bern," later). Looking upstream you can see the original Lindt chocolate factory, evoking an age when this stretch of river was lined with mills powering the industrial zone of Bern—tanneries, shipyards, lumber mills, and so on. The area is now routinely flooded when the river runs high. As you look upstream, notice the peaceful path along the left bank, a nice place for a walk.

• *Continue across the bridge, bear right, and look over the railings into...*

❷ Bear Park (BärenPark)

The symbol of Bern is the bear, and some lively ones frolic along this terraced hillside, to the delight of locals and tourists who

crowd along the rails. From 1857 to 2009, Bern housed its bears in two big, barren, concrete pits *(Bärengraben)*. But thanks to the agitation of the B.L.M. (Bear Liberation Movement), the city government was forced to replace the pits with posher digs. In 2009, the last of the pit bears died, and later that year, three-year-old brown bears Finn (a male from Finland) and Björk (a female from Denmark) moved to the big enclosure between the old pits and the river. Soon they welcomed their female cubs, Ursina and Berna. This ursine family enjoys much better conditions than their fore-bears, including a private fishing channel next to the river. In 2013, the surly teenager Berna was sent to a preserve in Bulgaria due to irreconcilable differences with her mother. Today Bern's bear family is happy, and Berna is shacked up with a new boyfriend in Bulgaria.

Concrete stairs lead down to the big historic pit. It's free to pop down and read the entertaining history boards (for more info, see www.baerenpark-bern.ch).

• *Above Bear Park is the...*

⓮ Old Tram Depot (Altes Tramdepot)

This used to be the garage for trams that ran across the bridge from the old town (the tracks are long gone). Now the depot hosts a brewery restaurant/café with a lively beer garden and terrace, as well as a TI, nice public WC, and Eiswerkstatt, a popular ice cream shop with creative flavors.

To continue this walk, you could take a seven-minute hike up the moderately steep, cobbled pathway to the left (with your back to the river). This takes you to the rose garden (a good picnic spot) and **Restaurant Rosengarten,** which offers a grand city view and grand prices (for details, see "Eating in Bern"). Or turn right and walk along the river, then return to the center via either Kirchen-feld or Dalmazi bridge.

To return directly to the train station, jump on bus #12 (runs every 6 minutes, get ticket from machine, 2.60 CHF). If wandering back through town on foot, be sure to get off into the quieter side lanes, which have a fascinating and entertaining array of shops and little eateries.

More Sights in Bern

▲▲The Berner Float and Marzilibad

For something to write home about, join Bern's merchants, students, and carp in a float down the Aare River. The Bernese, proud of their very clean river and their basic rud-diness, have a tradition—sort of a wet, urban *paseo.* On summer days, they hike upstream 5 to 30 minutes, then float back down to the excellent (and free) riverside baths and pools (Marzilibad) just below the parliament building.

The process is simple: Hike up the paved riverside sidewalk as far as you like, then take the steps leading into the water whenever you want to "put in." As you approach Marzilibad, just stroke over to the shore to grab one of the several poles placed to help people exit the river. The locals make it look easy, but it can be danger-ous—the current is swift. If you miss the last pole, you're history. The TI warns that this is only for strong, experienced swimmers.

If a float down the river is a bit much for you, enjoy the Mar-zilibad, a well-equipped public swimming pool and park with pic-nic spots, restaurant, lockers, wading pools, games, and more.

▲▲Museum of Fine Arts (Kunstmuseum)

Featuring 800 years of art, this three-story museum offers a unique opportunity to see not only the best of Swiss artists but works by other famous names as well. You'll find old masters from the 13th to 19th century—including Fra Angelico and Filippo Lippi—in the basement, 19th-century art by Manet, Monet, Cézanne, Van Gogh, Toulouse-Lautrec, and others on the ground floor, and 20th-century stuff upstairs, including works by Dalí, Picasso, and Miró.

Cost and Hours: 7 CHF, extra for temporary exhibits, covered by Swiss Travel Pass, Tue 10:00-21:00, Wed-Sun until 17:00, closed Mon, no English descriptions—get the worthwhile 5-CHF English audioguide, café, 4 blocks north of station at Hodlerstrasse 8, tel. 031-328-0944, www.kunstmuseumbern.ch.

▲▲Paul Klee Center (Zentrum Paul Klee)

With his wavy building mirroring the wavy landscape of the Bern countryside, Italian architect Renzo Piano celebrates the creative spirit of Swiss-born art-ist Paul Klee (1879-1940). Klee wasn't just a great painter—he was an inter-disciplinary explosion of creative energy. The cen-ter, which fosters music and theater as well as the visual arts, has a mission: to bring art to the people. For example, a huge zone is devoted to a children's creative work-shop that includes painting and a shadow theater.

Cost and Hours: 20 CHF, covered by Swiss Travel Pass, Tue-Sun 10:00-17:00, closed Mon, heavily academic audioguide-6 CHF, pick up free English-language booklet, mandatory lock-ers require refundable 1-CHF coin deposit, cafés, Monument im Fruchtland 3, tel. 031-359-0101, www.zpk.org.

Getting There: Take a 15-minute ride on frequent bus #12 from the train station to its last stop, Zentrum Paul Klee.

Parking: Museumgoers can park all day (until midnight) for 7 CHF—a great deal if you combine the museum visit with a trip into town afterward.

Children's Workshops: 15 CHF for 1-hour workshop at 12:00, 14:00, or 16:00, no reservations taken.

Visiting the Museum: The Klee collection is in the build-ing's middle wave. This cultural center keeps about 200 of Klee's pieces on display (out of a collection of 4,000). It's the best place in the world to experience and learn about this modernist painter of lively, almost childlike art. Artistically, you can't put Klee in a box. His paintings—mostly from the 1920s and 1930s—are playful yet enigmatic. His art is full of symbolism...or maybe we just think so. He experimented in pointillism, as you'll see in the piece *Ad Parnassum*.

Insula Dulcamara (Bittersweet Island) is a good example of Klee's enigmatic hieroglyph style. It's a puzzle—he pairs opposites: man, woman; air, water. It's 1938... is that a submarine on the horizon evoking the rise of fascism? Perhaps the black figures are death, floating in an eternal spring-like landscape. Kids love Klee, and they always teach the art snobs a thing or two with their interpretations.

Downstairs you'll find cafés, an art database, a movie about building the museum, a cozy hangout, and the children's workshop.

▲Einstein Museum

Fans of the genius will want to visit this "museum" (actually the second floor of Bern's Historical Museum) devoted to Einstein and his times. It's more interesting and informative than the Einstein House downtown, and has many more artifacts from Einstein's life. But it's also overpriced (as admission also includes the rest of the Historical Museum)—so unless you're a serious Einstein fan, have a Swiss Travel Pass, or are a Swiss history buff, it's probably not worth the money.

Photos and displays explain Einstein's accomplishments and complicated personal life, detail his travels after leaving Bern, and place him in historical context, with special emphasis on his Jewish identity (which for Einstein was more cultural than religious). Einstein's concepts are nicely illustrated, and everything is well-explained in English (the audioguide is not necessary). The mirrored stairway up to the second floor prepares your brain to expand your ideas about space and time.

Cost and Hours: 18 CHF, includes Historical Museum, covered by Swiss Travel Pass, Tue-Sun 10:00-17:00, closed Mon; across bridge from parliament at Helvetiaplatz 5—take tram #6, #7, or #8, or bus #19; tel. 031-350-7711, www.einsteinmuseum.ch.

Other Bern Museums

The Historical Museum and its Einstein exhibit are part of a larger ensemble that includes Alpine, Communication, Natural History, Rifle, and Kunsthalle (contemporary art) museums. All appeal mainly to visitors with specific interests. The Natural History Museum is fun for kids. The TI has a helpful pamphlet describing the museums (all covered by Swiss Travel Pass except Rifle Museum, most open Tue-Sun 10:00-17:00, closed Mon; see arrival instructions for Einstein Museum, above; www.museen-bern.ch).

Sleeping in Bern

As Switzerland's capital, Bern hosts not only tourists but also waves of businesspeople and politicians, keeping room rates rather high throughout the year. In general, prices rise during the week and drop on weekends. Conventions and other events, held about one out of every four nights, can drive demand and prices radically higher. Sleeping within walking distance of the train station is convenient and fun, but comes with compromises—noise, small rooms, and the highest prices. Swiss hotels generally don't have air-conditioning and don't appreciate Americans complaining about it being too hot. If you don't mind a short tram ride, you can find lower-priced lodgings in the neighborhood across the river to the north. Make sure you get your free Bern Ticket city transport pass at check-in.

NEAR THE STATION

These four places are within a 5- to 10-minute walk from the train station.

$$$ Hotel Goldener Schlüssel is the oldest inn in downtown Bern, but it's been completely and nicely renovated. Its 34 small, Euro-style rooms are fitted with prefab bathroom pods. The quieter, more expensive, high-ceilinged back rooms are worth reserving in warm weather, as the rooms facing Rathausgasse get café and disco noise from across the street. Rates are high for what you get, and the bare-bones breakfast is disappointing, but that's the norm at city-center hotels (RS%, family rooms, elevator, Rathausgasse 72, tel. 031-311-0216, www.goldener-schluessel.ch, info@goldener-schluessel.ch).

$$ Hotel National offers 46 rooms—some simple yet clean, others much nicer. It's a basic, old-school, creaky-hardwood-floor time warp of a place with a classic open elevator. There's some street noise in outward-facing rooms, and even inward-facing rooms can be noisy on Friday and Saturday due to the adjacent theater, so speak up when reserving if a quiet room is important. A few budget rooms have private bathrooms across the hall (family rooms, free welcome drink for guests arriving Mon-Fri; Hirschengraben 24, tel. 031-552-1515, www.nationalbern.ch, info@nationalbern.ch).

¢ Backpackers Hotel Glocke rents 77 of the cheapest beds in the old town. It's a mixture of small dorms and (on two upper floors) basic but adequate private rooms. All the rooms are stacked directly above a nightclub; fortunately, the reception desk provides

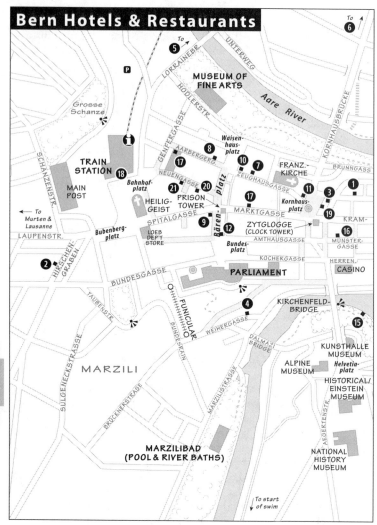

Bern Hotels & Restaurants

To 6

To 5

LORRAINEBR.

UNTERWEG

MUSEUM OF FINE ARTS

HODLERSTR.

Aare River

KORNHAUSBRÜCKE

Grosse Schanze

SCHANZENSTR.

TRAIN STATION

MAIN POST

Bahnhof-platz

GENFERGASSE

NEUENGASSE

AARBERGERG.

Waisen-haus-platz

8

17

10

7

FRANZ.-KIRCHE

BRUNNGASS.

ZEUGHAUSGASSE

11

3

1

18

21

20

platz

HEILIG-GEIST

PRISON TOWER

SPITALGASSE

9

Bären-platz

12

MARKTGASSE

17

Kornhaus-platz

19

KRAM-

ZYTGLOGGE (CLOCK TOWER)

16

To Murten & Lausanne

LAUPENSTR.

Bubenberg-platz

LOEB DEPT STORE

Bundes-platz

AMTHAUSGASSE

MÜNSTER-GASSE

HERREN-

2

HIRSCHENGRABEN

BUNDESGASSE

KOCHERGASSE

PARLIAMENT

CASINO

TAUBENSTR.

SÜLGENECKSTRASSE

FUNICULAR

BUNDESBAHN

WEIHERGASSE

4

KIRCHENFELD-BRIDGE

15

MARZILI

DALMAZI BRIDGE

KUNSTHALLE MUSEUM

BRÜCKENSTRASSE

MARZILISTRASSE

ALPINE MUSEUM

Helvetia-platz

HISTORICAL/EINSTEIN MUSEUM

AEGERTENSTR.

MARZILIBAD (POOL & RIVER BATHS)

NATIONAL HISTORY MUSEUM

To start of swim

a basket of free earplugs. The pleasant common room has a nice street view (no breakfast, elevator, no curfew, reception open 8:00-12:00 & 15:00-22:00, 10-minute walk from station or take tram #9 to Zytglogge stop, Rathausgasse 75, tel. 031-311-3771, www.bernbackpackers.ch, info@bernbackpackers.ch).

¢ **Bern Youth Hostel,** below the parliament building near the river, is a big institutional place that's well-run and adult-friendly (private rooms available, dinner available, game room, pay parking, reception open 7:00-12:00 & 14:00-24:00, Weihergasse 4, tel. 031-326-1111, www.youthhostel.ch/bern, bern@youthhostel.ch). To reach the hostel, walk three blocks south from the train station and

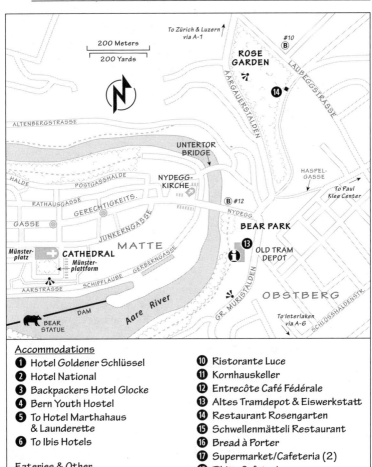

Accommodations

1 Hotel Goldener Schlüssel
2 Hotel National
3 Backpackers Hotel Glocke
4 Bern Youth Hostel
5 To Hotel Marthahaus
& Launderette
6 To Ibis Hotels

Eateries & Other

7 Restaurant Lötschberg
8 Gourmanderie Moléson
9 Mishio

10 Ristorante Luce
11 Kornhauskeller
12 Entrecôte Café Fédérale
13 Altes Tramdepot & Eiswerkstatt
14 Restaurant Rosengarten
15 Schwellenmätteli Restaurant
16 Bread à Porter
17 Supermarket/Cafeteria (2)
18 Tibits Cafeteria
19 Mekong & Bread à Porter
20 Meet Point
21 Stauffacher Bookstore

take the Marzilibahn funicular down to Weihergasse (1.40 CHF, free with hostel confirmation or Bern Ticket, runs until 21:00, after that use bus #30, www.marzilibahn.ch).

NORTH OF THE RIVER

These listings are an easy bus or tram ride from the center.

$$ Hotel Marthahaus is a better value than downtown hotels. Located two bus stops from the train station (walkable without luggage) in a quiet, elegant residential neighborhood north of the river, it's run as a fundraiser by a charitable organization that helps young people and seniors. Half of the 40 bright, simple rooms have shared bathrooms (family rooms, elevator, guest kitchen; take bus #20 from platform G at station to the Gewerbeschule stop, walk up the street to Wyttenbachstrasse and follow the yellow signs two short blocks to Wyttenbachstrasse 22a, tel. 031-332-4135, www.marthahaus.ch, info@marthahaus.ch).

Two **Ibis** hotels share the same entrance, check-in counter, and address: Am Guisanplatz 2. It's an easy 10-minute tram ride from the city center (take #9 from the station eight stops to Guisanplatz Expo, direction: Wankdorf Bahnhof). Look for the big metallic building by the Bern Convention Center (**$$ Ibis Bern Expo,** breakfast extra, tel. 031-335-1200, www.ibis.com, h5007@accor.com; **$ Ibis Budget Bern Expo** breakfast extra, pay parking, tel. 031-335-1212, www.ibisbudget.com, h5049@accor.com).

Eating in Bern

IN THE OLD TOWN

$$$$ Restaurant Lötschberg, a local favorite with a fun and youthful vibe, serves old-style Swiss cuisine in a modern space. One long wall is lined with the place's large variety of Swiss wines (Mon-Sat 10:00-24:00, Sun 11:00-23:00, Zeughausgasse 16, tel. 031-311-3455, www.loetschberg-aoc.ch).

$$$$ Gourmanderie Moléson is a long, skinny, classy bistro serving healthy and classic dishes with a French flair, including fondue and *tartes flambées* (like pizza without tomato sauce—known as *Flammkuchen* in German). It has a dressy and very Swiss interior with tables that tumble out onto the street (Mon-Sat 11:30-14:30 & 18:00-23:30, closed Sun, Aarbergergasse 24, tel. 031-311-4463, www.moleson-bern.ch).

$$$ Mishio is a mod pan-Asian place worth considering. The interior has an open kitchen, noisy acoustics, and plain furnishings. The trick here is to get an outside table on the terrace, which overlooks the lively Bärenplatz (Mon-Sat 11:00-22:00, closed Sun, Bärenplatz 2, tel. 031-313-1121).

$$$ Ristorante Luce brings the cooking of Italy's Emilia Romagna region (with lots of pastas and pizzas) to Bern. Choose between a venerable dining hall and great seating on the square (daily 11:30-14:00 & 18:00-23:00, reservations smart, Zeughausgasse 28, tel. 031-310-9999, www.ristoranteluce.ch).

$$$$ Kornhauskeller, in the palatial cellar of the old granary originally built to house the state's wine cellar, has vaulted archways decorated with colorful murals. This dressy, pricey Mediterranean (Swiss, French, Italian) place offers a fine antipasto bar: Make a meal out of the 19-CHF or 27-CHF plate, telling the man behind the buffet exactly what you'd like (daily 11:45-14:30 & 18:00-23:00, Kornhausplatz 18, tel. 031-327-7272, www.bindella.ch).

$$$$ Entrecôte Café Fédérale is a dressy and traditional bistro with a reputation for great steak. Very Swiss, it's a quiet place with more local politicians than tourists (daily 11:00-23:00, facing the parliament building at Bärenplatz 31, tel. 031-311-1624, www.entrecote.ch).

ACROSS THE RIVER, WITH VIEWS

$$$ Altes Tramdepot, in the Old Tram Depot above Bear Park, offers seating in its big, boisterous microbrewery (which was once the tram shed), or on a leafy terrace overlooking the town and river. It's popular, serving good-time food and Swiss specialties (fast and healthy 17-25-CHF weekday lunches, 20-CHF *Rösti* and wurst plates, daily 11:00-24:00, reserve in evening for outdoor view seating, bus #12 to Bärengraben stop, tel. 031-368-1415, www.altestramdepot.ch).

$$$$ Restaurant Rosengarten, perched at the edge of the city's rose garden atop the hill above the Bear Park, is good for city views. During the day, come for lunch, or for tea and cake amidst grannies (21-CHF two-course lunch special on weekdays). At night, you'll dine with couples enjoying the fresh seasonal menu (daily 9:00-24:00, Alter Aargauerstalden 31b, a moderately steep walk up from the Bear Park—or take tram #10 from the old town, tel. 031-331-3206, www.rosengarten.be).

$$$ Schwellenmätteli Restaurant is a chance to join trendy locals for a meal or drink while sitting directly over the river, next to the roar of water racing over the dam. The inside section is peaceful and open all year. The outside, open only in good weather, is loud—not good for conversation—but fun: At the tip of the platform is a lounge complete with sofas, mattresses, and a glass floor that lets you see the river racing underneath. This mod restaurant/lounge has a Swiss-Mediterranean menu (burgers, *Flammkuchen*, veggie dishes, and weekday lunch specials; daily 9:00-24:00; reservations smart for dinner, Dalmaziquai 11, cross Kirchenfeld Bridge from downtown and take path downhill to your left, or a pleasant 15-minute riverside stroll from Bear Park, tel. 031-350-5001, www.schwellenmaetteli.ch).

CHEAP EATS

Bakeries: Bern is very picnic-friendly. For a budget alternative to formal restaurant eating, small bakeries are all around town. One good option is **$ Bread à Porter,** which offers fresh sandwiches, quiches, salads, and usually a few small tables or stools at a bar (Kornhausplatz 11 and Münstergasse 74).

Supermarkets: Two large supermarkets are in the center—**Co-op** (Aarbergergasse 53, in the basement) and **Migros** (Marktgasse 40, ground floor). Both are open the same hours (Mon 9:00-

19:00, Tue-Wed 8:00-19:00, Thu 8:00-21:00, Fri 8:00-20:00, Sat 8:00-17:00, closed Sun). Outside of those hours, visit one of the midsize supermarkets in the **train station** (Migros on the upper level, daily 8:00-21:00; Co-op on the lower level, daily 6:00-22:00). You'll get a solid value on takeout food from the two **Migros Take-away** supermarket delis (bottom level of the train station and at Marktgasse 40). The staff will pack you up a hot lunch or dinner to take away for 10-15 CHF. Portions are big—often enough for two—and there are always several options on offer (such as lasagna with side salad or bratwurst with potatoes and veggies), as well as pizzas, quiches, and salads.

Self-Service Restaurants: The downtown **Co-op** and **Migros** supermarkets both run fine self-service restaurants with similar offerings. Aside from the typical Swiss cuisine, both have Asian food counters and kids' play zones. Co-op's cafeteria has a nice glassed-in terrace while Migros has a by-weight buffet and free tap water (hidden next to the tray-return conveyor belt). **$$ Tibits,** a busy buffet chain on the ground floor of the train station, offers a huge variety of vegetarian-only salads and sandwiches, plus two different hot dishes. Help yourself to a plate and pile it on. You'll pay by weight: An average helping will cost you about 20 CHF (free water, Mon-Sat 6:30-24:00, Sun 8:00-23:00, Bahnhofplatz 10, tel. 031-312-9111).

Ethnic Eateries: A few cheap ethnic takeout places hide deep under the arcades in the old town. **$ Mekong,** just 20 yards from the Zytglogge-Turm, has a daily selection of simple Asian dishes to go (2 CHF extra to eat in, Mon-Sat 11:30-14:30 & 17:30-23:00, closed Sun, Kornhausplatz 7, look for sign off Zibelegässli, tel. 031-311-2600). **$ Meet Point,** a Middle Eastern takeout counter with a couple of stools at Neuengasse 15, will sell you a *döner kebab* and a drink for 10 CHF (Mon-Sat 9:00-21:00, closed Sun).

Bern Connections

From Bern by Train to: Murten (hourly direct, 35 minutes, more with transfer), **Avenches** (4/day direct, 40 minutes, more with transfers), **Lausanne** (2/hour, 1 hour), **Interlaken** (2/hour, 1 hour, a few change in Spiez), **Luzern** (hourly direct, 1 hour), **Zürich** (3/hour, 1 hour), **Zürich Airport** (2/hour, 1.5 hours), **Zermatt** (2/hour, 2 hours, transfer in Visp), **Montreux** (2/hour, 1.5 hours, transfer in Lausanne), **Lugano** (hourly, 4 hours, transfer in Zürich or Luzern), **Appenzell** (hourly, 3 hours, transfer in Gossau), **Frankfurt** (3/day direct, 4 hours, more with change in Basel). Train info: Toll tel. 0900-300-300 (1.20 CHF/minute) or www.rail.ch.

ROUTE TIPS FOR DRIVERS

Interlaken to Bern: From Interlaken, catch the autobahn (direction: Spiez, Thun, then Bern). Circle Bern on the autobahn, taking the fourth Bern exit, *Neufeld Bern.* Signs to *Bern Zentrum* take you to Bern Bahnhof (train station). Turn right just before the station into the Bahnhof Parkplatz (described earlier, under "Arrival in Bern").

Bern to Murten: From the station, drive out of Bern following signs for *Lausanne,* then follow the green signs to *Neuchâtel* and *Murten.*

Murten

The finest medieval ramparts in Switzerland surround the old town of Murten (pop. 8,000; pronounced MOOR-ten; if you say MURR-ten, you get a quizzical look). You're on the linguis-

tic cusp of Switzerland: 25 percent of Murten speaks French; a few miles to the southwest, nearly everyone does (French-speakers call the town Morat).

Murten's old center is endearing. Its lively streets include a nicely arcaded main drag with breezy outdoor cafés and elegant shops (many closed Mon). Its castle is romantic, overlooking Lake Murten and the rolling vineyards of gentle Mont Vully in the distance. Spend a night here and have a local Vully wine (white, red, or rosé) with dinner. Murten is touristed, but mostly by locals, and never to the point of feeling overrun.

Make time for nearby Avenches (see end of chapter). Though quaint today, the town was once a powerful Roman capital—as its ruins attest.

Orientation to Murten

TOURIST INFORMATION

Murten's TI is just inside the city walls at the far end of town from the train station (April-Sept Mon-Fri 9:00-12:00 & 13:00-18:00, Sat-Sun 10:00-12:00 & 13:00-17:00; Oct-March Mon-Fri 9:00-12:00 & 14:00-17:00, closed Sat-Sun; Französische Kirchgasse 6, tel. 026-670-5112, www.murtentourismus.ch). Get a free map and walking guide, and ask about sights, biking, and boat trips.

ARRIVAL IN MURTEN

By Train: The train station is a five-minute walk from the center, and has a ticket office, free WC, and small pay lockers—the ticket office can store bigger bags (Mon-Fri 6:50-18:30, Sat 7:50-18:00, Sun 7:50-12:00 & 13:00-17:00). To reach the town from the station, exit to the right, take the first left, and walk uphill on Bahnhofstrasse, then turn right through the town gate. Murten's old center is tiny, and a delight on foot.

By Car: If you're overnighting here, get parking advice from your hotelier. You can park overnight in the old town for free (19:00-8:00). During the day, don't park inside the gates; metered prices are steep and there's a strict 75-minute time limit. Instead, park in the lot near the castle and Co-op supermarket (2 CHF/hour, pay at machine).

HELPFUL HINTS

Local Guide: Mary Brunisholz, an American who married into this part of Switzerland, is an excellent guide with a car (300 CHF/half-day, mobile 078-601-7040, mary.brunisholz@vtxnet.ch). The TI has a list of other guides.

Events: The town's **Youth Festival** commemorates the anniversary of the Battle of Murten each June 22. The **Murten Classics** music festival takes place in August and September, and there's a **Christmas market** on the second weekend in December.

Murten Walk

This self-guided introductory walk will give you the lay of the land and a lesson on the historic 15th-century Battle of Murten.

• *Start your walk just outside the town's main gate and TI, in front of the public school, where you see a statue of the feisty town hero...*

Adrian von Bubenberg

Burgundy was the aggressive power of the day, and this Murten native stopped a 15th-century Burgundian power grab by beating Charles the Bold. Adrian von Bubenberg (sent by Bern to hold the line against the expansionist Burgundians) stands here, looking across the lake at the distant peaks of the Jura Mountains—the historic border between the Swiss and the French (more on the battle a little later).

The earliest Swiss clockmakers were from those Jura Mountains. Look at the **clock tower**—where's the minute hand? As part of its lease, the restaurant below takes responsibility for hand-winding the clock each

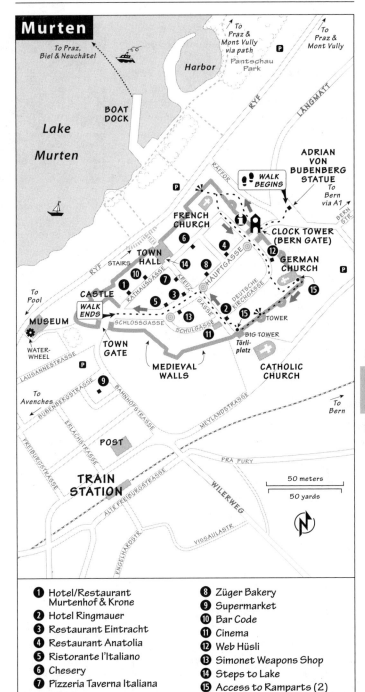

Murten

To Praz, Biel & Neuchâtel

To Praz & Mont Vully via path

To Praz & Mont Vully

Pantschau Park

Harbor

BOAT DOCK

Lake Murten

RYF

LÄNGMATT

ADRIAN VON BUBENBERG STATUE

To Bern via A1

WALK BEGINS

BERN STR.

FRENCH CHURCH

CLOCK TOWER (BERN GATE)

GERMAN CHURCH

TOWN HALL

STAIRS

RYF

CASTLE

WALK ENDS

RATHAUSGASSE

KREUZGASSE

HAUPTGASSE

DEUTSCHE KIRCHGASSE

To Pool

MUSEUM

WATER-WHEEL

SCHLOSSGASSE

SCHULGASSE

TOWER

BIG TOWER

Törli-platz

CATHOLIC CHURCH

TOWN GATE

LAUSANNESTRASSE

MEDIEVAL WALLS

To Avenches

BUBENBERGSTRASSE

BAHNHOFSTRASSE

ERLACHSTRASSE

MEYLANDSTRASSE

To Bern

POST

FREIBURGSTRASSE

TRAIN STATION

ALTE FREIBURGSTRASSE

FRA PURY

WILERWEG

ENGELHARDSTR.

VISSAULASTR.

50 meters

50 yards

N

BERN & MURTEN

① Hotel/Restaurant Murtenhof & Krone
② Hotel Ringmauer
③ Restaurant Eintracht
④ Restaurant Anatolia
⑤ Ristorante l'Italiano
⑥ Chesery
⑦ Pizzeria Taverna Italiana
⑧ Züger Bakery
⑨ Supermarket
⑩ Bar Code
⑪ Cinema
⑫ Web Hüsli
⑬ Simonet Weapons Shop
⑭ Steps to Lake
⑮ Access to Ramparts (2)

day, as it has since 1712. That's the Bern gate—so called because it opens up onto the road to Bern.

• Rather than enter the gate, go right instead (along the outside of the wall, not downhill). Head around the first turret, and look up at the cannon-balls, left in the wall from the 1476 Battle of Murten to remind townsfolk of their incredible victory over the Burgundians—like an Alamo with a happy ending.

   Turn the corner onto the...

Lakeview Terrace

Across the way is Mont Vully (mohn voo-YEE)—one big vineyard and a mecca for lovers of Swiss white wine. The lowlands to the right—a rich former lakebed—are the heart of the fertile Three Lakes Region (Lakes Biel, Neuchâtel, and Murten). The lush farmland is called the "vegetable garden of Switzerland" for its soil, which yields more than 60 varieties of produce.

The ancient Celtic Helvetii tribe settled here and took advantage of the fertility of this land. The Romans located their capital nearby (at Avenches) when they took over the region and established their colony of Helvetia (named after the Celtic tribe—the same word is the origin of Switzerland's official name, Confoederatio Helvetica).

• Behind you, check out the small...

French Church

Foreseeing a showdown with Burgundy, Adrian von Bubenberg had the town walls strengthened. As three-quarters of the townspeople were German-speaking, they took a vote and decided to tear down the French church to get more stones. (This little church was rebuilt for the French-speaking community six years after its big one was demolished.)

• Circle round the church, and if it's open, go inside.

As the Calvinist Reformation swept through Catholic Switzerland in the early 16th century, churches like this were stripped of their rich paintings, sculptures, and stained glass. Elaborate altars were replaced with simple, Bible-topped tables, and pulpits became the focus. The emphasis was teaching the word of God. In this church, about the only exceptions to the "no distractions" rule are the tiny stained-glass coats of arms—heraldry of the wealthy families who helped fund its construction. The church, still Protestant and serving its French community, is open sporadically.

• From here, leave the church and head straight toward the pointy spire of the German church across town. Walk along Französischer Kirchgasse

past the TI and the clock tower, and go up the lane to #26 (on left). The little **Web Hüsli** *is one of the few Murten buildings that survived a 15th-century fire that burned down the wooden town. Before the fire, most houses looked like this one. After the fire, building was limited to the characteristic yellow Jura stone (like the former library, across the street, at #31).*

• *Continue straight ahead to the...*

German Church

Murten's German church is also post-Reformation Protestant simple. Inside, in the center of the ceiling, notice the big stucco relief with two seals: the bear for Bern and the three castles for Fribourg. As the town is on the border between two cantons (Bern and Fribourg), for 400 years its rule was shared: Every five years, it would flip between cantons. Around 1800, when Switzerland was reorganized under Napoleonic rule, Murten became firmly a part of Fribourg.

The Protestant passion for Bible study is also evident in this church. Explore the choir (two rows of seats on each side for big shots) behind the altar. Find Adrian von Bubenberg's seat. (Hint: The window above shows the war hero in red, with his victorious local yokels in their alpine red-knit hats...underdogs whupping the Burgundians.) The old pulpit was carved in 1460 from a single oak tree. Notice the two prime seats on either side of the altar; the one to the preacher's right was for the leader of Bern or Fribourg—depending on who happened to be ruling that year. The front window (crucifixion) dates from 1926.

• *Leaving the church, hook left around the back. Finger the limestone and sandstone tombstones, quarried from Mont Vully for noble families. Then climb the two flights of creaky stairs and start walking along the...*

Ramparts

Strolling Murten's ramparts is a must (free, open daily until dusk). Survey the town, and note the uniformity of the town's architecture. Paint your place the wrong color, and you may be instructed to redo it—at your own expense. Scanning the countless chimneys and beavertail ceramic roof tiles, think of the enforced conformity that comes with living in a small town (and look to see if there are any oddballs). Telephone and electricity wires are all underground, as in Europe generally. Look back at the roof of the German church. The six-sided "star of David" isn't a Jewish symbol in this case,

but recalls the star that guided the wise men to Bethlehem on the first Christmas.

• *Continue 50 yards to the **tower with the staircase**. Climb the steps for a commanding town and lake view.*

Enjoy perhaps the ultimate view. The Jura Mountains in the distance (at the border with France) peek above vine-laden Mont Vully. On the right is the German church, Bern Tower, and French church. And to the far left is the castle tower—flying the black-and-white flag of Fribourg Canton—where this walk finishes.

With your back to the lake, look inland and imagine the action on June 22, 1476. Mighty Charles the Bold, with his 20,000 well-armed Burgundians, was camped on the hill (the one with the divided forest) for 10 days, laying siege to the town of 2,000. Runners were sent out from the town to gather help. A makeshift army of about 10,000 villagers gathered on the hills to the left. Just as George Washington attacked when the Redcoats were celebrating Christmas, the Swiss swooped in as the Burgundians were still hungover from a big Midsummer Night's Eve bash. The Battle of Murten was fought in pouring rain—a muddy, bloody mess. More than 10,000 Burgundians were slaughtered—many driven into the lake with their armor to drown (try swimming in a coat of mail). For centuries, French bones would wash ashore. Charles the (no-longer-so-) Bold barely got away on a very fast horse.

This victory demonstrated to the Swiss the advantages of *E Pluribus Unum,* and the gradual unification of the many still-fiercely independent Swiss cantons into the Helvetic Confederation snowballed. In this sweet little corner, an influential battle in European history had been fought. Burgundian power ebbed, and Europe got to know a new nation...Switzerland.

• *Walk a bit farther along the wall and descend at the next tower (across from Café-Pension Ringmauer).*

At the bottom of the stairs, study the fine old **clock** mechanism from 1816. It once powered the big clock in the City Hall tower. Later, it spent decades in a to-be-assembled pile, gathering dust in an attic. Finally, in 1991, a town resident—recognizing a good challenge—reassembled it into perfect working order. Notice how the gearbox powers three clock faces (as the tower had), and how the old hand crank raises the stones that power the clock, which rings on the quarter-hour. The white face displays the clock's time.

• *Step outside the wall, where you'll see the Catholic church (1886), private gardens along the wall, and evidence of how the wall was constructed in several distinct stages.*

The first phase was built with large river stones, some arranged in a neat fishbone pattern. Later, the town ran out of money, and the next stage shows pebbles and rubble mixed with a rough concrete. And finally, when the town prospered again, they finished the wall with finely cut sandstone. The former dry moat is now individual private gardens.

• *Walk back into town, stopping on the first corner at the fire station-turned-community-cinema.*

Contributors are thanked with their names on the door. Notice what's playing tonight (in Switzerland, movies are subtitled, not dubbed, to accommodate a two-language audience). At this corner, spin slowly, admiring the town's fine shutters.

• *Then, continue a block (noticing again that most buildings were stone—built after a fire) to the...*

Main Street (Hauptgasse)

In the 19th century, Murten's townsfolk got their water from the three fountains on this street. Turn left along the street and enjoy the colorful store signs—they still hang out their shingles in the traditional fashion. Bakery and *pâtisserie* competition on this street is fierce. Drop into one for regional specialties: *Nidlechueche,* a sweet, doughy cream tart; and *Seeländer Zwetschgen,* a chocolate-covered prune with liqueur.

Near the top of the main street, **Simonet Weapons** sells all the latest knives by Victorinox. There's the green "stay-glow," and even a model with a USB flash drive for the outdoorsman with a laptop (closed Sun-Mon). At the top of the street (#16), Murten's oldest house has fine paintings under its eaves.

• *Farther to the right, at the top of town, step into...*

Murten Castle and Town Museum

The town castle, which houses the police station in its former prison (closed to the public), shows off an impressive cannon from 1882 and a lovely lake view.

The nearby museum (6 CHF, generally Tue-Sun 14:00-17:00, closed Mon, described in German and French only—borrow English booklet) is a humble collection earnestly showing off the town history. It fills an old mill with modern displays and lots of artifacts. Outside is a functioning water mill, a WC, a lane leading down to the lake, and an elephant.

An elephant? Yes, in 1866 an elephant escaped from a traveling American circus. It rampaged (as if in heat) through Murten and was killed. To this day, one lane is nicknamed Elephant Alley.

Activities in Murten

Lake Activities

To get down to Murten's lazy lake-front, go out the gate by the TI and take a left down the hill. You'll see the boat dock first. Just beyond the grassy breakwater and the small-boat harbor is Pantschau, a big park, which is flanked by handy eateries. There's mini golf, windsurfing gear rental and instruction, a snack bar, and a fine lakeside promenade.

Lake Murten Cruises

Boats do a **75-minute loop cruise** at 12:00, 14:15, and 15:40. Consider stopping in the small town of Praz on the French-speaking shore. From there you could hike through vineyards up Mont Vully—where a pretty lake and Alp views await—and return on the lake with your same ticket. Or you can walk from Praz two hours back to Murten, clockwise around the lake.

Another option is the **Three Lakes cruise,** which covers all three of the region's lakes—connected by canals—and stops at several medieval villages on the way to the town of Biel (Bienne in French). The boat leaves Murten at 9:55, arrives in Biel at 14:10, then turns around and heads back along the same route, leaving Biel at 14:35 and arriving in Murten at 18:50. You can condense this full-day trip by taking the boat to Biel and a train back to Murten (train runs hourly, 45 minutes, change in Neuchâtel).

Cost and Hours: 75-minute loop cruise-22 CHF; boat from Murten to Praz-14.20 CHF; half-day Three Lakes cruise-61 CHF one-way, 122 CHF round-trip; all covered by Swiss Travel Pass and discounted 50 percent with Eurail pass, ask TI about boat-trip discount vouchers; buy tickets on board or at the kiosk at pier 1; boats run daily late May-late Sept, Fri-Sun only in off-season, no boats in winter; tel. 032-729-9600, www.navig.ch.

Swimming Pool

The Olympic-size public swimming pool is outside of town next to the lake, just past the castle (8 CHF; indoor pool Mon 14:00-21:00, Tue-Fri 9:30-21:00, Sat-Sun until 18:00; outdoor pool daily in summer; Lausannestrasse 2, tel. 026-672-3636, www.schwimmbad-murten.ch).

Biking

The Three Lakes region has 100 miles of signposted bike paths (well-described in the TI's brochures). Pick up a free map or buy a top-notch one at the TI. The best easy ride circles the lake and

Mont Vully (through vineyards and, if you like, to the summit for a good view). As elsewhere in Switzerland, you can rent **bikes** at train-station ticket counters, and usually for a small extra fee, drop them in another town; Murten, Avenches, and several nearby towns participate (for rates and specifics, see page 408).

Nightlife in Murten

Movies

Murten's cute little community co-op theater plays movies nightly (16 CHF, Schulgasse 18, www.kino-murten.ch). Movies are shown in their original language (capital letter indicates the soundtrack language, small letters indicate subtitles—e.g., "E/fd" means "English with *français* and *Deutsch* subtitles").

From early July to early August, an open-air cinema hosts a lakeside summer film festival (outside wall, past TI, details at www.open-air-kino.ch, then select "Murten").

Pubs

There are plenty of inviting pubs and nightclubs in town. **Bar Code** sells drinks with a lake view (Tue-Sun 18:00-24:00, closed Mon, Rathausgasse 9, between Hotel Murtenhof and Town Hall). The main street has an Irish bar and several other nightspots, and there's a popular bar just outside the clock tower.

Sleeping in Murten

This adorable town is no secret. The peak time is May through mid-September (especially on weekends)—make a reservation and expect maximum prices. The nearest youth hostel is in Avenches (see page 125).

$$$ Hotel Murtenhof & Krone offers elegance at fair-for-Switzerland prices in 57 nicely appointed rooms—each a stylish mix of old and new. There's a wide range of sleeping accommodations, so email them your needs in terms of size, view, and price (RS%, family rooms, elevator, pay parking, next to castle at Rathausgasse 3, tel. 026-672-9030, www.murtenhof.ch, info@murtenhof.ch, well-run by brothers Marc and Ariste Joachim). They have the best lakeview restaurant in town (described later, under "Eating in Murten").

$$ Hotel Ringmauer ("Ramparts") sits just under the wall in the quiet corner of town farthest from the lake. It rents 14 small, simple, slightly overpriced rooms, some with shared bath (family rooms, discount if you skip breakfast, attached restaurant, Deutsche Kirchgasse 2, tel. 026-670-1101, www.hotelringmauer.ch, info@hotelringmauer.ch, Padmakumara Nawarathna and family).

BERN & MURTEN

Eating in Murten

Eating in Murten is a joy. I'd stroll the main drag up one side and down the other to survey the action before making a choice. For elegance and a lake view, it's the restaurant at Hotel Murtenhof & Krone. There are several good options right on the lake a 10-minute walk down from the town center. Budget eaters can assemble a picnic at the Co-op grocery. Bakeries make good sandwiches, but they close by about 18:00.

RESTAURANTS

Anything called *Seeländer* or mentioning "three lakes" is typical of this Three Lakes region. Traditional restaurants serve *Egli-Filets*, the very popular perch "from the lake" (these days caught in the Bodensee—Lake Constance in English—up by the German border). As this is the "vegetable garden of Switzerland," restaurants pride themselves on offering good veggies. You'll want a glass of smooth and refreshing white Vully (voo-YEE) wine with your meal (about 4 CHF/glass).

$$$ Hotel Murtenhof & Krone's restaurant is perched high above the lake in the old town. Its covered terrace gives diners a comfortable and classy lake view regardless of the weather. Sipping a glass of local white wine with the right travel partner, while gazing across the lake at hillside vineyards as the sun sets, is one of Europe's fine moments. Choose from "updated Three Lakes cuisine" and several vegetarian choices. Reserve ahead for their limited lakeview seating. Their 10-CHF salad bar makes perhaps the best cheap light meal in town (Tue-Sun 11:00-23:00, closed Mon and Dec-Feb, tel. 026-672-9030, www.murtenhof.ch).

$$$ Restaurant Eintracht serves good-value, local cuisine from a fun and unpretentious menu, including old-time chef specials—even horsemeat (18-CHF lunch specials include soup and main course, half-portions available, healthy specials, generally 7:30-23:30, Sun until 18:00, closed Wed, streetside seating under arcades, Hauptgasse 19, tel. 026-670-2240, Ramseier family).

$$$$ Restaurant Anatolia features quality Turkish dishes made from fresh ingredients by the welcoming owner, Mehmet. Dine indoors with the fine mural of Istanbul, or watch the main-drag action from an outside table (daily 10:00-23:00, shorter hours and closed Wed off-season, Hauptgasse 45, tel. 026-670-2868, www.anatolia.ch).

$$$ Ristorante l'Italiano is the town choice for authentic Italian cuisine. The Prozzillo family emphasizes gastronomic simplicity. As its menu makes quite clear, they don't serve pizza (Tue-Sat 9:00-14:00 & 17:00-23:00, closed Sun-Mon; outside seating, Hauptgasse 11, tel. 026-672-2212).

$$ Chesery is both a café (with regional cheese plates, quiches, and other light meals), wine bar, and elegant secondhand store. This quirky spot is worth a peek even if you're not eating (daily 11:00-22:00, Rathausgasse 28, tel. 026-670-6577).

$$$ Pizzeria Taverna Italiana is one of two pizzerias in Murten's old town. The one on the main street has better views, but townsfolk say Pizzeria Italiana is a better value (daily 10:30-14:00 & 17:00-23:00, closed Feb-April, near Hotel Murtenhof at Kreuzgasse 4, tel. 026-670-2122).

CHEAP EATS

The main street has four **$ bakeries,** all with ample charm. **Züger** has indoor and outdoor seating, an inviting pastry and candy counter, and delicate open-face sandwiches typical of the region (8-CHF breakfast combo—coffee, croissant, and roll; generally 7:30-18:00, closed Tue, Hauptgasse 33, tel. 026-670-2253).

The Co-op **supermarket** towers between the train station and city center (Mon-Sat 7:00-20:00, Sun 8:00-18:00).

Murten Connections

From Murten by Train to: Avenches (hourly, 7 minutes, direction: Payerne), **Bern** (hourly, 35 minutes, more with change in Kerzers), **Lausanne** (3/hour, 1.5 hours), **Zürich** (hourly, 2 hours, transfer in Bern). Train info: toll tel. 0900-300-300 (1.20 CHF/minute) or www.rail.ch.

ROUTE TIPS FOR DRIVERS

Murten to Lake Geneva (50 miles): The autobahn from Bern to Lausanne/Lake Geneva makes everything speedy (see the Lake Geneva and French Switzerland chapter). Murten and Avenches are 10 minutes off the autobahn; Broc, Bulle, and Gruyères are within sight of each other and the autobahn. It takes about an hour to drive from Murten to Montreux. The autobahn (direction: Simplon) takes you high above Montreux (pull off at great viewpoint rest stop) and Château de Chillon. For the castle, take the first exit east of the castle (Villeneuve); signs direct you along the lake back to the castle.

Near Murten: Avenches

Avenches, four miles south of Murten, was once Aventicum, the Roman capital of Helvetia. Today, it's a quaint little French-speaking town with an ancient amphitheater taking a bite out of it. Below the town spreads a vast field of sparse Roman ruins.

With a pleasant, small-town French ambience, Avenches (ah-

VAHNSH) is quieter than Murten, and its old walls are mostly gone. Just a few minutes away by train, it makes an easy half-day trip. From the unstaffed Avenches train station, it's a seven-minute, somewhat steep walk to the town, amphitheater, and Roman museum. Exploring more of the ruins requires some outdoor walking. The **TI** is on the town's main square (Mon-Fri 8:30-12:00 & 13:30-17:30, Sat 9:30-12:30, closed Sun; Sept-April also closed Sat; Place de l'Eglise 3, tel. 026-676-9922, www.avenches.ch).

Sights in Avenches

Roman Avenches

Aventicum was a Roman capital, with a population of 20,000. The Romans appreciated its strategic crossroads location, fertile land, and comfortable climate (in modern times, it's been voted the "most livable place to retire"). While the population of today's Avenches could barely fill the well-worn ruins of their Roman amphitheater, Aventicum was once one of the largest cities of the Roman Empire. Everything sits on Roman ruins, which were quarried nearly to oblivion over several centuries; the scant remains were finally spared in the 19th century, and today, things are carefully preserved. Metal detectors must be registered here. Mothers, knowing that turning up anything ancient will bring on the archaeologists, yell at their kids, "Don't dig!" Even the benches on the main street are bits of a 2,000-year-old temple cornice.

The town has five Roman sights: the amphitheater, a lone tower, a sanctuary and a theater in a field outside of town, and a museum. While you'll pay to enter the museum, the ruins are free and always viewable.

The **amphitheater,** or arena, which once seated 18,000, is the largest Roman ruin in Switzerland (free, always open). There's no more gladiator action, but it's busy with an annual opera festival and other musical events. At the top of the amphitheater (just past the museum entrance), scan the surrounding countryside. The Roman town filled the low area in front of you (now partly farmland; Avenches' medieval residents retreated to the more easily defensible hilltop). The **tower** on the ridge (on left)—the only one remaining of the original 73 towers—marks where the wall once stood. In the middle, past the lone standing column of the **sanctuary,** you can see the small **theater** ruins (described later).

The **Roman museum,** next to the amphitheater, fills a medieval tower with three fascinating floors of Roman artifacts—such as gravestones, mosaics, glass, and fishing spears—which afford a fairly intimate look at domestic life back then. There's no English posted on the displays, so good students borrow the extensive English catalog. Don't miss the "gold" bust of Marcus Aurelius (A.D. 80) found in an old Roman sewer in 1939—it's actually a plastic copy; the original is in a bank in Lausanne (6 CHF, covered by Swiss Travel Pass; Tue-Sun 10:00-17:00; Oct and Feb-March Tue-Sun from 14:00; closed Tue and shorter hours Nov-Jan; closed Mon except in June; tel. 026-557-3300, www.aventicum.org).

Perhaps the best Aventicum experience is to spend some quiet time at sunset pondering the evocative **Roman theater** (Théâtre Romaine) and **sanctuary** in the fields, a half-mile walk out of town (free, always open, tiny free car park at the site). The single column marks "Du Cigognier"—nicknamed the "stork sanctuary" (c. 1700) for the stork nest it supported. The site was a quarry until the 19th century, so almost nothing remains.

Sleeping in Avenches

Sleeping in little Avenches makes the best sense if you have a car. It's not impossible by train, but schedules are sparse and hauling your bags uphill from the train station is a chore.

$$$ Hotel de la Couronne is an Old World, three-star place with a modern interior. Centrally set on the main square, it's unpretentious, with 21 bright, spacious rooms (free parking nearby, next to TI at Rue Centrale 20, tel. 026-675-5414, www.lacouronne.ch, info@lacouronne.ch).

¢ The Avenches **IYHF hostel,** the area's best option for travelers on a tight budget, fills a traditional building in a quiet setting on the far side of the town. It's a 15-minute walk from the train station if you take the stairs—longer route possible for those with wheeled bags. Run by the Dhyaf family, it has a homey TV room, table tennis, and a big backyard (private rooms available, dinner available, no curfew, reception open 7:00-10:00 & 17:00-22:00, pay parking, closed late Oct-March, Rue du Lavoir 5, tel. 026-675-2666, www.youthhostel.ch/avenches, avenches@youthhostel.ch).

BERN & MURTEN

GIMMELWALD & THE BERNER OBERLAND

Interlaken • Lauterbrunnen • Gimmelwald • Mürren

Frolic and hike high above the stress and clouds of the real world. Take a vacation from your busy vacation. Recharge your touristic batteries high in the Alps, where distant avalanches, cowbells, the fluff of a down comforter, the whistle of marmots, and the crunchy footsteps of happy hikers are the dominant sounds. If the weather's good (and your budget's healthy), ride a cable car from the traffic-free village of Gimmelwald to a hearty breakfast at the revolving Piz Gloria restaurant, on top of the 9,748-foot Schilthorn peak. Linger among alpine whitecaps before riding down 5,000 feet to the town of Mürren and then home to Gimmelwald.

Your gateway to the rugged Berner Oberland, the mountainous part of the canton of Bern, is the grand old resort town of Interlaken. Near Interlaken is Switzerland's open-air folk museum, Ballenberg, where you can climb through original traditional houses gathered from every corner of this diverse country.

Ah, but the weather's fine and the Alps beckon. Head deep into the heart of the Alps, and ride the cable car to the stop just this side of heaven—Gimmelwald.

PLANNING YOUR TIME

Rather than tackle a checklist of famous Swiss mountains and resorts, choose one region to savor: the Berner Oberland.

Interlaken is the region's administrative headquarters and transportation hub. Use it for business—banking, post office, laundry, shopping—and as a springboard for alpine thrills.

The highest-altitude lifts are very expensive, and it only makes sense to splurge if you have a good chance of seeing an alpine panorama instead of fog or clouds. Let your plans flex with the weather. If it's good—go! Ask at your hotel or the TI for the latest info or check www.jungfrau.ch, www.schilthorn.ch, or www.meteo.search.ch. Webcams showing live video from the famous (and most expensive-to-reach) peaks play just about wherever you go in the area.

If the weather's decent, explore the two areas that tower above either side of the Lauterbrunnen Valley, south of Interlaken: On

one side is the summit of Jungfrau (and beneath it, the tiny settlement of Kleine Scheidegg), and on the other is Schilthorn (overlooking the villages of Gimmelwald and Mürren).

Ideally, spend three nights in the region, with a day exploring each side of the valley. For accommodations without the expense and headache of mountain lifts, consider the valley-floor village of Lauterbrunnen. But for the best overnight options, I'd stay on the scenic ridge high above the valley, in the rustic hamlet of Gimmelwald or the resort town of Mürren. I've also listed a few options in other nearby mountain villages.

For a summary of the wildly scenic activities this region has to offer (from panoramic train rides and lifts to spectacular hikes and mountain biking), see "Activities in the Berner Oberland" on page 171.

If your time is very limited, consider a night in Gimmelwald, breakfast at the Schilthorn, an afternoon doing the Männlichen-Kleine Scheidegg hike, and an evening or night train out. What? A nature lover not spending the night high in the Alps? Alpus interruptus.

GETTING AROUND THE BERNER OBERLAND

For more than a century, this region has been the target of nature-worshipping pilgrims. And Swiss engineers and visionaries have made the most exciting alpine perches accessible.

By Lifts and Trains

Part of the fun here—and most of the expense—is riding the many mountain trains and lifts (gondolas and cable cars).

Trains connect Interlaken to Wilderswil, Lauterbrunnen, Wengen, Kleine Scheidegg, the Jungfraujoch, and also Grindelwald. Lifts connect Wengen to Männlichen and Grund (near Grindelwald); Grindelwald to First; Lauterbrunnen to Grütschalp (where a train connects to Mürren); and the cable-car station near Stechelberg to Gimmelwald, Mürren, and the Schilthorn.

For an overview of your many options, study the "Alpine

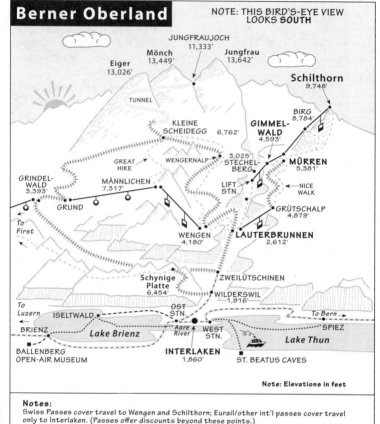

Berner Oberland

NOTE: THIS BIRD'S-EYE VIEW LOOKS **SOUTH**

JUNGFRAUJOCH 11,333'

Mönch 13,449' Jungfrau 13,642'

Eiger 13,026'

Schilthorn 9,748'

TUNNEL

KLEINE SCHEIDEGG 6,762'

BIRG 8,784'

GIMMEL-WALD 4,593'

GREAT HIKE WENGERNALP 3,025' STECHEL-BERG

MÜRREN 5,381'

GRINDEL-WALD 3,393'

MÄNNLICHEN 7,317'

LIFT STN.

NICE WALK

GRUND

GRÜTSCHALP 4,879'

To First

WENGEN 4,180' LAUTERBRUNNEN 2,612'

Schynige Platte 6,454'

ZWEILÜTSCHINEN

WILDERSWIL 1,916'

To Luzern ISELTWALD

OST STN.

To Bern

BRIENZ Lake Brienz

Aare River WEST STN.

SPIEZ

Lake Thun

BALLENBERG OPEN-AIR MUSEUM

INTERLAKEN 1,860' ST. BEATUS CAVES

Note: Elevations in feet

Notes:
Swiss Passes cover travel to Wengen and Schilthorn; Eurail/other int'l passes cover travel only to Interlaken. (Passes offer discounts beyond these points.)

BERNER OBERLAND

Lifts in the Berner Oberland" map and the "Berner Oberland at a Glance" sidebar in this chapter. Lifts generally go at least twice hourly, from about 7:00 until about 20:00 (sneak preview: www.jungfrau.ch or www.schilthorn.ch).

Beyond Interlaken, trains and lifts into the Jungfrau region are 25 percent off with a Eurail pass (doesn't require a flexi-day); with the **Swiss Travel Pass,** they're covered up to Wengen (above Wengen, passholders get 25-50 percent off) and all the way to the top of the Schilthorn. Ask about discounts for early-morning and late-afternoon trips, youths, seniors, families, groups (assemble a party of 10 and you'll save about 25 percent), and those staying awhile. Generally, round-trips are double the one-way cost, though some high-up trains and lifts are 10-20 percent cheaper. It's possible to buy a package covering all of your lifts at once, but then you don't have the flexibility to change with the weather.

Popular Passes: The Swiss Travel Pass is the best option (see

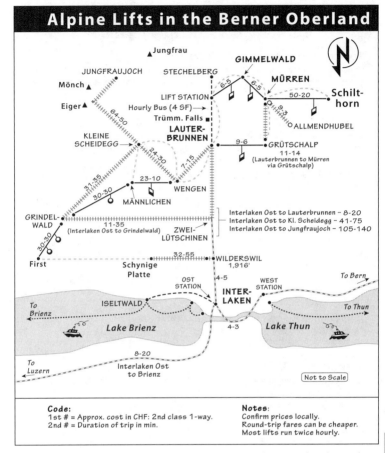

Alpine Lifts in the Berner Oberland

Jungfrau

JUNGFRAUJOCH   STECHELBERG   **GIMMELWALD**

Mönch   **MÜRREN**   Schilt-horn

Eiger   LIFT STATION   50-20

Hourly Bus (4 SF)→   6-5   6-5

Trümm. Falls   9-3   ○ ALLMENDHUBEL

LAUTER-BRUNNEN   64-50

KLEINE   9-6   GRÜTSCHALP
SCHEIDEGG   11-14
(Lauterbrunnen to Mürren
via Grütschalp)

24-30   7-15

23-10   WENGEN

31-35

30-30   MÄNNLICHEN

GRINDEL-   Interlaken Ost to Lauterbrunnen – 8-20
WALD   11-35   Interlaken Ost to Kl. Scheidegg – 41-75
(Interlaken Ost to Grindelwald)   ZWEI-   Interlaken Ost to Jungfraujoch – 105-140
LÜTSCHINEN

30-30   32-55   WILDERSWIL
First   Schynige   1,916'
Platte

OST   4-5   WEST
STATION   **INTER-**   STATION   To Bern
ISELTWALD   **LAKEN**

To   Lake Brienz   4-3   Lake Thun   To Thun
Brienz

8-20
To   Interlaken Ost
Luzern   to Brienz

Not to Scale

Code:
1st # = Approx. cost in CHF: 2nd class 1-way.
2nd # = Duration of trip in min.

Notes:
Confirm prices locally.
Round-trip fares can be cheaper.
Most lifts run twice hourly.

page 4), but travelers with limited time might consider these alternatives.

The **Berner Oberland Regional Pass** covers most trains, buses, and lifts in this area (and all the way to Bern, Luzern, Gstaad, and Brig) but isn't typically worthwhile since it costs almost the same as the Swiss Travel Pass (which offers bigger discounts on some high-mountain trips; for example, Mürren-Schilthorn cable car—fully covered with Swiss Travel Pass versus 50 percent off with Berner Oberland pass). The pass is only valid between late April and late October (4 days-250 CHF, 6 days-310 CHF, 8 days-350 CHF, 10 days-390 CHF, www.regiopass-berneroberland.ch).

The **Jungfrau Travel Pass,** available from three-day (180 CHF) up to six-day (255 CHF) versions, is more limited in scope, covering transportation on the east side of the valley, plus from Lauterbrunnen to Mürren via Grütschalp. With the pass, your ticket from Kleine Scheidegg to Jungfraujoch is 61 CHF (instead

Berner Oberland at a Glance

Towns, Villages, and Resorts

▲▲▲**Gimmelwald** Wonderfully rustic time-warp village—and a good home-base option—overlooking the Lauterbrunnen Valley. See page 153.

▲▲**Mürren** Pleasant resort town near Gimmelwald, midway up the Schilthorn cable-car line; a good high-mountain home base for those who find Gimmelwald too small and rustic. See page 162.

▲▲**Kleine Scheidegg** Small resort area with breathtaking views of Eiger, Mönch, and Jungfrau peaks; several hotels and restaurants (see page 188); and train station for pricey ride to the high-altitude Jungfraujoch (see page 173).

▲**Lauterbrunnen** Small town in the middle of the Lauterbrunnen Valley. From here, a cable car goes up to Grütschalp (with connections to Mürren and Gimmelwald), a train runs up to Wengen and Kleine Scheidegg, and the PostBus goes to Stechelberg (near the Schilthornbahn lift). See page 146.

▲**Interlaken** Big town between Lake Brienz and Lake Thun, at the "entrance" to the Berner Oberland. See page 133.

Top Lifts and Trains

▲▲▲**Schilthornbahn** Cable car soaring from Stechelberg in the Lauterbrunnen Valley to the 9,748-foot Schilthorn peak, with Piz Gloria revolving restaurant, James Bond exhibit, and stupendous views. Stops at Gimmelwald, Mürren, and Birg along the way. See page 155.

▲▲▲**Jungfraubahn** Train running from Kleine Scheidegg station and through tunnel inside Eiger and Mönch mountains to 11,333-foot Jungfraujoch saddle, with observation deck, restaurants, tip-top views, and snow activities. See page 173.

Walks and Hikes

▲▲▲**Männlichen-Kleine Scheidegg** Easy, mostly downhill ridge hike from cable-car station at Männlichen to Kleine Scheidegg, with spectacular views of Eiger and more. See page 180.

▲▲**Cloudy-Day Lauterbrunnen Valley Walks** Easy trails and pleasant walks along valley floor, plus short trail to Staubbach Falls at upper end of town. See page 176.

▲▲**North Face Trail** Relatively easy, view-filled hike from top of Allmendhubel funicular to villages of Mürren and/or Gimmelwald, passing farms with food service, Sprutz Waterfall, mountain huts, and meadows. See page 178.

▲▲**Schynige Platte to First** Demanding ridge walk from Schynige Platte train station to gondola station at First. Fabulous views of Jungfrau-area peaks and Lake Brienz. See page 183.

▲▲**Birg to Gimmelwald via Bryndli** High, scenic, moderately difficult hike from Birg cable-car station below Schilthorn summit to Gimmelwald. Trail winds past knobby summit of Bryndli, with nonstop views. See page 186.

▲**Sefinen Valley to Kilchbalm** Easy trail from village of Gimmelwald up Sefinen Valley to dramatic Kilchbalm, a glacier-carved bowl with streams, waterfalls, and meadows. See page 178.

▲**Allmendhubel to Grütschalp** Fairly easy walk from Allmendhubel down to Grütschalp, with views of the Jungfrau. See 179.

▲**Gimmelwald-Tanzbödeli-Obersteinberg-Stechelberg/Gimmelwald** Long, difficult, yet highly rewarding hike offering spectacular views and relative solitude (aside from goats, cows, chamois, and a cheesemaker). See page 184.

▲**Sprutz Waterfall** Moderately difficult hike from Gimmelwald up to and behind the waterfall (also a good stop on a hike down from Allmendhubel). See page 185.

▲**Grütschalp to Mürren** Super-easy, family-friendly stroll along the ridge with grand views of the Eiger, Mönch, and Jungfrau. See page 180.

More Sightseeing Options

▲▲**Ballenberg** Open-air folk museum near Interlaken, on Lake Brienz. See page 139.

▲**Trümmelbach Falls** Lauterbrunnen Valley's most powerful falls, accessed via elevator ride up into the mountain and dramatic walk through several wet caves. See page 149.

BERNER OBERLAND

of 128 CHF). But, this pass reduces your flexibility and it's hard to make it pay off (valid May-Oct only, tel. 033-828-7233, www.jungfrau.ch).

The **Junior Travelcard,** valid across Switzerland for families traveling with children, lets kids under 16 travel free with at least one parent (children under 5 already travel free). It's a great deal that pays for itself within the first hour of travel on trains and lifts (30 CHF/one child, 60 CHF/two or more children, buy at Swiss train stations).

By Car

Interlaken, Lauterbrunnen, and Stechelberg are accessible by car. You can't drive to Gimmelwald, Mürren, Wengen, or Kleine Scheidegg, but don't let that stop you from *staying* up in the mountains: Park the car and zip up on a lift. To catch the lift to Gimmelwald, Mürren, and the Schilthorn, park at the cable-car station near Stechelberg (4 CHF/2 hours, 10 CHF/day; for more on the cable car, see page 154). To catch the train to Wengen or Kleine Scheidegg, park at the train station in Lauterbrunnen (2.50 CHF/2 hours, 11 CHF/9-24 hours).

By Bus

A convenient local bus, called the PostBus, connects points along the valley and includes a stop at the Schilthornbahn cable-car station (www.postauto.ch).

HELPFUL HINTS IN THE BERNER OBERLAND

Closed Days: On Sundays and holidays (including lesser-known religious holidays), small-town Switzerland is quiet. Hotels are open and lifts and trains run, but many stores are closed.

Off-Season Closures: At higher altitudes many hotels, restaurants, and shops are closed between the skiing and hiking seasons: from late April until late May, and again from mid-October to mid-December.

Rainy-Day Options: When it rains here, locals joke that they're washing the mountains. If clouds roll in, don't despair. They can roll out just as quickly. With good rain gear and the right choice of trail, you can thoroughly enjoy a hike in the rain, with surprise views popping out all around you as the clouds break. Some good bad-weather options are the North Face trail, the walk from Mürren/Allmendhubel to Grütschalp, the Sefinen Valley hike, and the Lauterbrunnen Valley walk. Also consider a visit to Trümmelbach Falls, the Swiss Open-Air Museum at Ballenberg, or the Lauterbrunnen Valley Folk Museum. All are described in this chapter.

Visitor Cards *(Gästekarten):* Hotels here issue free Visitor Cards that include small discounts on some sights (paid for by your room tax).

Local Guidebook: For in-depth information on the area's history, folk life, flora, fauna, and hiking options, consider Don Chmura's *Exploring the Lauterbrunnen Valley* (available at Lauterbrunnen TI, 10 CHF).

Skiing and Snowboarding: The Berner Oberland is a great winter-sports destination, with good snow on its higher runs, incredible variety, relatively reasonable prices, and a sense of character that's missing in many swankier resort areas. You can even swish with the Swiss down the world's longest sledding run (9 miles long, out of Grindelwald, open only when snow's good). Three ski areas cluster around the Lauterbrunnen Valley: Mürren-Schilthorn (best for experts), Kleine Scheidegg-Männlichen (busiest, best variety of runs), and Grindelwald-First (best for beginners and intermediates, but lower elevation can make for iffier snowpack). For info and prices, see www.jungfrau.ch/winter. For more tips, see the Switzerland in Winter chapter.

Interlaken

When the 19th-century Romantics redefined mountains as something more than cold and troublesome obstacles, Interlaken became the original alpine resort. Ever since, tourists have flocked to the Alps "because they're there." Interlaken's glory days are long gone, its elegant old hotels eclipsed by the newer, swankier alpine resorts. Today, it's an alpine gateway town (rated ▲), with shops filled with chocolate bars, Swiss Army knives, trinkets, and sunburned backpackers.

While European jet-setters are elsewhere, Interlaken is cashing in on a huge interest from India and the Arab world. Indians come to escape their monsoon season—especially in April and May—and to visit places they've seen in their movies. (The Alps often stand in for Kashmir, which is less accessible to film crews.) There's even a restaurant called "Bollywood" atop the Jungfraujoch. People from the hot and dry Arabian Peninsula come here just to photograph their children frolicking in the mist and fog.

Efficient Interlaken (pop. 5,500) is above all a good administrative and shopping center. Take care of business, give the town a quick look, and view the webcam coverage (at the TI) of the weather higher up...then head for the hills.

BERNER OBERLAND

Orientation to Interlaken

Interlaken straddles a river that connects two alpine lakes: Lake Brienz and Lake Thun. The older part of town (called Unterseen) is on the right bank of the Aare River and has pockets of charm and a cute village square. The newer section (Interlaken proper), with most services and both train stations, is on the river's left bank.

TOURIST INFORMATION

A small TI operates at the Interlaken Ost train station in summer and is convenient if you're arriving there (June-Sept daily 8:30-18:30, though hours may vary; closed Oct-May).

Otherwise, visit the main TI, located by the post office at Marktgasse 1 (May-June and Sept Mon-Fri 8:00-18:00, Sat 9:00-16:00, closed Sun; July-Aug Mon-Fri 8:00-19:00, Sat 9:00-17:00, Sun 10:00-16:00; shorter hours and closed Sun Oct-April; tel. 033-826-5300, www.interlaken.ch). Pick up the timetable and the hiking guide published by the Jungfraubahn mountain railway (both include a good map of the area); and the *Here & Now* monthly entertainment guide. The TI also sells tickets for the Swiss rail system and books adventure sports. If you're planning to visit Kleine Scheidegg, the Jungfraujoch, or other destinations served by the Jungfraubahn, you can buy tickets for those at the TI, too.

ARRIVAL IN INTERLAKEN

Interlaken has two train stations: Ost (East) and West. Interlaken Ost is the name you'll see most often on train schedules, and it's the transfer point for narrow-gauge trains to the high mountains (to Lauterbrunnen, Gimmelwald, etc.) and to Luzern. Use this station if you're headed to those destinations or staying at the recommended Interlaken Hostel (next door). Interlaken Ost has free WCs, lockers, ticket counters (daily 6:00-19:30), and a summer-only branch TI.

If you're staying elsewhere in Interlaken, get off at Interlaken West, which is closer to my listed hotels and downtown shopping and services. All trains from western Switzerland—Bern, the Golden Pass, Basel—stop at Interlaken West, and then continue to Interlaken Ost. Interlaken West has free WCs, lockers (by track 1), and ticket counters (daily 6:40-19:00).

It's a pleasant 20-minute walk between the West and Ost train stations; an easy 3-minute trip by train (2-3/hour, 3.60 CHF); or a 10-minute trip on any of several local buses (3.60 CHF; #21, #102, #103, or #104).

HELPFUL HINTS

Laundry: Tiny self-service **Wäscherei** has a change machine, soap, English instructions, and a handy riverside location (daily 7:00-22:00; from the main street take Marktgasse over two bridges to Beatenbergstrasse 5, tel. 033-822-1566).

Bike Rental: The Interlaken West train station participates in the Swiss rail system's bike-rental scheme (see page 407). **Flying Wheels,** a short walk from the Ost train station, is a hip, well-organized, family-friendly outfit that specializes in electric bikes and guided bike tours. Its English-speaking staff give tips on where to go and can help you pick the right bike (bikes-35 CHF/half-day, 40 CHF/day; electric bikes-45 CHF/half-day, 55 CHF/day; includes helmet, daily May-Sept 9:30-20:00, shorter hours off-season, across street from northeast corner of Höhematte Park at Höheweg 133, tel. 033-557-8838, www.flyingwheels.ch). For info on their tours, see "Adventure Sports," later.

A short walk from the West train station, **Eiger Sport** rents bikes for a little less than Flying Wheels, but they charge for helmets (20 CHF/half-day, 30 CHF/day, helmets-5 CHF/day; Mon-Fri 8:30-12:00 & 13:30-18:30, Sat 8:30-16:00, closed Sun; from the West train station, cross the river—it's on the left at Bahnhofstrasse 2, tel. 033-823-2043, www.eiger-sport.ch).

Visitor Cards: If you're staying overnight in Interlaken, get a local Visitor Card from your hotelier—it lets you ride buses in town for free.

Interlaken Walk

Most visitors use Interlaken as a springboard for high-altitude thrills (and rightly so). But the town itself has history and scenic charm, and is worth a short walk. This 45-minute stroll circles from the West train station, down the main drag to the big meadow, past the casino, along the river to the oldest part of town (called Unterseen—historically a separate town), and back to the station.

• *From the West train station, walk along...*

Bahnhofstrasse: This main drag, which turns into Höheweg as it continues east, cuts straight through the town center from the West train station to the Ost train station. The best Swiss souvenir shopping is along this stretch (finer shops are on the Höheweg stretch, near the fancy hotels). At the roundabout is the handy post office (with free public WCs). At Höheweg 2, the TV in the window of the Schilthornbahn office shows the weather up top.

The 18-story **Metropole Hotel** (a.k.a. the "concrete shame of Interlaken") is by far the town's tallest building. Step right into the

BERNER OBERLAND

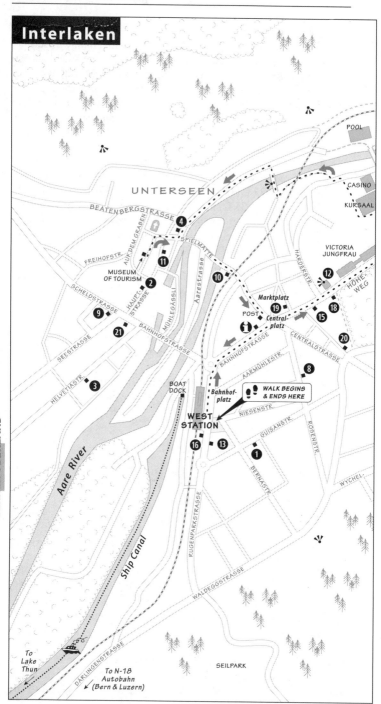

Interlaken

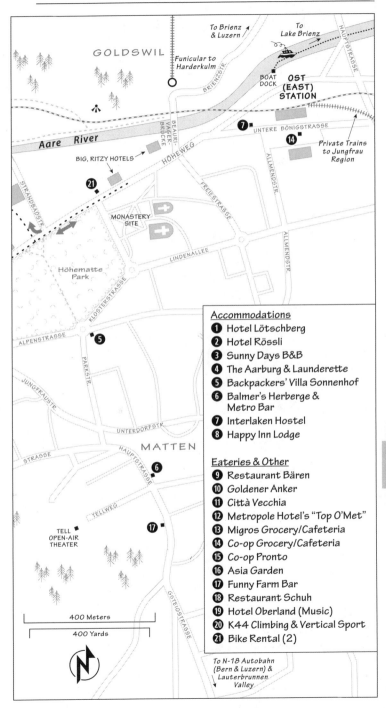

GOLDSWIL

To Brienz & Luzern

To Lake Brienz

Funicular to Harderkulm

BOAT DOCK

OST (EAST) STATION

BEAURIVAGE-BRÜCKE

BRIENZSTR.

UNTERE BÖNIGSTRASSE

7

14

HAUPTSTRASSE

Private Trains to Jungfrau Region

Aare River

ALLMENDSTR.

HÖHEWEG

BIG, RITZY HOTELS →

STRANDBADSTR.

21

MONASTERY SITE

FREISTRASSE

LINDENALLEE

ALLMENDSTR.

Höhematte Park

KLOSTERSTRASSE

ALPENSTRASSE

PARKSTR.

5

JUNGFRAUSTR.

UNTERDORFSTR.

MATTEN

STRASSE

HAUPTSTRASSE

6

TELLWEG

17

TELL OPEN-AIR THEATER

GSTEIGSTRASSE

To N-18 Autobahn (Bern & Luzern) & Lauterbrunnen Valley

400 Meters

400 Yards

N

Accommodations
- **1** Hotel Lötschberg
- **2** Hotel Rössli
- **3** Sunny Days B&B
- **4** The Aarburg & Launderette
- **5** Backpackers' Villa Sonnenhof
- **6** Balmer's Herberge & Metro Bar
- **7** Interlaken Hostel
- **8** Happy Inn Lodge

Eateries & Other
- **9** Restaurant Bären
- **10** Goldener Anker
- **11** Città Vecchia
- **12** Metropole Hotel's "Top O'Met"
- **13** Migros Grocery/Cafeteria
- **14** Co-op Grocery/Cafeteria
- **15** Co-op Pronto
- **16** Asia Garden
- **17** Funny Farm Bar
- **18** Restaurant Schuh
- **19** Hotel Oberland (Music)
- **20** K44 Climbing & Vertical Sport
- **21** Bike Rental (2)

BERNER OBERLAND

main lobby (through the second set of doors) and ride the elevator to the top for a commanding view of the "inter-laken" area, and gaze deep into the Jungfrau region to the scenic south. A meal or beverage here costs no more than one back on earth. Consider sipping a drink on the outdoor view terrace (or come back tonight—it's open very late).

• *On your right is...*

Höhematte Park: This "high meadow," or Höhematte (but generally referred to simply as "the park"), marks the beginning of Interlaken's fancy hotel row. Hotels like the Victoria-Jungfrau harken back to the late-19th-century days when Interlaken was *the* top alpine resort. The first grand hotels were built here to enjoy the views of the Jungfrau in the distance. (Today, the *junge Frauen* getting the most attention are next door, at Hooters.)

The park originated as farmland belonging to the monastery that predated the town (marked today by the steeples of both the Catholic and Protestant churches—neither are of sightseeing interest). The actual **monastery site** is now home to the courthouse and county administration building. With the Reformation in 1528, the monastery was shut down, and its land taken by the state. Later, as developers started to eye the parkland, the town's leading hotels and business families bought it and protected it from commercial use (a very early example of smart town planning). There was talk of building a parking lot under it, but the water table here, between the two lakes, is too high. (That's why the town cemetery is up on the hillside.) Today, this is a fine place to stroll, hang out on the park benches or at Restaurant Schuh, and watch the paragliders gracefully land.

• *Passing the Victoria-Jungfrau Hotel, follow the passage on your left (through a shopping arcade) into the grounds of the...*

Casino Kursaal: Here, at the top of each hour, dwarves ring the toadstools on the flower clock. The Kursaal, originally a kind of 19th-century fat farm, is now a convention center and casino (passport but no tie required to enter).

• *Follow the path left of the Kursaal to the river (note the huge public swimming pool across the river). Walk downstream along the riverside path, passing under the train bridge, and cross the pedestrian bridge, stopping in the middle to enjoy the view.*

Aare River: The Aare River is Switzerland's longest. It connects Lake Brienz and Lake Thun (with an 18-foot altitude difference that's controlled by sluices—this short stretch has quite a flow). From Lake Thun, it heads for Bern and ultimately into the Rhine. In the distance (looking downstream), a church bell tower marks a different parish and the technically separate town of Unterseen, across the river. Behind the spire is the pointy summit of the Niesen (like so many Swiss peaks, capped with a restaurant and accessible by a lift).

Stroll downstream along the far side of the river to the church spire. The delightful riverside walk is lined by fine residences. Notice that your Jungfrau view now includes the Jungfraujoch observation deck (the little brown bump in the ridge just left of the peak).

• *At the next bridge, turn right to the town square lined with 17th-century houses on one side and a modern strip on the other.*

Unterseen: This was a town when Interlaken was only a monastery, and preserves a little of its medieval layout and streetscape. A block away from the square, to the left, the worthwhile—but generally empty—**Museum of Tourism** (grandly named, but really a local history museum) shows off classic posters, fascinating photos of the construction of the Jungfraujoch, and exhibits on folk life, crafts, and winter sports (5 CHF, covered by Swiss Travel Pass, May-mid-Oct Thu-Sun 14:00-17:00, closed Mon-Wed and mid-Oct-April, Obere Gasse 28, tel. 033-826-6464, www.touristikmuseum.ch).

• *From Unterseen, cross the river on Spielmatte, and you're a few minutes' walk from your starting point.*

Return to the West Train Station: On the second bridge, notice the border between the two towns/parishes, marked by their respective heraldic emblems (each featuring an ibex, a wild mountain goat). A block or so later, on the left, is the Marktplatz. The river originally ran through this square. The settlement on this side of the river used to be called "Aarmühle" ("mill on the Aare"), after the mill that was here. But in the 19th century, town fathers mindful of the English tourists flocking here made a key marketing decision: They ditched the difficult-to-pronounce "Aarmühle" and changed the name to the romantic "Interlaken" ("between the lakes"). Judging from the throngs of tourists on the main drag, it worked.

Sights and Activities near Interlaken

For hikes and walks in the Berner Oberland, see page 175.

EASYGOING EXCURSIONS
▲▲Swiss Open-Air Museum at Ballenberg

At the far end of Lake Brienz from Interlaken, the Ballenberg open-air museum is a rich collection of more than 100 traditional and historic buildings brought here from every region of the country. All the houses are carefully furnished, and many feature traditional craftspeople at work. The sprawling 50-acre park, laid out roughly as a huge Swiss map (Italian Swiss in the south, Appenzell

BERNER OBERLAND

in the east, and so on), is a natural preserve providing a wonderful setting for this culture-on-a-lazy-Susan look at Switzerland.

Ballenberg has entrances at either end (east and west, about a mile apart, each served by the local bus). If you start in the east and go west, it's a generally downhill stroll. Pick up a daily craft demonstration schedule at the entry, and the free map/guide so you'll know where you are. There are daily events and demonstrations, hundreds of traditional farm animals (like very furry-legged roosters, near the merry-go-round in the center), and a chocolate shop (under the restaurant, just outside the park, on the east side).

There are more historic buildings than you can see in a single visit. Survey your map, note where the demonstrations are happening, and make a smart plan. Buildings I particularly enjoy are: #1361 (cheese upstairs, cow bells you can ring downstairs); #911 (a big Appenzell house); #611 (barbershop museum upstairs); #321 (sausages hanging from the ceiling); and #221 (a house and farm designed for hands-on fun).

There are several places to eat. Picnic tables and grills with free firewood are scattered throughout the park.

Cost and Hours: 24 CHF, covered by Swiss Travel Pass; houses open daily mid-April-Oct 10:00-17:00, grounds and restaurants 9:00-18:00; tel. 033-952-1030, www.ballenberg.ch.

Getting There: The trip from Interlaken to Ballenberg takes about 20 minutes by car (pay parking at either entrance), 50 minutes by train and bus, or 1.75 hours by boat and bus. By public transport, you'll first go to Brienz by train or boat, then from Brienz to Ballenberg by local bus. Trains for Brienz leave from the Interlaken Ost train station (2/hour, 15-20 minutes). Boats to Brienz leave from a dock just behind the Ost train station (every 1-2 hours, first boat leaves Interlaken at 9:07, last return from Brienz usually at 17:40—at 15:40 early April-mid-May, 75 minutes, 30 CHF one-way, 51 CHF round-trip, free with Swiss Travel Pass, early April-late Oct only, tel. 058-327-4811, www.bls.ch). From the Brienz station or boat dock, catch local bus #151 to either museum entrance (hourly, 20 minutes). Use the online timetables at www.rail.ch to plan your trip, and check bus return times carefully—after 18:00, buses back to Brienz leave only from the park's west entrance. Without a rail pass, ask for the Ballenberg combo-ticket when buying your train or boat tickets: This covers your whole trip from Interlaken or beyond, and saves about 10 percent off your fare and park entry.

Boat Trips

"Interlaken" is literally "between the lakes" of Thun and Brienz. You can explore these lakes on a lazy boat trip, hopping on and off as the schedule allows (free with Swiss Travel Pass or Eurail pass but uses a flexi-day, tel. 058-327-4811, www.bls.ch). Returning by train makes for a good plan, as boats run only a few times a day (5/day July-Aug, 2-4/day spring and fall).

Boats on **Lake Brienz** are a fun way to get to the town of Brienz (75 minutes, 32 CHF, get off here for the Ballenberg open-air museum); there's also a stop at the super-cute village of Iselt-wald on the way. These boats leave from near the Ost train station.

Boats on **Lake Thun** stop at the St. Beatus caves (30 minutes from Interlaken, 15 CHF, described next) and two visit-worthy towns: Spiez (80 minutes, 29 CHF) and Thun (2.25 hours, 45 CHF); these boats leave from near Interlaken's West train station.

The **St. Beatus caves,** named after a legendary medieval monk, can be visited on 1.25-hour guided tours (18 CHF, runs about hourly, mid-March-mid-Nov daily 9:45-17:00, closed off-season, tel. 033-841-1643, www.beatushoehlen.ch). If the caves are your objective, the best plan is to catch bus #21 from either Interlaken station (hourly, 15-25 minutes, 6.80 CHF, direction: Thun), get off at the Beatushöhlen stop; tour the caves; take the short, steep hike down to the lake; and return to Interlaken by boat.

ADVENTURE SPORTS

High-Adrenaline Trips

For the thrill-seeker with money, several companies offer trips such as rafting, canyoning (rappelling down watery gorges), bungee jumping, and paragliding. Costs range from roughly 150 CHF to 200 CHF—higher for skydiving and hot-air balloon rides. Interlaken's two dominant companies are **Alpin Raft** (tel. 033-823-4100, www.alpinraft.ch) and **Outdoor Interlaken** (tel. 033-826-7719, www.outdoor-interlaken.ch). Other companies are generally just booking agents for these two outfits. For an overview of your options, study the racks of brochures at most TIs and hotels.

Indoor Climbing

K44 is a breathtaking indoor climbing facility where you can join in, or enjoy a snack or nice cup of hot chocolate while watching hotshots practice their gravity-defying skills.

Cost and Hours: Free entry for viewing, 21 CHF to climb as long as you like, includes equipment but not instruction, family deals; daily 9:00-22:00; next to—and run by—**Vertical Sport,** at the back of the park across from Hotel Savoy at Jungfraustrasse 44, tel. 033-821-2821, www.k44.ch.

Rope Courses

Outdoor Interlaken's Seilpark offers eight rope courses of varying difficulty and height, giving you a tree-top forest adventure through a maze of rope bridges and zip lines.

Cost and Hours: 37 CHF, family deals, must weigh between 44 and 264 pounds; daily 10:00-18:00; April-May and Sept-Oct

Mon-Fri from 13:00, Sat-Sun from 10:00; closed Nov-March; from Interlaken's West train station, it's a 15-minute walk—head right up Rugenparkstrasse and into the park, then look for signs; tel. 033-826-7719, www.outdoor-interlaken.ch (select "Summer," "Earth Activities," then "Adventure Park").

Bike Tours

Flying Wheels offers bike tours of varying length and difficulty, including a three-hour Interlaken-only tour (79 CHF) and a tour of the Lauterbrunnen Valley (189 CHF, 6 hours, includes picnic and Trümmelbach Falls visit). For contact info, see page 135.

CASTLES

Three impressively well-kept and welcoming old castles in or near the town of Thun are worth considering for day trips (30 minutes from Interlaken by train or car, or about 2 hours by scenic boat ride).

Thun Castle (Schloss Thun)

Built between 1180 and 1190 by the Dukes of Zähringen, this castle in the center of Thun houses a five-floor historical museum offering insights into the cultural development of the region over some 4,000 years. From the corner turrets of the castle, you're rewarded with spectacular views of the city of Thun, the lake, and the Alps.

Cost and Hours: 10 CHF, daily 10:00-17:00, shorter hours off-season, Nov-Jan Sun only, tel. 033-223-2001, www.schlossthun.ch.

Hünegg Castle (Schloss Hünegg)

Located in Hilterfingen (on the outskirts of Thun), this castle-museum exhibits furnished rooms from the second half of the 19th century. The castle is situated in a beautiful wooded park by the lake, not far from the Hilterfingen boat dock and the #21 bus from Interlaken or Thun.

Cost and Hours: 10 CHF, mid-May-mid-Oct Tue-Sat 14:00-17:00, Sun from 11:00, closed Mon and off-season, tel. 033-243-1982, www.schlosshuenegg.ch.

Oberhofen Castle (Schloss Oberhofen)

A 20-minute walk along the lake from Hünegg Castle, this place is ideal for those interested in gardens. Its beautifully landscaped park with exotic trees is a delight. The museum in the castle depicts domestic life in the 16th to 19th centuries, including a Turkish smoking room and a medieval chapel.

Cost and Hours: Gardens—free, early April-late Oct daily 9:00-dusk; museum—10 CHF, mid-May-mid-Oct Tue-Sun 11:00-17:00, closed Mon; both closed off-season, by Oberhofen am Thunersee boat dock or take bus #21, tel. 033-243-1235, www. schlossoberhofen.ch.

Nightlife in Interlaken

Youthful Night Scenes

For counterculture with a reggae beat, check out **Funny Farm** (past the recommended Balmer's Herberge hostel, in Matten). The young frat-party dance scene rages at the **Metro Bar** at Balmer's (bomb-shelter disco bar, with cheap drinks and a friendly if loud atmosphere). And if you're into **Hooters,** you won't have a hard time finding it.

Mellower After-Dark Hangouts

To nurse a drink with a park view, the outdoor tables at **Restaurant Schuh** (on the edge of Höhematte Park) are convenient—if you don't mind the schlocky music. The **"Top O'Met"** bar and café in the Metropole Hotel skyscraper has great indoor and outdoor view seating with reasonable prices, 18 floors above everything else in town (open nightly until late, see "Eating in Interlaken," later). **Hotel Oberland** (near the post office) has live alpine music in its restaurant on Tuesdays at 19:00.

Sleeping in Interlaken

Interlaken is not the Alps. I'd sleep in Gimmelwald, or at least Lauterbrunnen (20 minutes away by train or car). In ski season, however, prices go down in Interlaken, while they shoot up at most mountain hotels. Prices listed here are for summer; they sag a bit in spring and fall, and plunge from November to March.

 $$$ Hotel Lötschberg, with a sun terrace, 24 rooms, and four apartments for longer stays, is run with lots of thoughtful touches by the English-speaking owners. Three of the cheaper rooms are in the building next door (closed Nov-mid-April, elevator in main building, free self-service laundry, free loaner bikes; lounge with microwave, fridge, and free tea and coffee; 3-minute walk from the West train station: turn right from the station, after Migros at the circle go left to General-Guisan-Strasse 31; tel. 033-822-2545, www.lotschberg.ch, hotel@lotschberg.ch).

 $$$ Hotel Rössli, across the river from the West train station, is nicely located, if a bit dated. Besides standard rooms, they offer "economy" rooms with a private bath down the hall and "budget" rooms with shared facilities (reserve on hotel website for best rates, closed Dec-mid-Jan, lots of stairs, comfy lounge, Hauptstrasse 10, tel. 033-822-7816, www.roessli-interlaken.ch, info@roessli-interlaken.ch).

$$ Sunny Days B&B is a homey, nine-room place in a quiet residential neighborhood (pay laundry, patio; from West train station: exit left and take first bridge to your left, after crossing two bridges turn left on Helvetiastrasse and go 3 blocks to #29; mobile 077-456-2338, www.sunnydays.ch, mail@sunnydays.ch).

$$ The Aarburg offers nine plain, peaceful rooms over a restaurant in a traditional-looking and beautifully located building in Unterseen, a 10-minute walk from the West train station (2 doors from launderette at Beatenbergstrasse 1, tel. 033-822-2615, www.theaarburg.ch).

¢ Hostels: Backpackers' Villa Sonnenhof is a creative 190-bed guesthouse affiliated with the Methodist church that's wholesome without being restrictive. It's fun, youthful, and great for families or travelers of any age (locker, sheets, and towel included, private rooms and family rooms available, view rooms have balcony and WC but shared shower, half-board dinner at nearby restaurant, kitchen, elevator, garden, movies, small game room, pay laundry, free entry to public swimming pool, no curfew, reception open 7:00-23:00, across park from TI at Alpenstrasse 16—a level 15-minute walk from either train station or take bus #102 to stop: Sonnenhof, tel. 033-826-7171, www.villa.ch, mail@villa.ch).

Balmer's Herberge is many people's idea of backpacker heaven. This 200-bed Interlaken institution comes with movies, table tennis, bar, restaurant, tiny grocery, kitchen, hot tub, swapping library, excursions, and friendly, hardworking staff. With all the youthful fun and activities, it can feel like a frat party, especially on summer weekends (sheets and breakfast included, reserve far in advance for private rooms, pay laundry; a 20-minute walk from either train station at Hauptstrasse 23, in Matten, tel. 033-822-1961, www.balmers.com, mail@balmers.com). More-expensive rooms in an adjacent building come with semiprivate kitchens and fewer beds per WC.

Interlaken Hostel is very convenient—right next to the Ost train station in a big, sterile modern building with 220 beds, including some private rooms. It's full of daylight and offers plenty of amenities (sheets and breakfast included, four-course dinner available, bike rental-25 CHF/day, pay laundry, game room, lockers, no curfew, check-in 15:00-24:00, Untere Bönigstrasse 3, tel. 033-826-1090, www.youthhostel.ch/interlaken, interlaken@youthhostel.ch).

Happy Inn Lodge, above the lively, noisy Brasserie 17 pub, has 16 cheap, conveniently located backpacker rooms, plus two basic doubles with private baths. It's a decent option for the young and scrappy—older folks and families will feel more comfortable elsewhere (breakfast extra, no curfew, microwave; 5-minute walk from West train station at Rosenstrasse 17, tel. 033-822-3225, www.happyinn.com, info@happyinn.com).

Eating in Interlaken

$$$ Restaurant Bären is across the river in Unterseen, in a classic low-ceilinged building with cozy indoor and fine outdoor seating. It's a great value for *Rösti*, fondue, raclette, fish, traditional sausage, and salads. Their chicken cordon bleu is popular (Tue-Thu 16:30-23:30, Fri-Sun 10:00-23:30 or later, closed Mon; from the West train station, turn left on Bahnhofstrasse, cross the river, and go a few blocks to Seestrasse 2; tel. 033-822-7526).

$$$ Goldener Anker, with its "melody rock and blues" ambience, is this town's local hangout. If you think Interlaken is sterile, you haven't been to the "Golden Anchor." Jeannette serves and René cooks, just as they have for 35 years. This place sometimes hosts small concerts and has launched some of Switzerland's top bands. The big, flexible menu seems designed to make a good hot meal affordable to travelers, with 15-CHF "backpacker specials" that include a main dish and salad (takeout available, Mon-Sat from 16:00, closed Sun, Marktgasse 57, tel. 033-822-1672).

$$$ Città Vecchia serves decent Italian with seating indoors or out, on Unterseen's leafy main square (lunch specials, Thu-Mon 10:30-14:00 & 18:30-23:00, Tue-Wed 18:30-23:00, Untere Gasse 5, tel. 033-822-1754).

$$$ Metropole Hotel's "Top O'Met," capping Interlaken's 18-story aesthetic nightmare, is actually a good café/restaurant serving traditional and modern food at down-to-earth prices, with no gouging on drinks. For 9 CHF, you can enjoy a glass of prosecco and awesome views from an indoor or outdoor table (daily lunch deals include two courses plus water and coffee, 50-CHF fondue for two; daily 8:00-23:00, Oct-May 10:00-22:00; hot food served 11:30-14:00 & 18:00-21:30, Höheweg 37, just step into the Metropole Hotel and go up the elevator as far as you can, tel. 033-828-6666).

Supermarkets and Cheap Eats: Interlaken's two big supermarkets sell picnic supplies and also have reasonable self-service restaurants. **Migros** is across the street from the West train station (Mon-Thu 8:00-19:00, Fri until 21:00, Sat until 18:00, closed Sun), with a ground-floor **$$** cafeteria (same hours plus Sun mid-July-mid-Aug 10:00-17:00, Rugenparkstrasse 1). The **Co-op** supermarket is across the square from the Ost train station and also has a good cafeteria (supermarket hours similar to Migros, cafeteria closes 30-60 minutes before store and open Sun 9:00-17:00, Untere Bönigstrasse 10). Smaller supermarkets in both train stations are

BERNER OBERLAND

open daily until 21:00; the only grocery store open late is the teeny **Co-op Pronto** (daily 6:00-22:30 at Höheweg 26).

Interlaken has many restaurants catering to its Asian tourists. One of the cheapest (though not the most elegant) is Chinese-run **$$ Asia Garden,** by the West train station (take out or eat in, daily 11:00-23:00, Rugenparkstrasse 4, tel. 033-821-2022).

Interlaken Connections

Interlaken is connected to Montreux (on Lake Geneva) and Luzern via the Golden Pass scenic rail route (see the Scenic Rail Journeys chapter). Interlaken, Bern, Basel, and Frankfurt are linked by an express train, but for most other destinations you'll change in Bern. Train info: Toll tel. 0900-300-300 or www.rail.ch.

From Interlaken Ost by Train to: Bern (1-2/hour, 1 hour), **Zürich** (2/hour, 2 hours, change in Bern, but 3-hour trip with change in Luzern is more scenic), **Zürich Airport** (2/hour, 2.5 hours, change in Bern), **Luzern** (hourly direct, 2 hours), **Lugano** (hourly, 4.5 hours, change in Luzern and sometimes Arth-Goldau), **Zermatt** (1-2/hour, 2 hours, change in Spiez and Visp), **Lausanne** (2/hour, 2 hours, change in Bern and sometimes Spiez; longer scenic route via Golden Pass—see the Scenic Rail Journeys chapter).

From Interlaken to the Lauterbrunnen Valley: Trains to **Lauterbrunnen** depart from Interlaken Ost (1-2/hour, 20 minutes). You can **drive** to Lauterbrunnen or Stechelberg, but not to Gimmelwald (park at the cable-car station near Stechelberg and ride up on the lift; see page 154) or to Mürren, Wengen, or Kleine Scheidegg (park in Lauterbrunnen and take the cable car to Mürren or the train to Wengen or Kleine Scheidegg). For more details, see "Lauterbrunnen Valley Connections" on page 152.

Lauterbrunnen

Lauterbrunnen is the valley's commercial center and transportation hub. Sitting under sheer cliffs at the base of the valley, with its signature waterfall spurting mightily out from the cliff (floodlit at night), Lauterbrunnen (rated ▲) is a fine springboard for Jungfrau and Schilthorn adventures. But for spending the night, I still prefer Gimmelwald or Mürren, perched on the ledge above the valley.

Orientation to Lauterbrunnen

In addition to its train station and cable car, the one-street town is just big enough to have all the essential services (grocery, bank, post office, bike rental, launderette, and so on)—plus several hotels and hostels. It's idyllic, in spite of the busy road that slices it in two.

Tourist Information: Stop by the friendly TI to check the weather forecast, find out about guided walks and events, and buy hiking maps or regional train or lift tickets (June-Sept daily 8:30-12:00 & 14:00-18:30; Oct-May Tue-Sat 9:00-12:00 & 13:30-17:00, closed Sun-Mon; on the main street a few houses up from the train station, tel. 033-856-8568, www.mylauterbrunnen.com).

Arrival in Lauterbrunnen: The small, modern train station has a ticket office (daily 6:00-19:30), a few small lockers (check larger bags at the ticket office), and free WCs, and is across the main street from the cable-car station. Go left as you exit the station to find the TI. Drivers can pay to park in the large multistory lot behind the station.

HELPFUL HINTS

Medical Help: Dr. Bruno Durrer has a clinic (with pharmacy) near the Jungfrau Hotel (look for *Arzt* sign). He and his associate both speak English (tel. 033-856-2626, answered 24/7).

Money: Several ATMs are along the main street, including one immediately across from the train station.

Wi-Fi: Cafés along the main street have Wi-Fi for customers.

Laundry: The **Valley Hostel** has coin-op machines (daily 9:00-21:00, Wi-Fi, tel. 033-855-2008).

Bike Rental: You can rent mountain bikes at **Imboden Bike** on the main street (30 CHF/4 hours, 40 CHF/day, includes helmet, Mon-Fri 8:30-18:30, Sat-Sun 9:00-17:00, tel. 033-855-2114, www.imboden-bike.ch).

Sports Gear: Hiking boots, skis, and snowboards are available to rent at the **Alpia Sports/Intersport** shop (winter daily 8:00-12:30 & 13:30-18:30, slightly shorter hours in summer, closed during Easter holiday, at Hotel Crystal, tel. 033-855-3292, www.alpiasport.ch).

Activities in and near Lauterbrunnen

For hikes and walks from Lauterbrunnen, including "Cloudy-Day Lauterbrunnen Valley Walks" that link Lauterbrunnen to Staubbach and Trümmelbach falls, see page 176.

BERNER OBERLAND

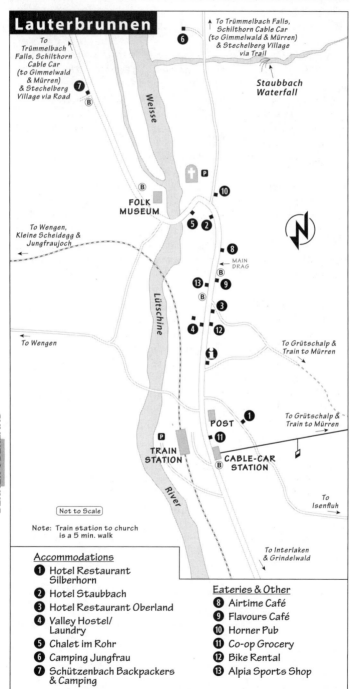

Lauterbrunnen

To Trümmelbach Falls, Schilthorn Cable Car (to Gimmelwald & Mürren) & Stechelberg Village via Trail

To Trümmelbach Falls, Schilthorn Cable Car (to Gimmelwald & Mürren) & Stechelberg Village via Road

Staubbach Waterfall

Weisse

P

FOLK MUSEUM

To Wengen, Kleine Scheidegg & Jungfraujoch

MAIN DRAG

Lütschine

To Wengen

To Grütschalp & Train to Mürren

To Grütschalp & Train to Mürren

POST

TRAIN STATION

CABLE-CAR STATION

River

To Isenfluh

Not to Scale

Note: Train station to church is a 5 min. walk

To Interlaken & Grindelwald

BERNER OBERLAND

Accommodations
1 Hotel Restaurant Silberhorn
2 Hotel Staubbach
3 Hotel Restaurant Oberland
4 Valley Hostel/Laundry
5 Chalet im Rohr
6 Camping Jungfrau
7 Schützenbach Backpackers & Camping

Eateries & Other
8 Airtime Café
9 Flavours Café
10 Horner Pub
11 Co-op Grocery
12 Bike Rental
13 Alpia Sports Shop

Staubbach Falls

The second highest waterfall in Switzerland (nearly 900 feet) is literally in Lauterbrunnen's backyard—just follow the trail past the church toward the sound of rushing water. Its spray looks like falling dust—*Staub*—hence the name. A trail is cut into the cliff that takes visitors up "behind" the falls (in winter, it's closed due to the danger of rock slides).

▲Trümmelbach Falls

If all the waterfalls have you intrigued, sneak a behind-the-scenes look at the valley's most powerful, Trümmelbach Falls. Ride the elevator up through the mountain, climb up to the upper falls, and then hike down through several caves (wet, with lots of stairs, and claustrophobic for some). You'll see the melt from the Eiger, Mönch, and Jungfrau grinding like God's band saw through the mountain at the rate of up to 5,200 gallons a second. The upper area is the best; if your legs ache, skip the lower falls and ride down on the elevator. A café (with WC) is directly across from the bus stop. The falls ticket kiosk is a three-minute walk beyond the café.

Cost and Hours: 11 CHF, daily July-Aug 8:30-18:00, early April-June and Sept-Oct 9:00-17:00, closed Nov-early April, opening date varies with ice conditions, tel. 033-855-3232, www.truemmelbachfaelle.ch.

Getting There: The falls are about halfway between Lauterbrunnen and the Schilthornbahn cable-car station; from either, it's a short ride on the PostBus or a 45-minute walk. Or combine a visit to Trümmelbach with a walk on the valley floor; see page 176.

Hang Out with BASE Jumpers

The Lauterbrunnen Valley has become an El Dorado of BASE jumping (parachuting off cliffs). Each season thrill-seekers hike to the top of a cliff, leap off—falling as long as they can (this provides the rush)—and then pull the ripcord to release a tiny parachute, hoping it will break their fall and a gust won't dash them against the walls of the valley. The Lauterbrunnen jumps are considered too tough for beginners—anyone considering BASE jumping should have extensive skydiving experience. (For a fascinating look at this sport, search for "BASE jumping Lauterbrunnen" on You-Tube, and read the FAQ at www.swissbaseassociation.ch).

To learn more about BASE jumping, talk with the jumpers themselves. They congregate at the ¢ **Horner Pub,** at the upper end of Lauterbrunnen (near the waterfall). This is the grittiest place in town, providing cheap beds and filling meals for BASE jumpers and the only real after-dark scene in town. Locals, jumpers, and stray tourists gather here in the pub each evening (dorm beds in 9 rooms, apartments available, no breakfast, disco Fri-Sat from 22:00 upstairs, tel. 033-855-1673, www.hornerpub.ch, mail@hornerpub.ch, run by Ferdinand Gertsch). Their kitchen sells cheap pastas, burgers, and raclette.

Lauterbrunnen Valley Folk Museum (Talmuseum Lauterbrunnen)

This interesting museum shows off the region's folk culture and two centuries of mountaineering from all the towns of this valley. You'll see lots of lace, old tools, exhibits on cheese and woodworking, cowbells, and classic old photos.

Cost and Hours: 5 CHF, free with hotel Visitor Card, June-mid-Oct Tue and Thu-Sun 14:00-17:30, off-season by appointment, closed Mon and Wed year-round, English handout, just over bridge and below church at the far end of Lauterbrunnen town, tel. 033-855-3586, www.talmuseumlauterbrunnen.ch.

Sleeping in Lauterbrunnen

The price ratings listed are typical for high summer (July-Aug). Expect lower prices in winter (many hotels close). Free parking is easy to find. For more peace, choose Gimmelwald or Mürren.

$$$ Hotel Silberhorn is a family-run, formal, 35-room hotel. It's in a very convenient location—a hundred yards uphill from the train station on a quiet side street. Almost every double room comes with a fine view and balcony, and some come clad in warm, knotty-pine woodwork (closed late Oct-mid-Dec, lots of stairs, dinner available, tel. 033-856-2210, www.silberhorn.com, info@silberhorn.com).

$$ Hotel Staubbach, a big, creaky Old World place, is one of the oldest hotels in the valley (1890). It has the casual feel of a national park lodge, with 33 simple and comfortable rooms. It's family-friendly and has a kids' play area. Rooms that face up the valley have fabulous views, though you may hear the happy crowd across the meadow at the Horner Pub or the church bells chiming on the hour. If the weather's bad, you can watch a DVD of my Switzerland TV show in the lounge (closed mid-Nov-March, airy breakfast room with great views, elevator, 10-minute walk up from station on the left, tel. 033-855-5454, www.staubbach.com, hotel@staubbach.com).

$$ Hotel Oberland is cheerfully located smack-dab in the center of town, with 28 tidy, bright rooms, most with balconies and views of the Staubbach waterfall or Jungfrau. It's run with pride by Australian Mark and lifelong Lauterbrunnen resident Ursula (closed mid-Oct-mid-Dec, family rooms and apartments available, 5 rooms are in nearby Crystal Hotel annex, popular with my tour groups, 5-minute walk up from station on the right, free parking, tel. 033-855-1241, www.hoteloberland.ch, info@hoteloberland. ch).

¢ **Hostels: Valley Hostel** is practical and comfortable, offering 92 inexpensive beds for quieter travelers of all ages, with a pleasant garden. This is a manageable budget option for families (private rooms available, breakfast extra, kitchen, pay laundry, reception open 8:00-12:00 & 15:00-22:00—shorter hours off-season, 5-minute walk up from train station, tel. 033-855-2008, www.valleyhostel.ch, info@valleyhostel.ch, Abegglen family: Martha, Alfred, Stefan, and Fränzi).

Chalet im Rohr—a creaky, flower-draped, woody firetrap of a place—has oodles of character (and lots of paragliders and BASE jumpers). It offers 56 beds in big one- to four-bed rooms that share six showers (no breakfast, cash only, common kitchen, across from church on main drag, tel. 033-855-2182, www.chaletimrohr.ch, info@chaletimrohr.ch, Hans and Elsbeth von Allmen-Müller).

¢ **Camping:** Two campgrounds just south of town provide beds in dorms and two- to four-bed bungalows (rentable sheets, kitchens, big English-speaking tour groups, local tax not included in price). This can be a good deal for families (or small groups) traveling by car who want to stay a few days and cook for themselves.

Camping Jungfrau, romantically situated along the small lane beyond Staubbach Falls, is huge (400 beds) and well-organized by Hans. Ample facilities include a grocery store (open daily), communal kitchen, a restaurant serving traditional fare that's also popular with locals, lounge, ATM, and playground (cabins and mobile homes available, 2-3-night minimum stay, 7-night minimum July-Aug, closed Nov; tel. 033-856-2010, www.campingjungfrau.swiss, info@camping-jungfrau.ch).

Schützenbach Backpackers & Camping, on the left as you drive out of Lauterbrunnen toward Stechelberg, is a very simple campground and hostel conveniently situated next to the Schützenbach PostBus stop (ages 18-35 only, reception open 8:00-11:00 & 16:00-20:00, linens included, often full with groups, tel. 033-855-1268, www.schutzenbach.ch, schutzenbach@yahoo.com).

Eating in Lauterbrunnen

At **$$$ Hotel Restaurant Oberland,** Ursula (Swiss) and Mark (Aussie) Nolan take pride in serving tasty, good-value meals from a fun menu, including traditional Swiss dishes. It's a high-energy place with lots of tourists and a huge front porch good for lingering on into the evening (pizzas, raclette, main courses, daily 11:30-21:00, tel. 033-855-1241).

$$$ Hotel Restaurant Silberhorn, with an elegant dining room, is the local choice for a fancy dinner out. Prices are reasonable, and they have all of the Swiss standards. Call to reserve a view table (lunch specials, daily 12:00-14:00 & 18:00-21:00, classy indoor and outdoor seating, above the cable-car station, tel. 033-856-2210).

$$ Airtime Café feels like an alpine Starbucks with hot drinks, homemade treats, breakfast, simple lunches, and light early dinners (sandwiches, meat pies). They have Wi-Fi, an English-language swap library, and can help you book adventure-sport activities such as tandem paragliding (daily 8:30-18:00, closed Nov, tel. 033-855-1515; Annette, Fred, and Beni).

$$ Flavours, a café without a hint of yodeling or cowbells, serves up full breakfasts, burgers, focaccia sandwiches, fresh-squeezed juices, and gelato (takeaway available, daily 9:00-18:00, shorter hours off-season, closed Nov-April, tel. 033-855-3652).

Supermarket: The small but well-stocked **Co-op** is on the main street across from the station (Mon-Fri 8:00-18:30, Sat until 17:00, closed Sun). The smaller grocery at **Camping Jungfrau** is usually open, even on off-season Sundays (call tel. 033-856-2010 to check before heading out).

Lauterbrunnen Valley Connections

The valley-floor towns of Lauterbrunnen and Stechelberg have connections by mountain train, bus, and cable car to the traffic-free villages, peaks, and hikes high above. Prices and trip durations given are one-way and per leg unless otherwise noted.

From Lauterbrunnen

By Train to: Interlaken Ost (1-2/hour, 20 minutes, 7.60 CHF), **Wengen** (2/hour, 15 minutes, 6.80 CHF), **Kleine Scheidegg** (2/hour, 45 minutes, 30.80 CHF), **Jungfraujoch** (2/hour, 1.5 hours, 94.80 CHF one-way, change in Kleine Scheidegg, see details on page 173); **Männlichen** (for hike to Kleine Scheidegg—take train to Wengen and change to cable car).

By Cable Car to: Grütschalp (2-4/hour, 6 minutes), where the train waits to take you to **Mürren** (another 15 minutes); total trip time 20 minutes, total one-way cost 11.40 CHF, www.jungfrau.ch.

By PostBus to: Schilthornbahn cable-car station (buses timed to depart a few minutes after trains arrive in Lauterbrunnen, 15-minute ride, 4.40 CHF, covered by Swiss Travel Pass), continues to the hamlet of **Stechelberg.**

By Car to: **Schilthornbahn cable-car station** (10-minute drive, pay parking lot).

From Schilthornbahn Cable-Car Station near Stechelberg

By Cable Car to: Gimmelwald (2/hour, 5 minutes, 6.20 CHF); **Mürren** (2/hour, 10 minutes, 11.40 CHF, change in Gimmelwald); and the **Schilthorn** (2/hour, 22 minutes, 105 CHF round-trip, change in Gimmelwald, Mürren, and Birg). Cable cars run up from the valley station—and down from Mürren—at :25 and :55 past the hour (5:55-19:55; then only once an hour until 23:45 Sun-Thu, until 24:55 Fri-Sat). From Gimmelwald to both Mürren and the valley station, the cable car runs at :00 and :30 (6:00-20:00; after 20:00 runs only once an hour).

Gimmelwald

Saved from developers by its "avalanche zone" classification, Gimmelwald was (before modern tourism) one of the poorest places in Switzerland. Its traditional economy was stuck in the hay, and its farmers—unable to make it in their disadvantaged trade—survived only on a trickle of visitors and Swiss government subsidies (and working the ski lifts in winter). For some travelers, there's little to see in a village. Others (like me) enjoy a fascinating day sitting on a bench and learning why they say, "If heaven isn't what it's cracked up to be, send me back to Gimmelwald."

Take a walk through the town. The huge, sheer cliff face that dominates your mountain views is the Schwarzmönch ("Black Monk"). The three peaks above (or behind) it are, left to right, the Eiger, Mönch, and Jungfrau. Although Gimmelwald's population dropped in the last century from 300 to about 120 residents, traditions survive. Most Gimmelwalders have one of two last names: von Allmen or Feuz. They are tough and proud. Raising hay in this rugged terrain is labor-intensive. One family harvests enough to feed only about 15 cows. But they'd have it no other way, and, unlike the absentee-landlord town of Mürren, Gimmelwald is locally owned. (When word got out that urban planners wanted to develop Gimmelwald into a town of 1,000, locals pulled some strings to secure the town's bogus avalanche-zone building code. Today, unlike nearby resort towns, Gimmelwald's population is the same all

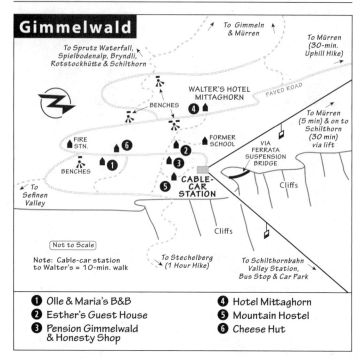

Gimmelwald

To Gimmeln & Mürren

To Mürren (30-min. Uphill Hike)

To Sprutz Waterfall, Spielbodenalp, Bryndli, Rotstockhütte & Schilthorn

WALTER'S HOTEL MITTAGHORN

PAVED ROAD

BENCHES

To Mürren (5 min) & on to Schilthorn (30 min) via lift

FIRE STN.

FORMER SCHOOL

VIA FERRATA SUSPENSION BRIDGE

BENCHES

CABLE-CAR STATION

Cliffs

To Sefinen Valley

Cliffs

Not to Scale

Note: Cable-car station to Walter's = 10-min. walk

To Stechelberg (1 Hour Hike)

To Schilthornbahn Valley Station, Bus Stop & Car Park

❶ Olle & Maria's B&B
❷ Esther's Guest House
❸ Pension Gimmelwald & Honesty Shop
❹ Hotel Mittaghorn
❺ Mountain Hostel
❻ Cheese Hut

year.) Those same folks are happy the masses go to commercialized Grindelwald, just over the Kleine Scheidegg ridge. Don't confuse Gimmelwald (rated ▲▲▲) and touristy Grindelwald—they couldn't be more different.

Thanks to local schoolteachers Olle and Maria and their son Sven, Gimmelwald has a helpful little website (www.gimmelwald.ch) where you can check out photos of the town in different seasons, get directions for 11 of the best hikes from town, and see all the latest on activities and rooms for rent. For more on hikes from Gimmelwald, see page 175.

In addition to my self-guided "Gimmelwald Walk," you can also download the free Schilthorn Explore App, which includes a Gimmelwald Audio Village Tour. It describes Gimmelwald's past and present in some detail at each of the eight stops along its route. Download the app via Apple's App Store or Google Play. When you open it on a mobile device, look for "Trip Suggestion" to find the Gimmelwald audio tour.

GETTING TO GIMMELWALD

To get from Lauterbrunnen to Gimmelwald, you have two options, outlined next. For times and prices, see "Lauterbrunnen Valley Connections" earlier.

1. Schilthornbahn Cable Car: The faster, easier way—best in bad weather or at the end of a long day with lots of luggage—is by road and then cable car. The cable-car station, near Stechelberg, is a 10-minute drive or 15-minute bus ride from Lauterbrunnen. Drivers can park at a pay lot at the cable-car station; otherwise, ride the PostBus from Lauterbrunnen (buses depart with the arrival of trains in Lauterbrunnen). The cable car whisks you in five thrilling minutes up to Gimmelwald.

Note that the Schilthornbahn cable car is closed for servicing for a week in late April or early May and for a month from early November through early December. If you're here during this time, you'll ride the cargo cable car from the valley floor directly up to Mürren, where a small bus shuttles you down to Gimmelwald.

2. Grütschalp Cable Car and Mürren Train: This is the more scenic route. Catch the cable car from Lauterbrunnen to Grütschalp. As you glide upward, notice the bed of the now-abandoned 100-year-old funicular train track below you. At Grütschalp, a special vintage train will roll you along the incredibly scenic cliffside to Mürren (the total trip takes 20 minutes). From there, either walk to the middle of Mürren and take a left down a moderately steep paved path 30 minutes to Gimmelwald, or walk 10 minutes across Mürren to catch the Schilthornbahn cable car down to Gimmelwald.

Gimmelwald Walk

Gimmelwald, though tiny, with one zigzag street, offers a fine look at a traditional Swiss mountain community.

• *Start this quick self-guided walk at the...*

Cable-Car Station: When the lift came in the 1960s, the village's back end became its front door. As you walk out of the station, pause at the big Infopoint map to orient yourself. Then turn right (uphill).

Gimmelwald was, and still is, a farm village. As you start up the street, you'll see a sweet little hut on the right. Set on stilts to keep out mice, the hut was used for storing cheese (the rocks on the rooftop here and throughout the town are not decorative—they keep the shingles on through wild storms). Behind the cheese hut stands the former village schoolhouse, long the largest structure in town (in Catholic Swiss towns, the biggest building is the church; in Protestant towns, it's the school). Gimmelwald's students now go to school in Lauterbrunnen, and the building is used as a cha-

BERNER OBERLAND

pel when the Protestant pastor makes his monthly visit. The little gray tower-like structure on the roof is the town fire siren. Now turn around: On the other side of the street, next to the little playground, is a bench with a nice view, and just beyond it is the recommended Mountain Hostel.

• *Walk up the lane 50 yards, past the town's Dalí-esque art gallery (who's showing in the phone booth?), to Gimmelwald's...*

"Times Square": The yellow alpine "street sign" shows where you are, the altitude (1,370 meters, or 4,470 feet), how many hours *(Std.)* and minutes it takes to walk to nearby points, and which tracks are serious hiking paths (marked with red and white, and further indicated along the way with red and white patches of paint on stones). You're surrounded by buildings that were built as duplexes, divided vertically right down the middle to house two separate families. Look for the Honesty Shop at Pension  Gimmelwald, which features local crafts and little edibles for sale (summer only).

Behind the sign, the lettering high up on the post office building is a folksy blessing: "Summer brings green, winter brings snow. The sun greets the day, the stars greet the night. This house will protect you from rain, cold, and wind. May God give us his blessings." Small as Gimmelwald is, it still has daily mail service. The postman comes down from Mürren each day (by golf cart in summer, sled in winter) to deliver and pick up mail. The date on this building indicates when it was built or rebuilt (1911). Gimmelwald has a strict building code: For instance, shutters can only be painted certain colors.

• *From this tiny intersection, walk away from the cable-car station and follow the town's...*

Main Street: Walk up the road past the garden-gnome greeting committee on the right. On the left, notice the announcement board: one side for tourist news, the other for local news (such as deals on chain-saw sharpening and upcoming shooting competitions). Cross the street and admire the big barn, dated 1995. At one front corner is a cow-scratcher. Swiss cows have legal rights (for example, in the winter they must be taken out for exercise at least three times a week). This big barn is built in a modern style. Traditionally, barns were small (like those on the hillside high above) and closer to the hay. But with trucks and paved roads, hay can be moved more easily, and farm businesses need more cows to be viable. Still, even a well-run big farm hopes just to break even. The industry survives only with government subsidies (see sidebar). As you wander, you'll also see private garden patches. Until recently, most locals grew their own vegetables—often enough to provide most of their family's needs.

• *Go just beyond the next barn. On your right is a...*

Water Fountain/Trough: This is the site of the town's historic water supply—still perfectly drinkable. Village kids love to bathe and wage water wars here when the cows aren't drinking from it.

• *Detour left down a gravel path (along a wooden fence). First you'll pass the lovingly tended pea-patch gardens of the woman with the best green thumb in the village (on your left). Continue along the path, which ends after 50 yards at another water trough in front of a house called...*

Husmättli: This is the oldest building in town, from 1658. (There are more 17th-century buildings on the road that zigzags down from Gimmelwald into the Sefinen Valley.) Study the log-cabin construction. Many old houses were built without nails. The wood was logged up the valley and cut on the water-powered village mill (also in the Sefinen Valley). Gimmelwald heats with wood, and since the wood needs to age a couple of years to burn well, it's stacked everywhere.

From here (at the water trough in front of Husmättli), look up to find a house with ten solar panels on the roof—it belongs to teachers Olle and Maria. As part of a green energy policy, a Swiss building code requires that new structures provide 30 percent of their own power. Switzerland is gradually moving away from nuclear power; its last reactor is supposed to close in 2034. The panels you see heat the water that Olle and Maria use for bathing and home heating; they fire up their furnace only from November to February.

• *Return to the main paved road and continue onward.*

Twenty yards along, on the left, look for the house with the *Self Service* sign. Open the door and you'll find a refrigerator with local cheese sold on the honor system by the Rubin family. Just outside the door, in the summer months, you may see a bunch of scythes hanging above a sharpening stone. Farmers pound, rather than grind, the blade to get it razor-sharp for efficient mowing on slopes too rocky or steep for machines or grazing animals. Feel a blade...carefully.

A few steps farther, notice the cute **cheese hut** on the right. This is where the cheese you saw on sale is produced. The hut's front wall is an alpine art gallery with nail-shoes used as flower pots. Nail shoes grip the steep, wet fields—this is critical for a farmer's

Swiss Cow Culture

Traditional Swiss cow farmers could make more money for much easier work in another profession. In a good year, farmers produce enough cheese to break even—they support their families on government subsidies of about $5,000 per cow. (Throughout the Alps, various governments support traditional farming as much for the tourism as for the cheese.) But these farmers have made a lifestyle choice to keep tradition alive and live high in the mountains. Rather than lose their children to the cities, Swiss farmers have the opposite problem: Kids argue about who gets to take over the family herd.

The cows' grazing ground can range in elevation by as much as 5,000 feet throughout the year. In the summer (usually mid-June), the farmer straps elaborate ceremonial bells on his cows and takes them up to a hut at high elevation. The cows hate these big bells, which weigh upward of 10 pounds and can cost more than 2,000 CHF apiece—a proud investment for a humble farmer. When the cows arrive at their summer home, the bells are hung under the eaves.

These high-elevation summer stables are called "alps." Try to find some on a Berner Oberland tourist map (such as Wengernalp, Grütschalp, or Schiltalp). The cows stay at the alps for about 100 days (roughly from June 10 to September 21). The farmers

safety, especially when carrying a sharp scythe. Even today, farmers buy metal tacks and fasten them to boots. The hut is full of strong cheese—up to three years old.

Look up. In the summer, a few goats are kept here behind the hut (rather than at a high alp) to provide families with fresh milk (about a half-gallon per day per goat). The farmers fence the goats in so they eat only this difficult-to-harvest grass.

On the left (at the *B&B* sign; see page 160) is Olle and Maria's home. They ran the local school until it closed in 2010. Now they both commute to teach at schools in other villages.

• *Fifty yards farther along on the right is the house called...*

Alpenrose: This is the old village school building, in use from about 1810 to 1930. Now it's a family home. You might see big ceremonial cowbells hanging under the eaves on the uphill side. These

hire a team of cheesemakers to work at each alp—mostly hippies, students, and city slickers eager to spend three summer months in mountainous solitude. Each morning, the hired hands get up at 5:00 to milk the cows; take them to pasture; and make the cheese, milking the cows again when they come home in the evening. In the summer, all the milk is turned into alp cheese (it's too difficult to get it down to the market in liquid form). In the winter, with the cows at lower altitudes, the fresh milk is sold as milk.

Every alp also has a resident herd of pigs. Cheesemaking leftovers (*Molke,* whey) can alter the ecosystem if thrown out—but pigs love the stuff. (The pigs parade up with the cows, but no one notices.) Cheesemakers claim that bathing in whey improves their complexion...but maybe that's just the altitude talking.

Meanwhile, the farmers, glad to be free of their bovine responsibilities in summer, turn their attention to making hay. The average farmer has a few huts at various altitudes, each surrounded by small hay fields. The farmer follows the seasons up into the mountains, making hay and storing it above the huts. In the fall, the cows come down from the alps and spend the winter moving from hut to hut, eating the hay the farmer spent the summer preparing for them.

Throughout the year you'll see farmers moving their herds to various elevations. If snow is in the way, farmers sometimes use tourist cable cars to move their cows. Every two months or so, Gimmelwald farmers bring together cows that aren't doing so well and herd them into the cable car to meet the butcher in the valley below.

swing from the necks of cows during the procession from town to the high Alps (mid-June) and back down (mid-Sept).

• *At the end of town, pause where a lane branches off to the left, leading into the dramatic...*

Sefinen Valley: At the bottom of this wild valley is a stream that rushes down toward Stechelberg. All the old homes in town are made from wood cut from the left-hand side of this valley (shady side, slow-growing, better timber) and milled on the valley floor.

• *A few steps ahead, the road switches back at the...*

Gimmelwald Fire Station (Feuerwehrmagazin): Peer through the windows in the door at the tractor-like engines. Then walk up around the hairpin bend to the notice board on the side of the building. The *Föhnwacht Reglement* sheet explains rules to keep the village from burning

down during the Föhn season, a period of fierce dry winds. During this time, there's a 24-hour fire watch, and even smoking cigarettes outdoors is forbidden. Mürren was devastated by a Föhn-caused fire in the 1920s. Villagers in Gimmelwald—mindful of the quality of their volunteer fire department—are particularly careful. The town hasn't had a terrible fire in its history (a rare feat among alpine villages).

Check out the other posted notices. This year's Swiss Army calendar tells reservists when and where to go (in all four official Swiss languages). Every Swiss male does a 22-week stint in the military, then serves three weeks a year in the reserves until age 34. The *Schiessübungen* poster details the shooting exercises required this year.

• *Unless you're really pooped, continue uphill along the road.*

High Road to Hotel Mittaghorn: The resort town of Mürren hovers in the distance. And high on the left, notice the hay field with terraces. These are from WWII days, when Switzerland, wanting self-sufficiency, required all farmers to grow potatoes. Today, this field is a festival of alpine flowers in season (best at this altitude in May and June).

• *In a couple of minutes, you'll reach a peaceful set of benches, just off the lane on the downhill side, which let you savor the view. Just beyond is the Hotel Mittaghorn and steps downhill, which bring you quickly back to Gimmelwald's "Times Square."*

Sleeping in Gimmelwald

Gimmelwald is my home base in the Berner Oberland. To inhale the Alps at 4,593 feet and really hold them in, you'll want to sleep high in Gimmelwald, too. Poor and pleasantly stuck in the past, the village has only a few accommodations options—all of them quirky and memorable. Rates here are listed without breakfast (except for the hostel) and include the local tax, which gives you free entry to the public swimming pool in nearby Mürren (at the Sportzentrum—see page 164).

Be warned: You'll meet a lot of my readers in this town. This is a disappointment to some; others enjoy the chance to be part of a fun extended family.

$$$ At Olle and Maria's B&B, the Eggimanns rent three rooms—Gimmelwald's most comfortable and expensive—in their quirky but alpine-sleek house. Having raised three kids of their own here, Maria and Olle offer visitors a rare and intimate peek at this community. Two rooms with shared bath are upstairs, while the "double" with private bath is a ground-level studio apartment with a kitchenette and a private entrance (family room available, breakfast extra, 3-night minimum, cash or PayPal only, nonrefundable 50 percent deposit via PayPal required, pay laundry service; from cable car, continue straight for 200 yards along the town's only road, look for *B&B* sign on left; tel. 033-855-3575, www.olleandmarias.ch, oeggimann@bluewin.ch).

$$ Esther's Guest House, overlooking the village's main intersection, rents seven clean, basic, and comfortable rooms with a two-night minimum. Three rooms have private bathrooms, and all share a generous lounge and kitchen (family rooms available—one sleeps up to 5, breakfast extra, sack lunches available, low ceilings, tel. 033-855-5488, www.esthersguesthouse.ch, info@esthersguesthouse.ch). Urs and Dana also rent two five-person **apartments** with kitchenettes next door (3-night minimum, see website for details).

$$ Pension Gimmelwald is an old, low-ceilinged farmhouse converted into a family-style inn, with 10 simple shared-bath rooms, 2 rooms with private bath, a restaurant, and a cozy bar. Aside from the rooms, they have a six-bed dorm (33 CHF) that attracts more mature guests than a typical youth hostel. Its terrace, overlooking the Mountain Hostel, has gorgeous views across the valley (RS% with 2-night stay if you book direct, family room available, breakfast extra, dinner available, open June-mid-Oct and late Dec-mid-April, 2-minute walk up from cable-car station, tel. 033-855-1730, www.pensiongimmelwald.com, pensiongimmelwald@gmail.com, Englishman David).

$ Hotel Mittaghorn is a classic, thin-walled, alpine-style place with superb views. It's run by Walter Mittler, an elderly Swiss gentleman, with help from trusty Tim. The hotel has three rooms with private showers and four rooms that share a coin-operated shower (2-night minimum, cash only, open mid-May-Oct, a 5-minute climb up the path from the village center, tel. 033-855-1658, www.mittaghorn.com, mittaghorn@gmail.com; reserve by e-mail—generally answered April-Oct only). If no one's there when you check in, look for a card in the hallway directing you to your room.

¢ Mountain Hostel is a beehive of activity, as clean as its guests, cheap, respectable, and friendly. The 50-bed hostel has low ceilings, a self-service kitchen, bar, pool table, and healthy plumbing. It's mostly a college-age crowd; families and older travelers will probably feel more comfortable elsewhere. Petra Brunner, who lines the porch with flowers, runs this relaxed hostel. Read the signs, respect Petra's rules, and leave it tidier than you found it (sheets and breakfast included, pay showers, pay laundry, closed Nov, from the lift station it's 20 yards up the path to the left, tel. 033-855-1704, www.mountainhostel.com, info@mountainhostel.com).

Eating in Gimmelwald

$$$ Pension Gimmelwald Restaurant has a good, simple menu featuring local produce served in a rustic indoor dining room or on a jaw-dropping view terrace. The atmosphere here is jazz-and-blues mellow (reservations required by phone if not staying overnight, daily mid-June-Sept and late Dec-mid-April 12:00-15:00 & 18:00-21:00, bar open until 23:00, closed off-season, tel. 033-855-1730, www.hotel-pensiongimmelwald.ch).

Picnics: Consider packing in a picnic meal from the larger towns. Mürren, a five-minute cable-car ride or a 30-minute hike up the hill, has a grocery store and good restaurants (see "Eating in Mürren," later). If you need a few groceries and want to skip the hike to Mürren, you can buy the essentials—noodles, spaghetti sauce, and candy bars—at the little Honesty Shop at Pension Gimmelwald (closed off-season). Farmers post signs to sell their produce. The Rubin family sells cheese and eggs in their house on the town's main street (see "Gimmelwald Walk," earlier).

Nightlife: For after-dark entertainment in Gimmelwald, **Pension Gimmelwald** offers a mellow scene with an old-time bar, cozy lounge, and view terrace. And from almost anywhere in Gimmelwald, you can watch the sun tuck the mountaintops into bed as the moon rises over the Jungfrau. If that's not enough nightlife, stay in Interlaken.

Mürren

Pleasant as an alpine resort can be, Mürren is traffic-free and filled with cafés, souvenirs, old-timers with walking sticks, employees enjoying incentive trips, and snap-happy tourists. Its chalets are prefab-rustic. With help from a cliffside train, a funicular, and a cable car, hiking options are endless from Mürren (rated ▲▲). Sitting on a ledge more than 2,000 feet above the Lauterbrunnen Valley, surrounded by a fortissimo chorus of mountains, the town has all the comforts of home (for a price) without the pretentiousness of more famous resorts.

Mürren dates from 1384, but its historic character has been

overwhelmed by development (unlike Gimmelwald). Still, it's a peaceful town, with 400 permanent residents. There's no full-time doctor, no police officer (they call Lauterbrunnen if there's a problem), and no resident priest or pastor. (The Protestant church—up by the TI—posts a sign showing where the region's roving pastor preaches each Sunday.) There's not enough business to keep a bank or proper bakery open (bread is baked down in Lauterbrunnen and shipped up). Depending on the time of year, Mürren is either lively (winter and summer, when the population swells to 4,000) or completely dead (spring and fall).

GETTING TO MÜRREN

There are two ways to get to Mürren: via the **Grütschalp cable car and train** from near Lauterbrunnen (the cable car connects to the train from Grütschalp; 20 minutes total) or on the **Schilthornbahn cable car** from near Stechelberg (10 minutes). The train and cable-car stations (which have lockers and free WCs) are at opposite ends of town. For several weeks in spring and fall, one (but never both) of these routes closes down for maintenance. For details, see "Lauterbrunnen Valley Connections" on page 152.

Orientation to Mürren

Mürren perches high on a ledge, overlooking the Lauterbrunnen Valley. You can walk from one end of town to the other in about 10 minutes.

Tourist Information: Mürren's TI, in the town sports complex, can help you find a room and gives hiking advice (daily 8:30-18:45, Dec-April until 20:00; May and Nov 8:00-12:00 & 13:00-17:00; above the village, follow signs to *Sportzentrum*, tel. 033-856-8686, www.mymuerren.ch). They also offer a walking tour of Mürren June-Oct and Dec-April Mon at 17:00; free with your hotel's Visitor Card, otherwise 20 CHF.

HELPFUL HINTS

Money: An ATM is at the cable-car station.

Wi-Fi: The **TI** has free Wi-Fi and a place to sit.

Laundry: Hotel Bellevue has a little self-service launderette in a shed on the side of the hotel (open 24/7 even when hotel is closed).

Bike Rental: You can rent mountain bikes at **Stäger Sport**—ask about returning the bike in Lauterbrunnen for an extra fee

BERNER OBERLAND

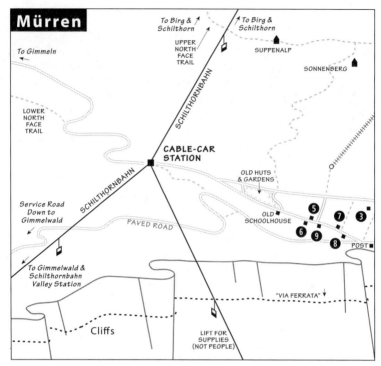

Mürren

To Gimmeln

To Birg & Schilthorn

To Birg & Schilthorn

SUPPENALP

SONNENBERG

UPPER NORTH FACE TRAIL

SCHILTHORNBAHN

LOWER NORTH FACE TRAIL

CABLE-CAR STATION

OLD HUTS & GARDENS

SCHILTHORNBAHN

Service Road Down to Gimmelwald

PAVED ROAD

OLD SCHOOLHOUSE

❺

❻ ❾ ❽

❼ ❸

POST

To Gimmelwald & Schilthornbahn Valley Station

"VIA FERRATA"

Cliffs

LIFT FOR SUPPLIES (NOT PEOPLE)

(30 CHF/half-day, 40 CHF/day, includes helmet, daily 9:00-12:00 & 13:00-17:00, closed late Oct-mid-May, in middle of town, tel. 033-855-2355, www.staegersport.ch). There's a bigger bike-rental place in Lauterbrunnen (Imboden Bike, described on page 147).

R & R: The slick **Sportzentrum** (sports center) that houses the TI offers a world of indoor activities, including a sauna, hot tub, and steam bath. A café offers a reasonably priced, basic menu, with indoor and outdoor seating (daily 10:00-18:00). The pool is 10 CHF with the Visitor Card given out by hotels and hostels (otherwise 12 CHF, daily 13:00-20:00, Dec-March until 21:00, April-May until 18:00, closed Nov, tel. 033-856-8686, www.sportzentrum-muerren.ch). In season, they offer minigolf, table tennis, and a fitness room.

Yoga: Denise (proprietor of the recommended Chalet Fontana) offers yoga classes at the sports center on Tuesdays in summer (mobile 078-642-3485).

Skiing and Snowboarding: The Mürren-Schilthorn ski area is the Berner Oberland's best place for experts, especially those eager to tackle the famous, nearly 10-mile-long Inferno run. The runs on top, especially the Kanonenrohr, are quite steep and have predictably good snow; lower areas cater to all levels,

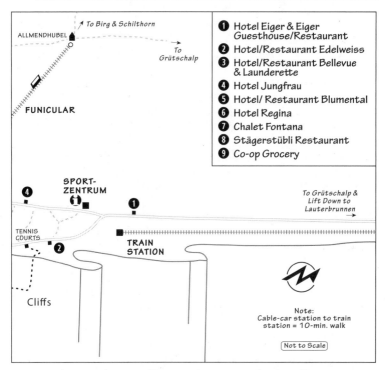

ALLMENDHUBEL

↗ To Birg & Schilthorn

→ To Grütschalp

FUNICULAR

1 Hotel Eiger & Eiger Guesthouse/Restaurant
2 Hotel/Restaurant Edelweiss
3 Hotel/Restaurant Bellevue & Launderette
4 Hotel Jungfrau
5 Hotel/ Restaurant Blumental
6 Hotel Regina
7 Chalet Fontana
8 Stägerstübli Restaurant
9 Co-op Grocery

SPORT-ZENTRUM

4

1

To Grütschalp & Lift Down to Lauterbrunnen →

TENNIS COURTS

2

TRAIN STATION

Cliffs

Note:
Cable-car station to train station = 10-min. walk

Not to Scale

but can be icier. For rental gear, try the friendly, convenient **Ed Abegglen** shop (best prices, next to recommended Chalet Fontana, tel. 033-855-1245), **Alfred's Sporthaus** (good selection and decent prices, between ski school and Sportzentrum, tel. 033-855-3030), or **Stäger Sport** (one shop in Sportzentrum and another in the town center, tel. 033-855-2330). For more info on snow sports, see the Switzerland in Winter chapter.

Mürren Walk

Mürren has long been a top ski resort, but a walk across town offers a glimpse into a time before ski lifts. This stroll takes you through town on the main drag, from the train station (where you'll arrive if coming from Lauterbrunnen) to the cable-car station, then back up to the Allmendhubel funicular station.

• *Start at the...*

Train Station: The first trains pulled into Mürren in 1891. (A circa 1911 car is permanently parked at Grütschalp's station.) A display case inside the station displays an original car from the narrow-gauge, horse-powered line that rolled fancy visitors from here into town. The current station, built in 1964, comes with impressive engineering for heavy cargo. Look out back, where a small truck can be loaded up, attached to the train, and driven away.

• *Wander into town along the main road (take the lower, left fork) for a stroll under the...*

Alpin Palace Hotel: This towering place was the "Grand Palace Hotel" until it burned in 1928. Today it's closed, and no one knows its future. The small wooden platform on the left—looking like a suicide springboard—is the place where snow-removal trucks dump their loads over the cliff in the winter. Look back at the meadow below the station: This is a favorite grazing spot for chamois (the animals, not the rags). Ahead, at Hotel Edelweiss, step to the far corner of the restaurant terrace for a breathtaking view stretching from the big three (Eiger, Mönch, and Jungfrau) on the left, past waterfalls gushing from the cliffsides (especially after a good rain), to the lonely cattle farm in the high alp on the right. Then look down.

• *Continue toward an empty lot with a grand view.*

Viewpoints: There are plans for a big apartment-hotel to be built here, but the project is waiting for investment money. Detour from the main street around the cliff-hanging tennis court. Stop at one of the little romantic shelters built into the far wall. Directly below, at the base of the modern wall, is the start of a 1.5-mile *via ferrata*, a "trail" with a steel-cable guide that mountaineers use to venture safely along the cliff all the way to Gimmelwald (see page 168). You can see the Gimmelwald lift station in the distance.

• *Return to the main street and continue to...*

"Downtown" Mürren: This main intersection (where the small service road leads down to Gimmelwald) has the only grocery store in town (the Co-op). A bit farther on, the tiny fire barn (labeled *Feuerwehr*) has a list showing the leaders of the volunteer force and their responsibilities. The old barn behind it on the right evokes the time, not so long ago, when the town's barns housed cows. Imagine Mürren with more cows than people, rather than with more visitors than residents.

About 65 feet beyond the fire barn (across the street from the old schoolhouse—Altes Schulhaus), detour right uphill a few steps into the oldest part of town. Explore the windy little lanes, admiring the ancient woodwork on the houses and the cute little pea patches.

• *Back on the main drag, continue to the far end of Mürren, where you come to the...*

Cable-Car Station: The larger cars that dock in the back of the station take hikers and skiers up to the Schilthorn and run down to the valley via Gimmelwald. The smaller cable car out front goes directly (and very steeply) to the valley floor. This was the main route down to Stechelberg until 1987, but today it is only

BERNER OBERLAND

for cargo, garbage, and backup passenger service in spring and fall when the newer cars are closed for maintenance.

• *Hiking back into town along the high road, you'll enter...*

Upper Mürren: You'll pass Mürren's two churches, the All-mendhubel funicular station, and the Sportzentrum (with swimming pool and TI).

• *Our walk is finished. Enjoy the town and the views.*

Activities in Mürren

During ski season and the height of summer, the Mürren area offers plenty of activities for those willing to seek them out. In spring and fall, Mürren is pretty quiet. For hikes from Mürren, see page 178.

Allmendhubel Funicular (Allmendhubelbahn)

A surprisingly rewarding funicular (built in 1912, renovated in 1999) carries nature lovers from Mürren up to Allmendhubel, a

perch offering a Jungfrau view that, though much lower, rivals the Schilthorn. At the station, notice the 1920s bobsled. Consider mixing a mountain lift, grand views, and a hike with your meal by eating at the restaurant on Allmendhubel (good chef, open daily until 17:00).

Allmendhubel is particularly good for families. The entertaining children's Adventure trail—with rough and thrilling kid-friendly alpine rides along the way—starts from here. This is also the departure point for the North Face hike and walks to Grütschalp (see page 178). While at Allmendhubel, consider its Flower trail, a 20-minute loop with nice mountain views and (from June through Sept) a chance to see more than 150 different alpine flowers blooming.

Cost and Hours: 8.80 CHF one-way, 14 CHF round-trip, half-price with Swiss Travel Pass, early June-mid-Oct daily 9:00-17:00, runs every 20 minutes, tel. 033-855-2042 or 033-856-2141, www.schilthorn.ch.

Tandem Paragliding

If you've ever wondered what it's like to soar like an eagle, a tandem paragliding flight will give you a pretty good idea. **Airtime Paragliding** offers a guided flight called "The Wall," which takes off near the Mürren cable car station and ends near the Stechelberg cable car station (flights last around 15 to 20 minutes, depending on conditions). After your pilot rigs you in the tandem harness and gives you a few brief instructions, he'll take you on a short run downhill and then you're both up, up, and away—flying gracefully over the Lauterbrunnen Valley, along cliff faces, past waterfalls, and over treetops.

Cost: 170 CHF for Mürren-Stechelberg flight, transport to Mürren not included; various other flight options available, no experience necessary, based at recommended Airtime Café in Lauterbrunnen, tel. 079-247-8463, www.airtime-paragliding.ch. Another longtime local outfit, Paragliding Jungfrau, also offers a variety of tandem flights at similar prices (tel. 079-779-9000, www. paragliding-jungfrau.ch).

Mürren *Via Ferrata* (Klettersteig Mürren)

Mountaineers and thrill-seekers can test their nerves on this 1.5-mile trail along the cliff running from Mürren to Gimmelwald. A *via ferrata* ("way of iron" in Italian) or *Klettersteig* ("climbing path" in German) is a cliffside trail made of metal steps drilled into the mountainside with a cable running at shoulder height above it. Equipped with a helmet, harness, and two carabiners, you are clipped to the cable the entire way. Experienced mountaineers can rent gear (from the Gimmelwald hostel or Mürren's Intersport) and do it independently; others should hire a licensed mountain guide. For a peek at what you're getting yourself into, search for *"Via Ferrata* Mürren Gimmelwald" on YouTube.

The journey takes about three hours. While half of the route is easily walked, several hundred yards are literally hanging over a 2,400-foot drop. I did it, and through the most dangerous sections, I was too scared to look down or take pictures. Along with ladders and steps, the trip comes with three thrilling canyon crossings—one by zip line (possible with guide only), another on a single high wire (with steadying wires for each hand), and a final stint on a terrifying suspension bridge (which you can see from the Gimmelwald-Mürren cable-car—look for it just above Gimmelwald).

Cost and Hours: 125 CHF, includes gear and donation to the Mürren Via Ferrata Association, guided tours in small groups of 4-8, accessible June-mid-Oct only, tel. 033-821-6100, www.klettersteig-muerren.ch.

Nightlife in Mürren

These are all good places for a drink after dinner: **Eiger Guesthouse** (a popular sports bar-type hangout with pool tables, games, and Wi-Fi), **Stägerstübli** (where old-timers nurse a drink and gossip), **Hotel Blumental** (with a characteristic cellar—lively when open), and **Hotel Bellevue** (with its elegant alpine-lounge ambience). All of these places are further described under "Sleeping in Mürren" or

"Eating in Mürren." In July and August, you can enjoy occasional folkloric evenings (some Wednesdays, at Sportzentrum).

Sleeping in Mürren

Mürren is about a mile high, so if you sleep here you may feel the altitude. These price rankings are based on summer room rates; they often rise during the ski season. Except where noted, all of the hotels and restaurants listed here close in spring (anywhere from Easter to early June) and again in fall (sometime between mid-Oct and mid-Dec). Half-board, if available, is a good idea in Mürren.

$$$$ Hotel Eiger, a four-star hotel dramatically and conveniently situated just across from the tiny train station, is a good but expensive bet. Family-run for four generations, Adrian and Susanna Stähli offer all the services you'd expect in a big-city hotel (plush lounge, elegant dining rooms, original art on the walls, indoor swimming pool, exercise room, and saunas) while maintaining an Old World, woody elegance in its 50 rooms. Their family suites, while pricey, include two double rooms and can be a good value for groups of four or five (grand breakfast, discounts for stays of 3 nights or more, email for best deals, elevator, tel. 033-856-5454, www.hoteleiger.com, info@hoteleiger.com).

At **$$$ Hotel Edelweiss,** it's all about the location—convenient and literally hanging on the cliff with devastating views. It's a big, modern building with 30 basic rooms (some with balconies) and a busy, recommended restaurant that's well-run by hardworking Sandra and Daniel Kuster-von Allmen (closed Nov-mid-Dec, half-board available, elevator, piano in lounge, self-serve pay laundry, tel. 033-856-5600, www.edelweiss-muerren.ch, info@edelweiss-muerren.ch).

$$$ Hotel Bellevue has a homey lounge, solid woodsy furniture, a great view terrace, the hunter-themed Jägerstübli restaurant, and 19 great rooms at fair rates—most with balconies and views (discount if staying 2 nights or more in early June or Sept-Oct, self-serve pay laundry, tel. 033-855-1401, www.bellevuemuerren.ch, bellevue@muerren.ch, Ruth and Othmar Suter).

$$$ Hotel Jungfrau offers 29 modern and comfortable rooms, and two apartments for up to six people (email for best deals, elevator, pay laundry service, pay Wi-Fi in rooms—free in common area, close to TI/Sportzentrum, tel. 033-856-6464, www.hoteljungfrau.ch, mail@hoteljungfrau.ch, Martin and Connie).

$$ Hotel Blumental has 16 rooms with woody accents and down comforters, a recommended restaurant in the main building, plus six modern rooms of equal quality in the chalet out back (RS%, half-board available, tel. 033-855-1826, www.hotel-blumental.

com, blumental@muerren.ch; Ralph and Heidi von Allmen are fourth-generation owners).

$$ Eiger Guesthouse offers 12 good, small, budget rooms across from the train station in a simply furnished, renovated older building with an easygoing ground-floor pub. Four of the rooms share two sets of bathroom facilities. Ema—born in Portugal but a longtime Switzerland resident—is your host (RS%, closed Nov, lots of stairs, game room, view terrace, tel. 033-856-5460, www. eigerguesthouse.com, info@eigerguesthouse.com).

$$ Hotel Regina, once a luxury hotel catering to posh English holiday-goers, may be a faded beauty but still has plenty of charm. It has 52 basic rooms (most with shared toilets and showers) and is conveniently located near the cable-car station. Management continues to revive the place bit by bit. For solo travelers, the single rooms are a decent value (family deals, tel. 033-855-4242, www. reginamuerren.ch, info@reginamuerren.ch).

$ Chalet Fontana, run by charming Englishwoman Denise Fussell, is a fine budget option, with five simple, crispy-clean, and comfortable rooms (cash only, closed late Oct-April, fridge in common kitchen, across street from Stägerstübli restaurant in town center, mobile 078-642-3485, www.chaletfontana.ch, chaletfontana@gmail.com). Denise also rents two family apartments with kitchen, bathroom, and breakfast (one in a separate building with a mountain view).

Eating in Mürren

Outside of summer and ski season, only a few places are open.

$$$ Hotel Edelweiss offers lunch and dinner with the most cliff-hanging dining in town—the views are incredible, and the prices are good, too (Swiss specialties, burgers, and salads; daily specials, family-friendly, tel. 033-856-5600).

$$$ Eiger Guesthouse Restaurant, a busy local hangout with a relaxed pub atmosphere, has long hours and a mostly Italian menu. They also do fondue, raclette, and *Rösti* (pizzas, meal-sized salads, main courses, inexpensive house wine, Wi-Fi and game room, daily 8:00-22:00, closed Nov, tel. 033-856-5460).

$$$ Stägerstübli, in the town center, is in a 1902 building that was once a tearoom for rich tourists. Locals were limited to the room in the back—which is now the nicer area to eat (look for grizzled regulars indoors). Sitting on its terrace, you know just who's out and about in town (*Rösti*, meat dishes, big portions, daily 11:30-20:30, closes for a week in early Sept, tel. 033-855-1316, Lydia).

$$$ Hotel Blumental's restaurant (called La Grotte) specializes in typical Swiss cuisine, but also serves fish, international, and vegetarian dishes in a stony and woody dining area. It's one of Mürren's most elegant, romantic settings (fondue served for one or more, pastas, daily from 14:00, tel. 033-855-1826).

$$$$ Hotel Bellevue's restaurant is atmospheric, with three dining zones: a spectacular view terrace, a sophisticated indoor area, and the Jägerstübli—a cozy, well-antlered hunters' room guaranteed to disgust vegetarians. This is a good bet for game, as they buy chamois, wild boar, and deer directly from local hunters (lamb and game, fondue, burgers, nonmeat dishes available, daily 11:30-14:00 & 18:00-21:00, tel. 033-855-1401).

Supermarket: The **Co-op** is the only grocery store in town, with good picnic fixings and sandwiches (Mon-Fri 8:00-12:00 & 13:45-18:30, Sat until 17:00, closed Sun, closed Tue-Thu afternoons in spring and fall). Given restaurant prices, this place is a godsend for those on a tight budget.

Activities in the Berner Oberland

Scenic Rides on Lifts and Trains

Many people enjoy a high-altitude thrill ride to one of the scenic viewpoints described here, but they're quite expensive. You can also enjoy the mountains on foot with the help of more modestly priced lifts (see "Hiking and Biking," later).

THE SCHILTHORN AND A SUMMIT-HIGH BREAKFAST

The Schilthornbahn cable car carries skiers, hikers, and sightseers effortlessly to the nearly 10,000-foot summit of the ▲▲▲ Schilthorn, where the Piz Gloria cable-car station awaits, with its solar-powered revolving restaurant, shop, and panorama terrace. At the top, you have a spectacular panoramic view of the Eiger, Mönch, and Jungfrau mountains, lined up on the horizon.

Times and Prices: You can ride to the Schilthorn and back from several points—the cable-car station near Stechelberg on the valley floor (105 CHF), cliff-hanging Gimmelwald (92.60 CHF), or the higher Mürren (82.20 CHF). If you have a Swiss Travel Pass, the ride to the summit is free. Without a pass, snare a 20 percent discount for early and late rides (leaving Stechelberg 7:25-8:55 and 15:25-16:25; no late discount in high season; if going late confirm last descent—generally 17:55) and in spring and fall (roughly May and Oct). If you have a Eurail pass (25 percent off the whole trip), you might as well go whenever you like, because you can't double up discounts. If you're staying a few days in Mürren or Gimmelwald and planning to go up, the Schilthornbahn's Holiday Pass starts to make sense (free travel on all routes between Lauterbrunnen and the peak, 140 CHF/4 days or 160 CHF/6 days, available May-Oct only).

Lifts go twice hourly, and the ride from Gimmelwald (including two transfers) to the Schilthorn takes 30 minutes. Lifts run all year, except during maintenance closures (a week in April and four weeks in Nov-Dec). Drivers can leave their cars at the pay lot at the valley station near Stechelberg. For more information, including current weather conditions, see www.schilthorn.ch or call 033-826-0007.

Ascending the Schilthorn: As the cable car floats between Gimmelwald and Mürren you'll see the metal bridge that marks the end of the *via ferrata*. You'll also see fields of wooden tripods, which serve two purposes: They stop avalanches and shelter newly planted trees. Made of wood, they're designed to eventually rot when the tree they protect is strong enough to survive the winter snowpack. From Mürren to Birg, keep an eye on the altitude meter. You can pause at Birg, where there's a café (not always open), the breezy Skyline Walk viewing platform that juts out over the cliff face, and the Thrill Walk—a 600-foot-long catwalk bolted to the cliffside. If walking the see-through metal catwalk seems tame to you, there are also opportunities to tightrope across a cable bridge (there's a net below), cross a section of glass flooring, or crawl through a chain-link tube—all with airy views to the valley far below.

At the Top: Head up two escalators to the Skyline View Platform. Outside, information boards identify the peaks, and directional signs point hikers toward some seriously steep downhill climbs. Watch paragliders set up, psych up, take off, and fly with the birds. Walk along the ridge out back and step onto the Piz Gloria view platform at the end of the fenced area. This is a great place for a photo of the mountain-climber you. Youth hostelers—not realizing that rocks may hide just under the snow—scream down the ice fields on plastic-bag sleds from the mountaintop. (There's an English-speaking doctor in Lauterbrunnen—see page 147.)

Back inside, peek in the Skyline Top Shop for souvenirs or head down the stairs and follow the maze that leads to the Bond World 007 exhibit and cinema. This interactive exhibit, well-signed in English, is worth a few minutes for even non-Bond fans. It takes you behind the scenes of the 1969 James Bond movie, *On Her Majesty's Secret Service,* which used the Schilthorn as one of its major locations (and financed the complex's completion). Step into the role of James Bond and try your hand at flying a helicopter to Piz Gloria or bobsledding down the Alps in the simulators. Don't miss the opportunity to morph your face onto one of several Bond stars (pictures available in the gift shop for a fee, of course). Even the WCs are Bond-themed—a sign in the men's room urged me to "Aim Like James."

At the end of the exhibit, the Bond World 007 cinema shows a 20-minute video of the natural wonders of the area, highlights a few activities (including racing down the famous Inferno ski run), briefly shares the story of the Schilthornbahn lift itself, and shows a substantial clip from *On Her Majesty's Secret Service.* If you haven't had enough Bond yet, peruse the 007 Walk of Fame, where cast and crew members from the film have left their handprints and personal messages (on the ridge to the Piz Gloria view platform).

You can hike down from the Schilthorn, but it's tough. (Hiking *up* from Gimmelwald or Mürren is easier on your knees...if you don't mind a 5,000-foot altitude gain.) For information on **hikes** from lift stations along the Schilthorn cable-car line, see "Hiking and Biking," later. My favorite "hike" from the Schilthorn is simply along the ridge out back, to get away from the station and be all alone on top of an Alp. (But if you need company, both Birg and the Piz Gloria have Wi-Fi.)

Summit-High Breakfast: The generous 33-CHF "007  Breakfast Buffet" is served starting at 8:00 on the top floor of the Piz Gloria. Save a few francs by adding the breakfast buffet to your lift ticket before heading up. The restaurant also serves salads, soups, and main dishes all day at prices that don't rise with the altitude.

JUNGFRAUJOCH

The literal high point of any trip to the Swiss Alps is a train ride through the Eiger mountain to the ▲▲▲ Jungfraujoch (the saddle between the Mönch and Jungfrau mountains). At 11,333 feet, it's

Europe's highest train station. (If you have a heart or lung condition, you may want to check with your doctor before making this ascent.) Keep in mind that you can enjoy the Berner Oberland without taking this trip—it's long, slow, expensive, crowded, and cold. But if the weather's good and you have a spare day and spare cash, the views are exhilarating and it's fun to be up on a snowy glacier in midsummer.

Planning Your Trip: Visiting the Jungfraujoch takes most of a day. The trip up from Lauterbrunnen takes a little under two hours each way, with a change of trains halfway at Kleine Scheidegg. If you're coming from Interlaken, Gimmelwald, or Mürren, add another half-hour. You'll want at least 1.5 hours at the top—more if you eat, hike, or sled. Expect outdoor temperatures to be around freezing in summer—so if you plan to go outside, bring a hat and gloves, as well as shoes with good traction, sunglasses, and sunscreen. Even if you stay inside, the train is chilly, and you'll need a jacket. It's smart to buy tickets the day before (they can sell out in peak season). Check the weather forecast at www.jungfrau.ch before committing. If it's cloudy, skip the trip.

Times and Prices: The train runs about twice hourly year-round. Round-trip fares are 211 CHF from Interlaken Ost, 190 CHF from Lauterbrunnen, 176 CHF from Wengen, and 128 CHF from Kleine Scheidegg. At peak periods (especially July-Aug), trains are standing-room only, and you shouldn't expect to get a seat. You can guarantee a seat (above Kleine Scheidegg only) for 5 CHF extra when you make your reservation.

From May to late October, a "Good Morning Ticket" saves you 25 percent on the 6:35/7:05 departures from Interlaken Ost, the 7:07/7:37 departures from Lauterbrunnen, and the 8:00/8:30 departures from Kleine Scheidegg. To get the discount you must leave the top by 13:00. Eurail pass holders get 25 percent off and can't combine discounts, so they should go whenever they want. The same goes for Swiss Travel Pass holders, who travel free as far as Wengen and pay only from there (also 25 percent off). For more information, visit www.jungfrau.ch or call 033-828-7233.

The **Jungfrau Travel Pass** (3-6 days, 180-255 CHF) offers discounted tickets to the Jungfraujoch as well as free rides on most other area trains and lifts (but not to Gimmelwald or up the Schilthorn). Buying this pass is a gamble on the weather, and it's usually hard to make it pay off unless you travel like mad.

Ascending the Jungfraujoch: The final 35 minutes of the trip—from Kleine Scheidegg—is mostly in a tunnel. On the ascent, the train makes two five-minute stops at two "stations"—one actually halfway up the notorious North Face of the Eiger. You have time to look out windows and marvel at how people could climb the Eiger—and how the Swiss built this train track more than a hundred years ago. Newer train cars run multilingual videos about the history of the train line.

At the Top: Once you reach the top, breathe deep, take it easy, and move slowly—you're way high up and your body isn't used to  such altitudes. Study the map to see your options. The main building has a reasonably priced self-service restaurant with expensive beverages, pricier restaurants with table service, luggage lockers, and touristy shops. A roped-in, snowy lookout plateau affords amazing views both north and south. Slip-slide along the corridors of the ice palace, which has some modest carvings. The "Alpine Sensation" is a cute, cheesy diorama with moving model trains.

You'll walk through a short tunnel to reach the most interesting parts of the complex. Take the elevator up to the Sphinx observation deck at 11,700 feet. (The Jungfrau Panorama is a 360-degree video that's pleasantly distracting while you wait in line for the elevator.) Here the views are truly astounding—deep below to the north are Kleine Scheidegg, Gimmelwald, and in the distance, Interlaken; to the south spreads the Aletsch Glacier—Europe's longest, at nearly 11 miles. The Sphinx has a tiny snack stand and a few benches where you can sit to munch a sandwich. There's a scientific measurement station here, and back downstairs by the elevator are some posters with interesting statistics on recent climate warming and the recovery of the ozone layer.

Just outside, a "Snow Fun Park" set up on the Aletsch Glacier offers skiing and snowboarding (35 CHF), sledding (20 CHF), and a zip line (20 CHF—prices include equipment; 45 CHF for all three activities, mid-May-mid-Oct). To get away from the Jungfraujoch crowds, you can hike an hour across the ice to Mönchsjochhütte (a mountain hut with a small restaurant).

You can combine one of the best hikes in the region—from Männlichen to Kleine Scheidegg—with your trip up to the Jungfraujoch (see page 173).

Hiking and Biking

This area offers days of possible hikes. Many are a fun combination of trails, mountain trains, and cable-car rides. The information below can help you decide which hike to tackle, but isn't intended as a turn-by-turn guide. Good hiking maps and more detailed trail descriptions than what I've provided here are essential and available from area TIs and hotels. Before setting out on any hike, check

Gimmelwald Area Hikes

Schilthorn 9,748'

BIRG

Wasenegg Ridge

Rotstock-hütte ❽

SCHILT-ALP

Ober-hornsee

TANZ-BÖDELI

Sefinen Valley

Kilch-balm

❶

BRYNDLI

OBER-STEINBERG

BUSEN-ALP

SPIEL-BODEN-ALP

GIMMELN

SUPPEN-ALP ❷

Hotel Tschingelhorn

❻

Sprutz Waterfall

Cable-car Station

Gimmel-wald 4,593'

❼

Walter's

Mürren 5,381'

Cable-car Station

VIA FERRATA

Weisse

Schilthornbahn Cable-car Station

Stechelberg 3,025'

❶ Sefinen Valley to Kilchbalm
❷ North Face Trail
❸ Allmendhubel to Grütschalp
❹ Allmendhubel to Grütschalp via Winteregg
❺ Grütschalp to Mürren
❻ Gimmelwald-Tanzbödeli-Obersteinberg-Stechelberg/Gimmelwald
❼ Sprutz Waterfall
❽ Birg to Gimmelwald via Bryndli

locally to be sure you've made the best match between your skills, gear, and trail conditions (snow can persist on trails even into summer).

EASIER HIKES
On the Valley Floor
▲▲Cloudy-Day Lauterbrunnen Valley Walks

Try the easy trails and pleasant walks along the floor of the Lauterbrunnen Valley. You don't ever need to (and shouldn't) walk along the main road, which parallels the river. A fine, paved, mostly vehicle-free farm lane (great for bikers) goes all the way along the valley on the opposite side of the river from the main road. Small bridges let you cross from the lane to the main road at various points. Near Lauterbrunnen, there's also a path right next to the river.

From Lauterbrunnen: For a smell-the-cows-and-flowers lowland walk—ideal for a cloudy day, weary body, or tight bud-

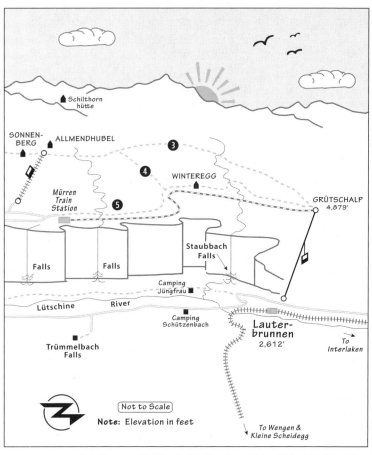

get—try this three-mile, basically level ramble: Take the PostBus from Lauterbrunnen town to the Schilthornbahn cable-car station and follow the river back to Staubbach Falls, near the town church (you can reverse the route, but it's a very gradual uphill to Stechelberg; see page 149 for more about Staubbach Falls).

As you amble back toward Lauterbrunnen, you can detour to Trümmelbach Falls (figure 45 minutes from the Schilthornbahn station to the falls, and another 45 minutes to Lauterbrunnen; see page 149). For a shorter walk back, ride the bus only as far as Trümmelbach and start from there.

Along the way between Trümmelbach Falls and Lauterbrunnen, look up to see BASE jumpers—parachutists who leap from cliffs. In this "Valley of Many Waterfalls" (literally—there are 72), you'll see cone-like mounds piled against the sides of the cliffs, formed by centuries of rocks hurled by tumbling rivers.

From Gimmelwald: If you're staying in Gimmelwald, try this plan: Take the Schilthornbahn lift down to the station near Stechelberg (5 minutes), then walk 1.5 hours along the river to Lauterbrunnen (side-tripping to Trümmelbach Falls after 45 minutes). To return to Gimmelwald from Lauterbrunnen, take the cable car up to Grütschalp (10 minutes), then either walk to Gimmelwald (1.5 hours) or take the train to Mürren (10 minutes). From Mürren, it's a downhill walk (30 minutes) to Gimmelwald. (This loop trip can be reversed or started at any point along the way—such as Lauterbrunnen or Mürren.)

From Gimmelwald
▲Sefinen Valley to Kilchbalm

The trail from Gimmelwald up the Sefinen Valley (Sefinental) is a good rainy-weather hike, as you can go as far as you like. After two hours and a gain of only 800 feet, you hit the end of the trail at Kilchbalm, a dramatic bowl of glacier fields. Snow can make this route unsafe, even into the summer, so confirm conditions locally before setting out. There's no food or drink along the way.

From the Gimmelwald fire station, walk about 100 yards down the paved road, following *Stechelberg* signs. Turn onto the dirt Sefinental road, which becomes a lane, then a trail. You'll cross a raging river and pass a firing range where locals practice their marksmanship (Fri and Sat evenings; the *danger of fire* sign refers to live bullets). Follow signs to Kilchbalm into a forest, along a river, and finally to the glacier fields.

From Mürren
▲▲North Face Trail

For a pleasant, fairly easy 2.5-hour hike, head out along this four-mile trail, starting at 6,385 feet and finishing at 5,375 feet (some stretches can be challenging if you're not in shape). As with any trail described here, before starting out, get a trail map from the Mürren TI or the cable-car station and confirm the route. The signed route loops counterclockwise around to Mürren. (You can also cut off at Spielbodenalp, near the end, and descend into Gimmelwald via the Sprutz Waterfall.)

To reach the trail, ride the Allmendhubel funicular up from Mürren (good restaurant at top, see page 167). Leaving the funicular, look for the children's play area and a blue *North Face Trail* sign. Follow the path uphill, skirting to the right around the play area, passing through small cattle gates, and past the chairlift station. From here, follow the blue signs down into the valley toward Sonnenberg. (Along the way, you'll see yellow directional signs pointing toward *Sonnenberg*, *Suppenalp*, and *Schiltalp*, as well as the blue *North Face Trail* signs.)

The hike offers great views, flowery meadows, mountain huts, and a dozen information boards, describing the fascinating climbing history of the great peaks around you. You'll also pass four farms (technically "alps," as they are only open in the summer) that serve meals and drinks. Sonnenberg was allowed to break the all-wood building code with concrete for protection against avalanches. Suppenalp is quainter. Lean against the house with a salad, soup, or sandwich, and enjoy the view. Just below Suppenalp is a little adventure park with zip lines and other kid-pleasing activities.

Notice how older huts are built into the protected side of rocks and outcroppings, in anticipation of avalanches. Above Suppenalp, Blumental ("Flower Valley") is hopping with marmots. Because hunters are not allowed near lifts, animals have learned that these are safe places to hang out—giving tourists a better chance of spotting them.

From Suppenalp, the trail leads up and over to a group of huts called Schiltalp (good food, drink, and service, and a romantic farm setting). In some spots along the way, where the path is not clearly defined, look for white and red stripes painted on rocks. At Schiltalp, if the poles under the eaves have bells, the cows are up here. If not, the cows are still at the lower farms. Half the cows in Gimmelwald (about 100) spend their summers here. In July, August, and September, you can watch cheese being made and have a snack or drink. Thirty years ago, each family had its own hut. Labor was cheap and available. Today, it's a communal thing, with several families sharing the expense of a single cow herder. Cow herders are master cheesemakers and have veterinary skills, too.

From Schiltalp, the trail winds gracefully down toward Spielbodenalp. From there, you can finish the North Face trail (continuing down and left through meadows and the hamlet of Gimmeln, then back to Mürren), or cut off right (descending steeply through a thick forest and under the dramatic Sprutz Waterfall into Gimmelwald—see Sprutz Waterfall, under "More Difficult Hikes," for details).

▲Allmendhubel to Grütschalp (a.k.a. Mountain View Trail)

For a not-too-tough two-hour walk with great Jungfrau views, ride the funicular from Mürren to Allmendhubel and walk to Grütschalp (a drop of about 1,500 feet), where you can catch the train back to Mürren. You'll see this route called the "Mountain View trail" on maps and brochures. An easier version goes from Allmendhubel to Grütschalp via Winteregg and its cheese farm.

BERNER OBERLAND

▲Grütschalp to Mürren

For a family-friendly, super-easy panorama stroll with grand views, walk either direction between Mürren (5,381 feet) and Grütschalp (4,879 feet)—roughly following the scenic train line between the same points. The trail from the tiny station at Grütschalp to Winteregg (5,177 feet) is a 30-minute scenic walk mostly on a gravelly lane. The trail between Winteregg and Mürren mostly parallels the train track—also scenic and gravelly, but less interesting. The highlight, along with the dramatic views of the Eiger, Mönch, and Jungfrau, is the wonderful restaurant/playground/cheese farm midway at Winteregg. (The Grütschalp-Mürren train also stops here.) The Alpkäserei Staubbach offers windows to peer into the cheese-making action, and they sell fresh yogurt and cheese. The Winteregg Restaurant has a dramatic view terrace and an extensive alp-happy playground.

From Lauterbrunnen
▲▲▲Männlichen-Kleine Scheidegg Hike

This is my favorite easy alpine hike (2.5 miles, 1-1.5 hours, 900-foot altitude drop to Kleine Scheidegg). It's entertaining all the way, with glorious mountain views. If you missed the plot, it's the Young Maiden (Jungfrau), being protected from the Ogre (Eiger) by the Monk (Mönch). The trail usually opens sometime in June and closes due to snow in October. Ask about conditions and get a map at the lift stations or at TIs; there are also useful webcams at www.maennlichen.ch and www.jungfrau.ch.

If the weather's good, start off bright and early. From the Lauterbrunnen train station, take the little mountain train up to Wengen. Sit on the right side of the train for great valley and waterfall views. In Wengen, buy a picnic at the Co-op grocery across the square from the station (daily 8:00-18:30 in summer), walk across town, and catch the lift to Männlichen, located on top of the ridge high above you (23 CHF one-way, half-price with Swiss Travel Pass, 3/hour, 2-minute trip, mid-May-mid-Oct first ascent at 8:30, at 8:10 July-mid-Sept, somewhat shorter hours off-season, tel. 033-855-2933, www.maennlichen.ch). The lift can be open even if the trail is closed; if the weather is questionable, confirm that the Männlichen-Kleine Scheidegg trail is open before ascending. Don't waste time in Wengen if it's sunny—you can linger back here after your hike.

Riding the gondola from Wengen to Männlichen, you'll go over the old lift station (inundated by a 1978 avalanche that buried a good part of Wengen—notice there's no development in the "red zone" above the tennis courts). Farms are built with earthen ramps on the uphill side in anticipation of the next slide. The forest of avalanche fences near the top was built after that 1978 avalanche.

As you ascend you can also survey Wengen—the bright red roofs mark new vacation condos, mostly English-owned and used only a few weeks a year.

When you get to the station at the top of the Wengen-Männlichen lift, see if they have any free "king for a day" envelopes by the ticket window; these fun souvenirs open up to make a panoramic crown that names the mountains you're seeing.

For a detour that'll give you an easy king- or queen-of-the-day feeling, turn left from the lift station, and hike uphill 10 minutes to the little peak (Männlichen Gipfel, 7,500 feet) topped with a crown-shaped viewpoint.

Then go back to the lift station (which has a great kids' area) and enjoy the walk—facing spectacular alpine panorama views—to Kleine Scheidegg for a picnic or restaurant lunch. To start the hike, leave the Wengen-Männlichen lift station to the right. Walk past the second Männlichen lift station (this one leads to Grindelwald, the touristy town in the valley to your left). Ahead of you in the distance, left to right, are the north faces of the Eiger, Mönch, and Jungfrau; in the foreground is the Tschuggen peak, and just behind it, the Lauberhorn. This hike takes you around the left (east) side of this ridge. Simply follow the signs for Kleine Scheidegg, and you'll be there in about an hour—a little more for gawkers, picnickers, and photographers. You might have to tiptoe through streams of melted snow—or some small snow banks, even well into the summer—but the path is well-marked, well-maintained, and mostly level all the way to Kleine Scheidegg.

About 35 minutes into the hike, you'll reach a bunch of benches and a shelter with incredible unobstructed views of all three peaks—the perfect picnic spot. Fifteen minutes later, on the left, you'll see the first sign of civilization: Restaurant Grindelwaldblick (the best lunch stop up here, open daily, closed Nov and May, described on page 189). Hike to the restaurant's fun mountain lookout to survey the Eiger and look down on the Kleine Scheidegg (rated ▲▲ for its spectacular panoramic mountain view). After 10 more minutes, you'll be at the Kleine Scheidegg train station, with plenty of lesser lunch options (including Restaurant Bahnhof, described on page 189).

Optional Add-Ons: From Kleine Scheidegg, you can catch the train up to "the top of Europe" (see Jungfraujoch listing, earlier), take the train back down to Wengen, or hike downhill (gorgeous 30-minute hike to the Wengernalp station, a little far-

BERNER OBERLAND

Hiking in the Berner Oberland

This region is a wonderful place to hike. I've listed my favorite excursions in this chapter. The super-scenic walk from Männlichen to Kleine Scheidegg is the best of all worlds: It's both dramatic and relatively easy (but doesn't open until June). Other relatively easy hikes include the North Face trail from Allmendhubel; various walks from Mürren or Allmendhubel to Grütschalp; the Sefinen Valley hike from Gimmelwald; and the stroll along the Lauterbrunnen Valley floor. More challenging routes include the spectacular hike from Schynige Platte to First and the hike from the Birg cable-car station down to Gimmelwald.

To do any serious hiking, invest in a good hiking map at any  TI, and ask about current weather and trail conditions. For easy hikes, it's usually enough to use the 3-D maps in the free brochures (called *Wandern/Hiking*) published by the Schilthornbahn (for the west side of the valley) and the Jungfraubahn (for the east side); they're available at stations, hotels, and TIs. These overview maps of the mountainsides also make attractive souvenirs.

Don't forget a water bottle and some munchies. In addition to a good map, for serious hikes it's wise to carry sun protection, an extra layer of clothing, and basic first-aid supplies. Know when the last lifts run in the afternoon. Trails are well-marked, with yellow signs listing destinations and the estimated time it'll take you to walk there. Once under way, don't mind the fences (although

ther to the Allmend stop; 60 more steep minutes from there into Wengen—not dangerous, but requires a good set of knees). The alpine views might be accompanied by  the valley-filling mellow sound of cow bells, alphorns, and distant avalanches. If the weather turns bad or you run out of steam, catch the train at any of the stations along the way. The boring final descent from Wengen to Lauterbrunnen is knee-killer steep—catch the train instead.

Hikers' Loop

If you're staying in Lauterbrunnen, are in good shape, and have only one full day here, consider this ambitious day plan: Ride the cable car to Grütschalp, walk along the ridge to Mürren, take the

be aware that wires can be solar-powered electric); a hiker has the right of way in Switzerland.

Weather Concerns: Locals always seem to know the weather report (as much of their income depends on it). Clouds can roll in anytime, but on warm summer days, skies are usually clearest in the morning. All over the region, TV sets are tuned to the local weather station, with real-time views from all the famous peaks. You can also check weather reports and view live webcams at www.jungfrau.ch and www.schilthorn.ch. For more detailed weather reports in English, visit www.meteoswiss.admin.ch.

In the Berner Oberland, snow can curtail your hiking plans, even in July. Before setting out on any hike, get advice from the TI or a knowledgeable local. The high trails (Männlichen to Kleine Scheidegg, Schynige Platte to First, and anything from Schilthorn or Birg) are typically passable only from June into October.

Wildlife: As hunting is not allowed in the vicinity of any lifts, animals find safe havens in places you're likely to be. Keep an eye out for chamois (called *Gemsen* here)—the sure-footed "goat antelopes" that live at the top of the treeline and go a little lower when hungry. Spotting an ibex—a wild goat with horns, scrambling along the rocky terrain—is another Berner Oberland thrill. You'll also encounter marmots—big alpine rodents (like 2-pound squirrels) that get really fat each summer, then sleep underground for six months through the winter. These burrowing critters are fun to watch, and if you sit still, they don't see you. You'll hear them whistle. The best viewing place is above Allmendhubel, in the meadow above the highest hut in Blumental.

For general tips about hiking in Switzerland's mountains, see page 201.

cable car up to the Schilthorn and back down to Mürren, ride the funicular up to Allmendhubel, hike the North Face trail to Gimmelwald, take the lift down to the Schilthornbahn station near Stechelberg, catch the PostBus to Trümmelbach Falls, and walk through the valley back into Lauterbrunnen. Make it more or less strenuous or time-consuming by swapping lifts and hikes (all described in this chapter). Or rent a mountain bike and do a wheeled variation on this (parking your bike in Mürren for the Schilthorn trip).

MORE DIFFICULT HIKES
Above Interlaken
▲▲Schynige Platte to First

The best day I've had hiking in the Berner Oberland was when I made this demanding six-hour ridge walk, with Lake Brienz on one side and all that Jungfrau beauty on the other. Start at the

Wilderswil train station (just outside Interlaken), and catch the little train up to Schynige Platte (6,454 feet; 32 CHF one-way, goes every 40 minutes and takes about an hour, runs late May-late Oct). The high point on the trail is Faulhorn (8,790 feet, with a famous mountaintop hotel). From here, hike on to First (7,110 feet), where you ride a small gondola down to Grindelwald (30 CHF; runs continuously—until at least 17:00 in summer) and catch a train back via Zweilutschinen to wherever you're staying. Or, if you have a regional lift pass (or endless money), you could finish the day by riding the lifts and trains from Grindelwald up to Kleine Scheidegg or Männlichen, then back down to Lauterbrunnen.

You can also do this hike in reverse, which means less climbing, from First (7,113 feet) to Schynige Platte (last train down at 17:53). The TI produces a great Schynige Platte map/guide narrating the train ride up and describing various hiking options from there (available at Wilderswil train station).

At the Schynige Platte station, look for a promotional booth run by Lowa, a local manufacturer of top-end hiking boots. They provide free loaners (already broken in) to hikers who'd like to give their boots a try.

Easier Options at Schynige Platte: For a shorter (3-hour) ridge walk, consider the well-signposted Panoramaweg, a loop from Schynige Platte to Daub Peak.

The alpine flower park at the Schynige Platte station offers a delightful stroll through several hundred alpine flowers (free, late May-late Oct daily 8:30-18:00, www.alpengarten.ch), including a chance to see edelweiss growing in the wild.

From Gimmelwald
▲Gimmelwald-Tanzbödeli-Obersteinberg-Stechelberg/Gimmelwald

This eight-hour, 11-mile hike can be extremely rewarding, offering perfect peace, very few people, traditional alpine culture, and spectacular views. (There's no food or drink for five hours, so pack accordingly.) The trail can be a bit confusing, so this is best done with a good, locally purchased map.

About 100 yards below the Gimmelwald firehouse, take the Sefinental dirt road (described earlier, in the Sefinen Valley to Kilchbalm hike). As the dirt road switches back after about 30 minutes, take the right turn across the river and start your ascent, following signs to *Obersteinberg*. After 1.5 hours of hard climbing, you have the option of a side-trip to Busenalp. This is fun if the goat-and-cow herder is there, as you can watch traditional cheese-making in action. (He appreciates a bottle of wine from hikers.) Trail markers are painted onto rocks—watch carefully. After visiting Busenalp, return to the main path.

At the *Obersteinberg 50 Min/Tanzbödeli 20 Min* sign-post, head for Tanzbödeli ("Dancing Floor"). This is everyone's favorite alpine perch—great for a little romance or a picnic with breathtaking views of the Obersteinberg valley.
From here, you enter a natural reserve, so you're likely to see chamois and other alpine critters. From Tanzbödeli, you return to the main trail (there's no other way out) and continue to Obersteinberg. You'll eventually hit the Mountain Hotel Obersteinberg (see "Sleeping in Obersteinberg," later; American expat Vickie will serve you a meal or drink).

From there, the trail leads to another mountain hotel at Tschingelhorn (www.tschingelhorn.ch). About an hour later, you hit a fork in the trail and choose where you'd like your hike to end: back to Gimmelwald (2 hours total) or Stechelberg (near the bottom of the Schilthornbahn cable car, 1.5 hours total).

▲Sprutz Waterfall

The forest above Gimmelwald hides a powerful waterfall with a trail snaking behind it, offering a fun gorge experience. The waterfall itself is not well-signed, but it's on the Gimmelwald-Spielbodenalp trail. It's steep, through a forest, and can be very slippery when wet, but the actual crossing under the waterfall is just misty.

The hike up to Sprutz from Gimmelwald isn't worth the trip in itself, but the trail is handy when combined with the hike down from Birg and Bryndli (described on the next page) or the North Face trail (see earlier, under "Easier Hikes"). As you descend on either of these hikes, the trail down to Gimmelwald splits at Spielbodenalp—to the right for the forest and the waterfall; to the left for more meadows, the hamlet of Gimmeln, and then gracefully back into Gimmelwald.

From Mürren

To arrange a guide for the white-knuckle, cliff-hugging *via ferrata* trail near Mürren, see page 168.

From the Schilthorn

Several tough trails lead down from the Schilthorn (there's a reason that virtually all visitors take the cable car down). Only a serious, experienced hiker should consider walking all or part of the way back into Gimmelwald. Proper shoes and clothing (weather can change quickly) and good knees are required. Don't attempt to hike down unless the trail is clear of snow. While it's possible to make the steep descent directly from the top of the Schilthorn, I prefer the less strenuous (but still challenging) hike from the intermediate cable-car station at Birg.

▲▲Birg to Gimmelwald via Bryndli

You can combine this difficult downhill hike from the Birg cable-car station with a visit to the Schilthorn by buying the round-trip excursion early-bird fare (it's cheaper than the Gimmelwald-Schilthorn-Birg ticket). Visit the summit first, then descend to Birg to hike down.

The most interesting trail from Birg to Gimmelwald is the high one via Grauseeli lake and Wasenegg Ridge to Bryndli, then down to Spielbodenalp and the Sprutz Waterfall. Warning: This trail drops 4,500 feet, is quite steep and slippery in places, and can take four hours. Locals take their kindergarteners on this hike, but Americans unused to alpine hikes shouldn't attempt it.

From the Birg lift station, hike toward the Schilthorn, taking your first left down and passing along the left side of the little Grauseeli lake. From the lake, a gravelly trail leads down rough switchbacks (including a stretch where the path narrows and you can hang onto a guide cable against the cliff face) until it levels out. When you see a rock painted with arrows pointing to Mürren and Rotstockhütte, follow the path to Rotstockhütte (traditional old farm with light meals and drinks), traversing the cow-grazed mountainside.

The safer, well-signposted approach to Bryndli is to drop down to Rotstockhütte, then climb back up to Bryndli. Thrill-seekers instead follow Wasenegg Ridge. It's more scary than dangerous if you're sure-footed and can handle the 50-foot-long "tightrope-with-handrail" section along an extremely narrow ledge with a thousand-foot drop. This trail gets you to Bryndli with the least altitude change. A barbed-wire fence leads you to Bryndli's knobby little summit, where you'll enjoy an incredible 360-degree view and a chance to sign your name on the register stored in the little wooden box.

From Bryndli, a steep trail winds directly down toward Gimmelwald and soon hits a bigger, easier trail. The trail bends right (just before the farm/restaurant at Spielbodenalp), leading to Sprutz. Walk under the Sprutz Waterfall, then follow a steep, wooded trail that deposits you in a meadow of flowers at the top side of Gimmelwald.

MOUNTAIN BIKING

Mountain biking is popular and accepted, as long as you stay on the clearly marked mountain-bike paths. You can rent bikes in Mürren (Stäger Sport, see page 163) or in Lauterbrunnen (Imboden Bike, see page 147). The Lauterbrunnen shop is bigger, has a wider selection of bikes, and is likely to be open when the Mürren one isn't. But if you pick up a bike in Mürren, you may be able to drop it at the Lauterbrunnen train station (ask).

As with any activity in the mountains, get maps and seek advice locally before venturing out. I've outlined some of the most popular bike rides next.

Lauterbrunnen to Interlaken: This is a gentle downhill ride on a peaceful bike path across the river from the road (don't bike on the road itself). You can re-turn to Lauterbrunnen by train (you'll have to buy a regular ticket for the bike). Or rent a bike at either Interlaken station, take the train to Lauterbrunnen, and ride back.

Lauterbrunnen Valley (between Stechelberg and Lauterbrunnen town): This delightful, easy bike path features plenty of diversions along the way (see "Cloudy-Day Lauterbrunnen Valley Walks" on page 176).

Mürren to Winteregg to Grütschalp and Back: This fairly level route takes you through high country, with awesome mountain views.

Mürren to Winteregg to Lauterbrunnen: This scenic descent, on a service road with loose gravel, takes you to the Lauterbrunnen Valley floor.

Mürren-Gimmelwald-Sefinen Valley-Stechelberg-Lauterbrunnen-Grütschalp-Mürren: This is rewarding but very demanding—with one very difficult stretch where you'll likely walk your bike down a steep gulley for 500 yards. While you'll be on your bike most of the time, to complete the loop take the cable car from Lauterbrunnen up to Grütschalp and then bike back to Mürren.

More Berner Oberland Towns

I'd sleep in Gimmelwald, Mürren, or Lauterbrunnen, but you could also consider overnighting in the following places.

Sleeping in Wengen

Wengen—a bigger, fancier Mürren on the east side of the valley at 4,180 feet—has plenty of grand hotels, restaurants, shops, diversions, and terrific views. This traffic-free resort is an easy train ride above Lauterbrunnen and halfway up to Kleine Scheidegg and Männlichen. From Wengen, you can catch the Männlichen lift (www.maennlichen.ch) up to the ridge and take the rewarding, view-filled, nearly downhill ▲▲▲ Männlichen-Kleine Scheidegg hike (described on page 180).

Wengen's **TI** is a two-minute walk from the station. When you get off the train, look for the yellow signs and big map and head up to the main drag (Dorfstrasse). Turn left on Dorfstrasse and you'll soon see the TI on the right (Tourist Center Wengen). They have info on hiking and sell trail maps (daily 9:00-18:00, closes for lunch Sat-Sun off-season, tel. 033-856-8585, www.wengen.ch).

The good-sized **Co-op grocery,** across the square from the train station, is great for picnic fixings (daily 8:00-18:30; closed Sun off-season).

Above the Train Station: **$$$$ Hotel Berghaus,** in a quiet area facing a pasture, is a five-minute uphill walk from the main street. They offer 19 rooms above a fine restaurant specializing in fish (family room available, elevator, open June-Sept and mid-Dec-early April, tel. 033-855-2151, www.berghaus-wengen.ch, info@berghaus-wengen.ch, Fontana-Fuchs family). At the train station, dial #25 on the hotel phone to request a free pickup. Or, to walk to the hotel from the main drag, head up the street across from Hotel Bernerhof, bear right at the fork, go 200 yards more past the church, and it's on the left.

$$$$ Romantik Hotel Schönegg, at the top end of Wengen's main road, is a centrally located splurge exuding a warm and woody ski-lodge ambience. Its 20 rooms are all designed in a cozy alpine style (all rooms have balconies and great views, family room with fireplace, sauna, half-board in good restaurant with big terrace available, tel. 033-855-3422, www.hotel-schoenegg.ch, mail@hotel-schoenegg.ch).

Below the Train Station: **$$$$ Bären Hotel,** run by friendly Therese and Willy Brunner, offers 17 tidy rooms with modern new bathrooms. Half-board is included in the rates; their restaurant is bright and inviting, offering garden-fresh Swiss cuisine (**$$** lunch specials; discount if you go without half-board; family rooms, elevator, kids' playroom, table tennis, closed mid-Oct-mid-Dec, tel. 033-855-1419, www.baeren-wengen.ch, info@baeren-wengen.ch). From the station, cross the street to the Co-op grocery, turn right and go under the rail bridge, and follow the road down the hill—the hotel will be on your right.

Sleeping and Eating at or near Kleine Scheidegg

This high settlement above the timberline (6,762 feet) is as close as you can stay to the Jungfraujoch. All of these places serve meals and let you sleep face-to-face with the Eiger. Confirm prices and availability before ascending. Note that the last train down to Lauterbrunnen leaves Kleine Scheidegg at 18:30. All of these places offer Wi-Fi only in common areas.

$$$$ Hotel Bellevue des Alpes, lovingly maintaining a 1930s elegance, is a very expensive but potentially worthwhile splurge. Since the 1840s, five generations of von Allmens have run this classic old 60-room alpine hotel (subsidized by the family income from Trümmelbach Falls). Every detail has been preserved, and filmmakers often use the hotel as a set for pre-WWII period shoots. The hallway is like a museum lined with old photos (breakfast and sumptuous four-course dinner included, four floors and no elevator, no TVs, closed mid-April-mid-June and mid-Sept-mid-Dec, tel. 033-855-1212, www.scheidegg-hotels.ch, welcome@scheidegg-hotels.ch).

¢-$$ Restaurant Bahnhof is a handy hostel in the train-station building (some private rooms with shared bath; breakfast included, dinner extra; open year-round, tel. 033-828-7828, www.bahnhof-scheidegg.ch, info@bahnhof-scheidegg.ch).

¢-$$ Restaurant Grindelwaldblick, a 10-minute hike up along the path toward Männlichen and visible from the train station, is more charming, romantic, and remote than Restaurant Bahnhof and has 90 beds. You can't get wheeled luggage up along the path by yourself, but for 10 CHF they'll bring it up for you (sheets and breakfast included, closed Nov and May, tel. 033-855-1374, www.grindelwaldblick.ch, grindelwaldblick@grindelwald.ch). The **$$$** restaurant, with a great sun terrace and a cozy interior, sells good three-course lunches and dinners, including a cheesy *Rösti.*

Sleeping in Stechelberg

Stechelberg, at 3,025 feet, is the hamlet at the end of the road up the Lauterbrunnen Valley; it's about a mile beyond the Schilthornbahn lift that goes up to Gimmelwald, Mürren, and the Schilthorn. From the lift station, it's a five-minute ride on the same PostBus that comes from Lauterbrunnen (1-2/hour) or a 20-minute walk. Beyond Stechelberg lies the rugged upper end of the Lauterbrunnen Valley, which is mostly a nature reserve with only a few scattered huts and a narrow service road.

$$ Hotel Stechelberg, at road's end, is surrounded by waterfalls and vertical rock, with a garden terrace, a good restaurant, and 16 quiet rooms—half in a functional old building, half in a concrete, no-character new building (free parking, bus stops right in front, hotel closed in Dec, restaurant closed Mon-Tue off-season, tel. 033-855-2921, www.hotel-stechelberg.ch, hotel@stechelberg.ch, Marianne and Otto).

¢ The **Alpenhof** fills a former "Nature Friends' Hut" with 44 cheap beds. Creaking like a wooden chalet built in 1926 should, and surrounded by a broad lawn, it provides a good, in-expensive base for drivers and families (each group gets a private room, breakfast extra, open nearly year-round, kitchen, no Wi-Fi, free parking, tel. 033-855-1202, www.alpenhof-stechelberg.ch, alpenhof@stechelberg.ch, Diane and Marc from England). From Hotel Stechelberg, head up the paved path, go right at the fork, and cross the river; it's on your left.

Sleeping in Obersteinberg

Here's a wild idea: ¢ **Mountain Hotel Obersteinberg** is a mile-high, working alpine farm with cheese, cows, a mule shuttling up food once a day, and an American (Vickie) who fell in love with a mountain man. It's a 2.5-hour hike from either Stechel-berg or Gimmelwald. They rent 12 primitive rooms and 30 loft beds. There's no shower, no hot water, and no electricity. Bring a battery-powered lamp; otherwise, candles light up the night. Ask for a hot-water bottle; first come, first served (sheets extra, break-fast and dinner included, discount if you go without meals; closed Oct-May, tel. 033-855-2033, more info under "Mountain Hotels" at www.stechelberg.ch). The place is filled with locals and Germans on weekends, but it's all yours on weekdays. Why not hike here from Gimmelwald and leave the Alps a day later?

ZERMATT & THE MATTERHORN

There's just something about the Matterhorn, the most recognizable mountain on the planet. Anyone who says, "You've seen one mountain, you've seen them all" hasn't laid eyes on this pointy, craggy peak. The Matterhorn seems to have a nearly mystical draw for people—it's the Stonehenge of Switzerland.

Oh, and there's a town, too. Zermatt, a little burg of about 5,800 people, might well be the most touristy resort in Switzerland. While the village has pockets of traditional charm, virtually everyone you meet in Zermatt earns a living one way or another from those who flock here for a peek at the peak. Aside from the stone quarries you'll pass on the way into town, tourism is Zermatt's only industry.

Many visitors find Zermatt touristy and overrated, especially considering its inconvenient location (at the dead-end of a long valley in the southwest corner of the country). And if you make the long trek and find only cloudy weather, you may end up shopping for a T-shirt that reads, "I went all the way to Zermatt and didn't even see the lousy Matterhorn." But in sunny weather, riding the high-mountain lifts, poking through lost-in-time villages, and ambling along on scenic hikes are all the more magical with that iconic triangular mountain nodding its white head in the background.

GETTING TO ZERMATT

Zermatt is barely two hours from Bern and Interlaken by train, thanks to the Lötschberg Base Tunnel. It's also easy to reach from Zürich or Lausanne (3 hours). Another popular way to reach Zermatt is from St. Moritz—this is an all-day ride on a historic narrow-gauge line that cuts across the country (see "Glacier Express" in the Scenic Rail Journeys chapter). You can also do just half of this route by connecting Zermatt with Luzern or Lugano (changing in Andermatt).

PLANNING YOUR TIME

High summer into early fall is the best time to come to Zermatt. On a two-week trip in Switzerland, I'd suggest two nights and the better part of two days here—if the weather's good.

Zermatt has earned its reputation for untrustworthy weather—the valley can get completely socked in at any time of year. While two good-weather days are enough to experience the highlights, add at least one buffer day, if you can, as insurance against rain. To get the latest weather report, check the webcams and forecast at www.zermatt.ch. In clear weather, you'll want to spend your daylight hours up above town.

With One Day: If you have just one good day in Zermatt in high season (when all the lifts are running), I'd catch the first train up to the high Gornergrat ridge, then do the gentle-but-gorgeous Riffelseeweg hike that connects the Rotenboden and Riffelberg train stops. From Riffelberg, take a gondola over and down to the stop called Furi, and, depending on your timing and interest, ride all the way up to the Matterhorn Glacier Paradise station at the Klein Matterhorn summit, then return via the Schwarzsee ridge (and perhaps hike part of the way back to Zermatt).

With a Second Day: If it's clear, I'd head up to the Rothorn summit, or at least to the midpoint lift station at Blauherd for the walk to the restaurant at Fluhalp, and then do one of the hikes from the Sunnegga ridge.

Other Options: If the Rothorn excursion sounds more appealing than the Klein Matterhorn, do the Rothorn as part two of your first good-weather day: After finishing your hike to Riffelberg, take the Gornergrat train down to Riffelalp, then do the two-hour Naturweg hike to Sunnegga, from where you can walk or take the funicular back to town. Then, if Mother Nature cooperates, you can do the Matterhorn Glacier Paradise and/or hikes from Schwarzsee on a second day.

Orientation to Zermatt

Zermatt (elevation 5,265 feet) lies at the end of the Nikolaital valley, in the shadow of the mighty Matterhorn (14,690 feet, "Cervin" in French, "Cervino" in Italian).

The train station is at the north end of the town's shopping zone, a few steps from the main drag, Bahnhofstrasse. As you stand in front of the station with the tracks at your back, the heart of the village is to your right. Lifts to thrilling Matterhorn viewpoints

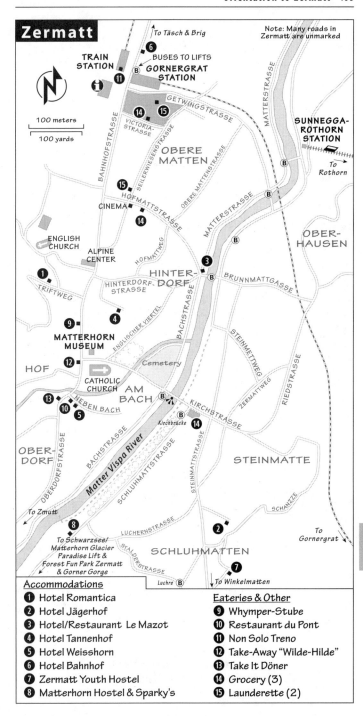

Zermatt

To Täsch & Brig

Note: Many roads in Zermatt are unmarked

TRAIN STATION

BUSES TO LIFTS

GORNERGRAT STATION

GETWINGSTRASSE

SUNNEGGA-ROTHORN STATION

To Rothorn

MATTERSTRASSE

100 meters

100 yards

VICTORIA-STRASSE

BAHNHOFSTRASSE

SEILERWIESENSTRASSE

OBERE MATTEN

OBERE MATTENSTRASSE

MATTERSTRASSE

OBER-HAUSEN

HOFMATTSTRASSE

CINEMA

ENGLISH CHURCH

ALPINE CENTER

HOFMATTWEG

HINTER-DORF

HINTERDORF-STRASSE

BRUNNMATTGASSE

BACHSTRASSE

TRIFTWEG

STEINMETTWEG

MATTERHORN MUSEUM

ENGLISCHER VIERTEL

Cemetery

ZERMATTWEG

RIEDSTRASSE

HOF

CATHOLIC CHURCH

AM BACH

NEBEN BACH

KIRCHSTRASSE

STEINMATTE

Kirchbrücke

OBER-DORF

OBERDORFSTRASSE

BACHSTRASSE

Matter Vispa River

SCHLUHMATTSTRASSE

STEINMATTSTRASSE

SCHANZZE

To Zmutt

To Schwarzsee/Matterhorn Glacier Paradise Lift & Forest Fun Park Zermatt & Gorner Gorge

LUCHERNSTRASSE

STALDERSTRASSE

SCHLUHMATTEN

To Gornergrat

Luchre

To Winkelmatten

ZERMATT

Accommodations

1 Hotel Romantica
2 Hotel Jägerhof
3 Hotel/Restaurant Le Mazot
4 Hotel Tannenhof
5 Hotel Weisshorn
6 Hotel Bahnhof
7 Zermatt Youth Hostel
8 Matterhorn Hostel & Sparky's

Eateries & Other

9 Whymper-Stube
10 Restaurant du Pont
11 Non Solo Treno
12 Take-Away "Wilde-Hilde"
13 Take It Döner
14 Grocery (3)
15 Launderette (2)

leave from near the train station: The cog railway up to Gornergrat leaves from across the street, the Sunnegga-Rothorn station for the funicular/gondola/cable car to Rothorn is a few blocks ahead along the river, and the gondola/cable car up to the Matterhorn Glacier Paradise (aside the Klein Matterhorn peak) is at the upper (southern) end of the village (about three-quarters of a mile away).

Zermatt bans cars within the town limits and brags that its streets are traffic-free. Well, not quite. Electric cars (resembling big golf carts) buzz around the streets like four-wheeled Vespas. Half of these cars are owned by hotels, which use them to shuttle guests and luggage to the train station; the other half operate as taxis.

In this small town, locals don't bother much with street names and house numbers. To find your hotel, use the map in this chapter, follow the free map from the TI, look for signs, or ask a local.

TOURIST INFORMATION

Zermatt's TI is right at the train station (late June-mid-Sept daily 8:30-18:00; rest of year Mon-Sat 8:30-12:00 & 13:30-18:00, Sun 9:30-12:00 & 16:00-18:00; tel. 027-966-8100, www.zermatt.ch). The unstaffed lobby stays open later and has essential brochures and maps.

The TI sells lift passes/tickets and hiking maps, including a detailed 1:25,000 map (25 CHF). They also offer two handy, free resources: an extremely detailed map that labels every building in town, and the thick *Adventure in the Mountains* information booklet with lift schedules and prices, hikes, and almost anything you could think to ask about (all info is also posted on their website).

Hiking and Lift Advice: The TI is well-versed in helping visitors weigh their options given current weather, time constraints, budgets, and hiking interests. If you're planning on doing more than one or two hikes, consider picking up their topographical hiking map, as the region's trail signs are often confusing. While you're unlikely to get stuck (all downhill trails eventually lead to Zermatt), the map can help you avoid taking a longer or steeper route than you intended.

Walking Tours: The TI offers a one-hour village walking tour in English once a week from mid-June through mid-August (10 CHF, usually Tue at 16:30). In July and August they also offer a tour (in English and German) that recalls village life of a century ago (15 CHF, Mon at 16:30, 1.5 hours, both tours depart from TI, confirm details and buy tickets online or at TI).

ARRIVAL IN ZERMATT

Zermatt's small **train station** is conveniently located in the middle of town. The ticket office is beside the tracks (daily 7:00-19:00); a free WC and pay lockers are down the stairs. The TI is immedi-

Zermatt at a Glance

In Zermatt

▲▲**Matterhorn Museum** Underground museum resembling archaeological dig covers history of Zermatt and its magic mountain. **Hours:** Daily July-Sept 11:00-18:00, Oct-June open afternoons only, closed Nov-mid-Dec. See page 198.

▲**Town Wander** Featuring the attractive old Hinterdorf quarter of Zermatt by the river, with antique chalets and traditional *mazots* (shacks on stone stilts). See page 197.

Klein Matterhorn

▲▲▲**Matterhorn Glacier Paradise Summit** Europe's highest cable-car station (12,739 feet), with jaw-dropping Alps view, year-round snow, and a "palace" carved into ice (but no hikes). See page 205.

▲**Schwarzsee Ridge** Hillside midpoint (8,474 feet) directly under the Matterhorn, with a welcoming sunbathing terrace and alpine lake. See page 205.

▲▲**Matterhorn Trail Hike** Deservedly popular trail from the Schwarzsee gondola station back to Zermatt. See page 206.

Gornergrat

▲▲**Gornergrat Top Station** Viewpoint (10,270 feet), reached by fun cogwheel train, that hovers above the Gorner Glacier with fantastic views of the Matterhorn and Switzerland's tallest mountain—Monte Rosa (15,200 feet). See page 207.

▲▲▲**Riffelseeweg Hike** Easy, mostly downhill walk with nonstop scenery between two mountain stations. See page 207.

Rothorn

▲▲**Rothorn Summit** Cable-car station at 10,180 feet with sweeping views of the Matterhorn and its valley. See page 209.

▲▲▲**Blauherd-Fluhalp Hike** Mostly level walk from the Blauherd lift station past a picturesque glacial lake (and great Matterhorn views). See page 209.

▲▲▲**Sunnegga Viewpoint** Best mountain destination for budget travelers, offering the ultimate Matterhorn views (7,506 feet). See page 209.

▲▲**Hikes from Sunnegga** Long, mostly gentle trail (Gourmetweg) back down to Zermatt, mixing hillside hamlets and lush forest, or a moderately strenuous walk (Naturweg) across to the Gornergrat's Riffelalp station. See page 210.

ately to the right as you leave the tracks, and lines of electric taxis wait right out front.

All the hotels I list are within walking distance of the train station, though Hotel Jägerhof and the two hostels are far enough away that you might want to take a taxi or the bus (see individual listings for directions). There are also free airport-style luggage carts at the train station (5-CHF deposit)—useful if it's a fairly level walk to your hotel.

Cars are not allowed in Zermatt. **Drivers** can park in the huge lot at Täsch, a few miles before Zermatt (15.50 CHF/day), then take the shuttle train into town (runs every 20 minutes until about 22:00, less frequent after that, 8.40 CHF one-way, www. matterhornterminal.ch).

GETTING AROUND ZERMATT

Even though Zermatt is "traffic-free," your feet aren't your only transportation option. Its buses are useful for hauling luggage to more distant lodgings or for saving the 20-minute walk between the station and the Matterhorn Glacier Paradise lifts. **Buses** depart across from the train station to the Matterhorn Glacier Paradise lifts at the top of town and make several stops along the way, including at the Sunnegga-Rothorn lift (about 2/hour, last buses leave around 18:00 or 19:00). The green Bergbahnen line goes more directly (2.50 CHF); the red line takes a more roundabout route via the Winkelmatten neighborhood (3.20 CHF). Both routes are covered by same-day mountain-train/lift tickets, the local Peak Pass, and the Swiss Travel Pass (but not Eurail passes), and charge extra for large luggage. Bus info: www.e-bus.ch.

You can also hire your own **electric taxi** from in front of the train station (about 12 CHF for a short ride in the heart of town, 22 CHF to either hostel, extra charge for luggage and rides at night, tel. 027-967-3333).

HELPFUL HINTS

Festivals: Folk troupes from all over western Switzerland converge on Zermatt for the **Folklore Festival,** usually on the second weekend in August. Sunday afternoon features a parade through town followed by free performances.

Goat Parade: Every day in summer (at about 9:00 and again at 17:00), a small flock of furry "blackneck" goats are herded through the center of town on the way to and from pasture. They're unique to the surrounding Upper Valais region, with a black head and shoulders, a white rear end, and long horns. Keep an eye out for this charming and unusual event.

Laundry: Waschsalon Doli is nice and central (drop-off service only, Mon-Sat 8:30-12:00 & 14:00-19:00, closed Sun, tel. 027-967-5100). To find it from the station, take the first left past McDonald's, turn right at the tennis courts, and go down the steps at their sign. **Womy Express** is in the Viktoria Center mall across from train station (drop-off service only, Mon-Fri 8:30-12:00 & 13:30-18:30, Sat 8:30-12:00, closed Sun, tel. 027-967-3242).

Cinema: The **Vernissage Cinema** in the Backstage Hotel plays a rotating schedule of historical Matterhorn-centric films in high season, but they also show first-run features (Hofmatt-strasse 4, tel. 027-966-6970, www.backstagehotel.ch).

Ski Rental: For equipment rental in town, try **Matterhorn Sport** (branch near Sunnegga-Rothorn lift, another at Bahnhof-strasse 78, tel. 027-967-2956, www.matterhornsport.ch), **Bayard Sports & Fashion** (branch on Bahnhofplatz, tel. 027-966-4960, www.bayardzermatt.ch), and **Dorsaz-Sport** (near Matterhorn Express lift, tel. 027-966-3810, www.dorsaz-sport.ch).

Sights in Zermatt

Consider the following options for when the weather is not coop-erating with an alpine adventure. Besides the sights listed below, other bad-weather options include joining a TI-sponsored town tour, walking up and out of town until you hit the cloud cover (Winkelmatten is a pleasant 20-minute stroll from the Catholic church), catching a movie, and/or taking a dip in one of the big hotel pools (nonguests can enjoy for a fee; get advice from TI).

▲Town Wander

Zermatt is charming enough, despite its single-mindedness about catching the tourist dollar. The streets may be lined with chalet after chalet, but all the dark wood and overflowing flower boxes lend this super-touristy town an authentic charm.

Just off the main drag, the **Hin-terdorf** quarter (see map), is a delight to explore. Narrow lanes are lined with traditional wooden buildings called *mazots,* built between the 16th and 18th centuries. They're set on stone stilts (to keep out mice) and topped by stone-slab roofs. Little more than a century ago, the *mazots* and the church were the only buildings standing in this town. A particularly scenic corner is along Hinterdorfstrasse, where several buildings are labeled according to their former purpose. You'll also see several *mazots* perched around Hotel Romantica and on the walk up to, and around, the Winkelmatten area. The valley's best and most scenically situated cluster of *mazots* might well be in Zmutt, an hour's walk up and along the western side of the valley; it's also walkable from the Furi and Schwarzsee gondola stations (see the listing for Matterhorn Trail Hike, later).

Out on the main street (Bahnhofstrasse), the big, landmark **Catholic church** (can't miss it) is ringed by mountaineers' tombstones, several inscribed in English. The lovingly tended graves are adorned with flowers and lit by glowing votive lanterns at night. A smaller English church, built for the many British mountaineers who have flocked to this region, is above and behind the post office, near Hotel Romantica.

Although Zermatt looks quintessentially Swiss, many of the workers who keep the hotels, restaurants, and lifts going are from other parts of Europe, particularly Portugal. Typically, hotel owners are local, and hotel staffers are foreign. In Täsch, the next village down the valley (where you park, and with more affordable housing than Zermatt), the majority of residents are Portuguese. While some Swiss feel that the current policy of free movement between Switzerland and the rest of Europe should be curtailed, no one has figured out how to square that vision with the needs of the hospitality industry.

▲▲Matterhorn Museum

This fun and interesting museum is the town's best indoor activity, and worth at least an hour of your time, especially on a rainy day.

Most of the museum is underground—the idea is that it's like an archaeological dig where you can unearth the history of Zermatt and its famous mountain. It brings you back to the 19th century, when Zermatt saw the advent of mountaineering and the Golden Age of tourism. Quite suddenly, what had been a tiny, backwater village became a major destination, known worldwide.

Cost and Hours: 10 CHF, covered by Swiss Travel Pass; daily July-Sept 11:00-18:00, Oct-June open afternoons only, closed Nov-mid-Dec; audioguide-5 CHF, under glass dome at Kirchplatz 11, across from Catholic church, tel. 027-967-4100, www. matterhornmuseum.ch.

Efficiency Tip for Glacier Express Travelers: In summer, when the early Glacier Express arrives in Zermatt at 16:10, consider going straight to the museum on arrival for an hour's visit before heading to your hotel. Leave your bags in the museum's free lockers.

Visiting the Museum: Pick up the free English flier, and consider paying for the excellent audioguide, which lets you hear Zermatt's history from two perspectives: that of native Zermatt alpinist Hannes Taugwalder or British mountaineer Edward Whymper. Then head downstairs.

The museum's main hall is filled with little *mazots* (those stone-roofed huts you've seen all around town). Each hut houses an exhibit. There are also reproductions of an old hotel and church from Zermatt's past, with fun sound effects. About half of the museum shows typical village furnishings, tools, and stuffed alpine fauna, and tells about the local prehistory and geology.

The rest of the museum focuses on Zermatt's mountaineering history. Reliefs of the Matterhorn (and the surrounding region) offer a helpful topographic overview. In the mountain guides' hut, press the buttons to see the different routes up the Matterhorn. Consider that even now, only about half the people who attempt this climb make it to the top. Find the picture of local hero Ulrich Inderbinden, who climbed the Matterhorn more than 370 times, the last when he was—no kidding—90 years old. (Inderbinden died in 2004 at age 104; a fountain in the Hinterdorf area of town honors him.)

Another hut displays artifacts found after deadly accidents, with a room dedicated to July 14, 1865—the day the Matterhorn was finally conquered by a team of seven climbers. (Four of them died on the descent, when the least-experienced among them fell, dragging three others to their deaths; you can see the snapped rope in a glass case.) Six short movies play in the "hotel." Be sure to check out the display case (near the WCs) that holds a collection of Matterhorn memorabilia and products.

Forest Fun Park Zermatt

This high-ropes park, located right under the gondola line to Furi (about 10 minutes past the Matterhorn Express station), has zip lines and a good range of ropes courses at various difficulty levels. Since it's open in all weather, the park is a great way to enjoy active fun on a rainy day.

Cost and Hours: 33 CHF, kids-23-28 CHF, daily 10:00-19:00, closed Nov-Easter, Zen Stechenstrasse 110, tel. 027-968-1010, www.zermatt-fun.com.

ZERMATT

Gorner Gorge (Gornerschlucht)

This special spot lets you peer into a narrow Ice Age gorge, complete with a waterfall, whirlpools, and wooden walkways that skirt the cliff edge. It's about 15 minutes beyond the end of the village on the path toward Furi, and worth considering when bad weather rules out a mountain excursion (or if you're already heading to or from Furi on foot). If you're here on a sunny day in early fall, try showing up in the mid-afternoon, when the sun's at just the right angle to set the water aglow in turquoise hues. Wear sturdy shoes, as the visit (allow 15-20 minutes) involves steep stairs and potentially slippery walkways.

Cost and Hours: 5 CHF, June-mid-Oct daily 9:15-17:45, closed off-season, tel. 027-967-2096, www.gornergorge.ch. It's well-signed, right under the gondola to Furi.

High-Mountain Activities in Zermatt

Think of the Zermatt region's many lifts and hikes in terms of the three high-mountain summit stations to which they're linked: **Matterhorn Glacier Paradise** (closest to the Matterhorn), **Gornergrat,** and **Rothorn** (farthest up the valley from the Matterhorn).

With at least two good-weather days, you can experience all three excursions. But if you have to choose just one, I'd go with the Gornergrat: It offers a fun train ride above the tree line, an up-close look at majestic glaciers, thrilling Matterhorn views, and one of my favorite hikes in the region. With more time, you can easily connect the Gornergrat via gondola with the Matterhorn Glacier Paradise lifts, or with a hike to the Rothorn hillside.

Weather Watch: Whichever excursions you opt for, pay close attention to the weather—the lifts aren't cheap, and none of them is worth it if the Matterhorn is completely socked in. If the weather's iffy, confirm that the entire route is open before you buy a summit ticket—upper segments can close if it's too windy (though the Gornergrat train and some Klein Matterhorn lifts usually keep running). That said, don't wait for perfectly clear skies to head into the hills—even in bright, sunny weather, the Matterhorn loves playing peek-a-boo behind the clouds. If it's at least sunny-ish, get up the mountainside.

Be Prepared: Even when it's balmy in the valley, take cold-weather gear if you're heading up the mountainside. It's cold up there (even at the lower elevations)—and can be windy to boot. For tips on prepping for mountain excursions, see "The Lowdown on High-Altitude Hiking" sidebar.

Passes and Tickets: It can be tricky to figure out the best ticketing option for your excursion. Basically you can either buy a pass that covers multiple lifts, or individual tickets for each one.

The Lowdown on High-Altitude Hiking

Here are some tips for staying safe and getting the most out of your Swiss mountain adventure:

- A waterproof/windproof outer layer will protect you from the Alps' unpredictable weather, and hiking boots are a must for navigating the rocky terrain. No matter how warm it might be in the valley, take extra layers for cold weather at the top.
- June through September are the best months for hiking in the Alps, though at high altitudes snow can make hiking difficult any time of year.
- The weather can be unpredictable, but locals can give you a general idea of what to expect. You can find weather reports in English at www.meteoswiss.admin.ch. It's also smart to check live webcams such as the ones at www.zermatt.ch.
- Know the symptoms of altitude sickness: shortness of breath, headaches, fatigue, and, in serious cases, confusion and ataxia (not being able to walk straight). Having plenty of water is a must, and ibuprofen, acetaminophen, or aspirin can combat headaches.
- A network of huts throughout the Swiss Alps provides meals and a place for hikers to sleep (see www.sac-cas.ch). But watch out, as they can be pricey.
- Many trails cross through fields of cattle. Hikers are expected to close gates after passing through. It's best to keep your distance from cows, especially if calves are nearby. If they're in your way, try to pass without making any sudden movements or loud noises.

A **Peak Pass** gives you unlimited access to all lifts in the area (1 day-170 CHF, 2 days-195 CHF, 3- to 5-day versions and non-consecutive passes available; cheaper in late spring and late fall; 5-CHF refundable card deposit, www.matterhornparadise.ch). You can purchase the pass online or in person at the Zermatt TI, the train station in Täsch, or the base stations for all three lifts/trains.

Another pass option is the **Peak2Peak** ticket: a one-day pass covering the trains/lifts for the Matterhorn Glacier Paradise and the Gornergrat, as well as the Riffelberg Express gondola (155 CHF, half-price with Swiss Travel Pass).

Even with the freedom and ease of a pass, it pays to consider **individual tickets** (lift prices are listed later). Keep in mind that Swiss Travel Pass holders pay half-price on full-fare individual tickets, but get only a 25 percent discount on the Peak Pass. All three mountain excursions offer ticket buyers some kind of dis-

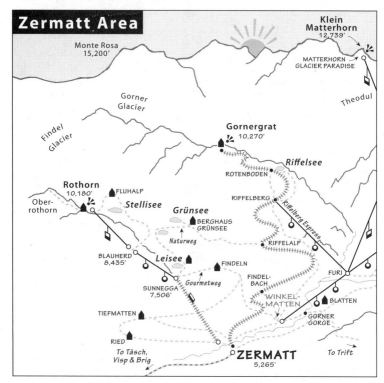

count in the later afternoon (though the Swiss Travel Pass discount beats these).

If, after reading the information in this chapter, you're still unclear on the best ticketing choice, consult with the staff at the TI. They expertly grapple with these questions every day on behalf of travelers.

Connecting the Mountainsides: I've described the three main excursions as separate experiences, but they can easily be combined to get the most out of a sunny day. The Gornergrat railway/hillside connects to the Klein Matterhorn hillside/Matterhorn Express lifts via the **Riffelberg Express** gondola, running between Riffelberg (on the Gornergrat side) and Furi (on the Klein Matterhorn slope). It operates only at the height of summer (24 CHF, 55 CHF round-trip, half-price with Swiss Travel Pass; July-mid-Aug 8:00-16:30, last descent at 16:45). If you're riding the Riffelberg Express to connect the Matterhorn Glacier Paradise and the Gornergrat on the same day (and don't have a Peak Pass), you may save money with the Peak2Peak ticket (see earlier).

Hikers can connect the Gornergrat hillside with Sunnegga, on the slopes of the Rothorn, via the moderately strenuous two-

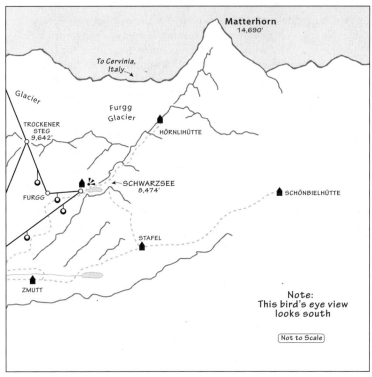

Matterhorn
14,690'

To Cervinia,
Italy

Glacier

Furgg
Glacier

TROCKENER
STEG
9,642'

HÖRNLIHÜTTE

FURGG

SCHWARZSEE
8,474'

SCHÖNBIELHÜTTE

STAFEL

ZMUTT

Note:
This bird's eye view
looks south

Not to Scale

hour Naturweg hike (works well in either direction; described later, under "Hikes from Sunnegga").

MATTERHORN GLACIER PARADISE

An excursion to what's branded as Matterhorn Glacier Paradise (the summit station for the Klein—"Little"—Matterhorn) has three main highlights: the summit (with views across the top of the Alps and a few fun indoor/outdoor activities), the halfway point at Schwarzsee (a nice spot to bask in Matterhorn views), and hikes down the mountainside (including my favorite, the Matterhorn Trail, from Schwarzsee). Note that you won't find any hiking paths from the very top of the Klein Matterhorn, since it's covered with snow year-round.

If you've been lucky enough to already visit the Berner Oberland's Schilthorn and/or Jungfraujoch (or France's Aiguille du Midi) in clear weather, the expensive trip up to this summit might not be worth it. But you should still consider the ride up to the Schwarzsee midpoint, with its lovely views and great hikes.

Lift Stages: The upward trip starts with a six-seat, five-minute gondola ride over glacier-carved foothills to **Furi**. Depending on the time of year, you may be able to transfer at Furi for the cable car

ZERMATT

to **Trockener Steg** (8 minutes, 6/hour)—if the weather's great, take this cable car, as it gets you to the summit faster (you can return via Schwarzsee). Otherwise, stay on the gondola and ride it for seven more minutes to the scenic ridge at **Schwarzsee.** From Schwarzsee, a second gondola dips down to the Furgg intermediary station, then soars up to Trockener Steg (9 minutes from Schwarzsee). From Trockener Steg, a cable car (8 minutes, 6/hour) takes you to the summit, with great views on the left side over glaciers and across to the Gornergrat train station.

Cost: A peak-season (July-Aug) round-trip ticket between Zermatt and the Matterhorn Glacier Paradise summit costs 110 CHF; Zermatt to Schwarzsee is 55 CHF round-trip (35 CHF one-way). All tickets are about 10 percent less in spring and fall, and half-price with the Swiss Travel Pass. An afternoon discount for the summit is available from mid-May through mid-Oct—be sure to ask.

Hours: The Klein Matterhorn lifts are open daily year-round. In summer (May-mid-Oct) they generally start running at 8:00, with the last ride up between 16:00 and 16:30, and the last ride down at 16:15-16:30 (from the summit) and 17:35-18:00 (from Furi). Note that the two stretches of gondola (from Furi to Schwarzsee, and from Schwarzsee to Trockener Steg) only run late June to mid-Oct, and the cable car between Furi and Trockener Steg runs all day only in spring (May-late June) and late summer (late Aug-mid-Oct); at the height of summer it runs only in the early morning (and is closed entirely for the last week of June). The Riffelberg Express gondola—a spur line connecting Furi up to Riffelberg, on the Gornergrat hillside—runs only in midsummer (see "Connecting the Mountainsides," earlier).

Information: For detailed schedule and price info, go to www.matterhornparadise.ch.

Getting There: The Matterhorn Express base station for the gondola to Furi (and Schwarzsee) is about three-quarters of a mile upriver from the Zermatt train station: Walk up Bahnhofstrasse to the Catholic church, head toward the bridge, and follow the river, or catch a bus (see "Getting Around Zermatt," earlier).

Trip Tips: It is always frigid at the summit and often windy—take cold-weather gear no matter how pleasant it might be in the valley. Since the area around the summit stays snow-covered all year long, you can even get in some summer skiing, but rent your gear in town—there are no rentals up top. Consider packing a lunch, as the summit's restaurant is particularly expensive, even by Swiss lift-station standards (picnicking is allowed on the summit's observation deck, but not in the café). And save money by using the free WCs at the Schwarzsee or Trockener Steg stations rather than the pay WCs at the summit.

▲▲▲Matterhorn Glacier Paradise Summit (12,739 feet)

To really get your high-altitude high, zip up to the highest cable-car station in Europe, the Matterhorn Glacier Paradise, on the side of the Klein Matterhorn. Be warned: Some visitors are disappointed by the view of the "real" Matterhorn from the summit, because it's not the classic postcard profile. (For views of the Matterhorn you imagined, visit the intermediate Schwarzsee stop.)

The best summit feature is the **observation deck,** with its stunning panoramas (access by elevator, then 42 steps). On a clear day, you can see Italy and France (including Mont Blanc, Europe's highest peak), as well as the Berner Oberland's Jungfrau and Mönch peaks (which you'll be viewing from the "back").

Inside, find the low-profile entrance of the **Glacier Palace,** marked *Gletschergrotte* (free with Peak Pass or full-price lift ticket,

8 CHF with discounted Swiss Travel Pass lift ticket, July-mid-Aug daily 8:15-16:00, rest of year 9:30-15:45). This place brags that it's the "highest glacial grotto in the world"—a claim that must make other high-altitude glacial grottos seethe with envy. The "palace" is basically a big hole dug into the glacier, allowing you to walk deep inside. As you wander, you'll see ice sculptures and some lackluster exhibits about glaciers, local wines, and "glacier fleas" (a.k.a. "springtails," little bugs that live up here).

Outside, you can trot across the snow, and young kids can take a turn on a very tame snow-tubing slope (free). Near the cable car's docking point is a darkened hall showing a range of exciting short films about high adventure in the local mountains.

Picnickers can take advantage of the observation deck; otherwise, your food options are limited to the **$$$** restaurant inside.

▲Schwarzsee Ridge (8,474 feet)

Roughly halfway to the Klein Matterhorn summit is the gondola station of **Schwarzsee** (named for the alpine lake nearby). When the gondola's running, you can detour here on your way back down the mountain—or come from Zermatt without going on to the summit. Though much lower in elevation, this area is the closest you can get to the Matterhorn. There's a lovely picnic spot near the station, making this a great place to pause on your way up or down the mountain. It's also the starting point for one of the best hikes in the area, including the Matterhorn Trail. Shorter walks back to town from the gondola station at Furi are also worthwhile.

▲▲Matterhorn Trail Hike (2-3 hours)

This moderately strenuous hike (#29 on local signs and maps) goes from Schwarzsee via Stafel to either Furi (2 hours), where you can ride the gondola back into town, or all the way to Zermatt (3 hours total), either via Zmutt or Furi. (From Schwarzsee, avoid the trail that leads directly down to Furi—it's much steeper than it is fun.)

From the Schwarzsee station, head down to the lake, then follow Matterhorn Trail signs to Stafelalp (the name of the hillside; also the name of a restaurant). A little farther down the path, ignore the red signs pointing to Stafelalp—red signs are for skiers—and stay on the main road. At the first major fork, about 30 minutes into your hike, a wooden sign off to the right points to the shortest path to Restaurant Stafelalp (20 minutes from here, near the mini village of Stafel), which takes you through a fascinating pocket of mossy hillocks, ponds, and bubbling streams.

From the restaurant, follow signs to Furi and Zmutt. After about 30 minutes you'll need to make a choice: Head downhill to cross over the Grande Dixence dam and on to the cute hamlet of Zmutt (25 minutes), or stay on the path to the gondola at Furi (which becomes hike #29a after the fork; about 40 mostly level minutes). I recommend taking the Zmutt fork, as it is a joy—an almost tourist-free time warp (with a restaurant or two as well as a fine cluster of traditional *mazot* buildings); from there, it's about an hour down to Zermatt. If going down via Furi, you can either take the gondola from Furi or hike a pleasant hour back to Zermatt, past the adorable village of Blatten (and its restaurant) and the Gorner Gorge (see listing under "Sights in Zermatt," earlier).

GORNERGRAT

The Gornergrat is my pick if you can fit in only one high-mountain excursion. Located between the Klein Matterhorn and the Rothorn, it's not inherently better than the neighboring peaks, but it's a best-of-all-worlds experience—and with more time, it's easy to combine with one of the neighboring hillsides.

This cogwheel-train excursion has two main highlights (aside from the train ride itself): the sweeping views from the top station, and the Riffelseeweg hike between the Rotenboden and Riffelberg stops.

Train Stations: A cogwheel train takes you from Zermatt steeply up to the Gornergrat summit (10,270 feet) in about 35 minutes, with stops at Findelbach, Riffelalp, Riffelberg, and Rotenboden. On the way up, sit on the right side for good Matterhorn vistas.

Cost: Peak-season (July-Aug) trips up to the Gornergrat station cost 57 CHF each way (49 CHF in May-June and Sept-Oct; no round-trip discount, half-price with Swiss Travel Pass). If going up in the late afternoon, get a discounted round-trip "Good Afternoon Ticket" (late April-Oct only, half-price with Swiss Travel Pass). If combining a Gornergrat trip and a Matterhorn Glacier Paradise visit on the same day via the Riffelberg Express, consider the Peak2Peak ticket (described earlier, under "Passes and Tickets").

Hours: Trains run daily year-round, departing 2-3/hour from early June to mid-Oct, with the first ascent at about 7:00 and the last descent at 19:00 or 20:00; off-season, trains run about once an hour with the last descent around 19:00. The Riffelberg Express gondola runs only in midsummer; see "Connecting the Mountainsides," earlier.

Information: Tel. 0848-642-442, www.gornergrat.ch.

Getting There: The Gornergrat train station is right across the street from Zermatt's train station.

▲▲Gornergrat Top Station (10,270 feet)

From the train platform, walk to the main building, where an elevator brings you to the observation platform. You'll be presented with a sweeping panorama, including great views of the Matterhorn (though it's not *quite* the perfect profile that you see from the Rothorn). You're also up close to the *other* big mountain in the neighborhood, Monte Rosa, the highest point in Switzerland (15,200 feet). And from here you have the best possible look at the Gorner glacier, a thousand-foot sheer drop below the platform.

There's also a chapel and a hotel, with a **$$$$** restaurant and a **$$$** self-serve buffet (in spring and fall, eating and shopping in the main building close down around 17:00).

▲▲▲Riffelseeweg Hike (1.5 hours)

Perhaps my favorite hike in the whole Zermatt region is the easy Riffelseeweg path (hike #21 on local signs and maps), which usually opens sometime in June. Take the train from the Gornergrat summit back down to the Rotenboden station. From there, be sure to follow the official Riffelseeweg trail (not route #23 down toward Riffelalp—don't confuse your Riffels!—which cheats you out of the nicest stretch of this walk). Just down the hillside from the Rotenboden station, you can also enjoy the pretty lake called Riffelsee—and, if you're lucky, catch the Matterhorn's reflection on its surface.

The trail leads over some gorgeous topography, ending at the Riffelberg station. You can continue by train back into Zermatt, or disembark at any point to hike down—or cross over to Sunnegga on the Rothorn (described next). Or you can head over to the

ZERMATT

Klein Matterhorn via the Riffelberg Express gondola, which whisks you efficiently over and down to the gondola station at Furi (described earlier, under "Connecting the Mountainsides").

ROTHORN

Of the main mountain options in the area, the Rothorn (ROTE-horn) hillside offers *the* classic Matterhorn view. It's also less crowded than the Gornergrat, has many good hiking options, and its first stage, at Sunnegga, offers the cheapest ride into the mountains—and arguably the single best Matterhorn vantage point anywhere.

The excursion has four main high-lights: the view from the Rothorn sum-mit, the hike from Blauherd to Fluhalp and back, the view from Sunnegga, and a variety of hikes from Sunnegga. The view from the summit is fantastic, but it's not that much better than what you see from Blauherd—if you don't have a Peak Pass, you might want to skip the summit and save your time and money for the lower stations.

Lift Stages: The lift system up to Rothorn has three parts: a frequent funicular (3-6/hour, 8 minutes) up to **Sunnegga,** a five-minute gondola ride to **Blauherd,** and, finally, a cable car (at least 3/hour) to **Rothorn.**

Cost: Peak-season (July-Aug) round-trip ticket between Zermatt and the Rothorn costs 74 CHF round-trip (49 CHF one-way); Zermatt to Blauherd is 53 CHF round-trip (33 CHF one-way), and Zermatt to Sunnegga is 27 CHF round-trip (18 CHF one-way). All full-fare tickets are about 10 percent less in spring and fall, and half-price with the Swiss Travel Pass. A round-trip ticket to the Rothorn summit is discounted in the later afternoon (July-Sept only, no Swiss Travel Pass discount).

Tip: If you intend to tackle the Naturweg hike but don't have a Peak Pass, you'll save money by getting the **Naturweg combo-ticket** in advance to cover your one-way rides between Zermatt and Sunnegga, and between Riffelalp and Zermatt (32 CHF; half-price with Swiss Travel Pass).

Hours: Daily lifts to the summit operate seasonally: The lower-elevation Sunnegga funicular operates late May-mid-Oct; the mid-dle lift (Sunnegga-Blauherd) runs late May-late Sept, and the top lift (Blauherd-Rothorn) goes from July until late Sept. From July to mid-Sept, the lifts start running at 8:00, with the last ride to the summit from Blauherd at 16:40, and the last ride down between 16:50 (from Rothorn) and 18:00 (from Sunnegga). Lifts operate on

ZERMATT

shorter schedules outside those months. The whole shebang is open again for skiers in winter, but closes entirely in the shoulder season.

Information: For detailed schedules and pricing, go to www. matterhornparadise.ch.

Getting There: The base station for the Sunnegga-Rothorn funicular is across the river from the Zermatt train station, just downstream from the Gornergrat train tracks.

▲▲Rothorn Summit (10,180 feet)

Atop the Rothorn, you have your choice of taking panoramic photos of the entire Matterhorn massif, watching paragliders step into thin air, eating at a fancy **$$$$** pizzeria, and/or picnicking on the rocks. Far below you'll see the Grünsee (lake with restaurant, more easily hikable from Sunnegga—you'll need strong knees to descend to the lake from here) and beyond it the Riffelalp station on the Gornergrat train line.

▲▲▲Blauherd-Fluhalp Hike (1.5 hours)

Perhaps the best hike on this mountainside is the easy, mostly level walk from the Blauherd station (8,435 feet) to the restaurant at Fluhalp, then back again (1.5 hours total). The start of the hike isn't well-signed: From behind the Blauherd station, walk up the gravel road in back of the "Blue Lounge" building. Continue for a few more yards toward the ski lift labeled *Hublot Express* to find a narrow hiking path on the right—look for the rock next to the path that's painted with an inconspicuous red-and-white trail marker. (You can also simply follow the road that curves to the right behind the Blue Lounge, but I prefer the smaller hiking path that parallels it.)

About 15 minutes into the hike, you hit its best part: the lake called Stellisee. It's pretty in its own right, but on calm days it becomes a reflecting pool for the Matterhorn—walk around to the far end to take in the view. If you're short on time, you can turn around here (which cuts the total hike time in half). Or push on to Fluhalp—the path climbs gently but steadily from here.

Note: From Blauherd, the 40-minute, 1,000-foot descent along the Murmelweg ("Marmot Path") to Sunnegga is a disappointment—just steep enough so you can't enjoy the view, and with no guarantee that you'll see the elusive rodents.

▲▲▲Sunnegga Viewpoint (7,506 feet)

This stop, just uphill from Zermatt, at the end of the in-mountain funicular, is the cheapest of all the lifts from Zermatt, but it's quite possibly the best spot anywhere to drink in the Matterhorn view. (It's also the starting point for several great hikes, described next.)

From the Sunnegga lift station, you can go through the tunnel (following the "Wolli" sheep signs) to take a free minilift down to a lakeside picnic-and-play area with nice views. Or you can eat at the self-service **$$$** Buffet-Bar Sunnegga.

▲▲Hikes from Sunnegga

Gourmetweg Hike (Sunnegga-Zermatt, 2.5 hours): This popular hike is mostly gentle, taking you through deserted villages, among larch forests, and past several restaurants. If you follow the official #6 path via the hamlet of Ried, it takes about 2.5 hours. You can cut the walk shorter by following signs off the route to steeper paths back to Zermatt.

The first part, leading through several sleepy hamlets, has fantastic Matterhorn views but is confusingly signed. Near the start of the hike, a fork points left (signed *Paradies*), but either path will take you to the same spot farther down the Gourmetweg trail. A little farther along (with the village of Findeln below you), a sign shows the Gourmetweg going downhill on a low road and also on a higher path—take the low road.

Not long after Findeln, with the ravine on your left, there are two spots where you can cut the walk short and hike steeply down into town via the Winkelmatten neighborhood (about 50 minutes to reach central Zermatt). If you continue on the Gourmetweg toward Ried, be warned that the trail turns into a relatively tedious forest walk, albeit over soft, fragrant pine needles. You have one last chance at a more direct route (via Tiefmatten) into town but after that, resist the urge to follow downhill paths off the main trail—some of these seeming shortcuts are knee killers, and ultimately won't save time.

Naturweg Hike (Sunnegga-Riffelalp, 2 hours): Level overall, but with enough up and down to get your heart pumping, the #19 Naturweg trail connects Sunnegga with Riffelalp. From the cute lake called Leisee, just under the Sunnegga station, go crosswise via the unremarkable Moosjisee, then up-up-up toward Grünsee. The path doesn't lead to the lake itself (though it's just a short detour off the trail), but rather to the pleasant Berghaus Grünsee restaurant and mountain refuge—perfectly placed for a well-earned break. From the refuge you're rewarded with an extra-scenic final stretch on to Riffelalp.

From Riffelalp you can either take the Gornergrat train back to town (25 CHF, half-price with a Swiss Travel Pass—or use the Naturweg combo-ticket described earlier, under "Cost"), or follow one of two good, relatively easy trails all the way into Zermatt (1.5 hours via the Arvenweg, hike #14, or 2 hours via the poorly signed Riffelalpweg, hike #20).

OTHER MOUNTAIN ACTIVITIES
Paragliding

Tandem paragliding down the mountainside is an expensive but unforgettable experience. You pick the altitude of your take-off point and land back in Zermatt (about 170 CHF from Blauherd or Riffelberg, 220 CHF from Gornergrat or Rothorn; contact Paragliding Zermatt/Air Taxi Tandem Flights, tel. 027-967-6744, www.paragliding-zermatt.ch; or FlyZermatt, tel. 027-967-2100, www.flyzermatt.com).

Mountain Biking

The hills above Zermatt are laced with great mountain-bike paths, ranging from easy to difficult. Bikers can buy a one- or two-day ticket for riding lifts and transporting bikes. For more information on trails and passes, or to connect with local guides who can take you touring, contact the TI.

Summer Skiing

Zermatt's high elevation and variety of runs—and, in winter, the chance to actually ski or snowboard from Switzerland to Italy—make this a popular skiing destination. Summer skiing is an option at Matterhorn Glacier Paradise (first lift starts at about 8:00, last lift stops around 14:00—after that the snow's too slushy, late April-mid-Oct, limited area in midsummer). A one-day summer lift ticket will run you about 90 CHF; for specifics, see www.matterhornparadise.ch.

For equipment rental in town, see "Helpful Hints," earlier. For more tips, see the Switzerland in Winter chapter.

Sleeping in Zermatt

Little Zermatt has more than a hundred hotels. This is a resort town, plain and simple, where building after building is for guests (many who rent by the week). You'll pay less at most places early and late in the season (June and Oct), and more during ski season (Dec-late March/early April). Many hotels close in the off-season (early spring and late fall). Of course, several hotels are open year-round.

$$$ Hotel Romantica, a flower-dappled, four-story chalet located one scenic (and steep) block up from the main street, offers 13 very comfortable rooms. They maintain plenty of rustic alpine-hut character while offering all the modern conveniences (and many have balconies). They also rent two tiny alpine huts (family room, often 2-night minimum, elevator, closed off-season, Chrum 21, tel. 027-966-2650, www.romantica-zermatt.ch, info@romantica-zermatt.ch, Cremonini family).

ZERMATT

$$$ Hotel Jägerhof has 51 homey rooms and common areas with lots of charm. It's a little farther from the center and across the river toward the Matterhorn Express lift, but they'll pick you up at the train station for no extra fee. The rustic lounge is plenty cozy on rainy days, and the rooms with views are worth the extra francs (some doubles have balconies, elevator, fitness room, open year-round, Steinmattstrasse 85, tel. 027-966-3800, www.jaegerhofzermatt.ch, jaegerhof@zermatt.ch, Perren family). From the train station, walk or take either the green or red bus to the Kirchbrücke stop (across the river from the Catholic church). From there, walk up Kirchstrasse (away from the river) one more block, then hang a right onto Steinmattstrasse (at the corner with Hotel Julen); at the building labeled *Zinnia,* take the left fork and look for the small wooden *Hotel Jägerhof* sign on your left.

$$ Hotel Le Mazot has nine cozy-if-basic rooms—four with Matterhorn-view balconies—in a central but quiet location next to the river and above an intimate restaurant (open mid-June-Oct only, Hofmattstrasse 23, tel. 027-966-0606, www.lemazotzermatt.ch, le.mazot@reconline.ch).

$$ Hotel Tannenhof hides a few steps off the main drag behind a fancy hotel that steals the Matterhorn views. Its 19 rooms are small, tight, and woody, without much character, but the location is good (thin walls, closed Oct, Englischer Viertel 3, tel. 027-967-3188, www.rhone.ch/tannenhof, hotel-tannenhof@rhone.ch, Christiane).

$$ Hotel Weisshorn offers 16 basic but comfortable rooms over a restaurant, right in the heart of town. The rooms are nothing special (even the four with mountain-view balconies), but the rates are reasonable (open year-round, Am Bach 6, tel. 027-967-1112, www.holidaynet.ch/weisshorn, hotel.weisshorn@bluewin.ch).

¢-$$ Hotel Bahnhof is a budget hotel and hostel in a respectable, remodeled building with four floors (but no elevator) across the street from the train station. There are 17 tidy, alpine-style rooms (those without bath have Matterhorn-view balconies) and three dorm rooms. The basement features a relaxing lounge, a dining room, and a large guests' kitchen (often dominated by big groups). It's well-run, but management is offsite at night—so if the younger crowd comes back late after partying, you're on your own (no breakfast, reception closes 12:00-16:00, nice showers, laundry facilities, lockers, closed for 4-5 weeks in shoulder season, Bahnhofplatz 54, tel. 027-967-2406, www.hotelbahnhof.com, welcome@hotelbahnhof.com, Lauber family).

¢-$$ Zermatt Youth Hostel looks over town from a perch high above the river and offers views of the Matterhorn. The super-modern hostel offers dorm beds and private rooms, most with bathrooms. Travelers of all ages will feel comfortable here, and the hostel's four-course dinner is a great value in expensive Zermatt (sheets included, towels extra for dorm rooms, laundry facilities, no curfew, reception open 7:00-10:00 & 16:00-22:00, Stalden-weg 5, tel. 027-967-2320, www.youthhostel.ch/zermatt, zermatt@youthhostel.ch). From the station, walk 15 minutes uphill toward the end of town or take the red-line bus marked *Winkelmatten* to the Luchre stop; the hostel is 50 yards uphill from there (follow signs with international hostel symbol).

¢ **Matterhorn Hostel** has 56 rock-bottom beds in a traditional building overlooking the river at the upstream end of town. Its mission is to provide cheap beds for young adults in an expensive town, and it delivers—but don't expect anything more. The floor plan is claustrophobic, with not an inch of wasted space: 10 dorm rooms with graffiti decor are upstairs (some with Matterhorn-view balconies); the lounge and showers are in the basement; and a tiny computer nook is tucked under the spiral staircase. It's hard to justify staying here if you can get a bed at the fine official youth hostel (simple breakfast extra, sheets and towels extra, reception open 7:30-10:00 & 16:00-21:00, Schluhmattstrasse 32, tel. 027-968-1919, www.matterhornhostel.com, info@matterhornhostel.com). It's a 15-minute walk from the train station on the way up to the Matterhorn Express lift station, above the river. Take the green- or red-line bus to the Kirchbrücke stop, then follow Schluh-mattstrasse upstream for a few minutes—look for signs for Sparky's restaurant, on the right.

Eating in Zermatt

Zermatt's restaurants are very expensive. But cheap takeout-type places aren't too hard to find, and you can easily assemble a picnic at one of the town's several bakeries and supermarkets.

$$$ Whymper-Stube, named for the first brave soul to conquer the Matterhorn, specializes in cheese dishes—that means fondue and raclette. While tourists photograph each other eating fondue, six barstools in the corner are warmed by local regulars. On evenings in peak season, reservations are smart (kitchen open daily 11:00-21:00 except no lunch service in winter, friendly staff, closed May and Oct-Nov, along the main drag at Bahnhofstrasse 80, across from the huge Zermatthof hotel, tel. 027-967-2296, www.whymper-stube.ch).

$$$ Restaurant du Pont claims to be the oldest restaurant in town. Note that it doesn't claim to be the best. Its ambience—with low ceilings and Swiss folk sayings on the walls—beats the food, which is fine, just simple (kitchen open daily 9:00-21:30, on Bahnhofstrasse at end of square with big Catholic church, tel. 027-967-4343, Evelin Kalbematten).

ZERMATT

$$$ Sparky's, in the same building as the Matterhorn Hostel, isn't very Swiss—Sparky himself is a friendly Brit who's lived in Zermatt for decades—but has a popular bar and serves Middle Eastern and Southeast Asian cuisine (kitchen open Tue-Sun 16:00-22:00, closed Mon and mid-Sept-mid-Nov, Schluhmattstrasse 32, tel. 027-968-1918).

$$$ Non Solo Treno, at the train station, isn't long on atmosphere but has ample indoor and outdoor seating, fine pizza, and long hours (daily 6:00-23:00—full menu available at 11:00, Bahnhofplatz 7, tel. 027-968-1968, www.restaurant-nonsolotreno.ch).

Sandwiches and Kebabs: Smack in the middle of town, across from the Catholic church, sits **$ Take-Away "Wilde-Hilde,"** a no-frills deli that makes fresh sandwiches on demand (Tue-Sun 9:00-19:00, closed Mon, Kirchplatz). It's the ground floor of the former home of the two Peter Taugwalders (father and son), mountain guides on the first Matterhorn ascent. Just a few more yards down Bahnhofstrasse, **$ Take It Döner** sells kebabs (daily 11:00-21:00, Oberdorfstrasse 24).

Supermarkets: A large **Co-op** is in the little mall across from the train station, **and Migros** is across from the tennis courts on Hofmattstrasse. The small **Pam,** along the river at the corner of Kirchstrasse and Schluhmattstrasse, is convenient if you're staying at the upper end of town. All are open daily about 8:00-19:00.

Zermatt Connections

Zermatt is at the end of the Nikolaital valley, which is reached on the narrow-gauge Matterhorn Gotthard Railway (MGB, www.mgbahn.ch). Swiss Rail (SBB) info: toll tel. 0900-300-300, www.rail.ch.

By Train: All of these trains from Zermatt transfer in Visp. Some have multiple transfers. Trains from Zermatt go to: **Bern** (1-2/hour, 2 hours), **Zürich** (hourly, 3.5 hours), **Montreux** (1-2/hour, 2.5 hours), **Lausanne** (2/hour, 3 hours), **Interlaken Ost** (1-2/hour, 2 hours, 2 transfers), **Luzern** (1-2/hour, 3.5 hours, 2 transfers).

By Glacier Express to Eastern Switzerland: This scenic train departs Zermatt (at least once daily through most of the year, more in summer) and arcs scenically on high-altitude tracks over the middle of Switzerland to the east. All of these Glacier Express trains go through **Chur** (6 hours), then continue either to **Davos** or **St. Moritz** (8 hours total to either). For details, see the Scenic Rail Journeys chapter.

APPENZELL

Appenzell Town • Ebenalp • Liechtenstein

Welcome to cowbell country. In the moo-mellow and storybook-friendly Appenzell region, you'll find the warm, intimate side of the land of staggering, icy Alps. With just one percent of Switzerland's territory and one percent of its population, the little canton of Appenzell stubbornly celebrates its way of life. You'll see its symbol everywhere: a scary bear walking upright, yielding its sharp claws and teeth. And yet the people here are mellow and welcoming. You'll savor Appenzell's cozy, small-town atmosphere—and if there's time, you can stop by one of Europe's smallest nations—Liechtenstein—for more off-the-grid ambience.

Appenzell is one of Switzerland's most traditional regions... and the butt of jokes because of it. Entire villages meet to vote in town squares such as Appenzell town's Landsgemeindeplatz (an event featured on most postcard racks). Until 1990, the women of Appenzell couldn't vote on local issues. But in a break from convention, in 2000 Appenzell's schools were the first in Switzerland to make English—rather than distant French—the mandatory second language.

A gentle beauty blankets this region of green, rolling hills, watched over by the 8,200-foot peak of Mount Säntis (Appenzell's highest point). As you travel, you'll enjoy an ever-changing parade of finely carved chalets, colorful villages, and cows mooing, "Milk me." While farmers' daughters make hay, old ladies with scythes walk the steep roads, looking as if they just pushed the Grim Reaper down the hill. When locals are asked about Appenzeller cheese, they clench their fists as they answer, "It's the best." (It is, without any doubt, the smelliest.)

If you're here in late August or early September, there's a good

Appenzell Region

Note: Not all rail lines are shown

GERMANY
To Munich
A-96
Lindau
Romanshorn
10 Kilometers
Lake Constance
10 Miles
13
Rorschach
Bregenz
A-1
Gossau
E-60
St.
St. Marg.
A-1
To Winterthur & Zürich
Gallen
A-13
Dornbirn
Herisau
Teufen
Altstätten
A-14
Stein
Stoss
Oberriet
A P P E N Z E L L
Gais
Ranksweil
Jakobsbad
Gonten-
(LUGE)
bad
Appenzell
Urnäsch
Town
AUSTRIA
(BAREFOOT HIKE)
Helmberg
Ebenalp
Brülisau
To Rapperswil & Luzern
See Ebenalp detail map
Wasserauen
Feldkirch
13
▲ Mt. Säntis
16
To Innsbruck via Arlbergpass
A-14
To Zürich & Luzern
Buchs
Schaan
S W I T Z E R L A N D
Vaduz
LIECHTEN-
A-3
Sevelen
STEIN
A-13
━━━━ Appenzeller Bahn
- - - - Other Rail
Sargans
Baby Rhine
To Chur & Pontresina
SWITZ.

chance you'll get to watch (or at least have to slow down for) the ceremonial procession of flower-be-decked cows and whistling herders in formal folk costumes. The festive march down from the high pastures is a spontaneous move by the herd-ing families, and when they finally do burst into town (like a slow-motion Swiss Pamplona), locals young and old become children again, running joyously into the streets.

PLANNING YOUR TIME

On a two-week trip through Switzerland, save a day for the Ap-penzell region. This pastoral area offers a good first look at Swit-zerland—but can be anticlimactic after the rugged Berner Ober-land or Matterhorn. If you have only a week or less in Switzerland, skip the subtle charms of Appenzell and head instead for the high mountains.

In the Appenzell region, I prefer overnighting up on Ebenalp to really get away from it all. But if that mountaintop retreat's rustic accommodations and steep hikes aren't your cup of tea, consider the comfort of sleeping in Appenzell town, which is also a more efficient base for getting around the region.

GETTING AROUND THE APPENZELL REGION

This area is a breeze by **car**—you could see everything in this chapter in one (very busy) day. Notice that the attractions in Stein and Urnäsch and the Kronberg luge ride form a handy little loop to the west of Appenzell town. The lift up to Ebenalp is just to the south.

The regional narrow-gauge **trains** are run by a private operator (Appenzeller Bahnen—Eurail and Swiss Travel passes valid). A very handy train generally runs twice an hour (except in the early afternoon and after 20:00, when it's hourly), connecting almost all of the destinations I describe. Starting up at Wasserauen (at the base of Ebenalp lift), it runs through Appenzell town (12 minutes), stopping at Gontenbad (one end of the Barefoot Walk, 16 minutes), Jakobsbad (luge ride and other end of the Barefoot Walk, 20 minutes), and Urnäsch (folk museum, 27 minutes), and then going north to Herisau (43 minutes; change here to reach Luzern) and Gossau (49 minutes; change here to reach Zürich). A separate line runs from Appenzell to the city of St. Gallen.

The one destination in this chapter not well covered by public transportation is Stein (with its folk museum and tourable cheese factory). It is reachable by taxi (for details, see the listing later in this chapter).

Appenzell Town

The center of this authentically Swiss town is a painfully cute pedestrian zone lined with colorful, patterned house fronts (rather than the white-painted or wooden facades favored elsewhere). This is a great spot to simply let your pulse slow and enjoy Swiss small-town life. The big square of Landsgemeindeplatz—at the far end of Hauptgasse from the town church and TI—is where residents gather on the last Sunday of each April to vote on local issues by show of hands. (The rest of the year, it's a parking lot.) A fountain on the square shows an Appenzeller raising his hand to be counted.

Appenzell town is touristy, sure. But from watching the locals robustly greet each other in the streets or laugh over a local beer in the pubs, it's clear this is also a real, living town.

Orientation to Appenzell Town

Appenzell town (pop. 6,000) clusters along its main street, Hauptgasse, which runs from the bridge over the Sitter River to the biggest square, Landsgemeindeplatz. From the middle of this colorful drag, Postgasse (which turns into Poststrasse) heads south to the train station. You can walk from one end of town to the other in about 10 minutes.

TOURIST INFORMATION

The TI is on the main street at Hauptgasse 4 (generally daily 10:00-17:00, may close for midday break; tel. 071-788-9641, www.appenzell.ch).

If you stay at least three nights in the region, your hotel or pension will give you an **Appenzell Card.** This covers all local train trips (on trains operated by Appenzeller Bahnen, as far as St. Gallen), free rides on three different cable cars, free admission to local museums, a free ride on the Kronberg luge, a day's free bike rental, discounted PubliCar taxi service, and more. It can be worth extending a two-night stay to three just to get the card.

ARRIVAL IN APPENZELL TOWN

The cute red **train** station has a ticket office (Mon-Fri 7:30-18:00, Sat-Sun 8:00-11:45 & 13:15-18:00), WCs, and small lockers (the ticket office can store larger bags). To reach the TI from the station, walk straight ahead up Poststrasse to Postplatz, and keep on going around to the right up to Hauptgasse. The TI is directly ahead.

If arriving by **car,** ask your hotel about parking. If you're just day-tripping here, leave your car in the pay lot by the brewery just across the river from downtown. Walk across the bridge and veer right onto the main drag, Hauptgasse; the TI is just past the church, on your right.

HELPFUL HINTS

Blue Monday: Most of Appenzell's museums are closed on Monday, but hiking and biking are good any day the sun shines. The folk museum in Urnäsch, the cheese factory in Stein, and (unless it's raining) the Kronberg luge in Jakobsbad are other good Monday options.

When the Cows Come Home: If you're here at the right time of year, you might luck into seeing the festive procession of cows heading up to the high-mountain pastures (*Alpfahrt,* generally

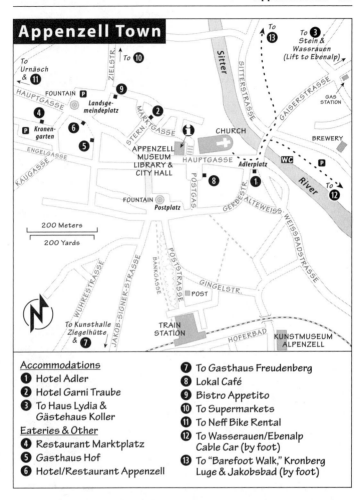

Appenzell Town

To Urnäsch & ⑪
FOUNTAIN P ⑨
HAUPTGASSE
④ Landsgemeindeplatz ②
ZIELSTR.
To ⑩
Sitter
To ⑬
To ③ Stein & Wassrauen (Lift to Ebenalp)
GAISERSTRASSE
GAS STATION
P Kronengarten
⑥
⑤
ENGELGASSE
KAUGASSE
STERNGASSE
MARKTGASSE
⑪
APPENZELL MUSEUM LIBRARY & CITY HALL
CHURCH
HAUPTGASSE
Adlerplatz
WC
P
BREWERY
River
To ⑫
⑧
POSTGASSE
GERBERSTR.
ALTEWEISS
WEISSBADSTRASSE
FOUNTAIN
Postplatz
200 Meters
200 Yards
WUHRESTRASSE
JAKOB-SIGNER-STRASSE
BANKGASSE
POSTSTRASSE
GINGELSTR.
POST
N
To Kunsthalle Ziegelhütte & ⑦
TRAIN STATION
HOFERBAD
KUNSTMUSEUM ALPENZELL

<u>Accommodations</u>
① Hotel Adler
② Hotel Garni Traube
③ To Haus Lydia & Gästehaus Koller

<u>Eateries & Other</u>
④ Restaurant Marktplatz
⑤ Gasthaus Hof
⑥ Hotel/Restaurant Appenzell
⑦ To Gasthaus Freudenberg
⑧ Lokal Café
⑨ Bistro Appetito
⑩ To Supermarkets
⑪ To Neff Bike Rental
⑫ To Wasserauen/Ebenalp Cable Car (by foot)
⑬ To "Barefoot Walk," Kronberg Luge & Jakobsbad (by foot)

late May-early June) or returning from a summer high in the Alps (*Alpabfahrt*, generally late Aug-early Sept). Unfortunately, the cows don't give much advance notice—announcements of the event pop up around town just a few days ahead. To be sure to fit some cows into your itinerary, catch them in the Appenzell cattle show, usually the first Tuesday in October.

Bike Rental: The **train station** has regular bikes (20 CHF/half-day, 25 CHF/day, return bike by 18:00) as well as electric bikes that can be reserved through the national rail system (see page 408). Most hotels rent bikes or can arrange a rental for you.

For mountain bikes, go to the garage of **Elmar Neff**, a five-minute walk beyond Landsgemeindeplatz (25 CHF/half-day, 35 CHF/day; Mon-Fri 7:30-12:00 & 13:15-18:30, Sat until 16:00, closed Sun, shorter hours off-season; Hauptgasse 58, tel. 071-787-3477, www.neff-zweirad.ch).

Sights in the Appenzell Region

The Appenzell region has three folk museums—one in Appenzell town, another in Stein, and a third in Urnäsch. All are good, and they're different enough that visiting all three is worth considering if you have ample time and interest. To be more selective, weigh these differences: Stein's is the biggest, most modern, and probably the best-presented (but also the most difficult to reach without a car); Urnäsch's is the most atmospheric, as it's in a creaky old house; and Appenzell town's is the most convenient, giving a good all-around look at the region (it's especially strong on local costumes) but lacking a bit of the charm of the other two.

APPENZELL TOWN
▲Appenzell Museum
This folk moo-seum, situated above the TI, provides a fine and efficient look at the local cow culture.

Cost and Hours: 7 CHF, covered by Swiss Travel Pass; Mon-Fri 10:00-12:00 & 13:30-17:00, Sat-Sun 11:00-17:00; Nov-March Tue-Sun 14:00-17:00, closed Mon; Hauptgasse 4, tel. 071-788-9631, http://museum.ai.ch.

Visiting the Museum: Buy your ticket, borrow the English translations, and ride the elevator five floors up. From the elevator, detour up the stairs to the attic for a collection of coins, measurement instruments, and torture devices. Check out the excellent collection of traditional costumes on the fifth floor, then work your way down, wandering through the rest of the exhibits as you go. You'll see old flags and banners, reconstructed rustic rooms, woodcarvings, 19th-century peasant art, handmade embroidery, and (oddly) an Egyptian coffin. One thought-provoking room displays boards called *Rebretter*, which were used to lay out the body of a recently deceased loved one. The boards were painted with the name and information of the deceased and, after the burial, displayed on the family's house.

▲Folk Music
The accordion never really caught on here, making Appenzell's folk music, which still uses older instruments (violin, dulcimer), unique in Switzerland. Free concerts take place every Thursday (early-June-mid-Oct) at 18:30 in the City Hall, and every Wednesday at 20:00

at the ritzy Hotel Hof Weissbad (about two miles out of town, on the way to Wasserauen, tel. 071-798-8080, www.hofweissbad.ch). You may also find live music at local restaurants—ask at the TI.

Modern Art Museums

Appenzell has a modern-/contemporary-art museum with two branches in great settings: **Kunstmuseum Appenzell** is a silver-clad modern building right behind the train tracks (Unterrain-strasse 5, tel. 071-788-1800), and **Kunsthalle Ziegelhütte** is a bit farther out (Ziegeleistrasse 14, tel. 071-788-1860).

Cost and Hours: Each costs 9 CHF, but a 15-CHF combo-ticket gets you into both; also covered by Swiss Travel Pass; Tue-Fri 10:00-12:00 & 14:00-17:00, Sat-Sun 11:00-17:00, shorter hours Nov-March, closed Mon year-round; www.h-gebertka.ch.

HIKING

Appenzell makes a good home base for hiking, with gentle hills and pastoral scenery all around. The TI can suggest several easy walks in the region. I recommend two possibilities here.

Appenzell to Wasserauen

This two-hour walk, which takes you to the foot of the Ebenalp cable car (described later) begins near the parish church in Appenzell and leads you along a creek through meadows and forests. The path is well-marked. Once you reach Wasserauen, you can take the cable car up to Ebenalp, or simply hop on the train back to Appenzell.

Barefoot Walk (Barfussweg)

This 1.5-hour walk between Jakobsbad and Gontenbad offers a surprising and unusual experience...yes, with your shoes off. The trail leads over meadows, through creeks, and on stretches of asphalted road, in a tranquil valley roughly parallel to the Appenzell-Urnäsch road and rail line. Two specially designed fountains along the way will refresh your feet. The path was inspired by the philosophy of 19th-century therapist Sebastian Kneipp, who sought to treat medical conditions with water of different temperatures and pressures.

To get from Appenzell to the trailhead, take the train to Jakobsbad (1-2/hour, 8 minutes, trailhead right across the street from the train station and the Kronberg luge ticket office—described later), and do the barefoot walk to Gontenbad. From Gontenbad, you can ride the train back to Appenzell (4 minutes), or keep on walking (about another hour).

NEAR APPENZELL TOWN
▲Stein

The unassuming, hill-capping village of Stein has two worthwhile attractions, side by side: a cheese production facility with a visitors center, and arguably the region's best folk museum. If you don't have a car, use the subsidized taxi service, **PubliCar,** which takes passengers to Stein and other locations not serviced by buses (each passenger pays a distance-dependent fare plus a flat fee—about 12 CHF from Appenzell to Stein). To reserve, ask at the TI, or call 0848-553-060 (more info at www.publicar.ch).

Appenzeller Dairy (Appenzeller Schaukäserei)

This is one of several dozen dairies in the area where the well-known Appenzeller cheese is made, and it's set up to explain the process to curious visitors. It's fast, smelly, and user-friendly.

Cost and Hours: Free admission to dairy, cheese tasting-8.50 CHF; daily 9:00-18:30, off-season until 17:30; videoguide-10 CHF for dairy only, 15 CHF for dairy and Folklore Museum (listed next); tel. 071-368-5070, www.showcheese.ch.

Visiting the Dairy: As you enter, pick up the English description of the cheesemaking process ("From Milk to Cheese"), and ask about the next English showing of the 10-minute video (which treads a fine line between being informative and promotional).

Large, colorful displays trace the cheesemaking process, and you can peer down into the production facility (cheese is generally being made 9:00-15:00—most interesting when they pour the contents of the giant vat into the long line of wheel molds). You'll learn how the special pungent flavor of Appenzeller cheese comes from an age-old, secret-recipe herbal brine mixture that's lovingly rubbed on each wheel as it ages. Down the long hallway, watch hundreds of wheels of cheese silently age. Then head into the tasting area, where you can nibble on the various types of Appenzeller-brand cheese. The ladies at the cheese counter love to cut it so you can sample it. Notice how the age affects the aroma and taste. The dairy also sells yogurt and cold drinks (the boxes of iced tea are cheap), and the restaurant serves powerful cheese specialties.

Appenzell Folklore Museum (Appenzeller Volkskunde Museum)

This excellent museum offers a modern, well-presented look at the folk culture in these parts.

Cost and Hours: 7 CHF, covered by Swiss Travel Pass; Tue-Sun 10:00-17:00, closed Mon; videoguide-10 CHF for museum only, 15 CHF for museum and Appenzeller Dairy (previous listing); tel. 071-368-5056, www.appenzeller-museum.ch.

Demonstrations: A visit to this museum is best on Saturdays

and summer Wednesdays, when demonstrations are going on (cheesemaking starts at 13:00, most interesting around 14:45). Call ahead to confirm the schedule.

Visiting the Museum: Borrow the essential English translations at the entry, then explore the three floors of exhibits. The ground floor is dedicated to local customs and lifestyles. The replica of the alpine cheesemaking hut is occasionally used for live demonstrations. There's a huge collection of cowbells, which, according to the explanation, are used for various purposes: to scare off evil spirits, to make the lead cow easier to follow in processions, to more easily find a lost cow..."and anyway, cows like them."

Upstairs is an art collection titled "Peasant Painting 1600-1900," with everything from huge murals from the sides of barns to delicate oil paintings to miniature wood carvings—virtually all featuring pastoral countryside scenes of cheesemaking huts, cows, and rolling meadows. Each of the "naive" (untrained) artists who created these works is explained in a short bio, which brings the collection to life. You'll see great examples of the brightly painted traditional regional furniture (also easy to find in local hotels and restaurants).

The basement shows off more furniture pieces (in the replica of a traditional bedroom, notice how the colorful paint makes the furniture stand out from the plain wooden walls). But the focus here is on two other local crafts: weaving and embroidery. The exhibit explains how embroidery gradually evolved from being simple and handmade to machine-made, as it went from a craft to an industry. The rustic loom and the giant embroidery machine are sometimes used for demonstrations.

▲Urnäsch

This appealing one-street town has Europe's cutest museum. It's a 15-minute train ride from Appenzell.

Museum of Appenzell Customs (Appenzeller Brauchtumsmuseum)

Located on the town square across from the church, this museum brings this region's folk traditions to life.

Cost and Hours: 6 CHF, covered by Swiss Travel Pass; daily 9:00-11:30 & 13:30-17:00 except closed Sun morning, shorter hours in off-season; tel. 071-364-2322, www.museum-urnaesch.ch.

Visiting the Museum: Exhibits are displayed on four floors of two adjacent, different-as-day-and-night buildings. The new building is slick and mostly used for temporary exhibits. The 400-year-old, aptly named "Old House" has low ceilings, dramatically sloping funhouse floors, and lots of creaks. Warm and homey, it's a happy little honeycomb of Appenzeller culture—you'll feel like a local invited you over for a visit.

First ask to watch an English showing of the 20-minute movie that explains four of the major regional festivals. The most memorable is Silvesterchläus—the Appenzell New Year, celebrated on January 13 per the old Julian calendar. On this date, local men celebrate by putting on gigantic, cartoonish headdresses and giant cowbells. You'll see some of those costumes—and others—then twist your way up through the tiny halls and staircases, pausing to look at replicas of local rooms, collections of handicrafts and tools, and other slices of Appenzell life. On the top floor of the new building, don't miss the music room, where you can try your hand at traditional musical instruments, including a hammered dulcimer and a coin-in-a-bowl (which, in the right hands, is more musical than you might think). There's no English, and barely any German, but it's still fun to explore.

Kronberg Luge Ride (Bobbahn)

Between Appenzell and Urnäsch, in the village of Jakobsbad, you can enjoy a bobsled ride that runs on steel rails from April through November. Each sled has seatbelts and can carry two people. Two side handles allow you to control the speed: Respect the *Bremsen!* signs—which suggest when to brake. The same entertainment zone includes a chairlift for hikes, as well as a high-ropes course.

Cost and Hours: 9 CHF per sled for adults—two adults can share one sled, 6 CHF per sled for kids—ditto, multiple-ride cards available and shareable; July-mid-Oct daily 9:00-18:00, April-June until 17:00, mid-Oct-Nov 10:00-16:00, closed Dec-March; no rides in rainy weather, tel. 071-794-1289, www.kronberg.ch.

Getting There: The luge is just across the tracks from the Jakobsbad station, which is an 8-minute train trip from Appenzell.

Sleeping in Appenzell Town

Sleep in touristy Appenzell town if you want comfort—but for a rustic, high-altitude thrill, I love the low-tech, no-shower dorms at Ebenalp (listed later). Appenzell town is small, and the hotels are central. The *B&Bs* are a 10- to 20-minute hike from the town center.

HOTELS

$$$ Hotel Adler rents 20 rooms above a delicious café/bakery with the best croissants in town (café closed Wed). The building dates from 1562 and boasts a historic wine cellar. The hotel has two types of rooms: modern or traditional Appenzeller. Helpful Franz Leu has decorated the halls with fun local and family memorabilia (elevator, pleasant garden lounge, small parking lot, a few loaner bikes for guests, closed Feb-mid-March, Weissbadstrasse 2, between TI and bridge on Adlerplatz, tel. 071-787-1389, www.adlerhotel.ch, info@adlerhotel.ch).

$$ Hotel Garni Traube, just off Hauptgasse near Landsgemeindeplatz, rents seven cozy, tastefully decorated, modern rooms in a very pretty building. The friendly Hunziker family has welcomed guests here for three generations, and they still do it with style (Marktgasse 7, tel. 071-787-1407, www.hotel-traube.ch, info@hotel-traube.ch).

B&BS

To experience a pleasant Swiss residential neighborhood, consider the following B&Bs, just east of Appenzell's pedestrian zone. To reach them from the town center (TI/town church), cross the bridge, pass the gas station, then take the next right. You'll reach Koller-Rempfler first (just a few houses down), then—after another 500 yards or so—Haus Lydia. To reach Haus Lydia by public transit, take the train to the Hirschberg station (2 minutes from Appenzell on the line to St. Gallen). From the station, it's a three-minute downhill walk.

$$ Haus Lydia, with six guest rooms on the upper floors of a large, traditional home, is filled with tourist information and a woodsy folk atmosphere. It has a garden and a powerful mountain view. (That's Ebenalp on the horizon.) Its crisp, nicely decorated rooms are a fine option if you have a car or don't mind a 20-minute walk from the town center (great breakfast, Eggerstandenstrasse 53, tel. 071-787-4233, www.hauslydia.ch, contact@hauslydia.ch, friendly Frau Mock-Inauen). She also rents two roomy apartments by the week (no breakfast).

$ At Gästehaus Koller, Stefan and Karin rent four comfortable rooms on the upper floor of their home. Stefan's father,

Niklaus, built all of the furniture, and his wife Karin makes traditional costumes (cash only, Eggerstandenstrasse 9, tel. 071-787-0222, www.gaestehaus-koller.ch, info@gaestehaus-koller.ch).

Eating in Appenzell

TRADITIONAL MEALS WITH TABLE SERVICE

Restaurants in Appenzell's old town cater to locals and day-trippers with classic Swiss-German menus and elaborate desserts. Almost every menu features (surprise) the heavenly but oh-so-smelly Appenzeller cheese. The Appenzeller beer is tasty, famous, and about the only thing cheap in the region. Many top restaurants cluster around the big main square (Landsgemeindeplatz). All of these places are open until about 23:00. Reservations are smart for dinner.

$$$ Restaurant Marktplatz is filled with locals playing cards in a genuine Appenzeller atmosphere. Enjoy the beautifully detailed inlaid tables and the wood-carved wall panels (closed Sun-Tue, Kronengarten 2, on small parking lot across from Landsgemeindeplatz fountain, walk around white building with horse head, tel. 071-787-1204, www.marktplatz-appenzell.ch).

$$$ Gasthaus Hof, which feels particularly local, offers a bewildering variety of specials (from "vitamin corner" to cold dishes to the *Fitnessteller*). There's a pleasant modern beer garden out back, and the cozy dining room is filled with the unforgettable aroma of Appenzeller cheese (daily, Engelgasse 4, tel. 071-787-4030, www.gasthaus-hof.ch).

$$$$ Hotel Appenzell serves from a large menu (with a long list of desserts—they run a pastry shop in one corner of the building) in a genteel dining room and at a few outdoor tables (daily, at corner of Landsgemeindeplatz closest to TI, tel. 071-788-1515, www.hotel-appenzell.ch).

With a View over Town: A steep 15-minute uphill walk or short drive from the town center, **$$$$ Gasthaus Freudenberg** has reasonably priced meals and sweeping panoramas over Appenzell's rooftops from outdoor tables. If you'd like to dine with a view, it's worth the effort (closed Wed and Nov; go under train station, turn right, and follow yellow *Freudenberg* signs through a residential zone, then up through the hills; Riedstrasse 57, tel. 071-787-1240, www.hotel-freudenberg.ch). Drivers can follow the yellow *Freudenberg* signs from near the train station.

CHEAP EATS

$$ Lokal is modern, Italian, and the opposite of every other eatery in Appenzell's old town. This low-key café serves made-to-order focaccia sandwiches, crêpes, and homemade gelato for takeaway or to eat in the mod interior or out front (Tue-Sat 9:00-18:00, Sun from 12:00, closed Mon, am Schmäuslemarkt, tel. 071-787-0115).

$$ Bistro Appetito has good, inexpensive pizzas. Take out or eat in their bright dining room just off Landsgemeindeplatz (closed Mon, Marktgasse 13, mobile 078/893-5676).

Supermarkets and Cafeterias: The **Migros** (with a self-service cafeteria) and **Co-op** supermarkets face each other along Zielstrasse, a five-minute walk downhill from Landsgemeindeplatz (both generally open Mon-Sat 8:00-19:00, closed Sun).

Appenzell Connections

For details on taking the train to destinations within this chapter, see "Getting Around the Appenzell Region" on page 217. For connections beyond the Appenzell region, you'll generally change in either Herisau or Gossau.

From Appenzell Town by Train to: Zürich (3/hour, 2 hours, change in Gossau), **Chur** (hourly, 2 hours, 1-3 changes), **St. Moritz** (hourly, 4.5 hours, change in St. Gallen and Chur), **Luzern** (2/hour, 3 hours, change in Herisau; more with changes in Gossau and Zürich), **Bern** (hourly, 3 hours, change in Gossau), **Interlaken** (hourly, 4.5 hours, change in St. Gallen and Bern), **Lausanne** (2/hour, 4.5 hours, change in Gossau), **Munich** (3/day, 4.5 hours, change in St. Gallen). Train info: Toll tel. 0900-300-300 or www.rail.ch.

Ebenalp

This mountain features wonderful views and a cliff-hanging, family-run hut, providing a lofty "hills-are-alive" alternative to Appenzell town. From Wasserauen—five miles south of Appenzell town by road or rail line—ride the lift up to Ebenalp (5,380 feet), a high, rocky ridge that drops off to vertical cliffs on the southern side. On the way up, you'll get a sneak preview of Ebenalp's cave church and the cliffside boardwalk that leads to the guesthouse (near the top, left side). From the top you'll enjoy a sweeping view north all the way to Lake Constance (Bodensee). Though this excursion is doable in so-so weather, clear skies really enhance the Ebenalp experience—ask in Appenzell before you head

up to the mountain, or check the webcam at www.ebenalp.ch. In any weather, sturdy shoes and rain gear are recommended—the weather can change in the blink of an eye.

Getting There: First, a train takes you from Appenzell to Wasserauen (1-2/hour, 12 minutes). Then, across the road from the Wasserauen station, the Ebenalp lift carries hikers to the summit and back every 15 minutes (20 CHF one-way, 31 CHF round-trip, half-price with Swiss Travel Pass, 6-minute trip, daily July-Aug 7:30-19:00, June and Sept until 18:00, May and Oct 8:00-17:30, mid-Dec-March 9:30-17:00, usually closed April and Nov-mid-Dec—call ahead, free and reportedly safe parking at lift, pick up free hiking map before you ascend, tel. 071-799-1212, www.ebenalp.ch).

Hiking from the Lift Station to Berggasthaus Aescher:

Leaving the lift, look for *Wildkirchli* and *Aescher* signs pointing to the 12-minute hike down to the mountain hut. First you'll hike steeply down under the cables, then you'll hook right and venture downhill through a good-sized natural cave where archaeologists once found the bones of prehistoric bears. It's fairly well-lit but slippery, so watch your step and use the railing—trust me, you'll soon return to daylight. As you emerge into the light, you'll pass a tiny museum (free and always open) in a hut built on the site where hermit monks lived from 1658 to 1853. A few yards farther along the cliff, in a separate cave, is the 400-year-old Wildkirchli church.

Next you'll follow the cliff-hugging path (not for those afraid of steep drop-offs—though there's a sturdy railing) to a 170-year-old, weathered-shingle guesthouse built snugly against the mountain. Originally a hut housing farmers, goats, and cows, it evolved into a guesthouse for pilgrims coming to the monks for spiritual guidance. Today, the recommended Berggasthaus Aescher welcomes tourists, offering cheap dorm beds and hot, hearty plates of *Rösti*. The region is a hit with hikers, who can trek between as many as 24 mountain hotels, each

Map legend:

Ebenalp

To Gais
To Stein
APPENZELL TOWN
To Gontenbad, Jakobsbad & Urnäsch
STEINEGG
WEISSBAD
To Brülisau & Hoher Kasten
Ebenalp 5,380
❶
To Säntis
❸
CAVE
Ⓟ
WASSERAUEN
▲❷
Seealpsee

Note: Appenzell Town to Wasserauen = 5mi / 8km   Not to Scale

❶ Berggasthaus Ebenalp
❷ Berggasthaus Seealpsee
❸ Berggasthaus Aescher

a day's hike apart. All originated as alpine farms. Of these, Berg-gasthaus Aescher is the oldest and smallest.

From the guesthouse's sunny cliffside perch, you can almost hear the cows munching on the far side of the valley. Only the paragliders tag your world as 21st century. In the distance, nestled below Säntis peak, are the isolated **Seealpsee** ("Lake-Alp Lake") and the recommended Berggasthaus Seealpsee.

Returning to the Ebenalp lift from Berggasthaus Aescher: Retrace your steps through the cave (allow 25 minutes for this up-hill hike). Or, for a different and more strenuous return, you can hike up around the back of the mountaintop: As you leave the Berggasthaus, continue straight on the path (skipping the first fork in the trail, which leads down to Seealpsee). After the fork, the path winds you steeply uphill, eventually arriving back at the top of the Ebenalp lift.

Hikes from Berggasthaus Aescher: The trail beyond Berg-gasthaus Aescher leads to a pair of rugged hikes that are worth considering: down to the al-pine lake called Seealpsee (and eventually all the way down to Wasserauen), or up for a steep-but-scenic route back to the Ebenalp lift.

The hike down to Seealp-see, which takes a little over an hour, is steep but rewarding: Take a left at the first fork beyond Berggasthaus Aescher. After some initial knee-jarring switchbacks, the trail gets easier, and as it flattens out, a fork to the right leads in about 10 minutes to the lake. To reach Wasserauen (45 minutes) and the train back to Appenzell, retrace your steps till you reach the nearest fork, but this time take the other path (to the right), which turns into a narrow road.

Sleeping and Eating on Ebenalp

Sleeping: Although Appenzell town offers all the predictable comforts, hardy travelers enjoy overnighting on Ebenalp instead. You'll live by the lift schedule, the facilities are limited (only rain-water), and reaching any of these accommodations involves some steep hiking. But it's an unforgettable place to sleep.

¢ **Berggasthaus Ebenalp** perches just a couple of min-utes' steep walk up from the upper lift station (200-foot eleva-tion gain). There's a paved path up, so it's actually just doable with wheeled luggage. Its rooms are booked long in advance for Saturdays, but are otherwise empty (coin-op rainwater shower, closed same months as lift—usually April and Nov-mid-Dec, restaurant open until 17:30, rooms available Sat only in winter, tel. 071-799-1194, www.gasthaus-ebenalp.ch, infos@gasthaus-ebenalp.ch, Sutter family).

¢ **Berggasthaus Seealpsee** is at a lower altitude on the idyllic alpine Seealpsee, most easily reached by a 50-minute hike up a private road from the Wasserauen train station (private rooms available, includes sheets and showers, closed Nov-mid-April, tel. 071-799-1140, www.seealpsee.ch, info@seealpsee.ch, Parpan-Dörig family).

Eating: Built in 1805, **$ Berggasthaus Aescher** is a memorable place to eat. The hut is actually built into the cliff; its back wall is the rock itself (see photo on page 228). The comfortable dining/living room is filled with happy hikers dining on *Rösti* and sipping coffee spiked with schnapps and topped with whipped cream. For a strenuous 45-minute pre-dinner hike, copy the goats: Take the high trail toward the lake, circle clockwise up toward the peak and the lift, then hike down the way you originally came (closed Nov-April, 12 minutes by steep trail below top of lift, tel. 071-799-1142, www.aescher-ai.ch, swiss@aescher-ai.ch, run by Nicole and Bernhard Knechtle).

You can also eat at the restaurant of the **Berggasthaus Ebenalp,** listed earlier.

Liechtenstein

Appenzell is just an hour away from the tiny and touristy country of Liechtenstein. This quirky remnant of medieval feudal politics is truly landlocked, without a seaport, or even an airport. Liechtensteiners—who number about 37,000—speak German, are mostly Catholic, and have a stubborn independent streak. Women weren't given the vote until 1984.

Liechtenstein is not worth going out of your way for (unless you collect stamps—postal or passport), but it's a no-brainer detour if you happen to be driving south from Appenzell toward Chur or the Upper Engadine (Pontresina/St. Moritz).

Vaduz

Low-key Vaduz, with about 5,000 people, feels basically like a midsized Swiss town. Its pedestrianized main drag is lined with modern art and hotels bordering a district of slick office parks.

Like other "micro-countries," Liechtenstein offers businesses special tax and accounting incentives. Many European companies establish their official headquarters here to take advantage of its low taxes.

Getting There: Heading south on the A-13 expressway from Appenzell, the road actually skirts Liechtenstein just across the Rhine (the border). For a 30-minute detour, exit at Buchs and turn toward Schaan. After crossing the border (without stopping, or likely even noticing), you'll wind up in the town of Schaan. Follow signs (south/right) toward Vaduz, the capital of the Principality of Liechtenstein (Fürstentum Liechtenstein, or FL for short on its sleek black license plates).

Visiting Vaduz: Various parking lots and garages are along the main street, Äulestrasse. Try to park directly under the looming castle. If you park at the Marktplatz garage, you can simply walk one block up to the pedestrian zone called Städtle, where you'll run right into the TI (at #39, tel. from Switzerland 00-423/239-6363, www.tourismus.li). The TI will stamp your passport for 3 CHF.

Go for a stroll along enjoyable Städtle street. Use Swiss francs or euros to buy a postcard and some Liechtenstein stamps to send to the collector in your life (but be sure to write and send it before leaving the country).

The prince's striking castle, a 20-minute hike above Vaduz, is closed to the public, but there's a fine view from the grounds (find the trail near Café Burg). The billionaire prince, who looks down on his six-by-twelve-mile country, wields more real political power in his realm than any other member of European royalty. The Liechtenstein family purchased this piece of real estate from the Holy Roman Emperor. In 1719, the domain was granted principality status, answering only to the emperor. In 1806, during the age of Napoleon, Liechtenstein's obligations to the Habsburg emperor disappeared, and the country was granted true independence.

The Liechtenstein princes, who lived near Vienna, saw their country merely as a status symbol, and at first didn't even bother to visit. In fact, it wasn't until the 20th century that the first Liechtenstein prince actually lived here. Later, after World War I, tough times forced the principality to enter an economic union with Switzerland. To this day Liechtenstein enjoys a very close working relationship with its Swiss neighbors—functioning in some ways like just another Swiss canton, with the same currency, international diplomacy, bus system, and even soccer league.

Leaving Vaduz: After visiting the castle grounds, you'll quickly run out of things to do. No problem—just head back to

Switzerland. Continue south through town on Äulestrasse, turn right at the well-marked *Schweiz* sign, cross back over the Rhine, and you're back in Switzerland (and on the A-13 expressway)... ready to check another country off your list. Or, if you're headed northeast toward Austria, drive back north through Schaan, then up to Feldkirch.

LAKE GENEVA &
FRENCH SWITZERLAND

Lausanne • Château de Chillon • Montreux • Gruyères • Diablerets Region

Lake Geneva, in the southwest corner of the country, is the Swiss Riviera. Separating France and Switzerland, the lake is surrounded by Alps and lined with a collage of castles, museums, spas, resort towns, and vineyards. The elegant French-style villas that grace the lakeshore—with pastel colors, frilly balconies, and characteristic mansard roofs—give it an air of gentility. This area is so beautiful that Charlie Chaplin and Idi Amin both chose it as their second home.

French is the predominant language at Lake Geneva ("Lac Léman" in French, "Genfersee" in German). To establish a better connection with the locals, see the "French Survival Phrases" in the appendix, *s'il vous plaît.*

Skip the big, dull city of Geneva; instead, sleep in fun, breezy Lausanne. Explore the romantic Château de Chillon and stylishly syncopated Montreux. It's also worth taking one day to delve into the French Swiss countryside, which offers up rolling green foothills topped with castles; chocolates, vineyards, and Gruyère cheese galore; a high-mountain excursion to give you a quick dose of the Alps; and picturesque towns tucked into the folds of the hillsides.

PLANNING YOUR TIME

On a quick trip, you can get a good overview of Lake Geneva's highlights in a day. Lausanne makes the best home base. If you're

Lake Geneva and French Switzerland at a Glance

▲▲▲**Château de Chillon** Medieval castle perched romantically on eastern shore of Lake Geneva, with climbable ramparts, damp dungeons, and literary history. See page 257.

▲▲**Lausanne** Twisty, 3-D city stretching up a steep hill from the lakefront, with pleasant old town, plenty of sights—most notably the Olympic and Art Brut museums—and easy boat and train connections to the surrounding area. See page 235.

▲▲**Gruyères** Storybook small town overlooking dreamy countryside, with worthwhile nearby sights, including a folk museum, cheese- and chocolate-making factories, and a mini mountain with views of the Lake Geneva basin. See page 263.

▲▲**Diablerets Region** Remote-feeling area high up in the hills, with the sloping little village of Gryon, and the majestic Les Diablerets mountaintop. See page 272.

▲**Montreux** Relaxed lakeside resort offering few sights—just sublime views of the misty lake and cut-glass peaks, and immediate access to the Golden Pass and Chocolate Train scenic rail lines. See page 261.

in a hurry, make a beeline for Château de Chillon. With more time, lazily float your way between Lausanne and Chillon on a scenic boat cruise, and get lost in Lausanne's old town and unique museums (the Art Brut and Olympic museums).

The French Swiss countryside to the east is worth exploring, especially if you have a third day for the region. It's most convenient by car, but also doable by train. If you're heading to the Berner Oberland from here with a car, carve out some time for the Gruyères region en route, or consider a longer detour via Gryon and Les Diablerets. Without wheels, you can get a good, quick taste of the Gruyères region's sights—and a peek at its scenery—on the convenient Chocolate Train, which departs from Montreux.

GETTING AROUND LAKE GENEVA

By Train: You can easily connect towns along Lake Geneva via train. Take a faster IR (interregional) train if you're going between larger cities, such as Lausanne or Montreux, or a slower "S" train (regional) if you're heading for a smaller destination, such as Château de Chillon.

By Boat: Daily boat trips connect Lausanne with Vevey (1 hour, 21 CHF), Montreux (1.5 hours, 27 CHF), Château de Chil-

lon (2 hours, 29 CHF), and points in between. These run about four times per day in each direction (late June-early Sept, fewer in shoulder season, virtually none mid-Oct-mid-April). First class costs about 40 percent more and gets you passage on the deck up top, where you should scramble for the first-come, first-served chairs. You can sail free with a Swiss Travel Pass (but it uses up a travel day of a flexipass) or get 50 percent off with a Eurail pass that includes Switzerland (does not use a day of pass); to avoid giving up a day just for the cruise, take an afternoon cruise on the same day you arrive by train in the morning (tel. 0848-811-848, www.cgn.ch).

Study the schedule (available online, at TIs, and in boat ticket windows) to find a cruise that appeals to you—there's a variety to choose from. For just a quick hop on the water, the 15-minute cruise between Montreux and Château de Chillon is fun. The pretty town of Vevey, between Montreux and Lausanne, is enjoyable for a short stop. A separate line runs from Lausanne directly across the lake to Evian-les-Bains, the French spa town famous for its mineral water (hourly, 35 minutes, passport required).

Lausanne

Lausanne is the most interesting city on the lake, proudly dubbing itself the "Olympic Capital" (it's been home to the International Olympic Committee since 1915). Amble along the serene lakefront promenade, stroll through the three-tiered, colorful old town, explore the sculptures at Olympic Park, and visit the remarkable Art Brut museum. Take a peek at

the Gothic cathedral, and climb its tower for the view.

The Romans founded Lausanne on the lakefront—but with the fall of Rome and the rise of the barbarians, the first Lausanners fled for the hills, establishing today's old town. The Roman site was abandoned (scant ruins survive), but in the age of tourism, the waterfront—a district called Ouchy—was revived. The city thus has a design problem that goes back 1,500 years: two charming zones separated by a nondescript residential/industrial section. Thank-

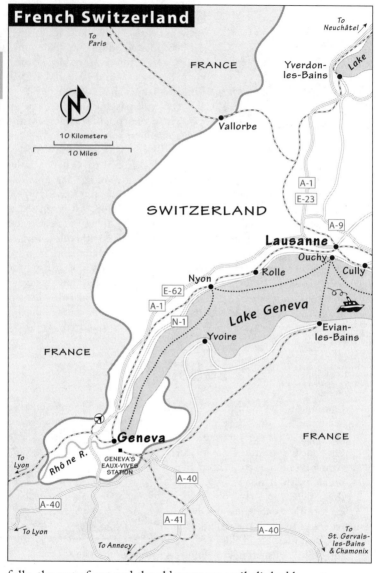

French Switzerland

fully, the waterfront and the old town are easily linked by a steep, handy Métro line (that runs every few minutes).

Lausanne has the energy and cultural sophistication of a larger city, but is home to only about 130,000 people (350,000 in the greater area). A progressive city government (with a mayor from the Green Party) that subsidizes art and culture, and a university with plenty of foreign students carbonate the place with a youthful spirit.

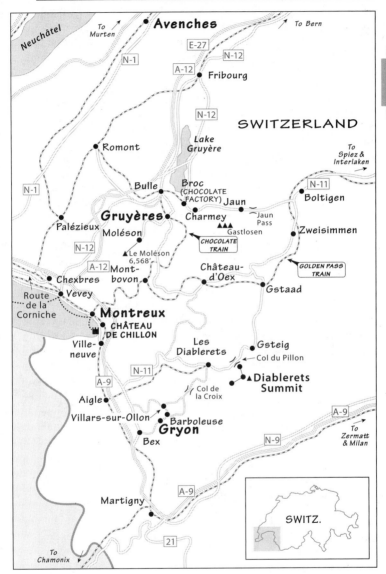

Orientation to Lausanne

The tourist's Lausanne has two parts: the lakefront **Ouchy** (oo-SHEE), with a breezy resort ambience and the Olympic Museum; and the **old town,** with creaky Old World charm and fine museums, directly uphill from the lake. The old town district is divided roughly into two adjacent parts: the true old town, or *vieille ville* (vee-yay veel), near the cathedral; and the city center, or *centre-ville*, with my favorite hotels and restaurants. The train station is located between Ouchy and the old town, and it's all connected by the slick Métro.

Walking around Lausanne's old town feels like a life-size game of Chutes and Ladders. Two-dimensional maps don't do justice to the city's bridges, underpasses, stairways, hills, and valleys. Even the Métro trains and platforms are on an incline. Plan to feel confused by the street plan at first. The model of old Lausanne in the City History Museum helps you understand how it developed.

Be careful to pronounce Lausanne correctly (loh-ZAHN), and don't confuse it with Luzern. Sundays are pin-drop quiet in the city. And more than just about anywhere I can think of, using public transit here is a joy.

TOURIST INFORMATION

Lausanne has two full-service TIs: One is at the train station's main entrance, and the other is at the lakefront Ouchy Métro stop, in a blue pavilion (both open daily 9:00-19:00, Oct-March until 18:00, tel. 021-613-7373, www.lausanne-tourisme.ch).

At the TI, ask about multilingual **walking tours** (10 CHF, pay guide directly, May-Sept Mon-Sat usually at 10:00 and 14:30, 2 hours, meet in front of Town Hall at Place de la Palud, www.lausanne-a-pied.ch). The language situation is potluck, depending on the guide and the tourists who show up. Most guides speak English, but not all; the TI has a list, so check with them in advance, or directly with Lausanne-à-Pied at tel. 021-320-1261. (If you have to share your tour with another language, my self-guided "Old Lausanne Walk," later, will probably be more informative.)

Be sure to ask about concerts (free and otherwise)—especially organ concerts at the cathedral. If you're here between mid-June and late September—prime time for cultural events—pick up the TI's free *Lausanne Estivale* program.

ARRIVAL IN LAUSANNE

By Train: The train station, with lockers, WCs, ticket office (Mon-Fri 6:00-20:30, Sat-Sun 6:30-20:00), late-night groceries, and a Métro stop, is midway between the old town and the lakefront. This sounds inconvenient, but the Métro takes you either up to the Old Town or down to the lake in less than five minutes, with constant departures. A **taxi** from the train station to your hotel runs a steep 15 CHF, and the Métro is probably faster anyway.

By Car: Driving is tricky in this nearly vertical city—especially in the twisty old town. Avoid headaches by leaving your car at a park-and-ride (labeled *P+R*); several flank the city and are well-connected by Métro to the old town (17 CHF/day covers parking

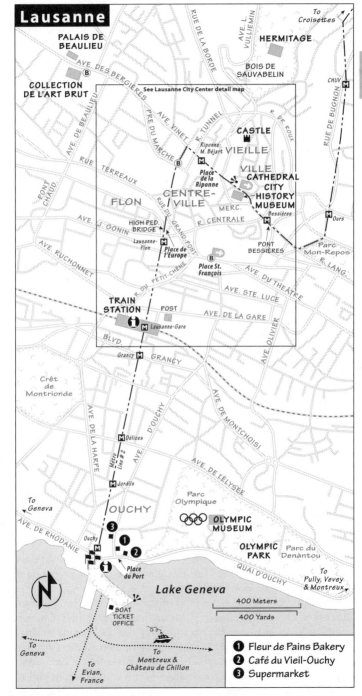

LAKE GENEVA

Lausanne

PALAIS DE BEAULIEU

COLLECTION DE L'ART BRUT

HERMITAGE

BOIS DE SAUVABELIN

AVE. DES BERGIÈRES

AVE. DE BEAULIEU

RUE TERREAUX

PONT CHAUD

AVE. J. GONIN

AVE. RUCHONNET

See Lausanne City Center detail map

RUE DE LA BORDE

AVE. L. VULLIEMIN

RUE DE BUGNON

CHUV

To Croisettes

AVE. YINET

R. TUNNEL

CASTLE

VIEILLE

R. DE ROUX

Riponne-M. Béjart

Place de la Riponne

VILLE

CATHEDRAL

CITY HISTORY MUSEUM

Ours

PRÉ DU MARCHÉ

FLON

CENTRE-VILLE

RUE DE GRAND-PONT

MERC.

R. CENTRALE

Bessières

Parc Mon-Repos

R. LANG.

HIGH PED. BRIDGE

Lausanne-Flon

Place de l'Europe

PONT BESSIÈRES

R. DU PETIT-CHÊNE

Place St. François

AVE. DU THÉÂTRE

AVE. STE. LUCE

TRAIN STATION

POST

Lausanne-Gare

AVE. DE LA GARE

AVE. OLIVIER

BLVD.

Grancy

GRANCY

Crêt de Montriond

AVE. DE LA HARPE

AVE. D'OUCHY

AVE. DE MONTCHOISI

Métro Line #2

Délices

Jordils

AVE. DE L'ÉLYSÉE

OUCHY

Parc Olympique

OLYMPIC MUSEUM

To Geneva

AVE. DE RHODANIE

Ouchy

OLYMPIC PARK

Parc du Denantou

To Pully, Vevey & Montreux

QUAI D'OUCHY

Place du Port

Lake Geneva

400 Meters

400 Yards

N

BOAT TICKET OFFICE

To Geneva

To Montreux & Château de Chillon

To Evian, France

❶ Fleur de Pains Bakery
❷ Café du Vieil-Ouchy
❸ Supermarket

and transit into center). If you're coming in on the freeway from the north (such as from Bern), get off at the *Vennes* exit and use the covered park-and-ride garage by the Vennes Métro stop. Or stay on the freeway as it loops down to *Lausanne Sud,* ending near the Ouchy park-and-ride, close to the base station of the Métro. If you're approaching on the lakeside road from the east (such as from Montreux), follow blue signs along the lakeshore directly to Ouchy. For more information, go to www.lausanne.ch/stationnement.

By Boat: From the dock, veer left toward the plaza with the flagpoles. Across the street is the TI and Métro station.

By Plane: Lausanne and the Lake Geneva area are served by the Geneva airport, at the lake's southwest corner. The airport sits on the western edge of Geneva, straddling the French border. For more on the airport, and how to get to town from there, see "Lausanne Connections," later.

HELPFUL HINTS

Market Days: On Wednesday and Saturday mornings, produce stands fill the pedestrian streets of the old town. Saturday is flea market day on Place de la Riponne.

Wi-Fi: Free city-run Wi-Fi is available at several points around town (such as Place de la Riponne, Place de la Palud, Place St-François, and the waterfront square in Ouchy)—look for the "Ville de Lausanne" network.

Laundry: Quick-Wash is well-run and handy to the train station (self-service, daily 8:00-22:00, English instructions, below station at Boulevard de Grancy 44, mobile 079-449-3761). Exit behind the train station (down the stairs past track 9), turn right, then head left down Passage de Montriond to the corner.

Bike Rental: A bike is pretty worthless in this steep city, but it's great for exploring the lakefront, vineyards, and nearby villages. It's a three-hour waterfront pedal from Ouchy to Montreux and back. A city-sponsored program offers cheap rental bikes; you can arrange this lakeside, at the Ouchy TI.

GETTING AROUND LAUSANNE

By Public Transport: Lausanne's nifty **Métro** and **bus** network makes it easy to get around. The Métro has two lines (converging at the Lausanne-Flon stop in the city center), but only line #2 is useful for travelers. Using it is simple: up (direction: Croisettes) or down (direction: Ouchy/Olympique). This inclined 14-stop line (which is completely automated—don't try to delay the doors from closing) climbs up from the lakefront to the old town, then all the way up to the freeway. The key stops are Ouchy (at the lakefront); Lausanne-Gare (at the train station); Lausanne-Flon (at the bottom end of the Old Town—exit into Place de l'Europe, ride the elevator up to the pedestrian bridge, and stroll straight into the town center); and Riponne-M. Béjart (at the top end of the old town, on Place de la Riponne). You're unlikely to need the bus, except to reach the Art Brut museum. For transit info, visit www.t-l.ch.

If you're sleeping in Lausanne, your hotel should give you a Mobilis Card, which covers local transit and is paid for by your hotel tax. Otherwise, unless you have a Swiss Travel Pass, you'll need to buy tickets from the friendly ticket machines (with English instructions). Tickets are valid on both Métro and buses. A short-ride ticket, valid for 30 minutes and up to three stops, costs 2.10 CHF. A single ticket is valid for an hour and costs 3.60 CHF, and an all-day ticket (valid 6:00-24:00) costs 9.30 CHF. Almost everything in this book is in the central zone 11. If you're headed a bit farther (such as to Lutry or the Vennes park-and-ride), you might cross into zone 12—this costs a bit more. But the Mobilis Card will take you well into the countryside and to some lakeside villages.

By Taxi: Cabs are pricey—figure 15 CHF for a short ride.

Old Lausanne Walk

There's no way to see this town without lots of climbing. Locals are used to it (enjoy the firm legs). This self-guided stroll introduces you to both parts of Lausanne's charming old town, starting in *centre-ville* near the Church of St. Francis and ending in *vieille ville near* the cathedral.

❶ Lausanne-Flon Métro Station
This is where you're most likely to arrive in town.
• *From the Métro stop, ride the elevator up to the high pedestrian bridge (Passerelle du Flon). Orient yourself from midway across the bridge, which leads to the city's main thoroughfare. Start by looking west (toward the solitary gray skyscraper)...*

❷ Passerelle du Flon View
Below you stretches Flon (the "Quartier du Flon")—once a ravine of the Flon River, then a down-and-dirty industrial zone, and

now—so typical of post-industrial 21st-century Europe—a thriving people zone. Its old warehouses are throbbing at night with trendy bars, restaurants, theaters, and discos. The recommended Vinothèque Nomade restaurant is immediately below. The only reminder of the mills that once churned here is the name of the hot-

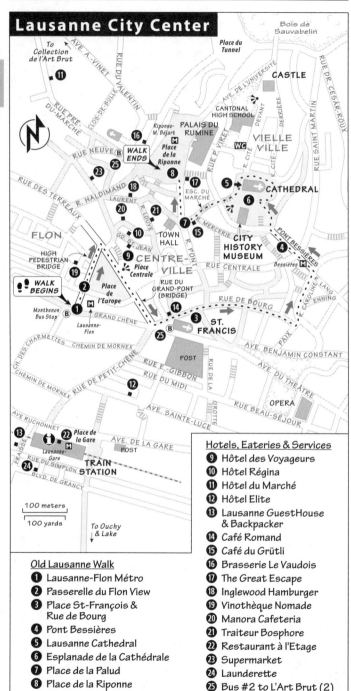

Lausanne City Center

Bois de Sauvabelin

Place du Tunnel

To Collection de l'Art Brut

11

CASTLE

CANTONAL HIGH SCHOOL

PALAIS DU RUMINE

Ripponne-M. Béjart

16

WALK ENDS

Place de la Riponne

25

23

VIELLE VILLE

WC

8

18

17

ESC. DU MARCHÉ

5

CATHEDRAL

6

RUE NEUVE

RUE DES TERREAUX

R. HALDIMAND

LAURENT

20

21

K. LOUVE

10

TOWN HALL

7

CITY HISTORY MUSEUM

15

PONT BESSIÈRES

4

Bessières

FLON

HIGH PEDESTRIAN BRIDGE

19

CENTRE-VILLE

9

Place Centrale

RUE CENTRALE

2

Place de l'Europe

RUE DU GRAND-PONT (BRIDGE)

RUE DE BOURG

WALK BEGINS

1

Montbenon Bus Stop

Lausanne-Flon

GRAND CHÊNE

14

3

ST. FRANCIS

25

CHEMIN DE MORNEX

POST

AVE. BENJAMIN CONSTANT

CH. DES CHARMETTES

RUE E. GIBBON

RUE DE PETIT-CHÊNE

RUE DU MIDI

12

AVE. SAINTE-LUCE

AVE. DU THÉÂTRE

RUE BEAU-SÉJOUR

OPERA

AVE. RUCHONNET

13

22

Place de la Gare

AVE. DE LA GARE

POST

FRAISSE

Lausanne-Gare

RUE DU SIMPLON

TRAIN STATION

24

BLVD. DE GRANCY

100 meters

100 yards

To Ouchy & Lake

Hotels, Eateries & Services

9 Hôtel des Voyageurs
10 Hôtel Régina
11 Hôtel du Marché
12 Hôtel Elite
13 Lausanne GuestHouse & Backpacker
14 Café Romand
15 Café du Grütli
16 Brasserie Le Vaudois
17 The Great Escape
18 Inglewood Hamburger
19 Vinothèque Nomade
20 Manora Cafeteria
21 Traiteur Bosphore
22 Restaurant à l'Etage
23 Supermarket
24 Launderette
25 Bus #2 to L'Art Brut (2)

Old Lausanne Walk

1 Lausanne-Flon Métro
2 Passerelle du Flon View
3 Place St-François & Rue de Bourg
4 Pont Bessières
5 Lausanne Cathedral
6 Esplanade de la Cathédrale
7 Place de la Palud
8 Place de la Riponne

test dance club in town: MàD (which stands for "Moulin à Danse" or "Dance at the Mill;" it's just out of sight at Rue de Genève 23). The Bel Air Tower (to the right) is famous as the country's first skyscraper (1932). The more elegant building, far to the left in the trees, was the 19th-century home of the Swiss Supreme Court.

Turn around and look down on the green rooftop of the Métro station (where different local plants grow all year). Scan this human coral reef of a city. Look for the viaduct, built in the 19th century as a double set of arches to cross the ravine. Now, as the city has evolved, only the top set of arches is visible.

• *Walk to where the pedestrian bridge hits the busy street, Rue du Grand-Pont. Head right toward the green copper spire of the Church of St. Francis. As you walk along Rue du Grand-Pont, enjoy lovely views of the cathedral on your left and the grassy Métro station on the right, with its vertical garden and colorful map of the Métro system. You'll soon reach...*

❸ Place St-François & Rue de Bourg

The Church of St. Francis marks the town's center and transportation hub. The square is lined with jewelry stores. Across the busy street stands the grand post office, a belle époque building from the days when post offices were a big deal. It's flanked by two also-grand banks (always a big deal in Switzerland). The church is Gothic, founded by Franciscans in the 13th century. But in 1536, it went Protestant—and was gutted of decorations. Later, a grand Baroque organ was installed. The church's locally quarried stones, laid 500 years ago, cleaned up quite nicely. The brass plaques in the pavement feature the names of children born in the city hospital on full-moon nights in the year 1998 (notice how multicultural the names are). These plaques celebrate the creation of the rustic fountain that replaced a much larger horse trough (this was once the wagon entry point of town).

As you leave the square, heading up the pedestrianized Rue de Bourg, the multiethnic makeup of today's Switzerland (one of the most multicultural countries in Europe) is on parade. At the first corner (Rue St. François), glance downhill—it's lined with circa 1960 St. Francis signposts. Rue de Bourg is lined with top-end shops. Blondels (on the left) is still hand-making chocolate in this location after 150 years. Notice the fine architecture above the noisy storefronts. On Wednesdays and Saturdays this street is filled with market stalls.

• *When the street ends, turn left, continuing uphill and over the bridge toward the cathedral.*

❹ Pont Bessières

Pause midbridge and enjoy the view—similar to the earlier Passerelle du Flon view but higher up. Find the skyscraper, the courthouse, and the Jura Mountains in the distance (border of France). And notice how the old river valley below is built over. The railing you may be leaning on is designed to discourage suicidal people from leaping. While Switzerland seems to have it all, its mindset can be conservative, and the orderliness can be stressful. For whatever reason, Switzerland illustrates how money doesn't always buy happiness.

Walking toward the cathedral, you'll notice that Lausanne's old town—filling the highest hill in town with administration buildings, offices, schools, and apartments—is subdued compared to the commercial center.

• *Climb up, with the patch of grass on your left, past the City History Museum to the cathedral. We'll enjoy the view terrace in a bit. But first, check out the biggest church in the country.*

❺ Lausanne Cathedral (Cathédrale de Lausanne)

Lausanne's cathedral is an Evangelical Reform Church, meaning that it belongs to the tradition of the early Protestant reformer John Calvin. Iconoclasm, the removal of religious symbols, suited the Calvinists well. The once-ornate cathedral, originally dedicated to Mary, was cleared of all its statues and decorations. Its frescoes were plastered over, and its colorful windows were trashed and replaced by plain ones. But, thankfully, there's still a lot to see.

Cost and Hours: Free, daily 9:00-19:00, Oct-March until 17:30; www.cathedrale-lausanne.ch.

Visiting the Church: Step inside. The **pipe organ** above the main door is American-made by Fisk, a Boston company that won the commission and installed it in 2003. Locals love their organ and figure its cost (four million CHF) was money well spent. Organ concerts here take place on some Friday evenings (check the schedule at www.grandesorgues.ch, or ask at the cathedral welcome center or TI). Look back at its 7,000 pipes: The "stiletto in Oz" design represents the wings of angels.

Admire the **stained glass.** The **rose window** in the south (right) transept has the church's only surviving 13th-century glass. The rest of the glass dates from the early 1900s. Don't miss the bold and clearly labeled scenes in the apse. The north (left) transept has some dreamy blue Art Nouveau scenes.

The **Mary Chapel,** below the rose window (and just to the left), was the most elaborate chapel in the church. In 1536, it was scraped clean of anything fancy or hinting of the Virgin Mary.

Look at the bits of surviving original paint, and imagine the church in its colorful glory six centuries ago. Also notice the stamp for the "pilgrims' passport." This church is a stop on one of the many pilgrimage routes across Europe that funnel hikers to the Camino de Santiago in northern Spain. If you're on a pilgrimage of any sort, take a stamp. But a much better pilgrim's experience is in the adjacent painted portal.

The painted portal (on the right side of the nave, as you face the altar) was the church's main entrance in the Middle Ages.

 Today, it's glassed in to protect its remarkable painted Gothic statuary. Imagine being a pilgrim approaching this beautifully painted main entrance to one of the great churches of Europe: On the left are six Old Testament prophets and on the right are six apostles—all standing upon symbols of evil and welcoming you with benevolent smiles; high above you, Jesus is about to crown Mary "Queen of Heaven." And then you step inside.

The Tower: In the back-right corner of the church you'll find a small **TI/welcome center** and gift shop, and the entrance to the tower climb (224 steps, grand lake views, lots of Alps, 5 CHF).

Since the Middle Ages, a **night watchman** has lived in the church's tower. As the city was originally built of wood, fire was a constant fear. His job: to watch for fires and to call out the hours. The city is made of stone today—so there's little danger of fire—and people wear their Swiss timekeepers on their wrists. Nevertheless, Lausanne's night watchman, the last one of his kind in Switzerland, still calls out the hours. Every night on the hour, from 22:00 to 2:00 in the morning, he steps onto his balcony and hollers. His first announcement: "I am the watchman. I am the watchman. We just had 10 o'clock. We just had 10 o'clock."

• *Back outside, belly up to the fine viewpoint immediately in front of the cathedral.*

➏ Esplanade de la Cathédrale

On a clear day, look beyond the spire of the Church of St. Francis to see the French Alps (Chamonix and Mont Blanc, over there somewhere, are just out of sight). Evian-les-Bains, the famous French spa town, is immediately opposite Lausanne. On the right, the soft, rolling Jura Mountains, which mark the border of France and Switzerland, stretch all the way from Lake Geneva to Germany.

• *Notice that across the square from the cathedral is the **City History Museum** (described later, under "Sights in Lausanne"). Now might be a good time to visit.*

A covered wooden staircase (Escaliers du Marché) leads down from the cathedral's front door. At the top of the stairs, a sign points to **Chemin de St. Jacques** *("The Way of St. James"—you'll see the stylized seashell icon of the Camino de Santiago pilgrimage near the next set of stairs). Head through the tunnel under the busy road (note the fine view back at the cathedral from just after the tunnel). Continue down the covered steps, pass the recommended Café du Grütli, and land on a long and narrow cobbled square.*

❼ Place de la Palud

This square is marked by its colorful Fountain of Justice. Since 1585 this blindfolded figure of Justice, holding her sword and scales, has commanded fairness as she stands triumphantly over kings and bishops. Imagine the neighborhood moms sending kids here to fetch water in the days before plumbing. Behind the fountain is a mechanical clock, which has animated figures that perform with recorded French narration every hour, on the hour (9:00-19:00). The Town Hall at the bottom of the square dates from 1685.

• *Uphill from Town Hall, Rue de la Madeleine leads to the vast and modern...*

❽ Place de la Riponne

The Palais du Rumine (former university), overlooking the square, now houses a collection of museums (all of which are skippable).

• *Your tour is over.* **The Great Escape,** *a fun hamburger bar with a nice selection of beers, fills the terrace a few steps above (between the square and the cathedral tower; see "Eating in Lausanne," later). There's a free WC on the first floor of the Palais du Rumine. To reach the* **Collection de l'Art Brut,** *walk about 10 minutes or catch bus #2 from Rue Neuve (a block west of Place de la Riponne, across the street from the blocky church). To head down to the lakefront* **Ouchy district,** *ride the Métro from this square (the Riponne–M. Béjart stop). Or simply enjoy poking around more of the old town's twisty lanes.*

Sights in Lausanne

IN AND NEAR THE OLD TOWN

▲City History Museum (Musée Historique de Lausanne)

This museum, housed in what was the bishop's residence (facing the cathedral), has nicely presented displays that trace life in Lausanne from Roman times to the present (look for English fliers in each room).

Cost and Hours: 8 CHF, covered by Swiss Travel Pass, Tue-Thu 11:00-18:00, Fri-Sun until 17:00, closed Mon except July-Aug 11:00-18:00, Place de la Cathédrale 4, tel. 021-315-4101, www.lausanne.ch/mhl.

Visiting the Museum: The highlight for many is the 1:200-scale model of Lausanne in the 17th century (when you enter the museum, request to hear the 18-minute recorded English commentary on the model, and they'll book you a time). While you wait for the commentary to begin, head downstairs and follow the one-way route of "Lausanne Through the Ages."

The model, in the last room of the bottom floor, is based on an engraving from 1638 (see copy on wall). It will give you a feel

for how this hilly city and its quirky street plan developed. You're viewing the town from the perspective of the lakefront district of Ouchy, with the Church of St. Francis in the foreground. You can see river valleys that have since been built over by the modern city. The little water mills mark the birthplace of industrial

Flon. Though the city's walls are long gone, its vineyards survive. The adjacent room shows the construction of the Grand-Pont.

Rounding out the collection are several rooms upstairs dedicated to the Bernese epoch (Protestant, 1536-1798), Lausanne silver from the 18th century, a collection of musical instruments, an exhibit about the beginnings of the modern era, and several temporary exhibits.

▲▲Collection de l'Art Brut

This well-displayed, thought-provoking collection shows art produced by untrained artists, many labeled (and even locked up) by society as "criminal" or "insane."

Cost and Hours: 10 CHF, covered by Swiss Travel Pass, Tue-Sun 11:00-18:00, closed Mon except July-Aug, bags must be checked in lockers, Avenue des Bergières 11, tel. 021-315-2570, www.artbrut.ch.

Getting There: From the Old Town, the museum is an easy 10-minute walk (west from Place de la Riponne) or bus ride (#2 to the Beaulieu-Jomini stop, direction: Désert, frequent service from Place St-François or from Rue Neuve near Place de la Riponne). From the train station, take bus #3 or #21 (also very frequent, direction: Bellevaux or Blécherette). The museum is across from the big building marked "Beaulieu."

Visiting the Museum: In 1945, artist Jean Dubuffet began collecting art he called "Brut"—created by untrained, highly original individuals who

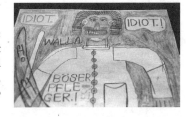

weren't afraid to ignore rules. In the 1970s, he donated his huge collection to Lausanne, and it has now expanded to 60,000 works by hundreds of artists—loners, mavericks, fringe people, prisoners, and mental-ward patients. Dubuffet said, "The art does not lie in beds ready-made for it. It runs away when its name is called. It wants to be incognito."

The works are displayed (perhaps fittingly) without much rhyme or reason on four floors. About 800 works are on display at any given time. Read thumbnail biographies of these outsiders (posted next to their works), and then enjoy their unbridled creativity. As you tour the thought-provoking collection and learn about the artists, ponder the fine line that separates sanity and insanity when it comes to creative output.

IN OUCHY, LAUSANNE'S WATERFRONT

The lazy resort charm of Lausanne lies on its lakefront. The place is lively from Easter through October, and dead otherwise. The handy Métro connects Ouchy with the train station and the old town every few minutes.

Before you leave the Métro, notice the parade of Olympic athletes literally hanging from the ceiling. Walk straight out (past a fine TI) to the main road (Quai d'Ouchy). There are several restaurants a block to the left. Also to the left, across the street, notice the grand Hotel Château d'Ouchy. It was built around a 13th-century tower—a reminder of Lausanne's importance in the Middle Ages. Before the hotel gates is an Olympic countdown clock (marking the days, and even seconds, remaining until both the next winter and summer games). Continuing past the hotel, you'll pass an elaborate kids' playground on the left and a sprawling festival zone on the right before reaching the lakefront. Environmentalism is popular in this city, which boasts 300 square feet of green space per inhabitant—more than nearly any city in Europe.

At the lake, you'll find the departure docks for various boat cruises (see below). The big C-shaped **weathervane** stands on the breakwater, indicating to sailors if the wind is *vaudaire* (roughly southeast, over the lake from Montreux), *bise* (northerly), *joran* (northwest), or *vent* (southwest). It's a puzzle, as the "C" is designed to line up with the semicircle cutouts in the four pillars. Crouch down, match the "C" with the pillar that creates an "O," then look down at the pavement for the corresponding name of today's wind. A five-minute stroll farther along the lake takes you to Ouchy's main attraction, the Olympic Museum and Park (described later).

Boat Rides

Several boat cruises leave from the dock at Ouchy. The solar-powered **Aquarel tour boats**—quiet, smooth, slow, and green—

run on the hour (12 CHF, 40-minute tours in good weather, no narration—chill out, May-Sept Wed-Sun 14:00-19:00, mobile 079-754-0535, www.lesaquarelsduleman.ch). Lake Geneva **cruise boats** leave from the piers just to the left (see "Getting Around Lake Geneva," earlier). Stop by dock 3, next to the main boat-ticket office, to find information about the eight still-steaming historic paddleboats (1904-1927).

▲▲Olympic Museum and Park
(Le Musée et Parc Olympique)

This museum celebrates the colorful history of the Olympic Games. It's set in a beautiful lakeside park where the Olympic flame flick-

ers between editions of the games. The exhibits and park celebrate the ideals of Pierre de Coubertin, who in 1894 founded the International Olympic Committee and restarted the games after a 1,500-year lapse. Coubertin acknowledged that to ask nations to love one another was naive, but to ask them to respect one another was a realistic and worthy goal.

The museum is a thrill for Olympics buffs—and plenty of fun for those of us who just watch every two years. This is your chance to see Jesse Owens' spiked jumping shoes, Katarina Witt's red skating dress, a basketball signed by the 1992 American "Dream Team," and Cathy Freeman's running shoes. The exhibits are lively (with plenty of fun, interactive stations designed to keep kids' attention), and stools scattered liberally throughout let you rest your feet while listening to the audioguide.

Cost and Hours: 18 CHF, family deals, free with Swiss Travel Pass, cash or Visa (an Olympic sponsor) only; daily 9:00-18:00, mid-Oct-April Tue-Sun 10:00-18:00, closed Mon; worthwhile audioguide-5 CHF, Quai d'Ouchy 1, tel. 021-621-6511, www.olympic.org/museum.

Getting There: From the Ouchy Métro stop, turn left and walk five minutes along the water to the big, white fountain, then walk up the stairs. On the way, you'll pass the Beau-Rivage Palace, Lausanne's venerable belle époque hotel, which, since 1857, has hosted a glamorous guest list that includes Winston Churchill, Woody Allen, Charlie Chaplin, Dizzy Gillespie, Liz Taylor, and, uh, Richard Nixon.

Visiting the Museum: Entering the building, you'll pass under a high-jump bar set at the current Olympic record level. Imagine trying to clear it yourself—these are no average feats.

The exhibits span three levels. You'll start on the upper floor (part 1), which covers the history of the games and their organization. You'll learn how the Olympics were born in ancient Greece, then reconceived by French aristocrat Pierre de Coubertin (1863-1937). Coubertin, a progressive thinker with socialist leanings, believed that strict French schools needed more physical education. He looked to British traditions as a model, and worked with British and Greek educators to hold the first modern games in Athens in 1896. Fourteen nations participated (more than 200 competed in Rio in 2016). The exhibit covers the different host cities since then, the complex politics involved, the tradition of the torch, and the games' planning and organizational challenges. You'll see past Olympic flags, torches, and mascots, and an audiovisual display of opening ceremonies throughout the years.

One level down, the ground-floor exhibit (part 2) covers the winter, summer, and Paralympic games. Displayed are uniforms, shoes, and other personal memorabilia of competitors through the decades. Sit riveted in the circular projection theater, which serves up a medley of dramatic replays of competition highlights.

The basement (part 3) is about the athletes' life in the Olympic village—what they eat, where they live, drug tests and anti-cheating measures, equipment, and the "Olympic Truce" that athletes from hostile nations commit to observe. A thought-provoking body-image wall shows the diverse bodies of Olympic athletes and how little they resemble fashion-model stereotypes. The exhibit concludes with a room of shiny replica medals from each of the modern games.

The museum's top-floor café has nice views and just-tolerable prices. Outside, in the park, there's a full-scale track on which you can measure your pace against the performance of Olympic athletes.

LAKESIDE AND VINEYARD EXCURSIONS NEAR LAUSANNE
Promenade Stroll to Pully
A delightful promenade stretches in both directions from the Ouchy Métro stop. From here, you can walk along the lakeshore until the Swiss cows come home. The best easy walk is east to Pully (left as you face the lake, about 1 hour). Along the way you'll meet locals strolling and jogging, and see birds and boats bobbing on the lake. At Pully, you can catch the train back to Lausanne (2/hour, 5 minutes).

Lavaux Wine Country
Beyond Pully are the terraced vineyards of the Lavaux wine country. These dreamy terraced banks—with farms and villages, winding lanes, and glorious mountain and lake views—are the quintessence of Lake Geneva's charms.

Hiking trails snake from Pully all the way to Montreux (a very full day's walk). The best stretch is between Lutry and Vevey. Parts of the trails are marked with plaques that explain in English the grape-growing process, as well as the local flora, fauna, and culture. There are countless options to mix and match boat rides, train rides, and scenic hikes here. Your Mobilis Card (from your hotel) covers public transit as far as Epesses. Trains generally go twice an hour. The TI is your best source for information and adept at reviewing options. Stop by, get their advice, and pick up the *Discover the Terraces of Lavaux* flier and the *Montreux Riviera Walks* map, which shows the various hiking routes. For tips on seeing this area by car, see "Route Tips for Drivers," later.

Chexbres-Village to St-Saphorin Hike: For a short and easy walk (less than an hour) that offers a superb sampling of the glories of the Lavaux region, take the hike from Chexbres-Village to St-Saphorin. From Lausanne, ride the train to Chexbres-Village (30 minutes, change in Vevey). At Chexbres, find the light-blue sign across the street from the TI pointing to St-Saphorin. You'll first wind down some village streets (following the blue signs), before being directed onto a concrete promenade that snakes scenically through the vineyards. It's all downhill from here, with gorgeous views of vineyards and villages, Lake Geneva, and France beckoning from across the water. At St-Saphorin, you can pause to sample some wines, then catch a train back to Lausanne.

Lavaux Express Tourist Train: A cutesy tourist choo-choo makes a one-hour loop, affording you an up-close look at the vineyards. Half the departures are from the boat dock at Lutry and half from the dock at nearby Cully—in both towns the boat dock is a short walk from the train station (15 CHF; runs April-Sept Tue-Sun at 13:30, 15:00, and 16:30; also Sat-Sun at 10:30; 25-CHF wine-tasting trip on Fri-Sun evenings, leaves at 18:30 and goes to a wine-cellar *cave;* tel. 0848-848-791, www.lavauxexpress.ch).

Bike to Morges

The best bike path goes west (after sharing with cars for a half-mile, the trail leaves the road and hugs the shoreline all the way to Morges). You'll pass Vidy (with its Roman ruins—just foundations, free), the headquarters of the International Olympic Committee (not open to the public), lots of sports facilities, and finally, just peaceful lakefront parkland stretching to Morges (about 6 miles away, easy return by boat or train).

Sleeping in Lausanne

Lausanne hotels are priciest between April and October, but with a summer lull in July and August. Prices also fall on weekends, as the city gets more business than leisure travelers. The only cheap doubles are at the Lausanne GuestHouse—which also has the best lake views but fills up fast in summer (hotels in the Old Town tend to be less full during this time). Along with your hotel room you'll get a Mobilis Card (courtesy of Lausanne's tourist tax), which gives you free access to the city's public transportation for the duration of your stay. Ask for yours when you check in.

IN THE OLD TOWN

To find Voyageurs and the Régina (which are across the street from each other), take the Métro to the Lausanne-Flon stop, ride the elevator up to the pedestrian bridge, cross Rue du Grand-Pont, walk up Rue Pichard, and take the first right. For the Marché, continue one more stop up on the Métro to Riponne-M. Béjart, then walk five minutes up Rue Pré-du-Marché. Because the Régina and Voyageurs are buried in Lausanne's old town, they can be challenging for drivers. You are allowed to drive through the pedestrian zone to your hotel to drop off your things, but you'll have to park the car at a nearby garage. Get careful instructions, or leave your car at a park-and-ride and arrive by Métro.

$$$ Hôtel des Voyageurs rents 35 cool, Swiss-modern rooms (elevator, Rue Grand Saint-Jean 19, www.voyageurs.ch, hotel@voyageurs.ch).

$$ Hôtel Régina, immersed in Old-Town charm on a steep pedestrian street, is a find: 35 comfy rooms, hospitable host (Patrick), and a great location (RS%, family rooms, ceiling fans, elevator, Bitcoin ATM in lobby, Rue Grand Saint-Jean 18, tel. 021-320-2441, www.hotel-regina.ch, info@hotel-regina.ch).

$$ Hôtel du Marché offers 41 nice, if plain, rooms (9 with private bath) in an inviting neighborhood. (It actually has 50 rooms, but some are rented to students.) It's a five-minute walk from Place de la Riponne in the Old Town, on the way to the Art Brut museum (breakfast extra, elevator, Rue Pré-du-Marché 42, tel. 021-647-9900, www.hoteldumarche-lausanne.ch, info@hoteldumarche-lausanne.ch).

NEAR THE TRAIN STATION

These are easier for drivers and offer rooms with lake views (unlike most hotels in the Old Town).

$$$ Hôtel Elite, run by the Zufferey family, is on a quiet, leafy, residential street just above the train station. Its 33 rooms are pleasant without being plush—a few have balconies (elevator, free parking; from station, cross the street and go uphill around McDonald's, take first right to Avenue Sainte-Luce 1; tel. 021-320-2361, www.elite-lausanne.ch, info@elite-lausanne.ch).

¢-$ Lausanne GuestHouse & Backpacker is a fine 80-bed hostel in a great location just three minutes from the station. The elegant, century-old, seven-story building—it used to house railway workers—turns its back on the train tracks. Its rooms are all on the quiet lake side, and the upper floors have a view. The bathrooms all face the tracks—so even if you have a "private" bathroom, you'll have to cross the hall to reach it. If traveling in summer, it's best to book ahead (private rooms available, sheets included, small breakfast extra, no curfew, reception open 7:30-12:00 & 15:00-22:00, elevator to upper floors only, lockers, laundry, kitchen, garden, reserve ahead for pay parking, Chemin des Epinettes 4, tel. 021-601-8000, www.lausanne-guesthouse.ch, info@lausanne-guesthouse.ch).

Eating in Lausanne

By Swiss standards, you can eat well and affordably here. Lausanne restaurants typically offer a weekday lunch deal for about 20 CHF (sometimes on Saturday, too). This usually just means a main course, perhaps with a side salad or coffee thrown in.

OLD TOWN
Restaurants with Table Service
$$$ Café Romand is a venerable, moderately priced, all-indoor restaurant filled with natives enjoying hearty Swiss home cooking—one of the last old-time brasseries still in business. The city's students, pensioners, and professionals sit under old-time photos in this characteristic yet simple eatery like they own the place (Swiss wines by the glass, Mon-Sat 11:45-23:00, closed Sun, Place St-François 2, tel. 021-312-6375, www.cafe-romand.ch).

$$$$ Café du Grütli, named for the meadow south of Luzern where Switzerland was born, offers typical French Swiss cuisine near Place de la Palud. While they have outside tables on a cozy cobbled lane, I prefer their 1850s-era dining room. It's a bit touristy, but the Prutsch family (Willi, Heiki, and Vanessa) are hands on, the food's fresh, and the service is very good. The family is into hunting, so you'll find game on the menu, good-value fondue, and plenty of salads (Mon-Sat 9:00-14:30 & 18:00-23:30, closed Sun, Rue de la Mercerie 4, tel. 021-312-9493, www.cafedugruetli.ch).

$$$ Brasserie Le Vaudois is a classic brasserie, with charm-

ing seating inside and out, serving all the traditional and local standards (long hours daily, Place de la Riponne, tel. 021-331-2222).

Burgers

$$ The Great Escape is a happening local spot (popular with ex-
pats but not touristy). The fun-loving crew cranks out great burgers
and a few other bar-food-type options. The restaurant is like a big
woody pub (with classic rock playing, one screen showing sports,
and a long bar). They have rickety tables outside on the gravelly
square and, when busy, people are perched with their little Great
Escape trays throughout the small park enjoying their meal (you'll
pay a 2-CHF deposit for your tray—don't forget to turn it in and
get your coin back). While quieter early, it gets loud and crazy
late—but remains welcoming for all ages. There's a good selection
of beer on tap; it's a great place to just pop in and have a drink (daily
11:00-23:00, Place de la Madeleine, just above the Métro stop on
Place de la Riponne).

$$ Inglewood Hamburger is a thriving joint in the old center near Place de la Palud, filled with happy locals munching on
creative burgers (beer on tap, Rue St. Laurent 14, Mon-Sat 18:30-
21:30, closed Sun).

TRENDY QUARTIER DU FLON

Flon, Lausanne's old industrial quarter, is dead by day and thriving at night. From the Flon Métro station, the main drag Voie
du Chariot leads to the central Flon square (following what was
the original train line serving all the warehouses). You'll pass
Vinothèque Nomade (described next), **The Bad Hunter** (a rare
vegetarian place in town), lively cocktail bars, and a trendy restaurant row lining the Main Square. Flon's central square also
has bowling, a cinema (multiplex; "VO" means it's playing in the
original language), and **MàD** (an iconic nightclub with four floors
of dancing and pricey cover, starting well after my bedtime). With
a beach bar in summer and skating in winter, it's well worth a look
whether eating or not.

$$$$ Vinothèque Nomade is primarily a wine bar, where
locals sip wine or their famous cocktails and hang out on the big,
modern sun terrace (40 wines available by the glass). They serve
family-style appetizers, or for a full meal, you can order tasty,
creative, and beautifully presented European and Mediterranean
dishes in a more formal dining room (Mon-Sat 19:00-22:00, closed
Sun, across from Flon Métro stop, Place de l'Europe 9, tel. 021-
320-1313, www.restaurantnomade.ch).

Self-Service and Cheap Eats

$$ Manora cafeteria, on the seventh floor of the downtown Manor department store, offers a quick and healthy series of lunch buffet lines where you can grab what looks good, including salads, hot meals, fancy fruit juices, desserts, and so on (Mon-Fri 9:00-19:00, Sat 8:00-18:00, closed Sun, hot food served until 15:00, air-con, free Wi-Fi, Rue St-Laurent 7). For even cheaper Manor eating, their food hall in the basement has a selection of ready-to-eat picnic meals.

$ Traiteur Bosphore, a cleaner and brighter-than-average kebab shop, is a good option for a quick and inexpensive takeaway lunch or early dinner. There's no seating—stand at the back counter or walk to the nearby Place de la Louve and find a bench (Mon-Fri 10:00-18:45, Sat until 17:00, closed Sun, Rue de la Louve 7).

$$$ Restaurant à l'Etage, owned by hardworking Hari, who came to Switzerland from Nepal, serves Indian and Nepali meals overlooking the grand hall of the Lausanne train station (enter up a stairway along track 1, Sun-Fri 11:30-14:00 & 18:30-21:00, closed Sat, Place de la Gare 9).

Supermarkets: The **Co-op** department store, in the center, has a big supermarket in the basement (there's also a lunch cafeteria upstairs; store open Mon-Fri 8:30-19:00, Sat until 18:00, closed Sun, Rue St-Laurent 24). The train station's small **Aperto** grocery store is open even longer hours (daily 5:30-24:00).

OUCHY

The lakeside Ouchy district is the place to relax in Lausanne. Immediately in front of the Métro stop is a fun zone with fountains, parks, playgrounds, promenades, and restaurants.

Picnics: The most affordable option is a picnic with the local office gang on any of the many inviting benches or scenic lakeside perches. Leaving the Métro station, head left one block to Avenue d'Ouchy, where you'll find several eateries including the **Co-op** supermarket (at #70, daily 6:00-22:00) and **Fleur de Pains,** a bakery offering sandwiches, quiche, and cakes, and a few humble tables (daily 6:00-19:00, at #73).

$$$ Café du Vieil-Ouchy, charming and reasonably priced, seems a bit out of place among all the fancy, expensive restaurants. It offers traditional Swiss cuisine, including cheese fondue and various versions of *Rösti* (main courses listed on chalkboard, daily 12:00-22:00, Place du Port 3, tel. 021-616-2194, www.vieilouchy. ch). If you want the local lake specialty, filet of perch, they have it.

Lausanne Connections

By Plane: If arriving by plane, you'll land at Geneva airport (airport code: GVA, www.gva.ch). It's straightforward and easy to manage. Exiting from the baggage claim area, you're met by various local TI desks. To the left is a bank of ATMs and beyond that, the airport's train station, with handy connections to points all over Switzerland. Trains leave for Lausanne about every 20 minutes (27 CHF, 50 minutes—much faster than driving). Geneva's city-center train station is the first stop on any train departing from the airport; you can get a free ticket for this short hop in the baggage-claim area (before customs—look for machines).

From Lausanne by Train to: Montreux (4/hour, 20-30 minutes), **Château de Chillon** (hourly, 30 minutes, station name: Veytaux-Chillon, more with change in Montreux), **Gruyères** (hourly, 1.5 hours, change in Romont and Bulle), **Geneva** (7/hour, 45 minutes), **Geneva Airport** (2-3/hour direct, 50 minutes), **Bern** (2/hour, 1 hour), **Murten** (2/hour, 1.5 hours, at least one change), **Interlaken** (2/hour, 2 hours, transfer in Bern and sometimes Spiez; or go by Golden Pass scenic route, with transfers in Montreux and Zweisimmen—see the Scenic Rail Journeys chapter), **Luzern** (hourly, 2 hours; or go by Golden Pass scenic route—see the Scenic Rail Journeys chapter), **Zürich** (hourly direct, 2 hours, more with change in Bern), **Zermatt** (2/hour, 3 hours, change in Visp), **Lyon** (every 2 hours, 3 hours, change in Geneva), **Chamonix** (6/day, 4 hours, at least three changes), **Paris** (4/day direct, 4 hours, more with change in Geneva). Train info: toll tel. 0900-300-300, www.rail.ch.

By Boat: For boat connections from Lausanne, see "Getting Around Lake Geneva" near the beginning of this chapter.

ROUTE TIPS FOR DRIVERS

If connecting the Lake Geneva sights by car, note the various routes. The expressway high above the lake zips you quickly between Lausanne and Montreux; although slower, the lakeside road provides great lake-and-vineyards views for about half of the drive (but also passes through several congested towns along the way).

For an even slower but more scenic approach, consider detouring to the **Corniche de Lavaux.** This rugged, sometimes frightening Swiss Wine Road swerves through picturesque towns and the stingy vineyards that produce Lake Geneva's tasty but expensive wine. It lies roughly between Lausanne and Montreux; to get a taste, detour from the lakeside road between Cully (near Lausanne) and Vevey (near Montreux). Going in either direction, follow signs for Chexbres to find the wine road. The Route de la Corniche between Chexbres and Cully is particularly well-known. Note that this isn't a tidy, straightforward route; expect lots of exploring on twisty vineyard roads. Getting lost is the point.

Château de Chillon

This medieval castle, set wistfully at the edge of Lake Geneva on the outskirts of Montreux, is a ▲▲▲ joy. Because it's built on a rocky island, it has a uniquely higgledy-piggledy shape that combines a stout fortress (on the land side) and a residence (on the lake side). Remarkably well-preserved, Château de Chillon (shee-yohn) has never been dam-aged or destroyed—always inhabited, always maintained. Today it's Switzerland's best castle experience. Enjoy the château's tingly views, dank prison, battle-scarred weapons, simple Swiss-style mobile furniture, and 800-year-old toilets. Stroll the patrol ramparts, then curl up on a windowsill to enjoy the lake.

GETTING THERE

The castle sits at the eastern tip of Lake Geneva, about 20 miles east of Lausanne and about 2 miles east of Montreux. From Lausanne, you can connect to the castle using a combination of methods. For a memorable outing, consider mixing and matching these options.

By Train Plus a Short Walk: The S3 regional train (7.40 CHF one-way, hourly, 30 minutes, direction: Villeneuve) takes you to the station at Veytaux-Chillon, a 10-minute walk along the lake (ideal for picnicking) from the castle.

By Train Plus a Bus Ride or Hike: The faster, more frequent IR (interregional) train whisks you to Montreux (14.80 CHF one-way, 2/hour, 20 minutes), where you transfer to a bus that takes you straight to the castle. From the Montreux station, escalate down to Avenue des Alpes, cross the street, and go down the stairs to Grand-Rue (or take the elevator down, marked *Ascenseur public Grand-Rue*). Cross the street and find the blue bus stop on your right, where you can hop bus #201 to Château de Chillon (3.50 CHF, 6/hour, 3/hour after 19:00 and Sun morning, 10 minutes, direction: Villeneuve Gare, stop: Chillon; buy tickets from driver—coins only, covered by Swiss Travel Pass, www.vmcv.ch). You can also hike the two miles from Montreux to Château de Chillon (figure about 45 minutes one-way).

To return to Lausanne, simply reverse the above directions (catch the regional train from the Veytaux-Chillon station back to Lausanne—trains leave hourly at :26 past the hour—or hop the bus from Château de Chillon to Montreux, direction: Vevey, stop: Escaliers de la Gare).

By Boat: A slower but more scenic route to Château de Chillon is to cruise there from Montreux (15 minutes), Vevey (30-60 minutes), or even Lausanne (2 hours). For details, see "Getting Around Lake Geneva," near the beginning of this chapter.

ORIENTATION TO CHÂTEAU DE CHILLON

Cost and Hours: 12.50 CHF, 6.25 CHF with Riviera Card (see "Sleeping in Montreux," later), free with Swiss Travel Pass, 29-CHF family ticket, daily 9:00-19:00, March and Oct 9:30-18:00, Nov-Feb 10:00-17:00, last entry one hour before closing, tel. 021-966-8910, www.chillon.ch.

Parking: There is free, easy parking along the road above the castle, but you'll need a blue cardboard clock (the ticket desk can give you one if necessary).

Tours: My self-guided tour in this chapter hits all the highlights, but for more depth, rent the excellent 1.5-hour audioguide (6 CHF, leave ID as deposit) or download the audioguide app (3 CHF) from the château's website.

Baggage Storage: The castle has free lockers (1-CHF deposit, off the first courtyard in the room with vending machines). The Veytaux-Chillon train station and boat dock don't have lockers, but the Montreux station has a few.

Eating: This is an ideal place to bring a picnic, which you can eat outside the castle on benches by the lake. Food at the basic garden **$$** café next to the castle is expensive, as are the drinks and snacks at the vending machines inside.

BACKGROUND

The aristocratic Savoy family (their seal is the skinny red cross on the towers) enlarged Château de Chillon to its current state in the 13th century. From the outside, the castle has looked pretty much the same for 800 years. The only major difference: In the Middle Ages, it gleamed with a bright whitewash.

This was the Savoys' fortress and residence, with four big halls (a major status symbol) and impractically large lake-view windows (because their powerful navy could defend against possible attacks from the water). But when the Bernese invaded in 1536, the castle was conquered in just two days, and the new governor made Château de Chillon his residence (and a Counter-Reformation prison). With the help of French troops, the French-speaking  Swiss on Lake Geneva finally kicked out their German-speaking Bernese oppressors in 1798. The castle became—and remains—the property of the canton of Vaud. It's been used as an armory, a warehouse, a prison, a hospital, and a tourist attraction. Jean-Jacques Rousseau's writings first drew attention to the castle, inspiring visits by Romantics such as Lord Byron and Victor Hugo, plus other notables, including Dickens, Goethe, and Hemingway.

❍ SELF-GUIDED TOUR

When you buy your ticket, ask for the free English brochure and map (there's also a kids' version). The numbers in my tour correspond to those in the brochure, on the audioguide, and posted at the site.

You'll cross a natural moat (the château is built on an island) and enter the **first courtyard** (#3, with handy fountains for your water bottle). In the room marked #4, you can pick up an audioguide and get oriented with a good model of the castle (in the off-season, audioguides may be in the gift shop—Room 2).

• *Start by heading down the stairs marked 5/9 to a series of...*

Cellars: You can see how the castle was built upon a foundation of jagged natural stone. In Room 8, look up to the right at the stone stairway—a secret escape route for the castle lord, who could (and did, in 1536) hightail it into a waiting boat from this hidden water gate. At the far end is Room 9, **Bonivard's Prison,** named for a renegade Savoyard who was tortured here for five years (lashed to the fifth column from the entrance). When the Romantic poet Lord Byron came to visit, Bonivard's story inspired him to write *The Prisoner of Chillon,* which vividly recounts a prisoner's dark and solitary life ("And mine has been the fate of those / To whom the goodly earth and air / Are bann'd, and barr'd—forbidden fare"; full text available in the gift shop). You can still see where Byron scratched his name in a column (third from entrance, covered by glass).

• *Head back out the way you came in and turn left through the big gate into the **second courtyard** (#12), which is dominated by the towering keep (more on that later). Just before the keep, on the left, go into the...*

Constable's Dining Room (#13): This is one of the château's finest halls. The gigantic fireplace was used to roast large animals (including bears and boars) for feasts. The opposite wall has the first of many grand lake-view windows you'll see in the castle. Look up to the six-centuries-old wooden ceiling.

• *Climb up the spiral staircase to the...*

Aula Nova (#14): This room has a striking barrel-vaulted ceiling that was restored in the 1920s. The collection of mobile furniture recalls a time when nobility traveled throughout their realm (and took their belongings with them) to keep an eye on things and collect taxes. In fact, in many European languages, the word for "furniture" implies that it's mobile—German *Möbel*, French *mobilier*, and so on. Enjoy the ornate decorations on each traveling chest.

• *Continue up to the...*

Private Quarters (#15-17): The **bedroom** (#16) has a short bed—only about five and a half feet long. Not only were people shorter back then, but they slept half-upright, propped up on pillows. The **coat-of-arms hall** (#18) is usually filled with temporary exhibits. The walls are lined with the family crests of some 50 "bailiffs" who governed this territory during Bernese rule. Capping this hall is another great wooden ceiling reminiscent of a waffle.

• *Exit at the far end of the hall, and turn right into the...*

Camera Domini (#19): This was the bedroom of the master of the house. Its location—at the farthest end of the castle from the entrance—was particularly secure. In the corner, notice the spiral stairs (closed to the public) that the lord could use to scamper down to Mass in his private chapel, or up to the ramparts. Under a sumptuous fleur-de-lis ceiling, wall paintings (imitating tapestries) illustrate various animals, including a camel, lion, griffin (with the body of a lion and the head and wings of an eagle), and the trademark Bernese bear. Study the model in the middle of the room, which helps you imagine what this room looked like in all its original colorful splendor.

• *Exit the room and turn right (following the 20/24 sign). In Room 21, make sure to see the* **medieval latrines,** *a feature that aims to please a certain class of traveler. Take the narrow stairs down and pass through Room 22. You'll end up in a* **small courtyard** *(#23), where stairs lead up to an observation post with good views. From the courtyard, squeeze into that* **private chapel** *(#24) where the lord's staircase ended up. Leave this room following the signs for 26, and you'll wind up in the...*

Third Courtyard (#25): Notice that the courtyard's irregular shape causes the angled walkways to focus your attention on the

grand window of the master's bedroom—the *camera domini* we visited earlier. There's no question who was the king of this castle.

• *Go in the door marked 26/33. The* **aula magna** *(#26) is yet another grand hall—this one for banquets—with spectacular (for their time) lake-view windows. Proceed through a few more rooms (including more latrines, #29) to the...*

Domus Clericorum (#31): In this "house of the clerks," the castle bean-counters kept meticulous records of all money and goods that passed through here, creating an invaluable historical record. In Room 32 you'll find a series of **models and illustrations** that explain the gradual construction of the château over time.

• *Climb back up into the third courtyard again, then pass through to the* ***fourth courtyard*** *(#34). Remember the grand views from the lakeside windows? Notice the small slits facing the road on the land side, which are more practical for defense.*

Now's the time to scramble along the ***sentry walk.*** *As you pass through various indoor rooms and outdoor galleries (marked 38/46), pretend that you're defending the château from invaders. Enjoy the castle courtyard and lake views. Circle all the way around, finally squeezing through the archway (rather than going down the wooden stairs) into the...*

Keep (#42): This was the last line of defense and final refuge in the event of a siege. To climb to the top of the eight-story

tower, you can scale 76 claustrophobic steps for views over the castle, lake, and surrounding mountains. From here you can see France (across the lake) as well as three different Swiss cantons.

Our tour is over. You may scramble the ramparts, enjoy the lake views, and play king of the castle at will.

Montreux

This expensive resort—primarily famous for its jazz festival each July—doesn't offer much to see, but its laid-back vibe and lake-

view accommodations help you remember that you're on vacation.

The **train station** (with a few storage lockers by track 1) is one steep block uphill from the main waterfront road. Exit the station via the escalator down to Avenue des Alpes. Then walk left 200 yards and cross the street by the post office to the stairs *(escalier)* and elevator *(ascenseur)* down to Grand-Rue, where you'll find the TI, boat dock, and my recommended hotel.

The wonderful Montreux **TI** has extensive information about the region and possible excursions (Mon-Fri 9:00-18:00, Sat-Sun until 17:00; shorter hours off-season; Place de l'Eurovision, tel. 0848-868-484, www.montreuxriviera.com). In summer you can take a two-hour walking tour of the city, though it's not always offered in English (10 CHF, April-Sept Wed-Sat at 10:00, meet in front of TI, call TI to confirm language).

Visiting Montreux: The lakeside promenade takes you along parks, palm trees, *crêperies*, ice-cream stands, modern sculptures, and the Friday produce market. In the center, meet the statue of Freddie Mercury, who had strong bonds with Montreux. His band, Queen, bought the local Mountain Recording Studios in 1978.

For an easy way to see several sights in the French Swiss countryside, including the town of Gruyères and the chocolate factory in Broc, take a ride from Montreux on the **Chocolate Train** (described later, under "Getting to Gruyères").

Sleeping in and near Montreux: All hotel guests receive a free Riviera Card, which gets you free passage on public transportation and discounts on boat cruises and museum admissions. **$$$ Hôtel Splendid** has genteel public spaces; it's worth paying extra for a bigger lake-view room (5-minute walk from train station, across the street from TI, Grand-Rue 52, tel. 021-966-7979, www. hotel-splendid.ch, info@hotel-splendid.ch). The very institutional **¢ Montreux Youth Hostel** is nicely situated near a lakeside park in the village of Territet (private rooms available; actually closer to Château de Chillon than to Montreux, and easily reachable by frequent buses; check-in 17:00-22:00, closed mid-Nov-mid-Feb, Passage de l'Auberge 8, tel. 021-963-4934, www.youthhostel.ch/ montreux, montreux@youthhostel.ch). On the main square of nearby Vevey, the **¢-$ Vevey Hotel and Guesthouse** offers "chic and cheap" beds in a 19th-century townhouse on the lake (private rooms available, 3-minute walk from station—cross Avenue de la Gare and head to the left of the big yellow building down Avenue Paul Cérésole to Place du Marché 5, tel. 021-922-3532, www. veveyhotel.com).

Montreux Connections: Trains go from Montreux to **Lausanne** (4/hour, 20-30 minutes), **Vevey** (4/hour, 10 minutes), **Gruyères** (hourly, 70 minutes, 1 change), **Bern** (3/hour, 1.5 hours, change in Lausanne), **Geneva** (3/hour direct, 70 minutes, more with change in Lausanne), **Zermatt** (2/hour, 2.5 hours, change in Visp). Montreux is also the first/last stop on the Golden Pass route to Interlaken and Luzern (see Scenic Rail Journeys chapter); note that the trip to Interlaken or Luzern on regular trains (changing in Visp or Lausanne, respectively) is faster, if less scenic.

Bus #201 goes from Montreux to Chillon and Vevey. Catch it on Grand-Rue; facing the lake, the Chillon bus (direction: Villeneuve Gare) is headed to the left, and the Vevey bus to the right

(6/hour, 3/hour after 19:00 and on Sun morning, 10 minutes to Chillon, 20 minutes to Vevey). The **boat** connecting Montreux to Lausanne, Château de Chillon, and several other Lake Geneva destinations departs from the big park next to the TI (see "Getting Around Lake Geneva," earlier).

French Swiss Countryside

The sublime French Swiss countryside is sprinkled with crystal-clear lakes, tasty chocolates, fragrant cheese, and sleepy cows. If you're passing through this enticing region, take time to sample a few of its sights, tastes, and smells.

I've divided these attractions into two groups. The **Gruyères area,** just north of Lake Geneva, is particularly handy if you're traveling between Lake Geneva and points north (e.g., Bern, Murten, or the Berner Oberland). The town of Gruyères, famous for cheesemaking, is charming but touristy; but outside of town, you can visit two very different cheesemakers, a chocolate factory, an appealing little mountain with surprisingly big views, and a workaday town with a fine folk museum.

Southeast of Lake Geneva is the mountainous **Diablerets region,** highlighted by a picturesque hillside village and a lift up to the icy peak that dominates the region. This area is ideal by car. By public transportation, it's a bit more challenging, but workable.

Gruyères

This ultratouristy town, famous for its cheese, fills its fortified hilltop like a bouquet. Its ramparts are now a park, and the ancient buildings serve tourists. Everything is expensive, from the museums to the food, but the town's magical ambience makes it worth a visit.

GETTING TO GRUYÈRES

The larger town of Bulle is the area's transit hub, with direct trains from Bern and easy connections from Lausanne (both about an hour away). From Bulle, local trains and buses connect easily to Gruyères (trains run hourly, 7 minutes).

To cram a visit to Gruyères and the Cailler Chocolate Factory into an easy all-day side-trip by public transportation from Lake Geneva, hop on the **Chocolate Train** in Montreux. The train carries either panoramic or old-time belle époque coaches. It leaves from Montreux shortly before 9:00. You'll be served coffee and a croissant while enjoying the scenic ride. At 10:15, the

train lets you off in Gruyères for a visit to the Maison du Gruyère cheese factory near the train station. An hour later, a bus drives you up to the picturesque old town of Gruyères, with plenty of time to explore and pause for lunch. Just before 14:00, the bus brings you downhill to Broc for a visit and tasting at the Cailler Chocolate Factory; after touring the factory, you board the train back to Montreux, arriving around 17:45 (99 CHF, first class only; 59 CHF with first-class Swiss Travel Pass or Eurail pass, 69 CHF with second-class pass; runs July-Aug daily; May-June Mon-Thu and Sept-Oct Mon, Wed, and Thu only; none Nov-April; tel. 021-989-8190, www.goldenpass.ch, info@goldenpass.ch).

Orientation to Gruyères

Tourist Information: The helpful TI is at the town entrance (daily 9:30-12:00 & 13:00-17:30, shorter hours Nov-April, Rue du Bourg 1, tel. 0848-424-424, www.la-gruyere.ch/gruyeres).

Arrival in Gruyères: The town's **train station** *(gare)* is at the foot of the hill, a steep 15-minute hike up to the village itself. A bus meets each train (just outside station shack, check timetable at www.rail.ch, 3 minutes, 2.90 CHF, covered by Swiss Travel Pass, get off at first stop: Gruyères Ville).

If you're **driving,** follow signs up to town and shoot for a spot in the P1 lot, right outside the town walls (free except Sat-Sun 10:00-17:00 and July-Aug daily 10:00-17:00 when it's 5 CHF). On your way uphill you'll pass P3 on the right, then P2 on the left—parking in either of these lower lots requires a steep walk up into town. Overnight guests who arrive in the evening and want to drop bags can often just drive (very, very slowly) toward the bollard that limits vehicular access to the main square—after a certain time in the evening, it's likely to lower for any car that gets close enough (but don't count on it).

Festivals: The town center hosts a one-day cheese festival in early May, and over a weekend in late June the castle goes full medieval with the midsummer festivities of La Saint-Jean. The region's most colorful autumn cow processions *(désalpes)* are in nearby Charmey, Albeuve, and Jaun (for festival information, go to www.

la-gruyere.ch, then search for the festival you want). If you're here on a summer weekend, you might happen to catch a free **alphorn concert** on the main square (about 10 performances a year, mostly on Sat or Sun, some on Thu, always 15:00-17:00—plus a longer, bigger show in mid-June; the TI has details).

Sights in and near Gruyères

IN THE TOWN CENTER

Gruyères' main attraction is the charming town itself. Wander around the manicured main square, which feels like a movie set. You'll see the town symbol—the crane (*grue* in French)—everywhere. Don't skip the castle's ramparts, which are free—you can walk all the way around to enjoy sweeping views of the surrounding countryside.

The following town center sights are all covered by the Swiss Travel Pass. Combo-tickets can save money if you visit more than one sight, or if you visit both the castle and the cheese factory—look for details at ticket desks.

Castle

Gruyères' castle has a fine setting and a ho-hum interior. While tidy and nicely restored, the place feels empty and could use a lively audioguide—it's not quite worth the cost of entry, but it merits a short stop if you have a Swiss Travel Pass. Admission includes a dull 18-minute audiovisual show about the town's history, heavy on myths and legends (you'll be assigned an entry time when you buy your ticket). Then, with the help

of the English brochure, you can explore the various halls and rooms of the castle itself. Spend some time poking around the grounds, including the view terrace and the manicured garden.

Cost and Hours: 12 CHF, daily 9:00-18:00, Nov-March 10:00-17:00, tel. 026-921-2102, www.chateau-gruyeres.ch.

H. R. Giger Museum

A spooky contrast to idyllic Gruyères, this museum is dedicated to the Swiss artist who designed the monsters in the *Alien* movies. Not for young kids or the easily creeped out, this museum shares those movies' dark aesthetic. It also displays temporary exhibits by other out-there artists.

Cost and Hours: 12.50 CHF; daily 10:00-18:00, Nov-March shorter hours and closed Mon-Tue; below the castle in the Château St. Germain, tel. 026-921-2200, www.hrgigermuseum.com.

Tibet Museum

This museum displays an offbeat but genuinely interesting collection of art and artifacts—statues, paintings, and other objects—from the top of the world. These prized Tibetan possessions of a Swiss collector are thoughtfully displayed inside a former church, making it feel as though the Tibetan deities are squatting in Jesus' old house. Dim lighting and mood music add to the mellow ambience. It's very small—especially considering its high price—but might interest anyone who enjoys Tibetan culture.

Cost and Hours: 10 CHF; daily 11:00-18:00, Nov-Easter shorter hours and closed Mon; 4 Rue de Château, tel. 026-921-3010, www.tibetmuseum.ch.

NEAR THE TRAIN STATION
▲La Maison du Gruyère Cheese Factory

Gruyères is justifiably famous for its Gruyère cheese (no "s" at the end when it's the cheese itself). The cheese is an A.O.C. *(appellation d'origine controlée)* product, meaning that to be called Gruyère, it must be made right here, according to exacting standards.

This modern cheese-production center at the foot of Gruyères is handy for train travelers (it's right across from the station). To see the same cheese made in a more traditional setting, head to the hillside *fromagerie* in Moléson (described later). Admission here includes a sample of three varieties of Gruyère cheese (aged different lengths of time), plus a cow-narrated audioguide, essential for understanding the otherwise sparse exhibits.

Cost and Hours: 7 CHF, 12-CHF family ticket, covered by Swiss Travel Pass; daily 9:00-18:30, Oct-May until 18:00; restaurant, well-stocked gift shop also serves as a decent minimart for travel essentials; straight ahead as you come down the road from Gruyères' hilltop, tel. 026-921-8400, www.lamaisondugruyere.ch.

Visiting the *Fromagerie:* A cow consumes 220 pounds of grass and 22 gallons of water each day to produce 6.5 gallons of milk, while 105 gallons of milk goes into making one 77-pound wheel of cheese. You'll come across these fun cheese facts and more en route to the viewing area. Smell the various alpine flowers and plants—see if you can discern the subtle flavors they lend the cheese—and hold some cheesemaking tools in your hands. Above the production floor, big windows give you a view down into the milky vats (most interesting when cheese production is going on, generally 9:00-11:00 and 12:30-14:30); the action peaks toward the end, when the curds are pulled from the vats. Even if cheesemakers aren't working during your visit, video screens show the process. The finale is the cellar (near the ticket desk), where long rows of cheese wheels age. Watch a robot cheesemaker move up and down the aisles, lovingly flipping and rubbing each wheel just right.

Sleeping and Eating in Gruyères

Sleeping: To sleep right on Gruyères' main square, consider **$$ Hostellerie Saint-Georges,** which has 14 comfortable, traditionally outfitted rooms above a restaurant (flexible rates, especially midweek and outside high season—but strict cancellation policies; reception available 9:00-12:00 & 15:00-18:30, Rue du Bourg 22, tel. 026-921-8300, www.hostelleriesaintgeorge-gruyere.com, hostelleriesaintgeorge@gmail.com.

Another option in the medieval center is **$$ Gruyère Rooms,** with 11 somewhat-rustic rooms upstairs from the Gruyère Traditions gift shop; some rooms have views, others have skylights instead of windows (Rue du Bourg 16, tel. 026-921-3090, www. gruyere-rooms.ch, info@gruyere-rooms.ch).

$ La Ferme du Bourgoz is a B&B with 3 homespun rooms in a quaint farmhouse (10-minute walk from Gruyères train station at Chemin du Bourgo 14, tel. 026-921-2623, www.lafermedubourgoz. ch, info@lafermedubourgoz.ch, Eliane and Jacques).

Eating: Gruyères' main square is surrounded by eateries with indoor and outdoor seating, serving (guess what?) all manner of Gruyère cheese dishes. These places are more or less interchangeable; pick the spot that looks best to you. **$$$ Chalet de Gruyères** looks like a giant cuckoo clock perched atop the square (on the way to the castle). With stuffy indoor seating or a fine terrace, this restaurant has a good reputation and serves up huge portions (open daily, tel. 026-921-2154, www.chalet-gruyeres.ch).

Near Gruyères

The following worthwhile sights are just a short hop from Gruyères in the towns of Moléson-sur-Gruyères, Bulle (pronounced "bool"), Broc, and Charmey. Bulle and Broc have train stations; Moléson and the baths in Charmey are served by buses. Drivers should consider the 2.5-hour scenic countryside loop drive from Gruyères (at the end of this section).

Moléson-sur-Gruyères

The sleepy vacation-home village of Moléson-sur-Gruyères, about five well-signed miles from Gruyères, has a very helpful **TI** (tel.

026-921-8500, www.moleson.ch). Hourly **buses** connect Gruyères and Moléson (15 minutes); drivers can park for free in the giant lot that stretches from the funicular's base station to the entrance to the village.

▲▲Le Moléson Mountain

The verdant hills and pastures immediately surrounding Gruyères are beautiful, but relatively undramatic, with one exception: the rocky-headed Moléson massif, which stretches up into the air over the hills behind Gruyères. At 6,678 feet, it's not much by Swiss standards, but its solitary prominence makes for incredible 360-degree views from its summit.

From the parking lot, a funicular takes you to the Plan-Francey transfer point (4,987 feet), where you can catch a cable car to the mountaintop perch. From here, it's a five-minute hike to the summit, where (weather permitting) you can see Lake Geneva, Mont Blanc, and even some peaks of the Berner Oberland. The mountain's hiking options include the 2.5-hour, not-as-steep-as-it-looks Panoramic Trail from the summit to Plan-Francey via Gros-Plané (from Plan-Francey, it's another hour down to the parking lot)—get details and free hiking maps from the TI before heading up.

Cost and Hours: 35 CHF round-trip to summit, cheaper for partial trips, 46 CHF day-ticket covers unlimited rides on funicular and cable car as well as the summer luge (described later), no discounts with Swiss Travel Pass or Eurail pass; lifts run daily 3/hour until 18:00 (last descent at 17:40), also Fri-Sat June-Oct 2/hour 18:00-23:00 for stargazing from observatory, closed Nov-mid-Dec and April-mid-May, www.moleson.ch.

Eating at the Top: Le Moléson's self-service **$$ Restaurant Le Sommet** offers a decent range of local dishes of higher quality than what you'll find at most cable-car stations.

▲Fromagerie d'Alpage du Moléson

A stark contrast to the sterile Maison du Gruyère's cheese factory, this rustic 17th-century farmhouse gives you an intimate look at the traditional, smelly method of crafting cheese in a huge cauldron over an open fire. There's no point venturing here unless you arrive by 10:00 to watch them make the cheese ye olde way (limited space, so best to reserve—see the next page).

Cost and Hours: 5 CHF for 45-minute cheesemaking demonstration, 13 CHF also includes a cheese platter afterward, May-Sept daily at 10:00, closed off-season, lunches served in restaurant; at Place de l'Aigle 12—

from the main Moléson parking lot, hike about 5 minutes up to the *fromagerie*—just follow the cartoon cows.

Reservations: Since space at the demos is limited to 50 people, it's wise to reserve a slot the day before. Use the email link from their website, or call—the staff speaks very limited English, so consider asking your hotelier or the Moléson TI to reserve for you (TI tel. 026-921-8500, farmhouse tel. 026-921-1044, www.fromagerie-alpage.ch).

Visiting the *Fromagerie:* A slow-moving video (with some English captions) traces the entire process. Then they repeat the whole thing in the flesh: First the milk is brought to the proper temperature and consistency. Then the cheesemaker skims out the curds with a cloth and packs it into a frame to drain and compress. Finally, he chops it into blocks and separates it into smaller circular frames that will turn it into wheels of cheese. Visitors are offered cups of the cheesemaking leftovers (milk minus curds, a.k.a. whey) to taste—it's like sweet skim milk. Then the cheesemaker takes buckets of whey out to feed to the pigs. Unfortunately, there's not a word of English during the presentation, but even for non-Francophones, it's still memorable.

Summer Luge

On the hillside adjacent to the *fromagerie* is a low-key luge ride—not Switzerland's best, but worthwhile for kids, luge aficionados, and anyone with the Moléson day-ticket, which covers unlimited rides (6 CHF/ride, daily 11:00-18:00, closed Nov-May and in bad weather, contact TI with questions).

Bulle

The small town of Bulle has its charms, but is only worthwhile if you're interested in the Musée Gruèrien folk museum or need supplies from a department store. The train station is just two blocks from the central square and its castle (closed to the public); the museum is just beyond the castle. A regional **TI** is located between the castle and the train station (closed Sun, Place des Alpes 26, tel. 0848-424-424, www.la-gruyere.ch).

Short-term pay street **parking** is available (up to an hour in the town square, 2 hours max near the station). If staying longer, use the Espace Gruyère garage; "blue zone" spots are available a short walk away (for details on how these work, see page 413 of the Practicalities chapter).

On Thursday mornings, a produce-and-craft **market** fills the center of town—and it's particularly big and colorful at the height of summer, when many vendors wear their traditional costumes and sell handmade crafts (and when most stalls stay open until 14:00).

▲Musée Gruèrien

Bulle's refreshing, cheery folk museum teaches you all about life in these parts and leaves you feeling good. A two-minute walk behind the castle (through the grounds and garden), the museum is located in the basement of the library, with thoughtfully selected pieces well-displayed in one large room. In this cheese-crazy region, cows are key—notice the many cowbells and the panels from barns painted with murals of the cows' twice-yearly procession up and down the Alps (called *poya* in the region's dialect).

Cost and Hours: 12 CHF, covered by Swiss Travel Pass; Tue-Sat 10:00-17:00, Sun from 13:30, Oct-May closes Tue-Fri 12:00-13:30, closed Mon year-round; Rue de la Condémine 25, tel. 026-916-1010, www.musee-gruerien.ch.

Broc

The sweet-smelling town of Broc is 25 minutes from Gruyères by an hourly train—which takes you right to the chocolate factory (use the Broc-Fabrique stop). If you're arriving by car on a weekday, park in the big lot that's a 5-minute walk from the entrance; on the weekend (when most of the factory staff is at home) you can drive past it and use the lot by the entrance (both lots are free).

Cailler Chocolate Factory

This factory's fun "Maison Cailler" visitors center features exhibits about the production and shipment of chocolate, a collection of old chocolate molds, and vintage films about chocolate production. This is more like a chocolate museum than a chocolate factory tour. Unlike the Alprose factory near Lugano, here you only get a glimpse of the production process.

Cost and Hours: 12 CHF, daily 10:00-18:00, Nov-March until 17:00, particularly busy in July-Aug, last entry one hour before closing, located at Rue Jules Bellet 7, follow signs to *Nestlé* and *Broc Fabrique*, tel. 026-921-5960, www.cailler.ch.

Visiting the Factory: Try to come in the morning, when it's less busy. On weekends and in summer, the wait to get in can reach three hours (they'll give you an estimated entry time when you arrive; no reservations taken). You'll taste almonds and hazelnuts, crumble a cocoa bean in the palm of your hand, and touch a block of cocoa butter. In the tasting room, friendly employees are happy to answer questions as visitors sample creations from elegant trays. Peek into the actual working factory, as video screens explain the process, before concluding in the chock-full-of-chocolate gift shop.

An alternative way to visit the factory is to sign up for one of the regularly offered multilingual workshops where you make your own chocolates under supervision in their "Atelier du Chocolat" (2-3-hour adult workshops-77 CHF, 1-1.5-hour kids' workshops-20-45 CHF, includes museum entry; schedule and reservations on website).

Bains de la Gruyère Thermal Spa (in Charmey)

This modern pool/sauna complex makes for a relaxing rainy-day retreat. On sunny days it offers expansive views from both the indoor and outdoor pools (3 hours-26 CHF, 5 hours-37 CHF, 5 CHF per additional half-hour, towel rental-6 CHF, swimsuits available in shop, family rates, Sun-Thu 9:00-21:00, Fri-Sat until 22:00, last entry 1 hour before closing, closed 2 weeks in late June; tel. 026-927-6767, www.bainsdelagruyere.ch).

Getting There: Charmey is a 20-minute drive from Gruyères' town center (and an easy stop along the Jaun Pass loop drive, described next). The spa is just off the main road—on the left and well-signed—at Gros-Plan 30.

Only serious spa fans will want to trek from Gruyères *sans* car, but here are options for nondrivers: Bus #260 leaves hourly from Epagny—the village at the northern foot of Gruyères' hill (20-minute walk down from the main square, direction: Jaun-Kappelboden, stop: Corbettaz, 40 minutes total for trip). It's also reachable by train from Broc (75 minutes).

▲▲Jaun Pass/Saane Valley Loop Drive

For a taste of Gruyères' gorgeous surroundings, take a 2.5-hour drive over the Jaun Pass (*Col de Bellegarde* in French; Jaun pronounced "yown"), then down the Saane Valley toward Gstaad, and back to Gruyères via the Intyamon Valley. The drive is still nice on a cloudy day, but I wouldn't bother if it's rainy enough to limit your long-distance views (like most alpine passes, the Jaun Pass is closed in bad weather, as well as most of winter).

From Gruyères, follow signs to Broc, then Charmey. The stretch between Gruyères and Broc has fantastic views back to Gruyères town (on the right). After passing Charmey's spa (listed earlier), head through the farmland toward Jaun. En route, you'll cross an invisible language divide into German-speaking territory (even though you're still in the Gruyères region); shortly after, the jagged limestone ridge called Gastlosen (the "Swiss Dolomite") can be seen jutting up on the right.

Uphill from Jaun, the road gets twisty, and guardrails are in short supply. Just after the summit (4,951 feet), there are several opportunities to pull over for views over the Simmental valley, which empties into the Berner Oberland's Lake Thun. As you descend to earth toward Boltigen, follow signs to Zweisimmen (not Interlaken/Bern), then Saanen. This stretch is relatively dull, but allows you to duck back into French-speaking Switzerland through a different valley.

From Saanen, you can either take a short detour to the ritzy resort of Gstaad (and even continue another 20 minutes to the base of the Diablerets cable car, described later) or just follow signs to Château-d'Œx, then toward Bulle. (For more on what you'll see between Saanen and the Intyamon Valley, see the Golden Pass section of the Scenic Rail Journeys chapter.) After Haut-Intyamon, consider a short detour (on the right) to the village of Grandvillard, which captures much of Gruyères' medieval charm, minus the tourists. The turnoff back toward Gruyères is shortly before Bulle.

Diablerets Region

Tucked in the slow-going mountainous countryside just southeast of Lake Geneva, this region is not in the immediate direction of other recommended destinations. It does, however, give you a French-flavored taste of high-altitude life in *les Alpes suisse*. The highlights of this region are the charming town of Gryon and the 10,000-foot Diablerets summit.

While Gryon and Les Diablerets (the town nearest the peak that shares its name) are easily reached by car, they're also served by narrow-gauge train lines that spur off the main line connecting Lake Geneva and Martigny (and farther to Zermatt). Guests spending the night in participating local hotels from late May to late October should ask for the **Free Access Card,** which covers local trains, buses, some lifts, and the Gryon village tour (www.villars-diablerets.ch/freeaccess).

▲▲Gryon

Gryon's cluster of traditional chalets tumbles down a hillside into the valley that separates it from the snowy Dents du Midi range. The place seems almost perpetually mist-shrouded, but that just adds to its charm. (Be warned: May and June are its wettest months.)

Gryon's **TI** is actually up the hill in La Barboleuse (a.k.a. Barboleusaz; two train stops away). Sitting right by the Barboleuse train stop, the helpful office has info on the whole Diablerets area, including tips on area hikes (Mon-Sat 8:00-12:00 & 13:30-17:30, Sun 9:00-12:00 & 15:00-17:30, tel. 024-498-0000, www.villars-diablerets.ch). The TI offers a 2.5-hour tour of Gryon in English at 14:00 on Tue (book ahead, leaves from TI, covered by Free Access Card).

Getting There: To reach Gryon by **train** from Lake Geneva or Zermatt, you'll hop on the BVB line (Bex-Villars-Bretaye) from Bex (hourly, 30 minutes; covered by Swiss Travel Pass, Eurail passes, and the Free Access Card). Gryon's station is on the road just above the heart of the village. **Drivers** can park free in the lot below the main road, marked by white lines (and the town dumpsters); "blue zone" parking is also available on the street.

Visiting Gryon: The town has zero "sights" and few eating options. But it's worth a stroll—or even an overnight—solely for its beauty. The **town church** (1215) is nothing special on the inside, but its humble spire looks majestic set against a backdrop of valley fog and snowy peaks. Free public WCs are in the salmon-colored library *(bibliothèque)*, just past the church and its gurgling fountain.

For a nice, **easy walk,** head to the church and continue downhill out of town along Le Vieux Chemin. You'll reach the hamlet of Les Posses-sur-Bex in about 30 minutes. From Les Posses, you can simply retrace your steps up the gentle slope, or hop the hourly BVB train back to Gryon.

The **thermal spa** in Villars-sur-Ollon (three train stops beyond La Barboleuse)—with pools, saunas, and views—makes a good rainy-day excursion (pool-10 CHF or covered by Free Access Card, whole spa complex-25 CHF, daily 9:00-20:00, Fri-Sat until 21:00, tel. 024-495-1221, www.bains-de-villars.ch).

Sleeping in Gryon: ¢-$ **Chalet Martin** is a friendly hostel with 25 beds spread across three dorms, along with four inviting, traditionally furnished private rooms (two with private bathrooms, two with balcony; one is outside in the secluded "Bell Tent," with electricity and a real bed). It's a mellow scene—the owners live on site with their family—and relaxed travelers of all ages can feel comfortable here. Common areas offer reading nooks, picnic tables, a fire pit, ping-pong, and can't-believe-I'm-here mountain views (breakfast not included, includes sheets, private rooms include towels, guest kitchen, coin-op laundry, Free Access Card available for 5 CHF, Route du Villars 3, mobile 079-724-6374, www.gryon.com, info@gryon.com). From the station, it's a five-minute walk: Follow the tracks uphill past the crosswalk, then look for signs pointing you to the gravel path on the left that zigzags up to the chalet. Drivers can do drop-offs near the hostel by following road signs (the lane doesn't show up on GPS), but there's no guest parking—leave your car in the city lot.

$$ B&B La Crémaillère, near Gryon, in La Barboleuse, has five woodsy, homey rooms in the top two floors of a three-story chalet just a few steps beyond the Place de la Barboleuse parking lot (less than 5 minutes from the train stop). All rooms have sinks, but share bathrooms with other rooms on that floor. One of the owners, who hails from Quebec, speaks fluent English (family rooms, free parking, tel. 024-498-2155, la.cremaillere@bluewin.ch).

Eating in Gryon: $ Café Pomme serves high-quality café fare (quiche, soup, etc.), plus craft beer, coffee, and homemade pastries in a cozy space in the heart of the village (Tue-Fri 8:00-20:00, Sat until 17:00, closed Sun-Mon, Rue du Village 9). **Marché Gryonnais,** the town grocery, stocks lots of local products—and can hook you up with a liter of fresh alpmilk for just 1 CHF if you request it 24 hours in advance (Mon-Fri 7:30-12:15 & 14:00-18:30, Sat until 17:00, Sun 8:00-12:00, Rue du Village 8). There's a picnic spot with great views on the tiny town square, just past the market.

La Barboleuse has a few more restaurant options, as does the resort of Villars-sur-Ollon, which also has shops with all the essentials.

▲▲▲Diablerets Summit (Glacier 3000)

For a grand alpine trip to the tip of a 10,000-foot peak, ascend to the top of the Diablerets massif, which does its icy thing high above the town of Les Diablerets. Up top you'll enjoy views of peaks all around and a vast glacier slowly oozing down below you. While similar lifts in the Lauterbrunnen Valley and Zermatt area are more thrilling, this is French Switzerland's answer to high-altitude fun. Allow about 1.5 hours total to get your money's worth.

Cost and Hours: 79 CHF round-trip, 40 CHF with Swiss Travel Pass or Eurail pass that includes Switzerland; cable car runs daily every 20 minutes early May-early Oct 9:00-16:50, off-season until 16:30 (but closed part of Oct for maintenance); these are last-descent times, tel. 024-492-3377, www.glacier3000.ch.

Getting There: Drivers can easily connect Gryon and Diablerets via a scenic 40-minute drive. Free parking is at the base of the Diablerets cable car (called Col du Pillon), about 10 minutes east of Les Diablerets town. (For a change of scenery on the way back, turn it into a loop drive by returning from Les Diablerets via Le Sépey and Aigle, which takes about an hour.) If connecting to Diablerets from Gruyères, consider going via Gstaad and my "Jaun Pass/Saane Valley Loop Drive," described earlier.

The trip is also doable by public transportation: To reach Les Diablerets from Lake Geneva, take the train, transferring at Aigle (covered by the Swiss Travel Pass, Eurail passes, and the Free Access Card). Hourly buses take train travelers from the town of Les Diablerets to the base station of the Diablerets cable car (Col du Pillon; about 10 minutes; exiting the Diablerets train station, the bus stop is across the street to the right). Col du Pillon is also served by the PostBus from points north.

LAKE GENEVA

If using Gryon as your base, you can reach the Diablerets summit with a train-and-bus combo: Take the BVB line 15 minutes uphill to Villars-sur-Ollon and catch bus #162 to Les Diablerets (2-3/day in summer, no buses off-season), which syncs up nicely with the shuttle bus to Col du Pillon (mentioned earlier). Note that only the first bus departure from Villars-sur-Ollon (around 9:00) allows you enough time to enjoy the Diablerets summit and get back to Villars by the same bus (figure around 1.5 hours from Gryon to the peak; entire trip covered by Free Access Card but not rail passes). Otherwise, it's a three-hour train journey with three transfers to reach the Col du Pillon cable-car station from Gryon (via Bex, Aigle, and shuttle bus from Les Diablerets).

Summiting Diablerets: At **Col du Pillon** you'll load into the cable car, ride five minutes up, switch to another car (follow *Glacier* signs), then ride another five minutes to the summit. In just 15 minutes total, you're standing on a perch overlooking a glacier, with panoramic alpine views.

The top of the lift is called **"Glacier 3000"** (as it's at nearly 3,000 meters). At your feet sprawls a glacier filled with skiers in cold weather (Oct-May), gray and gloomy in summer. The boxy gray tower adjacent to the cable car has an elevator zipping you to various services (shop, view terrace, cafeteria, restaurant). From the tower it's 98 steps up to the thrilling Peak Walk suspension bridge (free), which stretches 350 feet to the **Scex Rouge** summit. At the summit viewpoint, note that free telescopes have built-in labels identifying the peaks around you. You can see the Matterhorn, Jungfrau, and a bit of Mont Blanc, the Alps' highest peak.

Just outside the station's main building are several other activities. The most exciting is the **"alpine coaster"**—actually the world's highest summer luge course, perched on a rocky bluff (steeply pitched and priced—9 CHF/ride). You'll sit on a plastic sled and shoot down a 3,000-foot-long metal rail, with twists and turns that feel like they're about to send you over the edge (pull back on your handles to brake). At the end, you and your cart are pulled safely back up to the top. A **chairlift** (included in your lift ticket) takes you down to the glacier itself, where you can pay to ride a **"snow bus"** across its surface.

Town of Les Diablerets: The pleasant town of Les Diablerets has a good **TI** (open daily, tel. 024-492-

0010, www.diablerets.ch) and a range of decent sleeping options. My favorite is **$$ Auberge de la Poste,** which offers 10 comfortable rooms with plenty of rustic flavor despite its location in the center of town (short walk from the station and past the TI at Rue de la Gare 8, tel. 024-492-3124, www.aubergedelaposte.ch, fad@ bluewin.ch).

LUGANO

Lugano, the leading city of the Italian-speaking Swiss canton of Ticino, gives you Switzerland with an Italian accent. The town (population 60,000; metropolitan area 140,000) sprawls luxuriously along the shores of Lake Lugano. Just a short, scenic train ride over the Alps from the German and French regions of Switzerland, Lugano has a splashy, zesty, Mediterranean ambience. It attracts vacationers from the rainy north with its sunshine, lush vegetation, inviting lake, and shopping. While many travelers come here for the fancy boutiques, others make this a base for hiking, cruising the lake, and passing lazy afternoons in its many gardens. Its mountains aren't mighty, its beaches are lousy, the cityscape is nothing thrilling, and it can all feel a little geriatric, but Lugano is the best spot to enjoy palm trees in Switzerland, and its charm merits at least a short visit.

PLANNING YOUR TIME

Lugano lies conveniently at the intersection of the Gotthard Panorama Express and the Bernina Express—two of Switzerland's more scenic train rides. Blitz sightseers arrive along the Gotthard Panorama route one day and take off on the Bernina Express the next.

If relaxing is on your itinerary, spend two nights and a full day here, arriving and departing on the scenic trains. With a day, spend the morning exploring the old town with my self-guided walk, then do a boat cruise and ascend a mountain lift (San Salvatore is best) in the afternoon. Extra time—and you'll have some—can be spent relaxing in gardens and along the lakefront.

Orientation to Lugano

The old town is on Lake Lugano, which is bordered by promenades and parks. A funicular connects the old town with the train station above. Nearly everything in this chapter (with the exception of the mountain lifts) is within a five-minute walk of the base of the funicular. The town of Lugano fades into other, smaller waterfront communities all around the lake (much of which lies in Italy).

Italian is the language of Lugano and its region (Ticino), which is surrounded on three sides by Italy (see "Italian Survival Phrases" in the appendix). In this corner of Switzerland, a *Strasse* (street) becomes a *Via*, and a *Platz* (square) becomes a *Piazza*.

TOURIST INFORMATION

Lugano's main TI is in the **Town Hall** building, facing the boat dock (Mon-Fri 9:00-18:00, Sat until 17:00, Sun 10:00-16:00; shorter hours and closed Sun in off-season; Palazzo Civico, Riva Albertolli, tel. 058-866-6600, www.luganoturismo.ch). There's also a branch at the **train station** (Mon-Fri 9:00-19:00, Sat until 13:00, closed Sun, shorter hours in off-season).

The TI offers different **excursions,** such as to the fishing village of Gandria; to the top of San Salvatore; and to the top of

Monte Brè, including a short boat ride (all tours well described on the website). Tours are given in two languages at the same time (usually Italian and English), and depending on who signs up, may lean much more heavily toward one or the other (tours cost 10 CHF and include transport or lift tickets worth much more, reservations required, all tours leave from the TI).

ARRIVAL IN LUGANO

The train station is on a hill above downtown. It has pay lockers (in the underground passage), WCs, a ticket office (daily 7:00-19:00), ATMs, a convenient small grocery (Piccobello, open long hours daily), a surprisingly genteel restaurant (Buffet della Stazione, with affordable pizzas), and a branch TI. The easiest way to get to the town below is by **funicular** (look for *funicolare* sign—it's by track 1 in the middle of the station, departs every 5 minutes, daily 5:00-24:00, 1.30 CHF, free with Swiss Travel Pass). The funicular deposits you right in the heart of the old town, at Piazza Cioccaro and the start of my Lugano Walk.

You can also **walk** (but not with wheeled luggage) or take **bus** #2 or #4 down the hill (for bus details, see "Getting Around Lugano," later).

HELPFUL HINTS

Wi-Fi: The city operates free Wi-Fi along the waterfront and in Piazza della Riforma (look for the Wi-Fi Lugano network). To log in, you'll need a mobile phone that can receive texts.

Laundry: Il Girasole is a self-service launderette with English instructions a 15-minute walk away from the lake—or take bus #7 (direction: Pregassona) three stops from Lugano Centro to Piazza Molino Nuovo, then walk a block onward (daily 7:00-22:00, Via Giuseppe Bagutti 8, tel. 091-922-9900 or mobile 076-503-7964, www.lavanderiaselfservice.ch).

Local Guide: Lovely **Christa Branchi** teaches enthusiastically about her city and its history (180 CHF/1-3 hours, 220 CHF/half-day, 330 CHF/day, tel. 091-606-3302, christabranchi@hotmail.com).

GETTING AROUND LUGANO

The town center is easily walkable, and the two nearby hilltop excursions, San Salvatore and Monte Brè, start from funicular stations that are each a 20-minute lakeside stroll (in opposite directions) away from the center.

Buses can save time, though. All lines converge at the Lugano Centro terminal on the north edge of downtown. Bus #2 (2-4/hour) is the one to know: It conveniently links the Paradiso neighborhood (for San Salvatore), the train station, Lugano Centro,

Cassarate (for Monte Brè), and Castagnola (where the path to Gandria starts). Buy bus tickets from the English-speaking touchscreen machines at any bus stop (2-CHF "short-distance" ticket good for up to four stops, 2.50-CHF regular "Area 100" ticket valid for one hour; 7.50-CHF day pass—to buy, touch "Further Tickets," then "Day Pass," then select "Lugano"; all Lugano buses covered by Swiss Travel Pass, www.tplsa.ch).

Lugano Walk

Resorty Lugano hides some interesting history, but let's face it: You're here to relax. Consider taking this short self-guided stroll to get yourself oriented... or just grab a gelato and wind your own way through the city center's arcades and lakeside promenade.

Start on Piazza Cioccaro, at the base of the funicular that connects the train station with the town center.

• *With your back to the funicular, go down the narrow street to the right of the building at the bottom of the square.*

Via Pessina: In this tangled, colorful little corner are several small delicatessen-type shops run by Signor Gabbani. Stop in if you'd like to sample some of the best local cheese, bread, salami, and/or wine.

• *Bear right, and on your right, at Via Pessina 3, find the...*

Grand Café al Porto: This venerable, elegant institution is the most historic café in town. The *1803* above the fireplace is the date it opened—and also when Ticino joined the Swiss Federation. Once a convent (notice the fine *sgraffito* facade), the café evokes the 19th-century days when Giuseppe Mazzini and fellow Italian patriots would huddle here—safely over the border—planning their next move to unify Italy. Much later, as World War II wound down, US intelligence officer Allen Dulles (future head of the CIA) met right here with Nazi and Italian representatives to organize a graceful end to the war and prevent the Germans from ruining Italy with a scorched-earth retreat. And in more carefree times, this is where Clark Gable and Sophia Loren dipped cookies in their coffee.

• *Just past Grand Café al Porto, take a left at the fountain into...*

Piazza della Riforma: This square is Lugano's living room. With geraniums cascading on all sides, the square hosts an open-air cinema, markets (Tue and Fri mornings), and local festivals. The giant yellow building is the City Hall *(municipio).*

• *Facing the City Hall, make a 90-degree left turn and walk (between the* farmacia *and the white bank building) down...*

Via Canova: This street leads directly to the city park. Follow it for a few blocks, watching for the elegant gallery that burrows through a block (on your left after the second crosswalk). Just after that, on your right, you'll pass the **Palazzo Reali,** which displays ever-changing exhibits of primarily 19th- and 20th-century art (may be closed for renovation when you visit, main collection-8 CHF, covered by Swiss Travel Pass, Wed-Sun 10:00-17:00, Tue from 14:00, closed Mon, Via Canova 10, tel. 091-815-7971, http://masilugano.ch).

Next is the creamy little **Church of San Rocco.** Its rich frescoes celebrate the saint responsible for protecting the city against the plague.

Beyond the Church of San Rocco is the parklike **Piazza Indipendenza.** The giant head on its side is the work of Polish sculp-

tor Igor Mitoraj, who has decorated squares all over Europe with similar sculptures. On your right is the vast, sterile **casino** building. Though its blocky, modern style doesn't quite fit the otherwise elegant architecture of this area, it does have an elevator leading up to a fine lake view (lake side of building—we'll pass there later on this walk).

• *Continuing straight across the street from Piazza Indipendenza, pass through the gate to come face-to-face with the pink palace in the...*

City Park (Parco Civico Villa Ciani): The park's centerpiece, the Villa Ciani, houses a fine-arts museum. Sprawling from here along the lake is a lush park filled with modern art and exotic trees from around the world. Its water gate evokes the 19th century, when this was the private domain of aristocrats. The flower beds are organized to show off maximum color all year long. If the weather's nice, stow your guidebook

and remember you're on vacation as you explore this ingeniously

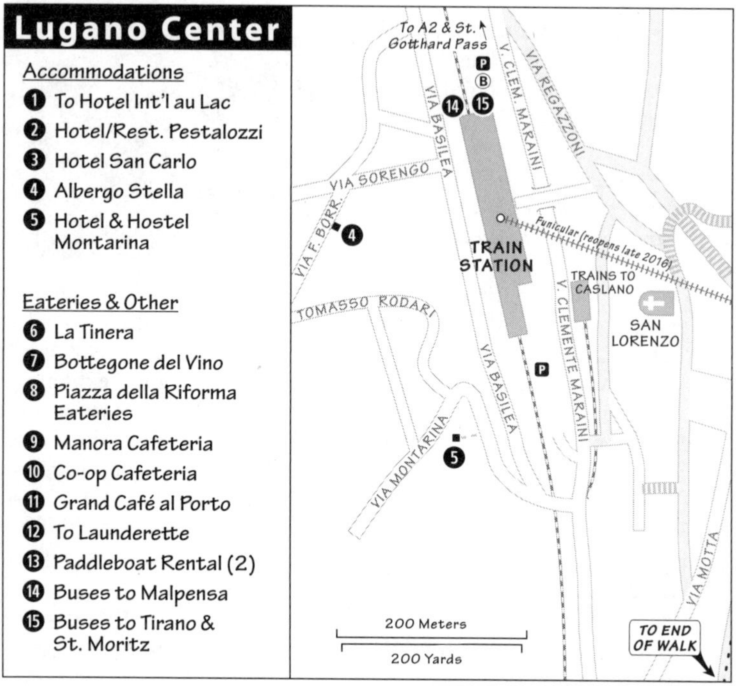

LUGANO

Lugano Center

Accommodations
1 To Hotel Int'l au Lac
2 Hotel/Rest. Pestalozzi
3 Hotel San Carlo
4 Albergo Stella
5 Hotel & Hostel Montarina

Eateries & Other
6 La Tinera
7 Bottegone del Vino
8 Piazza della Riforma Eateries
9 Manora Cafeteria
10 Co-op Cafeteria
11 Grand Café al Porto
12 To Launderette
13 Paddleboat Rental (2)
14 Buses to Malpensa
15 Buses to Tirano & St. Moritz

To A2 & St. Gotthard Pass

V. CLEM MARAINI

VIA REGAZZONI

VIA BASILEA

VIA SORENGO

VIA F. BORR

TRAIN STATION

Funicular (reopens late 2016)

TRAINS TO CASLANO

V. CLEMENTE MARAINI

SAN LORENZO

TOMASSO RODARI

VIA BASILEA

VIA MONTARINA

VIA MOTTA

200 Meters
200 Yards

TO END OF WALK

landscaped, people-friendly space. It's lit at night and particularly good for a late, romantic stroll (open long hours daily).

• *From the city park, walk back to the town center along the...*

Waterfront: This lovely promenade gets even nicer on Friday and Saturday evenings from late June through August (after 20:30), when the busy street is closed off to traffic and you'll find concerts and events in full swing.

On the right, the casino's top-floor restaurant overlooks the lake. If it's open, ride the glass *elevatore* up and down for a fun and free view (daily 12:00-15:00 & 19:30-24:00). Then continue strolling through the arcade or under the mulberry trees (a favorite of silk worms, dating from the time when silk was a local industry) until you reach the **TI** and the **boat dock** (for details on lake cruises, see "Cruising Lake Lugano," later). On the way, you'll pass several places to rent paddleboats (8 CHF/30 minutes).

Look across the lake for the village clustered around a huge, blocky, sand-colored building (lit up in bright colors at night). That's the Casinò di Campione, the largest casino in Europe, which

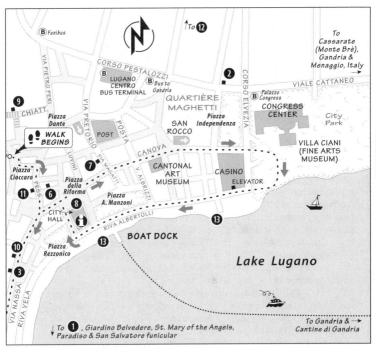

enjoys special legal privileges, granted by Mussolini when he saw what casino tourism had done for nearby Lugano. The casino dominates **Campione d'Italia**—a tiny enclave of Italy that's surrounded by Switzerland on all sides; residents use Swiss francs, have Swiss phone numbers and license plates, and pay Swiss taxes...but carry Italian passports.

• *Back at the yellow City Hall building, cross the busy road (notice the pedestrian underpass nearby). A block inland from the TI is Piazza della Riforma again. The first left off the square is...*

Via Nassa: This is one of Lugano's main shopping streets. For the next several blocks, just enjoy the wandering, window-shopping, and people-watching along this gauntlet of boutiques and jewelry shops under typical Lombardi arcades. On the right, at #22, the Co-op department store has a good selection of chocolates (just inside the door on the left), a basement supermarket, and a handy top-floor cafeteria with great views.

• *Follow Via Nassa until it dead-ends at the small but historic...*

Church of St. Mary of the Angels (Chiesa Santa Maria degli Angioli): This lakefront church, which dates from 1499, was part of a monastery (next door). Inside the church are the city's best frescoes.

The Passion and Crucifixion of Christ, the artistic highlight of all Ticino and the finest Renaissance fresco in Switzerland, is on the

LUGANO

The Story of Lugano

Lugano's history is tied to its strategic position: where the Italian world is pressed up against the Alps, and just below the most convenient alpine passes. The Celts crossed the Alps here and left their mark. The ancient Romans were here, too—the oldest sacred building in Switzerland is an early Christian baptistery on this lake.

In 1220, when the first road over the Gotthard Pass was built, the Swiss took an interest in acquiring the Italian-speaking region of Ticino, leading to a three-century-long battle for control. Several castles in the nearby town of Bellinzona recall a pivotal Swiss victory in 1513. With this success, the Swiss gained a toehold south of the Alps. At first, Ticino was ruled from farther north, as a sort of colony. But in 1798, after French troops invaded Switzerland and proclaimed the Helvetic Republic, locals stood up to Napoleon by creating an independent Republic of Ticino. The Ticinese couldn't rule themselves peacefully, though, and five years later (in 1803) they joined the reestablished Swiss Federation as a regular canton, on the same footing as the rest of Switzerland.

In the 19th century, Lugano—Italian-speaking, just a short trip from Milan, yet safely over the border in Switzerland—provided a refuge and staging ground for intellectual Italian revolutionaries. They'd meet here to plan the Risorgimento, the struggle for Italian unification (c. 1840-1869). Later in the 19th century, tourism arrived, and the grand lakefront hotels were built.

Today, Lugano is second among Swiss cities only to Zürich in its number of banks. It's easy for Italians and others with suitcases of hard cash—black money—to swing by and take advantage of the secret bank accounts. But the mentality here remains Italian. Rather than the Zürich model ("live to work"), the people of Lugano brag that they work to live.

wall that separates the nave from the altar area. Milanese Bernardino Luini, who painted it in 1529, is sometimes called the "Raphael of the North" for the gentle expressions and calm beauty of his art. Follow the action as the scenes from Christ's passion are played out, from Jesus being crowned with thorns (left) to the doubting apostle Thomas touching Jesus' wound after his Resurrection (right). The central dominating theme is the Crucifixion. The work is rife with symbolism. For instance, at the base of the cross, notice the skull and femur of Adam, as well as his rib (from which Eve was created). Worshippers saw this and remembered that without Adam

and Eve's first sin, none of the terrible action in the rest of the fresco would have been necessary. Luini spent a decade working on this fresco, applying his paints day by day, a section at a time, over thin layers of wet plaster.

Facing the giant fresco, look to your left to find the three smaller frames. This is Luini's *Last Supper,* which was sliced off a wall of the monks' dining hall and put on canvas to be hung here.

Finally, wander up to the front of the church. The altar is rich and unusual with its wooden inlay work.

• *Along the lakefront across from the church begins the...*

Giardino Belvedere: This delightful little garden park is an open-air modern-art museum. The building facing it was once a monastery, then the Grand Hotel Palace. This first grand hotel on the lake was radical in that it actually faced the lake. From here, survey the scene. Paradiso, the big hotel zone with its 80-foot-high fountain, is a 15-minute walk along the lakeside. From there, the San Salvatore lift zips sightseers to the summit. The ridge across the lake marks the border of Italy.

• *Our walk is finished. If you've got energy left, continue along the lakefront on the pleasant path to Paradiso; there you can summit San Salvatore, hop on a lake cruise, or do both.*

Sights near Lugano

MOUNTAIN LIFTS

Two handsome mountains (San Salvatore and Monte Brè) flank Lugano's city center, and you can conquer either one, sweat-free, by lifts. At about 3,000 feet, Lake Lugano's mountains are unimpressive compared with the mightier Alps farther north; if you've done some of the higher lifts in the Berner Oberland or Zermatt regions, nothing here will thrill you. Still, the commanding mountaintop views over the lake are enjoyable. Doing more than one is overkill; San Salvatore is best and relatively handy to Lugano town. Monte Generoso is a higher mountain that's a little farther from town.

▲San Salvatore

The easiest and most rewarding peak on the lake, thanks to its fine panoramic views, San Salvatore (2,990 feet) rockets up from the Lugano suburb of Paradiso.

Cost and Hours: 30 CHF round-trip, half-price with Swiss Travel Pass, 2/hour—departs on the hour and the half-hour, 12-minute ride, transfer to another funicular midway up; lift runs daily mid-July–mid-Aug

9:00-23:00; rest of year 9:00-18:00, Fri-Sat until 22:30, closed Nov-mid-March; these are last-ascent times—last descent generally 30 minutes later; tel. 091-985-2828, www.montesansalvatore.ch.

Getting There: To reach the base of the funicular, either walk along the water (about 20 minutes south of the city center; keep your eye out for brown *funicolare* signs), or take bus #2 (direction: Paradiso, get off at Paradiso/Geretta stop, rather than staying on until the Funicolare San Salvatore stop).

At the Summit: You'll find good viewpoints, as well as a playground and a restaurant (reasonably priced if you buy the daily special with your funicular ticket—menu posted at valley station, food served 11:00-15:00, in high season also 19:00-23:00).

From the lift, be sure to climb five more minutes to the actual summit. On the way up, pop into the Salvatore Museum, with its small collection of religious art and exhibits on local geology (included in funicular ticket, closed Mon-Tue). At the top of the mountain, there's a small church surrounded by a view terrace. For the best panorama, climb to the rooftop of the church (entrance around the right side) for a sweeping, nearly 360-degree view. Unfortunately, the bay directly in front of Lugano is just about the only thing you can't see from up here.

Monte Brè

Departing from the other end of Lugano, in the suburb of Cassarate, this funicular takes you to arguably the best view down on the lagoon of Lugano itself (3,005 feet). There's a restaurant up top.

Cost and Hours: 25 CHF round-trip, half-price with Swiss Travel Pass, 2/hour—generally at :15 and :45 after the hour, 33-minute trip; lift runs daily June-Oct 9:10-18:45 plus July-Aug Fri-Sat until 23:05, off-season until 16:45, closed Jan-Feb; these are last-ascent times—last descent generally 30 minutes later, restaurant has lunch-and-funicular combo offer, tel. 091-971-3171, www.montebre.ch.

Getting There: From Lugano's old town, you can take bus #2 (direction: Castagnola) to the Cassarate/Monte Brè stop. Getting off the bus, walk a little farther along the water, then follow brown *funicolare* signs uphill to the left. Don't dawdle—the turnstile gate closes with little warning shortly before the funicular departs. You can also reach Cassarate via the lake boat from downtown Lugano.

Monte Generoso

The tallest mountain but farthest from Lugano, Monte Generoso (5,590 feet) is high enough that you can see some of the more distant cut-glass peaks. A cogwheel train climbs up from the station at Capolago (at the south end of Lake Lugano) in 35 minutes, leaving you at Generoso Vetta, a 10-minute walk below the summit.

Cost and Hours: 54 CHF round-trip, half-price with Swiss Travel Pass, June-Sept roughly hourly 9:05-16:35, off-season until 15:35, few or no trains Nov-March, tel. 091-630-5111, www. montegeneroso.ch).

Getting There: From Lugano, take a regular train (15 minutes) to Capolago. You can also get there by boat, though it's slower and runs once a day.

CRUISING LAKE LUGANO WITH A STOP IN GANDRIA

Lake Lugano is made to order for a boat trip. The lake boats serve as regular public transport to a couple of car-free spots on the lake.

You can either ride the boat around the lake or hop on and off the boat to explore. There's also a dizzying array of more elaborate excursions to choose from (such as a lunch trip, a grand tour, a shopping excursion into Italy, and an evening dinner cruise).

Boats and Schedules

The basic one-hour boat cruise does a loop from Lugano. It stops at a few desolate restaurants and hamlets along the far side of the lake, visits Gandria (a peaceful and picturesque little fishing town with several romantic view restaurants), then returns to Lugano (27.40 CHF round-trip including stopovers, 16.60 CHF for one segment, free with Swiss Travel Pass).

You can get off at any point, look around, and wait for a later boat; from Gandria, you can also return to Lugano by foot or bus (explained later). Note that if you're hopping on and off the boat, you'll actually cobble together the trip from various longer cruises, each with different itineraries. Some circle the lake clockwise, others counterclockwise, and not every boat makes every stop (the boat serves only those parts of the lake within Swiss borders). Pick up the boat schedule *(orario)* or find it online (www.lakelugano.ch, tel. 091-222-1111). Study it carefully to note when the next boat comes and exactly where it stops. The schedule can be confusing, so ask at the TI or one of the boat docks if you need planning help.

Stops on the Lake

If you want to get off the boat, consider one of the following stops.

On the Far Side of the Lake

The best place to break your journey is at the adjacent stops of **Cantine di Gandria** and **Museo Doganale,** which are a quick walk from each other (boats dock at just one of these stops, not both). Cantine di Gandria has two traditional trattorias and wine grottos—great for a rustic meal or just a snack and a drink (daily 11:30-21:00, closed Oct-April, Grotto Teresa: tel. 091-923-5895, Grotto Descanso: tel. 091-922-8071). A five-minute walk from Cantine di Gandria takes you to the bright orange **Museo Doganale,** right on the Italian border, with underwhelming exhibits on customs and smuggling (3 CHF, no English but worth a quick visit, daily 13:30-17:30, closed mid-Oct-March, tel. 079-512-9907, www.zollmuseum.ch).

Gandria

This town, on the Lugano side of the lake, is the most popular stop. A dense cluster of houses hangs over the lake with a few lazy, romantic hotels and several inviting restaurants. The only "streets" are stairways and cool, narrow passageways between the lake below and the road above. Either of the two restaurants by the  boat dock will do for a meal or drink (**Ristorante Roccabella:** tel. 091-971-2722; and just up the stairs, **Ristorante Antico:** tel. 091-971-4871). But it's worth seeking out **$$$ Locanda Gandriesi,** deeper into the village, which has better food and a smaller, quieter terrace (pasta and polenta dishes, open daily—even in winter; go left from the dock—it's about a 5-minute walk, just below the church; tel. 091-971-4181).

Reaching Gandria by Bus: You can also connect Gandria and downtown Lugano by minibus (#490, 9/day Mon-Fri, 5/day Sat, none on Sun, 4.40 CHF, timetables at www.lakelugano.ch or www.rail.ch—search for stop "Gandria, Paese"). The bus stop in Lugano, called Al Forte, is across the street from Lugano Centro bus station, in front of Via Giovanni Nizzola 2. In Gandria, buses drop and pick up at the parking lot above the car-free village.

Returning to Lugano from Gandria: You can **walk** back to

Lugano along a great 45-minute lakeside path through restored olive groves, with multilingual signposts telling you all about olive cultivation (follow signs for *Sentiero dell'Olivo*). This path brings you to Castagnola, a suburb of Lugano; at the Castagnola post office, catch bus #2, #11, or #12 back into Lugano (or walk another 30 minutes).

You can also return to Lugano via **boat** or the **minibus** described above. Note that the last boat and bus depart from Gandria around 18:25 (confirm locally). If you miss these, you'll have to walk or fork over 40-50 CHF for a **taxi.**

Half-Day Plan

A pleasant way to spend a late afternoon and evening in summer is to catch a mid-afternoon boat (say 15:00) for the half-hour trip around the lake from Lugano to Gandria, and have a drink and appetizer—early diners always get lakeside tables. At around **17:00,** take the boat from Gandria to Paradiso, walk to the San Salvatore lift, and ride to the mountain summit (beautiful at twilight). Ride back down and walk along the lake back to Lugano. This plan works daily in the height of summer, and also Fridays and Saturdays in peak season, when the San Salvatore lift is open late (see listing earlier for details). Outside of those times, either go earlier in the day or skip the lift and just enjoy the walk back to Lugano.

CHOCOLATE EXCURSION
Alprose Chocolate Factory

On a rainy (or sweltering) day, a visit to this factory in Caslano, a small town near Lugano, makes a fun excursion (though it may be closed for renovation during your visit—call before you go). Alprose is one of Switzerland's smaller, less-well-known chocolate producers, but their factory is geared up for visitors and generous with free samples.

Cost and Hours: 3 CHF, no Swiss Travel Pass discount, Mon-Fri 9:00-17:30, Sat-Sun until 16:30, shop stays open a half-hour longer, Via Rompada 36, Caslano, tel. 091-611-8856, www.alprose.ch.

Getting There: The S60 suburban train runs from Lugano to Caslano (Mon-Fri 4/hour, Sat-Sun 2/hour, 20 minutes, direction: Ponte Tresa, covered by rail passes). The train leaves from the cute yellow antique train station across the street from Lugano's main station (marked *Ferrovie Luganesi;* go down the stairs). Machines and windows sell tickets (13.20-CHF day pass covers your return).

From Caslano station, cross the tracks and go one block downhill along Via Stazione, then turn right on Via Rompada (passing *Museo del Cioccolato* signs) a long block and a half to the factory.

Visiting the Factory: The machines are in operation Monday to Friday from 9:00 to 15:00, but you're always allowed a look at the factory. An elevated, enclosed, air-conditioned walkway lets you watch as big dollops of chocolate are dropped into plastic molds, cooled and popped out onto a conveyor belt, wrapped (mechanically), and packed (manually) into boxes. Next to the factory, a modest museum is set up in a tent. A 15-minute film describing the chocolate-making process runs continuously (ask for the English soundtrack). The shop sells fresh factory seconds for a reduced price. Picnickers can sit at tables next to a vending machine with drinks.

Sleeping in Lugano

Demand for hotel rooms in Lugano is more even than in other Swiss destinations, but prices are generally at their highest between April and October.

IN THE CITY CENTER

$$$$ Hotel International au Lac is a classic, elegant hotel with 78 rooms, old-school furnishings, some Lake Lugano views, and even a "museum" of relics from the hotel's Victorian past. It's conveniently and scenically located where pedestrian-only Via Nassa hits the lake. Four generations of Schmids have maintained the early-20th-century ambience since 1906, with old photos, inviting lounges, antique furniture, and, it seems, many of their original guests (family-friendly, air-con, elevator, terrace restaurant, fun view seats on balcony of bar, swimming pool, pricey parking, closed Nov-Easter, Via Nassa 68, tel. 091-922-7541, www.hotel-international.ch, info@hotel-international.ch). To reach the hotel from the station, either take the funicular down and walk (5 minutes), or take bus #4 (direction: Lugano Centro) four stops to Piazza Luini, right at the hotel's front door.

$$$ Hotel Pestalozzi Lugano, near the city park, is plain and vaguely institutional (it's run by a nonprofit foundation). It offers 55 fresh, modern, somewhat sterile rooms—some with lake views. Though it's a bit farther from the train-station funicular, this hotel is a better value (pricier rooms tend to have lake view and/or air-con—let them know what's important to you when reserving, elevator, recommended and affordable restaurant, Piazza Indipendenza 9—but GPS works better with "Via Pietro Bianchi," tel. 091-921-4646, www.pestalozzi-lugano.ch, info@pestalozzi-lugano.ch). From the station, you can reach the hotel quickly by taking bus #2 (direction: Castagnola) four stops to Palazzo Congressi.

$$ Hotel San Carlo, also on the pedestrian-only shopping street, is conveniently close to the train-station funicular, with 20 small, quiet rooms (elevator, no air-con but fans, breakfast smaller than at comparable hotels, Via Nassa 28, tel. 091-922-7107, www. hotelsancarlolugano.ch, sancarlo@ticino.com).

NEAR THE TRAIN STATION

$$$ Albergo Stella, a wonderful little oasis, offers 14 rooms between slick office buildings just behind the train station. Owners Daniel and Alexandra Hahne used to own an interior decorating store in Basel, and the hotel is their new playground. Enjoy the garden and the tiny swimming pool (RS%, some rooms have terraces, air-con, lots of stairs, Via Francesco Borromini 5, tel. 091-966-3370, www.albergostella.ch, info@albergostella.ch). From the station, find track 4 and walk to the end of the platform (keeping the station building on your right), turn left to cross the street by the big willowy tree, head uphill for a few yards, then turn left up Via Francesco Borromini.

Hotel & Hostel Montarina, a creaky pink mansion in a palm garden overlooking the lake, has to be one of Europe's most appealing hostels. It's a great hotel option as well. It has 120 **¢ dorm beds,** as well as 24 **$$ private rooms;** half of these are antique rooms with classic furniture and shared bathrooms, and the other half are modern "comfort" rooms, with private bathrooms and air-conditioning. Surrounded  by lush tropical gardens and an extremely inviting swimming pool, and with a helpful staff, this place is well worth consideration by those who usually don't stay in hostels (breakfast buffet extra, towels extra in dorm rooms, reception open 7:30-23:00, late-night train noise, lockers, small kitchen, pay laundry, free parking, closed Dec-Jan, Via Montarina 1, tel. 091-966-7272, www.montarina.ch, info@montarina.ch). At the train station, head to track 4, then walk along the platform with the station and lake on your left, and go through the parking lot toward the *Continental Parkhotel* sign. Just before the sign and a stone wall, take the sharp uphill turn to the right; halfway up the hill, go left through the gate marked *#1.*

Eating in Lugano

My recommended restaurants are all in the old town. You'll pay a premium to dine on Piazza della Riforma, but it can be worth the expense. Lugano is not the best place for lakeside dining—instead, cross the lake to the remote little grotto restaurants, or visit the town of Gandria (both options described earlier, under "Cruising Lake Lugano"). Good news for the wine-curious: You'll pay the same per liter for the little one-deciliter (about 3.5 oz) glasses as you do for the big half-liter (about 17 oz) carafes—so go with the small glasses and try several different wines. Experiment. The Ticino merlot is great.

IN THE OLD TOWN

$$$ La Tinera, beloved by locals, serves affordable, traditional Ticinese cuisine (such as *bollito misto*, a beef stew offered every Tue). It's tucked away in an old wine cellar, with heavy wooden furniture and decorated with wine bottles and antique copper cookware (air-con, Mon-Sat 11:30-15:00 & 17:30-23:00, closed Sun, Via dei Gorini 2, just a block behind Piazza della Riforma, tel. 091-923-5219).

$$$ Bottegone del Vino is a quality wine bar with indoor and outdoor ambience. There's a small, rustic food menu, too (just a few dishes). Sitting here, you feel in the know—but order carefully, as prices really add up (Mon-Sat 11:30-24:00, closed Sun, a block off Piazza della Riforma at Via Magatti 3, tel. 091-922-7689).

$$ Restaurante Pestalozzi, close to the city park and attached to the recommended hotel with the same name, cranks out reasonably priced Swiss, Italian, and vegetarian meals in an indoor, air-conditioned setting (daily 11:30-22:00, Piazza Indipendenza 9, tel. 091-921-4646, www.pestalozzi-lugano.ch).

Around Piazza della Riforma: Various restaurants offer decent but pricey food and great people-watching from outdoor tables on Lugano's main piazza. The ambience here is magical at twilight. At **$$$ Pizzeria Tango,** a helpful waitstaff serves pricey Italian cuisine with a Ticino influence. While many of its tables face the busy main piazza, its interior and the tables facing a quiet little square in the back are also inviting (daily 8:00-24:00, Piazza della  Riforma, tel. 091-922-2701, www.tango-ti.ch). Also consider **$$$ Sass Café** (a classy wine bar with food, too), **$$$ Olimpia** (the mayor's fave, below City Hall, with less expensive pizzas), and **$$$ Vanini Café** (tops for coffee and desserts; try the *marrons glacés*—candied chestnuts).

CHEAP EATS

Self-Service Cafeterias: Part of a chain, **$$ Manora** offers afford-able, healthy food—a salad bar, pasta bar, main-dish counter where meat or fish is cooked in front of you, and lots more. Sit inside or out on the covered terrace (with a playground). As it has its own entrance (on Salita Chiattone, up the stairs 100 yards from the bottom of the train-station funicular), it stays open later than the Manoras in other Swiss cities. During business hours, you can also enter via the bridge from the third floor of the Manor department store (daily until 22:00, last orders at 21:00, Piazza Dante 2).

The Co-op's fourth-floor cafeteria, midway along the Via Nassa pedestrian mall, has a pretty rooftop terrace, but is other-wise a poor second to Manora, with a smaller selection and shorter hours (hot food only at lunch, Mon-Sat 8:00-19:00, closed Sun, Via Nassa 22).

Supermarkets: Try the midrange **Co-op** on Via Nassa, or the more upscale **Manor** off Piazza Dante. Both share the same hours (Mon-Sat 8:15-19:00, Thu until 21:00, closed Sun) and are in the basements of their similarly named department stores. On Sunday, your only option is the small **Piccobello** at the train station (daily 6:00-22:00).

Lugano Connections

The opening of the world's longest railway tunnel—the **Gotthard Base Tunnel**—has shortened travel times between Lugano and Zürich, Luzern, and the rest of northern Switzerland.

If you're not in a hurry, though, knit Lugano into your Swiss itinerary with **scenic trains**—take the 5.5-hour **Gotthard Panorama Express** train-and-boat combination to Luzern, or the **Bernina Express** bus-and-train combination to eastern Switzer-land. More details about these trips are in the Scenic Rail Journeys chapter. Train info: toll tel. 0900-300-300, www.rail.ch.

Long-distance **buses** leave Lugano from various points around the train station. The Bernina Express and St. Moritz buses leave from the restaurant end of the station building (away from the lake), while airport buses leave from narrow streetside parking spaces at the end of track 4 (also going away from the lake). Allow extra time when departing, as you might need to ask for help, and bus stop locations may change due to construction work.

From Lugano by Train to: Luzern (every 2 hours, 2 hours, more with transfer), **Zürich** (2/hour, 2 hours, half with easy change in Arth-Goldau), **Interlaken Ost** (every 2 hours, 5 hours, change in Olten, more with additional transfers), **Bern** (hourly, 3.5 hours, change in Luzern or Zürich), **Milan** (hourly, 80 minutes).

From Lugano by Bus and Train to the Upper Engadine: The **Bernina Express** bus (#731) leaves from outside Lugano's train station at 10:00 (daily April-late Oct only), connecting in Tirano with trains heading over the scenic Bernina Pass to Pontresina, Samedan, St. Moritz, and Chur (reservations required, tel. 081-288-6565, www.berninaexpress.ch; see the Scenic Rail Journeys chapter). A less scenic but quicker option with no changes is the **Palm Express** bus to St. Moritz (#631), which leaves Lugano's train station at 12:05 daily in peak season (mid-June-mid-Oct) and on Saturdays, Sundays, and Mondays the rest of the year (4 hours to St. Moritz; reservations required, tel. 058-448-3535, www.postbus.ch, use webcode 10037 to reserve; bus from St. Moritz to Lugano runs Fri-Sun in off-season). You can always reach St. Moritz from Lugano via **regular train** to Bellinzona, then bus to Thusis, then train to St. Moritz (almost hourly, 4 hours total).

From Lugano by Bus to Italy's Lake Como: An Italian-run local bus (#C12) goes from Lugano to Menaggio on Lake Como (nearly hourly, fewer on Sun, 1 hour, www.asfautolinee.it). From Menaggio, you can take a ferry across the lake to Varenna. This bus leaves Lugano from a stop on Via Campo Marzio, by the corner of Via Pietro Capelli. This is near the Lido stop of bus #2, in the Cassarate neighborhood a little east of downtown. Tickets are sold at a newspaper kiosk on the far side of the Campo Marzio parking lot from the bus stop—not by the driver.

From Lugano to Milan's Airports: The closest major airports to Lugano are actually in Italy, near Milan: Malpensa Airport and Linate Airport (www.sea-aeroportimilano.it). The handiest way to reach Malpensa is to use the direct buses that leave from Lugano's train station—there are three competing operators, with stops right next to each other at the far end of track 4 (www.malpensaexpress.ch, www.jetbus.ch, and www.luganoservices.ch, about hourly, 80 minutes, 25 CHF, smart to reserve ahead). Alternatively, you can take the one-hour train to Milan's Central Station, from where a train (Malpensa Express) and/or shuttle buses leave frequently for Malpensa and Linate.

UPPER ENGADINE

Pontresina · Samedan · St. Moritz

Pontresina, Samedan, and St. Moritz are a trio of towns that anchor the Upper Engadine region, tucked away in an intriguing and picturesque fringe of Switzerland. Here you can ride a vintage funicular to a scenic hike along a mountain ridge, explore the unique townscapes of an exotically remote mountain valley, gaze on a local virtuoso's paintings that capture the region's grandeur, and hear enticing snippets of the obscure Romansh language.

Nestled in the southeast corner of the country, the time-passed Upper Engadine (Engiadin Ota in Romansh, Oberengadin in German) is arguably less thrilling—and certainly more difficult to reach—than the mountain resorts of the Berner Oberland and Zermatt. But this region, wedged in the Alps between Italy and Austria, offers rough-around-the-edges mountain culture that feels far from Germanic influence, and closer to the Latin roots that run deep beneath this part of Switzerland. It's also a more rugged landscape—less groomed by humanity, with more wildlife than you'll see elsewhere in Switzerland (the area is home to the largest colony of ibex in the Alps). And for train travelers riding the scenic Bernina Express or Glacier Express, or drivers keen to experience the country's most exciting roads, this area is an easy stopover.

On first glance, there may not seem to be much history here—but look closer. Celtic people inhabited this region centuries before Christ, and the hillsides are still terraced, recalling the hard work that came with farming up here in ancient times. History is in the region's unique language, too: Like French and Spanish, Romansh evolved from the Latin that arrived with Roman soldiers and settlers, who moved here as Rome expanded. Town names date back

UPPER ENGADINE

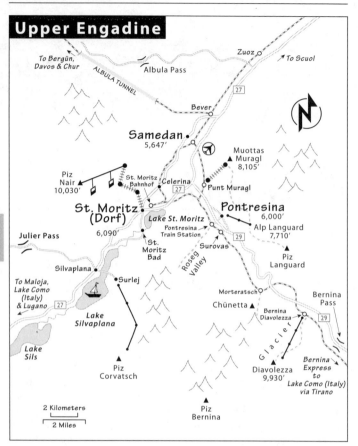

Upper Engadine

To Bergün,
Davos & Chur

ALBULA TUNNEL

Albula Pass

Zuoz

To Scuol

27

Bever

N

Samedan
5,647'

Muottas
Muragl
8,105'

Piz
Nair
10,030'

St. Moritz
Bahnhof

Celerina
27

Punt Muragl

Pontresina
6,000'

St. Moritz
(Dorf)
6,090'

Lake St. Moritz

Alp Languard
7,710'

Julier Pass

Pontresina
Train Station

29

St.
Moritz
Bad

Surovas

Piz
Languard

Silvaplana

Roseg Valley

Morteratsch

Bernina
Pass

To Maloja,
Lake Como
(Italy)
& Lugano

Surlej

Chünetta

Bernina
Diavolezza

27

Lake
Silvaplana

29

Lake
Sils

Glacier

Piz
Corvatsch

Diavolezza
9,930'

Bernina
Express
to
Lake Como (Italy)
via Tirano

2 Kilometers

2 Miles

Piz
Bernina

to various invaders. For instance, "Pontresina" comes from "Bridge of the Saracens."

Two valleys meet here, carving out a picturesque region dominated by three very different towns that form a convenient little triangle, each about 10 minutes apart by train or bus. The most famous is the ritzy ski resort of St. Moritz, where even summertime prices are unreasonably high (and the town's charm disappointingly low). Pontresina is a lower-key resort town that still has more than a few vestiges of its high-society past. With its relatively reasonable prices and proximity to my favorite hike, it's an ideal base for the region. And humble Samedan, with its cobbled lanes and cluster of lovingly painted facades, hoards most of the village charm (though there's little to do). If you can overlook the jet set comparing tans in St. Moritz, the Upper Engadine feels like a place where normal Swiss people go to find some high-altitude fun. English-language newspapers are in short supply, an indication that while there are many visitors, most are Swiss.

PLANNING YOUR TIME

Compared with the other high-mountain areas I recommend in this book (especially the Lauterbrunnen Valley and Zermatt), the Upper Engadine is pretty ho-hum. But *getting here* is anything but: Whether by a scenic rail journey or over some of Europe's most otherworldly mountain-pass roads, the trip alone—though time-consuming—makes a visit here worthwhile. And the free transit pass for overnight guests makes it worth staying two to three nights (see the "Engadin Card" sidebar, later). The chance to experience Switzerland's overlooked Romansh corner is a cultural bonus.

Conveniently, you can use the Upper Engadine to link two scenic rail trips: the Bernina Express and the Glacier Express (see the Scenic Rail Journeys chapter). And drivers should note that the valley lies right at the end of the stunning Julier Pass, a high-alpine wonderland of waterfalls and green ridges (take routes via Tiefencastel).

If staying two nights, with one full (good-weather) day, I'd do the Muottas Muragl panoramic hike to Alp Languard (above Pontresina) in the morning, head over to St. Moritz for a joyride up to Piz Nair, stroll Samedan in late afternoon, and, if it's still nice out, maybe head back up to Muottas Muragl to watch the sunset. (If the weather's bad, hit the Bellavita spa in Pontresina.) With two full days, you could do the Muottas Muragl hike one day, and hike around on Piz Nair the next (or take the Morteratsch glacier trail near Pontresina if it's cloudy), leaving you time to visit the Segantini Museum in St. Moritz before taking a leisurely wander around Samedan.

Like other mountain resort areas, this region has two distinct tourist seasons: summer (June-mid-Oct) and winter (Dec-March). Outside of these seasons, many places are closed and the area can feel dead.

GETTING AROUND THE UPPER ENGADINE

Pontresina, Samedan, St. Moritz, and Punt Muragl (the base of the funicular to Muottas Muragl) are all less than 10 minutes apart and well-connected by **bus** (about 2/hour, 5.60 CHF per trip, 11.20 CHF for 24-hour ticket). You can also take the **train** between towns (runs about hourly, same price), but the much more frequent buses take you up into each village center and save you the walk up from the train station down below. Bus rides within a town (such as between St. Moritz Bad and St. Moritz Dorf) cost 3 CHF. All local transport is covered by the Engadin Card and Swiss Travel Pass.

Allegra (Welcome) to Graubünden

Pontresina, Samedan, St. Moritz, and the rest of the Upper Engadine belong to Switzerland's biggest canton, Graubünden. Isolated by high mountain ranges, this canton is also one of the country's most conservative. The name Graubünden goes back to 1395, when a group of farmers wearing gray clothes organized themselves in the "Gray League" to fight for their autonomy. This fiercely independent region didn't join the Swiss Confederation until 1803.

People in Graubünden believe the best way to control nature is to obey it. Passionate about their environment, they purify all dirty water before returning it to the rivers. Engineers are currently going through the expensive process of removing canals (built to direct streams and rivers) and once again allowing the water to choose its own course. The natives love their beautiful countryside and cherish their customs—consistently voting against EU membership, immigration, and other issues that might compromise Swiss neutrality and self-determination. Many urban Swiss see this conservatism as narrow-minded and harmful to the country's economy, and support a more open, European Switzerland.

Graubünden cuisine is hearty. Try *Pizokel,* a *Spätzle*-like creation of cheesy flour dumplings. In fall you might find *Pizokel* made from chestnut flour and served with wild mushroom stew. Graubünden's air-dried beef, *Bündnerfleisch*—very expensive and sliced paper-thin—is popular throughout Switzerland. *Capuns* are cabbage leaves stuffed with a mix of dough, leeks, bacon, onion, and air-dried beef. *Bündner Gerstensuppe* is a creamy barley-and-vegetable soup. For a Graubünden dessert, it's got to be *Nusstorte,* a rich walnut cake.

Graubünden has three official languages: German, Italian, and Romansh (a descendant of Latin with its own independent history). You'll overhear conversations where one person speaks Italian, the other replies in German, a third butts in with Romansh...and everybody understands each other. On trains and buses, the announcements are in German and Romansh (which sounds a bit like Italian).

Most tourists here speak German (others Italian, others English), but if you'd like to please your Romansh hosts, try these phrases:

English	Romansh
Welcome.	*Allegra* (ah-LEY-grah)
Hello (Good day).	*Bun di.* (boon dee)
Good evening (after 17:00).	*Buna saira.* (BOO-nah SIGH-rah)
Please.	*Per plaschair.* (pehr plah-ZHAIR)
Thank you very much.	*Grazcha fich.* (GRAHTS-chah feech)
Goodbye.	*Arevair.* (ah-reh-VAIR)

Pick up the bus schedule *(Fahrplan/Urari)* at a TI, and study your options with the help of the map. Pay attention to which stop to use. For example, Pontresina Bahnhof is at the bottom of town, while Pontresina Post is near my recommended hotels. St. Moritz's most useful stops are Schulhausplatz (town center, near the Piz Nair funicular station) and Bahnhof (train station). In Samedan, the Chesa Planta stop is more central than the Bahnhof. If you're going, say, from St. Moritz to Samedan, save time by making sure you're not on a bus that travels via Pontresina. Bus info: tel. 081-837-9595, www.engadinbus.ch.

Considering the cost of parking, and the frequency of buses and trains, it makes little sense to drive between towns, especially with the Engadin Card.

HELPFUL HINTS

Altitude Alert: Even the valley floor here is at a high elevation (more than 6,000 feet), and you might feel dizzy and tired, especially on your first day. Top athletes from all over the world come here for altitude training before the Olympics.

Hiking Tips: Upper Engadine trails come with high altitudes. Hikers should bring the appropriate gear, including solid shoes, sun protection, windbreaker, hat, and water (for more hiking tips, see the sidebar on page 201). Even in summer, chill winds blow down from the snow-capped mountains, and it can get cold—especially on chairlifts. Here, and across the region, hiking trails are marked according to their difficulty. Yellow signs indicate easy hikes and walks. White-and-red signs signal more demanding hikes, where real hiking boots are in order. Blue signs are for alpine routes that require serious gear (these trails can be treacherous and include rock climbing and glacier crossings).

Keep in mind that in the Alps, some flowers are protected; pick one, and you may be fined. Some meadows are also protected for haymaking. Signs ask you to stick to the trails, as trampled grass is hard to cut.

Winter Activities: If you're here in winter and want to ski some of the most famous slopes in the world, head for Corviglia, the largest ski area in the region, which offers varied terrain, mostly intermediate runs, and good snowboarding (convenient from St. Moritz, or a bus ride from Pontresina). Other areas to consider are Corvatsch-Furtschellas (great views) and Diavolezza-Lagalb (smaller, less crowded, great for nonskiers who want views). Both cater mainly to intermediate and expert skiers. See www.bergbahnenengadin.ch for more information and to buy lift tickets in advance. Winter isn't just about hitting the slopes, though—the area has more than 100 miles of cross-country skiing trails, great sledding, Nordic walking, and spectator sports such as polo in the snow (horses and all). Ask at any TI for information; for more tips, see the Switzerland in Winter chapter.

Essential Brochures: Any TI can give you the local bus schedule *(Fahrplan/Urari);* the biweekly *Information for Visitors* guide, which includes a panoramic foldout map showing the lifts and hiking trails; and good maps of each town.

Pontresina

A popular winter and summer mountain resort with about 2,000 residents, Pontresina ("Puntraschinga" in Romansh) makes a good Upper Engadine home base. At 6,000 feet above sea level on a wind-protected terrace overlooking the Bernina Valley, Pontresina faces southwest and enjoys plenty of sunshine. Popular trails through its larch forests offer spectacular views of the 13,000-foot Piz Bernina peak and the immense Morteratsch glacier.

Pontresina's first tourists, mostly German and British, arrived in the 1850s. For a while, it was a summer-only destination. But by the early 1900s, the Muottas Muragl railway was inaugurated, the first grand hotels were built, and tourists began showing up in winter, too. Although a bit sterile and resorty—with not quite enough local charm or character—Pontresina offers more activities and services than Samedan, without being as glitzy as St. Moritz. This makes Pontresina the best compromise home base in this region.

Orientation to Pontresina

Pontresina sits on a ledge overlooking the confluence of two mountain streams, which then flow together across the valley to join the Inn River. Virtually everything of interest is along Via Maistra (maystrah)—Romansh for "Main Street." The post office and my recommended hotels are at the top end of Via Maistra, and the TI is near the bottom end. The train station sits in the valley floor a 10-minute walk below.

Engadin Card

Many tourist regions offer guest cards that grant discounts to overnighting tourists, but the Upper Engadine offers summer visitors something extraordinary: a guest card that covers all transportation in the region, including the pricey mountain lifts. In the rest of Switzerland, you have to factor in the price of a lift ticket when planning alpine excursions, even with a Swiss Travel Pass. Here, with an Engadin Card (Engadin is the German spelling), you can ride lifts to your heart's content, and it's free.

The pass is free (with a 10-CHF deposit) for anyone who stays at least two nights in a participating hotel in summer (May-Oct). The most common version is the "mountain railways inclusive" card, which covers local public trains and buses, mountain lifts, and even some guided hikes (see www. engadin.stmoritz.ch; select "Mountain Railways Included"). Most hotels in the region offer the pass, including those I recommend in Pontresina. However, not all hotels offer the pass, and some offer different versions of the card: Before you book, it's worth asking whether the pass is included, and which version you'll get. Versions include a card that covers just local transit, but not lifts (which is essentially useless); the "mountain railways all-inclusive" card (which lets you take a bike on board at no extra cost); and a card that covers all the mountain lifts, but not public transit between towns (not a big deal since local transit is pretty reasonable).

Tourist Information: The TI is in the heart of town in the slick Rondo Culture and Congress Center, right on Via Maistra. The staff is happy to suggest hikes and mountain lifts (Mon-Sat 8:30-18:00, Sun 16:00-18:00; shorter hours and closed Sun in mid-April-May and mid-Oct-mid-Dec, tel. 081-838-8300, www.pontresina.ch).

ARRIVAL IN PONTRESINA

The train station lies at the foot of the town, and has lockers and a ticket office. You can walk about 10 minutes steeply uphill to the town center, following the white signs to *Pontresina*. Or take bus #1 or #2 to Pontresina Post, near my recommended hotels (2-3/hour, buy ticket at counter inside train station or on bus, free with Swiss Travel Pass). To get straight to the TI, get off at Pontresina Rondo or Pontresina Punt Ota Sur. Walking the 10 minutes from Pontresina back down Via da Mulin to the train station offers dramatic gorge views.

All my recommended hotels (except the hostel) offer free or discounted parking, but drivers who aren't spending the night should head for the garage near the uphill end of Via da Mulin (1 CHF/hour) or the one near the TI (1.50 CHF/hour).

HELPFUL HINTS

Music: Free summer classical music concerts are offered in the Tais Forest across the river, and (on rainy days) in the Rondo Center or in the church next door (daily at 11:00, mid-June-mid-Sept, confirm and get details at TI).

Ski Rental: Try **Gruber Sport** (at Via Maistra 190, across from Hotel Schweizerhof, tel. 081-842-6236, www.gruber-sport.ch).

Shopping: Furniture and housewares store **Rominger Möbel** has an upstairs showroom that's like a modern Engadine home show: Walking among hand-carved beds, tables, and dressers—all made from the fragrant Swiss pine that's unique to this region—gives you a sense of good living high in this remote corner of Switzerland. You can find good souvenirs here (Mon-Fri 8:30-12:00 & 14:00-18:00, Sat until 17:00, closed Sun, Via Maistra 246, at the top end of town 5 minutes past Pontresina Post bus stop, tel. 081-842-6263, www.rominger.ch).

Sights and Activities in Pontresina

CHURCHES AND MUSEUMS

Church of St. Mary (Begräbniskirche Sta. Maria)

Above town, just beyond the five-sided, 13th-century Spaniola Tower, stands this remarkable little church. Inside, the wooden ceiling is entirely original. Faded 13th-century, Byzantine-inspired frescoes survive on the west wall (to the left as you enter). The other walls and ceiling were richly decorated by an Italian workshop (1497). The frescoes depict the legend of Mary Magdalene and (above) the story of Lazarus' resurrection. Imagine this church five centuries ago, packed with illiterate villagers who worshipped by following along with the pictures.

Cost and Hours: Free entry, but limited hours: generally opens Mon, Wed, and Fri at 14:30 or 15:30 and closes at 16:00 or 17:30; also open Tue and Thu in summer; closed altogether mid-Oct-mid-Dec and mid-April-May. For more information, contact the Pontresina TI.

Hiking Back to Town: For a quick (10-minute) hike, walk down from the church a different way: Follow the yellow sign for *Las Blais,* which takes you under the chairlift. Signs along the

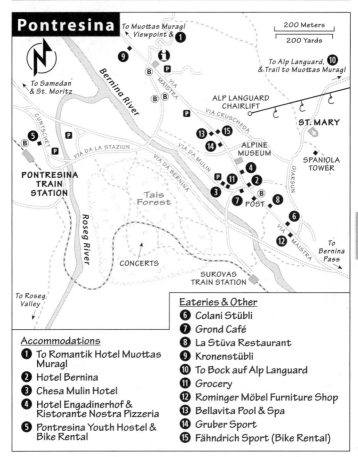

Pontresina

To Muottas Muragl
↑ Viewpoint & ❶

200 Meters

200 Yards

To Alp Languard, ❿
& Trail to Muottas Muragl

To Samedan
& St. Moritz

Bernina River

VIA MAISTRA

ALP LANGUARD
CHAIRLIFT

VIA CRUSCHEDA

ST. MARY

CUNTSCHET

VIA DA LA STAZIUN

VIA DA MULIN

VIA DA BERNINA

❺

❶❸

⓭ ⓯

⓮

ALPINE
MUSEUM

SPANIOLA
TOWER

GIARSUN

**PONTRESINA
TRAIN
STATION**

Tais
Forest

❹

❸ ❼

❶❶

❷

POST

❽

❻

VIA MAISTRA

Roseg River

CONCERTS

SUROVAS
TRAIN STATION

⓬

To
Bernina
Pass

To Roseg
Valley

Eateries & Other
❻ Colani Stübli
❼ Grond Café
❽ La Stüva Restaurant
❾ Kronenstübli
❿ To Bock auf Alp Languard
❶❶ Grocery
⓬ Rominger Möbel Furniture Shop
⓭ Bellavita Pool & Spa
⓮ Gruber Sport
⓯ Fähndrich Sport (Bike Rental)

<u>Accommodations</u>
❶ To Romantik Hotel Muottas Muragl
❷ Hotel Bernina
❸ Chesa Mulin Hotel
❹ Hotel Engadinerhof & Ristorante Nostra Pizzeria
❺ Pontresina Youth Hostel & Bike Rental

UPPER ENGADINE

way share interesting facts on ibex, which you may see from here if you look up the hillside. Eventually, head down to the left following the *Puntraschigna–Laret* sign; you'll come back into town near the TI.

Alpine Museum (Museum Alpin)

This little museum is worth a quick visit—it was founded by the local mountain guides' association. The exhibits fill three floors of an old Engadine town house, covering the development of alpine mountain climbing and skiing, the regional mining industry (with plenty of mineral samples), hunting, local animals, and replicas of traditional rooms (bedroom, kitchen, living room). About 130 of the 250 bird species found in the Upper Engadine are shown here. Listen to the recorded songs of 60 different birds on the primitive aviary jukebox. Find the slideshow room, where you can choose from four themes (mountains, flowers, butterflies, and a changing theme)—the mountain slides will make you feel like a wimp. Rounding out the space are temporary exhibits. Be sure to pick up the brief English descriptions when you enter.

Cost and Hours: 8 CHF, covered by Swiss Travel Pass, Mon-Sat 15:30-18:00, closed Sun, also closed mid-April-mid-June and mid-Oct-mid-Dec, Via Maistra 199, tel. 081-842-7273, www. pontresina.ch/museumalpin.

LIFTS AND HIKES

Pontresina is a hiker's paradise. The town boasts one of Switzerland's largest mountaineering schools and has a good reputation for adventure sports. Shops lining Via Maistra rent and sell all kinds of sports gear. The TI will help you find just the right hike. Their great, free foldout *Panorama* map is marked with hiking trails and lists details about each one. They also hand out a leaflet describing a few popular routes. (Most hikers agree that the Muottas Muragl-Alp Languard panoramic route is tops.) For a fee, you can hire an English-speaking mountaineer through the TI.

▲▲Muottas Muragl Viewpoint (8,105 feet)

This impressive alpine perch isn't as high as other spots mentioned in this chapter (Piz Nair, Diavolezza), but it's my favorite for its spectacular views over Pontresina and Samedan, and far away to the valleys and lakes beyond St. Moritz. To reach the viewpoint, ride the cute 1907 funicular from the **Punt Muragl** valley station. At the top of the funicular, you can rent a deck chair, have a meal, do an easygoing loop hike, or start a hike over to Alp Languard (described next). And since the funicular runs till late in the evening, it's the perfect place to watch the sunset. A pricey-but-good restaurant on the terrace is open late daily.

Getting There: Catch the funicular from the **Punt Muragl** valley station (25 CHF one-way, 35 CHF round-trip, 15 CHF after 18:00, covered by Engadin Card; runs early June-mid-Oct 2/hour 8:00-23:00—round-trip ticket lets you return on this funicular or on the Alp Languard lift described later; also runs late Dec-March; same contact info as recommended Romantik Hotel Muottas Muragl: tel. 081-842-8232, www.muottasmuragl.ch).

To reach the valley station from Pontresina, take bus #1 (in either direction—the bus stops at Punt Muragl both on the way into and out of town) or #2 (direction: Maloja). You can also catch the train between Pontresina and Samedan and get off at Punt Muragl (by request only—press the green button, or the train won't stop). You can park here for free—but if you're hiking to Alp Languard, it makes more sense to take the train or bus, as the hike ends back at Pontresina.

▲▲▲Muottas Muragl Panoramic Hike

This fantastic hike over to Alp Languard, directly above Pontresina, comes with grand views the entire way and a gradual descent of

about 400 feet. Midway, there's a great soup or coffee-and-cakes stop (ask for the WC key for a fun alpine memory). Keep your eyes open for ibex, bighorn stags, and marmots.

It's about four hours round-trip from Pontresina, including three hours of easy to moderately strenuous hiking. Leave Pontresina by 13:30 if you want to catch the chairlift down from Alp Languard. For extra credit, consider the more challenging upper route (the "Climate Trail") that climbs the mountainside above the main route via the Chamanna Segantini hut (adds about an hour to the hike).

▲▲Alp Languard Viewpoint (7,710 feet)

At Alp Languard, hovering right over the center of Pontresina, you can head out on a loop hike, bask in a lounge chair, unwind after your hike from Muottas Muragl, let the kids loose in the play area, and enjoy an affordable lunch with unbeatable views at the **$$ Bock auf Alp Languard** chalet (early June-mid-Oct daily 9:00-17:00, tel. 079-719-7810).

Getting There (and Back): A six-minute chairlift runs continuously between Alp Languard and a station a few minutes uphill from central Pontresina (early June-late Oct 8:30-17:30, 16.50 CHF one-way, 24 CHF round-trip—or, if coming from Muottas Muragl, use the return part of the round-trip ticket you bought there, covered by Engadin Card, tel. 081-842-6255). Don't worry if you arrive here after the lift's stopped running: It's only a 45-minute hike back into town. Where the path splits, take the left fork (the "Röntgenweg") for an easier descent on a zigzag path through the trees.

Morteratsch Glacier Walk

A popular, inexpensive excursion from Pontresina is by train to **Morteratsch,** partway up the Bernina Pass. From Morteratsch, an easy trail leads up-valley for 50 minutes to the tongue of the Morteratsch glacier, with signposts marking the glacier's reach in past decades. It's also a pleasant walk on a cloudy day. The whole round-trip from Pontresina is about two hours by train.

Following the glacial stream gently uphill, you first pass a field of dramatically lumpy glacier-hewn rocks. Farther along, you get the sense you're hiking on the bottom of a drained swimming pool—it's amazing (and alarming) to see, high up on the hillsides,

UPPER ENGADINE

the obvious former extent of the glacier (it hit the upper line in 1850). At the top of the trail, you're eye-to-eye with the snout of the glacier. Keep in mind that much of what looks like rock here is actually dirty ice. To extend the hike, you can scramble over the rock field past the end of the official path for a more up-close look, but be careful—the ground is very unstable beyond the groomed path.

Back at the trailhead, you can eat at the restaurant near the train stop, and also visit a traditional cheesemaker (also near train stop, mid-June-early Oct only, tel. 081-842-6273, www.alp-schaukaeserei.ch).

Getting There: The train drops you off right at the foot of the trail (hourly, 8 minutes from Pontresina, 5.60 CHF without Engadin Card). From the highway, drivers should follow signs for Morteratsch to the large parking lot at the end of the road (pay at machine). Walk from the lot toward the white Morteratsch Hotel, and then past it (with the hotel on the right) to the trailhead.

Diavolezza Peak (9,930 feet)

The 15-minute cable-car ride up to the peak called Diavolezza—the "she-devil"—takes you over an otherworldly, green landscape of babbling brooks, then past stark rock and ice to a ridgetop station. There you'll find a restaurant and terrace with expansive views of the top of the Morteratsch glacier. To turn this into a hiking excursion, return to the valley on foot (2 hours on a moderately difficult trail via Lake Diavolezza, or 3.5 hours on an easier trail past Lake Collinas).

Getting There: To reach the lift station from Pontresina, either take the train 10 minutes beyond Morteratsch to the Bernina Diavolezza stop or drive 12 minutes toward the Bernina Pass (free parking). The cable car is covered by the Engadin Card (otherwise 26 CHF one-way, 36 CHF round-trip, 3/hour, daily 8:30-17:00, tel. 081-838-7373, www.diavolezza.ch).

Roseg Valley Stroll

You can hike two easy hours up the Roseg Valley, directly opposite Pontresina (look for the trailhead behind the Pontresina train station) and marvel at its glacier (from a distance). Consider taking the fun **horse-drawn omnibus** back to Pontresina—or take the omnibus up and hike back (reservations required, June-Oct departures at fixed hours, 20 CHF one-way, 32 CHF round-trip, mobile 078-944-7555, www.engadin-kutschen.ch). You can also rent a private carriage (120 CHF one-way for up to 4 people, 220 CHF round-trip includes 1.5 hours for exploring; several coachmen offer this—try the Costa family, tel. 081-842-6057, www.stalla-engiadina.ch, office@stalla-engiadina.ch).

UPPER ENGADINE

OTHER ACTIVITIES
▲Bellavita Pool and Spa

This delightful pool complex is an ideal place to relax in any weather. The fun indoor-outdoor swimming-pool complex includes an enclosed, 250-foot-long spiral waterslide, an outdoor pool that stays at 93 degrees Fahrenheit year-round, and an indoor water playground for kids. There's also a spa (nudity required) with a series of saunas, steam baths, and more. (The spa is usually mixed-gender and adults-only, but it's women-only Mon 13:00-17:00 and Thu after 17:00; kids ages 6-15 allowed with parents Sat-Sun 12:00-16:00.)

Cost and Hours: Pool only-11 CHF, pool and spa-26.50 CHF; pool open Mon-Fri 10:00-22:00, Sat-Sun until 21:00, spa open similar hours; in the middle of town at Via Maistra 178, tel. 081-837-0037, www.pontresina-bellavita.ch. You can rent a swimsuit for a few francs, or buy one in the shop.

Biking

Several sports stores rent bicycles, easy-to-use electric-powered bikes, in-line skates, tennis rackets, and other gear. Riding the train to the Bernina Pass and biking nine miles back into town is just one of many fun biking options. In the town center, **Fähndrich Sport** rents good mountain bikes (25-38 CHF/half-day, 35-50 CHF/day, the higher price is for a full suspension) and electric bikes (39 CHF/half-day, 54 CHF/day; includes helmets, cheaper for multiple days; Mon-Fri 8:00-12:00 & 14:00-18:30, Sat until 17:00, closed Sun except July-Aug and Dec-March, closed most of May; Via Maistra 169, tel. 081-842-7155, www.faehndrich-sport. ch). Across the street from the train station, in the lower level of the big youth hostel building, **Bikezentrum Pontresina** rents a huge selection of bikes (mountain bikes-31 CHF/half-day, 43 CHF/day; electric bikes-39 CHF/half-day, 54 CHF/day; includes helmets; daily 8:30-12:00 & 13:30-18:00, closed Oct-mid-June; tel. 081-838-8388, www.pontresina-sports.ch).

Sleeping in Pontresina

The Romantik Hotel Muottas Muragl is perched on an alpine ledge above (and just barely outside) town—see its listing for directions. The other hotels listed here are within steps of Pontresina Post, the town's most convenient bus stop. All of these hotels, including the hostel, offer the Engadin Card free to guests staying at least two nights (see the "Engadin Card" sidebar, earlier in the chapter).

$$$$ Romantik Hotel Muottas Muragl offers a secluded overnight high in the Alps, with 16 elegant-rustic rooms furnished in the local Swiss pinewood. When the funicular takes the last tourist down, things become as peaceful as the Alps can be (cheaper for 3 or more nights, price includes funicular ticket, open mid-June–mid-Oct and mid-Dec–March only, free parking at base of funicular, tel. 081-842-8232, www.muottasmuragl.ch, info@muottasmuragl.ch).

$$$$ Hotel Bernina, a well-run and woody three-star place, picks up guests at the Pontresina station for free (let them know what time you'll arrive). Its 41 tidy, attractive rooms can be a fine value for this area, and come with nice touches (sauna, good restaurant serving Engadine specialties, Via Maistra 207, tel. 081-838-8686, www.hotelbernina.ch, info@hotelbernina.ch).

$$$ Chesa Mulin Hotel, below the main street, offers 30 modern, bright, and comfortable rooms, most with nature-based themes. The inviting sitting area with open fireplace and library makes bad weather tolerable. The friendly Isepponi-Schmid family takes good care of their guests (discounts sometimes available in shoulder season for guests over age 60, elevator, sauna, sundeck, free access to Bellavita pool and spa with 2-night stay, limited free parking, Via da Mulin 15, tel. 081-838-8200, www.chesa-mulin.ch, info@chesa-mulin.ch).

$$$ Hotel Engadinerhof, while less cozy, can be a good value. The hotel preserves a pre-WWII ambience, and its 88 rooms gather around a sprawling and classic Old World lounge. The three-night minimum is waived when business is slow. Cheaper sink-only rooms ("Category A") are clean and have well-preserved furniture from the 1930s. "Category B" offers the same old-fashioned rooms, plus antique bathrooms, and "Category C" gets you modern rooms (family deals, elevator, free pick-up from train station if staying at least 3 nights, pay parking, Via Maistra 203, tel. 081-839-3100, www.engadinerhof.com, info@engadinerhof.com).

¢ Pontresina Youth Hostel, across the street from the train station, rents 120 beds. There's no curfew, and guests have 24-hour access (though check-in times are limited; includes sheets and lockers, discount at Bellavita spa, four-course dinner available, pay laundry service, game and TV room, limited pay parking, closed early April–early June and mid-Oct–early Dec, Via da la Staziun 46, tel. 081-842-7223, www.youthhostel.ch/pontresina, pontresina@youthhostel.ch).

Eating in Pontresina

Virtually all restaurants in Pontresina are part of a hotel, apart from a few bakeries that serve reasonably priced meals. Except for the Grond Café, all the restaurants listed below are closed off-season, generally from early April to early June and again from mid-October to mid-December. And, the Muottas Muragl and Alp Languard viewpoints (described earlier, under "Sights and Activities in Pontresina") also have good eating options (though Alp Languard's closes before dinnertime).

$$$ Ristorante Nostra Pizzeria serves wood-fired pizzas as well as some local dishes in two pleasantly low-key rooms on the ground floor of Hotel Engadinerhof (pastas, meat dishes, fondue for two, daily 11:00-14:00 & 18:00-22:30, only pizza after 21:30, Via Maistra 203, tel. 081-839-3333, www.engadinerhof.com).

$$$$ Colani Stübli, a cozy, elegant eatery, serves regional and seasonal specialties, including meat dishes and local starchy dishes such as *Krautpizokel* and *Capuns* (67-75-CHF fixed-price meals, daily 12:00-14:00 & 18:00-21:00, limited menu available 14:00-18:00 and after 21:00, at Hotel Steinbock, Via Maistra 219, tel. 081-839-3626, www.hotelsteinbock.ch).

$ Grond Café is a bakery with great desserts, plus sandwiches and takeaway lunches (daily 7:00-18:30, Via da Mulin 29, tel. 081-838-8030).

$$ Pontresina Youth Hostel, by the train station, welcomes nonguests for its hearty four-course self-serve dinner (20 CHF includes soup, salad, main course, dessert, and tap water; daily 18:30-19:30, vegetarian option, reservations appreciated, Via da la Staziun 46, tel. 081-842-7223, www.youthhostel.ch/pontresina, pontresina@youthhostel.ch). They also serve a 12-CHF breakfast year-round and a 15-CHF, three-course lunch in winter (daily Dec-March 11:00-14:00).

$$$$ Elegant Five-Star Hotel Dining Rooms: Pontresina's two top hotels have wonderful restaurants in sumptuous dining rooms. **La Stüva Restaurant,** in the cellar of the fanciful faux-castle Hotel Walther at the top end of town, is expensive and exclusive, with a flair for serving inventive and light regional and international cuisine. Their multicourse fixed-price meals make a good splurge, but you'll be amazed at how well you can eat with only their inexpensive salad bar and cheese plate (Wed-Sun 19:00-21:30, closed Mon-Tue, Via Maistra 215, tel. 081-839-3636, www.hotelwalther.ch). **Kronenstübli** is in the Grand Hotel Kronenhof, which dominates the bottom end of town and has public rooms fit for a Viennese palace. It's less accommodating to anyone concerned about price, but if you've got francs to burn, its five-course fixed-price meal for 165 CHF is a memorable splurge (also has three-course meals, Tue-Sat 19:00-21:30, closed Sun-Mon, Via Maistra, tel. 081-830-3030, www.kronenhof.com).

Supermarket: Picnickers seek out the **Co-op grocery,** just below Via Maistra on Via da Mulin (Mon-Fri 8:00-19:00, Sat-Sun until 18:00).

UPPER ENGADINE

Samedan

Tiny Samedan (sah-MAY-den, population 3,000) is the prettiest—
and sleepiest—town of the three de-
scribed in this chapter. The historic
capital of the valley, it's stuffed with
traditional Engadine architecture,
and Romansh remains strong here.
Though charming, Samedan is also
humble, workaday, and even a bit
rough around the edges. Aside from
the grand Hotel Bernina, the town

seems almost untouched by the era of belle époque tourism. It was
primarily the region's transportation hub back then, when horse-
drawn carriages met arriving train passengers to cart them off to
fancy hotels in St. Moritz and Pontresina—and today it still feels
like the backwater cousin of its ritzy neighbors.

There's not much to do here after an hour or two, but it's worth
popping over from Pontresina for a quick taste of untouched Enga-
dine-village beauty.

Orientation to Samedan

Samedan is gently spread along the slope of a hill that rises from
the Inn River. The train station is at the bottom of town; the town
center clusters just above. The main street, called Plazzet, runs
through the middle of town parallel to the river (it's closed off on
market day—Tue, June-early Oct). All the streets seem to converge
at the main square, called Plaz, with its tall Protestant church.

Tourist Information: Samedan's TI is at Plazzet 3, by the
Chesa Planta bus stop (Mon-Fri 9:00-12:00 & 15:00-18:00, Sat
from 10:00, closed Sun, also closed Sat off-season, tel. 081-851-
0060, www.engadin.stmoritz.ch/sommer/en/samedan).

Arrival in Samedan: Whether you come by **bus or train,**
you'll stop at the train station, which has lockers, ticket windows,
and a free WC. Most buses do go up into the town itself after a
short wait (ask the driver); if you stay on, you'll want to get off in
two stops, at Chesa Planta. Or, from the train station, just hike up
the hill, bearing left on Via Mulin to reach the main square. **Drivers** who are here for just a quick visit can park free for one hour in
the big garage just off the roundabout into town (past the Co-op
and before the station). Pay street parking is usually easy to find
(maximum 2 hours within the town center or 12 hours at the top of
town); pay parking is also available at the train station.

Helpful Hints: If looking for a sit-down meal, **$$$ Restau-**

Traditional Engadine Architecture

Samedan and Pontresina both have fine old traditional houses. A short stroll in either town shows plenty of traditional elements and medieval ingenuity intended to keep inhabitants warm in the harsh mountain weather. Walls are thick—typically two feet—for insulation. Notice how windows are like the narrow end of a funnel—originally covered with animal skin rather than glass. Bay windows gathered maximum precious light and came with built-in seats where women sat to do handwork.

Even though they're thoroughly modernized, the structural essence of these grand farmhouses survives. You can still see the big lower door for animals and the big upper door for hay and the carriage—with a smaller door built into it for people to get in and out while minimizing heat loss. People had the animals sleep below in the hope their rising body heat would warm the living space above. Proud noble-family coats of arms still decorate buildings; many local families can trace their heritage to the Middle Ages.

Look for the traditional Engadine *sgraffito* ornamentation on exterior walls. To make *sgraffito,* facades are covered with a layer of dark plaster, which is then covered with white or colored plaster. Before the white plaster dries, decorative designs are scratched into it, so that the dark background appears. These rustic and crude decorations—much more durable than painted facades—look modern, but have a long history.

rant 1865, in the grand Hotel Bernina, is a decent value, with pizzas, calzones, and main courses (daily 18:00-22:00, Plazzet 20, tel. 081-852-1212.

Sights in Samedan

Samedan Town Walk

Samedan offers few activities other than relaxing and enjoying the town. For a start, follow this pleasant, self-guided stroll with nice views. The route described here takes you steeply up through town to a perch overlooking Samedan's magnificent setting, and offers a look at the local architecture.

Begin at the **main square (Plaz),** where all of Samedan's

(margin, vertical) **UPPER ENGADINE**

cobbled streets meet. Just downhill, the blocky, modern building with the colorful tiled window frames is Samedan's **"vertical spa,"** with several levels of pools (more expensive and less extensive than Pontresina's spa, www.mineralbad-samedan.ch).

From the square, walk uphill on Surtuor (leaving the steeple behind you on the left) to the fork in the road, and take the lane on the left, following the white sign for *Kath. Kirche.* Continue straight up the hill for a block to find (on the right) a 13th-century, castle-like **stone tower** that was the private tower of a noble family. From its wooden balcony, they'd oversee festivities in their little domain. It's now used for changing museum exhibits (www.latuor.ch).

Next door, the house at **#12** dates from 1656. The extended roof beams form an X-shaped St. Andrew's cross. This was a popu-

lar way to bless homes here. Notice the sturdy beam ends—roofs were built to support heavy stones and snow. Houses in the region are known by Romansh names: For example, you'll see houses marked *Chesa Juzi* (Juzi's House) and *Chesa dals 3 Frers* (House of the Three Brothers). A little farther up, across the street, look between Chesa Manzoni and Chesa Sleim to see an interesting modern house that's influenced by old local styles.

Continue uphill to the **Catholic Church** (Neo-Romanesque from 1910, with a bell dating back to 1505), at the top of the town. From here, survey the surrounding slopes and their ancient terracing, a vestige from Celtic peoples.

Carry on uphill, passing the ski lift. Yes, you can do it. Where the road swings right, pause at the wooden bench for the gorgeous **view.** Samedan overlooks the point where the Inn River (coming from St. Moritz) is joined by the Flaz (coming from Pontresina and the Bernina Pass). From here, the Inn continues through Innsbruck in Austria before joining the Danube.

Huff and puff the thin air (you're at 6,000 feet) to the dramatically situated Protestant **Church of St. Peter.** The Romanesque bell tower (c. 1100) predates today's late Gothic church (c. 1480; now a burial church, generally closed to tourists). Benches line the cemetery walls and offer sunny, wind-protected picnic spots. Beneath you stretches the highest-altitude airport in Europe, a favorite place to fly gliders (launched by a yellow truck with a huge winch). When you've had your fill of the views,

continue around the far side of the church, where the paved path leads quickly back down into town—steer for the tall steeple.

Chesa Planta

This interesting old mansion, just a block from the main square, shows off upper-crust lifestyles of the 18th and 19th centuries. This

former residence of the wealthy local Planta family is preserved just as it was when they lived here. It's rarely open, but the fascinating interior makes it worth considering if you happen to be here at the right time. You'll see some gorgeous wood-carved rooms, a beautifully painted dining room, original granite slab floors, and fancy ceramic stoves. Upstairs, the same building houses a Romansh library *(biblioteca rumauntscha),* where scholars collect Romansh literature. A copy of any new book published in the Romansh language is sent to this library.

Cost and Hours: 10-CHF German tour (with an English handout), covered by Swiss Travel Pass, 1.5-hour tour runs Thu at 16:30 in Jan-early April and July-mid-Oct; may open other weekdays and/or offer self-guided visit with tablet—check; tel. 081-852-1272, www.chesaplanta.ch.

St. Moritz

The oldest and perhaps best-known winter resort in the world, St. Moritz has long been the winter haunt of Europe's rich and

famous. It's said that in 1864, St. Moritz hotel pioneer Johannes Badrutt invented winter tourism in the Alps. To allay his British guests' skepticism, he offered them free accommodations if the winter weather was bad. They came and enjoyed fine weather. He

liquored them up, they had fun...and they brought their friends along the next year. St. Moritz hosted the Winter Olympics in 1928 and 1948.

Although St. Moritz might have been a real town once, today it's little more than a charmless cluster of luxury hotels and designer boutiques. (Think of it as the anti-Gimmelwald.) For the jet set, winter is prime time in St. Moritz, when celebrity-spotting and prices are at their peak. In summer, however, it's pretty quiet, and mostly attracts sporty Swiss vacationers of means who come for active recreation (in-line skating, polo, golf, paragliding, horseback riding, lake strolling, etc.).

For the rest of us, the town has little to offer—I don't recommend overnighting here (though nightlife seekers will find it livelier here than in surrounding towns). But those with the Engadin Card should consider a visit for the fun cable-car ride up to Piz Nair and its views, a hike or bike on the mountainside above town, and a quick look at the Segantini Museum.

Orientation to St. Moritz

The older section of St. Moritz (known as the "Dorf") sits on a steep slope above the lake. The train station *(Bahnhof)* is next to the lake at the base of the hill. The main bus stop (called Schulhausplatz) is at the top. Schulhausplatz is officially called "Plazza da Scoula" in Romansh (but you won't hear much Romansh in German-speaking St. Moritz).

From the center of town, the busy Via dal Bagn runs downhill to the modern suburb of St. Moritz Bad, which sprawls on a level plain at the far end of the lake. St. Moritz Bad has some sports facilities (covered pool, tennis courts, ice-skating hall, horseback riding, and so on) and a one-block shopping district (Via Salet), but it's mostly a characterless concrete town. Aside from its proximity to the lake, St. Moritz Bad is pretty, well, bad.

Tourist Information: The über-slick and helpful TI is along the main drag (Via Maistra) in the old center, a block from the main bus stop at Schulhausplatz. Swing by to get personalized advice on walks and hikes, check their cheap posters (see "Helpful Hints," later), and grab a free town map (Mon-Sat 9:00-18:30, closed Sun, Via Maistra 12, tel. 081-837-3333, www.stmoritz.ch). There's also a tiny branch TI next to the ticket office at the train station (daily 10:00-14:00 & 15:00-18:30).

ARRIVAL IN ST. MORITZ

St. Moritz's **train station** is near the lake, just below the Dorf. The station has lockers, ticket windows, a baggage-storage desk, an inexpensive café, and a branch TI.

The town center towers above the station. You can simply **walk** uphill for 15 minutes, but it's more fun (and less work) to head up via the Serletta parking garage: Exit the station to the left (look for *Zentrum/Dorf* signs with an escalator icon) and cross the footbridge into the garage. Inside, find the art-lined escalator (Switzerland's longest) that zips you up next to the Palace Hotel. Even ritzier, to enjoy your own private Swiss mountain lift for a couple of minutes, ride the elevator that runs next to the escalators (enter underneath the first stage). From the top, it's a relatively quick walk up to the center. To avoid walking from the station, hop on **bus** #3 up to Schulhausplatz (4/hour, 3 CHF, covered by Engadin Card).

If arriving by **car,** you can pay to park at the Serletta garage (near the train station) or at the more central Quadrellas garage (on Schulhausplatz). Street parking is a little cheaper.

UPPER ENGADINE

HELPFUL HINTS

Winter Activities: Ender Sport is one of many ski-rental shops (winter hours: Mon-Sat 8:00-19:00, Sun 10:00-13:00 & 15:00-18:00, just uphill from TI and recommended hotels at Via Maistra 26, tel. 081-833-3536, www.endersport.com). For a thrilling splurge you can take a ride—between a professional pilot and brakeman—on the mile-long Olympic **bobsled** course from St. Moritz to Celerina...in 75 seconds (250 CHF, open late Dec-early March, reserve ahead, www.olympia-bobrun.ch).

Bike Rental: To rent an e-bike or mountain bike, contact the St. Moritz sailing club, on the lakeshore just below the town center (helmets provided, open June-Oct, mobile 079-209-3899, www.scstm.ch). Mountain bikes are also rentable at the Chantarella funicular station above town.

Wi-Fi: Free public Wi-Fi is available in a few spots around town, including most of the pedestrian zone of St. Moritz Dorf, and the Chantarella and Corviglia funicular stations up on the mountainside (look for the "Free Wi-Fi Engadin" network).

Posters: St. Moritz's tourist board offers pre-WWII tourism posters for 5 CHF each. Buy from the main TI or order online (https://shop.stmoritz.ch).

Sights and Activities in St. Moritz

MUSEUMS

While the Berry Museum is just downhill from the center's pedestrian zone, the others are a 10- to 15-minute walk from the center of town, with the Segantini perched directly uphill from the Engadiner Museum. A steep, woodsy path connects the two—look for the path directly across the street from the Segantini Museum; leaving the Engadiner, head to the right to start the walk up.

▲▲Segantini Museum

This museum is dedicated to the ultimate painter of alpine life. Giovanni Segantini (b. 1858) came here to get away from the misty air of Milan, and to live more cheaply (in those days, Switzerland was a low-budget destination). The crisp alpine atmosphere was great for capturing the bright, sharp, crystal-clear mountain light. Painting in the open air with brushstrokes that invigorated his fascinating scenes, Segantini created works reminiscent of the French Impressionists. The tiny museum, which looks like a Neo-Byzantine church, is based on Segantini's design for the Swiss Pavilion at the 1900 World's Fair in Paris—but made of local stone rather than the originally intended steel. Segantini died young (at age 41,
in 1899), and money ran out before this grandiose pavilion could be built. Segantini's masterpiece, the *Alpine Triptych,* was also painted for the World's Fair, but not quite completed. Segantini's vision—both his pavilion and his life's major work—lives on here, near where he settled in his 30s.

Cost and Hours: 10 CHF, not covered by Swiss Travel Pass; Tue-Sun 10:00-12:00 & 14:00-18:00, closed Mon, also closed mid-Oct-mid-Dec and mid-April-mid-May; worthwhile 30-minute audioguide-3 CHF, Via Somplaz 30, tel. 081-833-4454, www.segantini-museum.ch.

Getting There: To reach the museum on foot you can simply follow signs along Via Somplaz, but for a nicer stroll, look for the "Segantiniweg" path that cuts through the woods just above the road. (Or take bus #2 or #5 one stop from Schulhausplatz to the Segantini Museum stop.) Drivers will find metered roadside parking just before the museum.

Visiting the Museum: The paintings are displayed on two floors. Begin by climbing the stairs to the round room on the top floor, where you can view the haunting *Alpine Triptych:* three paintings representing (left to right) life, nature, and death. Notice how, even in the death scene—as the body of a newly deceased loved one is brought out to a horse cart while mourning women look on—there's a glimmer of hope and faith in the swirling clouds above. Segantini even designed the *Triptych*'s frames, ornamented with the local five-needled Swiss pine.

Then head back to the entry level, and spend some time with the many smaller canvases here. Particularly notable is *Ave Maria at the Crossing,* where a man rowing a simple boat—laden with a flock of sheep and a mother and baby—pauses to pray at sunset as the church bells toll.

Engadiner Museum (Museum Engiandinais)

This four-story Engadine-style house, built in 1905 to house this museum, displays a collection of lovingly reassembled living areas *(stüvas)* from the region's surviving patrician houses of centuries past. Most of these interiors are entirely paneled in wood, much of it elaborately carved (especially in the Stüa de Gros). Following the well-done tablet guide (included with entry), you can also peek at a smoky farm kitchen and a nightmare-inducing four-poster bed that's overseen by a painted skeleton, just in case life in medieval Switzerland didn't provide enough reminders of one's mortality.

Cost and Hours: 13 CHF, covered by Swiss Travel Pass; open Wed-Mon 10:00-18:00 in summer, 14:00-18:00 in winter, Thu until 20:00 and closed Tue year-round; also closed mid-Oct-Nov and mid-April-mid-May; Via dal Bagn 39, walk 10 minutes downhill from town center, tel. 081-833-4333, www.museum-engiadinais.ch.

Berry Museum

Dedicated not to delicious little fruits, but to local painter Peter Robert Berry (1864-1942), this museum introduces visitors to another talented alpine artist. While Berry enjoyed neither the talent nor the fame of Segantini, and the entry price is steep, this is a suitable rainy-day activity for art lovers (and anyone with a Swiss Travel Pass).

Cost and Hours: 15 CHF, covered by Swiss Travel Pass, includes audioguide; hours uncertain but likely open in summer and winter Wed-Mon 10:00-18:00 with a midday break, closed Tue; also closed in spring and fall, confirm exact times locally; just below the center of St. Moritz Dorf at Via Arona 32, tel. 081-833-3018, www.berrymuseum.com.

LIFTS AND HIKES

▲▲▲Piz Nair (10,026 feet)

With an Engadin Card, the trip up to the Piz Nair station (at 9,915 feet) is the best reason to visit St. Moritz in the summer. (Without the card, your money's better spent on a visit to Muottas Muragl/Alp Languard—and I'd skip St. Moritz altogether.) The ride up is a treat, and from the top you get a sprawling, nearly 360-degree view across the region's rugged mountain rooftop and down to the lakes and valleys below. The view restaurant offers pleasant indoor and outdoor seating.

The ride up to Piz Nair has three stages: two funiculars, then a cable car, all of which leave every 20 minutes. From a station just uphill from Schulplatz, in the middle of St. Moritz Dorf, ride the first funicular to Chantarella (8:20-17:00, last ascent to Piz Nair at 16:00, last descent at 17:20). At Chantarella

(6,578 feet), change to a second funicular up to Corviglia (aim for a seat on the left, 8:30-16:50, last descent at 17:10). At Corviglia (8,156 feet), switch to the cable car for the last leg up to Piz Nair (8:45-16:25, last descent at 16:45). The entire ride up takes 30 minutes; riding all the way down can take a little longer, as the funicular isn't timed for the convenience of descending passengers.

The mountain's footpaths and bike trails are well-maintained. Experienced hikers up for a steep challenge can walk back to town in about four to five hours. For a much easier descent, ride the cable car down to the Corviglia ridge, then enjoy great views while hiking from there back into town (2 hours via Marguns—which also has eating options, fairly easy walk most of the way but with steep parts at the start and end). Corviglia is a lovely spot to hang out before heading down, with an alpine hut serving food (a short uphill walk from the station), and the absurdly swanky, crassly promotional Quattro Bar (as in the Audi model it's hyping), which perfectly captures the whole St. Moritz vibe. An even less strenuous walking option is "Heidi's Flower Trail," a relatively level one-hour loop through wildflower fields from the Chantarella funicular station.

Cost: 12.60 CHF for each leg, 69-CHF round-trip ticket, covered by Engadin Card. If you're taking a mountain bike, check your Engadin Card—if it's "all-inclusive," it includes the cost of the bike transport; otherwise it's 17.30 CHF for a day pass for the bike (cyclists without an Engadin Card pay 69.20 CHF for a day pass). Tel. 081-83-5020, www.mountains.ch.

Walk Around the Lake
The charming lake below St. Moritz is a delightful place for a stroll—especially on sunny summer days, when it's filled with sailboats. It takes about an hour to walk all the way around.

Eating in St. Moritz

As in Pontresina, most of St. Moritz's restaurants are in hotels.

$$$ Restaurant Hauser is the standard stop for locals who know where to find the best-value sit-down restaurant meal in town. Centrally located, this place has everything—restaurant, café, pastry shop, indoor and outdoor seating, and a vast menu—and you'll find everyone here (weekday lunch specials, sandwiches to go, daily 7:00-21:00, below Hotel Hauser at Via Traunter Plazzas 7, tel. 081-837-5050).

$$ Buffet Espresso café at the train station is a rare budget option in this pricey town, serving a couple of hot dishes daily until 17:00, as well as good Italian-style sandwiches (daily 6:00-20:00, tel. 081-834-4105).

Supermarket: There's a small, basic **Co-op** grocery right on the main square (Mon-Fri 8:00-19:00, Sat-Sun until 18:00, Schulhausplatz/Plazza da Scoula 12).

In St. Moritz Bad: $$$ Veltlinerkeller, decorated with a huge stuffed moose head, is a casual-feeling eatery—with the grill right in the dining area—that serves a variety of Italian specialties, including pastas and grilled meats (Mon-Sat 9:00-14:00 & 17:00-22:30, closed Sun in fall and spring, Via dal Bagn 11, 20-minute walk from St. Moritz Dorf or take bus #3 from Schulhausplatz to the Via Salet stop, tel. 081-833-4009, www.veltlinerkeller-stmoritz.ch).

A larger **Co-op** supermarket at Via dal Bagn 20 has a small, basic top-floor café with a limited menu, view terrace, and free Wi-Fi. It offers the cheapest meals in town (Mon-Fri 8:00-19:00, Sat-Sun until 18:00; 15-minute walk downhill from town center, just before you reach the St. Moritz Bad shopping street—get off bus #3 at the Via Aruons stop).

Upper Engadine Connections

BY TRAIN

From Pontresina to: **Chur** (hourly, 2 hours, change in Samedan), **Zürich** (hourly, 3.5 hours, change in Samedan and Chur or Landquart), **Luzern** (hourly, 4.5 hours, 3 changes), **Appenzell** (hourly, 5 hours, 3-4 changes), **Zermatt** (1-2 direct Glacier Express trains/day, 8 hours).

From St. Moritz and Samedan to: **Chur** (hourly direct, 2 hours, more with change), **Zürich** (hourly, 3 hours, change in Chur or Landquart), **Luzern** (hourly, 4 hours, 2 changes), **Appenzell** (hourly, 4.5 hours, 2-3 changes), **Zermatt** (1-2 direct Glacier Express trains/day, 8 hours), **Tirano** (hourly, 2.5 hours, in off-season leaves only from Pontresina), **Milan** (hourly, 5 hours, change in Tirano, in off-season leaves only from Pontresina).

For details on the Bernina Express to Tirano and the Glacier Express to Zermatt, see the Scenic Rail Journeys chapter. Train info: toll tel. 0900-300-300, www.rail.ch.

BY BUS

The Palm Express bus offers a connection-free trip over the Maloja Pass to **Lugano** once a day in summer (departs St. Moritz train station at 12:20, stops at Menaggio on Italy's Lake Como en route, arrives at Lugano's train station at 16:20; daily mid-June-mid-Oct, Fri-Sun-only mid-Oct-mid-June, reservations required at least 4 hours ahead, tel. 058-341-3492, www.postbus.ch, use Webcode 10037 to reserve, consider the audioguide—available via free PostAuto app). Otherwise, connect via train to Thusis, then bus to Bellinzona, then train to Lugano (hourly, 4 hours). To **Milan,** the quickest route is by bus from St. Moritz to Chiavenna in Italy, then onward by train (every 2 hours, 4.5 hours).

SCENIC RAIL JOURNEYS

Golden Pass • Gotthard Panorama Express •
Bernina Express • Glacier Express • Chur

Switzerland has one of the world's best rail networks, and many of its tracks run through dramatic and beautiful scenery. While just about any train ride in Switzerland is photogenic, four are aggressively marketed as the most spectacular: the Golden Pass, the Gotthard Panorama Express, the Bernina Express, and the Glacier Express. If you're looking for a scenic day enjoying the Alps from the window of your train, and would like to do it in a "panoramic" car (with huge windows that sweep halfway across the ceiling), these journeys can be great experiences. Though they aren't quite as "fantastic with countless highlights" as they're advertised to be (the high lifts in the mountains themselves are much higher and more breathtaking), the trains are a fun way to do some sightseeing while getting from point A to point B.

This chapter provides you with all the logistical, nuts-and-bolts information you'll need to splice each journey into your itinerary. Keep this in mind as you plan: You don't need to take a special train to enjoy the routes described in this chapter. Regular nonpanoramic trains also run along all these scenic routes. They go more frequently and cost less, but don't come with the expansive windows, special meals, and souvenirs that your scenic-train supplement pays for.

I've described highlights along each route, written in the direction that most travelers are likely to go. If you travel in the opposite direction, the same information still applies—just hold the book upside-down.

This chapter also includes information about Chur, a town that's not really worth a visit, except that it lies on both the Bernina Express and Glacier Express routes and can be handy for a pit stop or an overnight (especially if you're connecting to or from Zürich or Appenzell).

TICKETS

Schedules Can Change: In this chapter, I've listed specific departure and arrival times, but these schedules are always subject to change, so it's essential to confirm the times before you travel. Timetables for most of these trains appear on the Swiss Rail website: www.rail.ch. (You can also use Germany's all-Europe rail site, www.bahn.com, but it doesn't have Swiss price information.) Avoid calling the expensive Swiss Rail info line (tel. 0900-300-300). Any train station in Switzerland can provide you with free schedules. Each scenic rail line also operates its own website, with even more details.

Buying Tickets: Tickets and reservations for all these scenic rail lines are best purchased at any train station in Switzerland. Station staffers are familiar with the scenic routes and can help you sort through your options. These trips are covered by both Swiss Travel Passes and Eurail passes that include Switzerland, though reservations (required on some trains) cost extra.

While you can buy scenic-train tickets at the Swiss Rail website, there's a catch: Tickets bought online are unchangeable and nonrefundable, unlike tickets purchased at train stations in Switzerland. Also, the website only lets you purchase tickets within 30 days of travel. You may be able to buy tickets further in advance from the US—at www.raileurope.com or through your travel agent—but you'll pay a substantial markup.

Seat Reservations: Some scenic trains require seat reservations. Reservations are essentially scenic-train supplements that happen to come with a reserved seat. Be warned that many sell out several days ahead in high season. Reservations are required for all classes of the Glacier Express and Gotthard Panorama Express, the panoramic cars in all classes on the Bernina Express, and the bus segment of the Bernina Express. Reserve for the Golden Pass train between Zweisimmen and Montreux if you want a front-row VIP seat and during peak season. These options are explained in each section later.

If you're set on taking a panoramic train and your itinerary is already fixed, it makes sense to book your scenic-train seats as soon as you can. On most routes at most times, however, individual travelers usually book just a few days in advance—usually after they've seen a weather report. If your itinerary is flexible, I'd recommend you do the same: Keep an eye on the weather, pick a good travel day, and then reserve your seats at any train station. Only from mid-July to mid-August do trains (especially the über-promoted Glacier Express) book up further ahead.

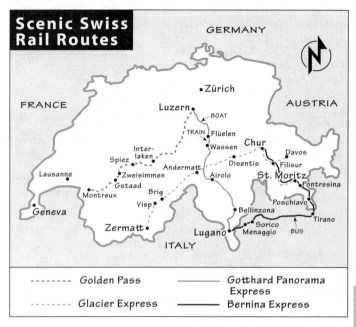

Scenic Swiss
Rail Routes

GERMANY

FRANCE

• Zürich

Luzern •
BOAT
TRAIN Flüelen
Inter-
laken
Wassen
Chur
Davos
Spiez
Andermatt
Disentis
Filisur
Lausanne
Zweisimmen
Airolo
St. Moritz
Gstaad
Brig
Pontresina
Montreux
Poschiavo
Visp
Geneva
Bellinzona
Tirano
Zermatt •
Sorico
Lugano
Menaggio
BUS

ITALY

AUSTRIA

- - - - - - - Golden Pass ——————— Gotthard Panorama
                                     Express
- - - - - - - Glacier Express ——————— Bernina Express

SCENIC RAIL JOURNEYS

Eurail Passes and Swiss Travel Passes: Rail passes cover travel on these four scenic trains. Seat reservations, though, always cost extra. You can skip reservations if traveling scenic routes on standard regional trains, rather than on the designated tourist departures.

When buying your ticket or making reservations, be sure the ticket agent understands what type of rail pass you have and exactly what trip you're taking. (Pass coverage varies on boats, buses, and mountain lifts, and is subject to change.) Confirm that you've purchased all of the reservations and other tickets you need to complete your trip.

TRAIN TYPES

Various types of trains, with various types of cars, run these routes. Here are the key distinctions to look for:

Classes: Most trains have both first- and second-class cars. The difference between the first- and second-class cars is generally the same on tourist trains as on standard trains (first class has somewhat wider seats, a little more legroom, and fewer passengers; second-class cars offer the same scenery, go just as fast, and usually still have plenty of room). If you have a second-class rail pass, you can always pay extra to sit in first on any given train. In bigger train stations, a digital panel on the tracks indicates departure time, destination, and at which part of the platform you'll find the first- or second-class cars.

Standard vs. Tourist Trains: Used by local commuters, standard trains may stop at more stations along the route than the designed-for-tourists panoramic trains. Many travelers enjoy the flexibility of following the scenic route on standard trains, enabling them to hop off and explore a village, then hop on the next standard train that comes through—without the headache of reservations (which are not necessary on standard domestic trains).

Panoramic vs. Standard Cars: All the tourist trains on the routes in this chapter offer special panoramic cars, usually in both first and second class, so there's no need to splurge for first class.

Panoramic cars have huge windows that curve back into the roof of the train car, allowing you to view high mountains from a wider angle than in a normal train car. The Golden Pass trains go one better: The driver sits in a little bubble upstairs, leaving the very front of the train open for VIP seating with completely unobstructed views of what's coming up. The windows in the panoramic cars generally can't open, meaning that photographs often suffer from glare, and there are no window shades, so the interior can heat up on sunny days even with air-conditioning. Bring sunglasses and a hat.

Since nonpanoramic cars have a smaller field of vision than the panoramic cars, these require a little more bobbing and weaving to enjoy the views. Aside from being cheaper, the chief advantage of standard cars is that the windows generally can be opened, for cool air and better photos. Passengers in panoramic cars are free to walk to the standard cars to open a window and snap a photo.

Golden Pass

The exceptionally picturesque Golden Pass train route cuts a swath diagonally across the pristine center of the country, connecting Luzern with Lake Geneva, German Switzerland with French. Of all the rail journeys in this chapter, it's the one you're most likely to

take, as it's central and laces together many of Switzerland's top sights.

ROUTE OVERVIEW

The Golden Pass officially runs between Luzern and Lake Geneva's Montreux in about five hours. The Golden Pass route has three distinct segments (Luzern-Interlaken Ost, Interlaken Ost-Zweisimmen, and Zweisimmen-Montreux). Because the tracks change from narrow to standard gauge to narrow again, you'll switch to a different train (waiting across the platform) at Interlaken Ost and Zweisimmen. You can lengthen your stop in Interlaken if you'd like to eat lunch there or walk around town.

The best stretch of the route is between Zweisimmen and Montreux. To enjoy just this part of the route, start in Interlaken (or in Bern—changing trains in Spiez). This is the stretch most likely to fill up, so it's worth reserving a seat, especially in summer.

The three trains that make up the full route are run by different companies and have different services. Here's the breakdown.

Luzern to Interlaken Ost: Regular trains, all with semi-panoramic windows (hourly, 2 hours).

Interlaken Ost to Zweisimmen: Regular trains (roughly hourly, 1.5 hours, sometimes with a change in Spiez).

Zweisimmen to Montreux: Specially designed tourist trains (8/day, 2 hours). Of the daily departures, four are panoramic trains, two are panoramic trains with VIP cars, and two are "classic" trains with vintage rail cars.

PLANNING YOUR TIME

Because it connects so many knockout Swiss destinations, the Golden Pass can be spliced into your itinerary in many different ways. I'd focus on the best stretch, using it to connect Interlaken and Lake Geneva (sleeping on the Lake Geneva end in either Montreux or Lausanne). Check schedules for the Zweisimmen-Montreux leg to pick the departure with your preferred type of train car. If you can avoid having to change trains in Spiez, that's a minor plus.

To go all the way from Luzern to Lake Geneva, here's a sample day plan: Take the 8:05 train from Luzern to Interlaken Ost (arriving at 9:55), wander Interlaken and have a quick lunch, catch the 13:08 train to Zweisimmen (arriving at 14:19), then change to a panoramic train and arrive in Montreux at 16:13.

You could also easily make a fuller day of the Golden Pass—starting in Zürich and ending in Lausanne—by tacking on standard trains from Zürich to Luzern, and from Montreux to Lausanne.

For onward train connections from major Golden Pass stops, see the Connections sections for Luzern (page 73), Interlaken Ost (page 146), and Montreux (page 262).

ORIENTATION TO THE GOLDEN PASS

Cost: The Golden Pass trip from Luzern to Montreux costs 91 CHF second class; the "best of" segment from Interlaken to Montreux is 54 CHF. The entire ride is covered by a Eurail pass or Swiss Travel Pass. Reservations, while not required, are recommended for the stretch from Zweisimmen to Montreux for summer departures and the super-scenic front seats (8 CHF, 15 CHF for front-row VIP seats; more details under "Seating," later).

Information: The three rail companies that operate the route (MOB, BLS, and the Zentralbahn) run an office and a website that can answer your questions (tel. 021-989-8190, www. goldenpassline.ch). A free booklet available on the train describes the route and includes a schedule.

Seating: Between Zweisimmen and Montreux, two panoramic trains have special VIP seats in the first car. On these trains, the driver sits in a little domed area upstairs—leaving both the front and back of

the train open for passengers. The first two rows of VIP seats offer an unobstructed view of the pristine alpine scenery coming right at you, but they usually book up fast.

Eating on the Golden Pass: The Luzern-Interlaken stretch is the only section with a restaurant car, but it may be closed on trains running early or late in the day. Snacks and bar service may be available between Zweisimmen and Montreux, but the menu is limited and pricey. Save your money and eat fresh by packing a picnic.

⊘ SELF-GUIDED TOUR

I've described only the best and most visually exciting portion of the Golden Pass journey, the five-hour stretch from Luzern to Lake Geneva, focusing on the *crème de la crème*—the two hours between Zweisimmen and Montreux (described from north to south).

As you leave Luzern (sit on the right side), you'll go along the lake to Alpnachstad, the starting point for the cogwheel train that climbs to the top of Mount Pilatus (the massive bulk on the right—see page 76). Then the train follows the Sarner Aa River through farmland, passing through the town of Sarnen and running along Lake Sarnen. Beyond the end of the lake is the town of Giswil, where the train begins its gradual ascent to the **Brünig Pass.** Eventually the train runs above the beautiful turquoise waters of the Lungernsee reservoir. After passing the resort of Lungern, the train climbs gradually through the forest to the summit station of Brünig-Hasliberg (keep an eye out for fake animal cutouts—lynx, ibex, deer—placed whimsically in the woods at eye level). After cresting the pass, the train descends to the Aare River valley, with its sheer cliffs and waterfalls. The arrow-straight river channel, straightened by the ever-efficient Swiss, slices through the broad valley. At Meiringen, the train reverses direction. (Sir Arthur Conan Doyle chose Meiringen and nearby Reichenbach Falls as the setting for the death of Sherlock Holmes.) The train then follows the river to beautiful **Lake Brienz** (Brienzersee; a bus runs from the town of Brienz to the remarkable open-air museum at Ballenberg—see page 139).

Beyond Brienz, the train follows the lakeshore to **Interlaken** ("between the lakes"), where the town sits between the big lakes of Thun and Brienz. As the train pulls out of Interlaken, you cruise along the south bank of **Lake Thun** (Thunersee). Before long, at the town of Spiez, you'll split off and head southwest to Zweisimmen—squeezing between two mountainsides and into the rolling, cow-speckled **Simmental** valley.

At **Zweisimmen,** you'll change to a panoramic train and continue through the Simmental, famous among American farmers for its top-end cows. Big farmhouses lie scattered in the lush meadows—an indication that the farmland is good here. The large wooden buildings are typical of Bernese farm architecture: housing the barn, sheltering the crops, and storing agricultural machines, all under one huge roof. Farming is heavily subsidized in Switzerland, and farmers form the strongest economic lobby. Trying to increase their income, many farmers have added exotic crops (like melons) or animals. Ostriches, yaks, bison, and highland cattle have become a common sight in the Swiss Alps lately.

Between Saanenmoser and Schonried, the train reaches its highest point (about 4,000 feet) and stops at the famous resort town of **Gstaad.** Although known as a favorite hangout for well-known rustic mountain folk such as Julie Andrews, Monaco's Princess Caroline, and Roman Polanski, the town doesn't offer much in the way of sights. In winter, its modest ski slopes are less crowded than the town's flashy nightspots. Sipping their cocktails, the *après*-skiers eye each other and discuss the latest trends in ski fashion. In summer, Gstaad hosts the Swiss Open tennis, polo, and golf tournaments, as well as high-quality music festivals.

Just south of Gstaad, say *auf Wiedersehen* to the German-speaking part of Switzerland and *bonjour* to **French Switzerland.** The mountains are jagged. In fact, many are called *dents,* French for "teeth." With the change in language comes a change in culture and architecture. French-style gray stone houses start to replace half-timbered, woody, German-style chalets. The mountain airstrips—generally made for the Swiss Air Force during World War II—are used today for sightseeing flights around the Alps. The cute village of Rougemont, with its fine church and traditional houses, is famous among the Swiss as the place where the wealthy send their girls to boarding school.

Happy **cows** spend their summers on the Alps, wandering freely and munching the fragrant herbs of these lush alpine meadows. The resulting milk is the secret ingredient for tasty Gruyère cheese. On steep hillsides here, the grass is still cut by hand. It dries in the summer sun, then is collected and stored in the barns to serve as cow salads through the winter.

You might consider interrupting your journey in **Château-d'Œx,** known for its Hot-Air Ballooning Week (last week of January). Bertrand Piccard and Brian Jones took off from here on March 1, 1999, and sailed their balloon all the way around the world. Below the train station, Le Chalet restaurant gives insight on Gruyère cheese production.

South of Château-d'Œx, the valley narrows to a deep gorge. The hillsides above were devastated by the 1999 winter storm **"Lothar."** Entire forests were leveled, aggravating an already precarious avalanche situation. Trees on steep slopes stop snow from sliding down and burying the villages, but once the trees are gone, artificial avalanche barriers need to be erected. Landslides and floods have been relatively common in recent years—an unfortunate consequence of deforestation and the construction of vacation homes in areas that traditionally served as pastures and forestlands.

The small **lake** is dammed and used for hydroelectric power. Switzerland makes good use of its Alps, with their fast-flowing streams. Although it has some nuclear power plants, 60 percent of Switzerland's energy is hydroelectric. The country exports its electricity to France and Italy.

Montbovon is the place to change trains if you're going to Bulle or Gruyères (see page 263). After the first tunnel, an inscription on the barn to the right welcomes you to the Gruyère region: *La Gruyère vous salue.*

The train winds its way uphill with more curves and tunnels than before. Passing through the **Jaman Tunnel,** you're engulfed in nearly two miles of darkness. When you emerge, you're in another world—you've left the feudal Middle Ages and entered the 19th-century belle époque. At the village of Les Avants, one of Switzerland's oldest winter resorts, the first glimpses of Lake Geneva sprawl deep underneath you. Beginning a steep descent, the train passes through a series of sharp bends in tunnels before delivering you from the mountains to lake level.

The architecture has even more of a French flair now that you've entered the **"Swiss Riviera."** Palm trees, vines, and many sanatoriums indicate that this is a warmer climate. You're surrounded by the vineyards of the Lavaux region, famous for its white wine. The view broadens to include the French Alps of Savoy across the lake, the lakeshore of the Swiss Riviera to the west, and the broad Rhône Valley to the east. As you approach Montreux—with its grand hotels—the train meanders its way intimately through private gardens.

Montreux is one of the only train stations in Europe with three different rail gauges: regular, narrow (which you're on), and very skinny (for the Rochers de Naye train, taking sightseers to a nearby peak with views less exciting than those you've just enjoyed).

From here, it's an easy train trip to Lausanne, or a quick bus ride or about a two-mile lakefront hike to Château de Chillon (see page 257).

SCENIC RAIL JOURNEYS

Gotthard Panorama Express

The journey marketed as the Gotthard Panorama Express is half by boat and half by train, from Luzern to the Italian-speaking region of Ticino (the towns of Bellinzona and Lugano). The boat ride passes the place where the first Swiss cantons pledged "all for one and one for all," the birthplace of the Confoederatio Helvetica in 1291.

Don't go out of your way to do this trip. The boat ride is more pastoral than thrilling, and the train ride is more interesting as a lesson in Swiss engineering than impressive for its views. (Because the train cuts through the highest mountains inside the old Gotthard Tunnel, it only reaches 3,600 feet above sea level.) But if you're connecting Luzern and Italian Switzerland in high season and have the time, this 5.5-hour boat-bus combination is undeniably scenic.

However, if you're in a hurry to get between Luzern and Lugano, it's possible to do the whole trip by train in only 2 hours via the new, 30-mile-long Gotthard Base Tunnel, which allows full-size freight trains to traverse the Alps and permits passenger-train speeds of up to 150 miles an hour. Most train schedules will route you through the new tunnel; to take the more scenic route, look for regional trains that require a transfer in Erstfeld.

Note that if you've already taken a boat trip on Lake Luzern, you won't see much more by taking the Gotthard Panorama Express boat. Conversely, if you're planning on doing the whole Gotthard Panorama trip, don't bother doing a boat trip while in Luzern.

ROUTE OVERVIEW

The Gotthard Panorama Express begins with a slow boat trip along the length of Lake Luzern from the city of Luzern to Flüelen (3 hours). There you'll switch to the train, and cut down into the Italian-speaking canton of Ticino (2.5 hours).

The boat trip from Luzern to Flüelen is lazy and very pretty. As the traditional steamer blows its old-time horn, you glide by idyllic lakeside resort towns and under mighty peaks. In Flüelen, you leave the boat and board the train. On weekends, you'll transfer in the town of Bellinzona to a second, nonpanoramic train to reach Lugano.

If you want to skip the reserved panoramic train, standard regional trains (without panoramic cars) make the scenic Luzern-Lugano trip with more options (3.5 hours total, 6/day with connection at Erstfeld, avoid nonstop trains if you want the scenic route).

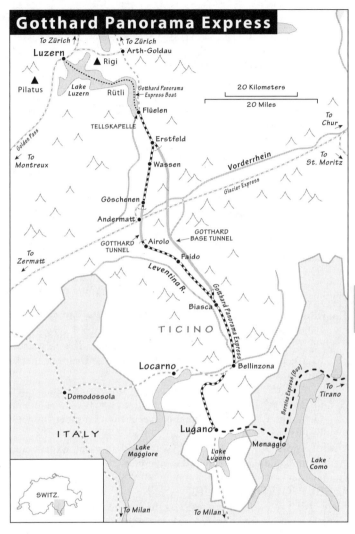

Gotthard Panorama Express

To Zürich
Luzern
To Zürich
Arth-Goldau
Rigi
Pilatus
Lake Luzern
Rütli
Gotthard Panorama Express Boat
Flüelen
TELLSKAPELLE
Erstfeld
Wassen
Vorderrhein
To Chur
20 Kilometers
20 Miles
Golden Pass
To Montreux
Göschenen
Andermatt
Glacier Express
To St. Moritz
GOTTHARD TUNNEL
Airolo
GOTTHARD BASE TUNNEL
Faido
To Zermatt
Leventina R.
Gotthard Panorama Express
Biasca
TICINO
Locarno
Bellinzona
Bernina Express (Bus)
To Tirano
Domodossola
Lugano
Menaggio
ITALY
Lake Maggiore
Lake Lugano
Lake Como
SWITZ.
To Milan
To Milan

SCENIC RAIL JOURNEYS

For onward train connections, see the Connections sections under Luzern (page 73) and Lugano (page 293).

ORIENTATION TO THE GOTTHARD PANORAMA EXPRESS

Cost: If you want a panoramic car, you must pay the first-class fare of 150 CHF; the second-class fare (without panoramic cars) is 92 CHF. Reservations are required for both classes.

Travelers using a Swiss Travel Pass pay a 24-CHF reservation fee in either class. Travelers with a Eurail pass pay the reservation fee plus a "supplemental" fare (23 CHF in second class, 34 CHF in first). If you have one of these passes, you may want to skip the package deal. All rail passes cover regular trains, Swiss Passes fully cover lake boats, and Eurail passes give you half off boat rides on Lake Luzern.

Schedule: The official package runs once daily in each direction between mid-April and late October. Going from north to south on weekdays, you'll leave Luzern on the 11:12 boat; after it docks in Flüelen, you have about 15 minutes before the 14:10 train leaves for Lugano. The total trip takes about 5.5 hours. Going from south to north on weekdays, you leave Lugano at 9:23 to make a Flüelen-Luzern boat departing at 12:00. On weekends, the reserved trains run only to/from Bellinzona, requiring extra connections to/from Lugano. As always, be sure to confirm all times.

Information: The boat and train companies both have brochures and websites about the Gotthard Panorama Express (boat: tel. 041-367-6767, www.lakelucerne.ch; train: www.rail.ch, choose "Leisure & Holidays," then "Travel in Switzerland," then "Panorama Trips").

Boarding the Boat and Train: If you're doing the full Gotthard Panorama Express route, board the boat at pier 1 across from the Luzern train station. Present your ticket. There's no real baggage check on the boat; travelers just stack their backpacks and suitcases in a corner.

As the train approaches the platform in Flüelen, watch for the car that corresponds to your reservation (the official Gotthard Panorama Express packet includes a sheet showing you where to stand for your car).

Useful Apps: Download the free Gotthard Panorama Express app from Apple's App Store or Google Play.

❍ SELF-GUIDED TOUR

Here's what you'll see if you're doing the entire Gotthard Panorama Express route. If you're taking only the train, skip to that section.

Boat Trip

The boat crisscrosses the **Vierwaldstättersee** (the "Lake of Four Forest Cantons"—let's call it "Lake Luzern"). The trip is popular with the older generation of European tourists, who eat and drink their way through the lazy route. On a sunny day, you can sit on the deck and enjoy the mountain views.

Survey the boat before you settle on a seat—consider sun, shade, and wind.

After two hours, you sail into the **canton of Uri,** and the landscape gets rougher, the slopes steeper, and the villages fewer and more rustic. Swiss patriots get excited as the boat approaches **Rütli.** The meadow above is the birthplace of the Swiss Confederation. In 1291, representatives of the three founding cantons met here and swore allegiance to each other, against their oppressive neighbors. More than 700 years later, Switzerland is still a confederation—but now its cantons number 26.

You may see hikers disembark at Rütli and head for the mystical meadow marked by a big Swiss flag. Then they follow the **Weg der Schweiz** ("Path of Switzerland"), a trail leading around the lake. Along the way, they contemplate stone signs representing each of the 26 cantons in the order they joined the union. The canton markers are spaced according to each canton's population (the 20-mile-long trail is designed to have exactly 5 millimeters for each Swiss citizen).

Later, the boat stops at **Tellskapelle.** This 16th-century frescoed chapel marks another legendary spot—where Swiss hero William Tell jumped ship on the way to prison and swam to freedom.

The last stop is **Flüelen,** where the panoramic train awaits.

Train Trip

From Flüelen, the train climbs from 1,540 feet up to 3,600 feet at the old Gotthard Tunnel—once the primary north-south transportation route through the Alps. You enter a classic alpine world of snowcapped mountains towering above wild valleys, with narrow gorges carved over eons by angry white water. Wooden chalets, pine forests, and lush meadows dotted with munching cows complete this image of picture-perfect Central Switzerland.

The train tracks are protected from avalanches, landslides, and waterfalls by concrete galleries. Gazing out the window, you'll see some of the greatest accomplishments of Swiss road-and-railroad engineering. **Wassen,** marked by its striking chapel, is the climax for trainspotters—it once had more trains passing per minute than just about anywhere else. First, the chapel is on your right. Then the train loops around the tiny town, and the chapel is on your left. Your train disappears into a tunnel, and when you emerge, the same chapel is still there. The train actually spirals up the slopes. Bring a compass and you can watch it spin 360 degrees.

Göschenen is the last stop before the 9.5-mile-long **Gotthard Tunnel.** After 10 minutes of rocketing through darkness, you emerge in a whole different world—a different climate (warmer), canton (Ticino), and language (Italian). Since the 13th century— long before this tunnel was built—the Gotthard Pass has been *the* major trade route over this part of the Alps, connecting northern and southern Europe. The trade continues to rumble under rather than over the pass, now by high-speed rail through the much longer Gotthard Base Tunnel.

Welcome to **Ticino,** Switzerland's botanical garden. While the weather around Lake Luzern is often iffy, Ticino feels Mediterranean—warm and southern—making it a favorite weekend destination for the Swiss. Rather than cuckoo-clock-like chalets, the houses are now plain, square, and made of stone. Instead of conifers, the forests are full of chestnut trees. You'll see vineyards, oleander, and even palm trees. And the upcoming train stops are announced in Italian now: *"Prossima fermata..."*

While life seemed almost too good in the pristine and touristic Lake Luzern region, here in the valley of **Leventina,** the economy is tougher. Unemployment rates are high, young folks have to commute into the cities farther south for a job, houses and roads aren't as well maintained, and window boxes no longer come with so many flowers. Before and after **Faido,** the train goes through four more spiral tunnels.

If heading to Lugano, you usually change trains in **Bellinzona** on weekends. By around 2020, the new, 10-mile-long Ceneri Tunnel will shoot straight under the high peaks between Bellinzona and Lugano. For now, the train to Lugano skirts the mountains, passes the northern tip of Lake Maggiore, and goes through a quiet, lush valley lined with picturesque villages and chestnut trees. Enjoy your time in Italian Switzerland!

Bernina Express

The Bernina Express is one of the more exciting rides through the Swiss Alps, thanks to its diversity: starting with the sunny, palm-tree ambience of Lugano, getting a taste of Italy along beautiful Lake Como, climbing up and over the twisting Bernina Pass, and seeing mountain towns like Pontresina before finishing up in eastern Switzerland. The first half of the trip is by bus; the second by rail. The little red train with panoramic cars spirals up to 7,380 feet, passing steep  mountains and cliffs, glaciers, waterfalls, and a wild, rugged landscape.

ROUTE OVERVIEW

The Bernina Express combines a bus trip through Italy with a train ride up and into the mountains. The bus begins in Lugano, but soon crosses the border to run along the west side of Italy's Lake Como, eventually arriving at Tirano, where passengers change to a train. From Tirano, the train crosses back into Switzerland and twists north up the steep mountainside, mastering a very steep grade on regular tracks (no cogwheels) en route to the most spectacular stretch: over the Bernina Pass. Then the train winds back down the other side and finally deposits you in one of several eastern Swiss towns, such as Pontresina, St. Moritz, Samedan, and Chur. (In summer, you can also finish in the resort town of Davos, home to the World Economic Forum.)

The route can be reversed (Chur or Pontresina to Tirano by train, then bus to Lugano). In fact, this way arguably provides an even better scenic experience.

PLANNING YOUR TIME

The trip between Pontresina and Lugano takes about six hours. Starting or finishing in Chur makes for a very long day (about nine hours). If you want to travel the whole route, split it up and do the Pontresina-Chur stretch on the way to destinations such as Zürich or Appenzell, or as part of the Glacier Express (which overlaps with the Bernina Express on this segment).

If you have more time, consider taking a standard regional train along the Pontresina-Tirano route (rather than the official Bernina Express train with panoramic cars). That way, you can get off as you like for hiking and exploring (see "Skipping the Official Panorama Train," later).

Also remember that you don't have to start or end the trip in Lugano. You could use the Pontresina-Tirano train as a way of connecting to Milan or Lake Como (see "Connecting to Towns in Italy," below). You could also make a day trip out of the Bernina Express, leaving Pontresina in the morning, exploring over the pass to Tirano (2.5 hours by train), then heading back.

Don't worry too much about which of the Upper Engadine towns your train stops in (Pontresina, St. Moritz, or Samedan)—the three towns are within 10 minutes of each other by local bus or train.

For onward train connections from the major Bernina Express stops, see the Connections sections for Lugano (page 293), and Chur (see end of this chapter).

ORIENTATION TO THE BERNINA EXPRESS

Cost: A one-way trip on the Bernina Express from Lugano to Pontresina costs 70 CHF second class, 92 CHF first class. Lugano to Chur costs more: 117 CHF second class, 165 CHF first class. St. Moritz is a few francs more expensive than Pontresina. The official Bernina Express trip requires a reservation for both the bus (14 CHF) and the panoramic train (14 CHF, 10 CHF in winter). The entire trip (including the bus) is covered by a Eurail pass or a Swiss Travel Pass, but passholders have to pay for reservations.

If you don't have a reservation for the bus, you may be allowed to board and pay if there's room, but there are no guarantees; if you don't have a reservation for the panoramic cars on the train, you can sit in the nonpanoramic cars without a reservation.

Schedule: The bus from Lugano to Tirano leaves daily at 10:00 (April-late Oct only) from outside Lugano's train station. Facing the lake with the Lugano station at your back, walk about 100 yards to the left to find the stop (look for yellow signs saying *Tirano, St. Moritz,* and *#731*).

About 13:00, you'll arrive in Tirano. Here, you'll board a panoramic train that continues north over the mountains. In summer, one train leaves Tirano at 14:03 and arrives in Pontresina at 16:00 and St. Moritz at 16:20; another leaves Tirano at 14:26 and arrives in Pontresina at 16:16 and Chur at 18:20. All trains follow the same tracks for most of the trip before fanning out at the end to different destinations.

If you're doing it the other way around, the train from St. Moritz leaves at 9:30, stops in Pontresina at 9:41, and arrives in Tirano at 12:00. From Chur, the train departs at 8:32 and stops in Pontresina at 10:19, arriving in Tirano at 12:45. The bus from Tirano leaves at 14:20 and arrives in Lugano at 17:30. Remember to confirm all times.

In winter (late Oct-March), the bus service stops, but the Bernina Express panoramic trains still run over the pass to Tirano a couple of times a day.

Information: The Bernina Express is operated by the Rhätische Bahn (RhB, tel. 081-288-6565, www.berninaexpress.ch). You can buy an English guidebook about the Bernina Express on the train or at gift shops along the way. Recorded English commentary plays on the train's loudspeaker.

Bring Food: Your time between bus and train in Tirano may be brief (especially if the bus is running late), so it makes good sense to bring an ample lunch along. The small supermarket at Lugano's train station is convenient.

Bus Tips: Make yourself comfortable on the bus leg of the Bernina trip. The seats recline, and the footrests, armrests, and individual fans give you more comfort than on a standard transit bus. There are no WCs on the bus, but it stops for a WC break in Italy (Swiss francs accepted). Bags can be put under the bus. The bus trip is almost entirely through Italy. If many people reserve the trip, a second bus may be added.

Train Tips: Once you reach Tirano, you'll switch to a train. For the first part of the ride, views are somewhat better on the right (though the left is better for seeing the train curve around the famous spiral viaduct at Brusio). After Poschiavo, views are better on the left.

Topless Trains: If traveling in July, August, or September, ask about sitting in the yellow "convertible" train cars with flip seats and no roof (but be aware that these go only on certain segments of the trip). The railway decides the day before—depending

on the weather—whether to add these cars to the train (available in both first and second class). Bring a jacket, hat, and sunscreen. If you get cold, you can move into a regular car when the train stops.

Skipping the Official Panorama Train: The train segment of the Bernina Express can be done on a standard regional train (with smaller windows that open, and possibly a car with larger-view windows). These trains stop at all stations along the line, giving you more options to hop off and walk around in the beautiful surroundings. (The regular Bernina Express only stops at three important stations—Poschiavo, Alp Grüm, and Ospizio Bernina.) You can get off at Poschiavo for a quick visit, at the Bernina Pass for hiking, or at Diavolezza to do a cable-car trip. Alp Grüm and Ospizio Bernina are starting points for several great hikes (at Ospizio Bernina, you can leave your bags at the restaurant near the station). Take advantage of the frequent and easy train connections to make as many short stops as time and interest allow. Not only do you save yourself the panoramic train supplement, but you have the flexibility of traveling without a seat reservation. The panoramic cars are indeed great—and this stretch is particularly well-suited for a panoramic car—but the trip is still very rewarding on a standard train.

Connecting to Towns in Italy: There are many other ways to reach Tirano than by bus from Lugano. For example, inexpensive, direct, hourly trains run to Tirano from both Milan (2.5 hours) and Varenna, a favorite stop on Lake Como (1.5 hours).

History Exhibit in St. Moritz: A small, free exhibit on the history of the Bernina Express rail line, including an English film, is in the St. Moritz train station. It's worth a look, though not a special trip.

❷ SELF-GUIDED TOUR
Bus Trip
The bus trip is more scenic than relaxing. Lakes Lugano and Como are almost fjord-like, lined with little Italian getaways. For the best views, sit on the right-hand side (if your reserved seat is on the left, change once the bus is under way).

At first, the bus takes you around Lake Lugano on narrow, winding roads, frequently honking its horn to warn oncoming traffic at tight passages. Leaving Lugano, you'll pass the town of Gandria (fun to visit from Lugano by boat and described in that chapter). Shortly after Gandria, you cross the border into **Italy** (it's a nonevent—bus doesn't stop, no need to show passports). You may notice changes in architecture and design: Whereas the Swiss love meticulously manicured gardens, painstakingly renovated houses, and clean, uncluttered lines, the Italians take things a bit easier.

Once the bus leaves Lake Lugano, the road broadens and takes you through modern Italian villages before hitting picturesque **Lake Como** (Lago di Como). Above the town of Menaggio are your first views of the lake. The village across the lake on the right (by the funny hump of land) is the *real* Bellagio. At the nearby village of Dongo, the Italian fascist dictator Mussolini was captured at the end of World War II. Tunnels occasionally disrupt your views, but you can catch glimpses of the lush lakefront. In Gravedona, the street narrows, and getting the bus through is a tight squeeze. Posh private villas and gardens line the street; look for the 12th-century Romanesque Church of Santa Maria del Tiglio. From here, the trip takes you to the tiny harbor town of Domaso, a touristy area with plenty of campgrounds, hotels, and swimming pools.

Shortly before noon, the bus stops for 15 dull minutes in **Sorico,** at the northern tip of Lake Como (no view). You'll have a chance to use the WC and buy a snack or drink (Swiss francs accepted).

The bus then crosses the **"Pian di Spagna"**—famous for a tense standoff between Spanish and Swiss troops during the religious wars of the Counter-Reformation. The trip continues up the fertile **Valtellina Valley,** where some of northern Italy's white wine is produced. The sunny slopes on the left side are reserved for vineyards, the right lower slopes are for woodland, and the bottom of the valley is occupied by apple plantations. For centuries (from 1512 until Napoleon in 1797) this region belonged to Switzerland's largest canton, Graubünden. This region is Italian today, but many Swiss are still nostalgic for the valley (called the *Veltlin* in German) and its wines. The white Grüner Veltliner grape is named after the valley, though it isn't actually grown here. In Tresivio (just after Sondrio, toward the end of the bus ride) you'll notice the creamy white, brown-trimmed 17th-century Baroque pilgrimage church of Santa Casa on the hill to your left.

Tirano is our last stop in Italy. In the old town, the bus passes an impressive Renaissance church (Madonna di Tirano, on the left) before arriving at the Italian Railways train station. Now you'll need to cross under the tracks to the separate, narrow-gauge, Swiss rail station. Go down the ramp or the stairs and through the tunnel, following *Retica* signs into the Swiss station building (which is still on Italian territory but inside the Swiss customs zone). You'll pass by a customs office, which will normally show no interest in you.

You may have time for lunch and some sightseeing in Tirano before hopping on the official Bernina Express trains. To cram in more sightseeing, take an earlier departure from Tirano on a regional train to gain time for a stopover in the fine town of Poschiavo (described later), and catch another train onward from Poschiavo later.

Train Trip
Part One: Tirano to Poschiavo

From Tirano, the train rolls streetcar-style through the center of Tirano, crosses the Italian-Swiss border, and then climbs up to **Brusio.** Here the train swirls up a circular viaduct—an ingenious construction allowing the train to reach higher altitudes without the help of a cogwheel mechanism. As the train spirals up, you can see the front and back cars curving in front of and behind you, riding over the viaduct.

Sit back and enjoy the most scenic part of the trip. You'll pass dark old pine forests with needle-and-moss-covered boulders. Chestnut forests, tobacco plantations, and vineyards contribute to the lush tableau. Wildflowers along the track include bright-orange lilies and mountain azaleas. The train slaloms up the steep mountain and offers more and more views of waterfalls, steep cliffs, and the Poschiavo valley and lake far below you.

If you're not stopping in Poschiavo, skip down to "Part Two."

Poschiavo

If you detour for a quick break in this cute town, check the time of the next train (posted on the wall) before you leave the station.

Deposit your bags at the station's luggage counter (small fee), just beyond the TI, where you can pick up a free map and the English translation for a short orientation walk (TI tel. 081-844-0571, www.valposchiavo.ch).

The best quick visit to Poschiavo includes a stroll to the main square (Piazza Comunale), with the Museo Casa Console and near the town's main church (St. Ignazio). From the station, walk straight out and down the main street until it ends at the river, then turn left, following signs for *Museo Casa Console.* Cross the river over the pedestrian bridge and continue left, then right, then left, following the *Museo* signs.

The main square, **Piazza Comunale,** is lined with Neoclassical and Neo-Gothic buildings, including an impressive Catholic church (Chiesa di San Vittore Mauro). A church stood here as early as 703, but the building has been rebuilt and renovated several times: The bell tower dates from 1202, and the Baroque front door was carved in the 1700s. Don't miss the little yellow building just before the church, with the intricate wrought-iron grills. Have a peek inside, and don't be startled by the skulls lining the walls—you're standing in front of the local ossuary.

If you have a Swiss Travel Pass, find the tiny **Museo Casa Console** in the old Town Hall, below the 12th-century church tower. It has a nice collection of Romantic-era paintings of this region—the sort that helped kick off the tourism boom and, in a sense, brought you here. Before becoming glamorized in the Romantic era, mountains were seen more as obstacles than objects of beauty (free with pass, otherwise overpriced at 10 CHF, Tue-Sun 11:00-16:00, closed Mon and Nov-mid-Dec, tel. 081-844-0040, www.museocasaconsole.ch).

Go from the main square a block north and find the **Church of St. Ignazio.** It's ironic that this Protestant church's namesake, St. Ignatius of Loyola, was the founder of the militant Jesuit order, whose main purpose was to fight "heretic" Protestants. Notice the inscription above the central pulpit, which is fervently Protestant: *Chiesa cristiana vangelica riformata da gli errori e superstizioni umane* ("Christian evangelical church, reformed from human errors and superstitions").

Then it's back to the station...you've got a train to catch.

Part Two: Poschiavo to Pontresina

Thirty minutes after leaving Poschiavo, just before the Alp Grüm station, you'll spot the first glacier, **Palü Gletscher** (on the left, above the little lake of Palüsee). It lies nestled between the peak of Piz Varuna (11,330 feet) on the left and the eastern summit of Piz Palü on the right (12,790 feet).

The screeching of the wheels is a reminder that this is the only train that crosses over the Alps without any tunnels. It goes right over the top. The Ospizio Bernina station marks the Bernina Pass and the highest point of this trip (7,380 feet, above the tree line). Next to the station, you'll see the White Lake (Lago Bianco), whose color comes from the snowmelt, also called "glacier milk." At the end of the lake, look to the left for a watershed sign (yellow, reading *Wasserscheide*), which explains that this is a European continental divide: From here, rivers flow either north (toward the Inn and Danube rivers, and finally to the Black Sea) or south (to the Adriatic Sea via the Adda and Po rivers).

Behind the White Lake, you can see the glaciers of **Sassal Masone** and **Piz Cambrena.** This mountain pass separates not only European drainage basins, but also cultures. In earlier decades, the train line was more susceptible to bad-weather closures. The Italian-speaking valley of Poschiavo was often cut off from Switzerland in the winter, and better connected to the valleys across the border in Italy (where you were just riding the bus).

The train crosses the barren landscape and descends into the **Engadine** valley. Tourists and convalescents discovered this part of Switzerland at the end of the 19th century. Imagine the gorgeous skiing here in the winter, which still attracts the rich and famous. After the railroad opened this secluded valley to the world, the first hotels and sanatoriums were built (the air and sunshine supposedly helped cure diseases like tuberculosis). Poets found their muse in the wild, romantic landscape, while painters flocked in, attracted by the quality of the light. Keep an eye out for typical Engadine architecture—small windows set in thick walls, etched *sgraffito* decorations, and carved wooden doors.

The **Montebello curve** offers you the best views over the Morteratsch glacier on the left, with impressive peaks in the background. From left to right: the Bellavista Range (12,770 feet), Crest Agüzza (12,690 feet), and the highest peak in the canton, Mount Bernina (13,280 feet). Mount Bernina was first climbed in 1850 by a team led by rangers from the village of Schanf. Their gear consisted only of thick woolen pants, a shirt and jacket, hobnailed shoes, and a hat with a black veil to shade them from the strong sunshine.

As you continue, the tracks are lined by more and more larch trees. The milky-white waters from Lago Bianco and the Morteratsch glacier run wild in a broad riverbed alongside the tracks, as satisfied cows chew away in the meadows while waterfalls tumble down the cliffs. From the Morteratsch station, there's a fine one-hour hike to the edge of the glacier, past posts tracking the glacier's recent retreat.

Next stop: **Pontresina.** This town is a good place to break the journey (see the Upper Engadine chapter). Consider spending a night or two in Pontresina, exploring the quaint village of Samedan, visiting the glitzy resort of St. Moritz, and maybe doing some hiking before continuing on your way.

If you're going to **St. Moritz,** your train trip is nearly over (about 10 minutes after Pontresina). If you're continuing to **Chur** (or, in summer, to **Davos**), there's more to see.

Part Three: Pontresina to Filisur

Although you're leaving the glaciers behind, your trip will still lead you through magnificent mountain scenery, with steep cliffs and deep gorges. (Note that from here on, the trip overlaps with the Glacier Express.)

First, you'll slide through the broad and mellow valley around

Samedan, following the shortest river in Switzerland, the Flaz-bach. On the right, look for the funicular heading up to **Muottas Muragl,** a viewpoint overlooking the valleys that come together in Samedan (described in the Upper Engadine chapter). Samedan is home to Europe's highest airport. It serves glider enthusiasts and vacationers in St. Moritz.

After Samedan, in **Bever,** the train leaves the Inn River valley and climbs to another spectacular leg of its journey. The section between Bever and Bergün boasts amazing engineering work. Technicians from all over the world come here to admire the diversity of spiral tunnels, looping viaducts, galleries, and bridges that span the Albula Gorge.

The train works its way up along a cheerfully splashing mountain creek, between the Swiss pine and larch trees and some isolated farmhouses. The **Albula Tunnel,** the highest subterranean alpine crossing in Europe, takes you up to 5,970 feet. This pass serves as another barrier between cultures and climate—it takes you from the valley of the Inn River (part of the Danube watershed) to the valley of the Albula, a tributary of the Rhine, and the weather is often quite different on either side of the tunnel. Hikers can follow the tracks and read the information panels about the construction of the train line.

From **Preda,** the train loops down through five spiral and two straight tunnels, crosses nine viaducts, and goes under two galleries—it's considered the most ingenious railway line ever built. It covers almost eight miles and descends more than 1,365 feet in altitude. The village of **Bergün** will be visible three separate times as you loop around the valley. Bergün greets you with a modern, public open-air swimming pool and an onion-shaped 17th-century "Roman tower." As the train continues winding down the pretty valley, you may be able to see other parts of the track below or next to you. Any track you see is one you've either already been on—or will soon be on. Every winter, the street along the tracks above Bergün is closed to cars, and 100,000 sled enthusiasts enjoy the ride of their lives on a winding three-mile stretch.

You'll pass through **Filisur,** where summer Bernina Express trains to Davos split off. If you're continuing to Chur, read on.

Part Four: Filisur to Chur

After Filisur, the train enters a tunnel, and an announcement reminds you to ready your camera and position yourself on the left side. Just after the tunnel, you'll cross the famous **Landwasser viaduct.** A masterpiece of engineering, its pillars were built without scaffolding. Iron towers, which formed the center of each pillar, were built first. With the help of cranes set up atop each pillar, materials were hoisted up and the brick was laid. The 425-foot-long

SCENIC RAIL JOURNEYS

viaduct curves elegantly in a radius of 330 feet. Below, the wild Albula River carves the dramatic gorge; above, your train's panoramic windows allow you to see the steep, rugged cliffs looming over the tracks (a particularly beautiful stretch is right after Solis). Notice how nicely the dark limestone masonry matches the surrounding landscape (it was quarried right here).

Thusis is the commercial hub of the broad and lush Domleschg valley. The trip takes you down along the Hinterrhein ("Back-Rhine") River. Notice the many fortresses, castles, towers, and ruins along the river, a reminder that taxes were levied on the traders traveling this major route between northern and southern Europe. One of Switzerland's most popular mineral waters originates in Rhäzüns. The 13th-century castle above the town now belongs to a local chemical company.

Reichenau marks the confluence of two arms of the Upper Rhine (the Hinterrhein and the Vorderrhein—"Front-Rhine"). This town became wealthy from the taxes it got from the passing merchants. The 17th-century Reichenau Castle, right where the rivers converge, was once used as a school, but is now a hotel.

The train follows the Rhine at the foot of Calanda Mountain to our final stop, **Chur.** You can catch the Glacier Express (explained next) from Chur or from St. Moritz.

Glacier Express

This most promoted of the Swiss scenic rail routes travels between Zermatt in the southwest of Switzerland and the best-known resort towns in eastern Switzerland (St. Moritz and Davos). If you stay on for the whole ride, you'll spend more than eight hours crossing 291 bridges, going through 91 tunnels, and reaching an altitude of 6,670 feet.

While it's an impressive and famous journey, the Glacier Express is not necessarily the be-all and end-all of Swiss rail trips. Much of the journey is down in valleys (as opposed to along the sides of cliffs), meaning that high-altitude views are a little lacking. And doing the whole route makes for a longer day than some wish. But the stark landscape, carved by the glaciers that gave the train its name, is striking. The trip offers a dramatic way to connect eastern Switzerland with tucked-away-in-the-mountains Zermatt.

ROUTE OVERVIEW

"Glacier Express" is a misnomer—you'll only glimpse glaciers at the two ends of the route, and it's hardly an express. Not only does it take its time (traveling at about 20 mph to make the full trip in

8 hours), but it also makes plenty of stops along the way. The route cuts along the southern part of Switzerland, between St. Moritz/Davos (in the east) and Zermatt (in the west). You can ride in either direction.

PLANNING YOUR TIME

Eight hours on a winding, jolting narrow-gauge train is a long time. If you don't want to commit to the whole eight hours, keep in mind that the most distinctive stretch of the trip is the high-mountain pass between Disentis and Brig. The stretch between St. Moritz and Filisur (which is also part of the Bernina Express route) is also a highlight. There are several ways of doing just a part of the route, though none is an obvious winner. Consider doing just St. Moritz to Chur (2 hours), then continuing to Zürich or Appenzell; St. Moritz to Brig (6.5 hours), then branching off to Interlaken, Bern, or Lausanne; Luzern or Lugano to Zermatt, connecting at Göschenen (6 hours); Luzern to St. Moritz, connecting at Andermatt (6.5 hours, see "**Luzern to St. Moritz Option**" later); or Lugano to Bern, via Göschenen and Brig (5.5 hours).

ORIENTATION TO THE GLACIER EXPRESS

Cost: You'll pay 150 CHF for second class, or 269 CHF for first class, between St. Moritz and Zermatt. The entire trip is covered by the Swiss Travel Pass or a Eurail pass (except the reservation fee of 33 CHF, or 13 CHF off-season). If you're riding the full length of the Glacier Express *sans* rail pass, the cost is high enough to warrant a look at the Half-Fare Travel Card, which can quickly pay for itself (see page 403).

All Glacier Express trains have panoramic first- and second-class cars with air-conditioning, headsets for commentary, and the option of an in-seat meal. Second-class seating can get extremely crowded in summer, so consider splurging on first class.

Schedule: The Glacier Express train runs at least once daily in each direction, except from late October to mid-December (when local trains are your only option). Going from east to west, the train begins in St. Moritz at 9:02 (Davos at 9:31) and arrives in Zermatt at 17:10. Going from west to east, the train departs Zermatt at 8:52 and arrives in St. Moritz at 16:58 (Davos at 16:29). In summer, one or two extra departures per day are added, an hour earlier and later than the times above. Confirm all times before your trip.

Information: The Glacier Express is operated jointly by the Matterhorn Gotthard Bahn (MGB), based in Brig (tel. 084-864-2442, www.glacierexpress.ch or www.mgbbahn.ch), and the Rhätische Bahn (RhB), based in Chur (tel. 081-288-6565, www.rhb.ch). For more detail than found here or in the headset narration, consider picking up a guidebook before you board, or buy the (overpriced) official guide on board.

Picking the Best Seat: For most of the trip—including the most dramatic stretch, between Disentis and Brig—it's slightly preferable to sit on the south-facing side of the train (generally seat numbers ending in 1 or 2 in both classes face south on this stretch; in second class, seats ending in 3 or 8 are along the aisle on the south-facing side). Coming from the east, even-numbered seats face forward for most of the trip. Keep in mind: Trains change directions in Chur—so if you start on the right side facing backward in Davos,  Samedan, or St. Moritz, you'll be on the (slightly preferable) left side facing forward for most of the trip. Conductors take reserved seat numbers seriously, but may allow you to switch into an unoccupied seat if you prefer.

Luggage: You'll keep your luggage with you (they don't check it through)—just slip it between the backs of the seats.

No-Show Bridges: Most promotional materials show the Glacier

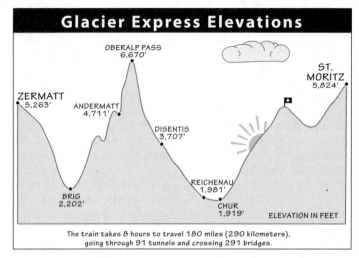

Glacier Express Elevations

OBERALP PASS
6,670'

ST. MORITZ
5,824'

ZERMATT
5,263'

ANDERMATT
4,711'

DISENTIS
3,707'

REICHENAU
1,981'

BRIG
2,202'

CHUR
1,919'

ELEVATION IN FEET

The train takes 8 hours to travel 180 miles (290 kilometers), going through 91 tunnels and crossing 291 bridges.

Express train venturing across ancient aqueducts and old stone bridges. It makes for picturesque publicity. But realize that you can barely see these bridges from the train itself...because you're on them.

Taking Regular Trains: This is the one scenic train where following the same route on regular trains is not a good option. While it can be done, and does save the hefty seat reservation fee, you'll need to change three times rather than enjoying the convenience of staying in one car the whole way. Regular trains are, however, the only option in late fall, when the express doesn't run.

Luzern to St. Moritz Option: An alternative, convenient way to connect visits to the Berner Oberland and the Upper Engadine regions is to go by train from Luzern to St. Moritz on a route that covers some of the nicest portions of the Glacier Express trip. Two trains leave Luzern every morning for St. Moritz with changes in Erstfeld, Göschenen, and Andermatt (see www.rail.ch for schedules).

Eating on the Glacier Express: The train has a fancy restaurant car that offers a **$$$$** lunch, which is handy if you're in for the full eight hours. The 43-CHF fixed-price meal includes a salad (summer) or soup (winter), a main dish, and a dessert (drinks cost extra). Their trademark gizmo: a tilted wine glass. Since lunch is generally served when the train is going up a steep incline (11:00-13:30), these gimmicky glasses always get a laugh.

To save a few francs, it's fine to bring your own **picnic,** and most seats have tables—perfect for a grocery-store feast.

● SELF-GUIDED TOUR

All Glacier Express trains—whether they begin in St. Moritz or Davos—go through Chur. I'll describe the route starting at Chur and heading toward Zermatt. (For details on the trip from St. Moritz to Chur, see parts three and four of the Bernina Express self-guided tour, earlier.)

Just outside Chur (near where the St. Moritz train line hits the Chur line), you'll be following the **Vorderrhein Gorge,** nicknamed "the Swiss Grand Canyon." It was carved by the Rhine River (though way up here in the Alps, this little "Front-Rhine" is not navigable). After about nine miles, the train diverges from the Rhine and enters a pastoral region called Surselva, centered on the town of Ilanz. This is Romansh country, where the fourth official language of Switzerland is kept alive—barely—in communities like this one. After headset commentary #33, keep an eye out on the right side of the train for three doors, under small brown roofs, tucked into a stone wall beneath a road along the bottom of the hillside. They're part of Switzerland's military defenses; access to this pass can be blown up on short notice. From this valley (Reichenau, roughly 2,000 feet above sea level and the lowest altitude of the route), the big climb begins.

As you approach **Disentis,** the tracks begin to twist along the edge of a canyon—making the scenery more dramatic (a taste of what's to come). Thirty years ago, those mountains above you were covered in snow year-round—but no longer. You'll pull into Disentis, with its big 17th-century Benedictine monastery looming in your window (first on the left side, then on the right). Your car will jiggle as a cogwheel engine (a.k.a. rack-and-pinion drive) is attached. This locomotive has gears that can lower to latch onto the cogs of an extra rail with grippable teeth. At a 10 percent incline (that's 100 meters of gain per kilometer, or about 500 feet per mile), conventional train wheels start to slip.

You'll work your way up the mountain alongside the Vorderrhein River. Just west of Sedrun was the staging ground for the excavation of the Gotthard Base Tunnel, which runs 30 miles under the mountain from Erstfeld to Bodio. Just past Rueras, the track steepens and the train slows to allow its gears to latch into the cog rail. After Tschamut, the last inhabited place before Oberalp Pass, you enter a long series of snow sheds—designed to protect the tracks (and trains) in case an avalanche strikes.

You'll emerge from the sheds at **Oberalp Pass,** the literal high point of this journey (6,670 feet), and glide along the Oberalp

Lake. Notice the extensive network of avalanche fences high above you—a reminder of the many generations of Swiss farmers who have learned to live on the land. The reddish streaks you might see on the snow? Believe it or not, that's sand from the Sahara Desert. It gets caught up in high-altitude winds and carried all the way to the Swiss Alps.

As you descend from the pass, you'll travel over, then through, the modern town of **Andermatt,** home to a Swiss Army base. Deep below you is the older, 9.5-mile-long Gotthard Tunnel, which takes trains unscenically from Göschenen to Airolo. The huge boulders seen throughout this desolate terrain were deposited by glaciers.

Soon after, you'll go through the 9.5-mile-long Furka Base Tunnel. While it might seem like a view killer, realize that this tunnel—finished in 1982—makes it possible for the Glacier Express to continue running through the winter. Automobiles are allowed onto the train to ride smoothly and safely between Realp and Oberwald. This is especially handy in the winter, when the road is closed.

You'll emerge into the region of **Goms,** with its pretty villages. The up-close view of the village of Reckingen is particularly fun as the train snakes through a narrow passage between the dark-wood houses. Along this stretch, the train joins up with another of Europe's great rivers, the **Rhône.** Just a bubbly little mountain stream here (originating from the once-mighty Rhône Glacier nearby), the Rhône flows all the way to Marseille, France, where it meets the Mediterranean. Some of the construction you may see in this area is part of a project to "correct" (channel and control) this upper stretch of the powerful river, which has a long history of flooding the valley.

As the valley gets rockier, consider that you're on the "back" side of the Berner Oberland. If you climbed up high enough to the north, you'd see the Jungfrau, Mönch, and Eiger mountains (from the village of Fiesch/Kühboden you can do just that, with the help of a cable car up to Eggishorn, which boasts views of the Matterhorn and Mont Blanc to boot).

Finally, you'll arrive at **Brig,** an ugly industrial town with good connections to other train lines (transfer here if you're not continuing to Zermatt). From Brig, it's 25 miles to Zermatt and the Matterhorn, following the craggy Nikolai Valley. You'll feel the tug as the train's cogwheel attaches again for another steep climb. Keep an eye out for vineyards—the highest in Europe. We're out of milk country and into wine country. At Stalden, a road leads up another valley to the resort of Saas-Fee. Along this section, the route closely follows the Vispa River as it scenically tumbles along. Shortly before the village of Randa, you pass a cone of rubble left by a huge avalanche that wiped out two miles of road and track here in 1991.

At **Täsch,** vast parking lots mark the end of the road for drivers. From here it's train-only into the traffic-free terminus of this line, Zermatt. Think about how much the terrain has changed since you started the trip: from remote valleys to fertile farmlands, to tundra above the tree line, to this rough and rocky terrain.

As you continue along the valley lined with quarries, you'll begin to get your first glimpses (provided the weather's clear) of the unmistakable shape of the **Matterhorn**—a fitting exclamation point marking the end of this long journey. **Zermatt**—with its bunker-like, avalanche-proof train station—lies just around the bend.

GLACIER EXPRESS CONNECTIONS

If you're not going all the way to St. Moritz or Zermatt, Chur and Brig are handy places to bail out of the Glacier Express.

From Brig by Train to: Bern (2/hour, 1 hour), **Lausanne** (2/hour, 2 hours), **Interlaken Ost** (1-2/hour, 70 minutes, change in Spiez), **Luzern** (hourly, 2.5 hours, change in Bern), **Zürich** (hourly, 2 hours, more with change in Bern).

For Chur connections, see the next page.

Chur

The routes of the Glacier Express and the Bernina Express both pass through Chur—supposedly Switzerland's oldest and warmest town. Fanning out over the foothills from the Rhine River, Chur is a handy transportation hub for these two scenic train lines and has a charming-enough old town. Overall, Chur (pronounced "khoor") is just a typical Swiss burg—fine for passing through, but not worth a detour.

Visiting Chur: Chur's train station is at the bottom (north end) of the town center, where it sits atop a long underground concourse housing the **TI** (tel. 081-252-1818, www.churtourismus.ch), shops, the handy Bahnhofplatz parking garage, and other services. To get to the old town, follow *Stadtzentrum* signs up the escalator, then walk straight up Bahnhofstrasse. In two blocks, you'll reach the big roundabout at Postplatz. The old town is straight ahead.

Public **WCs** are next to the cathedral. If you've got time to kill, you can wander up through the cobbled old town to two big churches (the Romanesque cathedral and the Gothic Church of St. Martin), some remains of the medieval city wall, and the town museum (Rätisches Museum, www.raetischesmuseum.gr.ch). Follow the handy red signs pointing you to the attractions.

Sleeping in Chur: Sleep in Chur only if you must, in order to connect to one of the scenic rail lines. Here are three moderately priced places in the atmospheric old town, an easy 10- to 15-minute walk from the train station: **$$$ Hotel Restaurant Rebleuten** (overlooking a quiet little square a block off Kornplatz at Pfisterplatz 1, tel. 081-255-1144, www.rebleutenchur.ch); **$$$ Hotel Freieck** (with a mod lobby and 39 rooms over a low-key café, Reichsgasse 44, tel. 081-255-1515, www.freieck.ch); and charming **$$$ Hotel Franziskaner** (with rooms above a popular restaurant, Kupfergasse 18, tel. 081-252-1261, www.hotelfranziskaner.ch).

Chur Connections: In addition to being a key stop for the Glacier Express and the Bernina Express, Chur also offers speedy, frequent connections to **Zürich** (3/hour, 1.5 hours), **Luzern** (2/hour, 2 hours, transfer in Thalwil), and **Appenzell** (hourly, 2.5 hours, 3 changes).

SWITZERLAND IN WINTER

One of my favorite Swiss memories happened one winter night on the snowy slopes of the Berner Oberland. My friend Walter (of Hotel Mittaghorn in Gimmelwald) and I, warmed by hot chocolate laced with schnapps, decided to go sledding between mountain-high villages. We strapped flashlights to our heads, miner-style, and zoomed through the crisp, moonlit night.

That said, this is a summertime book. I've included plenty of tips on hiking, while mostly ignoring the winter-sports scene. But winter activities are an important part of the Swiss culture (and tourist industry).

Just a century ago, clever entrepreneurs in the Swiss Alps realized that skiing (which began as a method of wintertime transportation in Scandinavia 4,000 years ago) could be a profitable extension of their resorts' spring and summer seasons. Telemark (cross-country) skiing came first, then alpine (downhill) skiing, and, more recently, snowboarding. Generations of Swiss skiers have honed their skills on these slopes. Big names include Erica Hess, Vreni Schneider, Maria Walliser, Carlo Janka, and the venerable 1948 Olympic champion Karl Molitor (whose  family currently runs a ski rental shop in Wengen in the Berner Oberland).

You don't have to be a skier or snowboarder to enjoy Switzerland in the winter. Ski resorts offer plenty of other activities, including snowshoeing, sledding, ice skating...and shopping. Or just ride up a lift, rent a chair in the sun, and warm up with a glass of *Pflümli* (plum liqueur).

TOP WINTER DESTINATIONS

The winter-sports season begins in early December and runs through Easter. Peak time hits at Christmas and New Year's—during this period, hotel prices in resort towns surpass summer highs.

While Switzerland's resorts vary greatly, they share a rich ski culture, an astounding variety of terrain, relatively mild temperatures (compared to many American destinations), and a lively après-ski scene. For those who can afford them, the best winter activities are in the Berner Oberland (Mürren, Wengen, Grindelwald, and Gstaad); the southern canton of Valais (Zermatt, Saas-Fee, Crans-Montana, and Verbier); and the eastern canton of Graubünden (St. Moritz, Davos, Klosters, and Arosa).

The **Berner Oberland** offers the ultimate diversity of terrain and character, as well as great sledding and stellar views (see the

Gimmelwald & the Berner Oberland chapter). The cliff-hanging town of Mürren is relatively uncrowded and a good home base for expert skiers, with the 10,000-foot Schilthorn peak as the backbone of its ski area. Across the valley, Wengen offers skiing for all skill levels, fine accommodations, and shopping, with a complex lift system connecting it to Kleine Scheidegg, Männlichen, and Grindelwald. Grindelwald, a little closer to Interlaken, is a bit pricier, but has the world's longest sled run and easy access to more than 100 miles of downhill trails, including the area's best range of beginners' runs. For a complete overview of these ski regions, see www.myjungfrau.ch.

The canton of **Valais** ("valley") is known for its excellent wine-making (in the Rhône River valley) as well as its ski slopes (www.valais.ch). Connected to Italy by several high-mountain passes, Valais is home to Switzerland's best-known sight: the Matterhorn (see the Zermatt & the Matterhorn chapter). The area around the Matterhorn, including the villages of Zermatt and Saas-Fee, enjoys a high elevation and good skiing.

The canton of Graubünden (www.graubuenden.ch) is home to **St. Moritz**—in the Upper Engadine valley—a resort town so well-known that it's a registered trademark (see the Upper Engadine chapter). St. Moritz offers designer boutiques, luxury accommodations, a natural mineral-spring spa...oh, and ski slopes, too (www.stmoritz.ch). In addition to skiing, winter visitors to St. Moritz play polo and cricket on snow, go bobsledding on natural ice, or try "skijoring"—skiing while being pulled by riderless horses.

TIPS FOR WINTER SPORTS

Expect to spend 60-80 CHF a day on lift tickets. You may find cheaper prices in the off-peak season (before mid-Dec and after Easter), if you buy a multiple-day pass, or if you have a Swiss Travel Pass. Prices may also be lower for seniors, teenagers, and kids (exact age cutoffs vary). Most ski areas offer half-day afternoon passes.

Rental prices are a bit higher than what you'd find in the US. Depending on the fanciness of the gear, you'll pay 50-80 CHF per day for skiing or snowboarding equipment. If you haven't packed ski wear, you'll pay about 50 CHF per day to rent ski pants, a jacket, and gloves.

Many rental shops in Switzerland belong to the Intersport rental network (www.intersportrent.ch), which sets fairly high standards for its member shops. Places outside this network can be cheaper, but Intersport shops are generally a safe bet and offer a useful bonus: Many of them let you pick up rental gear at one ski area and drop it off at another in the region for no charge (an especially handy option in the Berner Oberland).

Always ask your hotelier if they've arranged any special rental deals through local shops. Rental prices don't vary much (since so many shops are part of the Intersport network), so choose a place that's close to your hotel or convenient for getting up the mountain.

Swiss ski resorts are deservedly popular, and slopes can get crowded. Peak crowd times are Christmas, New Year's, mid-February to mid-March (when European school holidays hit), and Easter. The Berner Oberland also fills up in mid-January for world-class racing. Hit the slopes as soon as they open—the hordes don't usually arrive until 10:00 or later. This is especially true in swankier resorts, where well-heeled tourists enjoy long nights and short ski days.

For more in-depth information on the winter scene, see the winter sports section of the Swiss tourism website (www.myswitzerland.com).

CHRISTMAS CELEBRATIONS

Switzerland is an ideal place to celebrate the winter holidays. Imagine spending your days exploring Christmas markets in cozy Swiss cities, sipping hot mulled wine *(Glühwein),* picking out your favorite handmade ornaments, then relaxing at night in a warm little chalet, making figure-eights with your cube of bread through a steaming pot of cheese fondue.

Swiss Christmas markets are a treat, whether in big cities (such

as Bern, Zürich, and Basel) or smaller towns (Interlaken, Appenzell, Chur, and many others). While some of the bigger markets start at the beginning of December and run through Christmas Eve, smaller towns host markets for just one week or weekend. The Swiss Tourist Board's website gives specific dates (www.myswitzerland.com/christmas).

You'll find all cities festively decorated, but Zürich's remarkable display of tasteful, twinkling lights is arguably Switzerland's best. This being the land of Calvin—the most austere of Protestant Reformers—most Christmas decorations are relatively understated here, but they're still charming.

In the village of Gimmelwald, residents in each home adorn a window for Advent. Just as children open a different little paper window each day on an Advent calendar, Gimmelwald residents reveal a new decorated window on a different house each day. The debut of a new Advent window often comes with a party. Under a cold sky, with stars reflecting off the snow and the moon inside a halo, the village gathers. In a kind of roving block party, neighbors emerge to meet friends and enjoy grilled sausages, hot mulled wine, and folk music on the accordion. Men take sections of logs (the size of a four-foot chunk of telephone pole), cut the ends into a point, and plant them upright in the snow. Coated with tar, they're set ablaze—torches to light and warm the cozy yet frigid occasion. In the distance, children ride old-time wooden sleds, going up and down, up and down.

For the Swiss, a communal pot of fondue is purely a winter specialty. Invitations to a cozy Swiss party include the word

FIGUGEGL (fee-GOO-geck-ul), which stands for *Fondue isch guet und git e gueti Lune*—"Fondue is good and gives a good mood." According to tradition, if you drop your bread into the pot, you must kiss the person to your left.

Each Christmas season, usually on St. Nicholas Day (December 6), Swiss children receive a visit from Samichlaus—that's Swiss German for St. Nicholas. With his black-clad, soot-faced henchman, Schmutzli, by his side, Samichlaus goes door to door, visiting the town's children. He knocks on the door, and when the frightened-but-excited kids answer, Samichlaus consults his big book of sins—co-authored by parents—and does some lighthearted moralizing. Schmutzli stands by as a menacing enforcer, traditionally holding either a stick or switch for beating bad children, and a sack for carrying them away to be eaten (nowadays he only eats the really bad chil-

dren). Then Samichlaus asks the kids to earn a little forgiveness by reciting a poem. After the poems and assurances of reform, Samichlaus allows them to reach deep into his bag for a smattering of tangerines, nuts, gingerbread, and other treats.

Cutting and decorating the Christmas tree—traditionally on December 24—is a family affair. Real candles, kept upright by dangling ornamental counterbalances, are attached, then lit by the children. (Locals are bold with their candles; to me, it feels as if their pine houses, with open beams, are ready to go up in flames.) Presents are opened while the candles burn. The tree stays up after Christmas; candles are lit again on New Year's Eve for good luck. Some traditional rural Swiss churches also light candles on their trees for Christmas Eve services.

OTHER FESTIVITIES

Second only to Christmas is *Fasnacht,* the Germanic equivalent of Mardi Gras or Carnival. Traditionally celebrated in the days

before or after Ash Wednesday, *Fasnacht* features a parade of locals in traditional masks and garish, larger-than-life costumes. Quirky traditions vary from town to town (for example, in Basel—home to Switzerland's most outlandish *Fasnacht*—celebrations begin promptly at 4:00 in the morning, and feature

roving fife-and-drum bands). This pre-Christian ceremony likely dates from a pagan tradition to frighten away evil winter spirits and welcome the renewal of springtime. The most famous *Fasnacht* celebrations in Switzerland occur in Basel (www.fasnacht.ch), Bern (www.fasnacht.be), and Luzern (www.luzerner-fasnacht.ch). If you'll be in Switzerland at this time of year, it's worth the effort to catch one of these weird and wonderful celebrations.

SWITZERLAND: PAST & PRESENT

Switzerland has a unique and impressive story, forging unity from diversity and somehow remaining above the fray when Europe goes ballistic. Despite four languages, diverse geography, ill-defined borders, and many religious sects—and despite being surrounded by continental Europe's four big powers (France, Germany, Austria, and Italy)—the Swiss cantons banded together to form an independent federal system that still works today.

Even if you're not going to Switzerland for the history (who would?), you'll encounter it. You can play gladiator inside a fighting arena from Roman times or tour medieval castles and battlegrounds, left over from when the Swiss wrestled their independence from foreign rulers. Stripped-down cathedrals attest to the religious violence of the Reformation, which almost tore the country apart. You'll ride the ingenious cogwheel trains and cliff-climbing funiculars of Switzerland's progressive 19th century, when the country was at the forefront of the emerging Industrial Age. The specters of Nazi Germany and the Soviet Union arise in underground fortresses and bomb shelters now open to the public. And finally, you'll see the Switzerland of today—gleaming cities, state-of-the-art transportation, and happy citizens. I love to go a-wandering along the history path, so strap on your rucksack, and let's go.

EARLY HISTORY: CELTS AND ROMANS
(c. 500 B.C.-A.D. 500)

The Alps—Switzerland's star attraction—were born 500 million years ago, when the ocean floor was rocked by earthquakes that folded the earth's crust upward and created this long range of peaks (see the sidebar on page 18). The rugged landscape shaped the history and character of the Swiss people. It kept early populations physically isolated, leading to still-present cultural divisions and fostering an ethos of independence. Switzerland's location at the heart of Western Europe forced it to be international in outlook, yet the impregnable mountains allowed it to remain apart and neutral.

The first Swiss to appear in written records (c. 500 B.C.) were a Celtic tribe called the Helvetii. Their name survives today in the country's official title, Confoederatio Helvetica. "Helvetia," the female symbol of Switzerland, appears dressed in robes and armed with a spear and shield on coins, stamps, and statues.

In 58 B.C., the Helvetii were defeated by Julius Caesar, the Roman general and future ruler. The Romans established a capital at Avenches, near Murten (where evocative ruins remain); built the cities of Zürich, Geneva, Basel, and Lausanne; and assimilated the Helvetii into their Europe-wide empire. Roman culture thrived in Switzerland for almost 500 years.

As Rome fell (c. A.D. 400), the Alemanni and other Germanic tribes swarmed in from the north, snuffed out Roman culture, and established the German language. In the west, the Burgundians adopted Latin, which eventually evolved into French. But these tribes never penetrated the nooks and crannies of the most remote mountain areas, and in these regions, particularly in the southeast, people still converse in Romansh, a language that descends independently from the colloquial Latin spoken by Roman-era occupiers. South of the Alps, Latin gradually developed into modern-day Italian. These linguistic and cultural divides remain today.

THE MIDDLE AGES: THE HOLY ROMAN EMPIRE (c. 500-1291)

Like most of Europe during the dark medieval centuries, Switzerland was poor, feudal, and swept by barbarian invasions. The mostly pagan Swiss were slowly converted to Christianity by traveling Irish monks, including St. Gallus (seventh century), who gave his name to the canton of St. Gallen. Swiss lands became part of Charlemagne's empire (c. 800) and then of its successor to the east—the Holy Roman Empire.

Around the turn of the first millennium, Switzerland began to prosper. Cities such as Bern and Luzern were founded, welcoming skilled craftsmen and traders. High in the Alps, clever engineers built bridges and catwalks to open a vital north-south highway through the St. Gotthard Pass. Merchants bought luxury goods in Venice and shipped them over the high mountains to northern Europe. This trade route proved so lucrative that the Holy Roman

Emperor ensured access to it by granting the Swiss a measure of independence. Switzerland got a taste of freedom, and when the emperor (a member of the powerful Habsburg family) later tried to bring the country under tighter control, the Swiss had had enough.

THE OLD CONFEDERACY (1291-1500)

On August 1, 1291 (celebrated today as the country's national day), representatives of Switzerland's three original cantons (Uri, Schwyz, and Unterwalden) gathered together and swore an oath. "We will be a single nation of brothers..." they asserted, and joined together to oppose Habsburg rule. According to a famous legend, a Swiss man named William Tell refused to bow to the Habsburg hat, a symbol of their power. As punishment, he was forced to shoot an apple off his own son's head. His son lived to see another haircut, and Tell led the rebellion. (Sadly, historians say that Tell probably never actually existed.)

The Swiss had to battle the powerful Habsburg family for two full centuries to completely drive them out. Meanwhile, in the west, the Swiss fought Burgundy, trouncing them at the pivotal Battle of Murten. One by one, other cantons and cities (Luzern, Zürich, Bern) joined the confederacy. By around 1500, Switzerland's territory had grown to become roughly similar to its current bounds.

During these centuries of warfare, the Swiss earned a reputation as Europe's fiercest warriors. Swiss mercenaries became a valuable export, hired by foreign kings to fight their wars and de-

fend their palaces (think of the Swiss Guards, who still protect the Vatican today). During the French Revolution in 1792, when crowds stormed the king's palace in Paris, it was Swiss mercenaries who went through with the hopeless defense. Six hundred of them were killed—an event memorialized in Luzern's famous Lion Monument to fallen Swiss Guards.

REFORMATION AND ENLIGHTENMENT (c. 1500-1700)

The Protestant Reformation split Switzerland in two. Ulrich Zwingli preached Protestantism in Zürich (see sidebar on page 34), John Calvin brought his French flock to Geneva, and the Dutch humanist Desiderius Erasmus taught at Basel. While the cities went Protestant, the more rural cantons stayed true to the Catholic faith, plunging the country into religious warfare (1529-1531). Angry rioters stormed Catholic cathedrals, stripping them of their "graven images" and leaving the austere interiors travelers see today (including Zürich's Grossmünster, Bern's Münster, and Lausanne's cathedral).

While Europe suffered through a century of religious wars, Switzerland's struggles were relatively short-lived. Swiss mercenaries fought other countries' wars more than their own. When peace came to Europe with the Treaty of Westphalia (1648), the agreement also officially recognized Switzerland as a fully independent nation.

1700s AND 1800s

Through the Age of Enlightenment, Switzerland bucked the European trend toward absolute monarchs. As the country steadily advanced economically and technologically, it moved in a firmly democratic direction. However, internal conflict about how to organize the country's government made for a rocky transition. Swiss Protestants generally favored a strong central government and were more open to new political and social ideas. The more remote, more Catholic cantons wanted to keep power in local areas and preserve traditional ways of life. This tension continues in Swiss politics to this day.

Riding the wave of the French Revolution, Napoleon Bonaparte occupied Switzerland (1798) and tried (unsuccessfully) to establish a unified central government—called the Helvetic Republic—which fell apart within five years. With Napoleon's defeat (and the 1815 Congress of Vienna), the European powers restored Switzerland's old status. They also set it on its future political course—neutrality in all conflicts.

In 1847, the Swiss fought a four-week, not-very-bloody civil war which ended in a victory for the advocates of centralization. In 1848, amid a Europe-wide wave of liberal reforms, Switzerland crafted a constitution that struck a balance between the two camps. The constitution created a strong central government but also allowed each canton much more autonomy than the regions in other European countries. (It was partly modeled on America's, as the Swiss struggles with centralism and federalism mirror American debates over states' rights.) The country's national capital was established in the low-key town of Bern.

Around this time the country began to welcome hordes of tourists, beginning with French, English, and German aristocrats on the Grand Tour, who passed through Switzerland on their way to Italy. Next came the British mountaineers, whose reverence for the Alps was part of the Romantic outlook on nature: For the first time, Europeans looked at mountains as objects of beauty and inspiration, rather than as frustrating obstacles. Visitors marveled at the mountain scenery and the "sublime" rush it gave them. The new technology of rail travel made trips more comfortable and affordable. In this heyday of European travel, Switzerland virtually invented mass tourism as we know it—pioneering ways of marking its mountains, offering the first organized vacations, investing in a well-oiled infrastructure, and establishing a reputation for efficiency, cleanliness, quality, and ease (even inventing new names for places that had local names that were considered too intimidating for foreign visitors). Switzerland's system of high-altitude trains, funiculars, and mountain lifts was built to carry 19th-century tourists to previously unheard-of heights. Today's visitors stay in the same resort towns (Interlaken, Zermatt, Luzern, St. Moritz), ride the same kind of lifts, and see echoes of themselves in the stylized travel advertisements from that Romantic age.

As a neutral country, Switzerland fostered its reputation as a leader in international relations. Like tourists, politicians loved to meet amidst its clear air and alpine vistas. The world's diplomats descended on Geneva in 1863 and 1864, producing two landmark institutions: the International Red Cross (still run from Geneva) and the Geneva Conventions war treaties. The United Nations and other international organizations still maintain a large presence in Geneva. And when the modern Olympic Games were founded by a French aristocrat in 1894, nearby Lausanne became the movement's world headquarters.

20TH CENTURY: WORLD WARS

Switzerland entered the 20th century on the cutting edge of progress. Its trains and communications systems were top-notch. The artist Paul Klee (1879-1940), with his playful, eccentric style,

contributed to the Modernist movement (see his works at the Rosengart Collection in Luzern and at the Paul Klee Center in Bern). Europe's rich flocked to visit Swiss doctors at alpine sanatoriums. Carl Jung (1875-1961) pioneered the blossoming field of psychoanalysis. And in the quiet city of Bern, an anonymous patent clerk named Albert Einstein (1879-1955) was rewriting humankind's understanding of how the universe worked (see sidebar on page 100).

In World War I (1914-1918), Switzerland declared itself neutral and escaped the devastation that hit the rest of Europe. After the war, Geneva served as the seat of the League of Nations, a short-lived forerunner to the United Nations.

When World War II broke out (1939-1945), Swiss neutrality was not taken for granted. As Nazi Germany and fascist Italy flanked the country, 850,000 Swiss men grabbed their rifles and mobilized to protect the borders. Switzerland avoided invasion through military readiness and by trading with the Nazis—some would say "appeasing" the Nazis. Switzerland sheltered some refugees—and turned others away—and acted as a mediator between the Allies and the Axis.

Today, critics charge that, though neutral in the war, Switzerland actually helped the Nazi effort by continuing to do business with them. (It's no secret that a significant number of German-speaking Swiss weren't all that opposed to the Nazi regime.) They exchanged Swiss francs (the only currency accepted throughout Europe) for Nazi gold—knowing full well that the gold had been stolen from other nations and Holocaust victims. In the 1990s, lawsuits called Swiss banks to account for the ill-gotten bullion in their vaults. A 2002 commission formed by the Swiss government agreed that Switzerland could have done more to resist the Nazis and to help Jewish refugees...but restitution has been slow in coming.

After the war, Switzerland's policy of neutrality led the country to refuse membership in various international alliances and organizations, including the United Nations, NATO, and the European Union.

SWITZERLAND TODAY

Switzerland maintains a delicate balance between its traditional, neutral past and the high-tech, global future.

As it has been for 700 years, the government is a federalist democracy that gives considerable autonomy to each canton. On the national level, the executive branch is steered by a seven-member committee, and the presidency is just a figurehead position that rotates between the seven members. There's a strong bicameral parliament, in which no single political party has more than about a fourth of the seats. Since World War II, legislative power has been held by an ever-changing array of coalitions. No single point of view dominates, and collaboration is essential.

The federal government handles foreign affairs, national defense, currency, and the federal courts—and leaves most everything else to the 26 cantons. The man-on-the-street can always make his voice heard thanks to frequent referendums, held when citizens gather enough signatures to require a public vote on an issue. Unlike in most modern democracies, Swiss citizens have a direct say in many political matters and leave fewer decisions to elected representatives.

During the Great Recession, the euro zone's financial crisis posed a threat to Switzerland's financial stability by driving up demand for the Swiss franc—and making Swiss exports and tourism less competitive. Now, with Europe's economy on the rebound, Zürich continues to be a global center of banking and finance, and tourism remains a strong part of the economy. Stability is enhanced by strong social security and a collaborative approach to settling labor disputes between unions and employers.

In foreign affairs, Switzerland remains neutral…but ever-vigilant. Every able-bodied man serves in the army and stays in the reserves. Each house has a gun and a fully stocked bomb shelter. (Swiss vacuum-packed emergency army bread, which lasts two years, is also said to function as a weapon.) Altogether, the country bristles with 600,000 rifles in homes and 12,000 heavy guns in place. Airstrips are hidden inside mountains, accessed by  camouflaged doors. With the push of a button, all road, rail, and bridge entries to Swiss territory can be destroyed, sealing off the country from the outside world. Sentiments are changing, though, and Switzerland has come close to voting away its entire military. Today, you can visit once-hidden military installations, now open to the public as museums (for example, Fortress Fürigen—covered in the Luzern & Central Switzerland chapter).

The question of how closely to integrate with Europe has dominated political discussion in Switzerland for the last three decades. In 2002, the Swiss made a big step away from total neutrality when voters approved a referendum to join the United Nations. In 2008, Switzerland joined the Schengen Agreement, opening its borders to its neighboring countries and most of the EU. Is EU membership next? Probably not. In referendum after referendum the Swiss have strongly rejected the idea of full economic and political integration with the EU, judging the costs to be more significant than the huge potential gains. Still, they've seen benefits in collaborating with Europe on practical matters such as scientific research. For example, Switzerland is home to Europe's high-tech particle accelerator laboratory, called CERN (the place where the World Wide Web was invented by a British scientist).

PAST & PRESENT

While it's nice to think of Swiss neutrality as born of pacifism, many realists argue that it's more about money: Switzerland's neutrality policy was key to one of its main sources of income. Traditionally, many Swiss banks allowed foreigners to deposit money with few questions asked. Critics charge that these secret bank accounts have harbored the dirty money of mobsters, terrorists, dictators, guidebook authors, tax evaders, and sleazy businessmen. Switzerland also has a reputation as a safe haven from prosecution, harboring a long list of foreigners (from Hollywood sex offender Roman Polanski to Ugandan dictator Idi Amin). But times are changing. Recently, Swiss politicians and bankers have responded to outside pressure and introduced legislation that will require banks to share information on clients with the tax authorities in other countries.

Another big issue in Switzerland is how to deal with the rising tide of immigrants. The country's high standard of living makes it an appealing place to live, and Switzerland has more noncitizen residents than most countries (about 24 percent, compared with 7 percent in the US). Many of those immigrants are wealthy Europeans enjoying the country's easy tax laws. Others are young Germans, Italians, or Portuguese who have taken jobs in the hospitality industry. Still others are the Swiss-born, Swiss-raised children of an earlier generation of immigrants—who still don't have Swiss citizenship due to the complicated application requirements. It's the "less-desirable" immigrants who have drawn fire—those who arrive with little wealth and then rely on generous social services—but it's not clear that there are really that many of them.

Opinions on this and many other issues are generally divided along geographic/linguistic lines. City dwellers, along with French and Italian speakers, tend to favor immigrants' rights, EU membership, and other progressive issues; rural German speakers are more likely to be conservative. In 2009, when Switzerland voted to ban the construction of new minarets—sparking controversy across Europe—only four cantons opposed the initiative, all of them in French-speaking areas.

With 2,500 years of history, Switzerland has seen many shifts—from Celts to Romans to Habsburgs, from wars to neutrality to technological progress. But what's striking is how little Switzerland has changed. The Alps are still there, and they're still big and rugged. The government, after 700 years in existence, remains a model of democracy and international cooperation. Switzerland is fully modern, but you'll also encounter quaint pockets

of the past. Take time to see Swiss history alive today—from the cow parades of Appenzell to the Roman ruins in Avenches, and from the turrets of Château de Chillon to the farmers of Gimmelwald, who still make hay while the sun shines.

NOTABLE SWISS PEOPLE

William Tell (c. 1280-1354): On November 18, 1307, William (Wilhelm) Tell, a Swiss peasant, refused a bailiff's order to bow to a symbol of the Habsburg emperor. As punishment, Tell was forced to fire his crossbow at an apple resting on his son's head. He shot cleanly through the apple without injuring his son, and later ambushed and killed the bailiff—launching a revolt for Swiss independence. Though historians say the famous hero is fictional (a similar Danish legend predates the Swiss one), don't "tell" the Swiss—up to 60 percent still believe there was a real William Tell.

Huldrych Zwingli (1484-1531): The son of a farmer, Huldrych Zwingli started out as a Catholic true believer, but under the influence of Renaissance humanists, turned into a religious revolutionary. Known as the "third man of the Protestant Reformation" (the other two were Martin Luther and John Calvin), he used his position as the top pastor in Zürich to challenge Rome, insisting that Christians study the Bible to guide their beliefs. Many Protestant faiths, including the United Church of Christ and the Presbyterian Church, trace their theology back to Zwingli.

Jean-Jacques Rousseau (1712-1778): One of the most influential writers of the 18th century, Jean-Jacques Rousseau ran away from his humble Geneva home for France when he was 16, but he always considered himself Swiss, not French. His writings celebrated nature and human passion (over cold reason), unleashing forces that would result in the French Revolution, Romantic literature, and even a return to breastfeeding. Publishers couldn't print his books fast enough, so they rented them out by the day. Rousseau's descriptions of the Swiss countryside helped start the 19th-century craze for visiting the Alps.

Madame Tussaud (1761-1850): An entertainment empire began when Swiss-born Anna Maria Grosholtz moved to Paris and learned how to sculpt wax. It was an auspicious time and place—she was able to create figures of Voltaire, Jean-Jacques Rousseau, and Benjamin Franklin. Later, during the French Revolution, she made death masks from decapitated heads. After marrying François Tussaud (becoming "Madame Tussaud"), she moved to London and eventually opened a museum of wax figures, which still shows some of her original work.

Henri Dunant (1828-1910): In 1859, Geneva businessman Henri Dunant witnessed one of the bloodiest battles of the 19th century—the Battle of Solferino in northern Italy, where about 40,000 soldiers were killed or wounded. He wrote a book that not only described the carnage, but also proposed a neutral organization that would care for those wounded in wartime. His leadership led to the founding of the International Red Cross and the Geneva Conventions, which put humanitarian limits on the waging of war. He won the first Nobel Peace Prize in 1901.

Carl Jung (1875-1961): After Freud, Carl Jung had the greatest impact on modern psychology; there probably wouldn't be a New Age movement or the Myers-Briggs personality test without him. The Zürich psychologist popularized such terms as "introvert/extrovert," "personality complex," and "collective unconscious." He once said that the Swiss are a "primitive" people (their love of cows reminded him of African animism), and that under their legendary efficiency is a deeply buried "earth mysticism."

Hermann Hesse (1877-1962): German-born Hesse, who became a Swiss citizen in 1923, was into psychoanalysis, India, and Buddhism before they were cool. His writing was banned by the Nazis and later beloved by 1960s hippies for its themes of self-discovery and enlightenment. His best-known works—among them *Steppenwolf, Siddhartha,* and *Narcissus and Goldmund*—are still widely read today. He was particularly publicity-shy—upon winning the Nobel Prize for Literature in 1946, he wrote to a friend, "To hell with this damn business."

Paul Klee (1879-1940): Paul Klee's mastery of color and tone created highly individual art that critics have described as "musical" and "childlike." Born and raised in Bern, Klee became a teacher at the famous Bauhaus school in Weimar, Germany, but when Hitler came to power in 1933, he was fired. He returned to Switzerland as the Nazis stripped his paintings from museums and classified them as "degenerate." You can see his work at museums in Bern and Luzern—then decide for yourself.

Le Corbusier (1887-1965): "The house is a machine for living in." With this and other edicts, architect Charles-Edouard Jeanneret-Gris, better known as Le Corbusier, changed the shape of 20th-century cities. His plan for Paris' Marais district was emblematic—rows of identical towers set between freeways, replacing public squares and winding streets. The Parisians turned him down, but many office and housing projects in Europe and America followed his precepts. Le Corbusier was one of the most influential architects of his time, though today many regard his International Style as sterile and socially destructive.

Jean Piaget (1896-1980): According to *Time* magazine, Geneva psychologist Jean Piaget was "the first to take children's thinking seriously." Before the publication of his groundbreaking work, parents and teachers regarded children as empty vessels into which they poured knowledge. By studying his own three kids, Piaget deduced that children are constantly testing their own theories of how the world works, asserting that "children have real understanding only of that which they invent themselves."

Alberto Giacometti (1901-1966): The son of a post-Impressionist painter, sculptor/painter Alberto Giacometti was born in a Swiss alpine valley near the Italian border. Best known for his stylized, elongated figures, he was an important Surrealist sculptor in the 1930s, while his later work explored existentialism, evoking the melancholy and alienation of a post-WWII world.

Elisabeth Kübler-Ross (1926-2004): She grew up in a strict, Protestant family, but Elisabeth Kübler-Ross defied tradition and got her M.D. in 1957. A year later, she left Zürich for the US, where she was appalled by the way doctors and hospitals treated the dying. The five stages of grief she first explained in *On Death and Dying*—denial, anger, bargaining, depression, and acceptance—have become a modern touchstone, now commonly applied to any catastrophic personal loss.

Ursula Andress (born 1936): When the bikini-clad Andress walked out of the ocean in the first James Bond movie, *Dr. No,* the indelible image of the "Bond heroine" was born. Tough, smart, and outrageously beautiful, Andress was a great match for Sean Connery's 007, even though the producers dubbed her voice to mask her Swiss-German accent. Though many of her subsequent films were subpar, the list of her leading men is not: Laurence Olivier, Frank Sinatra, Marcello Mastroianni, Peter Sellers, and even Elvis Presley.

Roger Federer (born 1981): This Swiss ace was born and raised near Basel. By the age of 29, Federer had won a record 16 Grand Slam tennis titles, including all four majors. From 2003-2007, he reeled off five straight Wimbledon wins, and has since captured the title several more times. He also pulled off a five-peat at the US Open (2004-2008), making it clear why many regard him as one of the greatest tennis players of all time.

PRACTICALITIES

This chapter covers the practical skills of European travel: how to get tourist information, pay for things, sightsee efficiently, find good-value accommodations, eat affordably but well, use technology wisely, and get between destinations smoothly. To round out your knowledge, check out "Resources from Rick Steves." For more information on these topics, see www.ricksteves.com/travel-tips.

Tourist Information

The Swiss national tourist office in the US is a wealth of information (tel. 800-794-7795, www.myswitzerland.com). Before your trip, download or request brochures (including regional and city maps, festival schedules, and hiking information).

In Switzerland, a good first stop in every town is generally the tourist information office (abbreviated TI in this book). While you can get plenty of information online, I still make a point to swing by to confirm sightseeing plans, pick up a city map, and get information on public transit, walking tours, special events, and nightlife. Prepare a list of questions and a proposed plan to double-check. Throughout Switzerland, you'll find TIs are usually well-organized and always have an English-speaking staff. Most TIs are run by the government, which means their information isn't colored by a drive for profit.

Some TIs have information on the entire country or at least the region, so try to pick up maps for destinations you'll be visiting later in your trip. If you're arriving in town after the TI closes, call ahead or pick up a map in a neighboring town. Although TIs offer room-finding services, they're a good deal only if you're in search of summer and weekend deals on business hotels.

Travel Tips

Emergency and Medical Help: In Switzerland, dial 112 for medical or other emergencies. For police, dial 117. If you get sick, do as the locals do and go to a pharmacist for advice. Or ask at your hotel for help—they'll know the nearest medical and emergency services.

Theft or Loss: To replace a passport, you'll need to go in person to the US embassy (see page 417). If your credit and debit cards disappear, cancel and replace them (see "Damage Control for Lost Cards," later). File a police report, either on the spot or within a day or two; you'll need it to submit an insurance claim for lost or stolen rail passes or travel gear, and it can help with replacing your passport or credit and debit cards. For more information, see www.ricksteves.com/help.

Borders: Although Switzerland isn't in the European Union, it does belong to the Schengen Zone, which means border controls are a wave-through. Even so, remember that when you change countries, you also change currencies, country dialing codes, and *Unterhosen.*

Time Zones: Switzerland, like most of continental Europe, is generally six/nine hours ahead of the East/West Coasts of the US. The exceptions are the beginning and end of Daylight Saving Time: Europe "springs forward" the last Sunday in March (two weeks after most of North America), and "falls back" the last Sunday in October (one week before North America). For a handy online time converter, see www.timeanddate.com/worldclock.

Business Hours: In large cities, shops are generally open Monday through Friday 9:00-18:30, Saturday 8:00-17:00, and closed Sunday. They are often open later on Thursdays. Smaller shops, and all shops in villages, typically (and maddeningly) close for one or two hours at lunchtime—often from 12:00 to 14:00.

Saturdays are virtually weekdays, with earlier closing hours. Sundays have the same pros and cons as they do for travelers in the US: Sightseeing attractions are generally open, while shops and banks are closed, public transportation options are fewer, and there's no rush hour. Friday and Saturday evenings are lively; Sunday evenings are quiet. Many sights are closed on Monday (head for the hills).

Watt's Up? Europe's electrical system is 220 volts, instead of North America's 110 volts. Most newer electronics (such as laptops, battery chargers, and hair dryers) convert automatically, so you won't need a converter, but you will need an adapter plug with two round prongs, sold inexpensively at travel stores in the US. Sockets in Switzerland only accept plugs with slimmer prongs: Don't buy an adapter with the thicker ("Schuko" style) prongs—it won't work. Avoid bringing older appliances that don't automatically convert voltage; instead, buy a cheap replacement in Europe.

Switzerland uses its very own style of electrical plugs, not shared with any other country in Europe: three slim round prongs arranged in a triangular shape. You'll often see wall sockets with a three-plug cloverleaf pattern. If you already have an adapter for European plugs, you may not need another adapter for Switzerland— European plugs will fit in Swiss sockets if the prongs are of the slimmer type and ungrounded, and if the body of the adapter is small enough to fit in a recessed outlet.  If your adapter doesn't work in your hotel room's sockets, ask your hotelier if they have one you can borrow, or visit a department store; they're usually sold for about 5 CHF.

Discounts: Discounts for sights are generally not listed in this book. Youths (under 18) and students (with International Student Identity Cards) often get discounts—but only by asking. To get a teacher or student ID card, visit www.statravel.com or www.isic.org.

Online Translation Tips: Google's Chrome browser instantly translates websites. You can also paste text or the URL of a foreign website into the translation window at translate.google.com. The Google Translate app converts spoken English into most European languages (and vice versa) and can also translate text it "reads" with your smartphone's camera.

Money

Here's my basic strategy for using money in Europe:
- Upon arrival, head for a cash machine (ATM) at the airport and load up on local currency, using a debit card with low international transaction fees.

Exchange Rate

Switzerland, which isn't a member of the European Union, has retained its traditional currency, the Swiss franc. The international abbreviation for the Swiss franc is "CHF."

1 Swiss franc (CHF) = about $1

Check www.oanda.com for the latest exchange rates. One Swiss franc is broken down into 100 rappen (or centimes in French Switzerland). There are coins for one, two, and five francs, plus several coins for very small denominations of rappen. The small coin with real value is the 50-rappen (marked with "½" rather than "50"). It looks like a tiny dime, but is equivalent to a half-dollar. In a handful of change, it's easy to identify as the only one with ridges.

- Withdraw large amounts at each transaction (to limit fees) and keep your cash safe in a money belt.
- Pay for most items with cash.
- Pay for larger purchases with a credit card with low (or no) international fees.

PLASTIC VERSUS CASH

Although credit cards are widely accepted in Europe, day-to-day spending is generally more cash-based than in the US. I find cash is the easiest—and sometimes only—way to pay for cheap food, bus fare, taxis, tips, and local guides. Some businesses (especially smaller ones, such as B&Bs and mom-and-pop cafés and shops) may charge you extra for using a credit card—or might not accept credit cards at all. Having cash on hand helps you out of a jam if your card randomly doesn't work.

I use my credit card to book and pay for hotel reservations, to buy advance tickets for events or sights, and to cover major expenses (such as car rentals or plane tickets). It can also be smart to use plastic near the end of your trip, to avoid another visit to the ATM.

WHAT TO BRING

I pack the following and keep it all safe in my money belt.

Debit Card: Use this at ATMs to withdraw local cash.

Credit Card: Use this to pay for larger items (at hotels, larger shops and restaurants, travel agencies, car-rental agencies, and so on).

Backup Card: Some travelers carry a third card (debit or credit; ideally from a different bank), in case one gets lost, demagnetized, eaten by a temperamental machine, or simply doesn't work.

US Dollars: I carry $100-200 US as a backup. While you won't use it for day-to-day purchases, American cash in your money belt comes in handy for emergencies, such as if your ATM card stops working.

What NOT to Bring: Resist the urge to buy Swiss francs before your trip or you'll pay the price in bad stateside exchange rates. Wait until you arrive to withdraw money. I've yet to see a European airport that didn't have plenty of ATMs.

BEFORE YOU GO

Use this pre-trip checklist.

Know your cards. Debit cards from any major US bank will work in any standard European bank's ATM (ideally, use a debit card with a Visa or MasterCard logo). As for credit cards, Visa and MasterCard are universal, American Express is less common, and Discover is unknown in Europe.

Most credit and debit cards have chips that authenticate and secure transactions. In Europe, the cardholder inserts the chip card into the payment machine slot, then enters a PIN. (In the US, you provide a signature to verify your identity.)

Any American card, whether with a chip or an old-fashioned magnetic stripe, will work at Europe's hotels, restaurants, and shops. I've been inconvenienced a few times by self-service payment machines in Europe that wouldn't accept my card, but it's never caused me serious trouble.

If you're concerned, ask if your bank offers a true chip-and-PIN card. Cards with low fees and chip-and-PIN technology include those from Andrews Federal Credit Union (www.andrewsfcu.org) and the State Department Federal Credit Union (www.sdfcu.org).

Report your travel dates. Let your bank know that you'll be using your debit and credit cards in Europe, and when and where you're headed.

Know your PIN. Make sure you know the numeric, four-digit PIN for each of your cards, both debit and credit. Request it if you don't have one and allow time to receive the information by mail.

Adjust your ATM withdrawal limit. Find out how much you can take out daily and ask for a higher daily withdrawal limit if you want to get more cash at once. Note that European ATMs will withdraw funds only from checking accounts; you're unlikely to have access to your savings account.

Ask about fees. For any purchase or withdrawal made with a card, you may be charged a currency conversion fee (1-3 percent), a Visa or MasterCard international transaction fee (1 percent), and—for debit cards—a $2-5 transaction fee each time you use a foreign ATM (some US banks partner with European banks, allowing you to use those ATMs with no fees—ask).

If you're getting a bad deal, consider getting a new debit or credit card. Reputable no-fee cards include those from Capital

Why No Swiss Euros?

Though surrounded by countries enjoying the convenience of a shared currency, the Swiss have hung on to their old franc. They would have to be part of the European Union to join the euro zone—and compliance with European Union regulations would mean the end of Switzerland's fortress identity and subsidized agricultural system. Most Swiss are horrified by the idea of having to square their fiscal, military, and foreign policies with the cacophonous EU.

But it's not just fear of instability and loss of sovereignty that's kept the Swiss clinging to their francs. Having a separate currency helps bring business to Switzerland. A huge part of the Swiss economy is based on providing a safe and secret place for wealthy people from around the world to stash their money. When bank fees are figured in, people who "save" in Swiss banks actually earn negative interest—they pay the Swiss to keep their money. Switzerland's separate currency also means that residents enjoy lower mortgage interest rates than the rest of Europe.

Even though Switzerland hasn't adopted the euro, the majority of Swiss hotels, restaurants, and shops (especially in touristy areas) accept smaller euro bills. Most businesses will not take euro coins or larger bills, and you'll usually get bad rates (and your change in Swiss francs). But unless this is your last chance to use up leftover euros, spend francs in Switzerland instead—you'll save money, and they're prettier.

One, as well as Charles Schwab debit cards. Most credit unions and some airline loyalty cards have low-to-no international transaction fees.

IN EUROPE
Using Cash Machines

European cash machines have English-language instructions and work just like they do at home—except they spit out local currency instead of dollars, calculated at the day's standard bank-to-bank rate.

In most places, ATMs are easy to locate—in Switzerland, ask for a *Bankomat* or *Geldautomat* in German, or a *distributeur* in French. When possible, withdraw cash from a bank-run ATM located just outside that bank. Ideally use it during the bank's opening hours; if your card is munched by the machine, you can go inside for help.

If your debit card doesn't work, try a lower amount—your request may have exceeded your withdrawal limit or the ATM's limit. If you still have a problem, try a different ATM or come back later—your bank's network may be temporarily down.

Avoid "independent" ATMs, such as Travelex, Euronet, Moneybox, Cardpoint, and Cashzone. These have high fees, can be less secure than a bank ATM, and may try to trick users with "dynamic currency conversion" (see below).

Exchanging Cash

Avoid exchanging money in Europe; it's a big rip-off. In a pinch you can always find exchange desks at major train stations or airports—convenient but with crummy rates. Banks in some countries may not exchange money unless you have an account with them.

Using Credit Cards

European cards use chip-and-PIN technology, while most cards issued in the US use a chip-and-signature system. But most European card readers can automatically generate a receipt for you to sign, just as you would at home. If a cashier is present, you should have no problems. Some card readers will instead prompt you to enter your PIN (so it's important to know the code for each of your cards).

At self-service payment machines (transit-ticket kiosks, parking, etc.), results are mixed, as US chip-and-signature cards aren't configured for unattended transactions. If your card won't work, look for a cashier who can process your card manually—or pay in cash.

Drivers Beware: Be aware of potential problems using a credit card to fill up at an unattended gas station, enter a parking garage, or exit a toll road. Carry cash and be prepared to move on to the next gas station if necessary. When approaching a toll plaza, use the "cash" lane.

Dynamic Currency Conversion

Some European merchants and hoteliers cheerfully charge you for converting your purchase price into dollars. If it's offered, refuse this "service" (called dynamic currency conversion, or DCC). You'll pay extra for the expensive convenience of seeing your charge in dollars. Some ATMs also offer DCC, often in confusing or misleading terms. If an ATM offers to "lock in" or "guarantee" your conversion rate, choose "proceed without conversion." Other prompts might state, "You can be charged in dollars: Press YES for dollars, NO for Swiss francs." Always choose the local currency.

Security Tips

Pickpockets target tourists, even in safe Switzerland. To safeguard your cash, wear a money belt—a pouch with a strap that you buckle around your waist like a belt and tuck under your clothes. Keep

PRACTICALITIES

your cash, credit cards, and passport secure in your money belt, and carry only a day's spending money in your front pocket or wallet.

Before inserting your card into an ATM, inspect the front. If anything looks crooked, loose, or damaged, it could be a sign of a card-skimming device. When entering your PIN, carefully block other people's view of the keypad.

Don't use a debit card for purchases. Because a debit card pulls funds directly from your bank account, potential charges incurred by a thief will stay on your account while the fraudulent use is investigated by your bank.

To access your accounts online while traveling, be sure to use a secure connection (see page 400).

Damage Control for Lost Cards

If you lose your credit or debit card, report the loss immediately to the respective global customer-assistance centers. Call these 24-hour US numbers collect: Visa (tel. 303/967-1096), MasterCard (tel. 636/722-7111), and American Express (tel. 336/393-1111). In Switzerland, to make a collect call to the US, dial 0-800-890-011. Press zero or stay on the line for an English-speaking operator. European toll-free numbers (listed by country) can be found at the websites for Visa and MasterCard.

You'll need to provide the primary cardholder's identification-verification details (such as birth date, mother's maiden name, or Social Security number). You can generally receive a temporary card within two or three business days in Europe (see www.ricksteves.com/help for more).

If you report your loss within two days, you typically won't be responsible for unauthorized transactions on your account, although many banks charge a liability fee of $50.

TIPPING

Tipping in Switzerland isn't as automatic and generous as it is in the US. For special service, tips are appreciated, but not expected. As in the US, the proper amount depends on your resources, tipping philosophy, and the circumstances, but some general guidelines apply.

Restaurants: You don't need to tip if you order your food at a counter. At Swiss restaurants that have a wait staff, it's common to tip by rounding up (about 5-10 percent) after a good meal. For more details on tipping in restaurants, see the "Eating" section, later.

Taxis: For a typical ride, round up your fare a bit (for instance, if the fare is 13 CHF, pay 15 CHF). If the cabbie hauls your bags and zips you to the airport to help you catch your flight, you might want to toss in a little more. But if you feel like you're being driven in circles or otherwise ripped off, skip the tip.

PRACTICALITIES

Services: In general, if someone in the service industry does a super job for you, a small tip of a franc or two is appropriate...but not required. If you're not sure whether (or how much) to tip for a service, ask a local for advice.

GETTING A VAT REFUND

Wrapped into the purchase price of your Swiss souvenirs is a Value-Added-Tax (VAT) of about 8 percent (one of the lowest in Europe). You're entitled to get most of that tax back if you purchase more than 300 CHF (about $300) worth of goods at a store that participates in the VAT-refund scheme. Typically, you must ring up the minimum at a single retailer—you can't add up your purchases from various shops to reach the required amount. (If the store ships the goods to your US home, VAT is not assessed on your purchase.)

Getting your refund is straightforward...and worthwhile if you spend a significant amount on souvenirs.

Get the paperwork. Have the merchant completely fill out the necessary refund document. You'll have to present your passport. Get the paperwork done before you leave the store to ensure you'll have everything you need (including your original sales receipt).

Get your stamp at the border or airport. Process your VAT document at your last stop in Switzerland (such as the airport) with the customs agent who deals with VAT refunds. Arrive an additional hour before you need to check in to allow time to find the customs office—and to stand in line. Some customs desks are positioned before airport security; confirm the location before going through security.

It's best to keep your purchases in your carry-on. If they're too large or dangerous to carry on (such as Swiss Army knives), pack them in your checked bags and alert the check-in agent. You'll be sent (with your tagged bag) to a customs desk outside security, someone will examine your bag, stamp your paperwork, and put your bag on the belt. You're not supposed to use your purchased goods before you leave. If you show up at customs wearing your new Swiss watch, officials might look the other way—or deny you a refund.

Collect your refund. Many merchants work with services, such as Global Blue or Premier Tax Free, that have offices at major airports, ports, or border crossings (either before or after security, probably strategically located near a duty-free shop). These services, which extract a 4 percent fee, can usually refund your money immediately in cash or credit your card (within two billing cycles). If the retailer handles VAT refunds directly, it's up to you to contact the merchant for your refund. You can mail the documents from home or, more quickly, from your point of departure (using an envelope you've prepared in advance or one that's been provided by the merchant). You'll then have to wait—it can take months.

CUSTOMS FOR AMERICAN SHOPPERS

You can take home $800 worth of items per person duty-free, once every 31 days. Many processed and packaged foods are allowed, including vacuum-packed cheeses, dried herbs, jams, baked goods, candy, chocolate, oil, vinegar, mustard, and honey. Fresh fruits and vegetables and most meats are not allowed, with exceptions for some canned items. As for alcohol, you can bring in one liter duty-free (it can be packed securely in your checked luggage, along with any other liquid-containing items).

To bring alcohol (or liquid-packed foods) in your carry-on bag on your flight home, buy it at a duty-free shop at the airport. You'll increase your odds of getting it onto a connecting flight if it's packaged in a "STEB"—a secure, tamper-evident bag. But stay away from liquids in opaque, ceramic, or metallic containers, which usually cannot be successfully screened (STEB or no STEB).

For details on allowable goods, customs rules, and duty rates, visit http://help.cbp.gov.

Sightseeing

Sightseeing can be hard work. If you're spending time in urban Switzerland, use these tips to make your museum visits meaningful, fun, efficient, and painless.

MAPS AND NAVIGATION TOOLS

A good map is essential for efficient navigation while sightseeing. The maps in this book are concise and simple, designed to help you locate recommended destinations, sights, and local TIs, where you can pick up more in-depth maps. Maps with even more detail are sold at newsstands and bookstores.

You can also use a mapping app on your mobile device. Be aware that pulling up maps or looking up turn-by-turn walking directions on the fly requires an Internet connection: To use this feature, it's smart to get an international data plan (explained later, under "Staying Connected"). With Google Maps or City Maps 2Go, it's possible to download a map while online, then go offline and navigate without incurring data-roaming charges, though you can't search for an address or get real-time walking directions. A handful of other apps—including Apple Maps, OffMaps, and Navfree—also allow you to use maps offline.

PRACTICALITIES

PLAN AHEAD

Set up an itinerary that allows you to fit in all your must-see sights. Most sights keep stable hours, but you can easily confirm the latest by asking the TI or checking museum websites.

Don't put off visiting a must-see sight—you never know when a place will close unexpectedly for a holiday, strike, or restoration. Many museums are closed or have reduced hours at least a few days a year, especially on holidays such as Christmas and New Year's. A list of holidays is on page 417; check online for possible museum closures during your trip. In summer, some sights may stay open late. Off-season, many museums have shorter hours.

Going at the right time helps avoid crowds. This book offers tips on the best times to see specific sights. Try visiting popular sights very early or very late. Evening visits (when possible) are usually peaceful, with fewer crowds.

If you plan to hire a local guide, reserve ahead by email. Popular guides can get booked up.

Study up. To get the most out of the sight descriptions in this book, read them before your visit.

AT SIGHTS

Here's what you can typically expect:

Entering: Be warned that you may not be allowed to enter if you arrive 30 to 60 minutes before closing time. And guards start ushering people out well before the actual closing time, so don't save the best for last.

Some important sights have a security check, where you must open your bag or send it through a metal detector. Some sights require you to check daypacks and coats. (If you'd rather not check your daypack, try carrying it tucked under your arm like a purse as you enter.)

Photography: If the museum's photo policy isn't clearly posted, ask a guard. Generally, taking photos without a flash or tripod is allowed. Some sights ban selfie sticks; others ban photos altogether.

Temporary Exhibits: Museums may show special exhibits in addition to their permanent collection. Some exhibits are included in the entry price, while others come at an extra cost (which you may have to pay even if you don't want to see the exhibit).

Expect Changes: Artwork can be on tour, on loan, out sick, or shifted at the whim of the curator. Pick up a floor plan as you enter, and ask museum staff if you can't find a particular item.

Audioguides and Apps: Many sights rent audioguides, which generally offer excellent recorded descriptions in English. If you bring your own earbuds, you can enjoy better sound. To save money, bring a Y-jack and share one audioguide with your travel partner.

Museums and sights often offer free apps that you can download to your mobile device (check their websites).

Services: Important sights may have a reasonably priced on-site café or cafeteria (usually a handy place to rejuvenate during a long visit). The WCs at sights are free and generally clean.

Before Leaving: At the gift shop, scan the postcard rack or thumb through a guidebook to be sure you haven't overlooked something that you'd like to see.

Every sight or museum offers more than what is covered in this book. Use the information in this book as an introduction—not the final word.

Sleeping

I favor hotels and restaurants that are handy to your sightseeing activities. Rather than list hotels scattered throughout a city or town,

I choose hotels in my favorite neighborhoods. My recommendations run the gamut, from dorm beds to fancy rooms with all the comforts.

Accommodations in Switzerland are very expensive—but are normally very comfortable and come with a filling buffet breakfast. Plan on spending about $180-250 for a double room in a hotel or $120-150 for a double (with the bathroom down the hall) in a small guesthouse.

Extensive and opinionated listings of good-value rooms are a major feature of this book's Sleeping sections. I like places that are clean, central, relatively quiet at night, reasonably priced, friendly, small enough to have a hands-on owner and stable staff, and run with a respect for Swiss traditions. I'm more impressed by a convenient location and a fun-loving philosophy than flat-screen TVs and a fancy gym. Most places I recommend fall short of perfection. But if I can find a place with most of these features, it's a keeper.

Book your accommodations as soon as your itinerary is set, especially if you want to stay at one of my top listings or if you'll be traveling during busy times. See page 417 for a list of major holidays and festivals in Switzerland; for tips on reserving rooms, see the "Making Hotel Reservations" sidebar, later.

Some people make reservations as they travel, calling hotels a few days to a week before their arrival. If you anticipate crowds on the day you want to check in (worst weekdays at business destinations and weekends at tourist locales), call hotels at about 9:00 or 10:00, when the receptionist knows who'll be checking out and

PRACTICALITIES

Sleep Code

Hotels are classified based on the average price of a standard double room with breakfast in high season.

$$$$	**Splurge:**	Most rooms over 220 CHF
$$$	**Pricier:**	180-220 CHF
$$	**Moderate:**	120-180 CHF
$	**Budget:**	80-120 CHF
¢	**Backpacker:**	Under 80 CHF
RS%	**Rick Steves discount**	

Unless otherwise noted, credit cards are accepted, and free Wi-Fi is available. Prices generally do not include the hotel tax, which is assessed per person, per night. Comparison-shop by checking prices at several hotels (on each hotel's own website, on a booking site, or by email). For the best deal, always book directly with the hotel. Ask for a discount if paying in cash; if the listing includes **RS%,** request a Rick Steves discount.

which rooms will be available. If you encounter a language barrier, ask the fluent receptionist at your current hotel to call for you.

RATES AND DEALS

I've categorized my recommended accommodations based on price, indicated with a dollar-sign rating (see sidebar). The price ranges suggest an estimated cost for a one-night stay in a standard double room with a private toilet and shower in high season, include breakfast, and assume you're booking directly with the hotel (not through a booking site, which extracts a commission). Room prices can fluctuate significantly with demand and amenities (size, views, room class, and so on), but relative price categories remain constant. Part of the room price is a local tax (about $2-6 per person per night). In return, you get perks such as free local transport or museum discounts. In a few towns (and some types of accommodations) the tax is included in quoted room rates; in most others, it's broken out.

Room rates are especially volatile at larger hotels that use "dynamic pricing" to set rates. Prices can skyrocket during festivals and conventions, while business hotels can have deep discounts on weekends when demand plummets. Of the many hotels I recommend, it's difficult to say which will be the best value on a given day—until you do your homework.

Once your dates are set, check the specific price for your preferred stay at several hotels. You can do this either by comparing prices on Hotels.com or Booking.com, or by checking the hotels' own websites. To get the best deal, contact my family-run hotels directly by phone or email. When you go direct, the owner avoids

Making Hotel Reservations

Reserve your rooms as soon as you've pinned down your travel dates—particularly if you'll be traveling during peak times (especially for mountain destinations during summer weekends). For busy national holidays, it's wise to reserve far in advance (see page 417).

Requesting a Reservation: For family-run hotels, it's generally cheaper to book your room directly via email or a phone call. For business-class hotels, or if you'd rather book online, reserve directly through the hotel's official website (not a booking agency's site). For complicated requests, send an email. Almost all of my recommended hotels take reservations in English.

Here's what the hotelier wants to know:

- type(s) of rooms you need and size of your party
- number of nights you'll stay
- your arrival and departure dates, written European-style as day/month/year (for example, 18/06/19 or 18 June 2019)
- special requests (such as en suite bathroom vs. down the hall, cheapest room, twin beds vs. double bed, quiet room)
- applicable discounts (such as a Rick Steves reader discount, cash discount, or promotional rate)

Confirming a Reservation: Most places will request a credit-card number to hold your room. If you're using an online reservation form, look for the https or a lock icon at the top of your browser. If you book direct, you can email, call, or fax this information.

Canceling a Reservation: If you must cancel, it's courteous—and smart—to do so with as much notice as possible, especially

Don't confuse *Privatzimmer* with the *Ferienwohnung*, which is a self-catering apartment rented out by the week or fortnight.

Camping and Other Budget Beds

Campers can manage with listings at www.eurocampings.co.uk or with help from the local TI (ask for a regional camping listing). Your hometown travel bookstore should also have guidebooks on camping in Europe. You'll find campgrounds just about everywhere you need them. Look for *Campingplatz* signs. You'll meet lots of Europeans, as camping is a popular, middle-class-family thing to go. Campgrounds are cheap ($10 per person), friendly, safe, more central and convenient than rustic, and rarely full.

A fluffy straw bed awaits you at a number of farms that have opened their haylofts to sleepy tourists. It's a fun hostel alternative and more comfortable than you'd think (see www.schlaf-im-stroh. ch for details).

Some hotels and campsites provide dormitory-style accom-

the 20 percent commission, giving them wiggle room to offer you a discount, a nicer room, or free breakfast if it's not already included (see sidebar). If you prefer to book online or are considering a hotel chain, it's to your advantage to use the hotel's website.

Some hotels offer a discount to those who pay cash or stay longer than three nights. To cut costs further, try asking for a cheaper room (for example, with a shared bathroom or no window) or offer to skip breakfast (if included).

Additionally, some accommodations offer a special discount for Rick Steves readers, indicated in this guidebook by the abbreviation "RS%." Discounts vary: Ask for details when you reserve. Generally, to qualify you must book direct (that is, not through a booking site), mention this book when you reserve, show this book upon arrival, and sometimes pay cash or stay a certain number of nights. In some cases, you may need to enter a discount code (which I've provided in the listing) in the booking form on the hotel's website. Rick Steves discounts apply to readers with ebooks as well as printed books. Understandably, discounts do not apply to promotional rates.

TYPES OF ACCOMMODATIONS
Hotels

Swiss hotels are, generally speaking, clean, comfortable, and efficiently run by English-speaking staff.

A "twin" room has two single beds; a "double" has one double bed. If you'll take either, let the hotel know, or you might be needlessly turned away. Some hotels can add an extra bed (for a small charge) to turn a double into a triple; some offer larger rooms for four or more people (I call these "family rooms" in the listings). If there's space for an extra cot, they'll cram it in for you. In general, a triple room is cheaper than the cost of a double and a single. Three or four people can economize by requesting one big room.

Arrival and Check-In: Hotel elevators are becoming more common, though some older buildings still lack them. You may have to climb a flight of stairs to reach the elevator (if so, you can ask the front desk for help carrying your bags up). Elevators are typically very small—pack light, or you may need to send your bags up without you.

When you check in, the receptionist will normally ask for your passport and may keep it for anywhere from a couple of minutes to a couple of hours. Switzerland requires that hotels collect your name, nationality, and ID number. Relax. Americans are notorious for making this chore more difficult than it needs to be.

Smoking is prohibited in many Swiss hotels, sometimes by law (depending on the region) and sometimes by choice. Nearly all the hotels I list are completely nonsmoking, and all of them offer

Hotels vs. Booking Websites vs. Consumers

In the last decade it's become almost impossible for independent-minded, family-run hotels to survive without playing the game as dictated by the big players in the online booking world. Priceline's Booking.com and Expedia's Hotels.com take roughly 80 percent of this business. Hoteliers note that without this online presence, "We become almost invisible." Online booking services demand about a 20 percent commission. And in order to be listed, a hotel must promise that its website does not undercut the price on the third-party's website. Without that restriction, hoteliers could say, "Sure, sell our rooms for whatever markup you like, and we'll continue to offer a fair rate to travelers who come to us directly"—but that's not allowed.

Here's the work-around: For independent and family-run hotels, book directly by email or phone, in which case hotel owners are free to give you whatever price they like. Research the price online, and then ask for a room without the commission mark-up. You could ask them to split the difference—the hotel charges you 10 percent less but pockets 10 percent more. Or you can ask for a free breakfast (if not included) or free upgrade.

If you do book online, be sure to use the hotel's website (you'll likely pay the same price as via a booking site, but your money goes to the hotel, not agency commissions).

As consumers, remember: Whenever you book with an online booking service, you're adding a needless middleman who takes roughly 20 percent. If you'd like to support small, family-run hotels whose world is more difficult than ever, book direct.

nonsmoking rooms. If it's important to you to have a nonsmoking room, ask for one.

If you think that night noise might be a problem (if, for instance, your room is over a nightclub), ask for a quieter room in the back or on an upper floor.

If you're arriving in the morning, your room probably won't be ready. Check your bag safely at the hotel and dive right into sightseeing.

In Your Room: More pillows and blankets are usually in the closet or available on request. Towels and linens aren't always replaced every day. Hang your towel up to dry.

Most hotel rooms have a TV, telephone, and free Wi-Fi (although in old buildings with thick walls, the Wi-Fi signal doesn't always make it to the rooms; sometimes it's only available in the lobby). There's often a guest computer with Internet access in the lobby. Simpler places rarely have a room phone, but often have free Wi-Fi.

To guard against theft in your room, keep valuables out of sight. Some rooms come with a safe, and other hotels have safes at the front desk. I've never bothered using one and in a lifetime of travel, I've never had anything stolen from my room.

Breakfast and Meals: Some places offer "half-board," which means that dinner is included in the room price. This is often a good deal and gets you a hassle-free, value-priced three-course meal, but limits your choices. Swiss hotel breakfasts are usually excellent: fruit, eggs, muesli, cheese, fresh bread, and yogurt. Some places give you the option of skipping breakfast and paying less; you can buy breakfast items easily and cheaply at a bakery or supermarket—the savings add up, especially for families.

Checking Out: While it's customary to pay for your room upon departure, it can be a good idea to settle your bill the day before, when you're not in a hurry and while the manager's in. That way you'll have time to discuss and address any points of contention.

Hotelier Help: Hoteliers can be a good source of advice. Most know their city well, and can assist you with everything from public transit and airport connections to finding a good restaurant, the nearest launderette, or a late-night pharmacy.

Hotel Hassles: Even at the best places, mechanical breakdowns occur: Sinks leak, hot water turns cold, toilets may gurgle or smell, the Wi-Fi goes out, or the air-conditioning dies when you need it most. Report your concerns clearly and calmly at the front desk. For more complicated problems, don't expect instant results. Above all, keep a positive attitude. Remember, you're on vacation. If your hotel is a disappointment, spend more time out enjoying t' place you came to see.

Pensions

Compared to hotels, pensions (small guesthouses) and private homes give you double the cultural intimacy price. While you may lose some of the convenienc such as lounges, in-room phones, daily bedshe credit-card payments—I happily make the trad rates and personal touches.

Small guesthouses go by several inexac sion, Gasthaus, Gästezimmer, even "B&B" sion). In many parts of Switzerland, pe mer) in their homes to travelers. Look Frühstück, or Privatzimmer signs i chambres d'hôte in French Switzerland.

From:	rick@ricksteves.com
Sent:	Today
To:	info@hotelcentral.com
Subject:	Reservation request for 19-22 July

Dear Hotel Central,

I would like to stay at your hotel. Please let me know if you have a room available and the price for:
• 2 people
• Double bed and en suite bathroom in a quiet room
• Arriving 19 July, departing 22 July (3 nights)

Thank you!
Rick Steves

for smaller family-run places. Cancellation policies can be strict; read the fine print or ask about these before you book. Internet deals may require prepayment, with no refunds for cancellations.

Reconfirming a Reservation: Always call or email to reconfirm your room reservation a few days in advance. For B&Bs or very small hotels, I call again on my day of arrival to tell my host what time to expect me (especially important if arriving late—after 17:00).

Phoning: For tips on calling hotels overseas, see the "How to Dial" sidebar, later.

modations in bunk-bedded rooms. Also look for the word *Matratzenlager,* which usually indicates a loft lined with mattresses—common in mountain lodges. These slumber mills may be less charming than cozy hostels, but they're cheap and convenient.

For serious hikers and climbers, mountain huts and "refuges" are an essential alpine experience. Don't expect ski-lodge comfort: These practical, adventurous places are simple, offering a warm place to sleep and (usually) breakfast and dinner. Some mountain-hut guests are long-distance hikers, connecting one hut to another along an extended hiking trail. Others hike in from the parking lot one day and hike out the next, enjoying the fresh air and views for a night. You'll pay about $30 a night for your bunk and a little more for grub (see www.sac-cas.ch for a map and database of Swiss mountain huts).

Short-Term Rentals

A short-term rental—whether an apartment, house, or room in a local's home—is an increasingly popular alternative, especially if you plan to settle in one location for several nights. For stays longer than a few days, you can usually find a rental that's comparable to—and cheaper than—a hotel room with similar amenities. Plus, you'll get a behind-the-scenes peek into how locals live.

Many places require a minimum-night stay, and compared to hotels, rentals usually have less-flexible cancellation policies. And you're generally on your own: There's no hotel reception desk, breakfast, or daily cleaning service.

Finding Accommodations: Aggregator websites such as Airbnb, FlipKey, Booking.com, and the HomeAway family of sites (HomeAway, VRBO, and VacationRentals) let you browse properties and correspond directly with European property owners or managers. If you prefer to work from a curated list of accommodations, consider using a rental agency such as InterhomeUSA.com or RentaVilla.com. Agency-represented apartments typically cost more, but this method often offers more help and safeguards than booking direct.

Before you commit, be clear on the details, location, and amenities. I like to virtually "explore" the neighborhood using the Street View feature on Google Maps. Also consider the proximity to public transportation, and how well-connected the property is with the rest of the city. Ask about amenities (elevator, air-conditioning, laundry, Wi-Fi, parking, etc.). Reviews from previous guests can help identify trouble spots.

Think about the kind of experience you want: Just a key and an affordable bed...or a chance to get to know a local? There are typically two kinds of hosts: those who want minimal interaction with their guests, and hosts who are friendly and may want to interact with you. Read the promotional text and online reviews to help shape your decision.

Apartments and Rental Houses: If you're staying somewhere for four nights or longer, it's worth considering an apartment or rental house, called *Ferienwohnung* in German (shorter stays aren't worth the hassle of arranging key pickup, buying groceries, etc.). Apartment or house rentals can be especially cost-effective for groups and families. European apartments, like hotel rooms, tend to be small by US standards. But they often come with laundry machines and small, equipped kitchens, making it easier and cheaper to dine in. If you make good use of the kitchen (and Europe's great produce markets), you'll save on your meal budget.

Private and Shared Rooms: Renting a room in someone's home is a good option for those traveling alone, as you're more likely to find true single rooms—with just one single bed, and a price to match. Beds range from air-mattress-in-living-room basic to plush-B&B-suite posh. Some places allow you to book for a

The Good and Bad of Online Reviews

User-generated review sites and apps such as Yelp, Booking .com, and TripAdvisor can give you a consensus of opinions about everything from hotels and restaurants to sights and nightlife. If you scan reviews of a hotel and see several complaints about noise or a rotten location, it tells you something important that you'd never learn from the hotel's own website.

But as a guidebook writer, my sense is that there is a big difference between the uncurated information on a review site and a guidebook. A user-generated review is based on the experience of one person, who likely stayed at one hotel in a given city and ate at a few restaurants there (and who doesn't have much of a basis for comparison). A guidebook is the work of a trained researcher who, year after year, visits many alternatives to assess their relative value. I recently checked out some top-rated user-reviewed hotel and restaurant listings in various towns; when stacked up against their competitors, some were gems, while just as many were duds.

Both types of information have their place, and in many ways, they're complementary. If something is well-reviewed in a guidebook, and also gets good ratings on one of these sites, it's likely a winner.

single night; if staying for several nights, you can buy groceries just as you would in a rental house. While you can't expect your host to also be your tour guide—or even to provide you with much info—some may be interested in getting to know the travelers who come through their home.

Other Options: Swapping homes with a local works for people with an appealing place to offer, and who can live with the idea of having strangers in their home (don't assume where you live is not interesting to Europeans). A good place to start is HomeExchange. To sleep for free, Couchsurfing.com is a vagabond's alternative to Airbnb. It lists millions of outgoing members, who host fellow "surfers" in their homes.

Confirming and Paying: Many places require you to pay the entire balance before your trip. It's easiest and safest to pay through the site where you found the listing. Be wary of owners who want to take your transaction offline to avoid fees; this gives you no recourse if things go awry. Never agree to wire money (a key indicator of a fraudulent transaction).

Hostels

Switzerland has a wonderful network of official hostels (*Jugendherberge* in German, *auberge de jeunesse* in French) that charge $40-50 per night for beds (for a full list, see www.youthhostel.ch). Choose your hostel selectively: They can be cozy mountain chalets, serene lakeside villas—or antiseptic spaces overrun by noisy school groups. While official hostels are clean and predictable, they can also have an institutional feel.

Travelers of any age are welcome if they don't mind dorm-style accommodations and meeting other travelers. Most hostels offer kitchen facilities, guest computers, Wi-Fi, and a self-service laundry. Hostels almost always provide bedding, but the towel's up to you (though you can usually rent one for a small fee). Many hostels offer inexpensive evening meals (about 17-20 CHF), but there are also posh boutique hostels with in-house restaurants that are significantly more expensive. Expect youth groups in spring, crowds in the summer, snoring, and variability in quality from one hostel to the next. Family and private rooms are often available.

Independent hostels tend to be easygoing, colorful, and informal (no membership required; www.hostelworld.com or www.swissbackpackers.ch). You may pay slightly less by booking directly with the hostel. **Official hostels** are part of Hostelling International (HI) and share an online booking site (www.hihostels.com). HI hostels typically require that you either have a membership card or pay extra per night.

Eating

I look for restaurants that are convenient to your hotel and sightseeing. When restaurant-hunting, choose a spot filled with locals, not the place with the big neon signs boasting, "We Speak English and Accept Credit Cards." Venturing even a block or two off the main drag leads to higher-quality food for a better price.

The Swiss eat when we do and enjoy a straightforward, no-nonsense cuisine. Specialties include delicious fondue, rich chocolates, a melted cheese dish called raclette, *Rösti* (hash browns), fresh dairy products (try *Birchermüesli* for breakfast or an afternoon snack), 100 varieties of cheese, and Fendant—a good, crisp white wine.

The exorbitant prices at Swiss restaurants—up to double what you'd pay in neighboring Germany—mean that eating here demands some different strategies if you're on a budget. Think of restaurants with table service as a luxury for special occasions, and self-service cafeterias and supermarkets as your everyday options. Bakeries also sell sandwiches, quiches, and the like. If breakfast is included in your room price, don't miss it. But if your hotel gives

---

Restaurant Price Code

I've assigned each eatery a price category, based on the average cost of a typical main course. Drinks, desserts, and splurge items (steak and seafood) can raise the price considerably.

$$$$	**Splurge:** Most main courses over 30 CHF
$$$	**Pricier:** 20-30 CHF
$$	**Moderate:** 10-20 CHF
$	**Budget:** Under 10 CHF

In Switzerland, a kebab stand or other takeout spot is **$**; a self-service cafeteria or casual café is **$$**; a restaurant with table service is **$$$**; and a swanky splurge is **$$$$**.

---

you the option to skip an expensive breakfast and pay a lower rate, consider saying yes and eating more cheaply on your own.

Tipping: If you buy your food at a counter, don't tip. Service is included at Swiss restaurants with table service, but it's customary to round up the bill (5-10 percent; for a 19-CHF meal, pay 20 CHF). Give the tip directly to your server. Rather than leaving coins on the table, the Swiss usually pay with paper, saying how much they'd like the bill to be. For example, if paying for an 8.10-CHF meal with a 20-CHF bill, say "Nine francs" or *("Neun Franken")*. The server will keep a .90-CHF tip and give you 11 CHF in change. Rounding up isn't required, though, and no one will come running after you if you don't.

RESTAURANT PRICING

I've categorized my recommended eateries based on price, indicated with a dollar-sign rating (see sidebar). The price ranges suggest the average price of a typical main course—but not necessarily a complete meal. Obviously, expensive items (like steak and seafood), fine wine, appetizers, and dessert can significantly increase your final bill.

The categories also indicate a place's personality: **Budget** eateries include street food, takeaway, order-at-the-counter shops, and bakeries selling sandwiches. **Moderate** eateries are nice (but not fancy) sit-down restaurants or basic cafeterias, ideal for a straightforward, fill-the-tank meal.

Pricier eateries are a notch up, with more attention paid to the setting, presentation, and cuisine. These are ideal for a memorable meal that doesn't break the bank. This category often includes affordable "destination" or "foodie" restaurants. And **splurge** eateries are dress-up-for-a-special-occasion-swanky—typically with an elegant setting, polished service, pricey and intricate cuisine, and an expansive (and expensive) wine list.

I haven't categorized places where you might assemble a picnic, snack, or graze: supermarkets, delis, ice-cream stands, cafés or bars specializing in drinks, chocolate shops, and so on.

BUDGET OPTIONS

Grocery Stores: The midrange Migros and Co-op **grocery stores** are the hungry hiker's best budget bet. Larger stores have a great selection of prepared foods and picnic fixings. These include a huge variety of salads (green, potato, pasta, or meat—all sold with a plastic fork), decorated hard-boiled eggs (called *Picknickeier)*, sandwiches, delicious cheese, single portions of cake and ice cream, inexpensive chocolate bars, and sometimes, a hot-meal counter. You'll also see Manor ("mah-NOR"), a more elegant supermarket chain, and Aldi, a discount grocery store with a limited range. Manor is actually a department store (and many Migros and Co-ops are as well), with the supermarket typically hiding in the basement.

By law, most supermarkets are required to close on Sunday, with exceptions for stores in train stations and in some towns where grocery stores are allowed to open for a few hours on Sunday afternoons (a controversial issue in Switzerland). In larger cities, supermarket chains have skirted the law by building big stores in malls attached to train stations.

Self-Service Cafeterias and Buffets: Cafeterias have good food at much lower prices than restaurants with table service. You'll find them in most cities, usually at downtown branches of Manor, Co-op, and Migros supermarkets (in descending order of fanciness). Manor's cafeterias (called "Manora") feature lush salad bars, tasty entrées, and fresh-squeezed juices (I've listed several specific Manora locations in this book). A main course at a cafeteria is usually cooked to order in front of you and will cost 13-19 CHF; drinks and dessert run about 3 CHF each. Some self-service cafeterias have free tap water, often hidden in an inconspicuous place to encourage diners to pay for bottled drinks. Most have free Wi-Fi.

While cafeteria food may not be inventive, it is typical, fresh, and high-quality (these are supermarkets, after all); they're also popular with locals. Eating some of your meals at cafeterias can free up money for splurges on traditional dishes at fine restaurants with table service.

Another common type of self-service eatery is a gourmet buffet (often vegetarian) that is charged by weight. Look for Hiltl (in Zürich) and the Tibits chain (in Zürich and Bern).

Hostels: Swiss hostels that belong to the Hosteling International network usually offer a fine four-course dinner for 17-20 CHF, with free tap water—a great deal for guests. In a few cases this is open to nonguests, too, at a slightly higher price (call to reserve).

Ethnic Food: Asian and Middle Eastern restaurants abound, but are generally not as much of a bargain as in neighboring countries (a *döner kebab* costs around 9 CHF and a main course at an Asian restaurant about 20 CHF). The same goes for pizzerias, which are often upscale places with table service and 17-20-CHF pies; takeout orders are often slightly cheaper than the sit-down price.

RESTAURANTS

The cheapest main courses at Swiss restaurants start at just under 20 CHF—typically starchy dishes topped with meat or cheese (pasta, pizza, and potato dishes) or sausages with kraut or potato salad. Meat courses (served with a starch and vegetable) will run you 25-45 CHF at an average restaurant. Many restaurants offer a daily special—a main course for about 20 CHF (at least Mon-Fri at lunch, sometimes weekends and evenings, too). High-priced drinks can quickly run up the cost of a meal.

Different kinds of restaurants offer different experiences. Hotels often serve fine food. A *Gaststätte* is a simple, less expensive restaurant. A *Weinstübli* (wine bar) or *Bierstübli* (tavern) usually serves food. Mountain huts—called *Hütte*—generally have hot chocolate and hearty meat-and-potato meals. Smoking is no longer allowed inside Switzerland's eateries (though a few places skirt the laws with enclosed verandas for smokers). If you're not too hungry, order from the *kleine Hunger* (small hunger) section of the menu.

Most restaurants tack a menu onto their door for browsers and have an English menu inside. If you ask for the *Menü* (or *menu* in French), you won't get a list of dishes; you'll get a fixed-price meal of several courses. If you simply want a list of what's cooking, ask for *die Speisekarte* (dee SHPIE-zeh-kar-teh; *la carte* in French).

Only a rude waiter will rush you. Good service is relaxed (slow to an American). To wish others "Happy eating!" offer a cheery *"En Guete!"* When you want the bill, request *"Die Rechnung, bitte."* (See the survival phrases in the appendix for more tips.)

SWISS CUISINE

Here at this meeting point of European cultures, a region's food is heavily influenced by the cuisine of neighboring countries. You'll find heavy wurst-and-kraut fare in German-speaking areas; delicate, subtle French cuisine in the west; and pasta and polenta dishes *all'Italiana* in Ticino. In alpine regions, most meals are still built on the hardy ingredients that can be produced and stored in the mountains: cheese, potatoes, onions, cabbage, cured meat...and more cheese.

PRACTICALITIES

Traditional Dishes

Aside from clocks and banks, Switzerland is known for its cheese. Gruyère cheese is hard, with a strong flavor; Emmentaler is also hard, but milder (and looks like what we call "Swiss cheese"). Appenzeller is the incredibly pungent cheese from the northeast of Switzerland, with a smell that verges on nauseating...until you taste it.

Two of Switzerland's best-known specialties are cheese-based. *Käsefondue* is usually Emmentaler and Gruyère cheese melted with white wine, garlic, nutmeg, and other seasonings. You use a long fork to dip cubes of bread into it. The price for fondue is calculated per person (about 24-28 CHF), and many restaurants have a two-person minimum. While the Swiss consider fondue a winter-only meal, it's served year-round in touristed areas, and there's nothing silly about eating it "out of season." Note that "meat fondue" is an Asian-style hot pot (where you cook raw meat in broth at your table). This is sometimes also called *fondue chinoise* (Chinese fondue).

Raclette is cheese slowly melted on a special dish; as it softens, scrape a mound off and eat it with potatoes, pickled onions, and gherkins. (In restaurants, raclette often comes as little slices of cheese already melted.)

Another must-try dish, most typical in the mountains of the German-speaking areas, is *Rösti*—sort of like hash browns. The potatoes are grated coarsely, then often molded into a loose, round patty, and topped with alpine cheese, a bit of bacon or ham, or with an egg cracked over it...yum.

Each region has its own specialties. In French-speaking Switzerland, white wine and heavy cream are used in many dishes, and horsemeat (formerly imported from Eastern Europe, now imported from the US, New Zealand, and Australia) is common. The cuisine in eastern Switzerland (Pontresina, St. Moritz) uses chestnuts in many forms, wild mushrooms, and air-dried beef. Southwestern Switzerland (Zermatt area) specializes in all kinds of cheese, and their favorite white wine is Fendant.

Despite all the cheese and potatoes, the Swiss tend to be health-conscious; after all, they invented **muesli.** While the dry muesli served at every breakfast buffet is unremarkable, *Bircher-müesli*—a yummy mixture of fresh yogurt, fresh fruit, and juice-soaked oats—is worth seeking out in supermarket delis and on café menus. Menus often feature a *Fitnessteller* ("fitness plate")—usually a large mixed salad that comes with steak, chicken, or fish. *Bio* means organically grown (a *Biolädeli* is a store that sells organic products).

Of course, on the other end of the health spectrum, there's the famous **Swiss chocolate.** The vast variety of chocolate flavors available in any Swiss supermarket—let alone a specialty chocolate shop—is staggering. Only chocolate actually produced in the country is granted the honor of being called Swiss. Stroll the chocolate aisle of a grocery store and take your pick.

Beverages

Wine: Swiss wine is good, but expensive because of high production costs and mostly small vineyards. The Swiss certainly have plenty of winemaking experience—they've been growing grapes since Roman times. Since Swiss wine is not well-known outside of the country, and very little is exported, this is your chance to try the local *Wein/vin/vino.* About two-thirds of the production is white, and much of that is made from the Chasselas (a.k.a. Fendant) grape. Swiss specialties include the red Dole (a light-bodied blend of pinot noir and gamay grapes), Gutedel (or Chasselas; full, fruity, dry white); Fendant (a dry white that pairs well with cheese dishes), St. Saphorin (lovely, fruity white from Lake Geneva), and Merlot del Ticino (full-bodied red from Italian-speaking Switzerland).

Menus list drink size by the "deci"—a deciliter (dl, tenth of a liter). In German-speaking areas, order wine by the *Glas* (glass) or *Viertel* (quarter liter, or 8 oz.). Order it *süss* (sweet), *halb trocken* (medium), or *trocken* (dry); *weiss* (white), or *rot* (red). To order white wine, for instance, you can say, *"Ein Viertel Weisswein, bitte."* For fun, try ordering the same thing in colloquial Swiss German: *"Ä Viertel Wiisewyy, bitte"* (ih FEER-tehl VEE-seh-vee, BIT-teh).

In French Switzerland, wine comes either by *le verre* (a glass, 1-2 dl), *la carafe* (3 dl or 5 dl), or *la bouteille* (bottle). Order by requesting *"Un verre de vin blanc, s'il vous plaît"* (or *"vin rouge"* if you prefer red). In the Ticino region, *un boccalino* is a small, decorated 8-ounce ceramic jug filled with the local red wine.

Beer: Swiss beer is surprisingly good and inexpensive. Most of the beer is light, golden-colored lager, but you'll also find other types, such as *Hefeweizen* and *Dunkel* (dark) beers. Each pub has one brand of a local beer on tap, with others available in bottles. Feldschlössen is the largest brewery in the country, and you'll see its red-castle logo all over. But the Swiss are loyal to their local brews; for example, in the Appenzell region, Appenzeller is the beer of choice. The standard size, measured in centiliters (cl), is a *Stange* (33 cl); the smaller size is called a *Herrgöttli* (20 cl). Beer mixed with lemon-flavored soda or *Citro* (lemonade) is called a

Swiss Chocolate:
The Souvenir that Disappears

Of Switzerland's well-known icons—watches, banks, gadgety knives, booze-bearing mountain dogs—only one makes would-be visitors salivate in anticipation: chocolate. But why does Swiss chocolate hold such cachet? The answer dates back to 1819, when François-Louis Cailler figured out how to mechanize chocolate production and set up a factory near Lake Geneva. The Swiss also invented milk chocolate (in 1875) and conching, the process that makes solid chocolate smooth (1879).

The 1890s Golden Age of Swiss tourism spurred a Golden Age of Swiss chocolate, when vacationers returned home with a chocolate habit and chocolatey gifts for friends and family. By the 1910s, about 75 percent of the chocolate produced here was being exported. Today, Swiss chocolate is still a popular souvenir, what had been a small collection of "manufactories" has become a billion-dollar industry, and the Swiss people are among the world's top chocolate consumers.

When looking for high-quality chocolate, notice the way the chocolate breaks (a clean break with no crumbles is best), how it melts (like butter?), how it feels in your mouth (the smoother the better), and whether it leaves any gritty, unchocolatey aftertaste.

Of course, the only way to know what you like best is to try lots of different kinds (in the name of science!). The big-name brands—such as Lindt, Toblerone, and Cailler—are everywhere;

Panaché. In summer, this lightly sweet, sudsy drink is more refreshing than straight beer.

Water: Switzerland has a tradition of **free fountains,** with fresh, mountain-chilled water, in squares and other central points around cities and towns. I assume I can fill my bottle from any well-maintained public fountain unless I see a sign saying otherwise. At restaurants, tap water, which many waiters aren't eager to bring you, is *Leitungswasser* (*l'eau du robinet* in French). Ask for it by name, or you'll receive—and be charged for—*Mineralwasser* (*mit/ohne Gas,* with/without carbonation).

Other Nonalcoholic Drinks: Instead of Coke, try the local favorite, **Rivella,** a carbonated, vitamin-rich soft drink made with 35 percent whey (called "milk serum" on the label). Its unusual—but not unpleasant—taste isn't milky at all; it's more like chewable vitamins. It comes in four colors: Red is regular; blue is low-calorie; green is mixed with green tea; and yellow is soy-based. *Süssmost* is apple juice.

As an alternative to hot chocolate, try **Ovomaltine.** The Swiss have a fondness for this hot drink—a malt-derived vitamin supple-

keep your eyes peeled for lesser-known brands like Läderach, a high-end favorite among many Swiss. In his book *Swiss Watching*, Diccon Bewes reports on a blind taste test in which Prix Garantie, the Co-op house brand, came in a close second to Cailler—despite costing only a fraction of Cailler's price.

If you prefer milk chocolate, look for bars marked *Vollmilch* or *Alpenmilch;* dark chocolate fans want the *edelbitter* or *dunkeler* stuff, and *weisse Schokolade* is white chocolate. Bars with percentages printed on them are boasting their high cocoa content (the higher the number, the more bitter the chocolate). Common additions include *Haselnuss* (hazelnuts), *Mandeln* (almonds), *Trauben* (grapes/raisins), and *Joghurt* (guess). Connoisseurs watch for seasonal flavors.

Switzerland offers surprisingly few worthwhile sights for the choco-curious. You can ride the Chocolate Train, which combines three Swiss greats—rail travel, beautiful vistas, and chocolate noshing—and stops for a visit at the Cailler factory in the hills above Lake Geneva (both sights described in the Lake Geneva & French Countryside chapter). You can also visit the Alprose chocolate factory just outside Lugano (see the Lugano chapter). But my favorite Swiss chocolate experience is simply nibbling a bar on a high-mountain hike.

ment, flavored with chocolate so kids will drink it. (In the US, Ovaltine is an Asian variation on this drink—considered by the Swiss to be a cheap copy.)

Staying Connected

One of the most common questions I hear from travelers is, "How can I stay connected in Europe?" The short answer is: more easily and cheaply than you might think.

The simplest solution is to bring your own device—mobile phone, tablet, or laptop—and use it just as you would at home (following the tips below, such as connecting to free Wi-Fi whenever possible). Another option is to buy a European SIM card for your mobile phone—either your US phone or one you buy in Europe. Or you can use European landlines and computers to connect. Each of these options is described later, and more details are at www.ricksteves.com/phoning. For a very practical one-hour talk covering tech issues for travelers, see www.ricksteves.com/mobile-travel-skills.

PRACTICALITIES

Hurdling the Language Barrier

Switzerland has four official languages: German, French, Italian, and Romansh (a Romance language spoken in far-flung corners of Graubünden). Most of the destinations in this book are in the German-speaking territory. No matter where you are, most young or well-educated people—especially those in larger towns and the tourist trade—speak at least some English. Still, you'll get more smiles by using the local pleasantries. See the German, French, and Italian survival phrases at the end of the appendix.

In German-speaking Switzerland, locals speak sing-songy *Schwyzertütsch* (Swiss German) around the house, but in schools and businesses, they speak and write in the same standard German used in Germany and Austria (called "High" German, *Hochdeutsch*—though many Swiss prefer to call it *Schriftdeutsch,* "Written German"). The standard greeting is a hearty *Grüezi* (GRIT-see). "Thank you" is derived from French, but pronounced a little differently: *Merci* (MUR-see). They also sometimes use the more German-like *Dankche* (DAHN-kheh with a very guttural "kh"). The exact pronunciation of Swiss German words varies substantially by region, and there's no standard spelling.

English—like Dutch, Danish, Swedish, and Norwegian—is a Germanic language, making German easier on most American ears than Romance languages (such as Italian and French). High German is spelled phonetically—its pronunciation rules are regular, and there are no silent letters.

These tips will help you pronounce German words: The letter *w* is always pronounced as "v" (e.g., the word for "wonderful" is *wunderbar,* pronounced VOON-dehr-bar). The vowel combinations *ie* and *ei* are pronounced like the name of the second letter—so *ie* sounds like the letter *e* (as in *hier* and *Bier,* the German words for "here" and "beer"), while *ei* sounds like the letter *i* (as in *nein* and *Stein,* the German words for "no" and "stone"). The vowel combination *au* is pronounced "ow" (as in *Frau*). The vowel combinations *eu* and *äu* are pronounced "oy" (as in *neu, Deutsch,* and *Bräu,* the words for "new," "German," and "brew"). To pronounce *ö* and *ü,* purse your lips when you say the vowel; the other vowel with an umlaut, *ä,* is pronounced the same as *e* in "men." (In written German, these can be depicted without an umlaut as the vowel followed by an *e: oe, ue,* and *ae,* respectively.) Written German always capitalizes all nouns.

Give it your best shot. The locals will appreciate your efforts.

USING A MOBILE PHONE IN EUROPE

Here are some budget tips and options.

Sign up for an international plan. To stay connected at a lower cost, sign up for an international service plan through your carrier. Most providers offer a simple bundle that includes calling, messaging, and data. Your normal plan may already include international coverage (T-Mobile's does).

Before your trip, call your provider or check online to confirm that your phone will work in Europe, and research your provider's international rates. Activate the plan a day or two before you leave, then remember to cancel it when your trip's over.

Use free Wi-Fi whenever possible. Unless you have an unlimited-data plan, you're best off saving most of your online tasks for Wi-Fi. You can access the Internet, send texts, and even make voice calls over Wi-Fi.

Most accommodations in Europe offer free Wi-Fi, but some—especially expensive hotels—charge a fee. Many cafés (including Starbucks and McDonald's) have free hotspots for customers; look for signs offering it and ask for the Wi-Fi password when you buy something. You'll also often find Wi-Fi at TIs, city squares, major museums, public-transit hubs, airports, and aboard trains and buses.

Minimize the use of your cellular network. Even with an international data plan, wait until you're on Wi-Fi to Skype, download apps, stream videos, or do other megabyte-greedy tasks. Using a navigation app such as Google Maps over a cellular network can take lots of data, so do this sparingly or use it offline.

Limit automatic updates. By default, your device constantly checks for a data connection and updates apps. It's smart to disable these features so your apps will only update when you're on Wi-Fi, and to change your device's email settings from "auto-retrieve" to "manual" (or from "push" to "fetch").

When you need to get online but can't find Wi-Fi, simply turn on your cellular network just long enough for the task at hand. When you're done, avoid further charges by manually turning off data roaming or cellular data (either works) in your device's Settings menu. Another way to make sure you're not accidentally using data roaming is to put your device in "airplane" mode (which also disables phone calls and texts), and then turn your Wi-Fi back on as needed.

It's also a good idea to keep track of your data usage. On your device's menu, look for "cellular data usage" or "mobile data" and reset the counter at the start of your trip.

Use Wi-Fi calling and messaging apps. Skype, Viber, Face-Time, and Google+ Hangouts are great for making free or low-cost voice and video calls over Wi-Fi. With an app installed on your

How to Dial

International Calls

Whether phoning from a US landline or mobile phone, or from a number in another European country, here's how to make an international call. I've used one of my recommended Gimmelwald hotels as an example (tel. 033-855-1658).

Initial Zero: Drop the initial zero from international phone numbers—except when calling Italy.

Mobile Tip: If using a mobile phone, the "+" sign can replace the international access code (for a "+" sign, press and hold "0").

US/Canada to Europe

Dial 011 (US/Canada international access code), country code (41 for Switzerland), and phone number.

▸ To call the Gimmelwald hotel from home, dial 011-41-33-855-1658.

Country to Country Within Europe

Dial 00 (Europe international access code), country code, and phone number.

▸ To call the Gimmelwald hotel from Germany, dial 00-41-33-855-1658.

Europe to the US/Canada

Dial 00, country code (1 for US/Canada), and phone number.

▸ To call from Europe to my office in Edmonds, Washington, dial 00-1-425-771-8303.

Domestic Calls

To call within Switzerland (from one Swiss landline or mobile phone to another), simply dial the phone number, including the initial 0.

▸ To call the Gimmelwald hotel from Geneva, dial 033-855-1658.

More Dialing Tips

Swiss Phone Numbers: Swiss numbers that begin with 075 through 079 are mobile phones, which cost more to call.

phone, tablet, or laptop, you can log on to a Wi-Fi network and contact friends or family members who use the same service. If you buy credit in advance, with some of these services you can call any mobile phone or landline worldwide for just pennies per minute.

Many of these apps also allow you to send messages over Wi-Fi to any other person using that app. Be aware that some apps, such as Apple's iMessage, will use the cellular network if Wi-Fi isn't available: To avoid this possibility, turn off the "Send as SMS" feature.

USING A EUROPEAN SIM CARD

With a European SIM card, you get a European mobile number and access to cheaper rates than you'll get through your US carrier.

PRACTICALITIES

Toll and Toll-Free Calls: Numbers that begin with 0900, 0901, and 0906 are expensive toll numbers, which you should avoid using (they often cost over 1 CHF/minute). International rates apply to US toll-free numbers dialed from Switzerland—they're not free.

More Phoning Help: See www.howtocallabroad.com.

European Country Codes		Ireland & N. Ireland	353 / 44
Austria	43	Italy	39
Belgium	32	Latvia	371
Bosnia-Herzegovina	387	Montenegro	382
Croatia	385	Morocco	212
Czech Republic	420	Netherlands	31
Denmark	45	Norway	47
Estonia	372	Poland	48
Finland	358	Portugal	351
France	33	Russia	7
Germany	49	Slovakia	421
Gibraltar	350	Slovenia	386
Great Britain	44	Spain	34
Greece	30	Sweden	46
Hungary	36	Switzerland	41
Iceland	354	Turkey	90

This option works well for those who want to make a lot of voice calls or needing faster connection speeds than their US carrier provides. Fit the SIM card into a cheap phone you buy in Europe (about $40 from phone shops anywhere), or swap out the SIM card in an "unlocked" US phone (check with your carrier about unlocking it).

SIM cards are sold at mobile-phone shops, department-store electronics counters, some newsstands, and vending machines. Costing about $5-10, they usually include prepaid calling/messaging credit, with no contract and no commitment. Expect to pay $20-40 more for a SIM card with a gigabyte of data. If you travel with this card to the European Union, there may be extra roaming fees.

PRACTICALITIES

Tips on Internet Security

Make sure that your device is running the latest versions of its operating system, security software, and apps. Next, ensure that your device and key programs (like email) are password- or passcode-protected. On the road, use only secure, password-protected Wi-Fi hotspots. Ask the hotel or café staff for the specific name of their Wi-Fi network, and make sure you log on to that exact one.

If you must access your financial info online, use a banking app rather than accessing your account via a browser. A cellular connection is more secure than Wi-Fi. Avoid logging onto personal finance sites on a public computer.

Never share your credit-card number (or any other sensitive information) online unless you know that the site is secure. A secure site displays a little padlock icon, and the URL begins with *https* (instead of the usual *http*).

I like to buy SIM cards at a phone shop where there's a clerk to help explain the options. Certain brands—including Lebara and Lycamobile, both of which are available in Switzerland and elsewhere in Europe—are reliable and especially economical. Swisscom and Orange are the dominant Swiss providers. Ask the clerk to help you insert your SIM card, set it up, and show you how to use it. In some countries—including Switzerland—you'll be required to register the SIM card with your passport as an antiterrorism measure (which may mean you can't use the phone for the first hour or two).

Find out how to check your credit balance. When you run out of credit, you can top it up at newsstands, tobacco shops, mobile-phone stores, or many other businesses (look for your SIM card's logo in the window), or online.

PUBLIC PHONES AND COMPUTERS

It's possible to travel in Europe without a mobile device. You can make calls from your hotel (or the increasingly rare public phone), and check email or browse websites using public computers.

Most hotels charge a fee for placing calls—ask for rates before you dial. You can use a prepaid international phone card (available at post offices, newsstands, street kiosks, tobacco shops, and train stations) to call out from your hotel. Dial the toll-free access number, enter the card's PIN code, then dial the number.

You'll see Swisscom public pay phones in a few post offices and train stations. The phones generally come with multilingual instructions; most don't take coins but instead require insertable phone cards (called a "taxcard"; sold at post offices, newsstands, etc.); these work only within Switzerland.

Most hotels have **public computers** in their lobbies for guests to use; otherwise you may find them at Internet cafés and public libraries (ask your hotelier or the TI for the nearest location). On a European keyboard, use the "Alt Gr" key to the right of the space bar to insert the extra symbol that appears on some keys. If you can't locate a special character (such as @), simply copy and paste it from a web page.

MAIL

You can mail one package per day to yourself worth up to $200 duty-free from Europe to the US (mark it "personal purchases"). If you're sending a gift to someone, mark it "unsolicited gift." For details, visit www.cbp.gov and search for "Know Before You Go." The Swiss postal service works fine, but for quick transatlantic delivery (in either direction), consider services such as DHL (www.dhl.com).

Transportation

Because Switzerland's train network is excellent, I recommend using public transportation here. Only a few areas—like the Appenzell region and the French Swiss countryside—are better by car. Cars are an expensive headache in the bigger cities. For more detailed information on transportation throughout Europe, including trains, flying, renting a car, and driving, see www.ricksteves.com/transportation.

TRAINS

Trains are generally slick, speedy, and punctual, with synchronized connections. They're also clean, roomy, and, in Switzerland, entirely nonsmoking. Few places in Switzerland are out of reach of the train system—and nearly everywhere can be reached by Post Bus, which is also well-synchronized with Swiss Rail. However, due to frustrating schedules, some travelers might find a few out-of-the-way recommendations not worth the time or trouble.

Virtually all Swiss stations have luggage lockers. In smaller towns, lockers are sometimes too small to fit larger bags, but if asked nicely the ticket office will usually store bigger luggage for the same price.

Many Swiss trains and stations are marked "SBB CFF FFS." All those letters mean the same thing ("Swiss Federal Railways"), in three different languages: German, French, and Italian. Quite a few of Switzerland's trains are, however, run by small private companies—particularly in mountain areas. Though private, these companies all take part in the same website with schedule and pricing information.

Schedules

For timetables, visit the Swiss site (www.sbb.ch; www.rail.ch gets you straight to the English version; since the website is hard to navigate, use the search function for info on passes and scenic rail). Germany's excellent all-Europe timetable, www.bahn.com, also covers Switzerland, but doesn't give fare information. Although Switzerland has a 24-hour train-info number you can dial from anywhere in the country, it's so expensive that using it is a last resort (toll tel. 0900-300-300).

Oddly for a country that prides itself on timeliness, the touch-screen ticket machines at train stations and bus stops don't provide schedule information. Some train stations have a kiosk or two near the ticket office that lets you use the Rail.ch website. Also look for printed schedule booklets (in racks) showing major intercity connections, and yellow posters in stations that show departures. At the cost of waiting in line, ticket-office staff will print out a step-by-step itinerary for you, free of charge.

Intercity trains (IC, ICN, and EC) are the fastest, interregional trains (IR) come next, "regional expresses" (RE) skip minor stops, and most other trains (including those beginning with S) stop at all stops. Knowing these codes can help you save time by zeroing in on the fastest train available, as the yellow schedule posters at stations don't list arrival times at destinations.

Tickets

If you're traveling without a rail pass, get train tickets online or at the station—either at the ticket windows, or at the easy-to-use machines. You're not normally allowed to buy your ticket on the train. The penalty for boarding a train without a ticket is 90 CHF—which Swiss conductors strictly enforce.

The Swiss rail system's website lets you purchase train tickets no earlier than one month in advance, and tickets purchased online are nonrefundable and nonchangeable (with very few exceptions). Purchasing tickets at a station counter, which you can do up to three months in advance, lets you change or cancel them much more easily.

Unlike in neighboring countries, Swiss trains don't offer much in the way of advance purchase discounts, so there's little incentive to book far in advance. Also, tickets on fast trains usually cost the same as those on slower trains. Occasionally, though, you'll see discounts on particular departures offered on the website.

At larger stations, ticket offices have separate windows for international travel, which close earlier than the regular domestic sales windows.

The Swiss rarely make seat reservations on trains. Reservations are important only on certain special or international trains (for example, they're required on the Glacier Express, the Gotthard Panorama Express, and on TGV trains to France). They can also provide peace of mind at busy travel times (the www.rail.ch website helpfully indicates how crowded a train is expected to be). Get seat reservations at any ticket counter online.

If you're waiting on the platform for your train, and you have a reserved seat or are planning to sit in first class, look for blue diagrams that show the sector of the platform where the various cars in the train will stop (usually A through F). Stand in the appropriate sector to avoid a last-minute dash to your car or a long walk through the train to your seat.

Rail Passes

Because of high ticket prices, rail passes are a good deal in Switzerland, often even for just a three-day trip. For such a little country, Switzerland has a dizzying array of train passes and deals—but for most travelers, the Swiss Travel Pass is the way to go. For more detailed advice on figuring out the smartest rail pass options for your train trip, visit www.ricksteves.com/rail.

Swiss Travel Pass: The basic version covers all trains, boats, and buses, plus admission to most Swiss museums, and offers a half-price discount on most high-mountain trains and lifts (fully covers the trip up to the Schilthorn in the Berner Oberland). It comes in both consecutive-day and flexipass versions. Both versions cover the cost of most transportation options for a specified number of days (but do not cover seat reservations). Second class is 35 percent cheaper than first class.

The **Half-Fare Travel Card** gives you a 50 percent discount off all national and private trains, postal buses, boats, and many lifts ($125 for one month). This can save you money if your Swiss travel adds up to more than $250 in point-to-point tickets.

The **Swiss Transfer Ticket** covers two train rides within a month span: one ride from any point of entry (such as the German border or Zürich's airport) to any other point in Switzerland, and one back from that point to any border ($235 first class, $150 second class). Each direction must be completed in one calendar day by the fastest, most direct route (not a scenic detour).

If traveling with kids, look into the **Swiss Junior Travelcard.** This allows children ages 6-15 to travel free with their parents (30 CHF/1 child or 60 CHF/2 or more children at Swiss stations). The card is issued free on request to parents who purchase Swiss train

Rail Passes and Train Travel in Switzerland

A **Swiss Travel Pass** lets you travel by train in Switzerland for three to fifteen days (consecutively or not) within a one-month

period. This pass also covers boats, buses, many museum admissions, and gives discounts on mountain trains and lifts.

Switzerland can also be included in a Eurail **Select Pass,** which allows travel in two to four neighboring countries over two months, and it's covered (along with most of Europe) by the classic Eurail **Global Pass.**

Switzerland's many travel options also include a two-day **Swiss Transfer Ticket,** covering transportation to and from one destination, a one-month **Half-Fare Card** for discounts on individual point-to-point tickets, and various local or regional passes.

Most Eurail passes are sold only outside Europe (through travel agents or Rick Steves' Europe). The Swiss Travel Pass and related products are also sold at train stations in Switzerland and at *www.rail.ch* (search for "Swiss Travel Pass"). For more on the ins and outs of rail passes, including prices, download my **free guide to Eurail Passes** (*www.ricksteves.com/rail-guide*) or go to *www.ricksteves.com/rail.*

Use this map to add up approximate pay-as-you-go fares for your itinerary, and compare that to the price of a rail pass.

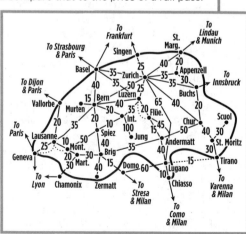

Map shows approximate costs, in $US, for one-way, second-class tickets.

Comparing Swiss Pass Coverage

All passes that include Switzerland cover national network trains and many sightseeing and private rail and boat discounts.

Here are the key routes where coverage varies:

Route or Bonus	Eurail/ Select or Two-Country Passes	Swiss Transfer Ticket	Swiss Travel Pass
Swiss Family Card (kids travel free)	No	Applies	Applies
Postal buses	No	Covered	Covered
Urban transport in 40 cities ($2/trip)	No	No	Covered
Swiss museum admissions	No	No	Covered
Glacier Express scenic train	Covered	Only if it's fastest, most direct route (from south border to south destination)	Covered
Brig-Zermatt private train to see the Matterhorn ($40 2nd class)	Covered	Only if Zermatt is final destination	Covered
Jungfrau Region Railways (e.g., from Interlaken: $10 to Lauterbrunnen, $11 to Grindelwald, $15 to Wengen; $200 round-trip to Jungfraujoch)	25% discount above Interlaken	No	25% discount above Grindelwald or Wengen
Mountain lifts Stechelberg-Schilthorn $105 roundtrip/$80 early bird	25% discount	No	Covered
Le Châtelard, Switzerland to Chamonix, France ($14)	Need France on pass	Covered (e.g., entering our exiting country via Chamonix)	Covered
All "covered" services start use of a travel day on a flexipass, but discounts do not.			

passes abroad (under a slightly different name, the "Swiss Family Card"). Children under 6 always travel free, so they don't need this benefit. There's a similar deal for grandchildren, too.

Eurail Passes: If you're also traveling to other countries, consider a Select Pass, which gives you up to 10 travel days (within a 2-month period) in up to 4 adjacent countries. Choose among Switzerland, Germany, Austria, Italy, France, and most other European countries (allow about $400 for 5 days in 3 countries, and up to about $650 for 10 days in 4 countries). A Global Pass is cost-effective only if you're doing a whirlwind trip of Europe (allow roughly $850 for 3 weeks). These rates are per person for two or more adults traveling together in first class; solo travelers age 28 or older will pay about 15 percent more. All Eurail passes allow up to two kids (ages 4-11) to travel free with each paying adult.

Rail Pass Bonuses and Discounts: If you buy a rail pass,

Public Transportation

Rail

Boat

Bus

Note: Not all transportation routes shown.

50 Kilometers

50 Miles

know what extras are included—for example, Swiss Travel Passes can get you free entry to many museums and discounts on many mountain lifts. Always ask. Eurail passes also include some deals in Switzerland beyond simple trains (such as discounts on lake boats and some mountain lifts), but the coverage and discounts aren't as extensive as the Switzerland-only passes. (For example, lifts in Zermatt are discounted and postal buses nationwide are free with a Swiss Travel Pass, but both are full price with a Eurail pass.)

If your rail pass is a flexipass (covering a certain number of days in a given span, rather than consecutive days), it's worth knowing when to activate your flexi-days (and when not to). With a flexi version of a Swiss Travel Pass, all coverage and discounts are offered only on the counted travel days. Any time you use the pass for a fully covered ("free") trip, it starts the use of a flexi-day. This can be fine and cost-effective if you're using the pass to cover other transportation that day. But if you've got no use for your pass that day other than that one "free" trip, it can make sense to pay out of pocket for it rather than use up a valuable day of your flexipass.

With a Eurail pass, discounted (but not free) trips—most notably many mountain lifts—are still offered at the lower price anytime within the two-month validity window (not just on a flexi-day).

Train Tips
Scenic Rail Journeys: In addition to being convenient for trans-portation, many of Switzerland's trains are also breathtakingly scenic. Several trips are particularly beautiful and billed as special "theme" routes for tourists. For many visitors, these are a Swiss highlight, and I've devoted an entire chapter to them (see the Scenic Rail Journeys chapter).

Using Rail Passes on Private Lines: Switzerland has some privately owned train lines. Most notably, the private Jungfrau Railway operates the trains from Interlaken up the Lauterbrunnen Valley and to the Jungfraujoch. In this region, Swiss Travel Pass coverage switches to just a discount above Wengen or Grindelwald, but Eurail pass coverage switches to a discount once you board a Jungfrau Railway train at Interlaken. If your rail pass doesn't cover an entire journey, pay for the "uncovered" portion at the station before you board the train.

Check Your Bags: If you're town- or mountain-hopping through Switzerland by train, a great way to lighten your load is by sending your baggage ahead (drop it off at the station before 19:00, pay 12 CHF with ticket or rail pass, maximum 55 pounds). Your bag will show up at the designated station within 36 hours of your arrival (usually faster) and will be held for two days (after that, you're charged a few francs a day). For an extra 30 CHF, you can

PRACTICALITIES

have same-day service for multiple bags to certain stations (in by 9:00, delivered by 18:00 or so). See www.rail.ch for details.

Bike 'n' Rail: You can rent a bike at more than 80 Swiss rail stations, usually at the baggage counter, for 35 CHF per day (30 CHF with Eurail pass or Swiss Travel Pass; 27 CHF/half-day, 22 CHF with rail pass, helmets included). You may be able to return the bike at another station (10 CHF extra). They also have electric bikes, tandem bikes, and kids' bikes. For more information, see www.sbbrail.ch/mobilitaet and search on "bike." Though not required, online reservations are encouraged. For general information on bike routes in Switzerland, visit www.veloland.ch.

TAXIS AND UBER

While most European taxis are reliable and cheap, Swiss taxis are expensive (Zürich's were recently ranked the priciest in the world). Public transit is extremely efficient; using it to get to outlying sights or an airport is still the best option. If you like ride-booking services like Uber, these apps work in Zürich, Lausanne, and Geneva just like they do in the US: You request a car on your mobile device (connected to Wi-Fi or a data plan), and the fare is automatically charged to your credit card.

RENTING A CAR

Swiss rental companies require you to be at least 20 years old and to have a valid license (age requirements vary by rental company). If you're also planning to drive in Austria or Italy, you're technically required to have an International Driving Permit—a translation of your driver's license (sold at your local AAA office for $20 plus the cost of two passport-type photos; see www.aaa.com). Drivers under the age of 25 may incur a young-driver surcharge, and some rental companies won't rent to anyone 75 or older. If you're considered too young or old, look into leasing (covered later), which has less-stringent age restrictions.

Research car rentals before you go. It's cheaper to arrange most car rentals from the US. Consider several companies to compare rates. Most of the major US rental agencies (including Avis, Budget, Enterprise, Hertz, and Thrifty) have offices throughout Europe. Also consider the two major Europe-based agencies, Europcar and Sixt. It can be cheaper to use a consolidator, such as Auto Europe/Kemwel (www.autoeurope.com or the often cheaper www.autoeurope.eu), which compares rates at several companies to get you the best deal—but because you're working with a middleman, it's especially important to ask in advance about add-on fees and restrictions.

Always read the fine print or query the agent carefully for add-on charges—such as one-way drop-off fees, airport surcharges, or

Lift Lingo

The Swiss have come up with an impressive variety of ways to conquer peaks and reach the best viewpoints and trailheads with minimum sweat. Known generically as "lifts," each of these contraptions has its own name and definition. Use the right terms, and impress your new Swiss friends.

Cogwheel Train: A train that climbs a steep incline using a gear system, which engages "teeth" in the middle of the tracks to provide traction. Also known as "rack-and-pinion train" or "rack railway." In German, it's a *Zahnradbahn* (*train à cremaillère* in French and *ferrovia a cremagliera* in Italian).

Funicular: A car that is pulled by a cable along tracks up a particularly steep incline, often counterbalanced by a similar car going in the opposite direction (meaning you'll pass the other car exactly halfway through the ride). Funiculars, like cogwheel trains, are in contact with the ground at all times. In German, it's a *Standseilbahn* (*funiculaire* in French and *funicolare* in Italian).

Cable Car: A large passenger car, suspended in the air by a cable, which travels between stations without touching the ground. A cable car holds a large number of people (sometimes dozens at a time), who generally ride standing up. When a cable car reaches a station, it comes to a full stop to allow passengers to get on and off. In German, it's a *Seilbahn* (*téléphérique* in French and *funivia* in Italian).

Gondola: Also suspended in the air by a cable, but smaller than a cable car—generally holding fewer than 10 people, who are usually seated. Gondolas move continuously, meaning that passengers have to hop into and out of the moving cars at stations. Also, while cable-car lines usually have two big cars—one going in each direction—gondolas generally have many smaller cars strung along the same cable. In German, it's a *Gondel* (*télécabine* in French and *telecabine* in Italian). Confusingly, the "car" compartment of a cable car is sometimes referred to as a "gondola."

mandatory insurance policies—that aren't included in the "total price."

For the best deal, rent by the week with unlimited mileage. I normally rent the smallest, least-expensive model with a stick shift (generally cheaper than an automatic). Almost all rentals are manual by default, so if you need an automatic, request one in advance; be aware that these cars are usually larger models (not as maneuverable on narrow, winding roads).

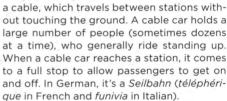

PRACTICALITIES

Figure on paying roughly $250 for a one-week rental. Allow extra for supplemental insurance, fuel, tolls, and parking. For trips of three weeks or more, leasing can save you money on insurance and taxes.

Picking Up Your Car: Compare pickup costs (downtown can be less expensive than the airport) and explore drop-off options. Always check the hours of the location you choose: Many rental offices close from midday Saturday until Monday morning and, in smaller towns, at lunchtime.

When selecting a location, don't trust the agency's description of "downtown" or "city center." In some cases, a "downtown" branch can be on the outskirts of the city—a long, costly taxi ride from the center. Before choosing, plug the addresses into a mapping website. You may find that the "train station" location is handier. Returning a car at a big-city train station or downtown agency can be tricky; get precise details on the car drop-off location and hours, and allow ample time to find it.

When you pick up the rental car, check it thoroughly and make sure any damage is noted on your rental agreement. Rental agencies in Europe tend to charge for even minor damage, so be sure to mark everything. Before driving off, find out how your car's lights, turn signals, wipers, radio, gearshift, and fuel cap function, and know what kind of fuel the car takes (diesel vs. unleaded). When you return the car, make sure the agent verifies its condition with you. Some drivers take pictures of the returned vehicle as proof of its condition.

Car Insurance Options

When you rent a car, you are liable for a very high deductible, sometimes equal to the entire value of the car. Limit your financial risk with one of these options: Buy Collision Damage Waiver (CDW) coverage with a low or zero deductible from the car-rental company, get coverage through your credit card (free, if your card automatically includes zero-deductible coverage), or get collision insurance as part of a larger travel-insurance policy.

Basic **CDW** includes a very high deductible (typically $1,000-1,500), costs $15-30 a day (figure roughly 30-40 percent extra), and reduces your liability, but does not eliminate it. When you reserve or pick up the car, you'll be offered the chance to "buy down" the basic deductible to zero (for an additional $10-30/day; this is sometimes called "super CDW" or "zero-deductible coverage").

If you opt for **credit-card coverage,** you'll technically have to decline all coverage offered by the car-rental company, which means they can place a hold on your card (which can be up to the full value of the car). In case of damage, it can be time-consuming to resolve the charges with your credit-card company. Before you

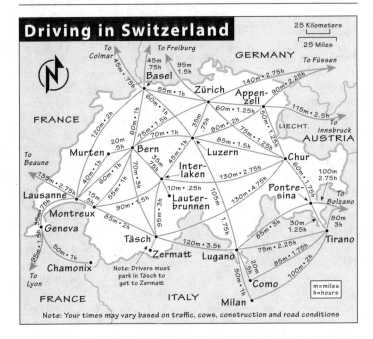

Driving in Switzerland

25 Kilometers

25 Miles

To Colmar

To Freiburg

GERMANY

To Füssen

45m · .75h

45m .75h

95m 1.5h

Basel

55m · 1h

Zürich

140m · 2.75h

Appen-zell

90m · 2.25h

FRANCE

60m · 1h

60m · 1h

35m .75h

60m · 1.25h

50m · 1.25h

115m · 2.5h

LIECHT.

To Innsbruck

AUSTRIA

120m · 2h

75m · 1.5h

70m · 1h

80m · 2h

75m · 1.25h

To Beaune

20m .5h

Murten

Bern

45m · 1h

Luzern

85m · 1.5h

Chur

40m · 1h

60m · 1h

35m .75h

Inter-laken

130m · 2.75h

60m · 1.75h

100m 2.75h

Lausanne

15m 5h

55m · 1h

70m · 3h

10m · .25h

105m

130m · 4.75h

Pontre-sina

To Bolzano

Montreux

85m · 2h

90m · 1.5h

Lauter-brunnen

95m · 3h

1.75h

85m · 3h

30m 1.25h

80m 3h

Geneva

Täsch

120m · 3.5h

75m · 2.25h

Tirano

35m · 1.5h

50m · 1h

Zermatt

Lugano

85m · 1.75h

100m · 2h

95m · 1.5h

Chamonix

Note: Drivers must park in Täsch to get to Zermatt

20m .5h

Como

m=miles h=hours

To Lyon

FRANCE

ITALY

Milan

50m · 1h

Note: Your times may vary based on traffic, cows, construction and road conditions

decide on this option, quiz your credit-card company about how it works.

If you're already purchasing a **travel-insurance policy** for your trip, adding collision coverage is an option. For example, Travel Guard (www.travelguard.com) sells affordable renter's collision insurance as an add-on to its other policies; it's valid everywhere in Europe except the Republic of Ireland, and some Italian car-rental companies refuse to honor it, as it doesn't cover you in case of theft.

For more on car-rental insurance, see www.ricksteves.com/cdw.

Leasing

For trips of three weeks or more, consider leasing (which automatically includes zero-deductible collision and theft insurance). By technically buying and then selling back the car, you save lots of money on tax and insurance. Leasing provides you a brand-new car with unlimited mileage and a 24-hour emergency assistance program. You can lease for as little as 21 days to as long as five and a half months. Car leases must be arranged from the US, and is most easily arranged through pickup/drop-off in Geneva. One of several companies offering affordable lease packages is Auto Europe (see www.autoeurope.com).

Navigation Options

If you'll be navigating using your phone or a GPS unit from home, remember to bring a car charger and device mount.

Your Mobile Device: The mapping app on your mobile phone works fine for navigation in Europe, but for real-time turn-by-turn directions and traffic updates, you'll generally need Internet access. And driving all day while online can be very expensive. Helpful exceptions are Google Maps, Here WeGo, and Navmii, which provide turn-by-turn voice directions and recalibrate even when they're offline.

Download your map before you head out—it's smart to select a large region. Then turn off your cellular connection so you're not charged for data roaming. Call up the map, enter your destination, and you're on your way. View maps in standard view (not satellite view) to limit data demands.

GPS Devices: If you prefer the convenience of a dedicated GPS unit, consider renting one with your car ($10-30/day). These units offer real-time turn-by-turn directions and traffic without the data requirements of an app. Note that the unit may only come loaded with maps for its home country; if you need additional maps, ask. Also make sure your device's language is set to English before you drive off.

A less-expensive option is to bring a GPS device from home. Be aware that you'll need to buy and download European maps before your trip.

Maps and Atlases: Even when navigating primarily with a mobile app or GPS, I always make it a point to have a paper map. It's invaluable for getting the big picture, understanding alternate routes, and filling in when my phone runs out of juice. The free maps you get from your car-rental company usually don't have enough detail. It's smart to buy a better map before you go, or pick one up at a European gas station, bookshop, newsstand, or tourist shop.

DRIVING

You can get anywhere quickly on Switzerland's fine road system, the world's most expensive per mile to build.

Road Rules: By law, you must use your headlights day and night in Switzerland (driving without them on will earn you a 40-CHF fine). Seat belts are required, and two beers under those belts are enough to land you in jail. Children under 12 (yes, 12) need to ride in a child-safety seat. Be aware of typical European road rules; for example, like many other European countries, Switzerland forbids drivers from talking on mobile phones without a hands-free headset. Ask your car-rental company about these rules, or check the US State Department website (www.travel.state.gov, search for

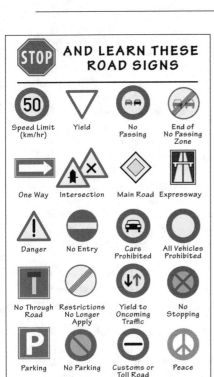

STOP AND LEARN THESE ROAD SIGNS

Speed Limit (km/hr)	Yield	No Passing	End of No Passing Zone
One Way	Intersection	Main Road	Expressway
Danger	No Entry	Cars Prohibited	All Vehicles Prohibited
No Through Road	Restrictions No Longer Apply	Yield to Oncoming Traffic	No Stopping
Parking	No Parking	Customs or Toll Road	Peace

your country in "Learn about your destination" box, then click on "Travel & Transportation").

Tolls: Drivers pay an annual 40-CHF fee for a permit to use Swiss autobahns. Check to see if your rental car already has one of these windshield stickers, called a "vignette"—if you picked it up in Switzerland, it most likely does. If not, buy it at border crossings, gas stations, post offices, or car-rental agencies. Anyone caught driving on a Swiss autobahn (indicated by green signs with a white expressway symbol) without this tax sticker is likely to be stopped and slapped with a steep fine (200 CHF plus the 40-CHF fee).

Fuel: Gas and diesel are both expensive—often around $6 per gallon. US credit and debit cards may not work at pay-at-the-pump stations, but are generally accepted (with a PIN code) at staffed stations. Diesel rental cars are common; make sure you know what type of fuel your car takes before you fill up.

Signage: Know the universal road signs (shown in this chapter and explained in charts in most road atlases and at service stations). *Dreieck* (literally, "three corners") means a Y in the road; *Autobahnkreuz* is an intersection (*carrefour* in French). Exits are spaced about 20 miles apart and often have a gas station (*bleifrei/sans plomb* are German/French for "unleaded"), a restaurant, a minimart, and sometimes a tourist information desk. Exits and intersections refer to the next major city or the nearest small town. Look at your map and anticipate which town names to watch out for. Know what you're looking for—miss it, and you're long autobahn-gone. When navigating, you'll see *Nord, Süd, Ost, West,* or *Mitte* (*nord, sud, est, ouest,* or *centre* in French).

To get to the center of a city, follow signs for *Zentrum* or *Stadtmitte* (or *centre-ville* in French). Ring roads go around a city.

Parking: Even in small towns, prime parking spots usually require payment. But it's easy to find free short-term parking in relatively central "blue zone" spaces, which require a blue cardboard "parking disc" clock (*Parkscheibe,* available free at TIs, gas stations, police stations, and *Tabak* shops). It's easy: Display your arrival time on the clock (you can scoot it up to the nearest full hour or half-hour) and put it on the dashboard, so parking attendants can see how long you've been there. Unless the sign indicates otherwise, you can park for free for an hour past the time set on your clock. If you arrive after 11:30, you can leave your car till 14:30, and if you arrive after 18:00, you're good until 9:00 the next day. Blue zones aren't patrolled overnight (19:00-8:00) or on Sundays, so you don't need to display a disc during those times.

FLIGHTS

While trains are usually the best way to connect places that are close together, if your trip extends beyond Switzerland, you may save time and money by flying.

The best comparison search engine for both international and intra-European flights is Kayak.com. An alternative is Google Flights, which has an easy-to-use system to track prices. For inexpensive flights within Europe, try Skyscanner.com.

Flying to Europe: Start looking for international flights four to five months before your trip, especially for peak-season travel. Off-season tickets can be purchased a month or so in advance. Depending on your itinerary, it can be efficient to fly into one city and out of another. If your flight requires a connection in Europe, see our hints on navigating Europe's top hub airports at www. ricksteves.com/hub-airports.

Flying Within Europe: If you're considering a train ride that's more than five hours long, a flight may save you both time and money. When comparing your options, factor in the time it takes to get to the airport and how early you'll need to arrive to check in.

Well-known cheapo airlines in Europe include Easyjet and Ryanair. But be aware of the potential drawbacks of flying with a discount airline: nonrefundable and nonchangeable tickets, minimal or nonexistent customer service, pricey and time-consuming treks to secondary airports, and stingy baggage allowances with steep overage fees. If you're traveling with lots of luggage, a cheap flight can quickly become a bad deal. To avoid unpleasant surprises, read the small print before you book. These days you can also fly within Europe on major airlines affordably—and without all the aggressive restrictions—for around $100 a flight.

Flying to the US and Canada: Because security is extra tight for flights to the US, be sure to give yourself plenty of time at the airport. It's also important to charge your electronic devices before you board because security checks may require you to turn them on (www.tsa.com for the latest rules).

Resources from Rick Steves

Begin your trip at www.ricksteves.com: My mobile-friendly **website** is *the* place to explore Europe. You'll find thousands of fun articles, videos, photos, and radio interviews organized by country; a wealth of money-saving tips for planning your dream trip; monthly travel news dispatches; a video library of my travel talks; my travel blog; and my latest guidebook updates (www.ricksteves.com/update).

Our **Travel Forum** is an immense yet well-groomed collection of message boards where our travel-savvy community answers questions and shares their personal travel experiences—and our well-traveled staff chimes in when they can be helpful (www.ricksteves.com/forums).

Our **online Travel Store** offers travel bags and accessories that I've designed specifically to help you travel smarter and lighter. These include my popular carry-on bags (which I live out of four months a year), money belts, totes, toiletries kits, adapters, other accessories, and a wide selection of guidebooks and planning maps (www.ricksteves.com/shop).

Choosing the right **rail pass** for your trip—amid hundreds of options—can drive you nutty. Our website will help you find the perfect fit for your itinerary and your budget: We offer easy, one-stop shopping for rail passes, seat reservations, and point-to-point tickets (www.ricksteves.com/rail).

Small Group Tours: Want to travel with greater efficiency and less stress? We offer more than 40 itineraries and have over 900 departures annually reaching the best destinations in this book...and beyond. We offer a 12-day Best of Switzerland tour; a 14-day Best of Germany, Austria & Switzerland tour; and a 12-day My Way: Alpine Europe "unguided" tour (covering hotel and transportation) of alpine destinations in Germany, Austria, Italy, Switzerland, and France. You'll enjoy great guides, a fun bunch of travel partners (with small groups of 24 to 28 travelers), and plenty of room to spread out in a big, comfy bus when touring between towns. You'll find European adventures to fit every vacation length. For all the details, and to get our Tour Catalog, visit www.ricksteves.com/tours or call us at 425/608-4217.

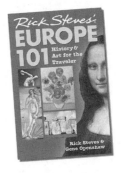

Books: *Rick Steves Switzerland* is one of many books in my series on European travel, which includes country guidebooks, city guidebooks (Rome, Florence, Paris, London, etc.), Snapshot guidebooks (excerpted chapters from my country guides), Pocket guidebooks (full-color little books on big cities), "Best Of" guidebooks (condensed country guides in a full-color, easy-to-scan format), and my budget-travel skills handbook, *Rick Steves Europe Through the Back Door*. Most of my titles are available as ebooks. My phrase books—for Italian, French, German, Spanish, and Portuguese—are practical and budget-oriented. My other books include *Europe 101* (a crash course on art and history designed for travelers), *Mediterranean Cruise Ports* and *Northern European Cruise Ports* (how to make the most of your time in port), and *Travel as a Political Act* (a travelogue sprinkled with tips for bringing home a global perspective). A more complete list of my titles appears near the end of this book.

TV Shows: My public television series, *Rick Steves' Europe*, covers Europe from top to bottom with over 100 half-hour episodes, including two on Switzerland, and we're working on new shows every year. To watch full episodes online for free, see www.ricksteves.com/tv.

Travel Talks on Video: You can raise your travel I.Q. with video versions of our popular classes (including talks on travel skills, packing smart, cruising, tech for travelers, European art for travelers, travel as a political act, and individual talks covering most European countries). See www.ricksteves.com/travel-talks.

Audio: My weekly public radio show, *Travel with Rick Steves*, features interviews with travel experts from around the world. It airs on 400 public radio stations across the US, and you can also listen to it as a podcast on iTunes, iHeartRadio, Stitcher, Tune In, and other platforms. A complete archive of programs (over 400 in all) is available at www.soundcloud.com/rick-steves. Most of this audio content is available for free through my **Rick Steves Audio Europe** app (see page 11).

APPENDIX

Useful Contacts

Police, Fire, and Ambulance: 112 (Europe-wide in English)
Medical/Ambulance: 144
Police: 117
Swiss Rescue: 1414
US Embassy in Bern: Tel. 031-357-7011, after-hours tel. 031-357-7777; services by appointment only Mon-Fri 9:00-11:30, closed Sat-Sun; Sulgeneckstrasse 19, http://bern.usembassy.gov
Canadian Embassy in Bern: Tel. 031-357-3200; passport services Mon-Fri 8:30-11:30, closed Sat-Sun; Kirchenfeldstrasse 88, http://switzerland.gc.ca

Holidays and Festivals

This list includes selected festivals in major cities, plus national holidays observed throughout Switzerland. Many sights and banks close down on national holidays—keep this in mind when planning your itinerary. However, not every canton celebrates all holidays (particularly religious ones); if you find yourself in a town closed down for an unexpected holiday, consider going on to your next stop (call ahead), where everything may well be in full swing. Before planning a trip around a festival, verify the dates with the festival website, the Switzerland tourist office (www.myswitzerland.com), or my "Upcoming Holidays and Festivals in Switzerland" web page (www.ricksteves.com/europe/switzerland/festivals).

Jan 1	New Year's Day
Jan 2	Berchtoldstag (St. Berchtold's Day), Harder-Potschete (parade), Interlaken
Jan 6	Epiphany (closings)
Mid-Jan	Lauberhorn ski race, Wengen; Inferno ski race, Mürren (www.inferno-muerren.ch)
Feb	Fasnacht (Carnival), especially celebrated in Luzern, Zürich, Bern, and Basel
March 19	Josefstag (St. Joseph's Day)
March-May	International Jazz Festival (www.jazzfestivalbern.ch), Bern
Late March-Early April	Lucerne Festival at Easter (classical and sacred music, www.lucernefestival.ch), Luzern
April	Easter Sunday-Monday: April 1-2, 2018; April 21-22, 2019
Mid-April	Sechseläuten (Spring Festival, www.sechselaeuten.ch), Zürich
Last Sun in April	Open-Air Parliament (public selection of delegates), Appenzell
May 1	Labor Day
May	Ascension (Christi Himmelfahrt): May 10 in 2018, May 30 in 2019
May or June	Pentecost and Pentecost Monday (Pfingsten and Pfingstmontag): May 20-21 in 2018, June 9-10 in 2019
May or June	Corpus Christi (Fronleichnam): May 31 in 2016, June 20 in 2019
June	Zürich Festival (www.zuercher-festspiele.ch)
Mid-June-Sept	William Tell Performance (open-air theater, www.tellspiele.ch), Interlaken
Late June-Early July	Montreux International Jazz Festival (www.montreuxjazz.com)
Early July	Estival Jazz (free open-air festival, www.estivaljazz.ch), Lugano
Early July	City Festival (www.festivalcite.ch), Lausanne

Mid-July	Gurten Open-Air Rock Festival (www.gurtenfestival.ch), Bern
Aug	Street Parade (citywide rave, www.streetparade.ch), Zürich
Aug 1	Swiss National Day (parades and fireworks)
Aug 15	Assumption of Mary (Maria Himmelfahrt)
Mid-Aug–Mid-Sept	Lucerne Festival in Summer (classical music, www.lucernefestival.ch), Luzern
Early Oct	Festa d'Autunno (food and wine festival), Lugano
Nov 1	All Saints' Day
Late Nov	Lucerne Festival at the Piano (www.lucernefestival.ch), Luzern
Late Nov	Traditional Onion Market Fair, Bern
Dec	Christmas fairs
Dec 6	St. Nicholas Day
Dec 8	Immaculate Conception
Dec 25	Christmas
Dec 26	St. Stephen's Day (Boxing Day)

Books and Films

To learn more about Switzerland past and present, check out a few of these books or films.

NONFICTION

Eiger Dreams (Jon Krakauer, 1990). In this collection of essays, Krakauer explores the trials and triumphs of mountaineering.

La Place de la Concorde Suisse (John McPhee, 1983). Following a mountain unit of the Swiss Army, this book explores how mandatory military service (for men) keeps Switzerland from breaking apart.

Scrambles Amongst the Alps (Edward Whymper, 1871). This mountaineering classic recounts adventure and tragedy in the life of the first climber ever to summit the Matterhorn.

Swiss History in a Nutshell (Gregoire Nappey, 2010). Nappey delivers information that's concise and enjoyable, yet not dumbed-down.

Swiss Watching (Diccon Bewes, 2010). This campy book covers all the basics in an easy-to-digest look at 21st-century Switzerland.

Target Switzerland: Swiss Armed Neutrality in World War II (Stephen P. Halbrook, 1998). Halbrook posits that Switzerland's robust preparation for armed resistance against the Nazis was a key to its success in maintaining neutrality.

A Tramp Abroad (Mark Twain, 1880). Twain humorously recounts his 1878 "walking tour" through the Alps.

The White Spider (Heinrich Harrer, 1959). This book chronicles the first successful ascent of the Eiger's north face in 1938.

Why Switzerland? (Jonathan Steinberg, 1976). Steinberg explains how a country with four official languages can still have a common culture.

FICTION

Einstein's Dreams (Alan Lightman, 1992). A young Albert Einstein wrests with his theory of relativity in turn-of-the-century Bern.

A Farewell to Arms (Ernest Hemingway, 1929). Two lovers struggle through the horrors of World War I, finding brief peace in Switzerland in the last act.

Hotel du Lac (Anita Brookner, 1995). A writer of romance novels attempts to recover from her own misguided love affair by fleeing to Switzerland.

Frankenstein (Mary Shelley, 1818). Set partially in Geneva, this novel explores the nature of humanity when scientist Victor Frankenstein creates a monster and brings it to life.

I'm Not Stiller (Max Frisch, 1954). In an attempt to reclaim his true identity, a prisoner in a small Swiss town recounts his adventurous life.

The Magic Mountain (Thomas Mann, 1924). An exclusive sanatorium high in the Alps is a microcosm for European society in the days before World War I.

The Night Manager (John le Carré, 1993). The fussy manager of a Swiss hotel is recruited by British intelligence to bring down a millionaire gunrunner.

The Watchers (Jon Steele, 2011). Three strangers in Lausanne must solve the mysteries haunting their town.

William Tell (Friedrich Schiller, 1804). William Tell, legendary Swiss marksman, fights for Swiss independence from the Habsburg Empire in the 14th century.

FILMS AND TV

The Bourne Identity (2002). This action movie, set mostly in Prague, pits an amnesiac spy against his pursuers in the heart of Zürich.

Clouds of Sils Maria (2014). Largely set (and filmed) in the Upper Engadine valley, this coming-of-middle-age drama stars Juliette Binoche as an aging actress and Kristen Stewart as the scandal-ridden young starlet who challenges her.

Dilwale Dulhania Le Jayenge (1995). In the longest-running film in

Indian cinema (600 weeks in the movie theaters), two young people fall in love on a trip to Switzerland.

The Eiger Sanction (1975). A man joins an expedition up the Eiger to avenge the murder of his friend in this film partially set in Kleine Scheidegg.

Five Days One Summer (1982). Sean Connery stars in the tale of an incestuous love triangle, offset by breathtaking climbing sequences in the Swiss Alps.

Jonah Who Will Be 25 in the Year 2000 (1976). A group of student activists living in Geneva face disillusionment during the late 1960s.

Journey of Hope (1990). Three members of a Kurdish family search for a better life in Switzerland.

North Face (2008). Based on a true story, this film chronicles the 1936 attempt by two Germans to scale the Eiger's "wall of death."

On Her Majesty's Secret Service (1969). James Bond goes undercover in the Swiss Alps, with action sequences set on the slopes of the Schilthorn.

The Swissmakers (1978). The most popular Swiss movie ever made showcases a group of foreigners trying to get Swiss citizenship.

Three Colors: Red (1994). In the Oscar-nominated final film of the acclaimed *Three Colors Trilogy,* a young model living in Geneva confronts interpersonal issues when she meets a cynical judge.

FOR KIDS

And Both Were Young (Madeleine L'Engle, 1983). In a tale for teens, Philippa struggles to find her place at a Swiss boarding school until she starts a secret romance and gains new friends.

Asterix in Switzerland (René Goscinny, 1970). Asterix and Obelix have adventures in Switzerland during Roman times in book number 16 of this beloved French cartoon series.

Banner in the Sky (James Ramsey Ullman, 1954). Young Rudi Matt tries to climb one of the world's most forbidding Alpine peaks in this Newbery Honor book.

A Bell for Ursli (Selina Chönz, 2007). High in the Alps, a boy named Ursli hikes alone into the snowy mountains to find a big bell with which to lead the spring procession.

Count Karlstein (Philip Pullman, 2000). Two girls escape the sinister plot of their uncle—an evil count—in this humorous middle-grade thriller set in a Swiss village in 1816.

Dear Alexandra: A Story of Switzerland (Helen Gudel, 1999). This charming picture book takes the form of letters from a grandmother who awaits her granddaughter's visit in a Swiss mountain village.

Heidi (Johanna Spyri, 1880). In the most famous novel about Switzerland, an orphan girl is sent to live with her grandfather in the Alps. A popular film version starring Shirley Temple was released in 1937.

Pitschi (Hans Fischer, 1947). In this Swiss children's classic, a kitten named Pitschi sets out to find her place among the animals on Old Lisette's farm.

A Tale of Two Brothers (Eveline Hasler, 2006). This Swiss-Italian folk tale of two brothers with vastly different worldviews delivers a moral about the power of positive thinking.

William Tell: One Against an Empire (Paul D. Storrie, 2008). This dynamic retelling of the legendary Swiss hunter's story is presented in graphic novel format.

Conversions and Climate

Numbers and Stumblers

- Europeans write a few of their numbers differently than we do. 1 = 1, 4 = 4, 7 = 7.
- In Europe, dates appear as day/month/year, so Christmas 2019 is 25/12/2019.
- Commas are decimal points and decimals are commas. A dollar and a half is $1,50, one thousand is 1.000, and there are 5.280 feet in a mile.
- When counting with fingers, start with your thumb. If you hold up your first finger to request one item, you'll probably get two.
- What Americans call the second floor of a building is the first floor in Europe.
- On escalators and moving sidewalks, Europeans keep the left "lane" open for passing. Keep to the right.

Metric Conversions

A kilogram equals 1,000 grams (about 2.2 pounds). One hundred grams (a common unit at markets) is about a quarter-pound. One liter is about a quart, or almost four to a gallon.

A kilometer is six-tenths of a mile. To convert kilometers to miles, cut the kilometers in half and add back 10 percent of the original (120 km: 60 + 12 = 72 miles). One meter is 39 inches—just over a yard.

1 foot = 0.3 meter	1 square yard = 0.8 square meter
1 yard = 0.9 meter	1 square mile = 2.6 square kilometers
1 mile = 1.6 kilometers	1 ounce = 28 grams
1 centimeter = 0.4 inch	1 quart = 0.95 liter
1 meter = 39.4 inches	1 kilogram = 2.2 pounds
1 kilometer = 0.62 mile	32°F = 0°C

CLOTHING SIZES

When shopping for clothing, use these US-to-European compari-
sons as general guidelines (but note that no conversion is perfect).

Women: For pants and dresses, add 30 in Switzerland (US
10 = Swiss 40). For blouses and sweaters, add 8 for most of Europe
(US 32 = European 40). For shoes, add 30-31 (US 7 = European
37/38).

Men: For shirts, multiply by 2 and add about 8 (US 15 = European 38). For jackets and suits, add 10. For shoes, add 32-34.

Children: Clothing is sized by height—in centimeters (2.5
inches = 1 cm), so a US size 8 roughly equates to 132-140. For
shoes up to size 13, add 16-18, and for sizes 1 and up, add 30-32.

Switzerland's Climate

First line, average daily high; second line, average daily low; third
line, average days without rain. For more detailed weather statistics
for destinations in this book (as well as the rest of the world), check
www.wunderground.com.

J	F	M	A	M	J	J	A	S	O	N	D
Bern											
38°	42°	51°	59°	66°	73°	77°	76°	69°	58°	47°	40°
29°	30°	36°	42°	49°	55°	58°	58°	53°	44°	37°	31°
20	19	22	21	20	19	22	20	20	21	19	21

Fahrenheit and Celsius Conversion

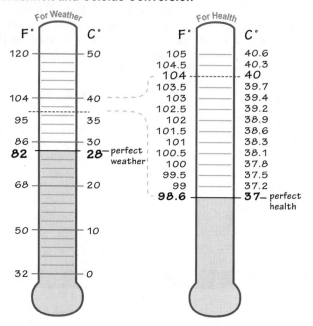

Europe takes its temperature using the Celsius scale, while we opt for Fahrenheit. For a rough conversion from Celsius to Fahrenheit, double the number and add 30. For weather, remember that 28°C is 82°F—perfect. For health, 37°C is just right. At a launderette, 30°C is cold, 40°C is warm (usually the default setting), 60°C is hot, and 95°C is boiling. Your air-conditioner should be set at about 20°C.

Packing Checklist

Whether you're traveling for five days or five weeks, you won't need more than this. Pack light to enjoy the sweet freedom of true mobility.

Clothing

- ❏ 5 shirts: long- & short-sleeve
- ❏ 2 pairs pants (or skirts/capris)
- ❏ 1 pair shorts
- ❏ 5 pairs underwear & socks
- ❏ 1 pair walking shoes
- ❏ Sweater or warm layer
- ❏ Rainproof jacket with hood
- ❏ Tie, scarf, belt, and/or hat
- ❏ Swimsuit
- ❏ Sleepwear/loungewear

Money

- ❏ Debit card(s)
- ❏ Credit card(s)
- ❏ Hard cash ($100-200 in US dollars)
- ❏ Money belt

Documents

- ❏ Passport
- ❏ Tickets & confirmations: flights, hotels, trains, rail pass, car rental, sight entries
- ❏ Driver's license
- ❏ Student ID, hostel card, etc.
- ❏ Photocopies of important documents
- ❏ Insurance details
- ❏ Guidebooks & maps
- ❏ Notepad & pen
- ❏ Journal

Toiletries Kit

- ❏ Basics: soap, shampoo, toothbrush, toothpaste, floss, deodorant, sunscreen, brush/comb, etc.
- ❏ Medicines & vitamins
- ❏ First-aid kit
- ❏ Glasses/contacts/sunglasses

- ❏ Sewing kit
- ❏ Packet of tissues (for WC)
- ❏ Earplugs

Electronics

- ❏ Mobile phone
- ❏ Camera & related gear
- ❏ Tablet/ebook reader/media player
- ❏ Laptop & flash drive
- ❏ Headphones
- ❏ Chargers & batteries
- ❏ Smartphone car charger & mount (or GPS device)
- ❏ Plug adapters

Miscellaneous

- ❏ Daypack
- ❏ Sealable plastic baggies
- ❏ Laundry supplies: soap, laundry bag, clothesline, spot remover
- ❏ Small umbrella
- ❏ Travel alarm/watch

Optional Extras

- ❏ Second pair of shoes (flip-flops, sandals, tennis shoes, boots)
- ❏ Travel hairdryer
- ❏ Picnic supplies
- ❏ Water bottle
- ❏ Fold-up tote bag
- ❏ Small flashlight
- ❏ Mini binoculars
- ❏ Small towel or washcloth
- ❏ Inflatable pillow/neck rest
- ❏ Tiny lock
- ❏ Address list (to mail postcards)
- ❏ Extra passport photos

German Survival Phrases for Switzerland

In the phonetics, ī sounds like the long i in "light," and bolded syllables are stressed.

English	German	Pronunciation
Hello.	Grüetzi.	**grewt**-see
Do you speak English?	Sprechen Sie Englisch?	**shprehkh**-ehn zee **ehng**-lish
Yes. / No.	Ja. / Nein.	yah / nīn
I (don't) understand.	Ich verstehe (nicht).	ikh fehr-**shtay**-heh (nikht)
Please.	Bitte.	**bit**-teh
Thank you.	Merci.	**mur**-see
I'm sorry.	Es tut mir leid.	ehs toot meer līt
Excuse me.	Entschuldigung.	ehnt-**shool**-dig-oong
(No) problem.	(Kein) Problem.	(kīn) proh-**blaym**
(Very) good.	(Sehr) gut.	(zehr) goot
Goodbye.	Ciao.	chow
one / two	eins / zwei	īns / tsvī
three / four	drei / vier	drī / feer
five / six	fünf / sechs	fewnf / zehkhs
seven / eight	sieben / acht	**zee**-behn / ahkht
nine / ten	neun / zehn	noyn / tsayn
How much is it?	Wieviel kostet das?	**vee**-feel **kohs**-teht dahs
Write it?	Schreiben?	**shrī**-behn
Is it free?	Ist es umsonst?	ist ehs oom-**zohnst**
Included?	Inklusive?	in-kloo-**zee**-veh
Where can I buy / find...?	Wo kann ich kaufen / finden...?	voh kahn ikh **kow**-fehn / **fin**-dehn
I'd like / We'd like...	Ich hätte gern / Wir hätten gern...	ikh **heh**-teh gehrn / veer **heh**-tehn gehrn
...a room.	...ein Zimmer.	īn **tsim**-mer
...a ticket to ___.	...eine Fahrkarte nach ___.	ī-neh **far**-kar-teh nahkh ___
Is it possible?	Ist es möglich?	ist ehs **mur**-glikh
Where is...?	Wo ist...?	voh ist
...the train station	...der Bahnhof	dehr **bahn**-hohf
...the bus station	...der Busbahnhof	dehr **boos**-bahn-hohf
...tourist information office	...das Touristen-informations büro	dahs too-**ris**-tehn-in-for-maht-see-**ohns-bew**-roh
...toilet	...die Toilette	dee toy-**leh**-teh
men	Herren	**hehr**-ehn
women	Damen	**dah**-mehn
left / right	links / rechts	links / rehkhts
straight	geradeaus	geh-**rah**-deh-**ows**
When is this open / closed?	Um wieviel Uhr ist hier geöffnet / geschlossen?	oom **vee**-feel oor ist heer geh-**urf**-neht / geh-**shloh**-sehn
At what time?	Um wieviel Uhr?	oom **vee**-feel oor
Just a moment.	Moment.	moh-**mehnt**
now / soon / later	jetzt / bald / später	yehtst / bahld / **shpay**-ter
today / tomorrow	heute / morgen	**hoy**-teh / **mor**-gehn

In a German-Speaking Restaurant

English	German	Pronunciation
I'd like / We'd like...	Ich hätte gern / Wir hätten gern...	ikh **heh**-teh gehrn / veer **heh**-tehn gehrn
...a reservation for...	...eine Reservierung für...	ī-neh reh-zehr-**feer**-oong fewr
...a table for one / two.	...einen Tisch für eine Person / zwei Personen.	ī-nehn tish fewr ī-neh pehr- zohn / tsvī pehr-**zoh**-nehn
Is this seat free?	Ist hier frei?	ist heer frī
Menu (in English), please.	Speisekarte (auf Englisch), bitte.	**shpī**-zeh-kar-teh (owf **ehng**-lish) **bit**-teh
service (not) included	Trinkgeld (nicht) inklusive	**trink**-gehlt (nikht) in-kloo-**zee**-veh
cover charge	Eintritt	**īn**-trit
to go	zum Mitnehmen	tsoom **mit**-nay-mehn
with / without	mit / ohne	mit / **oh**-neh
and / or	und / oder	oont / **oh**-der
menu (of the day)	(Tages-) Karte	(**tah**-gehs-) **kar**-teh
set meal for tourists	Touristenmenü	too-**ris**-tehn-meh-**new**
specialty of the house	Spezialität des Hauses	**shpayt**-see-ah-lee-**tayt** dehs **how**-zehs
appetizers	Vorspeise	**for**-shpī-zeh
bread / cheese	Brot / Käse	broht / **kay**-zeh
sandwich	Sandwich	**zahnd**-vich
soup	Suppe	**zoo**-peh
salad	Salat	zah-**laht**
meat	Fleisch	flīsh
poultry	Geflügel	geh-**flew**-gehl
fish	Fisch	fish
seafood	Meeresfrüchte	meh-rehs-**frewkh**-teh
fruit	Obst	ohpst
vegetables	Gemüse	geh-**mew**-zeh
dessert	Nachspeise	**nahkh**-shpī-zeh
mineral water	Mineralwasser	min-eh-rahl-**vahs**-ehr
tap water	Leitungswasser	**lī**-toongs-**vahs**-ehr
milk	Milch	milkh
(orange) juice	(Orangen-) Saft	(oh-**rahn**-zhehn-) zahft
coffee / tea	Kaffee / Tee	kah-**fay** / tay
wine	Wein	vīn
red / white	rot / weiß	roht / vīs
glass / bottle	Glas / Flasche	glahs / **flah**-sheh
beer	Bier	beer
Cheers!	Prost!	prohst
More. / Another.	Mehr. / Noch eins.	mehr / nohkh īns
The same.	Das gleiche.	dahs **glīkh**-eh
Bill, please.	Rechnung, bitte.	**rehkh**-noong **bit**-teh
Do you accept credit cards?	Akzeptieren Sie Kreditkarten?	ahkt-sehp-**teer**-ehn zee kreh-**deet**-kar-tehn
tip	Trinkgeld	**trink**-gehlt
Delicious!	Lecker!	**lehk**-er

For more user-friendly German phrases, check out *Rick Steves' German Phrase Book and Dictionary* or *Rick Steves' French, Italian & German Phrase Book*.

French Survival Phrases

When using the phonetics, try to nasalize the <u>n</u> sound.

English	French	Pronunciation
Good day.	*Bonjour.*	boh<u>n</u>-zhoor
Mrs. / Mr.	*Madame / Monsieur*	mah-dahm / muhs-yuh
Do you speak English?	*Parlez-vous anglais?*	par-lay-voo ah<u>n</u>-glay
Yes. / No.	*Oui. / Non.*	wee / noh<u>n</u>
I understand.	*Je comprends.*	zhuh koh<u>n</u>-prah<u>n</u>
I don't understand.	*Je ne comprends pas.*	zhuh nuh koh<u>n</u>-prah<u>n</u> pah
Please.	*S'il vous plaît.*	see voo play
Thank you.	*Merci.*	mehr-see
I'm sorry.	*Désolé.*	day-zoh-lay
Excuse me.	*Pardon.*	par-doh<u>n</u>
(No) problem.	*(Pas de) problème.*	(pah duh) proh-blehm
It's good.	*C'est bon.*	say boh<u>n</u>
Goodbye.	*Au revoir.*	oh ruh-vwahr
one / two	*un / deux*	uh<u>n</u> / duh
three / four	*trois / quatre*	trwah / kah-truh
five / six	*cinq / six*	sa<u>n</u>k / sees
seven / eight	*sept / huit*	seht / weet
nine / ten	*neuf / dix*	nuhf / dees
How much is it?	*Combien?*	koh<u>n</u>-bee-a<u>n</u>
Write it?	*Ecrivez?*	ay-kree-vay
Is it free?	*C'est gratuit?*	say grah-twee
Included?	*Inclus?*	a<u>n</u>-klew
Where can I buy / find...?	*Où puis-je acheter / trouver...?*	oo pwee-zhuh ah-shuh-tay / troo-vay
I'd like / We'd like...	*Je voudrais / Nous voudrions...*	zhuh voo-dray / noo voo-dree-oh<u>n</u>
...a room.	*...une chambre.*	ewn shah<u>n</u>-bruh
...a ticket to ___.	*...un billet pour ___.*	uh<u>n</u> bee-yay poor ___
Is it possible?	*C'est possible?*	say poh-see-bluh
Where is...?	*Où est...?*	oo ay
...the train station	*...la gare*	lah gar
...the bus station	*...la gare routière*	lah gar root-yehr
...tourist information	*...l'office du tourisme*	loh-fees dew too-reez-muh
Where are the toilets?	*Où sont les toilettes?*	oo soh<u>n</u> lay twah-leht
men	*hommes*	ohm
women	*dames*	dahm
left / right	*à gauche / à droite*	ah gohsh / ah drwaht
straight	*tout droit*	too drwah
When does this open / close?	*Ça ouvre / ferme à quelle heure?*	sah oo-vruh / fehrm ah kehl ur
At what time?	*À quelle heure?*	ah kehl ur
Just a moment.	*Un moment.*	uh<u>n</u> moh-mah<u>n</u>
now / soon / later	*maintenant / bientôt / plus tard*	ma<u>n</u>-tuh-nah<u>n</u> / bee-a<u>n</u>-toh / plew tar
today / tomorrow	*aujourd'hui / demain*	oh-zhoor-dwee / duh-ma<u>n</u>

In a French Restaurant

English	French	Pronunciation
I'd like / We'd like...	Je voudrais / Nous voudrions...	zhuh voo-dray / noo voo-dree-ohn
...to reserve...	...réserver...	ray-zehr-vay
...a table for one / two.	...une table pour un / deux.	ewn tah-bluh poor uhn / duh
Is this seat free?	C'est libre?	say lee-bruh
The menu (in English), please.	La carte (en anglais), s'il vous plaît.	lah kart (ahn ahn-glay) see voo play
service (not) included	service (non) compris	sehr-vees (nohn) kohn-pree
to go	à emporter	ah ahn-por-tay
with / without	avec / sans	ah-vehk / sahn
and / or	et / ou	ay / oo
special of the day	plat du jour	plah dew zhoor
specialty of the house	spécialité de la maison	spay-see-ah-lee-tay duh lah may-zohn
appetizers	hors d'oeuvre	or duh-vruh
first course (soup, salad)	entrée	ahn-tray
main course (meat, fish)	plat principal	plah pran-see-pahl
bread	pain	pan
cheese	fromage	froh-mahzh
sandwich	sandwich	sahnd-weech
soup	soupe	soop
salad	salade	sah-lahd
meat	viande	vee-ahnd
chicken	poulet	poo-lay
fish	poisson	pwah-sohn
seafood	fruits de mer	frwee duh mehr
fruit	fruit	frwee
vegetables	légumes	lay-gewm
dessert	dessert	day-sehr
mineral water	eau minérale	oh mee-nay-rahl
tap water	l'eau du robinet	loh dew roh-bee-nay
milk	lait	lay
(orange) juice	jus (d'orange)	zhew (doh-rahnzh)
coffee / tea	café / thé	kah-fay / tay
wine	vin	van
red / white	rouge / blanc	roozh / blahn
glass / bottle	verre / bouteille	vehr / boo-tay
beer	bière	bee-ehr
Cheers!	Santé!	sahn-tay
More. / Another.	Plus. / Un autre.	plew / uhn oh-truh
The same.	La même chose.	lah mehm shohz
The bill, please.	L'addition, s'il vous plaît.	lah-dee-see-ohn see voo play
Do you accept credit cards?	Vous prenez les cartes?	voo pruh-nay lay kart
tip	pourboire	poor-bwahr
Delicious!	Délicieux!	day-lees-yuh

For more user-friendly French phrases, check out *Rick Steves' French Phrase Book and Dictionary* or *Rick Steves' French, Italian & German Phrase Book.*

Italian Survival Phrases

English	Italian	Pronunciation
Good day.	*Buon giorno.*	bwohn **jor**-noh
Do you speak English?	*Parla inglese?*	**par**-lah een-**gleh**-zay
Yes. / No.	*Sì. / No.*	see / noh
I (don't) understand.	*(Non) capisco.*	(nohn) kah-**pees**-koh
Please.	*Per favore.*	pehr fah-**voh**-ray
Thank you.	*Grazie.*	**graht**-see-ay
You're welcome.	*Prego.*	**preh**-go
I'm sorry.	*Mi dispiace.*	mee dee-spee-**ah**-chay
Excuse me.	*Mi scusi.*	mee **skoo**-zee
(No) problem.	*(Non) c'è problema.*	(nohn) cheh proh-**bleh**-mah
Good.	*Va bene.*	vah **beh**-nay
Goodbye.	*Arrivederci.*	ah-ree-veh-**dehr**-chee
one / two	*uno / due*	**oo**-noh / **doo**-ay
three / four	*tre / quattro*	tray / **kwah**-troh
five / six	*cinque / sei*	**cheeng**-kway / **seh**-ee
seven / eight	*sette / otto*	**seh**-tay / **oh**-toh
nine / ten	*nove / dieci*	**noh**-vay / dee-**ay**-chee
How much is it?	*Quanto costa?*	**kwahn**-toh **koh**-stah
Write it?	*Me lo scrive?*	may loh **skree**-vay
Is it free?	*È gratis?*	eh **grah**-tees
Is it included?	*È incluso?*	eh een-**kloo**-zoh
Where can I buy / find...?	*Dove posso comprare / trovare...?*	**doh**-vay poh-soh kohm-**prah**-ray / troh-**vah**-ray
I'd like / We'd like...	*Vorrei / Vorremmo...*	voh-**reh**-ee / voh-**reh**-moh
...a room.	*...una camera.*	**oo**-nah **kah**-meh-rah
...a ticket to ____.	*...un biglietto per ____.*	oon beel-**yeh**-toh pehr ____
Is it possible?	*È possibile?*	eh poh-**see**-bee-lay
Where is...?	*Dov'è...?*	doh-**veh**
...the train station	*...la stazione*	lah staht-see-**oh**-nay
...the bus station	*...la stazione degli autobus*	lah staht-see-**oh**-nay **dehl**-yee **ow**-toh-boos
...tourist information	*...informazioni per turisti*	een-for-maht-see-**oh**-nee pehr too-**ree**-stee
...the toilet	*...la toilette*	lah twah-**leh**-tay
men	*uomini / signori*	**woh**-mee-nee / seen-**yoh**-ree
women	*donne / signore*	**doh**-nay / seen-**yoh**-ray
left / right	*sinistra / destra*	see-**nee**-strah / **deh**-strah
straight	*sempre dritto*	**sehm**-pray **dree**-toh
What time does this open / close?	*A che ora apre / chiude?*	ah kay **oh**-rah ah-**pray** / kee-**oo**-day
At what time?	*A che ora?*	ah kay **oh**-rah
Just a moment.	*Un momento.*	oon moh-**mehn**-toh
now / soon / later	*adesso / presto / tardi*	ah-**deh**-soh / **preh**-stoh / **tar**-dee
today / tomorrow	*oggi / domani*	**oh**-jee / doh-**mah**-nee

In an Italian Restaurant

English	Italian	Pronunciation
I'd like...	Vorrei...	voh-**reh**-ee
We'd like...	Vorremmo...	vor-**reh**-moh
...to reserve...	...prenotare...	preh-noh-**tah**-ray
...a table for one / two.	...un tavolo per uno / due.	oon **tah**-voh-loh pehr **oo**-noh / **doo**-ay
Is this seat free?	È libero questo posto?	eh **lee**-beh-roh **kweh**-stoh **poh**-stoh
The menu (in English), please.	Il menù (in inglese), per favore.	eel meh-**noo** (een een-**gleh**-zay) pehr fah-**voh**-ray
service (not) included	servizio (non) incluso	sehr-**veet**-see-oh (nohn) een-**kloo**-zoh
cover charge	pane e coperto	**pah**-nay ay koh-**pehr**-toh
to go	da portar via	dah **por**-tar **vee**-ah
with / without	con / senza	kohn / **sehnt**-sah
and / or	e / o	ay / oh
menu (of the day)	menù (del giorno)	meh-**noo** (dehl **jor**-noh)
specialty of the house	specialità della casa	speh-chah-lee-**tah** **deh**-lah **kah**-zah
first course (pasta, soup)	primo piatto	**pree**-moh pee-**ah**-toh
main course (meat, fish)	secondo piatto	seh-**kohn**-doh pee-**ah**-toh
side dishes	contorni	kohn-**tor**-nee
bread	pane	**pah**-nay
cheese	formaggio	for-**mah**-joh
sandwich	panino	pah-**nee**-noh
soup	zuppa	**tsoo**-pah
salad	insalata	een-sah-**lah**-tah
meat	carne	**kar**-nay
chicken	pollo	**poh**-loh
fish	pesce	**peh**-shay
seafood	frutti di mare	**froo**-tee dee **mah**-ray
fruit / vegetables	frutta / legumi	**froo**-tah / lay-**goo**-mee
dessert	dolce	**dohl**-chay
tap water	acqua del rubinetto	**ah**-kwah dehl roo-bee-**neh**-toh
mineral water	acqua minerale	**ah**-kwah mee-neh-**rah**-lay
milk	latte	**lah**-tay
(orange) juice	succo (d'arancia)	**soo**-koh (dah-**rahn**-chah)
coffee / tea	caffè / tè	kah-**feh** / teh
wine	vino	**vee**-noh
red / white	rosso / bianco	**roh**-soh / bee-**ahn**-koh
glass / bottle	bicchiere / bottiglia	bee-kee-**eh**-ray / boh-**teel**-yah
beer	birra	**bee**-rah
Cheers!	Cin cin!	cheen cheen
More. / Another.	Di più. / Un altro.	dee pew / oon **ahl**-troh
The same.	Lo stesso.	loh **steh**-soh
The bill, please.	Il conto, per favore.	eel **kohn**-toh pehr fah-**voh**-ray
Do you accept credit cards?	Accettate carte di credito?	ah-cheh-**tah**-tay **kar**-tay dee **kreh**-dee-toh
tip	mancia	**mahn**-chah
Delicious!	Delizioso!	day-leet-see-**oh**-zoh

For more user-friendly Italian phrases, check out *Rick Steves' Italian Phrase Book & Dictionary* or *Rick Steves' French, Italian, & German Phrase Book.*

INDEX

MAP INDEX

Start your trip at

Our website enhances this book and turns

Explore Europe

At ricksteves.com you can browse through thousands of articles, videos, photos and radio interviews, plus find a wealth of money-saving travel tips for planning your dream trip. And with our mobile-friendly website, you can easily access all this great travel information anywhere you go.

TV Shows

Preview the places you'll visit by watching entire half-hour episodes of Rick Steves' Europe (choose from all 100 shows) on-demand, for free.

ricksteves.com

your travel dreams into affordable reality

Radio Interviews

Enjoy ready access to Rick's vast library of radio interviews covering travel

tips and cultural insights that relate specifically to your Europe travel plans.

Travel Forums

Learn, ask, share! Our online community of savvy travelers is a great resource for first-time travelers to Europe, as well as seasoned pros. You'll find forums on each country, plus travel tips and restaurant/hotel reviews. You can even ask one of our well-traveled staff to chime in with an opinion.

Travel News

Subscribe to our free Travel News e-newsletter, and get monthly updates from Rick on what's happening in Europe.

Audio Europe™

Rick Steves has

Experience maximum Europe

Save time and energy

This guidebook is your independent-travel toolkit. But for all it delivers, it's still up to you to devote the time and energy it takes to manage the preparation and logistics that are essential for a happy trip. If that's a hassle, there's a solution.

Rick Steves Tours

A Rick Steves tour takes you to Europe's most interesting places with great

Credits

RESEARCHERS
Glenn Eriksen

A solo backpacking trip across Europe and Scandinavia back in the '70s turned out to be Glenn's first step on the road to Rick Steves' Europe. Today, as a guidebook editor and researcher, he indulges his love for the Old Country while helping Rick's readers to "keep on travelin'." When not on the road, Glenn lives in Seattle with his wife, Kathy, and enjoys hiking, photography, and keeping in touch with his Norwegian roots.

Gretchen Strauch

Before Gretchen became the online-content editor for Rick Steves' Europe, she spent three years in a town on the Swiss/German border teaching English and spending all her spare time and money on forays into the land of snowy peaks, melted cheese, and unpronounceable German.

Cary Walker

Cary discovered international travel during college and has been feeding her wanderlust ever since. A former teacher, she believes that Europe is the best classroom for those who travel with an open mind. When not researching guidebooks or leading Rick Steves' Europe tours, she resides in Dallas, where she enjoys playing baseball with nephews Tommy and Will.

CONTRIBUTOR
Gene Openshaw

Gene has co-authored a dozen Rick Steves books, specializing in writing walks and tours of Europe's cities, museums, and cultural sights. He also contributes to Rick's public television series, produces tours for Rick Steves Audio Europe, and is a regular guest on Rick's public radio show. Outside of the travel world, Gene has co-authored *The Seattle Joke Book*. As a composer, Gene has written a full-length opera called *Matter*, a violin sonata, and dozens of songs. He lives near Seattle with his daughter, enjoys giving presentations on art and history, and roots for the Mariners in good times and bad.

A Guide for Every Trip

BEST OF GUIDES

Full color easy-to-scan format, focusing on Europe's most popular destinations and sights.

Best of England
Best of Europe
Best of France
Best of Germany
Best of Ireland
Best of Italy
Best of Spain

COMPREHENSIVE GUIDES

City, country, and regional guides with detailed coverage for a multi-week trip exploring the most iconic sights and venturing off the beaten track.

Amsterdam & the Netherlands
Barcelona
Belgium: Bruges, Brussels, Antwerp & Ghent
Berlin
Budapest
Croatia & Slovenia
Eastern Europe
England
Florence & Tuscany
France
Germany
Great Britain
Greece: Athens & the Peloponnese
Iceland
Ireland
Istanbul
Italy
London
Paris
Portugal
Prague & the Czech Republic
Provence & the French Riviera
Rome
Scandinavia
Scotland
Spain
Switzerland
Venice
Vienna, Salzburg & Tirol

POCKET GUIDES

Compact, full color city guides with the essentials for shorter trips.

Amsterdam   Paris
Athens   Prague
Barcelona   Rome
Florence   Venice
Italy's Cinque Terre   Vienna
London
Munich & Salzburg

SNAPSHOT GUIDES

Focused single-destination coverage.

Basque Country: Spain & France
Copenhagen & the Best of Denmark
Dublin
Dubrovnik
Edinburgh
Hill Towns of Central Italy
Krakow, Warsaw & Gdansk
Lisbon
Loire Valley
Madrid & Toledo
Milan & the Italian Lakes District
Naples & the Amalfi Coast
Normandy
Northern Ireland
Norway
Reykjavík
Sevilla, Granada & Southern Spain
St. Petersburg, Helsinki & Tallinn
Stockholm

CRUISE PORTS GUIDES

Reference for cruise ports of call.

Mediterranean Cruise Ports
Scandinavian & Northern European Cruise Ports

Complete your library with...

TRAVEL SKILLS & CULTURE

Study up on travel skills and gain insight on history and culture.

Europe 101
Europe Through the Back Door
European Christmas
European Easter
European Festivals
Postcards from Europe
Travel as a Political Act

PHRASE BOOKS & DICTIONARIES

French
French, Italian & German
German
Italian
Portuguese
Spanish

PLANNING MAPS

Britain, Ireland & London
Europe
France & Paris
Germany, Austria & Switzerland
Ireland
Italy
Spain & Portugal

HE BEST OF ROME

ne, Italy's capital, is studded with
an remnants and floodlit-fountain
res. From the Vatican to the Colos-
, with crazy traffic in between, Rome
nderful, huge, and exhausting. The
ds, the heat, and the weighty history

of the Eternal City where Caesars walked
can make tourists wilt. Recharge by taking siestas, gelato breaks, and after-dark
walks, strolling from one atmospheric
square to another in the refreshing evening air.

ed *Pantheon*—which
est dome until the
ly 2,000 years old
over 1,500).

of Athens in the *Vat-
dies the humanistic
ce.

gladiators fought
nother, entertaining

s Rome *ristorante.*
ds at St. Peter's
seriously.

, toss in a coin

Rick Steves guidebooks are published by Avalon Travel, an imprint of Perseus Books, a Hachette Book Group company.

Rick Steves books are available from your favorite bookseller.
Many guides are available as ebooks.

ACKNOWLEDGMENTS

Thanks to Susana Minich for writing the original version of the Zürich, Central Switzerland, Lugano, Upper Engadine, and Scenic Rail Journeys chapters; and to Cameron Hewitt for writing the original versions of the Luzern and Zermatt chapters.

Avalon Travel
Hachette Book Group
1700 Fourth Street
Berkeley, CA 94710

Printed in Canada by Friesens.
Ninth Edition. First printing May 2018.

ISBN 978-1-63121-824-8

For the latest on Rick's talks, guidebooks, tours, public television series, and public radio show, contact Rick Steves' Europe, 130 Fourth Avenue North, Edmonds, WA 98020, tel. 425/771-8303, www.ricksteves.com, rick@ricksteves.com.

Rick Steves' Europe

Managing Editor: Jennifer Madison Davis
Special Publications Manager: Risa Laib
Assistant Managing Editor: Cathy Lu
Editors: Glenn Eriksen, Tom Griffin, Katherine Gustafson, Suzanne Kotz, Rosie Leutzinger, Carrie Shepherd
Editorial & Production Assistant: Jessica Shaw
Editorial Intern: Kevin Teeter
Researchers: Glenn Eriksen, Gretchen Strauch, Cary Walker
Contributor: Gene Openshaw
Graphic Content Director: Sandra Hundacker
Maps & Graphics: David C. Hoerlein, Lauren Mills, Mary Rostad

Avalon Travel

Senior Editor and Series Manager: Madhu Prasher
Editor: Jamie Andrade
Editor: Sierra Machado
Copy Editor: Maggie Ryan
Proofreader: Kelly Lydick
Indexer: Stephen Callahan
Cover Design: Kimberly Glyder Design
Production and Typesetting: Jane Musser, Lisi Baldwin, Kit Anderson, Rue Flaherty
Maps & Graphics: Kat Bennett

Photo Credits

Front Cover: © Blaine Harrington III/Getty Images
Title Page: p. i, Cow herder in Lauterbrunnen © Dominic Arizona Bonuccelli
Front Matter Color: p. viii, Mürren © Dominic Arizona Bonuccelli
Additional Photography: Dominic Arizona Bonuccelli, Julie Coen, Rich Earl, Glenn Eriksen, Trish Feaster, Simon Griffith, Cameron Hewitt, David C. Hoerlein, Sandra Hundacker, Rick Steves, Gretchen Strauch, Ian Watson, Wikimedia Commons (PD-Art/PD-US), Wikimedia Commons—Albert Einstein p. 98. Photos are used by permission and are the property of the original copyright owners.

More for your trip!
Maximize the experience with Rick Steves as your guide

Guidebooks
Make side trips smooth and affordable with Rick's Vienna and Germany guides

Phrase Books
Rely on Rick's French, Italian & German Phrase Book & Dictionary

Rick's TV Shows
Preview your destinations with a variety of shows covering Switzerland

Rick's Audio Europe™ App
Get free travel information for Switzerland

Small Group Tours
Take a lively, low-stress Rick Steves tour through Switzerland

For all the details, visit ricksteves.com